6—15—7

Religion in America

ADVISORY EDITOR

Edwin S. Gaustad

RELIGION

IN THE

UNITED STATES OF AMERICA

Robert Baird

ARNO PRESS & THE NEW YORK TIMES

New York 1969

Reprint edition 1969 by Arno Press, Inc.

*

Library of Congress Catalog Card No. 70-83411

*

Reprinted from a copy in the
Columbia University Libraries

*

Manufactured in the United States of America

RELIGION

IN THE

UNITED STATES OF AMERICA.

RELIGION

IN THE

UNITED STATES OF AMERICA.

OR AN ACCOUNT OF THE

Origin, Progress, Relations to the State, and Present Condition

OF THE

EVANGELICAL CHURCHES IN THE UNITED STATES.

WITH

NOTICES OF THE UNEVANGELICAL DENOMINATIONS.

BY THE

REV. ROBERT BAIRD;

AUTHOR OF "L'UNION DE L'EGLISE ET DE L'ETAT, DANS LA NOUVELLE ANGLETERRE."

BLACKIE AND SON; GLASGOW AND EDINBURGH.
DUNCAN AND MALCOLM; LONDON.
MDCCCXLIV.

GLASGOW:
W. G. BLACKIE AND CO., PRINTERS,
VILLAFIELD.

RECOMMENDATORY NOTICE.

HAVING had an opportunity of perusing a considerable portion of the following work while it was passing through the press, we have no hesitation in complying with a request made to us by the publishers, to recommend it to the attention of the British public. The Author is an esteemed minister of the American Presbyterian Church, and has had full access to the best and most authentic sources of information upon the various subjects which he discusses, while his personal acquaintance with the state of religion and the condition of the churches, both in Britain and on the Continent, has afforded him peculiar advantages in selecting the materials, with regard to the state of religion, and the efforts made for its promotion in America, which it might be most interesting and useful for the British churches to possess and to examine. The work contains a very large amount of interesting and valuable information with regard to the origin and history of the different religious bodies in the United States,—their doctrines, constitution, organization, and agency,—their relations with each other,—and the character and results of the efforts they are making to promote religion in their own country and in other lands. It supplies a larger amount of information upon all these important topics than any work with which we are acquainted; and there can be no reasonable doubt that the information it contains is well fitted to encourage the efforts of all churches which are similarly situated to those in America, and to afford some important practical lessons in the prosecution of those great objects which all Christian churches, in every variety of external circumstances, are bound to aim at. We do not agree in all the opinions which the esteemed Author has expressed, but we admire the judicious, benevolent,

b

candid, and catholic spirit by which the work is pervaded. We regard
the publication of this work in our own country as a boon conferred upon
the British churches, not merely because it gives a fuller view than could
any where else be obtained of "Religion in America;" but also, because
it is well fitted to promote a spirit of love and kindness among the churches
of Christ, and to diffuse more widely the benefits which may be derived
from a judicious use of the experience of the American churches, in the
peculiar circumstances in which, in providence, they have been placed,
and in connection with the peculiar way in which the Head of the church
has been pleased to make them instrumental in accomplishing his gracious
purposes. Whatever diversities of opinion may prevail in this country
on some important points connected with the condition and prospects of
religion in America, no candid man will deny, that religion has there been
placed in circumstances, and has appeared in aspects, which are well
worthy of serious consideration, and from a judicious investigation of
which, important practical lessons are to be learned. And on this ground
we hail with much satisfaction the publication of a work which contains
a very large amount of information upon this interesting and important
subject, and cordially recommend it to the perusal of British Christians.

                          DAVID WELSH, D.D.

                          WILLIAM CUNNINGHAM, D.D.

                          ROBERT BUCHANAN, D.D.

        Edinburgh, ⎱
        September, 1843. ⎰

PREFACE.

A few words about the circumstances which have led to the preparation and publication of the work now submitted to the reader, seem to be required by way of preface.

In the year 1835, at the instance of several distinguished Christian gentlemen of his native land, the Author visited the continent of Europe for the prosecution of certain religious and philanthropic objects, and in this pursuit he has been employed during the seven years that have since elapsed. He has had occasion, in the course of that period, to visit repeatedly almost every country on the continent, and has been led, also, to spend some time, more than once, in England and in Scotland, from the latter of which two countries his forefathers were compelled by persecution to emigrate two hundred years ago.

In the course of his continental journeys, his engagements introduced him to the acquaintance of a goodly number of distinguished individuals, belonging to almost all professions and stations in society. Among these are many who rank high in their respective countries for enlightened piety, zeal, and usefulness in their several spheres. From such persons the Author has had innumerable inquiries addressed to him, in all the places he has visited, sometimes by letter, but oftener in conversation, respecting his native country, and especially respecting its religious institutions. To satisfy such inquiries when

b 2

addressed to him by an illustrious individual,[1] whom God has called from the scene of her activity in this world to himself, he wrote a small work on the origin and progress of Unitarianism in the United States.[2] But that little work, while it so far satisfied curiosity on one subject, seemed but to augment it with regard to others; so that without neglecting what was by others as well as himself deemed a manifest duty, the Author had no alternative but to accede to the earnestly, though most kindly, expressed request of some distinguished friends in Germany, Sweden, France, and Switzerland, that he would write a work as extensive as the subject might require, on the origin, history, economy, action, and influence of religion in the United States. This task he has endeavoured to accomplish in the course of the summer and autumn that have just elapsed, and which he has been permitted to spend in this ancient city, whose institutions, and the influence of whose great Reformer, have, through their bearings on the history of England and Scotland, so greatly affected the colonisation, political government, and religious character of the greater part of North America.

His aim throughout this work has been, neither to construct a theory on any controverted point in the economy of the church, or its relations to the state, in any European country, nor to defend the political organisations of his own, or the conduct of its government, on any measure, properly political, whether of foreign or domestic policy. His sole and simple object has been to delineate the religious doctrines and institutions of the United States, and to trace their influence from their first appearance in the country down to the present time, with as little reference as possible to any other country.

The Author has mingled freely with his Protestant brethren in all the countries of Europe where Protestants are to be found, whatever might be their political leanings, and whatever the religious communions to which they belonged. He has received the utmost kindness from them all. And while it would be the merest affectation of impartiality, and most unbe-

---

[1] The late Duchess de Broglie.
[2] This work was published in Paris in 1837, under the title, "L'union de l'Eglise et de l'Etat dans la Nouvelle Angleterre."

coming in him as a Christian, to profess having formed no opinion on the various questions so warmly discussed among them, and especially on the relations which do, or ought to, subsist between the church and the state—a question so much agitated at the present moment in some countries, and which seems destined ere long to be so in many others; yet he can most conscientiously say that he has not allowed himself to be involved in any of them, nor is he conscious of having written a sentence in the present work with the view either of supporting or opposing any of them. He has endeavoured to confine himself throughout to a faithful exhibition of the religious institutions of his native country—their nature, their origin, their action, and their effects. His first desire has been to satisfy the reasonable curiosity of those at whose request he writes; his second and most strenuous endeavour has been to promote the extension of the Messiah's kingdom in the world, by communicating some information respecting measures which, through God's blessing, have proved useful in America without having anything to adapt them to that country more than to any other.

The more that the Author has seen of the Christian world, the more has he been impressed with the conviction that whatever relations the churches maintain with the civil powers, whatever their exterior forms or even their internal discipline, nothing in these respects can compensate for the want of soundness of doctrine and vital piety. Not that as some seem to do, he would treat those things as matters of indifference; for he firmly believes the maintenance and promotion of true religion to be much affected by them; but it is not in them that we are to find that *panacea* for all evils which many hope to find in them, or any substitute for the agency which God has appointed for securing the effectual reception of his glorious salvation. That agency, he humbly conceives, is the presentation of the gospel in all its fulness, in all proper ways, and on all proper occasions, by a spiritually-minded ministry, ordained and set apart to that work, combined with holy living, faithful co-operation in their proper spheres, and earnest prayer on the part of the members, in general, of the churches. The parts of his work, accordingly, that relate to this agency and its results in the experience of the churches in the United States, are those in which he himself feels most interest, and to which he would specially direct the attention of the reader.

The Author has divided his work into eight books or parts. The First is devoted to preliminary remarks intended to throw light on various points, so that readers the least conversant with American history and society may, without difficulty, understand what follows. Some of these preliminary remarks may be thought at first not very pertinent to the subject in hand, but reasons will probably be found for changing this opinion before the reader comes to the end of the volume.

The Second book treats of the early colonisation of the country now forming the territory of the United States; the religious character of the first European colonists—their religious institutions—and the state of the churches when the revolution took place by which the colonies became independent of the mother country.

The Third treats of the changes involved in and consequent upon that event—the influence of those changes—the character of the civil governments of the States—and the relations subsisting between those governments and the churches.

The Fourth exhibits the operations of the voluntary system in the United States, and the extent of its influence there.

The Fifth treats of the discipline of the churches—the character of American preaching—and the subject of revivals.

The Sixth is occupied with brief notices of the evangelical churches in the United States—their ecclesiastical polity and discipline—the doctrines peculiar to each—their history and prospects.

The Seventh treats in like manner of the unevangelical sects.

The Eighth shows what the churches are doing in the way of sending the gospel to other lands.

From the very nature of such a work it was requisite that the Author should consult many authorities. In order to procure the requisite materials he visited his native country last year, and so abundantly was he supplied with what he wanted, that in the actual execution of his task, he found himself in want of only one or two books and documents, and these of no essential importance.

But he should be guilty of great wrong were he not to acknowledge his obligations to many distinguished friends in America for their kind co-operation and aid. Without naming all who have anywise assisted him by furnishing necessary documents, or in communicating important facts, he cannot forbear to mention the names of the Rev. Drs. Dewitt, Hodge, Goodrich, Bacon, Anderson, Durbin, Emerson, and Schmucker, and the Rev. Messrs. Tracy, Berg, and Allen.[1] To the secretaries of almost all the religious societies and institutions in the country he is also greatly indebted for the reports, and in many cases, also, for the valuable hints they have furnished. Nor can he omit to acknowledge the kindness of Dr. Howe, Principal of the Institute for the Blind at Boston, the Rev. Mr. Weld, Principal of the Deaf and Dumb Asylum at Hartford, in Connecticut, and Dr. Woodward, Director of the Hospital for the Insane at Worcester, Massachusetts.

For the invaluable chapter on revivals, the reader as well as the Author, is indebted to the Rev. C. A. Goodrich, D.D., who has long been a distinguished professor in Yale college, at New-haven, in Connecticut, than whom no man in the United States is more capable of treating that subject in a judicious and truly philosophical manner.

Nor should the names of the Honourable Henry Wheaton, the Minister for the United States of America at the court of Prussia, and of Robert Walsh, Esq., now residing in Paris, be omitted. Among other obligations to the former of these gentlemen, the Author is indebted for some views which the reader will find in the Third book; and he has to thank the latter for many important suggestions which he has found much reason to appreciate in the course of his work. He makes this acknowledgement with the more pleasure, because Mr. Walsh is a Roman Catholic, and yet with a kindness and liberality in every way remarkable, he tendered his assistance with the full knowledge that the Author is a decided Protestant, and that his work, however liberal the spirit in which it is written, was to be of a thoroughly Protestant character.

---

[1] These gentlemen belong to the Reformed Dutch, Presbyterian, Congregational, Methodist, Lutheran, German Reformed, and Baptist churches, and are among the most distinguished ministers in the United States.

One word more to the English reader.   The Author deems it right to say, that his work was originally designed and primarily written for Germany and other countries on the continent of Europe.   Accordingly, it is fuller on some points than was absolutely requisite for British readers; these being, no doubt, better acquainted with the United States than are the inhabitants of the continent.

Deeply sensible that the work is far from perfect, he commends it nevertheless to the blessing of Him without whose favour nothing that is good can be accomplished.

GENEVA, (SWITZERLAND;)
    September, 1843.

CONTENTS.

BOOK I.

PRELIMINARY REMARKS.

BOOK II.

THE COLONIAL ERA.

BOOK III.

THE NATIONAL ERA.

BOOK IV.

THE VOLUNTARY PRINCIPLE DEVELOPED.

BOOK V.

THE CHURCH AND THE PULPIT IN AMERICA.

BOOK VI.

THE EVANGELICAL CHURCHES IN AMERICA.

BOOK VII.

BOOK VIII.

ERRATA.

Page   5, line 11, for *eastern*, read "western."

—   5, line 13, for *western*, read "eastern."

—   46, line 15, for *Chatta-Nootchee*, read "Chattahoochee."

—   50, line 14, for *Poiteoins*, read "Poitévins."

— 113, line 16, for *unrivalled*, read, "rivalled."

— 124, in Note 2, for *Huzzard*, read "Hazzard."

— 134, line 28, for *unsettlement*, read "unsettled state of the country."

— 159, line 19, for *waking*, read "making."

— 166, line 7, for *Dr. Millar*, read "D. Miller."

— 172, line 15, for *Littiz*, read "Lititz."

— 218, line 7, for *Charles I.* read "Charles II."

— 224, 3d Note, for *Dr. Schmuker*, read "Dr. Schmucker."

— 305, line 16, for 20,000, read "30,000."

— 328, line 15, after *Massachusetts*, add "who cannot read."

— 368, Union Theological Seminary was founded in 1821, not in "1812."

— 370, The Theological Seminary of the German Reformed Church is at *Mercersburg*, not "York."

— 385, line 19, for *Democratical*, read "Democratic."

— 388, Note, for *Turquei*, read "Turquie."

— 399, 1st line of 2d Note, for *expensive*, read "expansive."

— 408, line 5, for *Mr. Mill*, read "Mr. Will."

— 417, line 9, for *a few persons*, read "not a few persons."

— 438, 13th line of Note 1, for *devised*, read "denied."

— 449, last line but one, for *tribes*, read "whites."

— 521, lines 13 and 14 from bottom, instead of the words *differ both as to the proper mode of baptism, and its subjects, and also in church government*, read "differ from them on important, and in some cases, fundamental doctrines."

— 532, line 15, for *made members*, read "male members."

— 554, line 19, after the words *General Association*, add, " of Connecticut."

— 576, line 1, for *Pennsylvania*, read "Transylvania."

— 578, line 25, for *co-etus*, read "cœtus."

— 583, line 2, after the word *North*, add, "in the State of New York;" and in the 5th line, instead of *some state*, read "same state."

— 583, 11th line from bottom, for 35,000, read "3,500."

— 586, line 1, for *Mahlenburg*, read "Muhlenburg."

— 592, line 9 and 10, the words *American Education Society* are repeated.

— 593, line 21, for *Hans Honga*, read "Hans Houga."

— 630, line 14, for 1841, read "1842."

— 654, line 26, for *both which*, read "the latter of which."

— 669, line 16, for *Hitch*, read "Fitch."

— 671, line 21, for *Leisberger*, read "Zeisberger."

— 711, line 12 from the bottom, for *Rhenuis*, read "Rhenius."

— 714, line 7, instead of *ten millions*, read "tens of millions."

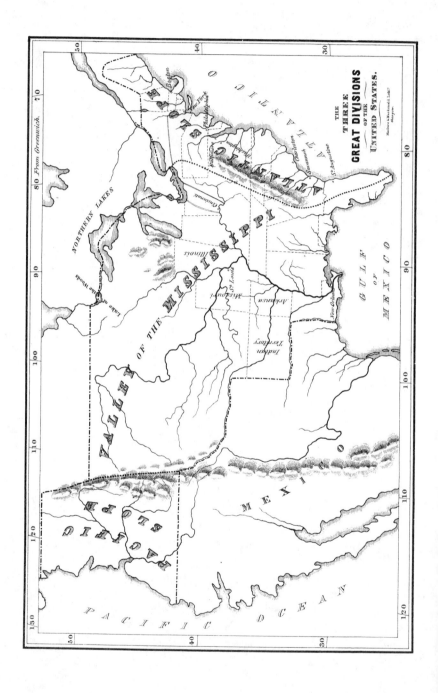

THE
THREE
GREAT DIVISIONS
OF THE
UNITED STATES.

Maclure & Macdonald Lith.rs Glasgow.

RELIGION IN AMERICA.

BOOK I.

PRELIMINARY REMARKS.

CHAPTER I.

GENERAL NOTICE OF NORTH AMERICA.

THE configuration of the continent of North America, at first view, presents several remarkable features. Spreading out like an open fan, with its apex towards the south, its coasts, in advancing northward, recede from each other with great regularity of proportion and correspondence, until, from being separated by only sixty miles at the isthmus of Darien, they diverge to the extent of 4500 miles; the east coast pursuing a north-eastern, and the west a north-western direction.

Parallel to these coasts, and at almost equal distances from them, there are two ranges of mountains. The eastern range, called the Alleghany or Apalachian, runs from south-west to north-east, at an average distance of 150 miles from the Atlantic. Its length is usually estimated at 900 miles.[1] Its greatest width, which is in Virginia and Pennsylvania, is about 120 miles. Rather a system than a range of mountains, it is composed of parallel ridges, generally maintaining the north-east and south-west direction of the whole range. But as it advances towards its northern extremity, and passes through the New England States, it loses much of its continuity, and gradually runs off into a chain of almost

[1] This is the length of the chain, considered as a continuous range, from the northern parts of Georgia and Alabama to the State of New York. Taken in the extensive sense in which it is spoken of in the text, the entire range exceeds 1500 English miles.

perfectly isolated mountains. The western or southern extremity, also, gradually sinks down into the hills of Georgia,
unless, indeed, we may consider it as disappearing in the low
central line of the peninsula of Florida. The north-eastern
end terminates in the ridges of Nova Scotia. The whole of
this range is within the limits of the United States, excepting
that part of it which stretches into the British provinces of
New Brunswick and Nova Scotia. We may remark, in passing, that although this mountain-range apparently separates
the waters which flow into the Atlantic ocean, from those which
fall into the Mississippi and the St. Lawrence, such is not
really the case. These mountains simply stand, as it were, on
the plateau or elevated plain on which those waters have their
origin. Rising often in the immediate vicinity of each other,
and often interlocking, these streams are not in the least affected
in their course by the mountains, the gaps and valleys of which
seem to have been made to accommodate them, instead of
their accommodating themselves to the shape and position of the
mountains. In a part of its northern extension, this range of
mountains seems to detach itself entirely from the plain where
those streams have their source, and lies quite east of it, so
that the streams that fall into the Atlantic, in making their
way to the south-east, as it were cut through the mountain
range, in its entire width.

When first discovered by Europeans, and for a century and
more afterwards, the long and comparatively narrow strip of
country between the Alleghany range and the Atlantic was
covered with an unbroken forest. The mountains, likewise,
up to their very summits, and the valleys that lay between
them, were clad with wood. Nothing deserving the name of a
field, or a prairie, was anywhere to be seen.

On the western side of the continent, as has been stated,
another range of mountains runs parallel to the coast of the
Pacific ocean. This range is a part of the immense system of
mountains, running from Cape Horn throughout the entire
length of the continent, and seems as if intended, like the back
bone in large animals, to give it unity and strength. It is by far
the longest in the world; [1] and bearing different names in differ-

----

[1] The entire length of this range is estimated to be 9000 English miles.

ent parts of its extent, it is the Andes in South America, the Cordilleras in Guatemala and Mexico, and the Rocky Mountains[1] in the north.

The long, and, in many parts, wide strip of land between the Oregon Mountains and the Pacific ocean, is claimed, on the north, by Russia; on the south, by Mexico; and in the middle, by England and the United States.

Between these two ranges of mountains, the Alleghany on the east, and the Oregon on the west, lies the immense Central Valley of North America,—wider in the north, than towards the south,—and reaching from the Northern ocean to the Gulf of Mexico. It is the most extensive valley in the world, and is composed of two vast sections, separated by a zig-zag line of table land. This ridge, which is of no great elevation, and which commences near the 42° of north lat. on one side, while it terminates near the 49° on the other, stretches across from the Alleghany system to the Oregon, and thus separates, also, the waters that flow southward into the Gulf of Mexico, from those flowing in the opposite direction into the northern seas. Thus the one section of this great valley inclines to the south, the other gently, nay, almost imperceptibly, descends towards the north. The former is drained by one great river and its numerous branches, called, in the pompous language of the aborigines of the country, the Mississippi, or Father of waters. The latter is drained by the river St. Lawrence, falling into the northern Atlantic; the Albany and other streams falling into Hudson's Bay; and by M'Kenzie's river, which falls into the Arctic ocean.

These great sections of this immense valley differ much in character. The northern possesses a considerable extent of comparatively elevated and very fertile land in its southern part; whilst towards the north it subsides to a low, monotonous, swampy plain, little elevated above the level of the ocean, and by reason of its marshes, bogs, and inhospitable climate, almost as uninhabitable as it is incapable of cultivation. The

---

[1] The proper name of this portion of the range is *Oregon*, a word of Indian origin, and which, whatever may be its original signification, is a much better name than what it has so long borne, and which has nothing distinctive about it, for all mountains are rocky.

A 2

southern section,—more commonly called the valley of the
Mississippi,—terminates on the low marshy coast of the Gulf
of Mexico; but, with the exception of the part of it which lies
on the upper streams of the Red river and La Platte, it everywhere abounds in fertile land, covered for the most part,
even yet, with noble forests, or adorned with beautiful prairies.
The St. Lawrence is the great river of the northern section or
basin, though not without a rival in the M'Kenzie's river;
whilst its southern rival, the Mississippi, flows almost alone in
its vast domain. There are, however, the Alabama and a few
small rivers on its left, and the Sabine, the Brazos, and some
others of lesser note on its right. The St. Lawrence boasts a
length of more than 2000 miles. That of the Mississippi exceeds
2500; and if the Missouri be considered the main upper branch,
as it ought to be, then it may fairly claim the honour of dragging
its vast length, with many a fold, through more than 4000 miles.
But though exceeded by the Mississippi in length, the St. Lawrence clearly has the advantage in the depth and noble expansion
of its waters towards its mouth, being navigable for the largest
ships of war as high as Quebec, 340 miles; and for large merchant
vessels to Montreal, 180 miles farther; whereas the Mississippi
does not reach the medium width of a mile, nor a depth in the
shallow places of the central channel, when the stream runs low,
of more than fifteen feet; so that, excepting when in flood, it is
not navigable by ships of 500 tons for more than 300 miles.
The St. Lawrence, and all the other considerable rivers of the
northern basin, pass through a succession of lakes, some of vast
extent, by which the floods caused by melting snows and heavy
rains, which otherwise, by rushing down in the spring, and
accumulating vast masses of ice in the yet unopened channel of
its lower and northern course, would spread devastation and
ruin over the banks, are collected in huge reservoirs, and permitted to flow off gradually during the summer months. Wonderful display of wisdom and beneficence in the arrangements
of divine creation and providence! But the Mississippi, as it
flows into the warmer regions of the south, needs no such provision; and hence with the exception of a few small lakes connected with the head streams of the upper Mississippi in the
west, and one or two connected with the Alleghany, a branch

of the Ohio, in the east, no lake occurs in the whole of the southern basin. Owing to this difference in these rivers, a sudden rise of three feet in the waters of the St. Lawrence would be more surprising than a rise of thirty feet in the Mississippi. But, in order that the country which borders upon the latter, may not be too much exposed to great and destructive inundation, the Creator has, in his wisdom, given to it a peculiar configuration. The inclined plane which slopes down from the Oregon mountains towards the east, is much wider than that sloping from the mountains on the opposite side. Hence the rivers from the eastern side of the valley have a much greater distance to traverse than those that drain the western slope, and the floods which they roll down in the spring, are of course proportionally later in reaching the lower Mississippi. . In fact, just as the floods of the Tennessee, the Cumberland, and the Ohio, have subsided, those of the Arkansas, the Missouri and upper Mississippi, begin to appear. If these all came down at once, the lower Mississippi, as the common outlet, by swelling to such an extent as to overflow its banks, would spread destruction far and wide over the whole delta. Such a calamity, or rather something approaching to it, does occasionally occur; but at long intervals, to teach men their dependence on divine providence, as well as to punish them for their sins.

Of the slope between the Oregon mountains and the Pacific, the northern part, occupied by Russia, is cold and little of it fit for cultivation; the middle, claimed by the United States and Great Britain, is said to be a fine country in many parts; whilst that occupied by Mexico has very great natural advantages. The country bordering on the Gulf of California is surpassed by none in North America for pleasantness of climate and fertility of soil.

On both sides of the upper Mississippi, as well as on both sides of the Missouri, there are extensive prairies,[1] as the

---

1 Much has been said and written on the origin of the prairies of North America; but after all, no perfectly satisfactory theory has yet been invented. The Indians know nothing on the subject. As to the barren prairies between the upper streams of the Red river and the Platte, mentioned in the text, under the name of the *Great American Desert*, the same cause produced them which produced the great Sahara in Africa, the utter sterility of the soil. But

French, who first explored that country, called them; that is, in many places there are districts, some of them very extensive, including hundreds and even thousands of acres of land, others smaller and resembling a field or meadow, which are covered in the summer with tall grass and a great variety of flowers; but on which scarcely anything in the shape of a tree is to be found. Many of these prairies possess a fertile soil; but others produce only a sort of stunted grass, and short weeds; and between the upper streams of the Red river and the La Platte, towards the Oregon mountains, there lies an extensive tract which has been called the great American Desert. The country there is covered with sand and detached rocks, or boulders, which have evidently come from the Oregon mountains, and is thinly clothed with a species of vegetation called buffalo grass. The prickly pear may often be seen spreading its huge leaves over the ground. Not a tree, and scarcely a bush, is to be met with in many places, for miles. Herds of buffalo sometimes traverse it, and a few straggling Indians are occasionally seen upon its outskirts. With these exceptions, the whole portion of North America, which is now either occupied or claimed by the people of the United States, was, when first visited by Europeans and for more than a century afterwards, one vast wilderness. The luxuriant vegetation with which it had been clothed, year after year, for ages, was destined only to decay and enrich the soil. Thus did the work of preparing it to be the abode of millions of civilized men, go silently and steadily on; the earth gathering strength, during this long repose, for the sustentation of nations which were to be born in the distant future. One vast and almost unbroken forest covered the whole continent, embosoming in its

as it relates to those fertile prairies which one finds in the States of Illinois and Missouri, and in the territories of Wisconsin and Iowa, the case is very different. In some respects, the theory that they owe their existence to the annual burning of the dry decayed grass, and other vegetable matter, in the autumnal months, seems plausible. It accounts well enough for the perpetuation of these prairies; but it fails to account for their origin. How is it that the same cause did not produce prairies in those parts of North America where none have ever existed; which yet have been, as far as we can learn, occupied by the aborigines as long as those in which the prairies are found. It is very likely that fire was one of the causes of their origin; but there may have been others not less efficient, as well as various concurring circumstances, with respect to which we are wholly in the dark.

sombre shadows alike the meandering streamlet and the mighty river, the retired bay and the beautiful and tranquil lake. A profound and solemn silence reigned everywhere, save when interrupted by the songs of the birds which sported amid the trees, the natural cries of the beasts which roamed beneath, the articulate sounds of the savage tribes around their wigwams, or their shouts in the chase or in the battle. The work of God, in all its simplicity, and freshness, and grandeur was seen every where; that of man almost no where; universal nature rested, and as it were kept Sabbath.

Two hundred years more pass away, and how widely different is the scene! Along the coasts, far and wide, tall ships pass and repass. The white sails of brig and sloop are seen in every bay, cove, and estuary. The rivers are covered with boats of every size, propelled by sail or oar. And in every water, the steam-boat, heedless alike of wind and tide, pursues its resistless way, vomiting forth steam and flame. Commerce flourishes along every stream. Cities are rising in all directions. The forests are giving way to cultivated fields, or verdant meadows. Savage life, with its wigwams, its blanket-covering, its poverty and its misery, yields on every side to the arts, the comforts, and even the luxuries of civilization.

CHAPTER II.

THE ABORIGINES OF NORTH AMERICA.

NORTH America, when discovered by Europeans, was in the occupancy of a great number of uncivilized tribes; some large, but most of them small, and although differing in some respects from one another, yet exhibiting indubitable evidence of a common origin. Under the belief that the country was a part of the East Indies, to reach which, by pursuing a westerly course, had been the object of their voyage, the companions of Columbus gave the name of Indians to those nations of the aborigines which they first saw. Subsequent, and more extensive exploration of the coasts of America, convinced them of their mistake, but the name thus given to the indigenous tribes has adhered to them to this day.

A striking similarity of organization pervades the tribes of North America.[1] All have the same dull vermilion, or cinnamon, or copper-colour complexion, differing wholly from the white, the olive, and the black varieties of the human family; all have the same dark, glossy hair, coarse, but uniformly straight. Their beards are generally of feeble growth, and instead of being permitted to grow long are almost universally eradicated. The eye is elongated, and has an orbit inclined to a quadrangular shape. The cheek-bones are prominent; the nose broad; the jaws projecting; the lips large and thick, though far less so than those of the Ethiopic race.

Yet there are not wanting considerable varieties in the organization and complexion of the aborigines of North America. Some nations are fairer skinned; some taller, and more slender than others; and even in the same tribe, there are often striking contrasts. Their limbs, unrestrained in childhood and youth by the appliances which civilization has invented, are generally better formed than those of the white men. The persons of the men are more erect, but this is not so with the women; these have become bowed down with the heavy burdens which, as slaves, they are habitually compelled to bear.

Their manner of life, when first discovered, was rude and barbarous. They had nothing that deserved the name of houses. Rude huts, mostly for temporary use, of various forms, but generally circular, were made by erecting a pole to support others leaning upon it as a centre, covering these with leaves and bark, and lining the interior with skins of the buffalo, the deer, the bear, &c. A hole at the top permitted the escape of the smoke; a large opening in the side answered the purpose of a door, a window, and sometimes of a chimney.

---

[1] This may be said also of all the aboriginal tribes of America entire, from the shores of the Northern ocean to the island of Terra del Fuego. But there was a vast difference in regard to civilization. The inhabitants of Mexico and Peru, when those countries were visited and conquered by Cortes and Pizarro, were far more civilized than the tribes of the portion of North America which we are considering. No remains of antiquity among the latter can be for a moment compared with those of the kingdom of Montezuma.

The skins of animals formed almost the whole covering of the body. Moccasins, and sometimes a sort of boot, made of the skins of the animals slain in the chase, were the only protection to their feet and legs in the coldest weather. The head was adorned with feathers and the beaks and claws of birds, the neck with strings of shells, and that of the warrior with the scalps of enemies slain in battle or in ambush.

Nothing like agriculture was known among them, save the planting of small patches of a species of corn which takes its name from them, and which, when parched, or when pounded, and made into paste and baked, is both palatable and nutritious. Having no herds, the use of milk was unknown. They depended mainly on the chase and on fishing for a precarious subsistence; not having the skill to furnish themselves with suitable instruments for the prosecution of either with much success. And when successful, as they had no salt, they could preserve an abundant supply of game, only by smoking it. Hence frequent famines among them, during the long cold months of winter.

Poets have sung of the happiness of the natural, in other words, of uncivilized life. But all who know anything of the aboriginal tribes of North America, even in the present times, when the Indians that border upon the abodes of civilized men live far more comfortably than their ancestors three hundred years ago, are well aware that their existence is a miserable one. During the excitements of the chase, there is an appearance of enjoyment; but such seasons are not long, and the utter want of occupation, and the consequent tedium of other periods, make the men in many cases wretched. Add to this the want of resources for domestic happiness; the evils resulting from polygamy; the depression naturally caused by the sickness of friends and relatives, without the means of alleviation; the gloomy apprehensions of death; and you cannot wonder that the red man should be miserable, and seek gratification in games of chance, the whiskey bottle, or the excitements of war. I have seen various tribes of Indians; I have travelled among them; I have slept in their poor abodes, and never have I seen them under any circumstances without being deeply impressed with the conviction of the misery of those especially who are not yet civilized.

They are not without some notions of a Supreme Power which governs the world, and of an Evil Spirit who is the enemy of mankind. But their theogony and their theology are alike crude and incoherent. They have no notion of a future resurrection of the body. Like children, they cannot divest themselves of the idea that the spirit of the deceased still keeps company with the body in the grave, or that it wanders in the immediate vicinity. Some, however, seem to have a confused impression that there is a sort of Elysium for the departed brave, where they will for ever enjoy the pleasures of the chase and of war. Even of their own origin they have nothing but a confused tradition, not extending back beyond three or four generations. As they have no calendars, and reckon their years only by the return of certain seasons, so they have no record of time past.

Though hospitable and kind to strangers to a remarkable degree, they are capable of the most diabolical cruelty to their enemies. The well authenticated accounts of the manner in which they sometimes treat their prisoners, would almost make us doubt whether they can belong to the human species. And yet we have only to recall to our minds scenes which have taken place in highly civilized countries, and almost within our own day, when Christian men have been put to death in its most horrible forms, by those who professed to be Christians themselves, to be convinced that when destitute of the grace of God there is nothing too devilish for man to do.

Some remains of the law written originally on the heart of man by his Creator, are to be found even among the Indian tribes. Certain actions are considered criminal and deserving of punishment, others are reckoned meritorious. The catalogue, it is true, of accredited virtues and vices is not extensive. Among the men, nothing can atone for the want of courage and fortitude. The captive warrior can laugh to scorn all the tortures of his enemies, and sing in the very agonies of a death inflicted in the most cruel manner, what may be termed a song of triumph, rather than of death! The narrations which the Jesuit (French) missionaries, who knew the Indian character better perhaps than any other white men that have ever written of them, have left, of what they themselves saw, are such as no civilized man can read without being perfectly appalled.[1] Roman fortitude never surpassed that displayed in innumerable instances, by the captured Indian warriors. In fact, nothing can be compared with it except that said to have been displayed by the Scandinavians, in their early wars with one another and with foreign enemies; and of which we have many accounts in the elder and younger Eddas, and in the Sagas.

Very many of the tribes speak dialects, rather than languages, distinct from those of their neighbours. East of the Mississippi river, and within the bounds of what is now the United States, when the colonization of the country by Europeans commenced, there were eight races or families of tribes, each comprehending those most alike in language and customs, and who constantly recognised each other as relatives. These were, 1. The ALGONQUINS, consisting of many tribes, scattered over the whole of the New England States, the southern part of New York, New Jersey, Pennsylvania, Delaware, Maryland, Virginia, and what is now Ohio, Indiana, Illinois, and Michigan. Being the most numerous of all the tribes, it occupied about half the territory east of the Mississippi, and south of the St. Lawrence and the lakes. 2. The SIOUX, or DACOTAS, living between lake Superior and the Mississippi. These were a small branch of the great tribe of the same name, to be found about the higher streams of that river, and between them and the Oregon mountains. 3. The HURON-IROQUOIS nations, who occupied all the northern and western parts of what is now the State of New York, and a part of Upper Canada. The most important of these tribes were the Five Nations, as they were long called, viz. the ·Mohawks, Oneidas, Onondagas, Cayugas, and Senecas. These were afterwards joined by the Tuscaroras from the Carolinas, a branch of the same great family, and then they

---

[1] The reader is referred to the work entitled: "Rélation de ce qui s'est passé en la Nouvelle France," in 1632, and the years following, down till 1660. Also to the work of Creuxius and the Journal of Marest. Much is to be found on the same horrible subject in Charlevoix's "Histoire de la Nouvelle France;" Lepage Dupratz's Histoire de la Louisiane; Jefferson's Notes on Virginia; Transactions of the American Philosophical Society, vol. i.; and the Letters of the late excellent Heckewelder, who was for forty years a missionary among the Delaware Indians, and whom the author of this work had the happiness of knowing intimately.

took the name of the Six Nations, by which title they are better known to history. 4. The CATAWBAS, who lived chiefly in what is now South Carolina. 5. The CHEROKEES, who lived in the mountainous parts of the two Carolinas, Georgia, and Alabama. Their country formed the southern extreme of the Alleghany mountains, and abounded in ridges and valleys. 6. The UCHEES, who resided in Georgia, in the vicinity of the site occupied at present by the city of Augusta. 7. The NATCHES, so famous for their tragical end, who lived on the banks of the Mississippi, in the neighbourhood of ,the present city of Natches. 8. The MOBILIAN tribes, or as Mr. Gallatin calls them, the MUSKHOGEE-CHOCTA, occupied the country which comprises now the States of Alabama and Mississippi, and the territory of Florida. The tribes which composed this family, or nation, are well known by the name of the Creeks, the Chickasas, the Choctas, and the Seminoles; to whom may be added the Yamasses, who formerly lived on the Savannah river; but exist no longer as a separate tribe.

The languages of these eight families of tribes are very different; and yet they are marked by strong grammatical affinities. It is most probable that the original colonies who settled America, come from whence they might, spoke different, though remotely related languages. All the languages of the aborigines of America are exceedingly complicated, regular in the forms of verbs, irregular in those of nouns, and admitting of changes by modifications of final syllables, initial syllables, and even, in the case of verbs, by the insertion of particles, in a way unknown to the languages of western Europe. They exhibit demonstrative proof that they are not the invention of those who use them, and that they who use them have never been a highly civilized people. Synthesis, or the habit of compounding words with words, prevails, instead of the more simple method of analysis, which a highly cultivated use of language always displays.[1] The Old English was much more clumsy than the modern. The same thing is true of the French and

---

[1] The reader who desires, may see much on the Indian languages in Humboldt's Voyages; Vater's Mithradates, vol. iii.; Baron Will. Humboldt; Publications of the Berlin Academy, vol. xliv.; Gallatin's Analysis; Duponceau, on Zeisberger; American Quarterly Review, vol. iii.; Heckewelder's two works respecting Indian manners, customs, etc.; and Mr. Schoolcraft's publications.

German—indeed of every cultivated language. The languages of the tribes bordering upon the frontier settlements of the United States, begin to exhibit visible evidences of the effect of contact with civilization. The half-breeds are also introducing modifications, which show that the civilized mind tends to simplify language; and the labours of the missionaries who have introduced letters among several tribes, are also producing great results, and leading to decided improvements.

A great deal has been said and written about the gradual wasting and disappearance of the tribes which once occupied the territories of the United States.

It is not intended to deny, that several tribes which figure in the history of the first settlement of the country by Europeans are extinct, and that several more are nearly so. Nor is it denied, that this has been partly occasioned by wars waged with them by the white or European population; still more, by the introduction of drunkenness and other vices of civilized men, and by the diseases incident to those vices. But whilst this may be all true, still the correctness of a good deal that has been said on this subject may well be questioned. Nothing can be more certain than that the tribes which once occupied the country now comprised within the United States, were at the epoch of the first settlement of Europeans on its shores, gradually wasting away, and had long been so; from the destructive wars waged with each other; from the frequent recurrence of famine, and sometimes from cold; and from diseases and pestilences against which they knew not how to protect themselves. If the Europeans introduced some diseases, it is no less certain that they found some formidable ones among the natives. A year or two before the Pilgrim Fathers reached the coast of New England, the very part of the coast where they settled was swept of almost its entire population by a pestilence. Several of the tribes which existed when the colonists arrived from Europe, were but the remnants, as they themselves asserted, of once powerful tribes, that had been almost annihilated by war, or by disease. This, as is believed, was the case with the Catawbas, the Uchees, and the Natches. Many of the branches of the Algonquin race, and some of those of the Huron-Iroquois, used to speak of the renowned days of their forefathers, when they were a powerful people. It is not easy, indeed, to estimate what was the probable number of the Indians who occupied, at the time of its discovery, the country east of the Mississippi and south of the St. Lawrence, comprising very nearly what may be called the settled portion of the United States; and from which the Indian race has disappeared in consequence of emigration, or other causes. But I am inclined to think with Mr. Bancroft, an American author who deserves the highest praise for the diligent research he has displayed in his admirable work on the United States, that there may have been in all not far from one hundred and eighty-thousand souls.[1] That a considerable number were slain in the numerous wars, carried on between them and the French and English, during our colonial days, and in our wars with them, after our independence; and that ardent spirits, also, have destroyed tens of thousands, cannot be doubted. But the most fruitful source of destruction to these poor "children of the wood" has been the occasional prevalence of contagious and epidemic diseases, such as the small pox, which a few years since cut off, in a few months, almost a whole tribe, the Mandans, on the Missouri.

Of the ALGONQUIN race, whose numbers two hundred years ago were estimated at ninety-thousand souls, only a few small tribes, and remnants of tribes, remain, probably not exceeding 20,000 persons. Of the HURON-IROQUOIS, not more probably than two or three thousands remain within the limits of the United States. The greater part who survive are to be found, I believe, in Canada. The SIOUX have not diminished. The CHEROKEES have increased. The CATAWBAS are nearly extinct as a nation. The remains of the UCHEES and NATCHES have been absorbed in Creeks and Choctas ; and indeed, it is certain, that not only straggling individuals, but also large portions of tribes, have united with other tribes, and so exist in a commingled state with them. It has happened that an entire conquered tribe has been compelled to submit to absorption among the conquerors. And finally, the MOBILIAN or MUSKHOGEE-CHOCTA tribes, taken as a whole, have decidedly increased, it is believed, within the last twenty-five years. They,

---

[1] Bancroft's History of the United States, vol. iii. p. 253.

with the Cherokees, and the remains of several tribes of the Algonquin race, are almost all collected together in the district of country assigned to them by the general government, west of the State of Arkansas. Respecting this plan, as well as respecting the general policy of the government of the United States towards the Indians, I shall speak fully in another place.

It is difficult to estimate with anything like absolute precision, the number of Indians that now remain as the descendants of the tribes which once occupied the country of which we have spoken. Without pretending to reckon those who have sought refuge with tribes far in the west, we may safely put it down at one hundred and fifteen thousand souls. Of what is doing to save them from physical and moral ruin, I shall speak hereafter.

The most plausible opinion respecting the origin of the aborigines of America is, that they are of the Mongolian race; and that they came to America from Asia, either by way of the Polynesian world,[1] or by Behring's Straits, or by the Aleutian islands, Mednoi island, and Behring group. Facts well attested prove this to have been practicable. That the resemblance between the aborigines of America and the Mongolian race is most striking, every one will testify who has seen both. "Universally and substantially," says the American traveller, Ledyard, respecting the Mongolians, "they resemble the aborigines of America."

CHAPTER III.

DISCOVERY OF THAT PART OF NORTH AMERICA WHICH IS COMPRISED IN THE UNITED
STATES.—THE EARLY AND UNSUCCESSFUL ATTEMPTS TO COLONISE IT.

As the American hemisphere had been discovered by expeditions sent out by Spain, that country claimed the entire continent as well as the adjoining islands; and to it a pope, as the vicegerent of God, had undertaken to cede the whole.

[1] Lang's View of the Polynesian Nations. Bancroft's History of the United States, vol. iii. p. 315—18.

But other countries having caught the spirit of distant adventure in quest of gold, these soon entered into competition with the nation whose sovereign had won the title of *Most Catholic Majesty;* and as all Christendom at that day bowed its neck to the spiritual dominion of the vicar of Christ, as the bishop of Rome claimed to be, they could not be refused a portion from the holy father, on showing that they were entitled to it. On the ground that Spain could not justly appropriate to herself any part of the American continent which she had not actually discovered, by coasting along it, by marking its boundaries, and by landing upon it, they created for themselves a chance of obtaining no inconsiderable share.

England was the first to follow in the career of discovery. Under her auspices, the continent itself was first discovered,[1] June 24, 1497, by the Cabots, John and Sebastian, father and son, the latter of whom was a native of that country, and the former a merchant adventurer from Venice, but at the time residing in England, and engaged in the service of Henry VII. By this event, a very large and important part of the coast of North America was secured to a country which, within less than half a century, was to begin to throw off the shackles of Rome, and to become, in due time, the most powerful of all Protestant kingdoms. He who "hath made of one blood, all nations of men, for to dwell on all the face of the earth, and hath determined the times before appointed, and the bounds of their habitation," had resolved in this manner to prepare a place to which, in ages then drawing near, those who should be persecuted for Christ's sake, might flee and find protection, and thus found a great Protestant empire. And yet, how near, if we may speak, was this mighty plan to be defeated. A Spanish discoverer, a year or two before, was diverted by some apparently trivial circumstance, from directing his course from Cuba, by the very coast which the Cabots afterwards sailed along. Had he done so, how different, in some momentous respects, might have been the state of the world at this day! We have here another illustration of the littleness of causes

---

1 Columbus had not at that epoch touched the continent, but had only discovered the West India islands.

with which the very greatest of human events are often connected, and of that superintending providence which rules in all things.

Spain, however, far from at once relinquishing her pretensions to a country thus discovered by England, insisted on claiming a large part of it, and for long extended the name of the comparatively insignificant peninsula with which she was compelled to be contented at last, over the whole tract reaching as far north as Chesapeake bay, if not farther. France, on the other hand, was not likely, under so intelligent and ambitious a monarch as Francis I., to remain an inactive spectator of maritime discoveries made by the nations on either side of her. Under her auspices Verrazzani, in 1524, and Cartier ten years afterwards, made voyages in search of new lands, so that soon she, too, had claims in America to prosecute. As the result of the former of those two enterprises, she claimed possession of the coast lying to the south of North Carolina, and extending, as was truly asserted, beyond the farthest point reached by the Cabots. Still more important were the results of Cartier's voyage. Having gone up the river St. Lawrence as far as the island on which Montreal now stands, he and Roberval made an ineffectual attempt to found a colony, composed of thieves, murderers, debtors, and other inmates of the prisons in France, on the spot now occupied by Quebec. Two other unsuccessful attempts at colonisation in America were made by France, the one in 1598, under the marquis de la Roche, the other in 1600, under Chauvin. At length, in 1605, a French colony was permanently established, under De Monts, a protestant, at the place now called Annapolis, in Nova Scotia, but not until after having made an abortive attempt within the boundaries of the present State of Maine. Quebec was founded in 1608, under the direction of Champlain who became the father of all the French settlements on North America. From that point the French colonists penetrated farther and farther up the St. Lawrence, until at length posts of their hunters and trappers, accompanied by Jesuit missionaries, reached the great lakes, passed beyond them, and descending the valley of the Mississippi, established themselves at Fort Du Quesne, Vincennes, Kaskaskia, and various other spots. Thus the greater part of the immense central valley of North America fell for a time into the hands of the French.

Nor was it only in the north that that nation sought to plant colonies. The failure of the French reformed in all their efforts even to secure for themselves mere toleration from their own government, naturally suggested the idea of expatriation, as the sole means that remained to them of procuring liberty to worship God according to his own Word. Even the prince of Condé, though of royal blood, nobly proposed to set the example of withdrawing from France, rather than be the occasion, by remaining in it, of perpetual civil war with the obstinate partisans of Rome; and in 1562, under the auspices of the brave and good Coligny, to whom, also, the idea of expatriation was familiar, two attempts were made by the Huguenots to establish themselves on the southern coast of North America. The first of these took place on the confines of South Carolina and seems at once to have failed. The second, which was on the river St. John's in Florida, survived but a few years. In 1565, it was attacked by the Spaniards, under Melendez, that nation claiming the country in right of discovery, in consequence of Ponce de Leon having landed upon it in 1512; and as religious bigotry was added to national jealousy in the assailants, they put almost all the Huguenots to death in the cruelest manner, "not as Frenchmen," they alleged, "but as Lutherans." For this atrocity the Spaniards were severely punished three years afterwards, when Dominick de Gourgues, a Gascon, having captured two of their forts, hanged his prisoners upon trees, not far from the spot where his countrymen had suffered, and placed over their bodies this inscription: "I do not this as unto Spaniards or mariners, but as unto traitors, robbers, and murderers."

With a view to encourage the colonisation of those parts of North America that were claimed by England, several patents were granted by the crown of that country, before the close of the sixteenth century. The enterprises, however, to which these led, universally failed. The most famous was that made in North Carolina, under a patent to Sir Walter Raleigh and others; it was continued from 1584 to 1588, but even the splendid talents and energy of its chief could not save his colony from final ruin. Though the details of this unsuccessful enterprise fill many a page in the history of the United States, strange to say, we are in absolute ignorance of the fate of the few remaining colonists that were left on the banks of the Roanoke; the most probable conjecture being, that they were massacred by the natives, though some affirm that they were incorporated into one of the Indian tribes. Two monuments of that memorable expedition remain to this day ; first, the name of Virginia, given to the entire coast by the courtier, in honour of his royal mistress, though afterwards restricted to a single province ; and next, the use of tobacco in Europe, Sir Walter having successfully laboured to make it an article of commerce between the two continents.

Some of the voyages made from England to America in that century for the mere purpose of traffic, were not unprofitable to the adventurers, but it was not until the following that any attempt at colonisation met with success. In this no one who loves to mark the hand of God in the affairs of men, and who has studied well the history of those times, can fail to be struck with the display it presents of the divine wisdom and goodness. For be it observed, that England was not yet ripe for the work of colonisation, and could not then have planted the noble provinces of which she was to be the mother country afterwards. The mass of her population continued until far on in the sixteenth century, to be attached to Rome ; her glorious constitution was not half formed until the century that followed. The Reformation, together with the persecutions, the discussions, and the conflicts that followed in its train, were all required, in order that minds and hearts might be created for the founding of a free empire, and that the principles and the forms of the government of England, might in any sense be fit for the imitation of her colonies.

Though England, when she first discovered America, thought only, as other nations had done, of enriching herself with mines of the precious metals and gems, on being undeceived by time, she indulged for a while the passion that followed for trafficking with the natives. But the commercial, as well as the golden age, if we may so speak, had to pass away, before men could be found who should establish themselves on that great continent with a view to agriculture as well as commerce; and who should look to the promotion of Christianity no less than to their secular interests. To this great and benevolent end, God was rapidly shaping events in the old world.

CHAPTER IV.

COLONISATION OF THE TERRITORIES NOW CONSTITUTING THE UNITED STATES, AT LENGTH ACCOMPLISHED.

THE first permanent colony planted by the English in America, was Virginia. Even in that instance, what was projected was a factory for trading with the natives, rather than a fixed settlement for persons expatriating themselves with an eye to the future advantage of their offspring, and looking for advantages which might reconcile them to it as their home. It was founded in 1607, by a company of noblemen, gentlemen, and merchants in London, by whom it was regarded as an affair of business, prosecuted with a view to pecuniary profit, not from any regard to the welfare of the colonists. These, consisting of forty-eight gentlemen, twelve labourers, and a few mechanics, reached Chesapeake bay in April, 1607, and having landed on the 13th of May, on the peninsula in the St. James's river, there they planted their first settlement, and called it James Town. There had been bestowed upon the company by royal charter, a zone of land, extending from the thirty-fourth to the thirty-eighth degree of north latitude, and from the Atlantic to the Pacific ocean, together with ample powers for administering the affairs of the colony, but reserving the legislative authority, and a control over appointments to the king—a species of double government under which few political privileges were enjoyed by the colonists.

What from the wilderness state of the country, the unfriendliness of the aborigines, the insalubrity of the climate, the arbitrary conduct of the company, and the unfitness of most of the settlers for their task, the infant colony had to contend with many difficulties. Yet not only did it gain a permanent foot-

ing in the country, but notwithstanding disastrous wars with
the Indians, insurrectionary attempts on the part of turbu-
lent colonists, misunderstandings with the adjacent colony of
Maryland, changes in its own charter and other untoward circumstances, it had become a powerful province long before the
establishment of North American independence. By a second
charter granted in 1609, all the powers that had been reserved
by the first to the king were surrendered to the company ; but
in 1624, that second charter was recalled, the company dissolved,
and the government of the colony assumed by the crown, which
continued thereafter to administer it in a general way, though
the internal legislation of the colony was left, for the most part,
to its own legislature.

Massachusetts was settled next in the order of time, and owed
its rise to more than one original colony. The first planted
within the province was that of New Plymouth, founded on the
west coast of Massachusetts bay, in 1620 ; but although it
spread by degrees into the adjacent district, yet it never acquired much extent. It originated in a grant of land from the
Plymouth company in England, an incorporation of noblemen,
gentlemen, and burgesses, on which King James had bestowed
by charter all the territories included within the forty-first and
forty-fifth degrees of north latitude, from the Atlantic to the
Pacific ocean. That company having undergone important
modifications, much more numerous settlements were made
under its auspices, in 1629 at Salem, and in 1630 at Boston,
from which two points colonisation spread extensively into the
surrounding country, and the province soon became populous
and powerful. A colony was planted in New Hampshire in
1631, and some settlements had been made in Maine a year or
two earlier ; but for long the progress of all these was slow. In
1636, the celebrated Roger Williams, being banished from Massachusetts, retired to Naragansett bay, and by founding there,
in 1638, the city of Providence, led to the plantation of a new
province, now forming the State of Rhode Island. In 1635,
the Rev. Thomas Hooker and John Haynes having led a colony
into Connecticut, settled at the spot where the town of Hartford
now stands, and rescued the valley of Connecticut from the
Dutch, who having invaded it from their province of New Ne-

therlands, had erected the fort called Good Hope on the right bank of the river. Three years thereafter, the colony of New Haven was planted by two puritan non-conformists, the Rev. John Davenport and Theophilus Eaton, who had first retired to Holland on account of their religious principles, and then left that country for Boston, in 1637. Thus, with the exception of Vermont, which originated in a settlement of much later date, drawn chiefly from Massachusetts and New Hampshire, we see the foundation of all the New England States laid within twenty years from the arrival of the pilgrim fathers at Plymouth.

Meanwhile Maryland, so called in honour of Henrietta Maria, daughter of Henry IV. of France, and wife of Charles I., had been colonised. The territory forming the present State of that name, though included in the first charter of Virginia, upon that being cancelled and the company being dissolved, reverted to the king, and he, to gratify his feelings of personal regard, bestowed the absolute proprietorship of the whole upon Sir Charles Calvert, the first Lord Baltimore, and his legal heirs in succession. Never was there a more liberal charter. The statutes of the colony were to be made with the concurrence of the colonists; thus securing to the people a legislative government of their own. Sir Charles was a Roman Catholic, but his colony was founded on principles of the fullest toleration; and though he died before the charter in his favour had passed the great seal of the kingdom, yet all the royal engagements being made good to his son Cecil, who succeeded to the title and estates, the latter sent out a colony of about two hundred persons, most of whom were Roman Catholics, and many of them gentlemen, accompanied by his brother Leonard. Maryland, though subjected to many vicissitudes, proved prosperous upon the whole. Though the Roman Catholics formed at first the decided majority, the Protestants became by far the more numerous body in the end, and, with shame be it said, enacted laws depriving the Roman Catholics of all political influence in the colony and tending to prevent their increase.

The first colony in the State of New York was that planted by the Dutch, about the year 1614, on the southern point, it is supposed, of the island where the city of New York now stands. The illustrious English navigator Hudson, having been in the

employment of the Dutch at the time of his discovering the
river that bears his name, Holland claimed the country bordering upon it, and gradually formed settlements there, the first
of which, called New Netherlands, was situate on an island
immediately below the present city of Albany. Hudson being
supposed to have been the first European that sailed up the
Delaware, the Dutch claimed the banks of that river also. But
their progress as colonists in America was slow. Though Holland was nominally a republic, yet the liberties of her people
were not sufficiently understood or regarded, to induce the
industrious artisan, or tiller of the ground, to emigrate to her
colonies,[1] nor has she ever abounded in the proper materials
for making good colonists. The country presentin : i ut a
limited scope for agriculture, the people are mostly en;a, (d in
trade or in the arts.

Pursuing in the new world the same selfish principles which
made the Dutch mercantile aristocracy the worst enemies of
their country in the old, the New Netherlands colonists were
allowed little or no share in the government, and accordingly,
notwithstanding the greatest natural advantages, the progress
of the colony was very slow. New Amsterdam, which, in consequence of such advantages, might have been expected even to
outstrip the mother city, as she has since done under the name
of New York, remained but an inconsiderable village. The
vicinity of New England provoked comparisons that could not
fail to make the Dutch colonists discontented with their institutions, At length, in 1664, the English conquered and took
possession of all the Dutch colonies in North America, which

---

[1] Here the author, if he refers to Holland, not her colonies, seems to forget
that not the enjoyment of civil and religious liberty, but the reverse was the
grand spur to emigration in the 17th century, and that the Dutch owed to their
decided superiority to other nations in that respect, so extraordinary a development of their resources at home, that not only was there no surplus population
to overflow into distant colonies, but foreigners had to be employed in their
armies, and even in carrying on the common useful arts. I have heard, for
example, that the bakers and chimney sweeps of Holland were mostly Italians
at one time. With the decline of Dutch prosperity and the almost total annihilation of some extensive manufactures, this state of things was much altered
towards the close of the eighteenth century, and as a remedy for the numerous
unemployed poor, a plan has been attempted in our own day for cultivating
poor soils by removing the pauper population from the cities and towns, and
employing them in tilling the ground. But these form too indigent a class for
distant colonisation, and the author has truly stated some of the causes that
make Holland still wanting in proper materials for that purpose.—Ed.

by that time, in addition to their settlements on the Hudson, extended to the eastern part of New Jersey, Staten Island, and the western extremity of Long Island, besides a detached settlement on the banks of the Delaware, with a population not exceeding in all ten thousand souls. New Netherlands was granted by Charles II. to his brother the Duke of York, from whom the colony and its capital took the name of New York. The voice of the people was now, for the first time, heard in its legislature; it began thenceforth to advance rapidly in population, and notwithstanding occasional seasons of trial and depression, gave early promise of what it was one day to become.

New Jersey was likewise granted to the Duke of York, who, in 1664, handed it over to Lord Berkeley and Sir George Carteret, both proprietors of Carolina. Difficulties, however, having arisen between the colonists and the lords superior with regard to the quit-rents payable by the former, that province was gladly surrendered by the latter upon certain conditions to the crown, and was for some time attached to New York, within twenty years after all the Dutch possessions had fallen into the hands of the English. West Jersey was afterwards purchased by a company of Friends, or Quakers, and a few years later, in 1680, William Penn, previous to his undertaking to plant a colony on a larger scale in Pennsylvania, purchased East Jersey, with the view of making it an asylum for his persecuted co-religionists. Finally, East and West Jersey being united as one province under the direct control of the crown, obtained a legislature of its own, and enjoyed a gradual and steady prosperity down to the revolution by which the colonies were severed from England.

Pennsylvania, as is indicated by its name, was founded by the distinguished philanthropist we have just mentioned, but he was not the first to colonise it. This was done by a mixture of Swedes, Dutch, and English, who had for years before occupied the right bank of the Delaware, both above the point where Philadelphia now stands, and many miles below. The charter obtained by William Penn from Charles II. dates from 1681. On the 27th of October in the following year, the father of the new colony having landed on his vast domain in America, immediately set about the framing of a constitution, and began to found a capital, which was destined to become one of the finest cities in the western hemisphere. The government, like that established by the Quakers in New Jersey, was altogether popular. The people were to have their own legislature, whose acts, however, were not to conflict with the just claims of the proprietor, and were to be subject to the approval of the crown alone. The colony soon became prosperous. The true principles of peace, principles that form so conspicuous a part of the Quaker doctrines, distinguished every transaction in which the aborigines were concerned. It was the glory of Pennsylvania that it never did an act of injustice to the Indians.

The territory belonging to the state of Delaware was claimed by Penn and his successors, as included in the domain described in their charter, and for a time formed a part of Pennsylvania, under the title of the Three Lower Countries. But the mixture of Swedes, Dutch, and English by whom it was occupied, were never reconciled to this arrangement, and having at last obtained a government of its own, Delaware became a separate province.

The settlement of the two Carolinas began with straggling emigrants from Virginia, who sought to better their fortunes in regions farther south, and were afterwards joined by others from New England, and also from Europe. At length, in 1663, the entire region lying between the thirty-sixth degree of north latitude, and the river St. John's in Florida, was granted to a proprietory company in England, which was invested with most extraordinary powers. The proprietors, eight in number, were Lord Ashley Cooper, better known as the Earl of Shaftesbury, Clarendon, Monk, Lord Craven, Sir John Colleton, Lord John and Sir William Berkeley, and Sir George Carteret. Their grand object was gain, yet the celebrated John Locke, at once a philosopher and a Christian, was engaged to make "constitutions," or a form of government, for an empire that was to stretch from the Atlantic to the Pacific. The result of the philosophical lawgiver's labours, was such as the world had never seen the like of before. The proprietors were to form a close corporation; the territory was to be partitioned out into counties of vast extent, each of which was to have an Earl or landgrave, and two barons or caciques, who as lords of manors, were to have judicial authority within their respective estates. Tenants of ten acres were to be attached as serfs to the soil, to be subject to the jurisdiction of their lords without appeal, and their children were to continue in the same degradation for ever! The possession of at least fifty acres of land was to be required, in order to the enjoyment of the elective franchise, and of five hundred acres in order to a man's being eligible as a member of the colonial parliament or legislature. These constitutions, into the further details of which we cannot enter, were attempted to be introduced, but were soon rejected in North Carolina; and after a few years' struggle, were thrown aside also in South Carolina, which had been separated from the northern province. The colonists adopted for themselves forms of government analogous to those of the other colonies; the proprietory company was after a while dissolved; the Carolinas fell under the direct control of the crown, but were governed by their own legislatures. Their prosperity was slow, having been frequently interrupted by serious wars with the native tribes, particularly the Tuscaroras, which, as it was the most powerful, was for long, also, the most mischievous.

Last of all the original thirteen provinces in the order of time, came Georgia, which was settled as late as 1732, by the brave and humane Oglethorpe. The colonists were of mixed origin, but the English race predominated. Although it had difficulties to encounter almost from the first; yet notwithstanding wars with the Spaniards in Florida, hostile attacks from the Indians, and internal divisions, Georgia acquired by degrees a considerable amount of strength.

Such is a brief notice of the thirteen original North American provinces, which by the revolution of 1775-1783, were transformed into as many states. They all touch more or less on the Atlantic, and stretch to a greater or less distance into the interior. Virginia, Georgia, Pennsylvania, and North Carolina, are the largest; Rhode Island and Delaware are the smallest.

In 1803, the French colony of Louisiana, now the State of that name, together with the territories since comprised in the States of Arkansas and Missouri, and an almost indefinite tract lying westward of these two last, was purchased by the United States for fifteen millions of dollars. And in 1821, the Spanish colony of Florida, comprising the peninsula which used to be called East Florida, and a narrow strip of land on the gulph of Mexico, called West Florida, was purchased by the same government for five millions of dollars.   Both purchases now form, of course, part of the great North American confederation.

CHAPTER V.

INTERIOR COLONISATION OF THE COUNTRY.

AFTER the short account we have given of the first establishment of the thirteen original provinces by successive arrivals of colonists from Europe, on the sea coast and the banks of the larger streams, we proceed to say something of the progress of colonisation in the interior of the country.

A hundred and twenty-five years, it will be observed, elapsed between the foundation of the first and the last of these provinces; also, that with the exception of New York and Delaware, which received their first European inhabitants from Holland and Sweden, they were all originally English; but that, eventually, these two were likewise included in English patents, and their Dutch and Swedish inhabitants merged among the English.

All these colonies were of slow growth, ten and even twenty years being required in several instances, before they could be regarded as permanently established.   Virginia, the earliest, was more than once on the point of being broken up.   Indeed, we may well be surprised, that when the colonists that survived the ravages of disease and attacks from the Indians, were still further reduced in their number by the return of a part of them to England, the remainder did not become disheartened and abandon the country in despair.   The Plymouth colonists lost upon the very spot where they settled, half their number within six months from their arrival; and terrible, indeed, must have been the sorrows of the dreary winter of 1620-21, as endured by those desolate yet persevering exiles.   But they had a firm faith in God's goodness ; they looked to the future; they felt that they had a great and a glorious task to accomplish, and that although they themselves might perish in attempting it, yet their children would enjoy the promised land.

Stout hearts were required for such enterprises. Few of the colonists were wealthy persons, and as those were not the days of fine packets, or of large and well appointed merchant vessels, the voyage had to be made in small and crowded ships. The inconveniences, to say nothing of the sickness that attended it, were but ill calculated to nerve the heart for coming trials; and as the colonists approached the coast, the boundless and solemn forests that stretched before them, the strangeness of every object that filled the scene, the absence of all tillage and cultivation, and of a village or house to give them shelter, and the uncouth and even frightful aspect of the savage inhabitants, must have damped the boldest spirits. In the case of Plymouth and some others, the settlers arrived during winter, when all nature wore her gloomiest attire. The rudest hovels were the only abodes that could be immediately prepared for their reception, and for weeks together there might only be a few days of such weather as would permit their proceeding with the operations required for their comfort. Not only conveniences and luxuries such as the poorest in the mother country enjoyed, but even the necessaries of life, were often wanting. Years had to be passed before any considerable part of the forest could be cleared, comfortable dwellings erected, and pleasant gardens planted out. Meanwhile disease and death would enter every family; dear friends and companions in the toils and cares of the enterprise, would be borne, one after another, to the grave. To these causes of depression there were often added the horrors of savage warfare, by which some of the colonies were repeatedly decimated, and during which the poor settler, for weeks and months together, would not know, on retiring to rest, whether he should not be awakened by the heart-quailing war-hoop of the savages around his house, or by finding the house itself in flames. Ah! what pen can describe the horror that fell upon many a family, in almost all the colonies, not once but often, when aroused by false or real alarms? Who can depict the scenes in which a father, ere he received the fatal blow himself, was compelled to see his wife and children fall by the tomahawk before his eyes, or be dragged into a captivity worse than death? With such depressing circumstances to try the hearts of the colonists,—circumstances that can be fully understood by those only who have passed through them, or who have heard them related with the minute fidelity of an eye-witness—who can wonder that the colonies advanced but slowly?

Still, as I have said, they gradually gained strength. At the revolution in England of 1688, that is, eighty-one years after the first settlement of Virginia, and sixty-eight after that of Plymouth, the population of the colonies, then twelve in number, was estimated at about two hundred thousand, which might be distributed thus: Massachusetts, including Plymouth and Maine, may have had forty-four thousand; New Hampshire and Rhode Island, including Providence, six thousand each; Connecticut, from seventeen to twenty thousand; making up seventy-five thousand for all New England; New York, not less than twenty thousand; New Jersey, ten thousand; Pennsylvania and Delaware, twelve thousand; Maryland, twenty-five thousand; Virginia, fifty thousand; and the two Carolinas, which then included Georgia, probably not fewer than eight thousand souls.

After having confined their settlements for many years within a short distance, comparatively speaking, from the coast, the colonists began to penetrate the inland forests, and to settle at different points in the interior of the country, in proportion as they considered themselves strong enough to occupy them safely. Where hostility on the part of the aborigines was dreaded, these settlers kept together as much as possible, and established themselves in villages. This was particularly the case in New England, where, from the soil being less favourable to agriculture, colonisation naturally assumed the compact form required for the pursuits of trade and the useful arts, as well as for mutual assistance when exposed to attack.[1] As the New England colonists had all along devoted themselves particularly to the

---

1 This clustering together of the colonists, and the title of *township* given to the parishes, or what the French call *communes*, seems to have given rise to the title of *city* being applied to so many towns in America.— ED.

fisheries and other branches of commerce, their settlements were for long to be found chiefly on the coast, and at points affording convenient harbours. But it was much otherwise in the south. In Virginia, in particular, the colonists were induced to settle along the banks of rivers to very considerable distances, their main occupation being the planting of tobacco, and trading to some extent with the Indians. In the Carolinas, again, most hands being employed in the manufacture of tar, turpentine, and rosin, or in the cultivation of rice, indigo, and eventually of cotton, the colonial settlements took a considerable range whenever there was peace with the Indians in their vicinity. Where there was little or no commerce, and agricultural pursuits of different kinds were the chief occupations of the people, there could be few towns of much importance; and so much does this hold at the present day, that there is not a city of twenty thousand inhabitants in all the five southern Atlantic States, with the exception of Baltimore in Maryland, and Charleston in South Carolina.

Even at the commencement of the revolutionary war, in 1775, the colonies had scarcely penetrated to the Alleghany or Appalachian mountains in any of the provinces that reach thus far, and their whole population was confined to the strip of land interposed between those mountains and the Atlantic ocean. It is true that immediately after the treaty of Paris in 1762, by which England acquired the Canadas and the valley of the Mississippi, excepting Lousiana, which remained with France, or rather, was temporarily ceded to Spain, a few adventurers began to pass beyond the mountains, and this emigration westward continued during the war of the revolution. But when peace came in 1783, I much doubt if there were twenty thousand Anglo-Americans in western Pennsylvania, western Virginia, Kentucky and Tennessee. These were but the advanced posts of the immense host about to follow, and for many years after the peace, the colonisation of the interior was slower than might be supposed. The population of the thirteen provinces at the commencement of the revolution, is not certainly known, but is believed to have exceeded three millions and a half, slaves included. No doubt, the population of the sea-board increased with considerable rapidity, and Vermont was not long of being added to the original thirteen states, making fourteen in all upon the Atlantic slope. They amount now to fifteen, by Maine, which was long a sort of province to Massachusetts, having become a separate state in 1820. After the establishment of independence, danger from the aborigines ceased to be apprehended throughout the whole country situate between the Alleghany mountains and the Atlantic ocean. The remains of the numerous tribes, its former inhabitants, had with some exceptions in New England, New York and the Carolinas, retired to the west, and there they either existed apart, or had become merged in other and kindred tribes.

But it was much otherwise in the great region to the west of the Appalachian range. There many of the Indian tribes occupied the country in all their pristine force, and were the more to be dreaded by settlers from the States, in as much as they were supposed to be greatly under the influence of the British government in Canada, and as unkindly feelings long subsisted between the Americans and their English neighbours, each charging the other, probably not without justice, with exciting the Indians, by means of their respective agents and hunters, to commit acts of violence. Excepting in some parts of western Pennsylvania and eastern Tennessee, there was little security for American settlers in the west, from 1783 until 1795. The first emigrants to Ohio suffered greatly from the Indians; two armies sent against them in the western part of that State under Generals Harmer and St. Clair, were defeated and shockingly cut to pieces; and not until they had received a dreadful defeat from General Wayne on the river Miami-of-the-lake, [1] was there anything like permanent peace established. But as a prelude to the war between the United States and Great Britain, commenced in 1812, and ended in 1815, the Indian tribes again became troublesome, particularly in Indiana, and in the south-eastern part of the valley of the Mississippi, forming now the State of Alabama. The Creeks, a powerful tribe of the Muskhogee race, then occupied that country, and it was not until defeated in many battles and skirmishes that they were reduced to peace. In point of fact, perfect security from Indian hostili-

[1] On the river Miami which flows into lake Erie, and so called to distinguish it from the Miami that falls into the Ohio.

ties has prevailed throughout the west only since 1815 ; since that, there have been the insignificant war with Black Hawk, a Sioux chief, which took place a few years ago, and the still more recent war with the Seminoles in Florida—exceptions not worth special notice, as they in no wise affected the country at large.

It is now (1842,) about sixty years since the tide of emigration from the Atlantic States set fairly into the valley of the Mississippi, and though no great influx took place in any one year during the first thirty-five of that period, it has wonderfully increased during the last twenty-five. When this emigration westward first commenced, all the necessaries that the emigrants required to take with them from the east, had to be carried on horseback, no roads for wheeled carriages having been opened through the mountains. On arriving at the last ridge over-looking the plains to the west, a boundless forest lay stretched out before those pioneers of civilisation, like an ocean of living green. Into the depths of that forest they had to plunge. Often would whole years of toil and suffering roll away before they could establish themselves in comfortable abodes. The climate and the diseases peculiar to the different localities, were unknown. Hence, fevers of a stubborn type cut many of them off. They were but partially acquainted with the mighty rivers of that vast region, beyond knowing that their common outlet was in the possession of foreigners, who imposed vexatious regulations upon their infant trade. The navigation of those long rivers could be carried on only in flat bottomed boats, keels, and barges. To descend them was not unattended with danger, but to ascend by means of sweeps and oars, by poling, warping, *bush-whacking*,[1] and so forth, was laborious and tedious beyond conception.

Far different are the circumstances of those colonists now!

---

[1] The word *bush-whacking* is of western origin, and signifies a peculiar mode of propelling a boat up the Mississippi, Ohio, or any other river in that region, when the water is very high. It is this : instead of keeping in the middle of the stream, the boat is made to go along close to one of the banks, and the men who guide it, by catching hold of the boughs of the trees which over-hang the water, are enabled to drag the boat along. It is an expedient resorted to more by way of change than anything else. Sometimes it is possible, at certain stages of the rivers, to go along for miles in this way. Even to this day, the greater portion of the banks of the rivers of the west are covered with almost uninterrupted forests.

The mountains at various points are traversed by substantial highways, and still further to augment the facilities for intercourse with the vast western valleys, canals and railroads are in progress. It is accessible also, from the south, by vessels from the gulf of Mexico, as well as from the north by the lakes, on whose waters from fifty to a hundred steamboats now pursue their foaming way. As for the navigable streams of the valley itself, besides boats of all kinds of ordinary construction, nearly, if not quite, four hundred steamboats ply upon their waters. [1] And now, instead of being a boundless forest uninhabited by civilised men, as it was a little more than sixty years ago, the far west contains no fewer than eleven regularly constituted States, and two Territories which will soon be admitted as States into the union, the population having meanwhile advanced from ten or twenty thousand Anglo-American inhabitants to above six millions.[2]

Generally speaking, the various sections of the valley of the Mississippi may be said to have been colonised from parts of the Atlantic coast, corresponding with them as nearly as possible in point of latitude. This is easily accounted for, emigrants from the east to the west naturally wishing to keep as much as they can within the climate which birth and early life have rendered familiar and agreeable, though a regard to their health may compel others to seek a change by passing to the south of their original latitude. Generally speaking, the New

[1] There are more than fifty on lake Erie alone.

[2] It may be worth while to give the names of those States and Territories, their extention in English square miles, and their population according to the census of 1840. They are as follows:

	Sqr. miles.		Pop. in 1840.
Ohio,	40,260	——	1,519,467
Indiana,	36,500	——	685,868
Michigan,	59,700	——	212,267
Illinois	57,900	——	476,183
Kentucky,	40,500	——	779,828
Tennessee,	40,200	——	829,210
Missouri,	63,800	——	383,702
Arkansas,	60,700	——	97,574
Alabama,	52,900	——	590,756
Mississippi,	47,680	——	375,651
Louisiana,	49,300	——	352,411
Territories,—			
Wisconsin,		——	30,945
Iowa,			43,112

Total, 6,376,972

York tide of emigration in its westward course, penetrated and settled the northern and western parts of that province, and advancing still farther in the direction of the setting sun, entered the northern parts of Ohio, Indiana, and Illinois, extended over the whole of Michigan, and is now stretching into the territory of Wisconsin. That from the southern counties of the same State, from New Jersey, and eastern Pennsylvania, first occupied western Pennsylvania, and then extended into the central districts of Ohio and Indiana. The Maryland and Virginian column colonised western Virginia and Kentucky, and then dispersed itself over the southern parts of Ohio, Indiana, and Illinois, while that from North Carolina, after colonising Tennessee, is reaching into Missouri and Iowa. The South Carolina column, mingling with that of Georgia, after having covered Alabama and a great part of the State of Mississippi, is now extending itself into Arkansas.

This account of the progress of colonisation westward, as a general statement, is remarkably correct, and it furnishes a better key to the political, moral, and religious character of the west than any other that could be given. The west, in fact, may be regarded as the counterpart of the east, after allowing for the *exaggeration*, if I may so speak, which a life in the wilderness tends to communicate for a time to manners and character, and even to religion, but which disappears as the population increases, and the country acquires the stamp of an older civilisation. Stragglers may, indeed, be found in all parts of the west, come from almost all parts of the east, and many emigrants from Europe too, Germans especially, enter by New Orleans, and from that find their way by steamboats into Indiana, Illinois, Missouri, Wisconsin, and Iowa. But all these form exceptions that hardly invalidate the general statement.

CHAPTER VI.

PECULIAR QUALIFICATIONS OF THE ANGLO-SAXON RACE FOR THE WORK OF
COLONISATION.

APART altogether from considerations of moral and religious character, and the influence of external circumstances, we may remark that the Anglo-Saxon race possesses qualities peculiarly adapted for successful colonisation. The characteristic perseverance, the spirit of personal freedom and independence, that have ever distinguished that race, admirably fit a man for the labour and isolation necessarily to be endured before he can be a successful colonist. Now, New England, together with the States of New York, New Jersey, Delaware, and Pennsylvania, with the exception of Dutch and Swedish elements too inconsiderable to affect the general result, were all colonised by people of Anglo-Saxon origin. And assuredly they have displayed qualities fitting them for their task, such as the world has never witnessed before. No sooner have the relations between the colonies and the aborigines permitted it to be done with safety, and sometimes even before that, than we find men and families ready to penetrate the wilderness, there to choose, each for himself or themselves, some fertile spot for a permanent settlement. If friends could be found to accompany him and settle near him, so much the better; but if not, the bold emigrant would venture alone far into the trackless forest, and surmount every obstacle single-handed, like a fisherman committing himself to the deep and passing the livelong day at a distance from the shore. Such was the experience of many of the first colonists of New England; such that of the earliest settlers in New York, New Jersey, Delaware, and Pennsylvania; such in our own day has been the case with many of the living occupants of Ohio, Indiana, Illinois, Michigan, and Wisconsin; and thus is colonisation advancing in all those territories at the present moment.

Living on the lands which they cultivate, the agricultural inhabitants of the New England and middle States are very much dispersed; the country far and wide is dotted over with the dwellings of the landholders and those who assist them in the cultivation of the soil. For almost every land-owner tills his property himself, assisted by his sons, by young men hired for that purpose, or by tenants who rent from him a cottage and a few acres. Field work in all those States is performed by men alone; a woman is never seen handling the plough, the hoe, the axe, the sickle, or the scythe, unless in the case of foreign emigrants who have not yet adopted American usages in this respect.

Now it is in this isolated and independent mode of life, that our men best fitted to penetrate and settle in the wilderness are trained; and from this, what may be emphatically called our frontier race, has sprung and is recruited from time to time.

Take the following case as an illustration of the process that is continually going on on the frontier. A man removes to the west, he purchases a piece of ground, builds a house, and devotes himself to the clearing and tillage of his forest acres. Ere long he has rescued a farm from the wilderness, and has reared a family upon it. He then divides his land among his sons, if there be enough for a farm to each of them; if not, each receives money enough to buy one, as he comes of age. Some may settle on lands bestowed on them by their father; others, preferring a change, may dispose of their portion and proceed, most commonly unmarried, to "the frontier country" as it is called, that is, to those parts of the west where the public lands are not yet sold. There he chooses out as much as he can conveniently pay for, receiving a title to it from the district land office, and proceeds to make for himself a home. This is likely to be in the spring. Having selected a spot for his dwelling, generally near some spring or where water may be had by digging a well, he goes round and makes the acquaintance of his neighbours, residing within the distance, it may be, of several miles. A day is fixed for building him a house, upon which those neighbours come and render him such efficient help, that in a single day he will find a log-house constructed, and perhaps covered with clap boards, and having apertures cut out for the doors, windows, and chimney. He makes his floor at once of rough boards riven from the abundant timber of the surrounding forest, constructs his doors and erects a chimney.

Occupying himself, while interrupted in out-door work by rainy weather, in completing his house, he finds it in a few weeks tolerably comfortable, and during fair weather he clears the underwood from some ten or fifteen acres, kills the large trees by notching them round so as to arrest the rise of the sap, and sows the ground with Indian corn, or maize as it is called in Europe.   He can easily make, buy, or hire a plough, a harrow, and a hoe or two.   If he find time, he surrounds his field with a fence of stakes.   At length, after prolonging his stay until his crop is beyond the risk of serious injury from squirrels and birds, or from the growth of weeds, he shuts up his house, commits it to the care of some neighbour, living perhaps one or two miles off, and returns to his paternal home, which may be from fifty to three hundred miles distant from his new settlement.   There he stays until the month of September, then marries, and with his young wife, a waggon and pair of horses to carry their effects, a few cattle or sheep, or none, according to circumstances, sets out to settle for life in the wilderness.   On arriving at his farm, he sows wheat or rye among his standing Indian corn, then gathers in this last, and prepares for the winter.   His wife shares all the cares incident to this humble beginning.   Accustomed to every kind of household work, she strives by the diligence of her fingers to avoid the necessity of going to the merchant who has opened his store at some village among the trees, perhaps some miles off, and there laying out the little money they may have left.   With economy and health they gradually become prosperous.   The primitive log-house gives place to a far better mansion, constructed of hewn logs, or of boards, or of brick or stone.   Extensive and well fenced fields spread around, ample barns stored with grain, stalls filled with horses and cattle, flocks of sheep and herds of hogs all attest the increasing wealth of the owners.   Their children grow up, perhaps to pursue the same course, or as their inclinations may lead, to choose some other occupation, or to enter one of the learned professions.

This sketch will give the reader some idea of the mode in which colonisation advances among the Anglo-Saxon race of the Middle and New England States of America.   Less Anglo-Saxon in their origin, and having all things modified by slavery, the Southern States exhibit colonisation advancing in a very

different style.   When an emigrant from those States removes
to the "Far West," he takes with him his waggons, his cattle,
his little ones, and a troop of slaves, so as to resemble Abraham when he moved from place to place in Canaan.   When he
settles in the forest he clears and cultivates the ground with the
labour of his slaves.   Every thing goes on heavily.   Slaves are
too stupid and improvident to make good colonists.   The country, under these disadvantages, never assumes the garden-like
appearance that it already wears in the New England and Middle States, and more and more of which is constantly to be seen
in the northern parts of the great central valley.   Slavery, in
fact, seems to blight whatever it touches.

Next to the Anglo-Saxon race from the British shores, the
Scotch make the best settlers in the great American forests.
The Irish are not so good; they know not how to use the
plough, or how to manage the horse and the ox, having had but
little experience of either in their native land.   None can han-
dle the spade better, nor are they wanting in industry.   But
when they first arrive they are irresolute, dread the forest, and
hang too much about the large towns, looking about for such
work as their previous mode of life has not disqualified them
for.   Such of them as have been bred to mechanical trades,
might find sufficient employment if they would let ardent
spirits alone, but good colonists for the forest they will never be.
Their children may do better in that career.   The few Welsh
to be found in America are much better fitted than the Irish
for the life and pursuits of a farmer.

The perseverance and frugality of the German, joined to other
good qualities which he has in common with the Anglo-Saxon
race, enable him to succeed tolerably well even in the forest,
but he finds it more his advantage to settle on a farm bought at
second hand and partially cultivated.   The Swiss are much the
same with the Germans.   The French and Italians, on the other
hand, are totally unfit for planting colonies in the woods.
Nothing could possibly be more alien to the usual habits of a
Frenchman.   The population of France is almost universally
collected in cities, towns, and villages, and thus from early
habit as well as constitutional disposition, Frenchmen love
society, and cannot endure the loneliness and isolation of the

settlements we have described.   When they attempt to form
colonies, it is by grouping together in villages, as may be seen
along the banks of the St. Lawrence and of the Lower Mississippi.   Hence their settlements are seldom either extensive or
vigorous.   French emigrants find themselves happier in the
cities and large towns.   If resolved to establish themselves in
the country, they should go to comparatively well settled
neighbourhoods, not to the forests of the far west.

CHAPTER VII.

ON THE ALLEGED WANT OF NATIONAL CHARACTER IN AMERICA.

FOREIGNERS who have written about the United States, have
often remarked that it is a country without a national character.
Were this the mere statement of an opinion, it might be suffered
to pass unnoticed, like many other things emanating from authors
who undertake to speak about countries which they have had
only very partial, and hence very imperfect, opportunities of
knowing.   But as the allegation has been made with an air of
considerable pretension, it becomes necessary that we should
submit it to the test of truth,

If oneness of origin be essential to the formation of national
character, it is clear that the people of the United States can
make no pretence to that character.   No civilised nation was
ever composed of inhabitants derived from such a variety of
sources; for in the United States we find the descendants of
English, Welsh, Scotch, Irish, Dutch, Germans, Norwegians,
Danes, Swedes, Poles, French, Italians, and Spaniards.   In some
few cases, it is admitted with pride, that the blood of an Indian
chief or princess mingles with that of the haughty Norman or
Norman-Saxon.   Many other nations are of mixed descent,
but where shall we find one derived from so many distinct races?

Neither if this national character depends upon the people
having all one language, can the citizens of the United States
make any claim to it; for the colonists from whom they are

descended brought with them the languages of the different countries from which they came, and these are retained in some instances to the present day. At least eleven of the different languages of Europe have been spoken by settlers in the United States.

But let us examine these two points somewhat more minutely, and we cannot fail to be struck with the facts that are thus brought before us.

And in the first, never has there been witnessed so rapid a blending of people from different countries and speaking different languages, as there may be seen in the United States. Within the last two hundred years, people have been arriving from some eleven or twelve different countries, and distinguished by as many different languages and customs, yet so singular a fusion has taken place, that in places where colonisation is at all compact, it would puzzle a stranger to determine the national origin of the people from any peculiarity of physiognomy or dialect, far less of language. Who can distinguish in New York the mass of persons of Dutch descent from those of Anglo-Saxon origin, unless, perhaps, by their retaining Dutch family names? Where discover by the indices of language, features, or manners, the descendants of the Swedes, the Welsh, with a few exceptions, the Poles, the Norwegians, the Danes, or the great body of French Huguenots? Almost the only exceptions to this universal amalgamation and loss of original languages, are to be found in the Germans and French, and even in regard to these, had it not been for comparatively recent arrivals of emigrants caused by the French revolution, the St. Domingo massacres, and various events in Germany, both the French and German languages would have been extinct ere now in the United States. The former is spoken only by a few thousands in the large cities, and some tens of thousands in Louisiana. In the cities, English as well as French is spoken even by the French, and in Louisiana, the only territory in the union which the French language has ever ventured to claim for itself, it is fast giving place to English. German also, spoken although it be by many thousands of emigrants arriving yearly from Europe, is fast disappearing from the older settlements. The children of these Germans almost universally acquire the English tongue in their infancy, and where located, as generally happens, in the neighbourhood of settlers who speak English as their mother tongue, learn to speak it well. Indeed, over nearly the whole vast extent of the United States, English is spoken among the well educated, with a degree of purity to which there is no parallel in the British islands. There, on a space not much larger than a sixth of the United States territory, no fewer than three or four languages are spoken, and in England alone, I know not how many dialects are to be found which a person unaccustomed to them can hardly at all comprehend, however familiar he may be with pure English. As for France, with its Gascon, Breton, and I know not how many other remains of the languages spoken by the ancient races scattered over its territories, the case is still worse.[1] Nor does either Germany or Italy present the uniformity of speech that distinguishes the millions of the United States, with the exception of the newly arrived foreigners; a uniformity which extends even to pronunciation, and the absence of provincial accent and phraseology. A well-educated American who has seen much of his countrymen, may, indeed, distinguish the southern from the northern modes of pronouncing certain vowels; he may recognise by certain shades of sound, if I may so express myself, the northern or southern origin of his countrymen, but these differences are too slight to be readily perceived by a foreigner.

Generally speaking, the pronunciation of well educated Americans is precisely that given in the best ortho-epical authorities of England, and our best speakers adopt the well established changes in pronunciation that from time to time gain ground there. A few words, however, are universally pronounced differently from what prevails in England. *Either* and *neither*, for example, are pronounced *eether* and *neether*, not *ither* and *nither*, nor will our lawyers probably ever learn to say *lien* for *leen*. There is a perceptible difference of accent between the English and Americans, particularly those of the Eastern or New England States. There may, also, be a difference of tone; in some parts

---

[1] I have been informed that there are twelve distinct languages and patois spoken in France, and that interpreters are needed in courts of justice within a hundred miles of Paris.—Ed.

of the States, there is more of a nasal inflexion of the voice than one hears in England.

English literature has an immense circulation in America, a circumstance which may be an advantage in one sense, and a disadvantage in another. We are not wanting, however, in authors of unquestionable merit, in almost every branch of literature, art, and science. Still, if a literature of our own creation be indispensable to the possession of a national character, we must abandon all claim to it.

It may be added, that we have no fashions of our own. We follow the modes of Paris. But in this, Germans, Russians, Italians, and English, without any abatement of their claims to national character, do the like.

Amalgamation takes place, also, by intermarriages to an extent quite unexampled anywhere else; for though the Anglo-Saxon race has an almost undisputed possession of the soil in New England, people are everywhere else to be met with, in whose veins flows the mingled blood of English, Dutch, Germans, Irish, and French.

Nor has the assimilation of races and languages been greater than that of manners, customs, religion, and political principles. The manners of the people, in some places less, in others more refined, are essentially characterised by simplicity, sincerity, and kindness. The religion of the overwhelming majority, and which may therefore be called the national religion, is in all essential points what was taught by the great Protestant reformers of the sixteenth century. With respect to politics, with whatever warmth we may discuss the measures of the government, but one feeling prevails with regard to our political institutions themselves. We are no propagandists; we hold it to be our duty to avoid meddling with the government of other countries; and though we prefer our own political forms, would by no means insist on others doing so too. That government we believe to be the best for any people under which they live most happily, and are best protected in their rights of person, property, and conscience; and we would have every nation to judge for itself what form of government is best suited to secure for it these great ends.

Assuredly no country possesses a press more free, or where,

notwithstanding, public opinion is more powerful; but on these points we shall have more to say in another part of this work.

The American people, taken as a whole, are mainly characterised by perseverance, earnestness, kindness, hospitality, and self-reliance,—that is, by a disposition to depend upon their own exertions to the utmost, rather than look to the government for assistance. Hence, there is no country where the government does less, or the people more. In a word, our national character is that of the Anglo-Saxon race, which still predominates amongst us, in consequence of its original preponderancy in the colonisation of the country, and of the energy which forms its characteristic distinction.

Has the reader ever heard Haydn's celebrated oratorio of the Creation performed by a full orchestra? If so, he cannot have forgotten how chaos is represented at the commencement, by all the instruments being sounded together without the least attempt at concord. By and by, however, something like order begins, and at length the clear notes of the clarionet are heard over all the others, controlling them into harmonious concert. Something like this has been the influence in America, of the Anglo-Saxon language, laws, institutions, CHARACTER.

But if when it is alleged that we have no national character, it be meant that we have not originated any for ourselves, it may be asked what nation has? All owe much to those from whom they have sprung; this we, too, have done, although what we have inherited from our remote ancestors, has unquestionably been much modified by the operation of political institutions which we have been led to adopt by new circumstances, and which probably were never contemplated by the founders of our country.

CHAPTER VIII.

THE ROYAL CHARTERS.

FEW points in the colonial history of the United States, are more interesting to the curious inquirer than the royal charters, under which the settlement of the country first took place.

These charters were granted by James I., Charles I., Charles II., James II., William and Mary, and George I. They were very diverse both in form and substance. Some were granted to companies, some to single persons, others to the colonists themselves. Most of them preceded the foundation of the colonies to which they referred; but in the cases of Rhode Island and Connecticut, the territories were settled first, while Plymouth colony had no crown charter at all, and not even a grant from the Plymouth company in England, until the year after its foundation.

The ordinary reader can be interested only in the charters granted by the crown of England; those from proprietory companies and individuals, to whom whole provinces had first been granted by the crown, can interest those readers only who would study the innumerable law-suits to which they gave occasion. Such in those days was the utter disregard for the correct laying down of limits and boundaries, that the same district of country was often covered with two or more grants made by the same proprietors to different individuals, thus furnishing matter for litigations which lasted in some colonies more than a century, and sometimes giving rise to law-suits even at the present day.

The royal charters give us an amusing idea of the notions with respect to North American geography, entertained in those days by the sovereigns of England, or by those who acted for them. The charter of Virginia not only included those vast regions now comprised in the States of Ohio, Indiana, Illinois, and Michigan, but the northern and southern bounding lines, if extended according to the terms of the charter, would have terminated the one in the Pacific ocean, and the other in Hudson's bay; yet by the same charter, they were both to terminate at the South sea, as the Pacific ocean was then called.

The North Carolina and Georgia charters conveyed to the colonists provinces that were to extend westward to the South sea.

The Massachusetts and Connecticut charters made these colonies also reach to the South Sea; it never appearing to have entered the royal head that they must thus have interfered with the claims of Virginia. New York, which they must also have traversed, seems never to have been thought of, though claimed and occupied at the time by the Dutch. Indeed, considering the descriptions contained in their charters, it is marvellous that the colonies ever ascertained their boundaries. Looking at the charter of Massachusetts, for example, and comparing it with that State as laid down on our maps, we are amazed to think by what possible ingenuity it should have come to have its existing boundaries, especially that on the north-east. Still more confounding does it seem, that Massachusetts should have successfully claimed the territory of Maine, and yet have had to relinquish that of New Hampshire.

The charter granted to William Penn for Pennsylania was the clearest of all, yet it was long matter of dispute whether or not it included Delaware. On the other, Delaware was claimed by Maryland, and with justice, if the charter of the latter province were to be construed literally. Still Maryland did not obtain Delaware.

Such charters, it will be readily supposed, must have led to serious and protracted disputes between the colonies themselves. Many of these disputes were still undetermined at the commencement of the revolutionary war; several remained unadjustified long after the achievement of the national independence; and it was only a few years ago, that the last of the boundary questions was brought to a final issue before the supreme court of the United States.

After the revolution, immense difficulties attended the settlement of the various claims preferred by the Atlantic States to those parts of the west which they assumed to have been conveyed to them by their old charters, and into which the tide of emigration was then beginning to flow. Had Virginia successfully asserted her claims, she would have had an empire in the valley of the Mississippi, sufficient, at some future day, to counterbalance almost all the other States put together. North Carolina and Georgia also laid claim to territories of vast extent. The claims of Connecticut and Massachusetts directly conflicted with those of Virginia. Accordingly it required a great deal of wisdom and patience to settle all these claims, without endangering the peace and safety of the confederacy. All at length were adjusted except that of Georgia, and it too was arranged at a later date. Virginia magnanimously relinquished all her claims in the west; a spontaneous act, which immediately led to the establishment of the State of Kentucky, followed in due time by Ohio, Indiana, Illinois, and Michigan, in what was long called the north-western territory. The relinquishment by North Carolina of her claims to the west of the Alleghany mountains, led to the creation of the State of Tennessee. But Connecticut refused to abandon her claim to the north-eastern part of Ohio, often called to this day New Connecticut, without receiving from the general government a handsome equivalent in money, which has been safely invested, and forms the basis of a large capital, set apart for the support of the common schools of the State.[1] Georgia also ceded her claims in the west to the general government, on this condition, that it should obtain for her from the Indians, a title to their territory lying to the east of the Chatta-Nootchee river, now the western boundary of that State. Out of the cession thus made by Georgia, have been formed the States of Alabama and Mississippi.

The United States have had to struggle with still further serious difficulties, originating in the old royal charters. Small regard was paid to the prior claims of the Indians in the extensive grants made by those charters, directly or indirectly, to the colonists. The pope had set the example of giving away the aborigines with the lands they occupied, or rather of giving away the land from under them; and although in all the colonies founded by our English ancestors in America, there was a kind of feeling that the Indians had some claim on the ground of prior occupation, yet these, it was thought, ought to give place to the rights conferred by the royal charters. The colonists were subject to the same blinding influence of selfishness that affects other men, and to this we are to ascribe the importunity with which they urged the removal of the prior occupants from the land conveyed by the royal charters, and which they had long been wont to consider and to call their own. In no case, indeed, did the new comers seize upon the lands of the aboriginal occupants without some kind of purchase; yet unjustifiable means were often employed to induce the latter to make over their claims to the former, such as excessive importunity, the bribery of the Indian chiefs, and sometimes even

[1] Amounting to 2,040,228 dollars.

threats. Thus, although with the exception of lands obtained by right of conquest in war, I do not believe that any whatever was obtained without something being given in exchange for it; yet I fear that the golden rule of "doing to others as we would that they should do unto us," was sadly neglected in many of those transactions. In Pennsylvania and New England, unquestionably, greater fairness was shown than in most, if not all the other States; yet even there, full justice, according to the above rule, was not always practised. Indeed, in many cases it was difficult to say what exact justice implied. To savages roaming over vast tracts of land which they did not cultivate, and which, even for the purposes of the chase, were often more extensive than necessary, to part with hundreds or even thousands of square miles could not be thought a matter of much importance, and thus conscience was quieted. But although our forefathers may not have done full justice to the poor Indians, it is by no means certain that others in the same circumstances would have done better.

The impatience of the colonists to obtain possession of lands which their charters or arrangements consequent thereon led them to regard as their own, has at times thrown the general government into much embarrassment and difficulty. Thus in the case of the conflict betwixt it and the State of Georgia a few short years ago, congress had agreed to buy up the claims of the Indians still remaining within that State, and to provide for their removing beyond its limits, in return for the relinquishment of its claims in the west. But this removal of the Indians, it had been expressly stipulated, was to be effected "peaceably," and with their own consent. Time rolled on, the population of Georgia increased, the settlements of the white men had begun to touch upon those of the red men, and the latter were urged to sell their lands and to retire farther to the west. But to this they would not consent. Thereupon the general government was called on to fulfil its engagement. It exerted itself to the utmost to persuade the Indians to sell their lands; but neither would it employ force itself, nor allow Georgia to do so, though much was done by the colonists, and something too, by the State, indirectly, to worry the Indians into terms. The chiefs, however long held back. But at length the lands were sold at a great price, and their occupants received others west of the Mississippi, and have removed to these. There, I doubt not, they will do better than in their former abodes.

To rid itself of such embarrassments created by the old charters, the general government, at the instance of great and good men, adopted some years ago the plan of collecting all the tribes still to be found within the confines of any of the States, upon an extensive district to the west of Arkansas and Missouri, claimed by no State, and therefore considered as part of the public domain. There it has already collected the Cherokees, the Choctaws, the Chickasas, the Creeks, and several smaller tribes. Soon the territories of all the States will be cleared of them, except in so far as they choose to remain and become incorporated with the colonists as citizens. Nor can I but cherish the hope that the great Indian community now forming, as I have said, westward of Missouri and Arkansas, will one day become a State itself, and have its proper representatives in the great council of the nation.

I may conclude these remarks by observing, that the late painful dispute between the United States and Great Britain, now so happily terminated, relative to the boundaries between the State of Maine on the one hand, and Lower Canada and New Brunswick on the other, originated in the geographical obscurity of certain limits, described in one of these old charters.

CHAPTER IX.

HOW A CORRECT KNOWLEDGE OF THE AMERICAN PEOPLE, THE NATURE OF THEIR GOVERNMENT, AND OF THEIR NATIONAL CHARACTER, MAY BEST BE ATTAINED.

He who would obtain a thorough knowledge of the people of the United States, their national character, the nature of their government, and the spirit of their laws, must go back to the earliest ages of the history of England, and study the character of the various races that from early times have settled there. He must carefully mark the influences they exerted on each other, and upon the civil and political institutions of that country. He must study the Saxon conquest, followed by the introduction of Saxon institutions, and Saxon laws and usages; the trial of an accused person by his peers; the subdivision into small districts, called townships or hundreds; the political influence of that arrangement; and the establishment of seven or eight petty kingdoms, in which the authority of the king was shared by the people, without whose consent no laws of importance could be made, and who often met for legislation in the open fields, or beneath the shade of some wide-spreading forest, as their Scandinavian kinsmen met, at a much later period, round the Mora stone. [1] He must next study the modifications afterwards introduced during the subjugation of the Saxons by the North-men or Danes, extending over 261 years,[2] and which, though both partial in extent, and interrupted in its continuance, left not a few monuments of its existence, and gave a name to one of the orders of the English nobility.[3]

But, above all, he must study the influence of the Norman conquest, which was completed within twenty years from the battle of Hastings, fought A. D. 1066. Without extirpating all the Saxon institutions, that event reduced the Anglo-Saxons of England to the condition of serfs; gave their lands to sixty thousand warriors, composing the conqueror's army; established an absolute monarchy, surrounded by a powerful landed aristocracy; and thus introduced an order of things wholly new to the country and foreign to its habits.

He must attentively mark the influence exercised by the Anglo-Saxon and Norman races upon each other, during the period that has since elapsed, of nearly eight hundred years, and will there find a clue to many transactions which appear obscure and mysterious in the common histories of England. The reciprocal hatred of the two races will explain the affair of Becket, the first archbishop of the Saxon race after the conquest, and Henry II., the fifth of the Norman kings; that national animosity leading Becket to resist the demands of the king, as calculated to extend the tyranny of a hated race of conquerors,

[1] On the plains of Upsala in Sweden. The *mora stone* signifies the stone on a moor.
[2] From A. D. 787, to A. D. 1048.
[3] That of *Earl*, from the Danish and Norwegian Iarl, who was at once the civil and military governor of a province.

and the king to humble the conquered by crushing their haughty representative, That this, not the diminution of the power of the pope, as is commonly believed, was Henry's object, may be seen from the fact of his being no less earnest in calling for assistance from Rome, than Becket was in invoking her protection.

He will perceive this mutual animosity manifesting itself in innumerable instances, and in apparently contradictory conduct. At one time the Anglo-Saxons side with the nobility against the monarch, as in the wars between the barons and king John, and also Henry III., not because they loved the barons, who were of the same detested Norman race, but because they dreaded the consequences to themselves of another conquest, by a king who had invited over the Poiteoins, the Aquitains, and the Provençals, to help him against his own subjects in England. At other times they sided with the king against the barons, when they saw that the triumph of the latter was likely to augment their burdens.

And although, as M. Thierry remarks,[1] the bitter hostility which had lasted for four centuries, seemed to be extinct in the fifteenth, when the wars between the houses of York and Lancaster ranged the two races promiscuously on each side, yet traces of their distinct existence are to be found at this day, in the language, in the customs, and in the institutions of England. Although the monarch no longer employs the ancient formula, as it occurs in royal ordinances and proclamations for four hundred years after the conquest, such as " Henry V.,Henry VII. of that name since the conquest,"[2] yet to this day a Norman phraseology is sometimes employed by the monarch, as, for instance, *le roy le veult ; le roy s'advisera'; le roy merciè ses loyaux subjets.*[3] To this day the nobility of England, though recruited from time to time from the rich, the talented, and the ambitious commoners of Saxon blood, remains essentially Norman in spirit and in character. The same may be said of the gentry, or proprietors of landed estates, whereas the great bulk

---

1 "Conquête de l'Angleterre," vol. iv., pp.366-368. Brussels edition.
2 Henry VIII. was the last monarch who used this formula in his proclamations, and styled himself Henry, Eighth of the name since the conquest.
3 " The king wills ;" "the king will consider ;" "the king thanks his loyal subjects."

of the remaining population is of Anglo-Saxon origin. In Wales, and in Ireland, the races of the conquerors and the conquered appear still more distinct, and in the latter, mutual antipathy is far from having ceased. In Scotland, there is comparatively little Norman blood, the Normans never having conquered that country.[1]

To the resistance of the Anglo-Saxon race in England to the domination of the Norman aristocracy, that kingdom was ultimately indebted for the free institutions it now enjoys. The oppressions of the nobility and of the crown were checked by the cities and boroughs, in which the Anglo-Saxon commons became more and more concentrated with the advance of civilisation and population. The nobles themselves, on occasions when they too had to contend for their rights and privileges against the sovereign, would give a helping hand to the people; and in later times especially, after the people had established the power of their Commons, or third estate, on an immovable foundation, would aid the sovereign against alleged encroachments on the part of the people. Thus the cause of liberty gained ground both among the nobility and the commonalty.

With the progress of the Reformation, the strife betwixt the two races became exasperated; the nobility and gentry desiring little more than the abatement or rejection of the papal usurpation; the Saxon race, led by men whose hearts were more deeply interested in the subject, desiring to see the Church rid of error and superstition of every form. From the discussion of the rights of conscience, the latter went on to examine the nature and foundations of civil government, and being met with violent opposition, they proceeded to lengths that they never dreamed of when they first set out. In the fearful struggle that followed, both the national church and the monarchy were for a time completely overthrown.

It was just as this grand opposition of sentiment was drawing on to a direct collision, and when men's minds were engrossed with the important questions that it pressed upon them, that

---

[1] I apprehend there is *not a little* Norman blood in Scotland; but what of it is to be found in the aristocracy, came by intermarriages or by Normans who recommended themselves by their talents and courage to the favour of the Scottish monarchs, not by conquest.—Ed.

the two colonies destined to exercise a predominant influence in America, left the British shore. The first of the two in point of date, sought the coasts of southern, the second sailed to those of northern Virginia, as the whole Atlantic slope was then called. The one settled on James's river in the present State of Virginia, and became, in a sense, the ruling colony of the south; the other established itself in New England, there to become the mother of the six northern States. Both, however, have long since made their influence to be felt far beyond the coasts of the Atlantic, and are continuing to extend it towards the Pacific, in parallel and clearly defined lines. And both retain to this day the characteristic features that marked their founders when they left the shores of England.

If not purely Norman in blood, the southern colony was entirely Norman in spirit; whereas the northern was Anglo-Saxon in character, and in the institutions which it took to the New World. Both loved freedom and free institutions, but they differed as to the extent to which the people should enjoy them. The one had sprung from the ranks of those in England who pleaded for the prerogatives of the crown, and the privileges of the nobility; the other, from the great party that was contending for popular rights. The one originated with the friends of the Church as left by Queen Elizabeth; the other, with those who desired to see it purified from what they deemed the corruptions of antiquity, and shorn of the exorbitant pretensions of its hierarchy. The one, composed of a company of gentlemen, attended by a few mechanics or labourers, contemplated an extensive traffic with the natives; the other, composed, with a few exceptions, of substantial farmers of moderate means, and industrious artisans, contemplated the cultivation of the ground, and the establishment of a state of society in which they might serve God according to his Word. The one had no popular government for some years after its foundation; the other was self-organised and self-governed, before it disembarked upon the shores that were to be the scene of its future prosperity. Finally, the religion of the one, though doubtless sincere, and so far as it went, beneficial in its influence, was a religion that clung to forms, and to an imposing ritual; the religion of the other was at the farthest possible remove from the church of

Rome, both in form and spirit, and professed to be guided by the Scriptures alone.

Such was American colonisation in its grand origin. But widely different has been the subsequent histories of those English colonies from that of England herself. The former carried out to their legitimate extent the great principles of civil and religious liberty, which they had learned in England, in the school of oppression and of long and fierce discussion. The latter, after rushing on for a time in the same career, carried those principles to such a length, as to subvert the government and plunge the country into all the horrors of revolution and misrule, ending at last in the despotism of a military chief. The former went on gradually improving the forms of popular government which they had originally adopted, in the face of all the efforts of the crown of England to destroy them. The latter provoked, by their excesses, a revulsion, from which, even after the lapse of two centuries, they are still suffering. The former, although never were there subjects more loyal to a crown, or a people more sincerely attached to their fatherland, were compelled, as they believed, by the unkind and almost unnatural course pursued by that fatherland, to sever the bonds that bound them to it, and to establish an independent government of their own. The latter have had to fight the battles of liberty over and over again, and have not even yet obtained for the people all the rights which are considered, in America, their proper inheritance from the hand of their Creator.

I speak not here of the form of government. The founders of the American colonists, and their descendants for several generations, were monarchists, as they would doubtless have been to this day, had they not been compelled, while struggling against injustice and oppression, to dissolve their political connection with the mother country. In all essential points, colonial freedom differed not from that which their independent existence has given them; and the people of the United States enjoy little more liberty at present, than what the fathers of the Revolution maintained that they ought to have enjoyed under the British constitution and crown.

CHAPTER X.

HOW TO OBTAIN A CORRECT VIEW OF THE SPIRIT AND CHARACTER OF THE RELIGIOUS
INSTITUTIONS OF THE UNITED STATES.

THUS, too, if we would have a thorough knowledge of the spirit
and character of the religion of the United States, we must
study the history of religion in England first, and then in those
other countries whose religious institutions must have considerably influenced those of America, in consequence of the numerous emigrations from them that have settled there. Indeed, it
is very certain that the religious institutions of America have
been far more affected than the political, by colonists from Holland, France, and other parts of the continent of Europe, as
well as from Scotland and Ireland.

Men of speculative habits may indulge many plausible *a
priori* reasonings, on the kind of religion likely to find favour
with a people of democratic feelings and institutions; but in
these the conclusions will probably be found very much at variance with facts. M. de Toqueville presents a striking instance
of this in the first few chapters of his second work on democracy in America.[1] A purely abstract argument, or rather a
mere fanciful conjecture, might in this case interest by its ingenuity and even be believed as true, in the absence of facts.
But when he proceeds to establish an hypothesis by an appeal

---

[1] Both of M. de Toqueville's works intituled, Democracy in America, unquestionably possess great merit; the earlier publication, however, is much superior to the later. But the author's great fault is, that he puts his theory uniformly before his facts, instead of deducing, according to the principles of the
Baconian philosophy, his theory from his facts. The consequence of this fatal
mistake, is, that having advanced a theory, and shown by argument its plausi-
bility, he immediately goes to work to support it by facts, and in doing so, often
distorts them badly. For the object for which he wrote, that of arresting the
progress of democracy in Europe, by reading lectures to it from American
democracy, as from a text-book, his works certainly correspond to his purpose.
But, however able they may be, it is absurd to say that his volumes give a just
view of American institutions on all points. On many subjects he has said
some excellent things; and indeed no other foreigner has come so *near* to comprehending the spirit of our institutions. But no man ever will, no man ever
can understand them perfectly, unless he inhaled their spirit as it were with
his mother's milk.

to facts, it is hard to say whether he is oftener right or wrong. Take one or two paragraphs.   " In the United States," says he, " the majority undertakes to furnish individuals with a multitude of ready-made opinions, and thus to relieve them of the necessity of forming their own.   There are many theories in philosophy, morals, and politics, which every one there adopts without examination, upon the faith of public opinion; and upon a closer inspection, it will be found that religion itself reigns there much less as a doctrine of revelation than as a commonly admitted opinion."[1]

Now, democratic as America may be, it would be impossible to find a country in which the last assertion in the above paragraph is less true, for no where do people demand reasons for everything more frequently or more universally; no where are the preachers of the gospel more called upon to set forth, in all their variety and force, the arguments by which the divine revelation of Christianity is established.

Again, he says: " In the United States the Christian sects are infinitely various, and incessantly undergoing modifications; but Christianity itself is an established and irresistible fact, which no one undertakes either to attack or to defend."

Again: "The Americans, having admitted without examination the main dogmas of the Christian religion, are obliged, in like manner, to receive a great many more truths flowing from and having relation to it."[2]

Now, hardly any assertions concerning his country, could surprise a well-informed American more than those contained in these paragraphs, nor could M. de Toqueville have made them,

---

[1] Aux Etats-Unis, la majorité se charge de fournir aux individus une foule d'opinions toutes faites, et les soulage ainsi de l'obligation de s'en former qui leur soient propres.   Il y a un grand nombre de théories en matière de philosophie, de morale, ou de politique que chacun y adopte ainsi sans examen, sur la foi du public ; et si l'on regarde de très-près on verra que la religion ellemême y règne bien moins comme doctrine révélée que comme opinion commune. —" Démocratie en Amérique," Seconde Partie.   Tome I. Chapitre 2.

[2] Aux Etats-Unis, les sectes chrétiennes varient à l'infini et se modifient sans cesse; mais le christianisme lui-même est un fait établi et irrésistible qu'on n'entreprend point d'attaquer ni de défendre.

Les Américains, ayant admis sans examen les principaux dogmes de la religion chrétienne, sont obligés de recevoir de la même manière un grand nombre de vérités qui en découlent et qui y tiennent.—"Democratie en Amérique," Seconde Partie.   Tome I., chapitre 1.

had he not been carried away by certain theories, with respect to the influence of democratic institutions upon religion.

M. de Toqueville does not forget that religion gave birth to Anglo-American society, but he does forget for the moment what sort of religion it was; that it was not a religion that repels investigation, or that would have men receive any thing as truth, where such momentous concerns are involved, upon mere trust in public opinion. Such has never been the character of Protestantism, rightly so called, in any age.

Nor is this distinguished author nearer the truth when, giving way to the same speculative tendency, he asserts, that "the human mind in democratic countries must tend to pantheism." [1] But enough: all that I have wished to show in referring to M. de Toqueville's work, in many respects an admirable one, is, that the religious phenomena of the United States are not to be explained by reasonings *a priori*, however plausible and ingenious.

No; we must go back to the times when, and the influences under which, the religious character of the first colonists from England was formed, and then trace its effects upon the institutions that were established by those colonists in the new world.

It is interesting to investigate the history of Christianity in England from the earliest ages; its propagation by missionaries from Asia Minor; its reception by the Celtic races; the resistance made by the British Christians, in common with those of Ireland and France, to the claims of Rome; the conquest of England by the Saxons, and the advantage taken of that event by Rome to subdue the native Christians, whom it accused of heresy; the conversion of the Anglo-Saxons to Christianity, and their subsequent dissatisfaction with the Romish hierarchy; the Norman conquest, and the efforts of the popes to take advantage of that also, in seeking to establish a complete ascendency over the British and Irish Christians; the witnesses to the truth raised up by God from the ancient Anglo-Saxon churches; the influence of Wickliffe and other opponents of Rome; and, finally, the dawn of the Reformation. That event, there can be no doubt, was connected, in the providence of

---

[1] "Democratie en Amérique," Seconde Partie. Tom. i., chapitre 7.

God, with the long-continued and faithful resistance of the ancient churches of England to error. Some remains of truth had doubtless lain concealed, like unextinguished embers beneath the ashes, but the clearing away of the accumulated rubbish of ages, and the contact of God's word, sufficed to revive and make it spread anew throughout the nation.

But the grand means employed by God in preparing a people who should lay the foundation of a Christian empire in the New World, was the Reformation. To their religion the New England colonists owed all their best qualities. Even their political freedom they owed to the contest they had waged in England for religious liberty, and in which, long and painful as it was, nothing but their faith could have sustained them. Religion led them to abandon their country, rather than submit to a tyranny that threatened to enslave their immortal souls, and made them seek in the New World the freedom of conscience that was denied to them in the old.

They have been justly accused, indeed, of not carrying out their principles to their legitimate results, and of being intolerant to each other. Still, be it remembered to their honour, that both in theory and in practice, they were in these respects far in advance of all their contemporaries; still more, that their descendants have maintained this advanced position; so that the people of the United States of America now enjoy liberty of conscience to an extent unknown in any other country. Persecution led the Puritan colonists to examine the great subject of human rights, the nature and just extent of civil government, and the boundaries at which obedience ceases to be a duty. What Sir James Mackintosh has said of John Bunyan, might be applied to them: "The severities to which he had been subjected had led him to revolve in his own mind the principles of religious freedom, until he had acquired the ability of baffling, in the conflict of argument, the most acute and learned among his persecutors." The clear convictions of their own minds on this subject they transmitted to their posterity, nor was the inheritance neglected or forgotten.

The political institutions of the Puritan colonies of New England are to be traced to their religion, not their religion to their political institutions, and this remark applies to other colonies also. Now if the reader would know what the religious character of those Puritans was, let him peruse the following eloquent eulogy upon them, from a source which will not be suspected of partiality to their religion, whatever opinions may be attributed to it in relation to their political principles.

"The Puritans were men whose minds had derived a peculiar character from the daily contemplation of superior beings and eternal interests. Not content with acknowledging in general terms an over-ruling Providence, they habitually ascribed every event to the will of the Great Being for whose power nothing was too vast, for whose inspection nothing was too minute. To know Him, to serve Him, to enjoy Him, was with them the great end of existence. They rejected with contempt the ceremonious homage which other sects substituted for the pure worship of the soul. Instead of catching occasional glimpses of the Deity through an obscuring veil, they aspired to gaze full on the intolerable brightness, and to commune with Him face to face. Hence originated their contempt of earthly distinctions. The difference between the greatest and meanest of mankind seemed to vanish, when compared with the boundless interval which separated the whole race from Him on whom their own eyes were constantly fixed. They recognised no title to superiority but His favour; and, confident of that, they despised all the accomplishments and all the dignities of the world. If their names were not found in the registers of heralds, they felt assured that they were recorded in the Book of Life. If their steps were not accompanied by a splendid train of menials, legions of ministering angels had charge over them. Their palaces were houses not made with hands; their diadems, crowns of glory which should never fade away. On the rich and the eloquent, on nobles and priests, they looked down with contempt; for they esteemed themselves rich in a more precious treasure, and eloquent in a more sublime language; nobles by the right of an earlier creation, and priests by the imposition of a mightier hand. The very meanest of them was a being to whose fate a mysterious and terrible importance belonged—on whose slightest action the spirits of light and darkness looked with anxious interest; who had been destined, before the heavens and the earth were created, to enjoy a felicity which should continue when heaven and earth should have passed away. Events, which short-sighted politicians ascribed to earthly causes, had been ordained on his account. For his sake empires had risen, and flourished, and decayed. For his sake the Almighty had proclaimed his will, by the pen of the evangelist, and the harp of the prophet. He had been rescued by no common Deliverer from the grasp of no common foe. He had been ransomed by the sweat of no vulgar agony, by the blood of no earthly sacrifice. It was for him that the sun had been darkened, that the rocks had been rent, that the dead had arisen, that all nature had shuddered at the sufferings of her expiring God."[1]

CHAPTER XI.

A BRIEF NOTICE OF THE FORM OF GOVERNMENT IN AMERICA.

Some knowledge of the civil and political structure of the government, is almost indispensable to a correct investigation of the religious economy of the United States; for although there is no longer a union there between Church and State, still the interests of religion come into contact, in many ways, with the political organisations of the General and State governments.

The government of the United States must appear extremely complicated to a foreigner accustomed to the unity that distinguishes most monarchical polities, and complicated it is in fact. We will endeavour to describe its leading features as briefly as possible.

The whole country, then, is subject to what is called the National or General government, composed of three branches: I. The Executive; II. The Legislative; III. The Judicial.

The executive power is lodged in one man, the president; who is appointed for four years, by electors chosen for that purpose; each State being allowed as many as it has members of Congress. These are chosen differently in different states, but

1 Edinburgh Review, vol. xlii. 339.

generally by districts, each district choosing one elector, and that for the sole purpose of electing the president and vice-president. The latter presides over the senate, but his office is almost nominal: should the president die, the vice-president immediately steps into his place.

The president appoints the secretaries of state, or ministers of the various departments of the administration, such as the treasury, navy, war office, &c., and, directly or indirectly, he appoints to all offices in the national or general government; in the case of the more important offices, however, only with the consent and approbation of the Senate.

The legislation of the national government is committed to the Congress, and that has two branches, the Senate and the House of Representatives. The Senate is composed of two persons from each state in the Union, chosen by the legislatures of those states respectively, and for the period of six years. The House of Representatives is chosen by the people of the states, generally by districts, and for the period of two years. [1] Their number is, from time to time, determined by law. The House of Representatives represents the people; the Senate represents the States. No act of Congress has the force of law without the president's signature, unless when two-thirds of each house has voted in favour of an act which he refuses to sign. All matters falling within the legislative jurisdiction of the Congress, are specified in the constitution of the United States: such as are not specifically mentioned there, are reserved for the legislation of the individual States.

The judicial power is vested in a supreme court, consisting at present of nine judges, appointed by the president, with consent of the Senate. They can be removed only by impeachment before the Senate, and hold a yearly winter session at Washington, the capital of the United States. When not thus united there, they hold circuit courts in different parts of the country. The whole country is divided, also, into districts, each having a judge appointed by the president, for the decision of causes that fall within the cognisance of the United States' courts, and from whose decisions an appeal lies to the

[1] By a very recent law the members of the House of Representatives are hereafter to be chosen for districts.

supreme courts.   That court decides how far the laws passed by the national Congress, or by the legislatures of the different States, are consistent with the constitution; also, all questions between individual States, or between the United States and an individual State, and questions arising between a foreigner, and either the United States, or any one State.

The government of the States individually, closely resembles that of the confederation, the jurisdiction of each being confined. of course, to its own territory.   Each has its own governor and its own legislature, the latter in all cases but one,[1] consists of a senate, and house of representatives, besides a supreme law court, with subordinate district and county courts.   The legislature of each State embraces a vast variety of subjects, falling within the compass of its own internal interests.   The different States vary materially on several points, such as the term during which the governor holds office, and the extent of his power; the terms for which the senators and representatives are elected, and for which the judges are appointed; the salaries of those functionaries, and so forth.

With the exception of South Carolina and Louisiana, in which the territorial divisions are called districts, all the States are subdivided into counties, having courts of justice attached to each, and officers likewise, for a great many local objects, such as upholding the roads, providing for the poor, &c., &c.   These counties are subdivided into what are called townships, averaging six or eight miles square in New England, New York, New Jersey, Pennsylvania, and all the Mississippi states; in Delaware they are called hundreds, and in Louisiana parishes; whilst in Maryland, Virginia,[2] the two Carolinas, Georgia, Kentucky, and Tennessee, the counties form the smallest territorial divisions.   In the three Territories, the subdivision into townships has been adopted.

These townships form important political and civil districts and corporations; the inhabitants meet once a year, or oftener, for local purposes, and for the appointment of local officers and

---

[1] Vermont has but one house in its legislature.
[2] In the eastern part of Virginia, and a great part of Maryland, the parochial subdivisions that existed previous to the revolution are still retained for many local purposes, and are even recognised by the law.

committees. At these primary assemblies the people acquire habits of transacting public business, which are of the greatest importance in fitting them for legislation and government, both in national and local affairs. As for the larger towns, they are incorporated as cities and boroughs, and have municipal governments of a threefold kind;—legislative, executive, and judicial.

The separation of the colonies from Great Britain, and the re-organisation of their respective governments, produced changes less essential than at first view might be supposed. The King, Parliament, and Justiciary of England, were superseded by the President, Congress, and Supreme Court of America, the nature of the government remaining essentially the same. For an hereditary sovereign we have a President, chosen once in four years; for an hereditary House of Peers, a Senate, the members of which are chosen for six years; the powers of the President and Senate being almost identical in most things with those of the corresponding branches of the British constitution. As for the several colonies, these the revolution transformed into States, and the old royal charters were, with one exception,[1] superseded by constitutions. Beyond this there was no essential change, and but little alteration even in forms. Instead of being appointed by the British crown, or by proprietory companies, or individuals, the governors were chosen by the people themselves. The legislative and judicial branches underwent very little modification.

There are now in the American Union twenty-six organised States, three Territories, and one District. The Territories are now under the government of the president and Congress of the United States, but will become States as soon as the amount of their population entitles them, in the opinion of Congress, to be represented in the national legislative. They have a legislature of their own, but their governors are appointed by the president. Two, namely, Wisconsin and Iowa, will soon have a sufficient population to entitle them to a place among the

---

[1] Rhode island, until this day, has had no government but that given to her in the charter of Charles the Second, but it seems high time that that ancient instrument should be superseded by something better adapted to the present state of that commonwealth. This feeling has prevailed among many of the people, but their strenuous efforts to obtain a constitution have been very unwisely directed.

States.   And when these are admitted, Florida will probably be so too.

Under the impression that the national government should be removed from the immediate influence of any one State, the district called Columbia, ten miles square, was taken from Virginia and Maryland, and set apart as the seat of the national government, and to it, immediately, that is, to the President, Congress, and Supreme Court, it is immediately subject.   Experience has hardly approved of this measure as either wise or necessary.   No part of the country is worse governed, Congress being too much occupied with other matters to pay much attention to so insignificant a territory.

The preceding outline will suffice to give the reader some idea of the government of the United States, and prepare him for understanding many things which might otherwise be obscure in the further course of this work.

CHAPTER XII.

A BRIEF GEOGRAPHICAL NOTICE OF THE UNITED STATES.

IN like manner, a short account of the physical character and resources of the United States will be found useful to the reader.

The United States lie between the parallels of 24° 27′ and 54° 40′ north latitude, and 19° 20′ and 126° west longitude from Greenwich, and are bounded as follows: On the east, by the Atlantic, and the British provinces of New Brunswick; on the south, by the gulph of Mexico, Texas, and the Republic of Mexico; on the west, by the Pacific ocean; and on the north, by the British possessions, from which they are separated, partly by the river St. Lawrence, and the great chain of lakes that flow into, or rather, that form a series of expansions of that river, and partly by a conventional line west of the Oregon mountains, which line has not been determined.   The United States' government claims up to latitude 54° 40′ but this is resisted by

England. The 49° of north latitude will most probably be agreed to, that being the latitude of the boundary eastward of those mountains to the Lake of the Woods, after which it pursues a south-east direction through some small lakes, and across an intervening portage to Lake Superior, which is the uppermost of the chain of lakes through which the St. Lawrence flows.

A glance at the map will show that this vast territory consists of three grand sections; the Atlantic slope, the Pacific slope, and the intermediate valley of the Mississippi. The whole is computed by Mr. Tanner, a distinguished American geographer, to contain 2,037,165 square miles.

The outlines of the entire territory may be given as follows:

	MILES.
On the North, from the mouth of the St. Croix river to the Oregon mountains	3,000
From the Oregon mountains to the Pacific ocean	600
Along the Pacific, from lat. 54° 40′ to lat. 42°	625
Along the Mexican and Texian territories, from the Pacific to the mouth of the Sabine river	2,300
Along the Gulph of Mexico to Florida Point	1,100
Along the Atlantic ocean	1,800
Making a total outline of	9,425

Of the 2,037,165 square miles, constituting, according to Mr. Tanner, the area of the United States, about 400,000 are found on the Atlantic slope, including East Florida, 1,341,649 in the valley of the Mississppi,[1] and 295,516 on the Pacific slope. Hence it appears that nearly two-thirds of the whole territory of the United States lie in the valley of the Mississippi, a fact which shows the vast relative importance of that section of the country.[2]

Upon a survey of the whole of this territory it will be found to possess physical advantages, such as few other countries enjoy. While, with the exception of Florida, all parts of it comprise a large proportion of excellent soil, many exhibit the most astonishing fertility. It abounds in the most valuable minerals. Iron is found in several states in great abundance. At various points, but particularly in the middle States, there

---

[1] According to Mr. Darby's estimate, the valley of the Mississippi contains 1,341,649.

[2] The accompanying map will give the reader a good idea of these several parts of the area of the United States.

are vast deposits of coal, which is easily conveyed by water-carriage to other parts of the country. Even gold is found in considerable quantities in the western parts of North Carolina, the adjacent parts of South Carolina and Georgia, and some in Virginia and Tennessee. The almost boundless forests of the interior furnish timber suited to all purposes. Navigable rivers everywhere present facilities for trade. On the Atlantic slope, beginning from the east and advancing south-west, we find in succession the Penobscot, the Kennebec, the Merrimac, the Connecticut, the Hudson, the Delaware, the Susquehanna, the Potomac, the Rappahannock, the James's river, the Roanoke, the Neuse, the Fear, the Pedée, the Santee, the Savannah, the Altamaha, and the St. John's, without reckoning many smaller but important streams, navigable by common boats and small steamers. Many of these rivers, such as the Delaware, the Potomac, the Rappahannock, the James's, and the Roanoke, expand into noble estuaries before they fall into the ocean, and the coast is indented, also, with many bays, perhaps unrivalled in point of extent and beauty. Beginning from the east we have Portland or Casco bay, Portsmouth bay, Newburyport bay, Massachusetts bay, Buzzard's bay, Narragansett bay, New York bay, Amboy bay, Delaware bay, Chesapeake bay, into which twelve wide-mouthed rivers fall, Wilmington bay, Charleston bay, &c., &c.

With the exception of part of the eastern coast of Connecticut, a chain of islands, some inhabited, many not, runs parallel to the shore, beginning at Passamaquoddy bay, and extending to the southern extremity of Florida, and thence round into the gulph of Mexico, and along its coast, to beyond the western limit of the United States. Thus are formed some of the finest channels for an extensive coasting trade, such as Long island sound, Albemarle sound, Pamlico sound, and many others. To increase these facilities, canals and railroads have been extended along the coast from Portland in Maine, to Charleston in South Carolina, and even farther.

Immediately off the sea coast of the western part of New Jersey, there commences a belt of sand, which extends along the whole margin of the southern states, forming an almost uninterrupted forest of pines, and enlarging as it advances south-

E

ward, from twenty to nearly a hundred miles broad, the latter being its breadth opposite to North Carolina. Between this sandy tract and the Alleghany mountains, the land is generally fertile and produces various crops according to the climate, such as fine wheat, and the other grains in New Jersey, Pennsylvania, Maryland, and Virginia; in which last State, tobacco is also largely cultivated, cotton in the Carolinas and in Georgia, and on the rich bottom lands along the bays and streams of the sandy tract, rice and indigo.

As we advance northward along this fertile tract intervening between the sand and the mountains, we gradually leave the region of transition and secondary rocks, and enter on that of granite, so that before reaching the state of Maine, primitive rocks abound everywhere, even on the surface of the ground.

But in point of fertility the Atlantic slope bears no comparison with the valley of the Mississippi, embracing a territory about six times as large as that of France, and likely, ere long, to be the abode of many millions of the human race. Fifty years ago it contained little more than a hundred thousand inhabitants; the population of the settled part of it, amounted, as we have seen, in 1840[1] to above six millions, and this, it is calculated from the data supplied in the last forty years, will have increased in thirty-five years hence, to not much under thirty millions. By the end of the century, it will probably be not less than fifty or sixty millions.

The tabular view on page 33 shows the immense size of the eleven States and two Territories already organised in this vast valley, let us now look for a moment to their natural resources.

Ohio, lying between the beautiful river of that name and lake Erie, comprises 40,260 square miles, and a population of above a million and a half. As England and Wales have 57,929 square miles, and 15,906,829 inhabitants; Ohio, at the same ratio, would have 11,055,066, but the latter having a far larger proportion of fertile land than the former, even in that case it could not be thought so densely inhabited. With the exception

---

[1] The exact population of the eleven States and two Territories of the valley of the Mississippi was, without including western Virginia, Pennsylvania, and Florida, in 1840, 6,376,972; in 1830, it was 3,342,680; in 1820, it was 2,237,454; in 1810, it was 1,099,180; and in 1800, it was 385,647; in 1790, it was 109,888.

of a part of it in the south-east, on the Hockhocking river, there is little poor land in the State. Vast forests cover the greater part of it to this day. Lake Erie on the north, the river Ohio on the south, and several navigable streams flowing from the interior, both to the north and the south, give it great natural advantages for commerce, in addition to which, two important lines of communication, made at great expense, traverse it from lake Erie to the Ohio. Cincinnati, its commercial capital, has a population of not less than fifty thousand inhabitants. Indiana and Illinois are scarcely, if at all, inferior to Ohio in natural advantages; and considering its proportion of first-rate land, Michigan is perhaps the best State in the Union. Kentucky and Tennessee abound both in good land and in mineral resources. Missouri, the largest State in the Union, possesses a vast extent of excellent land, besides rich mines of iron and of lead. The two territories, Iowa and Wisconsin, lying northward of Missouri and Illinois, the former on the west, and the latter on the east of the Upper Mississippi, are large and fertile districts of country, besides abounding in lead mines. Both are evidently destined to become great States. Arkansas having a great deal of inferior, as well as of fertile land, is considered one of the poorest States on the Mississippi. The large State of Alabama, with the exception of a small part in the south, about Mobile, and another part in the north near the Tennessee river, was in 1815, in the occupancy of the Creek, Choctaw, and Chickasaw Indians, chiefly the first of those tribes; but is now rapidly increasing in population. The State of Mississippi has also much land of the very best quality, and although its financial affairs are at present in a deplorable condition from bad legislation, it may be expected, in a few years, to emerge from its embarrassments. Humanly speaking, it must be so, for its resources are enormous. And as for Louisiana, the rich alluvial soil of the banks of its rivers, and the advantages for commerce, derived from its position in the lowest part of the great valley of the Mississippi, must eventually make it a rich and powerful State. But it would require the perseverance shown in similar circumstances by the people of Holland, to defend with dykes the greater part of the State territory, to recover from the sea the mass of the delta of the Mississippi, and to make the whole the valuable country into which it might be converted.

An immense tract of almost unexplored country lies to the north-west of the State of Missouri and the territories of Iowa and Wisconsin, much of which is believed to be fertile. What new States may yet be formed there, time alone will show.

Nearly the whole of this vast valley is drained by one great river and its branches, of which no fewer than fifty-seven are navigable for steam boats. Indeed, the Missouri, the Arkansas, the Red river, and the White river, flowing from the west, and the Illinois, the Ohio, the Cumberland, and the Tennessee, from the north and east, are themselves great rivers. On the north the great lakes, and on the south the gulph of Mexico, form openings into this vast region for the commerce of the world. But besides those two great inlets from the north and south, communication with the Atlantic slope has been opened up at various points of the Alleghany chain, by means of substantial roads of the ordinary construction, and also by canals and railways. Thus a railway above six hundred miles in length, unites the town of Buffalo on lake Erie with Boston; a canal unites it with Albany, and from that the North river connects it with New York. Buffalo communicates, again, with all the northern parts of Ohio, Indiana, Michigan, and Illinois, and with the eastern side of the Wisconsin territory, by fifty steam boats which ply between it and the ports of those regions. To all these advantages we must ascribe the rapid appearance of so many large cities in this great western valley, such as New Orleans, St. Louis, Louisville, Cincinnati, and Pittsburg, to say nothing of smaller towns on spots, which, with the exception of New Orleans, may be said to have been covered by the forest only fifty years ago.

I conclude this chapter, by remarking for a moment on the kind and wise Providence which kept the great valley of the Mississippi from the possession, and almost from the knowledge of the colonists of the United States, for more than one hundred and fifty years. By that time they had so far occupied and reduced to cultivation the less fertile hills of the Atlantic slope, and there had acquired that hardy, industrious, and virtuous character, which better fitted them to carry civilisation and religion into the vast plains of the west. So that, at this day, the New England, and other Atlantic States, whilst all increasing in population themselves, serve at the same time as nurseries, from which the West derives many of the best plants that are transferred to its noble soil.

CHAPTER XIII.

OBSTACLES WHICH THE VOLUNTARY SYSTEM IN SUPPORTING RELIGION HAS HAD TO ENCOUNTER IN AMERICA; 1. FROM THE ERRONEOUS OPINIONS ON THE SUBJECT OF RELIGIOUS ECONOMY WHICH THE COLONISTS BROUGHT WITH THEM.

SOME persons in Europe entertain the idea, that if the American plan of supporting religion by relying, under God's blessing, upon the efforts of the people, rather than upon the help of the government, has succeeded in that country, it has been owing, in a great measure, to the fact that the country presented an open field for the experiment; that every thing was new there; that no old establishments had to be pulled down; no deep-rooted prejudices to be eradicated; no time-honoured institutions to be modified; but that all was favourable for attempting something new under the sun. Now it is hardly possible to entertain an idea more remote from the truth than this.

What follows will demonstrate, that so far from committing religion to the spontaneous support of persons cordially interested in its progress, the opposite course was pursued from the first in all the colonies, excepting such as had been founded expressly to afford an asylum for persons coming from countries, or even from other colonies, in which they were compelled to support a worship which they disapproved, and in which they could not conscientiously bear a part. In the greater number of the colonies, in fact, men looked to the civil government for the support of the Christian ministry and worship. Now, what we have here to consider is not the question whether they were right or wrong in doing so, but the simple fact that they actually did so; and accordingly, that so far from what has been called the voluntary principle having had an open field in America, in those very parts of the country which now perhaps best illustrate its efficiency, it had long to struggle with establishments founded on the opposite system, and with strong prepossessions in their favour.

In all such parts of the country many obstacles were opposed to the abandonment of the old system. Good and great men made no secret of their fears that the cause of religion would thus be ruined; that the churches would be forsaken by the people, whose unaided efforts would prove unequal to the expense of maintaining them, and that they could never be induced to attempt it. In fact, as they had never been accustomed to rely upon their own exertions in that matter, and were not aware how much they could do, they were at first timid and discouraged. Another obstacle lay in the unwillingness of those who had enjoyed the influence and ascendancy conferred by the old system, to surrender those advantages. Such persons were prone to believe, and naturally sought to impress others with the conviction, no doubt very sincerely, that their resistance to the proposed change was the legitimate fruit of their zeal for the cause of God, and of their dread lest that cause should suffer.

Other obstacles, and those not inconsiderable, had to be encountered, all resulting directly, or indirectly, from the old system. It will be shown in due time, that some of the worst heresies in the United States were originated and propagated by measures arising out of the old system. Not that such results flowed inevitably from an union of Church and State, for I would not even say that they were the legitimate consequences of the peculiar kind of union that subsisted in the quarter where those evils manifested themselves. What I mean to say is, that truth has there encountered powerful obstacles, which we have every reason to believe would not have existed but for that union. Other evils there might have been in the absence of any such union, but, be that as it may with the obstacles to which I refer, it could not be said that the field was entirely new, far less open.

Still more; some of the greatest obstacles which the "American plan," as it has sometimes been called in Europe, of supporting religion had to overcome, arose from the erroneous views of the colonists on the subject of religious liberty. The voluntary system rests on the grand basis of perfect religious freedom. I mean a freedom of conscience for all; for those who believe Christianity to be true, and for those who do not; for those who prefer one form of worship, and for those who prefer another. This is all implied, or rather it is fully avowed, at the first step in supporting religion upon this plan.

Now it so happened,—nor ought we to wonder at it, for it would have been a miracle had it been otherwise,—that very many of the best colonists who settled in America had not yet attained to correct ideas on the subject of religious toleration, and the rights of conscience. It required persecution, and that thorough discussion of the subject which persecution brought in its train both in the Colonies and in England, and other European countries, to make them understand the subject. And, in point of fact, those who first understood it had learned it in the school of persecution. Such was Roger Williams; such were Lord Baltimore and the Roman catholics who settled in Maryland; such was William Penn. Accordingly, the three colonies that they founded, Rhode island, Maryland, and Pennsylvania, including Delaware, were the first communities, either in the new or the old world, that enjoyed religious liberty in the fullest extent.

I am sure indeed, that, as I have already said, the founders of the first American colonies, and those of New England in particular, did as much for freedom of conscience as could have been expected, and were in that respect in advance of the age in which they lived. If they were intolerant, so were others. If they would not allow Roman catholics to live among them, the most dreadful examples, be it remembered, of Roman catholic intolerance were forced upon their attention, and that their policy was merciful in the extreme compared with that of Roman catholic countries in those days. They merely refused to receive them, or to allow them to remain among them, whereas the poor Huguenots were not permitted so much as to retire from amid their enemies. If, in some of the colonies, Quakers were treated with great harshness and shocking injustice, what treatment did the members of that sect receive at the same period in England? If the colonists burned witches,

was not that done also in Scotland, England, and other countries ?

I may therefore repeat that the colonists were in advance of
their cotemporaries in their views of almost all questions relating to human rights, and that they maintained this advance is
attested by the institutions that arose among them. But the
intolerance with which they were chargeable at first, may be
traced to their opinions with regard to the relations which
the Church ought to sustain towards the State. And their
erroneous views on that subject created obstacles which were
with difficulty overcome by the principle of leaving religion,
not to the support as well as protection of the State, but to the
hearts and hands of persons who have truly received, and are
willing to sustain it. These remarks will suffice to show that
the field was not so open to that principle in America as some
have thought.

CHAPTER XIV.

OBSTACLES WHICH THE VOLUNTARY SYSTEM HAS HAD TO ENCOUNTER IN AMERICA ;
2. FROM THE NEWNESS OF THE COUNTRY, THE THINNESS OF THE POPULATION, AND
THE UNSETTLED STATE OF SOCIETY.

A second class of obstacles which the voluntary system, or, I
should rather say, which religion in general has had to encounter in America, comprehends such as are inseparable from its
condition as a new country.

From its very nature, the life of a colonist presents manifold
temptations to neglect the interests of the soul. There is the
separation of himself and his family, if he has one, from old
associations and influences; and the removal, if not from
abundant means of grace, at least from the force of that public
opinion which often powerfully restrains from the commission
of open sin. Now though many of the American colonists fled
from persecution and from abounding iniquity. Such was not
the case with all. Then, there is the entering into new and
untried situations; the forming of new acquaintanceships, not

always of the best kind; and even that engrossment with the
cares and labours attending a man's removal into a new country, especially in the case of the many who have to earn their
bread by their own strenuous exertions.   All these things
hinder the growth of piety in the soul, and form real obstacles
to its promotion in a community.

And if such hindrances had a baneful effect at the outset,
they have never ceased to operate injuriously down to this day.
To say nothing of the foreigners who come, year after year, to
the American shores on their way to the *Far West*, thousands
of the natives of the Atlantic slope leave their houses every
year to settle amid the forests of that vast western region.   In
their case there is peculiar exposure to evil; their removal
almost always withdraws them from the powerful influence of
neighbourhoods where true religion more or less flourishes.
Such of them who are not decidedly religious in heart and life,
greatly risk losing any good impressions they may have
brought with them, amid the engrossing cares and manifold
temptations of their new circumstances — circumstances in
which even the established Christian will find much need of
redoubled vigilance and prayer.

The comparative thinness, also, of the population in the
United States now is, and must long continue to be, a great
obstacle to the progress of religion in that country.   I have
already stated, that the area of all the territories claimed by
its government is somewhat more than 2,000,000 of square
miles.   Now, leaving out of view the vast region on the upper
Missouri and Mississippi rivers, west and north of Iowa and
Wisconsin, and reaching to the Oregon mountains; leaving
out of view also the Pacific slope, and looking only to the
twenty-six States, three Territories, and one District, we have a
country of somewhat more than 1,000,000 of square miles, over
which the Anglo-American race has more or less diffused
itself.   But the whole population, including the African race
among us, in 1840, was just 17,068,666.   That is, upon an
average, about seventeen souls to the square mile.   If this
population were equably diffused over the entire surface of the
organised States and Territories, even then it would be difficult
enough to establish and maintain churches and other religious

institutions among so sparse a population. Still, perhaps, it could be done. A parish of thirty-six square miles, which would be large enough in point of extent, would contain 612 souls. One twice as large would contain 1224 souls. But although a country would be considered well supplied if it had a pastor for every 1224 souls, still the dispersion of these over seventy-two square miles would necessarily very much curtail the pastor's capacity for doing good, and prevent the souls under his charge from enjoying the full influence of the gospel. But the population of the United States is far from being thus equally distributed. Some of the older States are pretty densely settled; not more, however, than is necessary for the easy maintenance of churches, and of a regular and settled ministry. Massachusetts, the most densely settled of them all, has 102 souls to the square mile; some others, such as Connecticut and Rhode island, have from seventy to eighty; others, such as New Jersey, Delaware, Maryland, and New York, will average from forty to fifty. Taking the whole Atlantic slope, with the exception of Florida, which is but little inhabited, the average is twenty-eight, whilst in the eleven States and two Territories in the valley of the Mississippi, it is less than ten souls to the square mile.

It is manifest, therefore, that while the population of a large proportion of the Atlantic States, and of parts of the older ones in the west, is hardly dense enough to render the support of gospel ordinances easy, the difficulty of effecting this is immensely increased in many quarters, but especially in the west, by the inhabitants being much more widely scattered. I shall show in another place how this difficulty is, in a good measure at least, overcome; here it is enough that I point to its existence.

Personal experience alone can give any one a correct idea of the difficulties attending the planting and supporting of churches and pastors in that vast frontier country in the west, where the population, treading on the heels of the Indians, is, year after year, advancing into the forests. A few scattered families, at wide intervals, are engaged in cutting down the huge trees, and clearing what at first are but little patches of ground. In a year or two the number is doubled. In five or six years the country begins to have the appearance of being inhabited by civilised men. But years more must roll away before the population will be dense enough to support churches at convenient distances from each other, and to have ministers of the gospel to preach in them every Sabbath. Yet this work must be done, and it is doing to an extent which will surprise many into whose hands this book may fall.

But if the thinness of the population be an obstacle, how great must be its rapid increase in the aggregate? I say in the aggregate; for it is manifest that its increase in the thinly settled districts must so far be an advantage. But with this increase diffusing itself into new settlements, we have a double difficulty to contend with,—the increase itself demanding a great augmentation of churches and ministers, and its continued dispersion rendering it difficult to build the one and support the other, even were a sufficiency of pastors to be found. This difficulty would be quite appalling, if long contemplated apart from the vast efforts made to meet and overcome it. The population of the United States was in 1790, 3,929,827; in 1800, 5,305,925; in 1810, 7,239,814; in 1820, 9,638,131; in 1830, 12,866,920; and in 1840, 17,068,666.[1] The reader may calculate for himself the average annual increase during each of the five decades which have elapsed since 1790. But it is not so easy so ascertain the yearly increase. From 1830 to 1840 it was 4,201,746, being at the average rate of 420,174 souls per annum. During the decade from 1840 to 1850, it will unquestionably much exceed an average of 500,000 per annum, unless checked by some great calamity, of which there is no prospect.

Now, to provide churches and pastors for such an increase as this is no very easy matter, yet it must either be done, or, sooner or later, the great bulk of the nation, as some have predicted, will sink into heathenism. How far this is likely, judging from what has been done and is now doing, we shall see in another place. Here I simply state the magnitude of the difficulty.

---

[1] Including seamen in the government service, not included in the enumerations commonly published. Hence the difference between the statements in the text and those the reader may meet with elsewhere. But the difference is only 6,100.

Finally, the constant emigration from the old States to the new, and even from the older to the newer settlements in the latter, is a great obstacle to the progress of religion in all places from which part of the population is thus withdrawn. It occasionally happens in one or other of the Atlantic States, that a church is almost broken up by the departure for the western States of families, on whom it mainly depended for support. Most commonly, however, this emigration is so gradual, that the church has time to recruit itself from other families, who arrive and take the place of those who have gone away. Thus, unless where a church loses persons of great influence, the loss is soon repaired. In the cities of the east, and their suburban quarters especially, from the population being of so floating a character, this evil is felt quite as much as in the country.

But it must not be forgotten, that what is an evil in the east, by withdrawing valuable support from the churches there, proves a great blessing to the far west, by transferring thither Christian families, to originate and support new churches in that quarter.

CHAPTER XV.

OBSTACLES WHICH THE VOLUNTARY PRINCIPLE HAS HAD TO ENCOUNTER IN AMERICA; 3. FROM SLAVERY.

That the co-existence in one country of two such different races as the European or Caucasian, and the African, standing to each other in the relation of masters and slaves, should retard the progress of true religion there, it requires but little knowledge of human nature to believe.

Slavery has been a curse in all past time, and by no possibility can it be otherwise. It fosters a proud, arrogant, and unfeeling spirit in the master, and naturally leads to servility and meanness, to deceitfulness and dishonesty, in the slave. Either way it is disastrous to true religion.

But, I have no intention to speak here of the nature of slavery, its past history, present condition, or future prospects in

the United States. My object is simply to show how it operates as one of the greatest obstacles to the promotion of religion; and, as such, militates against the success of the voluntary system there. Slavery, indeed, may easily be shown to
be peculiarly an obstacle to that system.

I might mention that the fact of the reluctance of slaves to
worship in the same congregation with their masters, is unfavourable to the interests of true piety. That there is such a
reluctance, every one knows who has had much to do with the
institution of slavery. It often shows itself in the hesitation of
slaves to come to the family altar, even in families which are
known to treat them with kindness.

This fact is easily accounted for. Human nature, however
degraded, and whether wearing a black or a white skin, has still
some remains of pride, or rather some consciousness of what is
due to it, and it is not wonderful that it avoids as much as
possible coming into contact with persons, however worthy and
kind they may be, yet to whom it feels itself placed in ignoble
subjection. Therefore it is, that the negro of our southern
States prefers going to a church or meeting composed of people
of his own colour, and where no whites appear. Slaves, also,
sometimes prefer places of worship where greater latitude is
allowed for noisy excitement, to whatever denomination of
Christians they may belong, than would be tolerated in the
religious assemblies of white people.

I am not aware that I have exaggerated, as some may think,
the repugnance of the slaves to join in religious worship with
their masters. One thing is certain, that whether from such
repugnance, or some other cause, the slaves like better to meet
by themselves, wherever allowed to do so.

That the separation of the two classes thus occasioned is
injurious to the spiritual interests of both, must be evident from
a moment's consideration. So long as slavery exists in the
world, the gospel enjoins their appropriate duties upon both
masters and slaves, and they should be made to hear of those
duties in each other's presence. This should be done kindly
but also faithfully. And no Christian master can excuse himself from doing this duty he owes to his slave, in relation to his
spiritual and immortal interests, by saying, that he permits him

to go he hardly knows whither, and to be taught those things which concern his highest happiness by he knows not whom. Where, indeed, the master himself is wholly indifferent to the subject of religion, as alas! is too often the case, it is well that the slave is allowed and disposed to seek religious instruction anywhere.

But one of the greatest evils of slavery, as respects the maintenance of Christian institutions, is, that it creates a state of society extremely unfavourable to the providing of a sufficient number of churches and pastors for the spiritual wants of all classes—rich and poor, slaves and free. This holds especially in the case of large landed estates, with many hundred slaves in the possession of a small number of rich proprietors. In such circumstances, a church capable of containing one or two hundred persons might perhaps accommodate all the masters and their families within the compass of a very large parish, whereas an immense edifice would be required for the accommodation of all their slaves. Now, where this is the state of things, there is danger that the landowners, being few in number, may grudge the expense of maintaining a church and pastor at all, however well able to do so; or, that with horses and carriages at their command, all the rich within one vast district, will join in having public worship at some central point, where few, comparatively, of the slaves and labouring white population will find it possible to attend. Where even a few of the rich proprietors are religious men, there is no difficulty in having the gospel brought, not only to their own doors, but also to those of their slaves and other dependents. But where they are indifferent, or opposed to religion, then, not only does the gospel not reach them, but if it reaches their slaves, it must be with great difficulty, and often very irregularly. For, be it remembered, that a slave population is generally too poor to contribute anything worth mentioning for the support of the gospel. Blessed be God there is a way, as I shall show hereafter, by which some of the evils here spoken of may be mitigated;—and that is by the system of itinerant preaching employed in the United States, so extensively, and so usefully, by the Methodists.

Contemplating these difficulties, we shall come to the conclusion that if, in any part of the United States, the support of the gospel by taxation enforced by law is better adapted to the circumstances of the people than the voluntary plan, it is in the sea-board counties of Maryland, Virginia, and the two Carolinas. Still, it will be found that even there the voluntary system has not been inefficient, but that through the ministry either of fixed or itinerant preachers of righteousness, it has carried the gospel to the inhabitants of all classes, to an extent which, under such adverse circumstances, might seem impracticable.

It must be noted that while such are the difficulties that. oppose the maintenance of a Christian ministry in the slaveholding States, there is a special necessity for the *preaching* of the gospel there. It is emphatically by the "hearing" of the word that the slaves can be expected to come to the knowledge of salvation. A most unwise and iniquitous legislation has, in most of those States, forbidden the teaching of the slaves to read! And although, doubtless, this law is not universally obeyed, and here and there a good many slaves can both read and teach others to do so privately, yet it is from the voice of the living teacher that the great bulk of that class in the United States must receive instruction in divine things. Thanks be to God! no legislature in any State has forbidden the preaching of the gospel to those who are in the bonds of slavery; and many thousands of them, it is believed, have not heard it in vain.

I conclude by stating that slavery exists in thirteen States, —those which form the southern half of the Union, and in one Territory, that of Florida. It does not exist in the other thirteen, nor in the two important Territories of Wisconsin and Iowa. The States in which it exists are Delaware, Maryland, Virginia, North Carolina, South Carolina, Georgia, Kentucky, Tennessee, Missouri, Arkansas, Louisiana, Mississippi, and Alabama.

CHAPTER XVI.

OBSTACLES WHICH THE VOLUNTARY SYSTEM HAS HAD TO ENCOUNTER IN AMERICA ;
4. FROM THE VAST EMIGRATION FROM FOREIGN COUNTRIES.

It is superfluous to say that the emigration from Europe of
such excellent persons as many of those were who founded the
American colonies, or who joined them in the days of their
infancy, could not fail to be a blessing to the country. But
the emigration into the United States at the present day is of
a very different character. Whatever violent persecution there
may have been in Europe during the last seventy years, has
been limited in extent and of short duration, so that the emigrations from the old world to America, during that period,
must be referred to worldly considerations, not to the force of
religious convictions leading men to seek for the enjoyment of
religious liberty. In fact, to improve their worldly condition,
to provide a home for their children in a thriving country, to
rejoin friends who had gone before them, or to escape from
what they deemed civil oppression in Europe,—such, generally,
have been the motives that have prompted the recent emigrations to America. To these we must add a different class—
that of men who have left their country, as has been said,
"for their country's good;" nor is the number of such inconsiderable.

It is difficult to discover to what extent emigrants have
poured into the United States since the Revolution, and especially since the close of the second war with Great Britain in
1815. Our custom-house books do not sufficiently distinguish
between emigrants, properly so called, and American citizens
returning from abroad. Again, many of the emigrants enter
the United States by way of Canada, those especially who come
from the British islands,[1] and no exact enumeration of these,
it is believed, is kept on the frontier. 60,000 foreigners, it
has been supposed, have annually entered the United States

[1] I apprehend that a far greater number go to Canada by the way of the
United States, particularly by New York.—ED.

for several years past with the view of settling there. According to the report of the secretary of state, 70,509 foreigners arrived in 1839, of whom 34,213 were from Great Britain, and 30,014 from the continent of Europe. The remainder were from South America, Texas, the West Indies, &c. This is probably too low an estimate. From tables published in England, it appears that from 1825 to 1837 inclusive, no fewer than 300,259 left Great Britain and Ireland for the United States, and, also, that the number had increased every year until 1836, when it reached 37,774. In 1837 the number was 36,770.

It is quite certain, I think, that the emigrants from the continent of Europe, consisting almost entirely of Germans from Germany proper and Alsace, Swiss, and French, are nearly if not quite as numerous as those from the British islands, and if so, the total number of emigrants into the United States, from all quarters, must be nearer 70,000 than 60,000.

It must not be supposed, however, that all the foreigners who come to the United States are emigrants. Many come only to make a longer or shorter stay, as merchants and traders, and some, after having arrived with the intention of remaining, become dissatisfied and return to their native country. In short, it is impossible to discover, with any degree of accuracy, the real yearly augmentation of the population of the United States arising from emigration. I am inclined to believe that it is greatly over-rated, and that it does not exceed 50,000, or at most 60,000.

Now, although among these emigrants there are many respectable people, and some who bring with them no inconsiderable amount of property, duty compels me to say that the great majority of them are not only very poor, but ignorant also and depraved. Of those from Ireland, very many are intemperate and ill qualified to succeed in a new country. Should the Temperance cause, indeed, continue to prosper in Ireland, as it has done for some years past under Father Matthew's efforts, we may hope for an improvement in the "Irish importation." Of the Germans, likewise, a great many are poor, and some are of improvident and depraved habits; although, in the mass, they are much superior to the Irish in point of frugality and sobriety. Many of the Germans have of late years brought with them considerable sums of money, and though a good many are Roman Catholics, yet the majority are Protestants. A large proportion of them now come from the kingdoms of Wurtemburg and Bavaria, and from the duchy of Baden, whereas, in former times, they came chiefly from the eastern and northern parts of Germany.

Now, although, no doubt, the mortality among these emigrants from Europe, caused by exposure, anxiety, fatigue, diseases incident to a strange climate, and so forth, is far greater than among native Americans, yet the yearly accession of so many people, ignorant in a great degree of the nature of our institutions, about half of them unable to speak English, and nearly half of them, also, Roman Catholics, must impose a heavy responsibility, and a great amount of labour upon the churches in order to provide them with the means of grace. Everything possible must be done for the adults among them, but hope can be entertained chiefly for the young. These grow up speaking the language and breathing the spirit of their adopted country, and thus the process of assimilation goes steadily on. In a thousand ways the emigrants who are, as it were, cast upon our shores, are brought into contact with a better religious influence than that to which many of them have been accustomed in the old world. From year to year, some of them are gathered into our churches; whilst, as I have said, their children grow up Americans in their feelings and habits. All this is especially true of the emigrants who, meaning to make the country their home, strive to identify themselves with it. There are others, however, and particularly those who, having come to make their fortunes as merchants and traders, calculate upon returning to Europe, that never become American in feeling and spirit. From such no aid is to be expected in the benevolent efforts made by Christians to promote good objects among us.

I have been struck with the fact that, generally speaking, our religious societies receive their most steady support from our Anglo-American citizens. The emigrants from the British realm, English, Welsh, Scotch, and Irish, rank next in the interest they take in our benevolent enterprises, and in readiness to contribute to their support.   The Germans rank next, the Swiss next, and the French last.   There is most infidelity among the French, yet it prevails also, to a considerable degree, among the Swiss and Germans, among the better-informed classes of whom it is sometimes to be found.   There is no want of infidelity and indifference to religion among emigrants from the British islands, but they are chiefly to be found among the lowest class of them.

Thus, as I remarked before, while the emigration from Europe into the United States brings us no inconsiderable number of worthy people, it introduces also a large amount of ignorance, poverty, and vice.   Besides this, it is difficult to supply with religious institutions, and it takes long to Americanise, if I may use the expression, in feeling, conduct, and language, those multitudes from the continent of Europe who cannot understand or speak English.   Many of the Germans, in particular, in consequence of the impossibility of finding a sufficient number of fit men to preach in German, were at one time sadly destitute of the means of grace in their dispersion over the country.   But within the last fifteen years, a brighter prospect has opened upon that part of our population, as I shall have to show in its place.

I have not charged upon the ordinary emigration to the shores of America the great amount of crime in the United States, which may be traced to the escape thither of criminals from Europe; for these cannot, with propriety, be regarded as constituting a part of that emigration.   Nevertheless, it is the case that much of the crime committed in America, from that of the *honourable* merchant who scruples not to defraud the custom-house if he can, down to the outrages of the man who disturbs the streets with his riots, is the work of foreigners.

It may be said, I am sure, with the strictest truth, that in no country is a foreigner who deserves well, treated with more respect and kindness than in America; in no country will he find less difference between the native and the adopted citizen; in no country do men become more readily assimilated in principle and feeling to the great body of the people, or more fully realise the fact that they form a constituent part of the nation.

I have now finished the notice which I intended to take of

some of the obstacles which the voluntary system has had to encounter in the United States. I might mention others were it necessary; but I have said enough to show that it is a mistake to suppose that it has had an open field and an easy course there. I am far from saying that if the experiment were to be made in an old country, where the population is established and almost stationary—where it is homogeneous and indigenous—there would not be other obstacles to encounter, greater perhaps than those to be found among us, and in some respects peculiar to America. I only wish these difficulties not to be lost sight of as we advance in this work, and that they should be appreciated at their just value when we come to speak of subjects upon which they bear.

Such are some of the topics which I thought it of consequence to treat beforehand, that the reader might be prepared for a better comprehension of the grand subject of this work. Upon the direct consideration of that subject we are now ready to enter.

BOOK II.

CHAPTER I.

I HAVE already remarked, that if we would understand the civil and political institutions of the United States of America, we must trace them from their earliest origin in Anglo-Saxon times, through their various developments in succeeding ages, until they reached their present condition in our own days.

In like manner, if we would thoroughly understand the religious condition and economy of the United States, we must begin with an attentive survey of the character of the early colonists, and of the causes which brought them to America.

Besides, as has been elsewhere said,[1] a striking analogy may be traced between natural bodies and bodies politic. Both retain in manhood and old age, more or less of the characteristic traits of their infancy and youth. All nations bear some marks of their origin, the circumstances amid which they were born, and which favoured their early development, and leave an impression which stamps their whole future existence.

We begin our inquiry, therefore, into the religious history and condition of the United States, by pourtraying, as briefly as possible, the religious character of the first colonists who may be regarded as the founders of that commonwealth. We shall

---

[1] See M. de Toqueville, "Démocratie en Amérique," Première Partie. Tome i. chap. 1. Also Lang's " Religion and Education in America." Chap. 1. page 11.

follow neither the chronological nor the geographical order, but shall first speak of the colonists of New England, next of those of the south, and finally of those of the middle States. This gives us the advantage at once of grouping and of contrast.

How wonderful are the events that sometimes flow from causes apparently the most inadequate, and even insignificant! The conquest of Constantinople by the Turks in 1453, seemed to be only one of the ordinary events of war, and yet it led to the revival of letters among the higher classes of society throughout Europe. The invention of the art of printing by an obscure German, two years later, gave immense facilities for the diffusion of knowledge among all classes of people. The discovery of America by a Genoese adventurer towards the close of the same century (A. D. 1492), produced a revolution in the commerce of the world. A poor monk in Germany, preaching (A. D. 1517,) against indulgences, emancipated whole nations from the domination of Rome. And the fortuitous arrival of a young French lawyer who had embraced the faith of the Reformation at an inconsiderable city in Switzerland, situated on the banks of the Rhone, followed by his settling there, and organising its ecclesiastical and civil institutions, was connected, in the mysterious providence of Him who knows the end from the beginning, and who employs all events to advance His mighty purposes, with the establishment of free institutions in England, their diffusion in America, and their triumph in other lands.

The way had long been preparing for the Reformation in England by the opinions avowed by Wickliff and his followers, and by the resistance of the government to the claims and encroachments of the ecclesiastical authorities. The light, too, which had begun to appear in Germany, cast its rays across the North sea, and men were ere long to be found secretly cherishing the doctrines maintained by Luther. At length an energetic, but corrupt and tyrannical prince, after having been rewarded for writing against Luther, by receiving from the pope the title of "Defender of the Faith," thought fit to revenge the refusal of a divorce from his first wife, by abolishing the papal supremacy in his kingdom, and transferring the headship of the church, as well as of the state, to himself. But Henry VIII. desired to have no reformation either in the doctrines or the worship of the church;

and in his last years he revoked the general permission that he had granted for the reading of the scriptures, being all that he had ever done in favour of the Reformation among the people, and confined that privilege to the nobles and merchants. A tyrant at once in spiritual and temporal matters, he punished every deviation from the ancient usages of the church, and every act of non-compliance with his own arbitrary ordinances.

The reign of Edward VI. (1547-1553,) forms a most important era in the history of England. Partly through the influence of the writings of Calvin, which had been circulated to a considerable extent in that country; partly through that of his public instructions, which had been frequented at Geneva by many young English students of divinity; but still more by the lectures of those two eminent continental divines, Peter Martyr and Martin Bucer, who had been invited to England, and made professors of theology at Oxford and Cambridge; many persons had been prepared for that reformation in the church which then actually took place under the auspices of Cranmer, and was carried to the length, in all essential points, at which it is now established by law. Hooper, and many other excellent men, were appointed to the most influential offices in the church, and much progress was made in resuscitating true piety among both the clergy and the people.

But the Protestants of England soon became divided into two parties. One headed by Cranmer, then archbishop of Canterbury, consisted of such as were opposed to great changes in the discipline and government of the church, and wished to retain, to a certain degree, the ancient forms and ceremonies, hoping thereby to conciliate the people to the Protestant faith. To all the forms of the Romish church the other party bore an implacable hatred, and insisted upon the rejection of even a ceremony or a vestment, that was not clearly enjoined by the word of God. Wishing to see the church purified from every human invention, they were therefore called Puritans, a name given in reproach, but by which, in course of time, they were not averse to being distinguished. With them the Bible was the sole standard, alike for doctrines and for ceremonies, and with it they would allow no decision of the hierarchy, or ordinance of the king, or law of parliament to interfere. On that great foundation they planted their feet, and were encouraged in so doing by Bucer, Peter Martyr, and Calvin himself.[1] The Churchmen, as their opponents were called, desired, on the other hand, to differ as little as possible from the ancient forms, and readily adopted things indifferent; but the Puritans could never sever themselves too widely from every usage of the Romish church. For them the surplice and the square cap were things of importance, for they were the livery of superstition, and tokens of the triumph of prescription over the word of God— of human over divine authority. And though then but a small minority, even thus early there was evidently a growing attachment to their doctrines in the popular mind.[2]

During the bloody reign of Edward VI.'s successor, Mary, that is, from 1553 to 1558, both parties of Protestants were exposed to danger, but especially the Puritans. Thousands fled to the continent, and found refuge chiefly in Frankfort-on-the-Maine, Emden, Wesel, Basel, Marpurg, Strasbourg, and Geneva. At Frankfort the dispute between the two parties was renewed with great keenness; even Calvin vainly attempted to allay it. In the end, most of the Puritans left that city and retired to Geneva, where they found the doctrine, worship, and discipline of the church to accord with their sentiments. While residing there, they adopted for their own use a liturgy upon the plan suggested by the great Genevese reformer, and there also they translated the Bible into English.[3] Persecution, meanwhile, prevailed in England. Cranmer, to whom the queen in her early years had owed her life, Hooper, Rogers,

---

[1] Strype's Memorials, vol. ii., chap. xxviii. Hallam's Constitutional History of England, vol. i., p. 140.

[2] The Puritans have been often and severely blamed for what some have been pleased to call their obstinacy, in regard to things comparatively indifferent. But it has been well remarked by president Quincy, in his Centennial Address at Boston, that " The wisdom of zeal for any object is not to be measured by the particular nature of that object, but by the nature of the *principle*, which the circumstance of the times, or of society, have identified with such objects."

[3] This version was first published in 1560. So highly was it esteemed, particularly on account of its notes, that it passed through thirty editions. To both the translation and notes King James had a special dislike, alleging that the latter were full of " traitorous conceits." In the conference at Hampton Court, " he professed that he could never yet see a Bible well translated in English, but worst of all his Majesty thought the Geneva to be." This version was the one chiefly used by the first emigrants to New England, for that of King James, published in 1611, had not then passed into general use.—(Strype's Annals ; Barlow's Sum and Substance of the Conference at Hampton Court.)

and other distinguished servants of Christ, suffered death. Many of the clergy again submitted to the Roman see.

On the death of Queen Mary, many of the exiled Puritans returned, with their hatred to the ceremonies and vestments inflamed by associating them with the cruelties freshly committed at home, and by what they had seen of the simple worship of the reformed churches abroad. But they struggled in vain to effect any substantial change. Elisabeth, who succeeded her sister Mary in 1558, would hear of no modifications of any importance in doctrine, discipline, or worship, so that in all points the church was almost identically the same as it had been under Edward VI. While Elisabeth desired to conciliate the Romanists, the Puritans denounced all concessions to them, even in things indifferent. Though by profession a Protestant, she was much attached to many of the distinguishing doctrines and practices of the papacy, and she bore a special hatred to the Puritans, not only because of their differing so much from her in their religious views, but also because of the sentiments they hesitated not to avow on the subject of civil liberty. The oppression of the government was driving them, in fact, to scrutinise the nature and limits of civil and ecclesiastical authority, and to question the right of carrying it to the extent to which the queen and the bishops were determined to push it. The popular voice was becoming decidedly opposed to a rigorous exaction of conformity with the royal ordinances respecting the ceremonies. Parliament itself became imbued with the same spirit, and showed an evident disposition to befriend the Puritans, whose cause began to be associated with that of civil and religious liberty. The bishops, however, and most of the other dignified clergy, supported the views of the queen. Whitgift, in particular, who was made archbishop of Canterbury in 1583, vigorously enforced conformity. The court of High Commission compelled many of the best ministers of the established church to relinquish their benefices, and to hold private meetings for worship as they best could; very inferior and worthless men being generally put into their places.

Still, the suppression of the Puritans was found a vain attempt. During Elisabeth's long reign their numbers steadily increased. The services they rendered to the country may be so far estimated by the verdict of an historian, who has been justly charged with lying in wait, through the whole course of his history, for an opportunity of throwing discredit upon the cause of both religion and liberty, and who bore to the Puritans a special dislike. Mr. Hume says: "The precious spark of liberty had been kindled and was preserved by the Puritans alone." [1]

As a body, the Puritans studiously avoided separation from the established church. What they desired was reform, not schism. But towards the middle of Elisabeth's reign, a party arose among them that went to an extreme in their opposition to the high churchmen, and refused to hold communion with a church whose ceremonies and government they condemned. These were the Independents, or Brownists, as they were long improperly called, from the name of one who was a leading person among them for a time, but who afterwards left them and ended his days in the established church. The congregation which Brown had gathered, after sharing his exile, was broken up and utterly dispersed. But the principles which, for a time, he had boldly advocated, were destined to survive his abandonment of them in England, as well as to flourish in a far distant region, at that time almost unknown.

From that time forward the Puritans became permanently divided into two bodies—the Nonconformists, constituting a large majority of the body, and the Separatists. The former saw evils in the established church, and refused to comply with them, but at the same time acknowledged its merits and desired its reform; the latter denounced it as an idolatrous institution, false to truth and to Christianity, and, as such, fit only to be destroyed. Eventually the two parties became bitterly opposed to each other; the former reproached the latter with precipitancy; the latter retorted the charge with that of a base want of courage.

The accession of King James gave new hopes to the Puritans, but these were soon completely disappointed. That monarch, though brought up in Presbyterian principles in Scotland, no sooner crossed the border than he became an admirer of

---

[1] Hume's History of England, iii. 76.

Prelacy, and although a professed Calvinist, allowed himself to become the easy tool of the Arminian sycophants who surrounded him. Having deceived the Puritans, he soon learned to hate both them and their doctrines. His pedantry having sought a conference with their leaders at Hampton Court, scenes took place there which were as amusing for their display of the dialectics of the monarch as they were unsatisfactory to the Puritans in their results. " I will have none of that liberty as to ceremonies; I will have one doctrine, one discipline, one religion in substance and in ceremony. Never speak more on that point, how far you are bound to obey." [1] 'And verily it was a point on which such a monarch as James I. did not wish to hear anything said. The conference lasted three days. The king would bear no contradiction. He spoke much, and was greatly applauded by his flatterers. The aged Whitgift said: " Your Majesty speaks by the special assistance of God's Spirit." And bishop Bancroft exclaimed on his knees, that his heart melted for joy, " because God had given England such a king as, since Christ's time, has not been." [2]

The Parliament was becoming more and more favourable to the doctrines of the Puritans; but the hierarchy maintained its own views, and was subservient to the wishes of the monarch. Conformity was rigidly enforced by Whitgift's successor, Bancroft. In 1604, three hundred Puritan ministers are said to have been silenced, imprisoned, or exiled. But nothing could check the growth of their principles. The Puritan clergy and the people became arrayed against the established church and the king. The latter triumphed during that reign, but very different was to be the issue in the following. So hateful to the court were the people called Brownists, Separatists, or Independents, that efforts were made, with great success, to root them out of the country. Some remains of them, however, outlived for years the persecutions by which they were assaulted.

In the latter years of Elisabeth, a scattered flock of these

[1] In the second day's conference his Majesty spoke of the Puritans with little ceremony. " I will make them conform, or I will harry them out of the land, or else worse." " Only burn them, that's all."—(Barlow's Sum and Substance of the Conference at Hampton Court, p. 71, 83.)

[2] Barlow's Sum and Substance of the Conference at Hampton Court, p. 93, 94 ; Lingard, ix. 32 ; Neal's History of the Puritans, iii. p. 45.

Separatists began to be formed in some towns and villages of Nottinghamshire, Lincolnshire, and the adjacent borders of Yorkshire, under the pastoral care of John Robinson, a man who has left behind him a name admitted, even by his bitterest enemies, to be without reproach. This little church was watched and beset day and night by the agents of the court, and could with difficulty find opportunities of meeting in safety. They met here or there, as they best could, on the Sabbath, and thus strove to keep alive the spirit of piety which united them. They had become "enlightened in the word of God," and were led to see, not only that "the beggarly ceremonies were monuments of idolatry," but also "that the lordly power of the prelates ought not to be submitted to." Such being their sentiments, no efforts, of course, would be spared to make their lives miserable, and if possible to extirpate them.

At last, seeing no prospect of peace in their native land, they resolved to pass over to Holland, a country which, after having successfully struggled for its own independence and for the maintenance of the Protestant faith, now presented an asylum for persons of all nations when persecuted on account of their religion. After many difficulties and delays, a painfully interesting account of which will be found in their annals, they reached Amsterdam in 1608. There they found many of their brethren who had left England for the same cause with themselves. The oldest part of these exiled Independents was the church under the pastoral care of Francis Johnson. It had emigrated from London about the year 1592. There was also a fresh accession composed of a Mr. Smith's people. Risk of collision with these induced Mr. Robinson and his flock to retire to Leyden, and there they established themselves.

CHAPTER II.

RELIGIOUS CHARACTER OF THE FOUNDERS OF NEW ENGLAND.—PLYMOUTH COLONY.

THE arrival of Mr. Robinson's flock in Holland was destined to be the beginning only of their wanderings. "They knew that they were PILGRIMS and looked not much on those things, but lifted up their eyes to heaven their dearest country, and quieted their spirits." 1   "They saw many goodly and fortified cities, strongly walled and guarded with troops and armed men. Also, they heard a strange and uncouth language, and beheld the different manners and customs of the people, with strange fashions and attires; all so far differing from that of their plain country villages, wherein they were bred and born and had so long lived, as it seemed they were come into a new world.   But those were not the things they much looked on, or that long took up their thoughts; for they had other work in hand," and " saw before long poverty coming on them like an armed man, with whom they must buckle and encounter, and from whom they could not fly.   But they were armed with faith and patience against him and all his encounters; though they were sometimes foiled, yet by God's assistance they prevailed and got the victory."

On their removal to Leyden, as they had no opportunity of pursuing the agricultural life they had led in England, they were compelled to learn such trades as they could best earn a livelihood by for themselves and their families. Brewster, a man of some distinction, who had been chosen their ruling elder, became a printer.   Bradford, afterwards their governor in America, and their historian, acquired the art of dying silk.   All had to learn some handicraft or other.   But notwithstanding these difficulties, after two or three years of embarrassment and toil, they "at length came to raise a competent and comfortable living, and continued many years in a comfortable condition, enjoying much sweet and delightful society, and spiritual comfort together in the ways of God, under the able ministry and prudent government of Mr. John Robinson and Mr. William Brewster, who was an assistant unto him in the place of an elder, unto which he was now called and chosen by the church; so that they grew in knowledge, and other gifts and graces of the Spirit of God; and lived together in peace, and love, and holiness.   And many came unto them from divers parts of England, so as they grew a great congregation."2   As for

1 See Governor's Bradford's History of Plymouth Colony.
2 Governor Bradford's History of New England. It has been calculated

Mr. Robinson, we are told that the people had a singular affection for him, and that "his love was great towards them, and his care was always bent for their best good, both for soul and body. For, besides his singular abilities in divine things, wherein he excelled, he was able also to give direction in civil affairs, and to foresee dangers and inconveniences; by which means he was every way as a common father unto them." Not only so; besides writing several books and preaching thrice a-week to his own flock, Mr. Robinson entered warmly into the Arminian controversy, which was raging during his residence at Leyden, and disputed often with Episcopius and other champions of the Arminian side.[1]

Although they had begun to enjoy some degree of comfort in Holland, still they did not feel themselves at home there. Accordingly, they began to agitate the question of removing to some part of America. Their reasons for thinking of such a step, as stated in the words of their own historian, give us new proof of the excellent character of this simple-hearted and excellent flock.

I. "And first, they found and saw by experience the hardness of the place and country to be such, as few in comparison would come to them, and fewer that would bide it out and continue with them. For many that came to them could not endure the great labour and hard fare, with other inconveniences which they underwent and were contented with. But though they loved their persons, and approved their cause, and honoured their sufferings, yet they left them, as it were, weeping, as Orpah did her mother-in-law Naomi; or as those Romans did Cato in Utica, who desired to be excused and borne with, though they could not all be Catos.[2] For many, though they desired to enjoy the ordinances of God in their purity, and the liberty of the gospel with them, yet alas! they admitted of bondage with

from data to be found in other histories of that colony, that so much had Mr. Robinson's church increased, that it had three hundred "communicants" before any of them embarked for America.

[1] Besides the testimony of Winslow in his "Brief Narrative," which might be suspected of being partial, we have that of the celebrated professor Hornbeck, in his "Summa Controversiarum Religionis," respecting Mr. Robinson, whom he calls "Vir ille (Johannes Robinsonus,) gratus nostris, dum vixit, fuit, et theologis Leidensibus familiaris et honoratus."

[2] See Plutarch's Life of Cato the Younger.

danger of conscience, rather than endure those hardships; yea, some preferred and chose prisons in England rather than liberty in Holland, with these afflictions. But it was thought that if a better and easier place of living could be had, it would draw many, and take away these discouragements; yea, their pastor would often say that many of those that both writ and preached against them, if they were in a place where they might have liberty, and live comfortably, they would then practise as they did.

II. "They saw that although the people generally bore all their difficulties very cheerfully and with a resolute courage, being in the best of their strength, yet old age began to come on some of them; and their great and continual labours, with other crosses and sorrows, hastened it before the time; so as it was not only probably thought, but apparently seen, that within a few years more they were in danger to scatter by necessity pressing them, or sink under their burdens, or both; and therefore, according to the divine proverb, that 'a wise man seeth the plague when it cometh, and hideth himself,'[1] so they, like skilful and beaten soldiers, were fearful either to be entrapped or surrounded by their enemies, so as they should neither be able to fight nor fly; and therefore thought it better to dislodge betimes to some place of better advantage and less danger, if any could be found.

III. "As necessity was a taskmaster over them, so they were forced to be such not only to their servants, but in a sort to their dearest children; the which, as it did a little wound the tender hearts of many a loving father and mother, so it produced also many sad and sorrowful effects. For many of their children, that were of best dispositions and gracious inclinations, having learned to bear the yoke in their youth, and willing to bear part of their parents' burden, were oftentimes so oppressed with their heavy labours, that although their minds were free and willing, yet their bodies bowed under the weight of the same, and became decrepit in their early youth; the vigour of nature being consumed in the very bud as it were. But that which was more lamentable, and of all sorrows most heavy to be borne, was,

---

[1] Quoted from the Geneva version.

that many of their children by these occasions, and the great
licentiousness of youth in the country, and the manifold temptations of the place, were drawn away by evil examples into
extravagant and dangerous courses, getting the reins on their
necks, and departing from their parents.   Some became soldiers,
others took them upon far voyages by sea, and others some
worse courses, tending to dissoluteness and the danger of their
souls, to the great grief of their parents and dishonour of God;
so that they saw their posterity would be in danger to degen-
erate and be corrupted.

IV. " Lastly, (and which was not the least,) a great hope
and inward zeal they had of laying some good foundation, or at
least to make some way thereunto, for the propagating and
advancing the gospel of the kingdom of Christ in these remote
parts of the world; yea, though they should be but as step-
ping-stones unto others for performing of so great a work."

Besides these reasons, mentioned by Governor Bradford in
his History of Plymouth colony, the three following are adduced
by Edward Winslow, who also was one of its founders: 1.
Their desire to live under the protection of England, and to
retain the language and the name of Englishmen.   2. Their
inability to give their children such an education as they had
themselves received.   And, 3. Their grief at the profanation of
the Sabbath in Holland.

Such were the considerations that induced the pilgrims to
send over to England a deputation, with the view of ascertaining what kind of reception their project might meet with from
the king, and whether the London Company, or as it was most
commonly called, the Virginia Company, would sanction their
settling as a colony on any part of its possessions in America.
With all his detestation of the Independents, the king felt
rather gratified than otherwise at the prospect of extending
colonisation—that being an object in which he had long felt an
interest.   Many years before this he had encouraged colonisation in the Highlands and western islands of Scotland, and the
north of Ireland has long been indebted for a prosperity and
security, such as no other part of that island has enjoyed, to
the English and Scotch plantations which he had been at great
pains to form on lands laid waste during the desolating warfare

of his predecessor, Elisabeth, with certain Irish chieftains in those parts.[1] To extend the dominions of England he allowed to be "a good and honest motion." On his inquiring what trade they expected to find in the northern part of Virginia, [2] being that in which they thought of settling, they answered, "fishing;" to which the monarch replied with his usual asseveration: "So God have my soul, 'tis an honest trade; 'twas the apostles' own calling." [3] But as the king wished to consult the archbishop of Canterbury and the bishop of London, the delegates were recommended not to press the matter, but to trust to his connivance rather than to look for his formal consent. This they resolved to do, rightly concluding that "should there be a purpose to wrong us, though we had a seal as broad as the house-floor, there would be found means enough to recall it."

The Virginia Company showed the most favourable dispositions. They said "the thing was of God," and granted a large patent, which, however, proved of no use. One of them, to help on the undertaking, lent the sum of £300, without interest, for three years, and this was afterwards repaid. This advance must have been a seasonable encouragement, for a hard bargain had to be struck with some London merchants, or "adventurers," as they are called by the colonial historians, in order to raise what further money was required. At length, two ships, the Speedwell of sixty, and the Mayflower of a hundred and eighty tons, were engaged, and everything else arranged for the departure of as many as the ships could accommodate. Those went who first offered themselves, and Brewster, the ruling elder, was chosen their spiritual guide. The other leading men were John Carver, William Bradford, Miles Standish, and Edward Winslow. Mr. Robinson stayed behind, along with the greater part of the flock, with the intention of joining those who went first at some future time, should such be the will of God. A solemn fast was observed. Their beloved pastor afterwards delivered a farewell charge, which must be regarded as a remarkable production for those times.[4]

1 See Robertson's History of Scotland, chap. viii.
2 The reader will remember that the whole Atlantic coast was then called Virginia by the English.
3 Edward Winslow's Brief Narrative.
4 This charge is related in Edward Winslow's " Brief Narrative." It is

All things being now ready, the emigrants, after being "feasted at the pastor's house, for it was large," by those who were to remain behind, and having been "refreshed after their tears by the singing of psalms," set out for Delft-haven, where the ships then lay. There they were again "feasted," and prayer having been made, they were accompanied on board by their friends, but "were not able to speak to one another for the abundance of sorrow to part." The wind being favourable, they were soon on their way.

here subjoined in the language in which it is given by that author—from whom alone it became known to the world :—

"We are now ere long to part asunder, and the Lord knoweth whether ever he should live to see our faces again. But whether the Lord had appointed it or not, he charged us before God and his blessed angels to follow him no further than he followed Christ ; and if God should reveal anything to us by any other instrument of His, to be as ready to receive it as ever we were to receive any truth by his ministry ; for he was very confident the Lord had more truth and light yet to break forth out of his holy word. He took occasion, also, miserably to bewail the state and condition of the Reformed Churches, who were come to a period in religion, and would no further go than the instruments of their reformation. As, for example, the Lutherans, they could not be drawn to go beyond what Luther saw ; for whatever part of God's will He had further imparted and revealed unto Calvin, they will rather die than embrace it. And so also, saith he, you see the Calvinists, they stick where he left them, a misery much to be lamented ; for though they were precious shining lights in their times, yet God hath not revealed His whole will to them ; and were they now living, saith he, they would be as ready and willing to embrace further light as that they had received. Here, also, he put us in mind of our church covenant, at least that part of it whereby we promise and covenant with God and one another, to receive whatsoever light or truth shall be made known to us from his written word ; but withal exhorted us to take heed what we received for truth, and well to examine and compare it, and weigh it with other scriptures of truth before we received it. For, saith he, it is not possible the Christian world should come so lately out of such thick antichristian darkness, and that full perfection of knowledge should break forth at once.

"Another thing he commended to us was that we should use all means to avoid and shake off the name of Brownist, being a mere nickname and brand to make religion odious, and the professors of it to the Christian world. And to that end, said he, I should be glad if some godly minister would go over with you before my coming ; for, said he, there will be no difference between the unconformable [nonconforming—but who had not actually separated from the church] ministers and you, when they come to the practice of the ordinances out of the kingdom. And so advised us by all means to endeavour to close with the godly party of the kingdom of England, and rather to study union than division, viz. how near we might possibly, without sin, close with them, than in the least measure to affect division or separation from them. And be not loth to take another pastor or teacher, saith he ; for that flock that hath two shepherds is not endangered but secured by it."

Such is this remarkable farewell address, as reported by Winslow. "Words," says Prince in his "Annals," speaking of it, "almost astonishing in that age of low and universal bigotry which then prevailed in the English nation ; wherein this truly great and learned man seems to be the only divine who was capable of rising into a noble freedom of thinking and practising in religious matters, and even of urging such an equal liberty on his own people. He labours to take them off from their attachment to him, that they might be more entirely free to search and follow the Scriptures."

They left Holland on the 22d of July, 1620, followed by the respect of the people among whom they had lived. We learn from Winslow that the Dutch, on learning that they were about to leave their country, urged them much to settle in Zealand, or if they preferred America, to seek a home for themselves on the Hudson, within the territory discovered by the navigator who gave his name to that river while in their service, and which they therefore claimed and had resolved to colonise. But the liberal inducements then offered to the emigrants, could not alter their sweet purpose of settling in a country which should be under the government of their native land.

A few days brought them safely to Southampton in England. On learning that the captain of the smaller of the two vessels was found unwilling to prosecute so long a voyage in her, so that after putting back, first to Dartmouth and then to Plymouth, they were compelled to send the Speedwell with part of the company to London, and it was not until the 6th of September that the Mayflower finally sailed across the Atlantic with a hundred passengers. The voyage proved long and boisterous. One person died and a child was born, so that the original number reached the coast of America. On the 9th of November they entered the harbour of cape Cod, and after that spent fully a month in looking about for a place that seemed suitable for a settlement, they fixed at last on the spot now bearing the name of the town where they had received the last hospitalities of England. There they landed on the 11th of December, old style, or the 22d of December, according to the new; and to this day the very rock on which they first planted their feet at landing, is shown to the passing stranger as a cherished memorial of that interesting event. On that rock commenced the colonisation of New England.

On the day before the arrival of the Mayflower in cape Cod harbour, the following document was signed by all the male heads of families, and unmarried men not attached to families, represented by their respective heads.

" In the name of God, Amen. We, whose names are underwritten, the loyal subjects of our dread sovereign lord, King James, by the grace of God, of Great Britain, France, and Ireland, king, defender of the faith, &c., having undertaken, for the glory of God, and advancement of the Christian faith, and honour of our king and country, a voyage to plant the first colony in the northern parts of Virginia, do, by these presents, solemnly and mutually, in the presence of God and one of another, covenant and combine ourselves together into a civil body politic, for our better ordering and preservation, and furtherance of the ends aforesaid, and by virtue hereof to enact, constitute, and frame such just and equal laws, ordinances, acts, constitutions, and offices, from time to time, as shall be thought most meet and convenient for the general good of the colony; unto which we promise all due submission and obedience. In witness whereof we have here under subscribed our names, at cape Cod, the 11th of November,[1] in the year of the reign of our sovereign lord, King James, of England, France, and Ireland the eighteenth, and of Scotland the fifty-fourth, anno domini 1620."

Here may be said to have been the first attempt made by an American colony to frame a constitution or fundamental law—the seminal principle, as it were, of all that wonderful series of efforts which have been put forth in the new world, towards fixing the foundations of independent voluntary self-government. John Carver was chosen governor of the colony, and to assist him in administering its affairs, a council of five, afterwards increased to seven members, was appointed.

After fixing upon what they considered to be the best spot for a settlement, as the ship's boat could not come close to the water's edge, they suffered much in their health by having to wade ashore. The few intervals of good weather they could catch between snow and rain, they spent in erecting houses; but before the first summer came round, nearly half their number had fallen victims to consumptions and fevers, the natural effects of the hardships to which they had been exposed. What may we not imagine must have been the distress they suffered during that dreary winter, passed beneath unknown skies, with a gloomy unbroken forest on the one hand, and the dreary ocean on the other!

[1] Here there is a discrepancy in the date, as they are said to have entered the harbour on the 9th. Hutchinson makes them enter it on the 11th, that is, the day of signature.—Ed.

But with the return of spring came health, and hope, and courage. The colony took root. The ground it occupied had been cleared for it by the previous destruction by pestilence of the tribe of Indians which had occupied it. Of course the colonists could not buy land which there was nobody to sell. They soon made the acquaintance of the neighbouring tribes, acquired their friendship, and entered into treaty with them. Their numbers were in course of time increased by successive arrivals of emigrants, until in 1630 they exceeded 300. After the second year they raised grain not only to supply all their own wants but with a surplus for exportation.[1] They soon had a number of vessels employed at the fisheries. They even planted a colony on the Kennebec in Maine, and extended their trade to the Connecticut river, before the close of the first ten years of their settlement, and before any other English colony had been formed on the coast of northern Virginia, or New England, the name given to it by Captain Smith in 1614, and by which it was ever after to be distinguished.

The governor and council were chosen every year. At first, and for above eighteen years, "the people" met as in Athens of old, for the discussion and adoption of laws. But as the colony extended, and towns and villages rose along the coasts and in the interior, the "democratic" form of government gave place to the "republican," by two delegates being chosen from each township to form "the general court," or legislature of the commonwealth.

For some time they had no pastor or preaching elder, but Mr. Brewster conducted their public devotions until they came to have a regular minister. Their affairs as a church were con-

---

1 During the first two or three years they suffered greatly at times for want of food. Sometimes they subsisted on half allowance for months. They were once saved from famishing by the benevolence of some fishermen off the coast. "I have seen men," says Winslow, "stagger by reason of faintness for want of food." "Tradition declares, that at one time the colonists were reduced to a pint of corn, which being parched and distributed, gave to each individual only five kernels: but tradition falls far short of reality; for three or four months together they had no corn whatever. When a few of their old friends arrived to join them, a lobster, or a piece of fish, without bread or any thing else but a cup of fair spring water, was the best dish which the hospitality of the whole colony could offer. Neat cattle were not introduced till the fourth year of the settlement. Yet, during all this season of self-denial and suffering, the cheerful confidence of the pilgrims in the mercies of Providence remained unshaken."
—(Bancroft's History of the United States vol. i., p. 315.)

ducted with the same system and order that marked their civil economy.

Such is a brief account of the founding of Plymouth colony, the earliest of all that were planted in New England. Placed on a sandy and but moderately productive part of the coast, and commanding a very limited extent of inland territory from which to derive the materials of commerce and wealth, it could never be expected to become a great and important colony, like others of which I have yet to speak. But it was excelled by none in the moral worth of its founders. All professing godliness, they almost without exception, as far as we know, did honour to that profession. True religion was with them the first of all possessions. They feared God, and He walked among them and dwelt among them, and his blessing rested upon them. The anniversary of their disembarkation at Plymouth has long been regularly celebrated upon the yearly return of the 22d of December, in prose and in verse, in oration and in poem;—a patriotic and religious duty, to which have been consecrated the highest efforts of many of the noblest and purest minds ever produced by the country to whose colonisation they led the way.

CHAPTER III.

RELIGIOUS CHARACTER OF THE EARLY COLONISTS—FOUNDERS OF NEW ENGLAND—
COLONY OF MASSACHUSETTS BAY.

THE first English settlements actually formed in America, arose, it will be remembered,[1] from James I. investing two companies, the one formed at London, the other at Bristol and other towns in the west of England, each with a belt of territory extending from the Atlantic to the Pacific ocean; the one lying between the 34th and 38th, the other between the 41st and 48th degrees of north latitude. Both companies were formed in a purely commercial spirit; each was to have its own

1 Book i., chap. iv.

council, but the royal council was to have the superintendence
of their whole colonial system.   The London company was dissolved, we have seen, after an existence of eighteen years.   The
other accomplished nothing beyond giving encouragement to
sundry trading voyages to the coast of the country made over
to it by its charter.

At length, at the repeated instance of Captain Smith, the
Western company sought a renewal of their patent with additional powers, similar to those of the London company's second
charter in 1609, with the view of attempting an extensive plan
of colonisation; and notwithstanding opposition from the parliament and the country at large, they succeeded in their request.
On November 3d, 1620, the king granted a charter to forty of
his subjects, among whom were members of his household and
government, and some of the wealthiest and most powerful of
the English nobility, conveying to them in absolute property,
to be disposed of and administered as they might think proper,
the whole of that part of North America which stretches from
the Atlantic to the Pacific, between the 40th and 48th degrees
of north latitude, under the title of "The Council established
at Plymouth, in the county of Devon, for the planting, ruling,
ordering, and governing New England in America."   Under
the auspices of a vast trading corporation, invested with such
despotic powers, the colonisation of New England commenced.
While this charter was in course of being granted, the pilgrims
were fast approaching the American coast.   No valid title had
given them, as yet, any legal right to set their feet upon it,
but this they obtained a few years after from the newly formed
Plymouth company.

From its very commencement the new company began to
lavish away grants of the immense territory which had been
conveyed to it, so that during the fifteen years of its existence,
it had covered with its patents the whole country now comprising Massachusetts, New Hampshire, Maine, and the vast region
westward of these, as far as the Pacific ocean.   Such was the
utter disregard shown in those grants for anything like clear
and precise boundaries, that we cannot so much wonder at the
number of lawsuits that arose from them, as that these were
ever terminated.   To Mason and Gorges were granted the ter-

ritories now forming the States of New Hampshire and Maine; to Sir William Alexander the country between the river St. Croix and the mouth of the St. Lawrence, notwithstanding that it was all well known to be claimed by the French, who had even planted a colony upon it, called by them Acadie, but ultimately destined to receive the name of Nova Scotia.

But the most important grant made by the Plymouth company, often called in history the Council for New England, was one conveying the Massachusetts territory to a body organised in England in 1628, for the purpose of at once providing an asylum for persons suffering for conscience sake in the old world, and of extending the kingdom of Christ in the new, by founding a colony on a large scale. With this view six Dorchester gentlemen bought from the company a belt of land stretching from the Atlantic to the Pacific, between three miles south of Charles river and Massachusetts bay, and three miles north of every part of the river Merrimac. Of these six, three, namely, Humphrey, Endicot, and Whetcomb, retained their shares, while the other three sold theirs to Winthrop, Dudley, Johnson, Pynchon, Eaton, Saltonstall, and Bellingham, so famous in colonial history, besides many others, men of fortune and friends to colonial enterprise. Thus strengthened, this new company sent out 200 colonists under Endicot, a man every way fitted for such an enterprise, courageous, cheerful, and having firmness of purpose and warmth of temper, softened by an austere benevolence. These arrived in Massachusetts bay in September, 1628, and settled at Salem, where several members of the Plymouth colony had already established themselves.

The news of this still farther augmented the now growing interest felt in England on the subject of colonising America. In the painful circumstances in which the Puritans were placed, they could not fail to have their attention drawn to the continued prosperity of the Plymouth settlement, and naturally rejoiced to hear of a land towards the setting sun, where they might enjoy a tranquillity to which they had long been strangers in the land of their fathers. Such was the interest felt throughout the kingdom, that not only in London, Bristol, and Plymouth, but at Boston, and other inland towns, influential persons were found ready to risk their fortunes in the cause.

Efforts were made to procure the royal sanction for the patent granted by the Plymouth to the Massachusetts company, and a royal charter in favour of the latter, after much trouble and expense, passed the seals on the 4th of March, 1629.

This charter, bearing the signature of Charles I., was evidently granted under the idea that the persons whom it incorporated were to be rather a trading community than a civil government. They were constituted a body politic by the name of " The Governor and Company of Massachusetts bay in New England." The administration of its affairs was committed to a governor, deputy-governor, and thirteen assistants, elected by the shareholders. The freemen were to meet four times a year, or oftener if necessary, and were empowered to pass laws for the regulation of their affairs, without any provision rendering the royal assent indispensable to the validity of their acts. Strictly considered, the patent simply conferred the rights of English subjects, without any enlargement of religious liberty. It empowered, but did not require, the governor to administer the oaths of supremacy and allegiance. The persons in whose favour it was granted were still members of the church of England—not Independents or Separatists—and probably neither the government, nor the first patentees, foresaw how wide a departure from the economy of that church would result from the emigration that was about to take place under its provisions.

It is surprising that a charter which conferred unlimited powers on the corporation, and secured no rights to the colonists, should have become the means of establishing the freest of all the colonies. This was partly owing to its empowering the corporation to fix what terms it pleased for the admission of new members. The corporation could increase or change its members only by its own consent, and not being obliged to hold its meetings in England, it was possible for itself to emigrate, and thus to identify itself with the colony which it was its main object to found. This was actually done. As the corporation was entirely composed of Puritans, it was not difficult, by means of resignations and new elections, to choose the governor, deputy-governor, and assistants, from among such as were willing to leave England as colonists.

The first object of the new company, on obtaining a royal

charter, was to re-inforce the party who had gone out with
Endicot and settled at Salem.   The re-inforcement consisted of
200 emigrants, under the pastoral care of the Rev. Francis
Higginson, an eminent non-conformist minister, who was delighted to accept of the invitation he received to undertake that
charge.   By their arrival, which happened in June, the colony
at Salem was increased to 300 persons, but diseases and the
hardships incident to new settlements cut off, during the following winter, eighty of that number, who died only lamenting
that they were not allowed to see the future glories of the colony.
Among these was their beloved pastor, Mr. Higginson, whose
death was a great loss to the little community.

The year following, namely, 1630, was a glorious one for the
colonisation of New England.   Having first taken every preparatory measure required for self-transportation, the corporation itself embarked, accompanied by a body of from 800 to
900 emigrants, among whom there were several persons of large
property and high standing in society.   John Winthrop, one
of the purest characters in England, had been chosen governor.
Taken as a whole, it is thought that no single colony could ever
be compared with them.   One may form some idea of the elevated piety that pervaded the higher classes among the Puritans
of that day from the language of the younger Winthrop: " I
shall call that my country," said he to his father, " where I
may most glorify God, and enjoy the presence of my dearest
friends.   Therefore herein I submit myself to God's will and
yours, and dedicate myself to God and the company with the
whole endeavours both of body and mind.   The ' conclusions'
which you sent down are unanswerable; and it cannot but be a
prosperous action which is so well allowed by the judgments of
God's prophets, undertaken by so religious and wise worthies in
Israel, and indented to God's glory in so special a service."[1]

Governor Winthrop had a fine estate which he sacrificed, as
did many others, what were considered good estates in England
in those days.   One of the richest of the colonists was Isaac
Johnson, "the father of Boston," as a proof of which it may be
mentioned, that by his will his funeral expenses were limited to

---

[1] Winthrop's Journal, i. pp. 359, 360.

£250. His wife, the lady Arabella, was a daughter of the Earl of Lincoln. In her devotedness to the cause of Christ, "she came from a paradise of plenty into a wilderness of wants." [1] They were almost without exception godly people, and when they embarked for America were members of the church of England, being that in which they had been born and brought up. Though of the party that were opposed to what they considered Romish superstitions and errors, still cleaving in their conscientious convictions to the national church, and though they could not in all points conform to it, yet they had not separated from it, but sought the welfare of their souls in its ministrations, whenever they possibly could hope to find it there. They lamented what they regarded as its defects, but not in a spirit of bitter hostility. This very plainly appears from the following letter addressed to the members of the church of England, by Governor Winthrop and others, immediately after their going on board, and when they were about to bid a long farewell to their native shores. It is conceived in a noble spirit :—

"The humble request of his majesty's loyal subjects, the Governor and the Company, late gone for New England; to the rest of their brethren in the church of England.

"*Reverend Fathers and Brethren.* The general rumour of this solemn enterprise wherein ourselves with others, through the providence of the Almighty, are engaged, as it may spare us the labour of imparting our occasion unto you, so it gives us the more encouragement to strengthen ourselves by the procurement of the prayers and blessings of the Lord's faithful servants; for which end we are bold to have recourse unto you, as those whom God hath placed nearest his throne of mercy, which affords you the more opportunity, so it imposeth the greater bond upon you to intercede for his people in all their straits; we beseech you, therefore, by the mercies of the Lord Jesus, to consider us as your brethren, standing in very great need of your help, and earnestly imploring it. And howsoever your charity may have met with some occasion of discouragement, through the misreport of our intentions, or through the disaffection, or indiscretion of some of us, or rather amongst us—for

[1] Judge Story's Centennial Discourse.

we are not of those that dream of perfection in this world—yet we desire you would be pleased to take notice of the principles and body of our company, as those who esteem it our honour to call the church of England, from whence we rise, our dear mother, and cannot part from our native country, where she specially resideth, without much sadness of heart, and many tears in our eyes; ever acknowledging that such hope and part as we have obtained in the common salvation, we have received in her bosom, and sucked it from her breasts; we leave it not, therefore, as loathing that milk wherewith we were nourished there, but blessing God for the parentage and education, as members of the same body shall always rejoice in her good, and unfeignedly grieve for any sorrow that shall ever betide her; and while we have breath, sincerely desire and endeavour the continuance and abundance of her welfare, with the enlargement of her bounds in the kingdom of Christ Jesus.

"Be pleased, therefore, fathers and brethren, to help forward this work now in hand, which if it prosper, you shall be the more glorious; howsoever, your judgment is with the Lord, and your reward with your God. It is an usual and laudable exercise of your charity to commend to the prayers of your congregations, the necessities and straits of your private neighbours; do the like for a church springing out of your own bowels. We conceive much hope that this remembrance of us, if it be frequent and fervent, will be a most prosperous gale in our sails, and provide such a passage and welcome for us from the God of the whole earth, as both we which shall find it, and yourselves, with the rest of our friends who shall hear of it, shall be much enlarged to bring in such daily returns of thanksgivings, as the specialities of his Providence and goodness may justly challenge at all our hands. You are not ignorant that the Spirit of God stirred up the apostle Paul to make continual mention of the church of Philippi, (which was a colony from Rome,) let the same Spirit, we beseech you, put you in mind that are the Lord's remembrancers, to pray for us without ceasing, (who are a weak colony from yourselves,) making continual request for us to God in all your prayers.

"What we entreat of you that are the ministers of God, that we also crave at the hands of all the rest of our brethren, that they would at no time forget us in their private solicitations at the throne of grace.

"If any there be, who through want of clear intelligence of our course, or tenderness of affection towards us, cannot conceive so well of our way as we could desire, we would entreat such not to despise us—nor to desert us in their prayers and affections, but to consider rather that they are so much the more bound to express the bowels of their compassion towards us, remembering always that both nature and grace doth ever bind us to relieve and rescue with our utmost and speediest power, such as are dear to us when we conceive them to be running uncomfortable hazards.

"What goodness you shall extend to us on this or any other Christian kindness, we, your brethren in Christ Jesus, shall labour to repay in what duty we are or shall be able to perform, promising, so far as God shall enable us, to give him no rest on your behalf, wishing our heads and hearts may be as fountains of tears for your everlasting welfare, when we shall be in our poor cottages in the wilderness, overshadowed with the spirit of supplication, through the manifold necessities and tribulations which may not altogether unexpectedly, nor we hope, unprofitably befal us.   And so commending you to the grace of God in Christ, we shall ever rest."

The ships that bore Winthrop and his companions across the Atlantic, reached Massachusetts bay in the following June and July. After having consoled the distresses and relieved the wants of the Salem colonists, the newly arrived emigrants set about choosing a suitable spot for a settlement; a task which occupied the less time, as the bay had been well explored by preceding visitors. The first landing was made at the spot where Charleston now stands. A party having gone from that up the Charles river to Watertown, there some of them resolved to settle, others preferred Dorchester; but the greater number resolved to occupy the peninsula upon which Boston now stands, the settlement receiving that name from part of the colonists having come from Boston in England. For a while they were lodged in cloth tents and wretched huts, and had to endure all kinds of hardship. To complete their trials, disease made its attacks and carried off 200 of them at least before De-

cember.   About a hundred lost heart and went back to England.   Many who had been accustomed in their native land to
ease and plenty, and to all the refinements and luxuries of cultivated life, were now compelled to struggle with unforeseen
wants and difficulties.   Among those who sank under such
hardships and died, was the lady Arabella Johnson.   Her husband too, "the greatest furtherer of the plantation," was carried
off by disease; but "he died willingly and in sweet peace," making "a most godly end."[1]   These trials and afflictions were
borne with a calm reliance on the goodness of God, nor was
there a doubt felt but that in the end all would go well.   They
were sustained by a profound belief that God was with them,
and by bearing in mind the object of their coming to that wilderness.

Amid all this gloom light began to break in at last.   Health
returned, and the blanks caused by disease were filled up by
partial arrivals of new emigrants from England in the course of
the two following years.   On the colony becoming a little settled,
measures were taken to introduce a more popular government
by extending the privileges of the charter, which had established
a kind of close corporation.   By it all fundamental laws were to
be enacted by general meetings of the freemen, or members of
the company.   One of the first steps accordingly was to convene
a general court at Boston, and admit above a hundred of the
older colonists to the privileges of the corporation; and from
that they gradually went on, until instead of an aristocratic
government conducted by a governor, deputy-governor, and
assistants, holding office for an indefinite period, these functionaries were elected annually, and the powers of legislation
were transferred from general courts of all the freemen joined
with the assistants, to a new legislature, or "general court,"
consisting of two branches, the assistants constituting the upper,
and deputies from all the "towns" forming the lower branch.
Within five years from the foundation of the colony, a constitution was drawn up which was to serve as a sort of Magna
Charta, embracing all the fundamental principles of just government; and in fourteen years from its foundation, the colonial

[1] Governor Winthrop's Journal.

government was organised upon the same footing as that on which it rests at the present day.

But with these colonists the claims of religion took precedence of all other concerns of public interest. The New England Fathers began with God, sought his blessing, and desired first of all to promote his worship. Immediately after landing they appointed a day for solemn fasting and prayer. The worship of God was commenced by them not in temples built with hands, but beneath the wide-spreading forest. The Rev. Mr. Wilson, the Rev. Mr. Philips, and other faithful ministers had come out with them; and for these, as soon as the affairs of the colony became a little settled, a suitable provision was made.

In the third year of the settlement there came out among other fresh emigrants, two spiritual teachers who were afterwards to exercise a most extensive and beneficial influence in the colonies. One of these was the eminently pious and zealous Cotton, a man profoundly learned in the holy scriptures, as well as in the writings of the fathers and the schoolmen; in the pulpit rather persuasive than eloquent, and having a wonderful command over the judgments and hearts of his hearers. The other was Hooker, a man of vast endowments, untiring energy, and singular benevolence; the equal of the reformers, though of less harsh a spirit than that which marked most of those great men. These, and other devoted servants of God were highly appreciated, not only for their works' sake, but also for their great personal excellencies.

Ere long the colony began to extend in all directions, from Boston as a centre and capital; and as new settlements were made additional churches were also planted, for the New England fathers felt that nothing could be really and permanently prosperous without religion.[1] Within five years a considerable

[1] Several of these new and feeble churches actually supported two ministers, one called the "Pastor" and the other the "Teacher." The distinction between these offices is not very easily expressed, and must have been more difficult to maintain in practice. Thomas Hooker, in his "Survey of the Summe of Church Discipline," &c., declares the scope of the pastor's office to be "to work upon the will and the affections;" that of the doctor or teacher, "to informe the judgment, and to help forward the work of illumination in the minde and understanding, and thereby to make way for the truth, that it may be settled and fastened on the heart." The former was to "wooe and win the soul to the love and practice of the doctrine which is according to godlinesse;" the latter to dispense "a word of knowledge." I need hardly say that this duplicate of the ministerial office, though much liked by the early colonists, did not long survive their day.

population was to be found scattered over Dorchester, Roxbury, Watertown, Cambridge, Charlestown, Lynn, and other settlements. Trade was spreading wide its sails; emigrants were arriving from Europe; brotherly intercourse was opened up with the Plymouth colony, by the visits of Governor Winthrop and the Rev. Mr. Wilson. Friendly treaties were made not only with the neighbouring Indian tribes, the Nipmucks and Naragansetts, but also with the more distant Mohigans and the Pequods in Connecticut. God was emphatically honoured by the great bulk of the people, and everything bore the aspect of prosperity and happiness. Such was the origin of the colony of Massachusetts bay—a colony destined to exercise a controlling influence over all the other New England plantations.

CHAPTER IV.

RELIGIOUS CHARACTER OF THE EARLY COLONISTS—FOUNDERS OF NEW ENGLAND—
COLONIES OF CONNECTICUT, RHODE ISLAND, NEW HAMPSHIRE, AND MAINE—GENERAL
REMARKS.

PLYMOUTH[1] colony had been planted only three years when it began to have off-shoots, one of which in 1623, settled at Windsor, on the rich alluvial lands of the Connecticut, led thither, however, more by the advantages of the spot as a station for trading in fur, than by the nature of the soil. The report of its fertility having at length reached England, the Earl of Warwick bought from the Council for New England, as we have seen that the Plymouth company was sometimes called, the whole valley of the Connecticut, which purchase was, the year following, transferred to Lord Say and Seal, Lord Broke, and John Hampden. Two years later, the Dutch, who, in right of discovery, claimed the whole of the Connecticut territory, sent an expedition from their settlement at Manhattan up the river

[1] Plymouth in America is often called New Plymouth by early writers in speaking of New England. I prefer the name by which exclusively the town is now known. The context will always enable the reader to distinguish it from Plymouth in England.

Connecticut, and attempted to make good their claim by erecting a block-house, called Good Hope, at Hartford.   In 1635, the younger Winthrop, the future benefactor of Connecticut, came from England with a commission from the proprietors to build a fort at the mouth of the river, and this he did soon after. Yet even before his arrival, settlers from the neighbourhood of Boston had established themselves at Hartford, Windsor, and Weathersfield.   Late in the fall of that year a party of sixty persons, men, women, and children, set out for the Connecticut, and suffered much from the inclement weather of the winter that followed.   In the following June, another party, amounting to about a hundred in number, and including some of the best of the Massachusetts bay settlers, left Boston for the valley of the Connecticut.   They were under the superintendence of Hayes, who had one year been governor of Boston, and of Hooker, who as a preacher, was unrivalled in the new world by none but Cotton, and even Cotton he excelled in force of character, kindliness of disposition, and magnanimity.   Settling at the spot where Hartford now stands, they founded the colony of Connecticut.   They too carried the ark of the Lord with them, and made religion the basis of their institutions.   Three years sufficed for the framing of their political government. First, as had been done by the Plymouth colony, they subscribed a solemn compact, and then drew up a constitution on the most liberal principles.   The magistrates and legislature were to be chosen every year by ballot, the "towns" were to return representatives in proportion to their population, and all members of the "towns" on taking the oath of allegiance to the commonwealth, were to be allowed to vote at elections.   Two centuries have since passed away, but Connecticut still rejoices in the same principles of civil polity.

But before this colony had had time to complete its organisation, the colonists had to defend themselves and all that was dear to them against their neighbours, the Pequods.   This was the first war that broke out between the New England settlers and the native tribes, and it must be allowed to have been a just one on the part of the former, if war can ever be so.   The Pequods brought it upon themselves by the commission of repeated murders.   In less than six weeks hostilities were brought to a close by the annihilation of the tribe. Two hundred only were left alive, and these were either reduced to servitude by the colonists, or incorporated among the Mohigans and Narragansetts.

The colony of New Haven was founded in 1638 by a body of Puritans, who, like all the rest, were of the school of Calvin, and whose pastor at that time was the Rev. John Davenport. The excellent Theophilus Eaton was their first governor, and continued to be annually elected to that office for twenty years. Their first sabbath, in the yet cool month of April, was spent under a branching oak, and there their pastor discoursed to them on the Saviour's " temptation in the wilderness." After spending a day in fasting and prayer, they laid the foundation of their civil government by simply covenanting that " all of them would be ordered by the rules which the scriptures held forth to them." A title to their lands was purchased from the Indians. The following year these disciples of " Him who was cradled in a manger," held their first constituent assembly in a barn. Having solemnly come to the conclusion that the scriptures contain the perfect pattern of a commonwealth, according to that they constructed theirs. Purity of religious doctrine and discipline, freedom of religious worship, and the service and glory of God, were proclaimed as the great ends of the enterprise. God smiled upon it, so that in a few years the colony could show flourishing settlements rising along the sound, and on the opposite shores of Long island.

While the colonisation of Connecticut was in progress, that of Rhode island commenced. Roger Williams, a Puritan minister, had arrived in Boston the year immediately following its settlement by Winthrop and his companions, but there he soon advanced doctrines on the rights of conscience, and the nature and just limits of human government, which were unacceptable to the civil and religious authorities of the colony. For two years he avoided coming into collision with his opponents, by residing at Plymouth, but having been invited to become pastor of a church in Salem, where he had preached for some time after his first coming to America, he was ordered at last to return to England; whereupon, instead of complying, he sought refuge among the Narragansett Indians, then occupying a large part of the present State of Rhode island.   Having ever been the steady friend of the Indians, and defender of their rights, he was kindly received by the aged chief, Canonicus, and there, in 1636, he founded the city and plantation of Providence.   Two years afterwards, the beautiful island, called Rhode island in Narragansett bay, was bought from the Indians by John Clarke, William Coddington, and their friends, when obliged to leave the Massachusetts colony, in consequence of the part which they had taken in the Antinomian controversy, as it was called, and of which we shall yet have occasion to speak.   These two colonies of Providence and Rhode island, both founded on the principle of absolute religious freedom, naturally presented an asylum to all who disliked the rigid laws and practices of the Massachusetts colony in religious matters; but many, it must be added, fled thither only out of hatred to the stern morality of the other colonies.   Hence Rhode island, to this day, has a more mixed population, as respects religious opinions and practices, than any other part of New England.   Though there is no inconsiderable amount of sincere piety in the State, the forms in which it manifests itself are multiform.

As early as 1623, small settlements were made, under the grant to Mason, on the banks of the Piscataqua, in New Hampshire; and, in point of date, both Portsmouth and Dover take precedence of Boston.   Most of the New Hampshire settlers came direct from England, some from the Plymouth colony. Exeter owed its foundation to the abandonment of Massachusetts by the Rev. Mr. Wheelwright and his immediate friends, on the occasion of the Antinomian controversy.

The first permanent settlements made on " the Maine," as the continental part of the country was called, to distinguish it from the islands, and hence the name of the State, date as early, it would appear, as 1626.   The settlers were from Plymouth, and no doubt carried with them the religious institutions cherished in that earliest of all the New England colonies.

Within twenty years from the settlement of that first colony at Plymouth, all the other chief colonies of New England were founded, their governments organised, and the coast of the Atlantic, from the Kennebec river in Maine almost to the Hudson in New York, marked by their various settlements.   Off-shoots from these original stocks gradually appeared both at intervening points near the ocean, and at such spots in the interior as attracted settlers by superior fertility of soil, or other physical advantages.   From time to time, little bands of adventurers would leave the older homesteads, and wander forth in search of new abodes.   Carrying their substance with them in waggons, and driving before them their cattle, sheep, and hogs, these simple groups would wend through the tangled forest, cross swamps and rivers, and traverse hill and dale, until some suitable resting-place appeared; the silence of the wilderness, meanwhile, broken by the lowing of their cattle and the bleating of their sheep, as well as by the songs of Sion, with which the pilgrims beguiled the fatigues of the way.   Every where nature had erected Bethels for them, and from beneath the overshadowing oak, morning and night, their orisons would ascend to the God of their salvation.   Hope of future comfort sustained them amid present toils.   They were cheered by the thought that the extension of their settlements was promoting also the extension of the kingdom of Christ.

This rapid advance of the New England settlements, during the first twenty years of their existence, must be ascribed, in a great measure, to the troubled condition and lowering prospects of the mother-country during the same period.   The despotic principles of Charles I. as a monarch, still more perhaps the religious intolerance of Archbishop Laud and his partisans, so fatally abetted by the king, drove thousands from England to the colonies, and hurried on the revolution that soon followed at home.   The same oppressive and bigotted policy, indeed, that was convulsing Great Britain, threatened the colonies also; but in 1639, just as they were on the eve of an open collision with the government, that government found itself so beset with difficulties at home, that New England, happily for its own sake, was forgotten.

Nor does the prosperity of the colonial settlements, during those twenty years, seem less remarkable than their multiplication and extension over the country.   The huts in which the emigrants first found shelter gave place to well-built houses. Commerce made rapid advances.   Large quantities of the country's natural productions, such as furs and lumber, were exported; grain was shipped to the West Indies, and fishing employed many hands. Ship-building was carried to such an extent, that within twenty-five years from the first settlement of New England, vessels of 400 tons were constructed there. Several kinds of manufactures even began to take root in the colonies.

It is calculated that 21,200 emigrants had arrived in New England alone before the Long Parliament met. "One hundred and ninety-eight ships had borne them across the Atlantic; and the whole cost of the plantations had been 1,000,000 of dollars—a great expenditure, and a great emigration, for that age; yet in 1832, more than 50,000 persons arrived at the single port of Quebec in one summer, bringing with them a capital exceeding 3,000,000 of dollars." [1]

A great change, in this respect, took place during the next twenty years, embracing the period of the civil war, and the protectorate of Oliver Cromwell and his son. Not only were there few arrivals of emigrants during that interval, but some fiery spirits in the colonies returned to the mother-country, eager to take part in the contest waging there. This, indeed, some of the leading men in New England were earnestly pressed to do by letters from both houses of parliament, but they were unwilling to abandon the duties of the posts they occupied in the new world. Upon the whole, from 1640 to 1660, the population of New England was rather diminished than augmented.

But while such, during the early years of their existence, was the temporal prosperity of these colonies, not less was their spiritual. In 1647, New England had forty-three churches united in one communion; in 1650, the number of churches was fifty-eight, that of communicants 7,750; and in 1674, there were more than eighty English churches of Christ, composed of known pious and faithful professors only, dispersed through the wilderness. Of these twelve or thirteen were in Plymouth colony, forty-seven in Massachusetts and the province of New Hampshire, nineteen in Connecticut, three in Long island, and one in Martha's Vineyard.[2] Well might one of her pious historians say: "It concerneth New England always to remember

[1] Bancroft's History of the United States, vol. i. p. 415.
[2] Prince's Christian History; Emmerson's History of the First Church.

that they are a religious plantation, and not a plantation of trade. The profession of purity of doctrine, worship, and discipline, is written upon her forehead."[1]

The New England colonists may have been "the poorest of the people of God in the whole world," and they settled in a rugged country, the poorest, in fact, in natural resources of all the United States' territories; nevertheless, their industry and other virtues made them increase in wealth, and transformed their hills and valleys into a delightful land. Their commerce soon showed itself in all seas; their manufactures gradually gained ground, notwithstanding the obstacles created by the jealousy of England, and with the increase of their population, they overspread a large extent of the space included in their charters.

Many, indeed, affect to sneer at the founders of New England, but the sneers of ignorance and prejudice cannot detract from their real merits. Not that we would claim the praise of absolute wisdom for all that was done by the "New England fathers." Some of their penal laws were unreasonably and unjustly severe, some were frivolous; some were even ridiculous.[2] Some of their usages were dictated by false views of propriety. Nor can it be denied that they were intolerant to those who differed from them in religion; that they persecuted Quakers and Baptists, and abhorred Roman Catholics. But all this grew out of the erroneous views which they, in common with almost all the world at that time, entertained on the rights of human conscience and the duties of civil government, in cases where those rights are concerned. We shall see, likewise, that they committed a few most serious mistakes, resulting from the same erroneous views, in the civil establishments of religion adopted in most of the colonies. Notwithstanding all this, they will be found to have been far in advance of other nations of their day.

---

[1] Prince in his Christian History, p. 66.

[2] A great deal of misrepresentation and falsehood has been published by ignorant and prejudiced persons at the expense of the New England Puritans. For example, pretended specimens of what are called "the blue laws of Connecticut" have appeared in the journals of certain European travellers, and have been received by credulous readers as perfectly authentic. Yet the greater part of these so-called "laws" are the sheerest fabrications ever palmed upon the world, as is shown by professor Kingsley in his Centennial Discourse, delivered at New Haven a few years ago.

With respect to their treatment of the native tribes, they were led into measures which appear harsh and unjust by the circumstance of their laws being modelled upon those of the Jews. Such, for example, was their making slaves of those Indians whom they made prisoners in war. There were cases also of individual wrong done to the Indians. Yet never, I believe, since the world began, have colonies from civilised nations been planted among barbarous tribes with so little injustice being perpetrated upon the whole. The land, in almost all cases where tribes remained to dispose of it, was taken only on indemnification being given, as they fully recognised the right of the natives to the soil. The only exceptions, and these were but few, were the cases in which the hazards of war put them in possession of some Indian territory. Nor were they indifferent to the spiritual interests of those poor people. We shall yet see that for these they did far more than was done by any other colonies in the whole American continent, and I shall explain why they did not do more.

Let us now, in conclusion, contemplate for a moment the great features that mark the religious character of the founders of New England, leaving our remarks on their religious economy to be introduced at another place.

First, then, theirs was a religion that made much of the BIBLE;—I should rather say, that to them the Bible was everything. They not only drew their religious principles from it, but according to it, in a great degree, they fashioned their civil laws. They were disposed to refer everything " to the law and to the testimony." And although they did not always interpret the scriptures aright, yet no people ever revered them more, or studied them more carefully. With them the famous motto of Chillingworth had a real meaning and application: THE BIBLE IS THE RELIGION OF PROTESTANTS.

Second. The religion of the founders of New England was friendly to the diffusion of knowledge, and set a high value on learning. Many of their pastors, especially, were men of great attainments. Not a few of them had been educated at the universities of Oxford and Cambridge in England, and some had brought with them a European reputation. John Cotton, John Wilson, Thomas Hooker, Dunster and Chauncey, which last two were presidents of the college at Cambridge, Thomas Thatcher, Samuel Whiting, John Sherman, John Elliot, and several more of the early ministers, were men of great learning. All were well instructed in theology, and thoroughly versed in Hebrew, as well as in Greek and Latin. Some, too, such as Sherman of Watertown. were fine mathematical scholars. They were the friends and correspondents of Baxter, and Howe, and Selden, and Milton, and other luminaries among the Puritans of England. Their regard for useful learning they amply proved, by the establishment of schools and academies for all the youth of the colonies, as well as for their own children. Only eight years after the first settlement of Massachusetts colony, they founded, at a great expense for men in their circumstances, the university of Harward at Cambridge, near Boston, an institution at which, for a period of more than sixty years, the most distinguished men of New England spent their college life.

Third. Their religion was eminently fitted to enlarge men's views of the duty of living for God, and promoting his kingdom in the world. They felt that Christianity was the greatest boon that mankind can possess; a blessing which they were bound to do their utmost to secure to their posterity. In going to a new continent they were influenced by a double hope, the enlargement of Christ's kingdom by the conversion of heathen tribes, and by the founding of an empire for their own children, in which his religion should gloriously prevail. Their eyes seemed to catch some glimpses of Messiah's universal reign, when " all nations shall be blessed in him, and call him blessed."

Fourth. Their religion prompted to great examples of self-denial. Filled with the idea of an empire in which true religion might live and flourish, and satisfied from what they had seen of the old world, that the truth was in bondage there, they sighed for a land in which they might serve God according to his blessed word. To secure such a privilege to themselves and their children, they were willing to go into a wilderness, and to toil and die there. This was something worth making sacrifices for, and much did they sacrifice to obtain it. Though poor in comparison with many others, still they belonged to good families, and might have lived very comfortably in England, but they preferred exile and hardship in the hope of

securing spiritual advantages to themselves and their posterity.

Fifth. There was a noble patriotism in their religion. Some
of them had long been exiled from England; others had found
their mother-country a very unkindly home, and yet England
was still dear to them. With them it was not: Farewell, Babylon! farewell, Rome! but, Farewell, dear England![1] Though
contemptuously treated by James I. and Charles I., yet they
spoke of being desirous of enlarging his majesty's dominions.
The Plymouth settlers did not wish to remain in Holland,
because "their posterity would in a few generations become
Dutch, and so lose their interest in the English nation; they
being desirous to enlarge his majesty's dominions, and to live
under their natural prince." And much as they had suffered
from the prelacy of the established church, unnatural stepmother
as she had been to them, nothing could extinguish the love that
they felt for her, and for the many dear children of God whom
she retained in her communion.

Sixth and last. Their religion was favourable to liberty of
conscience. Not that they were all sufficiently enlightened to
bring their laws and institutions into perfect accordance with
that principle at the outset; but even then they were, in this
respect, in advance of the age in which they lived, and the
spirit of that religion which had made them and their fathers in
England the defenders of the rights of the people, and their
tribunes, as it were, against the domination of the throne and
the altar, enabled them at last to admit the claims of conscience
in their full extent.

No! the fathers of New England were no mean men, whether
we look to themselves or to those with whom they were associated in England—the Lightfoots, the Gales, the Seldens, the
Miltons, the Bunyans, the Baxters, the Bates, the Howes, the
Charnocks, the Flavels, and others of inferior standing, among
the two thousand who had laboured in the pulpits of the established church, but whom the Restoration cast out.

Such were the men who founded the New England colonies,
and their spirit still survives, in a good measure, in their

[1] See Mather's Magnalia, b. iii. c. i. s. 12.

descendants through six generations. With the exception of a few thousands of recently arrived Irish and Germans in Boston, and other towns on the sea-board, and of the descendants of those of the Huguenots who settled in New England, that country is wholly occupied by the progeny of the English Puritans who first colonised it. But these are not the whole of their descendants in America, for besides the 2,234,202 souls, forming the population of the six New England States in 1840, it is supposed that an equal, if not a still greater number, have gone off into New York, the northern parts of Ohio, Indiana, and Illinois, and into all parts of Michigan and Wisconsin, carrying with them, in a large measure, the spirit and the institutions of their glorious ancestors. Descendants of these Puritans are also to be found scattered over all parts of the United States, and many of them prove a great blessing to the neighbourhoods in which they reside.

How wonderful, then, was the mission of the founders of New England! How gloriously accomplished! How rich in its results!

CHAPTER V.

RELIGIOUS CHARACTER OF THE EARLY COLONISTS—FOUNDERS OF THE SOUTHERN STATES.

WIDELY different, I have already remarked, were the early colonists of the southern from those of the northern States. If New England may be regarded as colonised by the Anglo-Saxon race, with its simpler manners, its equal institutions, and its love of liberty, the south may be regarded as colonised by men very much Norman in blood, aristocratic in feeling and spirit, and pretending to superior dignity of demeanour and elegance of manners. Nor did time ever efface this original diversity. On the contrary, it has been increased and confirmed by the continuance of slavery in the south, which never prevailed much at any time in the north, but has immensely influenced the tone of feeling and the customs of the southern States.

If the New England colonies are chargeable with having allowed their feelings to become alienated from a throne, from which they had often been contemptuously spurned, with equal truth might those of the south be accused of going to the opposite extreme, in their attachment to a line of monarchs, alike undeserving of their veneration, and incapable of appreciating their generous loyalty.

We might carry the contrast still farther. If New England was the favourite asylum of the Puritan roundhead, the south became in its turn the retreat of the "cavalier," upon the joint subversion of the altar and the throne in his native land. And if the religion of the one was strict, serious, in the regard of its enemies unfriendly to innocent amusements, and even morose, the other was the religion of the court, and of fashionable life, and did not require so uncompromising a resistance "to the lust of the flesh, the lust of the eyes, and the pride of life."

Not that from this parallelism, which is necessarily general and extreme, the reader is to infer that the northern had exclusive claims to be considered as possessing a truly religious character. All that is meant is to give a general idea of the different aspects which religion bore in the northern and southern colonies.

Virginia was the first in point of date of the southern, and indeed of all the colonies. Among its neighbours in the south, it was what Massachusetts was in the north—the mother in some sense of the rest, and the dominant colony. Not that the others were colonised chiefly from it, but because from the prominence of its position, the amount of its population, and their intelligence and wealth, it acquired from the first a preponderating influence which it retains as a State to this day.

The records of Virginia furnish indubitable evidence that it was meant to be a Christian colony. The charter enjoined that the mode of worship in the intended colony should conform to that of the established church of England. In 1619, for the first time, Virginia had a legislature chosen by the people; and by an act of that body, the Episcopal church was, properly speaking, established. In the following year the number of boroughs erected into parishes was eleven, and the number of pastors five; the population at the time being considerably under 3000. In

1621-22, it was enacted that the clergymen should receive from their parishioners 1500 pounds of tobacco, and sixteen barrels of corn each, as their yearly salary, estimated to be worth in all £200. Every male colonist of the age of sixteen or upwards, was required to pay ten pounds of tobacco and one bushel of corn.

The company under whose auspices Virginia was colonised, seems to have been influenced by a sincere desire to make the plantation a means of propagating the knowledge of the gospel among the Indians. A few years after the first settlement was made, in the body of their instructions they particularly urged upon the governor and assembly, "the using of all probable means of bringing over the natives to a love of civilization, and to the love of God and his true religion." They recommended the colonists to hire the natives as labourers, with the view of familiarising them with civilised life, and thus to bring them gradually to the knowledge of Christianity, that they might be employed as instruments "in the general conversion of their countrymen so much desired." It was likewise recommended, "that each town, borough, and hundred, should procure by just means a certain number of Indian children, to be brought up in the first elements of literature, that the most towardly of these should be fitted for the college, in building of which they purposed to proceed as soon as any profit arose from the estate appropriated to that use; and they earnestly required their earnest help and furtherance in that pious and important work; not doubting the particular blessing of God upon the colony, and being assured of the love of all good men upon that account." [1]

Even the first charter assigns as one of the reasons for the grant, that the contemplated undertaking was "a work which may, by the providence of Almighty God, hereafter tend to the glory of his divine majesty, in the propagating of the Christian religion to such people as yet live in darkness, and miserable ignorance of the true knowledge and worship of God.[2]

The company seems early to have felt the importance of pro-

[1] Burk's "History of Virginia," pp. 225, 226.
[2] 1 Charter.—1. Huzzard's State Papers, 51. This work of the late Mr. H. contains all the charters granted by the sovereigns of England for promoting colonisation in America.

moting education in the colony.   Probably at their solicitation the king issued letters to the bishops throughout England, directing collections to be made for building a college in Virginia.   The object was at first stated to be "the training up and educating infidel (heathen) children in the true knowledge of God.[1]   Nearly £1500 had already been collected, and Henrico had been selected as the best situation for the building, .when at the instance of their treasurer, Sir Edwin Sandys, the company granted 10,000 acres to be laid off for the new "university of Henrico;" the original design being at the same time extended, by its being resolved that the institution should be for the education of the English, as well as the Indians.   Much eagerness was felt throughout England for the success of this undertaking.   The bishop of London gave £1000 towards its accomplishment, and an anonymous contributor £500, exclusively for the education of the Indian youth.   It had warm friends in Virginia also.   The minister of Henrico, the Rev. Mr. Bargave, gave his library, and the inhabitants of the place subscribed £1500, to build a hostelry for the entertainment of strangers and visitors.[2]   Preparatory to the college or university, it was proposed that a school should be established at St. Charles' city, to be called the East India School, from the first donation towards its endowment having been contributed by the master and crew of an East Indiaman on its return to England.

But the whole project received its death-blow by the frightful massacre perpetrated by the Indians on the 22d of March, 1622, when, in one hour, 347 men, women, and children, were slaughtered without distinction of sex or age, and at a time too, when the Indians professed perfect friendship.   For four years, nevertheless, they had been maturing their plan, had enlisted thirty tribes in a plot to extirpate the English, and might have succeeded in doing so but for the fidelity of a converted Indian named Chanco.   The minds of the colonists were still further estranged from the idea of providing a college for the Indian youth, by the long and disastrous war that followed.   At a much later date, a college for the education of the colonial youth

1 Stith's " History of Virginia," pp. 162, 163.
2 Holmes' Annals, p. 173.

was established at Williamsburg, which was for long the capital of the colony.[1]

In proportion as the population began to spread along the large and beautiful streams that flow from the Alleghany mountains into Chesapeake bay, more parishes were legally constituted, so that in 1722 there were fifty-four, some very large, others of moderate extent, in the twenty-nine counties of the colony. Their size depended much on the number of titheable inhabitants within a certain district. Each parish had a convenient church built of stone, brick, or wood; and many of the larger ones had also chapels of ease, so that the places of public worship were not less than seventy in all. To each parish church there was a parsonage attached, and likewise, in almost all cases, a glebe of 250 acres and a small stock of cattle. But not more than about half, probably, of these established churches were provided with ministers; in the rest the services were conducted by lay readers, or occasionally by neighbouring clergymen. When the war of the revolution commenced there were ninety-five parishes, and at least a hundred clergymen of the established church.

We shall yet have occasion to speak of the church establishment in Virginia and its influence upon the interests of religion, as well as of the character of the clergy there during the colonial period. I cannot, however, forbear saying that although the greater number of the established ministers seem, at that epoch, to have been very ill qualified for their great work, others were an ornament to their calling. I may mention as belonging to early times the Rev. Robert Hunt and the

[1] This was the college of William and Mary, established in 1693, and in the order of time, the second that appeared in the colonies. It owed its existence, under God, to the great and long continued exertions of the Rev. Dr. Blair. It ought to be mentioned that in the former part of the last century, a number of Indian youths were educated at it. The celebrated Robert Boyle presented it with a sum of money to be applied to the education of the Indian tribes. At first, efforts were made to procure for this purpose children that had been taken in war by some victorious tribe; but during the administration of Sir Alexander Spottswood, which commenced in 1710, that plan was relinquished for a far better. The governor went in person to the tribes in the interior, to engage them to send their children to the school, and had the gratification of seeing some arrive from a distance of four hundred miles in compliance with his request. He also, at his own expense, established and supported a preparatory school on the frontiers, at which Indian lads might be prepared for the college, without being too far removed from their parents.—(See Beverley's " History of Virginia.")

Rev. Alexander Whitaker.   The former of these accompanied the first settlers—preached the first English sermon ever heard on the American continent, and by his calm and judicious counsels, his exemplary conduct, and his faithful ministrations, rendered most important services to the infant colony.   The latter was justly styled "the apostle of Virginia."   At a later period we find among other worthies the Rev. James Blair, whose indefatigable exertions in the cause of religion and education, rank him among the greatest benefactors of America. Nor were there laymen wanting among those who had the cause of God at heart.   Morgan Morgan, in particular, was greatly blessed in his endeavours to sustain the spirit of piety, by founding churches and otherwise, more especially in the northern part of the great valley.   In later times Virginia has produced many illustrious men, not only in the Episcopalian, but in almost every other denomination of Christians.

In point of intolerance the legislature of Virginia equalled, if it did not exceed, that of Massachusetts.   Attendance at parish worship was at one time required under severe penalties; nay, even the sacramental services of the church were rendered obligatory by law.   Dissenters, Quakers, and Roman Catholics, were prohibited from settling in the province.   People of every name entering the colony, without having been Christians in the countries they came from, were condemned to slavery. Shocking barbarity! the reader will justly exclaim; yet these very laws prove how deep and strong, though turbid and foul, ran the tide of religious feeling among the people,   As has been justly remarked; "If they were not wise Christians, they were at least strenuous religionists."

I have said enough to show that in the colonisation of Virginia, religion was far from being considered as a matter of no importance; its influence, on the contrary, was deemed essential to national as well as individual prosperity and happiness.

Maryland, we have seen, though originally a part of Virginia, was planted by Lord Baltimore as a refuge for persecuted Roman Catholics.   When the first of its colonists landed in 1634, under the leadership of Leonard Calvert, son of that nobleman, on an island in the Potomac, they took possession of the province "for their Saviour," as well as for "their lord the King."

They planted their colony on the broad basis of toleration for all Christian sects, and in this noble spirit the government was conducted for fifty years. Think what we may of their creed, and very different as was this policy from what Romanism elsewhere might have led us to expect, we cannot refuse to Lord Baltimore's colony the praise of having established the first government in modern times, in which entire toleration was granted to all denominations of Christians; this too, at a time when the New England Puritans could hardly bear with one another, much less with "papists;" when the zealots of Virginia held both "papists" and "dissenters" in nearly equal abhorrence; and when, in fact, toleration was not considered in any part of the Protestant world to be due to Roman Catholics. After being thus avowed at the outset, toleration was renewed in 1649, when, by the death of Charles I., the government in England was about to pass into the hands of the extreme opponents of the Roman Catholics. "And whereas the enforcing of the conscience in matters of religion," such is the language of their statute, "hath frequently fallen out to be of dangerous consequence in those commonwealths where it has been practised, and for the more quiet and peaceable government of this province, and the better to preserve mutual love and amity among the inhabitants, no person within this province professing to believe in Jesus Christ, shall be any way troubled, molested, or discountenanced, for his or her religion, or in the free exercise thereof." Meanwhile Protestant sects increased so much, that the political power of the State passed at length entirely out of the hands of its founders, and before the war of the revolution, many churches had been planted in it by Episcopalians, Presbyterians, and Baptists.

North Carolina was first colonised by stragglers from Virginia settling on the rivers that flow into Albemarle sound, and among these were a good many Quakers, driven out of Virginia by the intolerance of its laws. This was about the middle of the seventeenth century. Puritans from New England, and emigrants from Barbadoes, followed in succession, but the dissenters from Virginia predominated. Religion for a long while seems to have received but little attention. William Edmunson and George Fox visited their Quaker friends among the pine groves of Albemarle in 1772, and found "a tender people." A quarterly meeting was established, and thenceforward that religious body may be. said to have organised a spiritual government in the colony. But it was long before any other made much progress. No Episcopalian minister was settled in it until 1703, and no church built until 1705.

The proprietaries, it is true, who obtained North as well as South Carolina from Charles II., professed to be actuated by a "laudable and pious zeal for the propagation of the gospel;" but they did nothing to vindicate their claim to such praise. In their constitution they maintained, that religion and the profession of it were indispensable to the well-being of the State and privileges of citizenship;—vain words, as long as no measures were taken to promote what they thus lauded. But we shall yet see that little as true religion owed in North Carolina to the first settlers, or to the "proprietories," that State eventually obtained a large population of a truly religious character, partly from the emigration of Christians from France and Scotland, partly from the increase of Puritans from New England.

South Carolina began to be colonised in 1670 by settlers shipped to the province by the "proprietaries," and from that time forward it received a considerable accession of emigrants almost every year. Its climate was represented as being the finest in the world: under its almost tropical sun flowers were said to blossom every month of the year; orange groves were to supplant those of cedar, silk-worms were to be fed on mulberry trees introduced from the south of France, and the choicest wines were to be produced. Ships arrived with Dutch settlers from New York, as well as with emigrants from England. The Earl of Shaftesbury when committed to the tower in 1681, begged for leave to exile himself to Carolina.

Nor were they churchmen only who emigrated thither from England. Many dissenters, disgusted with the unfavourable state of things in that country, went out also, carrying with them intelligence, industry, and sobriety. Joseph Blake in particular, brother of the gallant admiral of that name, having inherited his brother's fortune, devoted it to transporting his persecuted brethren to America, and conducted a company of them from Somersetshire thither. Thus the booty taken from

New Spain helped to people South Carolina.[1] A colony from Ireland also, went over, and were soon merged among the other colonists.

Such was the character of what might be called the substratum of the population in South Carolina. The colonists were of various origin, but many of them had carried thither the love of true religion, and the number of such soon increased.

Georgia, of all the original thirteen colonies, ranks latest in point of date. The good Oglethorpe, one of the finest specimens of a Christian gentlemen of the cavalier school, one who loved his king and his church, led over a mixed people to settle on the banks of the Savannah. Poor debtors taken from the prisons of England, formed a strange medley with godly Moravians from Herrnhut in Germany, and brave Highlanders from Scotland. To Georgia, also, were directed the youthful steps of those two wonderful men, John and Charles Wesley, and the still more eloquent Whitefield, who made the pine forests that stretch from the Savannah to the Altamaha resound with the tones of their fervid piety. In Georgia, too, was built the "Orphan House," for the erection of which so much eloquence was poured forth both in England and in the Atlantic cities of her American colonies, but which was not destined to fulfil the expectations of its good and great founder.

Thus we find that religion was not the predominating motive that led to the colonisation of the southern States, as was the case with New England; and yet it cannot be said to have been altogether wanting. It is remarkable that in every charter granted to the southern colonies, "the propagation of the gospel" is mentioned as one of the reasons for their being undertaken. And we shall see that that essential element of a people's prosperity, ultimately received a vast accession of strength from the emigrants whom God was preparing to send from the old world to those parts of the new.

---

[1] Bancroft's " History of the United States," vol. ii., pp. 172, 173.

CHAPTER VI.

RELIGIOUS CHARACTER OF THE EARLY COLONISTS OF NEW YORK.

WE now proceed to give some account of the intermediate States between New England and those in the south, comprising New York, New Jersey, Delaware, and Pennsylvania. We begin with New York, which, as we have seen, was first colonised by the Dutch.

"The spirit of the age," says an eloquent author,[1] to whom we have often referred, "was present when the foundations of New York were laid. Every great European event affected the fortunes of America. Did a State prosper, it sought an increase of wealth by plantations in the west. Was a sect persecuted, it escaped to the new world. The reformation, followed by collisions between English dissenters and the Anglican hierarchy, colonised New England. The reformation, emancipating the United Provinces, led to European settlements on the Hudson. The Netherlands divide with England the glory of having planted the first colonies in the United States; they also divide the glory of having set the example of public freedom. If England gave our fathers the idea of a popular representation, Holland originated for them the principle of federal union."

It was the Dutch, we remarked, who first discovered the rivers Hudson and Connecticut, and probably the Delaware also. In 1614, five years after Henry Hudson had sailed up the first of those streams, and to which he gave his name, they erected a few huts upon Manhattan island, where now stands the city of New York.

The first attempts to establish trading stations, for they hardly could be called settlements, were made by the merchants of Amsterdam. But when the Dutch West India company was formed, in 1621, it obtained a monopoly of the trade with all parts of the Atlantic coast claimed by Holland in North America. Colonisation on the Hudson does not appear to have

[1] Mr. Bancroft's "History of the United States," vol. ii. p. 256.

I 2

been the main object of that company. The territory of New Netherlands was not even named in the charter, nor did the states-general guarantee its possession and protection. Trade with the natives in skins and furs was, in fact, the primary and almost exclusive object.

But in a few years, as the families of the company's factors increased, what was at first a mere station for traders gradually bore the appearance of a regular plantation; and New Amsterdam, on Manhattan island, began to look like some thriving town, with its little fleet of Dutch ships almost continually lying at its wharves. Settlements were also made at the west end of Long island, on Staten island, along the North river up to Albany, and even beyond that, as well as at Bergen, on the Hackensack, and on the Raritan, in what was afterwards New Jersey.

Harmony at this time subsisted between the Dutch and their Puritan neighbours, notwithstanding the dispute about their respective boundaries. In 1627, we find the governor of New Netherlands, or New *Belgium*, as Holland was sometimes called in America, paying a visit of courtesy and friendship to the Plymouth colony, by whom he was received with "the noise of trumpets." A treaty of friendship and commerce was proposed. "Our children after us," said the pilgrims, "shall never forget the good and courteous entreaty which we found in your country, and shall desire your prosperity for ever."

The colony, as it extended, gradually penetrated into the interior of East Jersey, and along the shores of the Delaware. Still, receiving neither protection nor encouragement from the fatherland, and abandoned to the tender mercies of a low-minded commercial corporation, its progress was not what might have been expected. It had not always wise governors. The infamous Kieft, neglecting to conciliate the Indians, allowed the settlers on Staten island to be destroyed by the savages of New Jersey; and having in a most wanton attack upon a tribe of the friendly Algonquins, massacred many of them in cold blood, the colony lay for two whole years (1643-1645) exposed to attack at all points, and was threatened with absolute ruin. From the banks of the Raritan to the borders of the Connecticut not a "bowery" (farm-house) was safe. " Mine eyes," says an eye-witness, " saw the flames of their towns, and the flights and hurries of men, women, and children, the present removal of all that could to Holland!" In this war the celebrated Anne Hutchinson, one of the most extraordinary women of her age, was murdered by the Indians, together with all her family, with but one exception.

Next to this disastrous war, the colony was most retarded by the want of a popular form of government, and by the determination of the West India company not to concede one.

The first founders of New Netherlands were men of a bold and enterprising turn, whose chief motive in leaving Holland was, no doubt, the acquisition of wealth. But educated in the national Dutch church, they brought with them a strong attachment to its doctrines, worship, and government, and however deeply interested in their secular pursuits, they unquestionably took early measures for the gospel being preached purely among them, and to have the religious institutions of their fatherland planted and maintained in their adopted country. A church was organised at New Amsterdam, now New York, not later probably than 1619; and there was one at Albany as early, if not earlier. The first minister of the gospel established at New York was the Rev. Everardus Bogardus.

The Dutch language was exclusively used in the churches until 1764, being exactly a century after the colony had fallen into the hands of the English. As soon as that event took place, the new governor made great efforts to introduce the language of his own country, by opening schools in which it was taught and otherwise. This, together with the introduction of the English Episcopal church, and the encouragement it received from governor Fletcher, in 1693, made the new language come rapidly into use. The younger colonists began to urge that, for a part of the day at least, English should be used in the churches; or that new churches should be built for those who commonly spoke that tongue. At length, after much opposition from some who dreaded lest together with the language of their fathers, their good old doctrines, liturgy, catechisms, and all should disappear, the Rev. Dr. Laidlie, a distinguished Scotch minister who had been settled in an English Presby-

terian church at Flushing, connected with the Dutch reformed
church, was invited to New York, in order to commence divine
service there in English. Having accepted this call, he was,
in 1764, transferred to that city, and in his new charge his
labours were long and greatly blessed. From that time the
Dutch language has gradually disappeared, so that hardly a
vestige of it now remains.

The population of New Netherlands, when it fell into the
hands of the English, is supposed to have been about ten thousand, or half as many as that of New England at the same
date. There has been a slight emigration to it from Holland
ever since, too small to be regarded as of any importance. But
all the emigrants from Dutch ports to America were not Hollanders. The reformation had made the Dutch an independent
nation, and the long and bitter experience they had had of
oppression, led them to offer an asylum to the persecuted Protestants of England, Scotland, France, Italy, and Germany. [1]
Among others who thus came by way of Holland to America
was Robert Livingston, ancestor to the numerous and distinguished family of that name to be found in various parts of
America, but particularly in the State of New York, and son
of that pious and celebrated minister, the Rev. John Livingston
of Scotland, who after being eminently blessed in his labours
there in his native country, was, in 1663, driven by persecution
into Holland, where he spent the remainder of his life as minister of the Scotch church at Rotterdam.

Several causes retarded the progress of religion among the
Dutch colonists in America. One was the unsettlement caused

---

[1] This has often been made an occasion of reproach and ridicule to the good
Dutch by men of more wit than grace or sense.
Beaumont and Fletcher, in their Maid of the Inn, introduce one of their
characters as saying :—

> " I am a schoolmaster, Sir, and would fain
> Confer with you about erecting four
> New sects of religion at Amsterdam."

And Andrew Marvell, in his " Character of Holland," writes :—

> " Sure when religion did itself embark,
> And from the east would westward steer its bark,
> It struck ; and splitting on this unknown ground,
> Each one thence pillaged the first piece he found,
> Hence Amsterdam, Turk, Christian, Pagan, Jew,
> Staple of sects, and mint of schism, grew :
> That bank of conscience, where not one so strange
> Opinion, but finds credit and exchange.
> In vain for Catholics ourselves we bear ;
> The universal church is only there."

by actual or dreaded hostilities with the Indians; another lay in the churches being long unnecessarily dependent for their pastors on the classis, or presbytery, of Amsterdam; a body which, however well disposed, was at too remote a distance to exercise a proper judgment in selecting such ministers as the circumstances of the country and the people required; a third is to be found in the late introduction of the English tongue into the public services of the churches; it ought to have been introduced at least fifty years sooner.

Notwithstanding these hindrances, the blessed gospel was widely and successfully preached and maintained in the colony, both when under the government of Holland and afterwards. Its beneficial influence was seen in the strict and wholesome morals that characterised the community, and in the progress of education among all classes, especially after the adoption of a more popular form of government. Many faithful pastors were either sent over from Holland, or raised up at later periods in the colony, and sent over to Holland for instruction in theology. Among the former I may mention the Rev. T. J. Frelinghuysen, who came from Holland in 1720, and settled on the Raritan. As an able, evangelical, and eminently successful preacher, he proved a great blessing to the Dutch church in America. He left five sons, all ministers, and two daughters who were married to ministers.[1] To this testimony we may add that of the Rev. Gilbert Tennent, who, in a letter to Mr. Prince of Boston, says: " The labours of Mr. Frelinghuysen, a Dutch minister, were much blessed to the people of New Brunswick and places adjacent, especially about the time of his coming among them. When I came, which was about seven years after, I had the pleasure of seeing much of the fruits of his ministry: divers of his hearers, with whom I had opportunity of conversing, appeared to be converted persons, by their soundness in principle, Christian experience, and pious practice; and these persons declared that his ministrations were the means thereof." [2] Among the latter was the late J. H. Liv-

1 Christian Magazine, quoted in Dr. Gunn's Memoirs of Dr. Livingstone, p. 87.
2 I may add that the Mr. Frelinghuysen, spoken of in the text, was the ancestor of three brothers of the same name, who have adorned the profession of the

ingston, D.D., who died in 1825, after being for long one of the most distinguished ministers in the United States. On his return from Holland, he was for many years a pastor in New York, and thereafter divinity professor in the theological seminary of the Dutch reformed church at New Brunswick, in the State of New Jersey. He was one of those who, though born to fill a large space in the history of the church, yet spend their lives in the calm and unostentatious discharge of the duties of their calling. The impress of his labours and character will long be felt in the church of which he was so distinguished an ornament.

The descendants of the Dutch are numerous and widely dispersed in America. They constitute a large proportion of the inhabitants of the southern part of the State of New York, and eastern part of New Jersey, besides forming a very considerable body in the north and west of the former of these States. But they are to be found also in larger or smaller numbers in all parts of the confederacy. Though often made the butts of ridicule for their simplicity,[1] slowness of movement, and dislike to innovation of every kind, yet, taken as a whole, they have been uniformly a religious and virtuous people, and constitute a most valuable part of the American nation. Some have found a place among our most illustrious statesmen. Emigrants from the country of Grotius and John de Witt have furnished one president, and three vice-presidents, to the republic which they have done so much to establish and maintain. They have preserved to this day the church planted by their forefathers in

law in the present generation, one of whom, the Hon. Theodore Frelinghuysen, was for several years a distinguished member of the senate of the United States, and is now chancellor of the university of New York.—(Prince's Christian History.)

[1] Their Yankee neighbours, as the New England people are called, tell a thousand stories showing the simplicity of the Dutch. One of the best which I have heard is that a wealthy Dutch farmer, in the State of New York, who had erected a church in his neighbourhood at his own expense, was advised (probably by some very sensible Yankee) to attach a lightning-rod to it. But he received the suggestion with displeasure, as if God would set fire to his own house! Another is as follows:—Shortly after the arrival of the Rev. Dr. Laidlie, and the commencement of his labours, he was thus addressed by some excellent old people, at the close of a prayer-meeting one evening, in which he had most fervently addressed the throne of grace : " Ah, Dominie ! (the title which the Dutch in their affection give to their pastors) we offered up many an earnest prayer in *Dutch* for your coming among us ; and truly the Lord has heard us in *English*, and sent you to us."

America; but although a very respectable part of them still adhere to it, a still greater number have joined the Episcopal church, and many belong to other denominations.

CHAPTER VII.

RELIGIOUS CHARACTER OF THE EARLY COLONISTS.—FOUNDERS OF NEW JERSEY.

HOLLANDERS from New Amsterdam were the first European inhabitants of New Jersey, and, during the continuance of the Dutch dominion in America, it formed part of New Netherlands.   The first settlement was at Bergen, but the plantations extended afterwards to the Hackensack, the Passaic, and the Raritan.   It is probable that a few families had settled even on the Delaware, opposite Newcastle, before the cession of the country to the English in 1664.

But the Dutch were not the only colonists of New Jersey. A company of the same race of English Puritans that had colonised New England, left the eastern end of Long island in 1664, and established themselves at Elisabeth-town. They must have been few in number, for four houses only were found there the following year, on the arrival of Philip Carteret as governor of the province.   Woodbridge, Middleton, and Shrewsbury, were founded about the same time by settlers from Long island and Connecticut.   Newark was founded in 1667 or 1668 by a colony of about thirty families, chiefly from Brandon in Connecticut.

The Newhaven colonists bought land on both sides of the Delaware in 1640, and fifty families were sent to occupy it, but their trading establishments were broken up, and the colony dispersed, in consequence of the Dutch claiming the country. There are extant memorials, however, in the records of Cumberland and Cape May counties, that colonies from New England established themselves in these not very long after the province changed its masters.   The middle parts were gradually occupied by Dutch and New England settlers in their progress westward, and also by a considerable number of Scotch and Irish emigrants—all Protestants, and most of them Presbyterians.

It will be remembered that by the gift of his brother, Charles II., the duke of York became "proprietary" of all that part of America ceded by the Dutch to the English in 1664. That same year the duke sold New Jersey to Sir George Carteret and Lord Berkeley, in honour of the former of whom it took the name that it bears to this day. They immediately appointed a governor, and gave the colonists a popular form of government. The legislature, however, soon became the organ of popular disaffection; few were willing to purchase a title to the soil from the Indians, and to pay quitrents to the proprietaries besides. After some years of severe struggles between the colonists and their governors, Lord Berkeley became tired of the strife, and in 1674 sold the moiety of New Jersey to Quakers for £1000, John Fenwick acting as agent in the transaction for Edward Byllinge and his assigns. Fenwick left England the following year, accompanied by a great many families of that persecuted sect, and formed the settlement of Salem on the Delaware. Lands in West Jersey were now offered for sale by the Quaker company, and hundreds of colonists soon settled upon them. In 1676 they obtained from Carteret the right, so far as he was concerned, to institute a government of their own in West Jersey, and proceeded, the year following, to lay the groundwork in the "Concessions," as their fundamental deed was called. Its main feature was that "it put the power in the people." Forthwith great numbers of English Quakers flocked to West Jersey, with the view of permanently settling there. A title to the lands was purchased from the Indians, at a council held under the shade of the forest, at the spot where the town of Burlington now stands; there the tawny children of the wood conveyed to the men of peace the domain which they desired. "You are our brothers," said the Sachems, "and we will live like brothers with you. We will make a broad path for you and us to walk in. If an Englishman falls asleep in this path, the Indian shall pass him by and say: He is an Englishman; he is asleep; let him alone. The path shall be plain; there shall not be in it a stump to hurt the feet."[1] And they kept their word.

---

[1] Smith's " History of New Jersey."

In November, 1681, Jennings, who acted as governor for the proprietaries, convened the first Quaker legislature ever known to have met. The year following, by obtaining the choice of their own chief ruler, the colonists completed the measure of their self-government. In the year following that again, William Penn and eleven others bought East New Jersey from Carteret's heirs, and from that time a Quaker emigration set into that division of the province, but never to such a degree as to change the general character of the inhabitants. The population, upon the whole, remained decidedly Puritan, though combining the elements of a Scotch, Dutch, and New England Presbyterianism. It was much otherwise with West New Jersey. With the exception of a few churches planted here and there by other denominations, and standing like islands in this sea of the religion of George Fox, Salem, Gloucester, and Burlington counties were peopled almost entirely with Quakers, and continue to be so to this day.

After about twelve years of embarrassment, commencing with the revolution of 1688 in England, the proprietaries of both East and West New Jersey surrendered "their pretended right of government" to the British crown, and in 1702, both provinces, united into one, were placed for a time under the governor of New York, retaining, however, their own legislature. The population, notwithstanding the difficulties and irritation caused by political disputes intimately affecting their interests, steadily increased. Taken as a whole, few parts of America have been colonised by a people more decidedly religious in principle, or more intelligent and virtuous; and such, in the main, are their descendants at the present day. No where in the United States have the churches been supplied with a more faithful or an abler ministry. New Jersey was the scene of the excellent David Brainerd's labours among the Indians, during the latter years of his short but useful life. There, too, laboured the celebrated William Tennent, and those other faithful servants of God, in whose society Whitefield found so much enjoyment, and whose ministrations were so much blessed. There, and particularly in the eastern section of the province, many have been witnesses of those outpourings of the Holy Spirit, which we shall have occasion yet to speak of. And, lastly, in

New Jersey was planted the fourth, in point of date, of the American colleges, commonly called Nassau hall, but more properly the college of New Jersey. That college has had for its presidents some of the greatest divines that have ever lived in America,—Dickinson, Burr, the elder Edwards, Finley, Witherspoon, Smith, Green, &c., and it is still as flourishing as ever, although a sister institution has arisen at New Brunswick, to co-operate in diffusing blessings throughout the State. I may add, that no State in the American union has more decidedly proved the importance of having a good original population, nor has any State done more, in proportion to its population and resources, to sustain the honour and promote the best interests of the American nation.

CHAPTER VIII.

RELIGIOUS CHARACTER OF THE EARLY COLONISTS—FOUNDERS OF DELAWARE, AT FIRST CALLED NEW SWEDEN.

THOUGH of all the States Delaware has the smallest population, and is the least but one in territorial extent, yet its history is far from uninteresting. Fairly included within the limits of Maryland, it never submitted to the rule of Lord Baltimore's colony; subjected for a time to the dominion of the Quaker province of William Penn, from that it emancipated itself in time to be justly ranked among the original thirteen States, which so nobly achieved their independence.

This small province was claimed by the Dutch in right of discovery, as well as the country on the other side of Delaware river and bay; and in 1631, a colony under De Vries actually left the Texel for the south shore of that bay, and settled near the present site of Lewestown, on lands acquired the year before by Godyn and his associates Van Ranselaar, Bloemart, and De Lact. That colony, consisting of above thirty souls, was, in the absence of De Vries, utterly destroyed by the Indians towards the close of the following year; yet its priority in point of date saved it from being included in Lord Baltimore's charter, and secured for subsequent settlers the benefits of a separate colony and independent State.   Before, however, it could be rescued from the Indians, and colonised a second time by the Dutch, it fell to the possession of a Scandinavian prince.

Gustavus Adolphus, justly pronounced the most accomplished prince of modern times, and the greatest benefactor of humanity in the line of Swedish kings, had early comprehended the advantages of foreign commerce and distant colonisation.   Accordingly in 1626, he instituted a commercial company, with exclusive privileges to trade beyond the Straits of Gibraltar, and with the right of planting colonies.   The stock was open to all Europe.   The king himself pledged 400,000 dollars from the royal treasury; the chief seat of business was Gottenburg, the second city in the kingdom, and the best situated for commerce in the open sea.   The government of the future colonies was committed to a royal council, and colonists were to be invited from all Europe.   The new world was described as a paradise, and the hope of better fortunes on its distant shores was strongly excited in the Scandinavian mind.   The colony proposed to be planted there, was to be a place where "the honour of the wives and daughters" of those whom wars and bigotry had made fugitives, might be safe; a blessing to the "common man," as well as to the "whole Protestant world."[1]   As opening an asylum for persecuted Protestants of all nations, the project was well worthy of the great champion of Protestant rights.

But Gustavus Adolphus did not live to carry his favourite scheme into effect.   On the Protestant princes of Germany being compelled to defend their violated religious privileges by taking up arms against the emperor, they made the first offer of the command of their armies to Christiern IV. of Denmark; but when on that prince proving unequal to the task, they turned their regards to the youthful king of Sweden, who hesitated not to accept their summons.   Crossing the Baltic with his small army of 15,000 faithful Swedes, Finns, and Scotch, he put himself at the head of the confederate troops, and within eighteen months gained the series of splendid victories that

[1] Argonautica Gustaviana, pp. 11, 16.

have placed him in the highest rank of warrior-princes.   Having driven the imperial troops from the walls of Leipsic to the southern extremity of Germany, he fell at last on the plains of Lützen, on the 16th of October, 1632, victory even there crowning his efforts, while his body, covered with wounds, lay undistinguished among the slain.   Yet even the toils and the horrors of that war could not make the brave young monarch forget his favourite project.   A few days before that last fatal battle, where it has been beautifully said that "humanity won one of her most glorious victories, and lost one of her ablest defenders," he recommended to the people of Germany the colonial project, which he still continued to regard as "the jewel of his kingdom."[1]

The enterprise, however, which his premature death prevented Gustavus Adolphus from carrying into effect, fell into the hands of his minister Oxenstiern, the ablest statesman of that age. Emigrants for Delaware bay, furnished with provisions for themselves, and with merchandise for traffic with the Indians, accompanied also by a religious teacher, left Sweden in 1638, in two ships, the Key of Calmar and the Griffin.   Upon their arrival they bought the lands on the Delaware, from its mouth up to the falls where Trenton now stands; and near the mouth of Christiana creek they built a fort, to which they gave that name, in honour of their youthful queen.   Tidings of their safe arrival, and encouraging accounts of the country, were soon carried back to Scandinavia, and naturally inspired many of the peasantry of Sweden and Finland with a wish to exchange their rocky unproductive soil for the banks of the Delaware.   More bands of emigrants soon went thither, and many who would fain have gone, were prevented only by the difficulty of finding a passage.   The plantations gradually extended along the Delaware, from the site of Wilmington to that of Philadelphia. A fort constructed of huge hemlock logs, on an island a few miles below Philadelphia, defended the Swedish settlements, and became the head quarters of Prints, their governor.   The whole country, as above described, was called New Sweden, and the few families of emigrants from New England that happened

---

[1] Bancroft's " History of the United States," vol. ii. p. 285.

to be within its boundaries, either submitted to the Swedish government, or else withdrew and established themselves elsewhere.

Meanwhile the Dutch re-asserted their old claims to the country, planted a fort at Newcastle, and ultimately reduced New Sweden under their dominion by means of an expedition of six hundred men, under the famous Peter Stuyvesant, governor of New Netherlands. Thus terminated in 1655, the power of Sweden on the American continent, after it had lasted above seventeen years. The Swedish colonists probably did not much exceed seven hundred, and as their descendants in the course of some generations became widely scattered, and blended with emigrants of a different lineage, they are supposed to constitute one part in 200 of the present population of the United States. [1]

Interesting as this colony is from its early history, it becomes still more so because of its practical worth. The colonists were invariably amiable and peaceable in their deportment; they maintained the best terms with the Indians; they were frugal and industrious; they were attentive to the education of their children, notwithstanding the want of schools and the difficulty of procuring books in their mother tongue; and above all, they were careful in upholding religious institutions and ordinances. Lutherans, as their kindred in Sweden are to this day, they long preserved their national liturgy and discipline, besides keeping up a most affectionate intercourse with the churches in their mother country; and from these they often received aid in bibles and other religious books, as well as in money. Having established themselves in the southern suburb of Philadelphia, previous to the colonisation of Pennsylvania by William Penn, they have always had a church there, known as the "Swedes' church" to this day, and which with two or three more in Delaware and Pennsylvania, now belongs to the Protestant Episcopal communion. The late Dr. Colin was the last of the long line of Swedish pastors.

Taken possession of by the Dutch in 1655, New Sweden was, nine years after that, ceded by them to the English. It was then placed for some time under the administration of the gover-

[1] See Bancroft's " History of the United States."

nor of New York; was afterwards attached to Pennsylvania, but ultimately became first a separate colony, and then an independent State.   Meanwhile its population, composed of the descendants of Swedes, of Quakers who accompanied William Penn, of settlers from New England, and of Scotch, Irish, and a few emigrants from other parts of Europe, steadily increased. Religion has ever had a happy, and not an inconsiderable influence in this little commonwealth.   It would, no doubt, have been greater still had slavery never existed in the colony.   But though Delaware is still a slave-holding State, it scarcely deserves the name, from the number of slaves being so small.

CHAPTER IX.

RELIGIOUS CHARACTER OF THE EARLY COLONISTS—FOUNDERS OF PENNSYLVANIA.

THE history of William Penn, the Quaker philosopher and lawgiver, is very generally known.   The son of a distinguished English admiral, heir to a fortune considered large in those days, accustomed from his youth to mingle in the highest circles, educated at the university of Oxford, rich in the experience and observation of mankind acquired by much travelling, and versed in his country's laws, he seemed fitted for a very different course from that which he considered marked out for him in after life.   He inherited from his parents a rooted aversion to the despotism of a hierarchy, and having, when a student at Oxford, ventured to attend the preaching of George Fox, he was for this offence expelled from the university.   After his expulsion, from a desire to make himself acquainted with the doctrines and spirit of the French Reformed, he spent some time at Saumur, one of their chief seats of learning, and there he attended the prelections of the gifted and benevolent Amyrault.   From that time he returned to England, and in 1666 visited Ireland, where he heard Thomas Loe preach of "the faith that overcomes the world," whereupon he was immediately filled with peace, and decided upon following out his future

plans of benevolence.   In the autumn of that year he was imprisoned for conscience sake.   "Religion," said he to the Irish
viceroy, "is my crime and my innocence; it makes me a pri-
soner to malice, but my own free man."   On returning to England, he became the butt of unmeasured ridicule from the wit-
lings of the court, which was that of one of the most dissolute
monarchs that ever lived.   Driven penniless from his father's
house, he found compassion where it takes up its last abode, if
it ever leaves this world, in a mother's heart.   Her bounty
kept him above want, while he was preparing, in God's providence, to become an author, and a preacher of the doctrines of
peace to princes, priests, and people.   Experience of persecution
had prepared him for the great mission of helping sufferers from
persecution.   He could truly say:—

" Haud ignarus mali miseris succurrere disco.

He had become a member of the ever-" suffering kingdom" of
righteousness.

William Penn's personal interests, in the course of providence, coincided with his benevolent views, in leading him to
think of founding the colony to which he so assiduously devoted
himself.   His father having had a large sum due to him by the
crown, this not very hopeful debt he left as a legacy to his son.
But the son proposed to his royal creditor an easy mode of paying it; the king had only to make him a grant of waste land
in the new world, and the suggestion was favourably received,
for the profuse and profligate Charles II. had been his father's
friend.   On the 5th of March, 1681, he received a title to a
territory which was to extend from the Delaware river five
degrees of longitude westward, and from the 39° to the 42°
N. latitude.   The whole of this, with the exception of a few
previous grants, of no great extent, made by the Duke of York,
was to be his; and thus all that remained of the territory
claimed by the Dutch, but which they had been compelled to
cede to the English, became not a place of refuge merely, but
the absolute property and sure abode of a sect which had probably been loaded with as much contempt and ridicule as had
ever fallen to the lot of any portion of the human race.   Their
peculiar dress and modes of speech, no doubt, so far invited this

treatment, while their principles secured impunity to such as meanly chose to attack with such weapons what they deemed absurdity and fanaticism.

Nor was it only for the persecuted "Friends" in England that William Penn founded his colony; it was to be open also to members of the same society in America. Incredible as it may appear, they were persecuted in New England by the very men who themselves had been driven thither by persecution. Twelve Quakers were banished from Massachusetts by order of the general court in 1656, and four of these who had returned were actually executed in 1669. That same year an act was passed by the legislature of Virginia, to the effect, "that any commander of any shipp, or vessell, bringing into the collonie any person or persons, called Quakers, is to be fined £100; and all Quakers apprehended in the collonie are to be imprisoned till they abjure this countrie, or give securitie to depart from it forthwith. If they return a third time, they are to be punished as felons."[1]

After making all necessary arrangements, Penn left England for his ample domain in America, and arrived there on the 27th of October, 1682. Having landed at Newcastle, he went from that to Chester, and thence, by boat, up the Delaware to the spot where now stands the city of Philadelphia. His first care was to acquire, by fair purchase, a title from the Indians to as much land, at least, as might be required for his projected colony, and this transaction took place at a famous council, held under a large elm-tree at Shakamaxon, on the northern edge of Philadelphia. There the hearts of the congregated chiefs of the Algonquin race were captivated by the simplicity and sincerity of Penn's manners, and by the language of Christian affection in which he addressed them. "We will live," said they in reply to his proposals, "in love with William Penn and his children, and with his children's children, as long as the moon and sun endure."

The year following was devoted by the philosopher to the founding of a city, to be called Philadelphia, between the Delaware and the Schuylkill rivers, and to the establishing of a

---

[1] Hening's Collection of the laws of Virginia.

government for his people.   Hardly could a pleasanter situation have anywhere been found than what he selected for his capital, which was destined to become one of the largest and finest cities in America, and to be the birth-place of national independence, where union among the liberated colonies was to be secured by the framing of a federal constitution for the whole. Nothing could have been more popular than the constitution laid down for his own colony, with the exception of his *veto* as proprietary, which was what he could hardly have abandoned, and an acknowledgment of the supremacy of the English crown and government.   Council, assembly, judges, and petty magistrates,—all were to be appointed by the colonists themselves.

The first emigrants to Pennsylvania were, for the most part, Quakers; but the principle of unlimited toleration, upon which it was established, made it a resort for people of all creeds and of none.   Swedes, Dutch, and New Englanders, had previously established themselves within its limits, and not many years had elapsed when the Quakers, whom Penn had specially contemplated as the future citizens of his colony, were found to be a minority among the inhabitants.   This, however, has not marred the harmony and tranquillity of the province.   No act of persecution or intolerance has ever disgraced its statute-book. The rights of the Indians have been almost always respected; their friendship has hardly ever been interrupted.

Friends' meeting-houses, and churches of other denominations, soon increased with the population, which spread by degrees into the interior, and reached the most western limits of the colony within a century from its commencement.

It were superfluous in me to pronounce any eulogium on the morality of the Quakers.   The foundations of the colony of William Penn were laid in the religion of the Bible, and to the blessed influence of that religion it is unquestionably indebted for much of the remarkable prosperity which it has enjoyed. But the Quaker population now forms only a small minority in the State of Pennsylvania, especially in its central and western parts.   I shall yet have occasion to show what were the original seats of the emigrants who constitute the remaining population of those parts.

Thus have I completed my promised notice of the religious

K 2

character of all the original colonies, which by settling on the
Atlantic slope, may be said to have founded the nation, by
founding its civil and religious institutions; or rather, I should
say, I have spoken of the colonies that had territorial limits as
such, and were established under charters from the crown of
England. I have treated of the bases—the lowest strata, so to
speak, of the colonisation of the United States. I have yet to
speak of the superadded colonies, which dispersed themselves
over the others, without having any territorial limits marked
to them by charters, but which settled here or there as individuals or groups might prefer. It will be seen that this secondary, but still early colonisation, exerted an immense influence
upon the religious character of the country, and in many cases,
through the wonderful providence of God, supplied what was
wanting in the religious condition of the primary and territorial
colonisation.

CHAPTER X.

RELIGIOUS CHARACTER OF THE EARLY COLONISTS—EMIGRANTS FROM WALES.

PRESBYTERIANISM is said to have had many zealous adherents in
Wales, in the time of the commonwealth, or from 1648 to 1660,
and when the restoration came, many Welsh Presbyterians,
including both pastors and people, sought a refuge from the
persecution that ensued by emigrating to America. On reaching the new world many of these wandered over the country,
and were glad to avail themselves of a resting-place wherever it
could be found. But a natural predilection for their own people, language, and customs, led others to keep together and
settle on the same spots; a course almost indispensable in the
case of some who could neither understand nor speak English.
Hence we find that towards the close of the seventeenth century, no fewer than six townships on the left bank of the
Schuylkill, were in the occupation of Welsh colonists.[1]

1 Proud's "History of Pennsylvania," vol. i. p. 221.

The success of those earlier emigrations, led to a steady and even copious transference of the inhabitants of the principality to America, long after open persecution had ceased to drive them from their native hills and valleys. About the beginning of the present century a colony from Wales settled in the mountains of Pennsylvania, on a large tract of land which they had bought before leaving home, and gave the name Cambria, the ancient appellation of Wales, to a whole county. A pretty large part of their settlement lies on a kind of table land, in the centre of the Alleghany mountains, and the chief villages were Armagh and Ebensburg, the latter of which is the seat of justice for the county. Two or three faithful pastors accompanied them from Wales, and to this day, I believe, they conduct their religious services in Welsh. There are several congregations, likewise, of Welsh Baptists in the State of New York, and throughout the United States not fewer than twenty-five churches of Calvinistic Welsh Methodists.

I have no means of knowing how numerous the emigrations from Wales from first to last have been; doubtless they have been far from unimportant in point of numbers. What, however, is of most consequence is, that they were good in point of character, and have already given to America many distinguished men. The Rev. Mr. Davies, of whom I shall have some notice to give hereafter, probably the most eloquent preacher in America of his day, and at his death president of the college of New Jersey, was, if I mistake not, of Welsh ancestry. The Morris family, so numerous, and in many of its members so distinguished, is of Welsh origin. So, also, are the Morgans. Besides these, we find many persons of the name of Jones, Griffiths, &c., all of Welsh descent, several of whom have risen to eminence in the church and state. Let me add that Roger Williams, the founder of Rhode island, whom I have had occasion already to notice, was a native of Wales.

CHAPTER XI.

RELIGIOUS CHARACTER OF THE EARLY COLONISTS OF AMERICA—EMIGRANTS FROM
SCOTLAND AND IRELAND.

NEXT to the Puritans of England we must unquestionably
rank the Scotch, as having largely contributed to form the religious character of the United States.   A few words, then, as
to the causes that have, at different times, led so many of the
natives of Scotland to pass over to America, will not be out
of place, and will prepare the reader for the remarks to be made
on the religious character of emigrants from that part of the
united kingdom.   James I., before he left Scotland, when called
to the throne of England in 1603, assured his countrymen of
his love to their church, and his determination to support it;
but no sooner had he crossed the Tweed than he manifested a
predilection for Prelacy, and a decided aversion to Presbytery,
as being of an essentially republican tendency.   Flattered and
caressed by the aged Whitgift, by Bancroft, and other bishops,
he soon learned to hate the Presbyterians of Scotland, as well
as to despise the Puritans of England; nor was it long before
he showed a fixed purpose to change, if possible, the ecclesiastical government of his northern kingdom, notwithstanding
that prudence and natural timidity deterred him from abrupt
measures.

It was otherwise with his unfortunate son.   Charles I. resolved to snatch at results to which caution and cunning might
in time have conducted his arbitrary but timid father.   He
began with ordering the publication of a book of canons, essentially altering the constitution of the church of Scotland, and
these he tried to enforce by his own authority.   He next caused
a liturgy to be drawn up and published, copied in a great measure from that of the church of England, but brought by Laud
into a closer agreement with the Romish missal; and this he
commanded all the Scotch ministers to use on pain of suspension.   These proceedings led, at last, to open resistance on

political as well as religious grounds; for they involved an
assumption of powers denied to the king by the Scottish constitution, and it was seen and felt that if he could introduce the
English liturgy, he might at some future time force upon the
country the Romish mass.   The wrong attempted in Scotland
roused the sympathy of England, and the upshot was, as Hallam remarks, "the liberties of England were preserved, but her
monarchy was overthrown."

But Charles II. behaved a great deal worse than his father
had done.   When that father was beheaded the son was a
friendless fugitive.   The Scotch offered to receive him as their
king, and to assist him in recovering the throne of England,
on his pledging himself by oath to maintain their presbyterian
form of church government.   This he engaged to do, and on his
arriving among them he subscribed the covenant.   The Scotch
thereupon took up arms in his cause, but were defeated by
Cromwell, so that Charles was driven a second time to the continent.   When restored, in 1660, to the crown of England, he
voluntarily renewed his former promise to the Scotch, to whom
he was greatly indebted for his restoration; but no sooner was
he seated on the throne than his oaths and promises were all
forgotten.   Presbyterianism was almost immediately abolished,
and Episcopacy restored in Scotland; that, too, in the most
repulsive form.   The bishops were invested by royal mandate
with the utmost plenitude of prelatical power, and a new law
forbade speaking against the king's ecclesiastical supremacy, or
the government of the church by bishops and archbishops.   A
court of high commission, partly composed of prelates, and armed
with inquisitorial powers, was set up, and was followed by scenes
of persecution and oppression, unparalleled except by the worst
doings of Rome.   Numbers of learned and godly ministers were
ejected, and though their places were filled for the most part by
ignorant and godless men,[1] the people were compelled under

---

[1] The author would not be understood for a moment to place in the same category, all the prelates, and all the parish clergy, introduced into the Scottish
established church by the measures mentioned in the text.   He is well aware
that among the former there was a Robert Leighton, who was forced, however,
by the atrocities of his associates to relinquish an office which his gentle spirit
would no longer suffer him to hold, and a Henry Scougall among the latter.
Such beautiful characters were enough to redeem, if that were possible, the
worthlessness of a whole generation, composed of such men as the greater num-

severe penalties to attend the ministrations of such worthless persons. The ejected ministers were not allowed to preach even in the fields, under pain of death. They might pray in their own houses, but none of the neighbours were allowed to attend. Even the nearest relations were forbidden to afford shelter to the denounced, or in any way to succour them. All landowners were required to give bonds that neither they nor their dependents should attend "conventicles," as the forbidden meetings were called. The laws were enforced by torture, fines, imprisonment, banishment, and death. Soldiers were quartered upon defenceless families, and allowed to harass them as they pleased; men were hunted down like wild beasts, and shot or gibbetted upon the highways, and this dreadful state of things lasted nearly thirty years, for the sole object of forcing upon the Scotch a form of church government which they conscientiously disliked. Can we wonder that the Scotch Presbyterians of that day detested Prelacy, as not the occasion only, but the cause of their sufferings? In their experience it was identified with despotism, superstition, and irreligion, whereas Presbyterianism was associated with the love of liberty and truth.

ber of the intruded clergy are known to have been. The author could not avoid referring to the arbitrary principles and horrible cruelties of the Scottish prelates and statesmen who patronised them, and he has not done so with the intention of casting odium on Episcopacy in general—the odium being due to the men and their principles, not to their office. Should it be supposed that stronger terms than the truth of history will warrant, have been employed in speaking of those men and their doings, let the reader consult Burnett's "History of his own Times;" Dr. Cook's "History of the Church of Scotland;" or M. Hallam's "Constitutional History of England." Let two short extracts from the last of these authorities suffice:

"The enormities of this detestable government are far too numerous, even in species, to be enumerated in this slight sketch, and of course, most instances of cruelty have not been recorded. The privy council was accustomed to extort confessions by torture; that grim divan of bishops, lawyers, and peers, sucking the groans of each undaunted enthusiast, in the hopes that some imperfect avowal might lead to the sacrifice of other victims, or at least warrant the execution of the present." And again: "It was very possible that Episcopacy might be of apostolical institution; but for this institution houses had been burned and fields laid waste, and the gospel had been preached in the wilderness, and its ministers had been shot in their prayers, and husbands had been murdered before their wives, and virgins had been defiled, and many had died by the executioner, and by massacre, and in imprisonment, and in exile, and slavery; and women had been tied to stakes on the sea-shore till the tide rose to overflow them, and some had been tortured and mutilated; it was a religion of the boots and the thumbscrew, which a good man must be very cool-blooded indeed, if he did not hate, and reject from the hands which offered it. For, after all, it is much more certain, that the Supreme Being abhors cruelty and persecution, than that he has set up bishops to have superiority over presbyters."
—Const. Hist. vol. iii. pp. 435, 442.

The Scottish parliament being then so constituted and regulated as to be a very imperfect exponent of the will, and advocate of the rights of the nation, it was the general assembly of the church, therefore, which it regarded as the best guardian of its dearest interests and privileges.   In the suppression of free assemblies, the body of the nation probably felt themselves more grievously wronged than had parliament itself been suppressed, and such upon the whole was the state of the law, and the oppressive manner in which it was administered, that none can reasonably wonder that the most loyal people to be found anywhere, should have attempted to rid themselves of their oppressors by rising against them.   The attempts of this kind, however, whether made in England or Scotland, led only to the sacrifice of some valuable lives, nor was it until by the revolution of 1688, so bloodless, yet so complete, that the Stuarts were again removed from the throne, that a better era dawned upon both kingdoms.

Such was the severity, however, of the nation's griefs while they lasted, that it seems strange that the Scotch Presbyterians did not abandon their country *en masse*.   But they were withheld by the hope of better times—a hope that even sometimes arrested plans of extensive emigration.   Thus, after a company of thirty-six noblemen and gentlemen had contracted for a large tract of land in the Carolinas, as an asylum for their persecuted countrymen, the project was relinquished in hopes of the success of the abortive attempt for which Russel and Sidney suffered in England.   Many, nevertheless, went over from Scotland into Ireland; many emigrated to America; and a large proportion of the former, or of their descendants, subsequently sought a resting-place in the new world.   This emigration from Scotland and Ireland, after it had thus commenced in the reigns of Charles II. and James II.. was continued, from other causes, down to the American revolution, and consisted almost exclusively of Presbyterians.   It was not until a later epoch that the emigration of Roman Catholics to America properly commenced; at least, until then it was too inconsiderable to merit notice.

Let us now see to what parts of America this emigration was directed, and which have enjoyed most of the happy effects of its moral influence.

New England did not on many accounts present the most attractions to Scotch emigrants. Not only were its best districts already occupied, but in almost all its colonies a church was established, between which and the Presbyterian there might not be all the harmony that was to be desired. Some, nevertheless, did go to New England, and received a kind welcome there. According to Cotton Mather, even previous to 1640, 4000 Presbyterians had arrived in that province, but what proportion of these came from Scotland and Ireland we have no means of ascertaining. At a later period, Londonderry, in New Hampshire, was founded by a hundred families of Irish Presbyterians, who having brought their pastor with them, organised a Presbyterian church there. Another church of that denomination was formed at Boston in 1729, and such it remained until 1786, when it became congregational. Other Presbyterians settled at Pelham and Palmer.

Neither was New York, for some time at least, an inviting quarter to Presbyterian emigrants; the establishment of the Episcopal church in that colony towards the close of the seventeenth century, and the intolerance to which it led, would naturally deter them from making it their choice. Some, indeed, had arrived previous to that epoch, and many Scotch and Irish settled in the province in the following century, particularly as the American revolution was drawing on. Between 400 and 500 emigrants from Scotland alone, arrived at New York in 1737, and twenty years later, Scotch and Irish colonists established themselves in Ulster county, and also at Orange and Albany.

In 1682, William Penn, and eleven other Quakers, having bought the claims of Lord Carteret's heirs, associated with themselves twelve other persons, a large proportion of whom were Scotch, with the view of securing as extensive an emigration as possible from Scotland, as well as other places. Nor were they disappointed; many were induced to leave that country and the north of Ireland, and to settle in East New Jersey, from the favourable accounts they heard of that colony. "It is judged the interest of the government," said George Scot of Pitlochie, a Scotchman of rank and influence, "to suppress Presbyterian principles altogether; the whole force of the law of this kingdom is levelled at the effectual bearing of them down. The rigorous putting of these laws in execution has, in a great part, ruined many of those who, notwithstanding hereof, find themselves in conscience obliged to retain their principles. A retreat, where by law a toleration is allowed, doth at present offer itself in America, and is no where else to be found in his majesty's dominions."[1] "This is the era," says Mr. Bancroft, "at which East New Jersey, till now chiefly colonised from New England, became the asylum of Scottish Presbyterians." "Is it strange," asks that author, "that many Scottish Presbyterians of virtue, education, and courage, blending a love of popular liberty with religious enthusiasm, came to East New Jersey in such numbers as to give to the rising commonwealth a character which a century and a half has not effaced?"[2] Many of the more wealthy of these emigrants brought with them a great number of servants, and, in some instances, transported whole families of poor labourers, whom they placed on their lands.[3] And in speaking of the town of Freehold, in Monmouth county, one of the earliest settlements in New Jersey, the Rev. William Tennent, long pastor of the Presbyterian church in that place, observes: "The settling of that place with a gospel ministry was owing, under God, to the agency of some Scotch people that came to it; among whom there was none so painstaking in this blessed work as one Walter Ker, who, in 1685, for his faithful and conscientious adherence to God and his truth, as professed by the church of Scotland, was there apprehended and sent to this country under a sentence of perpetual banishment. By which it appears that the devil and his instruments lost their aim in sending him from home, where it is unlikely he could ever have been so serviceable to Christ's kingdom as he has been here. He is yet (1744) alive; and, blessed be God, flourishing in his old age, being in his 88th year."[4]

But it was to Pennsylvania that the largest emigrations of Scotch and Irish, particularly of the latter, though at a later

---

[1] Bancroft's "History of the United States," vol. ii. p. 411.
[2] Ibid. vol. ii. p. 414.
[3] Gordon's "History of New Jersey," p. 51.
[4] The Rev. William Tennent, quoted by Dr. Hodge in his "Constitutional History of the Presbyterian Church in the United States."

period, took place. About the commencement of last century
they began to arrive in large numbers. It is said that nearly
6000 Irish arrived in 1729; and that up to the middle of the
century as many as 12,000 came over every year. Speaking
of that period, Proud, in his History of Pennsylvania, says,
" they have flowed in of late years from the north of Ireland in
very large numbers." They settled in the eastern and middle
parts of the State,—the only parts then inhabited by white
men. Cumberland county was filled with them.

From Pennsylvania they emigrated in great numbers into
the western parts of Maryland, the central portions of Virginia,
and the western counties of North Carolina. A thousand
families are said to have left the northern colonies for the last
of these provinces in the single year 1764. There their descendants now constitute a dense homogeneous population,
occupying the whole western section of the State, and distinguished by the strict morality and unbending principles of
their forefathers. Five or six hundred Scotch settled near
Fayetteville, N. C. in 1749, and there was a second arrival
from the same country in 1754, after which a steady yearly
emigration of the same hardy and industrious people was kept
up for a long period.[1]

But besides the emigration of Scotch and Irish colonists from
Pennsylvania into Maryland, the latter province received emigrants direct from Scotland and Ireland. Colonel Ninian
Beall, a native of Fifeshire, who had been implicated in some
of the disturbances in his native country, fled first to Barbadoes, and removed from thence to Maryland, where he bought
an immense estate, including much of the ground now occupied
by Washington and Georgetown. About 200 of his friends
and neighbours joined him at his request about the year 1690,
and brought along with them the Rev. Nathaniel Taylor, their
pastor.

In 1684, a small colony of persecuted Scotch settled, under

[1] The Scotch settlers near Fayetteville, in North Carolina, are said to have
been almost without exception from the Highlands. Gaelic is still spoken by
some of the old colonists, and I understand that it is still used in some of the
churches in that quarter for public worship, which, I may add, is in every
respect conducted as in Scotland.—(See Hodge's " Constitutional History of
the Presbyterian Church," vol. i. p. 66.)

Lord Cardross, in South Carolina.[1] In 1737, multitudes of husbandmen and labourers from Ireland embarked for that province,[2] and within three years before 1773 no fewer than 1600 emigrants from the north of Ireland settled there. Indeed, of all European countries, Ireland furnished South Carolina with the greatest number of inhabitants;[3] they not only settled in the interior, but also on Edisto and the other islands on the coast.

Georgia, too, was partly colonised by Scotch and Irish, who emigrated south-westward from Pennsylvania, across Maryland, Virginia, and North Carolina, besides receiving no small proportion of its first settlers directly from the Highlands of Scotland.

Thus it is manifest that Presbyterians from Scotland and the north of Ireland have largely contributed to form the religious character of the United States; particularly in the middle and southern parts of the country, and by consequence the corresponding parts of the valley of the Mississippi which have been colonised from them. As the early emigrants from Scotland and Ireland were not only Protestants but decidedly religious people, they did much to give a religious tone to the districts in which they established themselves, being those precisely that most stood in need of such an influence. So that in this we have another instance of the divine interposition in behalf of a country, whose whole history is a continued illustration of the mercy and the goodness of our God.

I may add, in concluding this chapter, that America owes to the early emigrations from Scotland and Ireland not a few of the men who have risen to the highest eminence both in church and state. The Tennents, the Blairs, the Allisons, were of Scoto-Irish origin; Dr. Witherspoon, one of the most valuable men in America of his day, both as a divine and as a statesman, Dr. Nisbet, and many others, were from Scotland.

The son of a poor Irish emigrant, who had settled in North Carolina, has been president of the United States.[4] The son of

---

[1] Bancroft's " History of the United States," vol. ii. p. 173.
[2] Holme's Annals, vol. ii. p. 145.
[3] Ramsay's " History of South Carolina," vol. i. p. 20; vol. ii. pp. 23, 548.
[4] General Andrew Jackson.

a Scoto-Irish emigrant, who had settled first in Pennsylvania and removed afterwards to South Carolina, has been vice-president.[1]

CHAPTER XII.

RELIGIOUS CHARACTER OF THE EARLY COLONISTS—HUGUENOTS FROM FRANCE.

NEXT to the English Puritans and Scotch Presbyterians we must rank the exiled Huguenots, or French Reformed, as having done most to form the religious character of the United States.

The Reformation found its way into France in the reign of Francis I., but was hated by that monarch on a double account. First, it placed man at once before his Creator and his Judge, without the intervention of human proxies, or the possibility of standing there in the ground of human merit. It placed the sinner at once in presence of the God against whom he had sinned. Second, because, in Calvin's hands the natural development of its principles, threatened the questioning of the rights of despotic power. Hence, although the king's love of literature, and his patronage of learned men, led him for a time to defend the chiefs of the Reformation in France on account of the interest they showed in the revival of letters, and his hatred of the scholastic and fanatical theologians of the Sorbonne; Francis distinguished himself by being almost the first ruler that put a Protestant to death. His successors but too closely followed his example. Persecution, though intermitted at times, owing to the pressure of circumstances, was resumed when that pressure ceased; until 1598, when Henry IV. granted the edict of Nantes—a measure which far from accorded the full measure of Protestant rights, but which at length was sacredly observed, at least during the remainder of that monarch's reign. But during that of his successor Louis XIII., and the early years of Louis XIV., that famous ordinance was no better than an ill-observed truce.

Louis XIV. after having come to the crown in his minority,

[1] Hon. John C. Calhoun.

was now approaching his fiftieth year, and had begun to feel the decline of passions which he had long indulged without regard for the restraints of religion and morality, beyond a habitual compliance with the outward forms of the Romish church, and occasional fits of remorse that were soon forgotten amid the excitement of new pleasures. In proportion as his relish for a voluptuous life became blunted by increasing age and satiety, he became more and more anxious to atone in some way for long years of sinful indulgence by acts of extraordinary devotion, without altogether sacrificing, however, either his love of pleasure or the pursuit of glory. He was thus in a state of mind admirably calculated to make him the tool of an order of men, who have acquired the highest celebrity for their profound knowledge of the human heart, and their consummate skill in making alike its strength and its weakness subserve the advancement of their power, more especially in the case of persons placed in stations of authority and influence. A Jesuit skilled in casuistry, and a fascinating and ambitious woman, were bent, the one on waking the king, who had been brought up in moderate sentiments towards the Reformed, and had long provoked their enemies by his respect for the edict of Nantes, become the instrument of Rome in utterly suppressing the Reformation in France, and if possible, throughout Europe; the other, on making herself the now widowed monarch's wife. To attain these ends they played into each other's hands, with an unrivalled mastery of all the arts usually employed on such occasions. The confessor used his influence in confirming the favourite's ascendancy in the king's affections—the favourite, though educated a Protestant, and under early and deep obligations to a Protestant relation, sacrificed her friends, and perhaps her convictions, by professing an extravagant zeal for the universal reign of the Roman Catholic religion, and by suggesting that in no way could the king better atone for his past irregularities, or promote his own glory, than by labouring "for the conversion of heretics." Both succeeded, but not to the full measure of their desires. Madame de Maintenon was privately married to Louis XIV., but never became the acknowledged queen of France. The edict of Nantes was revoked, bnt the Reformation survives in the French dominions to this day.

The king had come under too many solemn obligations to observe that edict, and had a conscience too little sophisticated by Jesuit morality in early life, to be brought into a direct revocation of Protestant privileges. The mode by which his scruples were overcome was exceedingly ingenious. His consent was first obtained to a multitude of indirect methods of diminishing the numbers of the Reformed; much violence and fraud unknown to him were mingled with the execution of those measures, and he was then persuaded that the edict of Nantes was unnecessary, since those in whose favour it had been granted had ceased to exist in his dominions. Favours of every kind were promised to those who would recant the alleged errors transmitted to them from their ancestors, or embraced by themselves; offices were held out as the reward of such meritorious recantations, while on the other hand, all hope of public employment, and even of public favour in any form, was denied to such as refused to be converted. Not only were they excluded from every post of honour or place of trust, but even the guilds and trades' corporations were closed against them. No Protestant was to be allowed to marry a Roman Catholic. Bribery was also employed, and converts were purchased for gold.

Proselytism nevertheless went on slowly, and death threatened to overtake its illustrious apostle, before he should see his subjects united again under the crosier of the successor of Peter the fisherman. The enterprise must needs be hastened forward. The sacredness of the family sanctuary is next invaded. Children of seven years of age are invited to abjure the faith of their parents. Protestant ministers begin to be tormented in every way: Protestant chapels are pulled down, or confiscated to other uses; Protestant schools are shut up; Protestant funds are seized and diverted from their legitimate ends; those that attempt to fly are forbidden to leave France under pain of being sent to the galleys. Vain attempt! The conversions still proceed very slowly.

Next come scenes of violence. Instead of Jesuit missionaries, or rather along with those missionaries, dragoons are sent into the Protestant districts, to be quartered on the inhabitants, and to worry them into conversion. Ferocity and lust are let loose under every roof and escape is hopeless.

At length the edict of Nantes was formally revoked. All public worship among the Protestants was suppressed; their places of public worship existed no more for them at least. The old Chancellor le Tellier, could exclaim, "Now, Lord, lettest thou thy servant depart in peace," and the royal dupe believed that he had united all dissenters with the Roman church.

But what pen can describe the results of this pretended union? Property plundered, books destroyed, children torn from their parents, faithful pastors who would not abandon their flocks, broken on the wheel, the bodies of all who died unreconciled to the church, thrown to the beasts, estates given up to relations who conformed to the Romish church, and protracted tortures employed to extort recantations of Protestantism! Men were even roasted at slow fires, plunged into wells, and wounded with knives and red hot pincers. The loss of life cannot now be computed, but it has been asserted that ten thousand persons perished at the stake alone, or on the gibbet and the wheel.[1]

In consequence of these proceedings it is believed that no fewer than half a million of Protestants left France. It was in vain that the frontiers were guarded. Despair was more ingenious in devising means of evasion, than bigotry was in its endeavours to prevent it. Another half million, unable to escape, remained in France, yet could not be reduced to absolute conformity with the established creed and worship. Fanaticism grew weary in hunting down its victims, and found nothing harder to subdue than the human mind when once disenthralled by truth.

Those Huguenots that escaped sought refuge in all the Protestant countries of Europe—at the Cape of Good Hope and in America, carrying with them the useful arts wherever they went, and founding many new manufactures in Germany, Holland, and the British islands. A whole suburb of London came to be inhabited by French mechanics, and they had six churches at one time in that city. The Prince of Orange took whole regiments of brave refugees into his service, and retained them after he became William III. of England. Most affecting nar-

---

1 De Rulhière Œuvres, v. p. 221.

ratives have come down to our times from the actors in those
scenes, and yet filial piety has not been so diligent as it ought
to have been in collecting and preserving them.

"In our American colonies," says the eloquent historian to
whom I have been so often indebted, "they were welcome every
where. The religious sympathies of New England were awakened. Did any arrive in poverty, having barely escaped with
life? the towns of Massachusetts contributed liberally to their
support, and provided them with lands; others repaired to New
York; but a warmer climate was more inviting to the exiles of
Languedoc, and South Carolina became the chief resort of the
Huguenots. What though the attempt to emigrate was by
the law of France a felony? in spite of every precaution of the
police 500,000 souls escaped from the country. The unfortunate
were more wakeful to fly than the ministers of tyranny to restrain.

"'We quitted home by night, leaving the soldiers in their
beds, and abandoning the house with its furniture,' said Judith,
the young wife of Pierre Manigault; 'we contrived to hide ourselves for ten days at Romans, in Dauphiny, while a search was
made for us; but our faithful hostess would not betray us.'
Nor could they escape to the sea board, except by a circuitous
journey through Germany and Holland, and thence to England,
in the depths of winter. 'Having embarked at London, we
were sadly off. The spotted fever appeared on board, and many
died of the disease; among these our aged mother. We touched
at Bermuda, where the vessel was seized. Our money was all
spent; with great difficulty we procured a passage in another
vessel. After our arrival in Carolina, we suffered every kind
of evil. In eighteen months, our eldest brother, unaccustomed
to the hard labour which we were obliged to undergo, died of a
fever. Since our leaving France we had experienced every sort
of affliction—disease, pestilence, famine, poverty, hard labour.
I have been six months without tasting bread, working like a
slave; and I have passed three or four years without having it
when I wanted it. And yet,' adds the excellent woman in the
spirit of grateful resignation, 'God has done great things for us
in enabling us to bear up under so many trials.'

"This family was but one of many that found a shelter in
Carolina, the general asylum of the Calvinist refugees. Escap-

ing from a land where the profession of their religion was a felony, where their estates were liable to become confiscated in favour of the apostate, where the preaching of their faith was a crime to be expiated on the wheel, where their children might be torn from them to be subjected to their nearest Catholic relation,—the fugitives from Languedoc, on the Mediterranean, from Rochelle, and Saintonge, and Bordeaux, the provinces on the Bay of Biscay, from St. Quentin, Poictiers, and the beautiful valley of Tours, from St. Lo, and Dieppe, men who had the virtues of the English Puritans without their bigotry, came to the land to which the tolerant benevolence of Shaftesbury[1] had invited the believer of every creed.   From a land that had suffered its king in wanton bigotry to drive half a million of its best citizens into exile, they came to the land which was the hospitable refuge of the oppressed; where superstition and fanaticism, infidelity and faith, cold speculation and animated zeal, were alike admitted without question, and where the fires of religious persecution were never to be kindled.   There they obtained an assignment of lands, and soon had tenements; there they might safely make the woods the scene of their devotions, and join the simple incense of their psalms to the melodies of the winds among the ancient groves.   Their church was in Charleston; and thither on every Lord's day, gathering from the plantations on the banks of the Cooper, and taking advantage of the ebb and flow of the tide, they might all regularly be seen, the parents with their children, whom no bigot could wrest from them, making their way in light skiffs through scenes so tranquil, that silence was broken only by the rippling of the oars, and the hum of the flourishing village at the confluence of the rivers.

"Other Huguenot emigrants established themselves on the south bank of the Santee, in a region which has since been celebrated for affluence and refined hospitality.

"The United States are full of monuments of the emigrations from France.   When the struggle for independence arrived, the son of Judith Manigault entrusted the vast fortune he had

---

[1] The "Constitutions" which Mr. Locke prepared for Carolina, and to which Mr. Bancroft alludes, promised not equal rights, but "toleration" to "Jews, heathens, and other dissenters," to "men of any religion."   The Episcopal church was to be established by law.

acquired to the service of the country that had adopted his mother; the hall in Boston where the eloquence of New England
rocked the infant spirit of independence, was the gift of the son
of a Huguenot; when the treaty of Paris for the independence
of our country was framing, the grandson of a Huguenot, acquainted from childhood with the wrongs of his ancestors, would
not allow his jealousies of France to be lulled, and exerted a
powerful influence in stretching the boundary of the States to
the Mississippi. On our north-eastern frontier State, the name
of the oldest college bears witness to the wise liberality of a
descendant of the Huguenots. The children of the Calvinists
of France have reason to respect the memory of their ancestors." [1]

The emigration of the Huguenots to America, is an exceedingly interesting event in the history of that country. It commenced earlier, and was more extensive than is generally supposed. Even previous to the massacre of St. Bartholomew's
day, some of the Protestant leaders, as we have seen, whether
from feeling their position to be even then intolerable, or from
their anticipations of a still darker futurity, proposed to establish a colony and a mission in Brazil—the mission being the
first ever projected by Protestants. The admiral of France,
de Colligny, who was afterwards a victim in the above massacre,
entered warmly into the undertaking, and Calvin urged it on
with all his might, and selected three excellent ministers, who
had been trained under his own eye at Geneva, to accompany
the emigrants. The expedition set out in 1556, but proved
peculiarly disastrous. The commander relapsed to the Roman
Catholic faith, and having put the three ministers to death,
returned to France, leaving the remains of the colony to be
massacred by the Portuguese! Nor did better success attend
two attempts made by the good admiral to plant colonies in
North America, the one in South Carolina, the other in Florida.
It seemed as if the time had not yet come for the planting of
good colonies, and that neither religion·nor persecution had as
yet sufficiently *ripened* the Protestants for the enterprise.

From the time of the siege of Rochelle to that of the revocation of the edict of Nantes, there had been a continual emigra-

---

[1] Bancroft's "History of the United States," vol. ii. pp. 180—183.

tion of French Protestants to the English colonies in America, which after the last of these two events was greatly augmented, as is abundantly proved by the public acts of those colonies. The first notice of the kind to be found in an act of the colony of Massachusetts bay, in 1662, to this effect, "that John Touton, a French doctor and inhabitant of Rochelle, made application to the general court of Massachusetts in behalf of himself and other Protestants, expelled from their habitations on account of their religion, that they might have liberty to live there, which was readily granted to them."[1] In 1686, a grant of 11,000 acres was made to another company of French Protestants who had settled at Oxford, in the same colony.[2] In that year, too, a French Protestant church was erected at Boston, which, ten years after, had the Rev. Mr. Daillé for its pastor. A century later, when the French Protestants had ceased to use the French language, and had become merged in other churches, their place of worship fell into the hands of some French Roman Catholic refugees.

In 1666, an act for the naturalisation of French Protestants was passed by the legislature of Maryland; acts to the like effect were passed in Virginia in 1671; in the Carolinas in 1696, and in New York in 1703.[3]

New York became an asylum for the Huguenots at a very early date, for even before it was surrendered to England, namely, about 1656, they were so numerous there that the public documents of the colony had to be published in French as well as in English;[4] and in 1708, Smith, the historian of that colony, says, that next to the Dutch they were the most numerous and the wealthiest class of the population. From an early period they had in that city a church, which exists at the present day. I understand that it has long been attached to the denomination of the Protestant Episcopal church, and has a Frenchman for its rector.

New Rochelle, about sixteen miles above the city of New

[1] Holme's "American Annals" for that year.
[2] Ibid.
[3] Huguenots had long been settled in both Carolinas and New York before they were naturalised. This arose solely from internal difficulties, which rendered their naturalisation for the moment impossible, not from any unwillingness to receive them.
[4] Bancroft's "History of the United States," vol. ii. p. 302.

York, on the East river, or sound, as it is more commonly called, was settled solely by Huguenots from Rochelle in France, and the French tongue, both in public worship and common parlance, was in use even until after the American revolution. There are many of the descendants of French Huguenots in Ulster and Duchess counties in the State of New York.

The Rev. Dr. Millar, professor of Church History in the theological seminary at Princeton, New Jersey, had the following interesting facts respecting the early inhabitants of New Rochelle communicated to him: "When the Huguenots first settled in that neighbourhood their only place of worship was in the city of New York. They had taken lands on terms that required the utmost exertions of men, women, and children among them to render tillable. They were, therefore, in the habit of working hard till Saturday night, spending the night in trudging down on foot to the city, attending worship twice the next day, and walking home the same night to be ready for work in the morning. Amid all these hardships they wrote to France, to tell what great privileges they enjoyed."[1]

In 1679, Charles II. sent, at his own expense, in two ships, a company of Huguenots to South Carolina, in order that they might there cultivate the vine, the olive, &c., and from that time there was an extensive emigration of French Protestants to the colonies. Collections were made for them in England in the reign of James II., and the English parliament at one time aided them with a grant of £15,000.[2] In 1690, William III. sent a large colony of them to Virginia, in addition to which that colony received 300 families in 1699, followed successively by 200 and afterwards by 100 families more. In 1752 no fewer than 1600 foreign Protestants, chiefly French, settled in South Carolina, and above 200 more in 1764.

In 1733, 370 Swiss Protestant families settled in South Carolina, under the conduct of Jean Pierre Pury of Neuchâtel; the British government granting them 40,000 acres of land, and £400 Sterling for every hundred adult emigrants landed in the colony.[3]

[1] "History of the Evangelical churches of New York."
[2] Holme's "American Annals."
[3] Ibid.

In some of the colonies where an established church was supported by a tax, special acts were passed for relieving French Protestants of that burden, and for granting them liberty of worship.   Thus, in 1700, the colony of Virginia enacted as follows: "Whereas a considerable number of French Protestant refugees have been lately imported into this his majesty's colony and dominion, several of which refugees have seated themselves above the fall of James's river, at or near the place commonly called and known by the name of the Monacan towns, &c., the said settlement be erected into a parish, not liable to other parochial assessments,"   This exemption was to last for seven years, and was afterwards renewed for seven more. [1]

These Huguenots, whenever sufficiently numerous, at first used their own language in public worship, and had churches of their own, until, with one or two exceptions, and those only for a time, they fell into either the Presbyterian or Episcopal denominations.   This must be taken as a general statement, for their descendants may now be found in almost all-communions, as well as in all parts of the United States.   Many members, too, of the Dutch reformed churches are descended from Huguenots, who had first taken refuge in Holland, and afterwards emigrated to America.   Nor must we forget the descendants of Huguenots who found their first asylum in England and Scotland.   Among these was the late excellent Divie Bethune, whose ancestors came originally from the town of Bethune, not far from Calais.

On looking over the roll of the Presbyterian churches of Charleston, South Carolina, there may be found the Huguenot names of Dupré, Du Bosse, Quillin, Lanneau, Legaré, Rosamond, Dana, Cousac, Lequeux, Bores, Hamet, Rechon, Bize, Benoist, Berbant, Marchant, Mallard, Belville, Molyneux, Frabrique, Chevalier, Bayard, Sayre, De Saint Croix, Boudinot, Le Roy, Ogier, Janvier, Gillet, Purviance, Guiteau, Boyer, Simon, &c., &c. [2]

As the entire population of the American colonies amounted only to about 200,000 souls in 1701,[3] more than forty years after the commencement of the Huguenot emigrations, a large propor-

1 Holme's "American Annals," pp. 432, 472, 492.   Henning's "Statutes," p. 201.   Dr. Hawk's "Virginia," p. 79.
2 Lang's "Religion and Education in America," p. 24.
3 Holme's "Annals."

tion of that number must have been French Protestants, and Huguenot blood accordingly must be extensively diffused among the citizens of the United States at the present day.[1] It is very obvious that so large an accession of people, whose very presence in America proved the consistency of their religious character, and who were generally distinguished by simple and sincere piety, must have been a great blessing to the land of their adoption, especially to the southern States, where it was most required. Their coming to America, on the other hand, has been blessed, under God, to them and their descendants. Many of the first families in New York, Maryland, Virginia, and the Carolinas, as well as other States, are to be found among the latter, as may be seen in many cases from their names, although these have often been lost through intermarriages, or can with difficulty be recognised, owing to their being spelt as they are pronounced by Anglo- Americans. Some of the most eminent persons that have ever adorned the United States were of Huguenot descent. Such were no fewer than three out of the seven presidents of congress, and in a sense of the whole nation, during the war of the Revolution, namely John Jay, Henry Laurens, and Elias Boudinot,—all excellent men.

I conclude this chapter in the words of a distinguished clergymen of the Episcopal church in America.[2] "And never, probably, did any people better repay the hospitable kindness of the land which afforded them a refuge. Many of their descendants are still left in New York, Virginia, the Carolinas, and other parts of our country; and among the brightest ornaments of the State, in the halls of legislation and of justice, as well as in the sacred office, may be found the names of some of the French refugees. No man in America need ever blush to own himself one of their descendants; for observation has more than once been made, and it is believed to be true, that among their descendants the instances have been rare indeed, of individuals who have been arraigned for crime before the courts of the country."

[1] Lang's "Religion and Education in America," pp. 22, 23.
[2] Rev. Dr. Hawk's "History of the Episcopal Church in Virginia."

CHAPTER XIII.

RELIGIOUS CHARACTER OF THE EARLY COLONISTS—EMIGRANTS FROM GERMANY.

GERMANS began to emigrate to America in the latter part of the seventeenth century, and the first comers were probably sufferers in the devastations committed by the French under Turenne in the Upper Palatinate, a country lying on both sides of the Rhine, having Manheim for its capital, and including territories which have since been transferred from the German empire to France.   In 1674 the whole of it was rendered almost utterly desolate by the troops of Louis XIV., who had no better motive for perpetrating such atrocities, than that the invaded province was part of the empire with which he was then at war, and next, that its inhabitants were almost all Protestants.   So effectually did these troops do their master's bidding, that the elector palatine could at one time see, from his palace at Manheim, two cities and twenty-five villages in flames!   In this work of horror Turrene, no doubt, proved to his royal master's satisfaction, the sincerity of his conversion from Protestantism to Romanism, but he for ever tarnished by it his own great reputation.

As persecution continued what war and rapine had begun, on the palatinate falling under the government of a bigot, many German Protestants emigrated to the English colonies in America; and it may be remarked, that previous to the American revolution, the German emigration, though not always confined to the palatinate, and though many of the emigrants came from the north-west of Germany, continued to be almost purely Protestant.

About 2700 "palatines," as they were called, who had sought refuge in England, were sent out by the British government under Col. Hunter in 1710, when that officer was transferred from the governorship of Virginia to that of New York, and German settlements were formed about that time, and some years following, on the "German flats," and some other parts of that province.

In Pennsylvania this emigration is said to have commenced in 1682 or 1683, when Germantown, near Philadelphia was founded, and in subsequent years, such was the influx of those emigrants that they and their descendants were estimated in 1772, at a third of the whole population of that province, then amounting to between 200,000, and 300,000.[1] In a letter dated Oct. 14th 1730, Mr. Andrews says: "There is besides in this province a vast number of palatines, and they come in still every year.   Those that have come of late are mostly Presbyterians, or as they call themselves, Reformed; the palatinate being about three-fifths of that sort of people."   There were, however, many Lutherans mixed with them, as Mr. A. afterwards remarks, whilst he adds: "In other parts of the country they are chiefly Reformed, so that, I suppose, the Presbyterian party are as numerous as the Quakers, or near it.[2]   In the year 1749, 12,000 Germans arrived in that colony, and for several years thereafter nearly the same number came.[3]

From Pennsylvania they spread into Maryland and Virginia.   "The year 1713 was rendered memorable by an act of kindness shown to certain emigrants, similar to that which had been manifested towards the French refugees.   It seems that a small body of Germans had settled above the falls of the Rappahannock, on the southern branch of the river, in the county of Essex.   This was at that period the frontier of civilisation; and therefore, it was alike the suggestion of interest and humanity to afford protection and encouragement to these foreigners. Accordingly they were exempted, as the French had been, from all ordinary taxes for the term of seven years, and were formed into the "parish of St. George," with power to employ their own minister and upon their own terms."[4]

Many Germans emigrated to the Carolinas also.   In 1709 above 600 arrived, and from the name of their settlement, Newbern, they are supposed to have been Swiss-Germans from the

---

[1] Proud's " History of Pennsylvania," vol. ii. p. 273.
[2] Dr. Hodge's " Constitutional History of the Presbyterian Church," vol. i. p. 50.
[3] Proud's " History of Pennsylvania," vol. ii. pp. 273, 274.
[4] Dr. Hawk's " History of the Episcopal Church in Virginia," p. 81.

canton of Berne.[1]   From 1730 to 1750, South Carolina received
large accessions from .Switzerland, Holland, and Germany, and
a great many "palatines" arrived every year.[2]   In 1764, 500
or 600 were sent over from London, and had a township set
apart for them.[3]   Some years later a considerable number of
German families, after having settled in Maine, left that province to join their countrymen at Londonderry in South Carolina, but most of these repented having taken that step, and
returned to Maine, where their descendants are to be found at
this day.[4]

Georgia had Germans among its very first colonists.   A band
of these were led thither by Col. Oglethorpe, and reinforcements
from time to time arrived from Europe.

The Germans who emigrated to America during the colonial
era, being almost all Protestants, organised upon their arrival two
communions, or churches, upon the great doctrinal principles
which had divided them into two denominations in Germany,—
the Reformed, or the Calvinists, who are Presbyterians, and the
Church of the Augsburg Confession, or Lutherans.   The history
of these churches down to the present day will fall under notice
elsewhere.   But although difference of language compelled them
in the first instance to have churches of their own, many of their
descendants, partly from having adopted the English tongue,
partly from their wide dispersion over the country, are now
members of the Presbyterian, Episcopal, Methodist, and Baptist churches.

Among the Germans who settled in America, were two small
but interesting portions of the ancient Sclavonic churches of
Bohemia, as if to show that even the great Eastern branch of
the Christian church was to have its representatives also in the
new world, and to contribute to lay the foundations of a Christian empire there.   These were the United Brethren, or Mora-

---

[1] Williamson's "History of North Carolina," vol. i. p. 184.

[2] Ramsay's "History of South Carolina," vol. i. p. 11.

[3] Holme's "American Annals," vol. ii. p. 268.

[4] There is an interesting account of this colony in the American Quarterly
Register for Nov. 1840.   It was commenced, it would seem, in 1739, and received several accessions from Germany, but never became very strong.   It
suffered much in its early days from the Indians, and also from lawsuits about
the titles to the lands occupied by the emigrants.   The chief place in the colony
is called Waldoborough, where there is a church and a pastor, but the German
language is now disused.

vians as they are more commonly called, and some members of the churches of Bohemia. The Moravians came direct from Herrnhut, the mother city of the whole fraternity that adopt the renovating system, received by some of the remains of the ancient race from Count Zinzendorf, in the early part of last century. The Bohemians came in a dispersed state by way of Holland, but not having organised themselves as a distinct communion, these children of John Huss and Jerome of Prague were soon merged in the Protestant churches of the land of their adoption. Not so with the United Brethren, who preserve their own organisation and peculiar institutions to this day. Besides a few churches in such large cities as Philadelphia and New York, and some scattered throughout the interior, they are chiefly to be found in the three settlements of Bethlehem, Nazareth, and Littiz in Pennsylvania, and Salem in North Carolina. But I shall speak of their history and present numbers in another part of this work.

Previous to the revolution the German emigration was not only extensive but also, to a considerable degree at least, pure. The emigrants had left Europe on account of their religion, and brought with them into America the simple and tranquil habits, and the frugal industry that characterise the nation from which they came. Not only was their general standard of morality high, but there was not wanting among them a goodly number of sincere Christians, distinguished for the cultivation of all the Christian virtues. But ever since the revolution, and especially during the last thirty years, a very numerous emigration from Germany to the United States has taken place, consisting both of Protestants and Roman Catholics, influenced in expatriating themselves chiefly by worldly considerations, and much inferior in point of religious character to those godly emigrants of the same race who had been driven to our shores by persecution and oppression at home.

The descendants of German settlers are very numerous in Pennsylvania, Maryland, Virginia, and the other southern States, as well as in New York, Ohio, Indiana, Illinois, Michigan, Missouri, and the Territories of Wisconsin and Iowa. Indeed they are by far the most numerous of all the emigrants to America that are not of the British stock. But their influence on the religious character of the nation has not been equal to that of the Puritans, the Scotch, or the Huguenots. The first bible printed in America was Luther's version.

CHAPTER XIV.

RELIGIOUS CHARACTER OF THE EARLY COLONISTS—EMIGRANTS FROM POLAND.

EVEN Poland was called upon to furnish her contingent towards the colonisation of America, and sent over some excellent people, whose descendants are now dispersed over the country.

I know not whether the traditional fact I am about to mention stands recorded in any history, but it may, without hesitation, be received as true in all material points. I received it myself from some excellent ministers of the Dutch Reformed Church, who are personally acquainted with a considerable number of the descendants of the colonists to whom it relates. They state that in the early part of the 18th century, a Count Sobieski, a lineal descendant of the famous John Sobieski III., who routed the Turks at the battle of Choczin in 1673, and chased them from the walls of Vienna in 1683, led a colony of about 200 Protestants from Poland to the shores of America, there to enjoy a religious freedom which was not to be found in their native country.

In this tradition there is nothing strange. The doctrines of the Reformation made a considerable progress for a time in Poland, and one or two of the kings of that country were well disposed to it. Stipulations somewhat like the edict of Nantes were even made, for securing liberty of conscience and of worship to the Protestants. But these were afterwards disregarded, the Protestants persecuted, and their doctrines so effectually suppressed, that a Protestant Pole is hardly to be found now in the whole kingdom; for those that you meet with there are Protestants from Germany, not of Polish race. Thus there is nothing incredible in Poland, too, being represented in a country where the persecuted of every land have found a home.

This Polish colony settled in the valleys of the Passaic and Raritan rivers in New Jersey, where there are some of their descendants at the present day, while others are dispersed over various parts of the country. The name of Sobieski, corrupted into that of Zabriskie, is retained by a highly respectable family, many members of which are to be found in one part of New Jersey and others in the city of New York.

How wonderful are the ways of God! Poland chose to cleave to Romanism and rejected the Protestant reformation, and how has Romanism served her in her recent dreadful struggle for national independence? This question is best answered by the pope's bull,[1] addressed to the bishops of the kingdom in relation to that war.

CHAPTER XV.

RELIGIOUS CHARACTER OF THE EARLY COLONISTS—EMIGRANTS FROM THE VALLEYS OF PIEDMONT.

WHILE even Bohemia, Moravia, and Poland, thus sent forth their little bands of faithful men to America, it is not to be supposed that we should find no such witnesses to the truth proceeding from the valleys of Piedmont, to place themselves in the ranks of those whom God was thus calling out from so many nations to take part in peopling the new world with pure professors of the gospel. It was most fitting that among those there should be some at least to represent that martyr-people, veritable living relics of those churches in the north of Italy and south-west of France, which had remained faithful to the truth during long ages of apostacy, and whose preservation was so appropriately symbolised by "the bush unconsumed in the midst of the flames."

These had heard in the recesses of their valleys of the wonderful movement of the reformation in Germany and France.

[1] This bull is given at length in the work of the Abbé de la Mennais intituled " Rome."

They sent a deputation to Geneva to learn from Calvin what were his and Luther's views, and what those doctrines were which were turning the world upside down.   They heard with joy that the faith of the Reformers was the same as their own, and hastened, accordingly, to unite themselves to the general body of faithful men, who through much tribulation were casting off the yoke of that spiritual Babylon, drunk with the blood of saints, which had been endeavouring for so many ages to crush their forefathers.

But ere long the persecution which was to fall upon the whole Protestant body reached them also, and with fresh violence. Neither the seclusion of their valleys, nor the insignificance of their numbers, could save them from this stroke.   Then it was that the voice of Cromwell spoke for them with a power which even the emperor of Germany dared not disregard.   And then the pen of England's greatest poet was no less ready to teach a persecuting prince the duty that he owed to suffering humanity, than it was "to assert eternal providence, and justify the ways of God to man."   Those valleys contain enduring monuments of British benevolence; the fund contributed at that time by the Christians of England has aided the preaching of the gospel to their poor inhabitants ever since.   But those who had fled from persecution before the voice of Britain was thus lifted up, had to be provided with an asylum, and for this they were indebted to the city of Amsterdam, which offered them a free passage to America.   There the few hundreds that embraced the offer found a welcome reception awaiting them.[1]

1 "Albany Records," vol. iv. p. 223.   Lambrechtsten, p. 65, without quoting his authority, says 600 came over. Mr. Bancroft, vol. ii. p. 322, thinks this overstated.   A second emigration was proposed in 1663, but the project failed.

CHAPTER XVI.

SUMMARY.

SUCH, as respects the religious character of the colonists was the early colonisation of the United States, and well may it excite our wonder as altogether without a parallel in the history of the world. What were the colonies of Egypt, of Phœnicia, of Greece, and Rome?—what those of Spain and Portugal, when compared with those we have been considering? Before leaving the subject let us take a general survey of their character.

1. They were not composed of the rich, the voluptuous, the idle, effeminate, and profligate. Neither were they, generally speaking, composed of poor, spiritless, dependent, and helpless persons. They rather came from that middle class of society, which is placed in the happy medium between sordid poverty and overgrown wealth. They knew that whatever comfort or enjoyment they could look for in the new world, was only to be attained by the blessing of God upon their industry, frugality, and temperance.

2. They were not an ignorant rabble, such as many ancient and some modern States have been obliged to expel from their borders. Taken in the mass they were well informed—many of them remarkably so for the age in which they lived—and which in the case of none of them was an age of darkness. Letters had revived; the art of printing had diffused a great amount of valuable knowledge among the middle, and was fast carrying it down to the lowest ranks of society. With few exceptions they had acquired the elements of a good education. There were few persons in any of the colonies that could not read. They were moreover a thinking people, and very unfit to be the slaves of despotic power.

3. They were a virtuous people—not a vicious herd, such as used to be sent out by ancient states, and such as chiefly colonised South America and Mexico—men of unbridled passions and slaves to the basest lusts. The morality of the United

States' early colonists was unexampled in any community of equal extent, and has been lauded by almost all who have written about them, as well as by those who governed them.

4. They were religious men. They believed and felt that Christianity is no vain fancy—a fact that holds true even as respects those of them with whom religious motives were not the chief inducement for expatriating themselves. The overwhelming majority stood acquitted of the slightest approach to infidelity. Neither were they what are called "philosophers," attempting to propagate certain new theories respecting human society, and suggesting new methods for rendering it perfect. By far the greater number of them were simple Christians, who knew of no way by which men can be good or happy, but that pointed out by God in his word. There was not a single St. Simon or Owen to be found among them. Many of them, indeed, were irreligious men; some were even openly wicked, and opposed to all that is good. But these, in most of the colonies, formed a small minority.

Nor was their religion inoperative. It produced the fruits of righteousness. They have been blamed for their conduct to the Indians, but not with so much justice as has been supposed. No doubt there were instances of individual wrong, but they cannot be charged with any general want of justice or kindness to the aborigines. Except in war, and in one or two cases where no claimants appeared, they bought from those prior occupants the lands on which they settled. But on this and some other points of a general nature, I shall have more to say at another place.

5. With few exceptions the first colonists were Protestants; indeed, Lord Baltimore's was the only Roman Catholic colony, and even in it the Romanists came to form a small minority long before the revolution of 1775. The great mass had sacrificed much—some their all, for the Protestant faith. They were Protestants in the sense of men who took the bible for their guide, who believed what it taught, not what human authority put in its place. "What saith the Lord?" this was what they desired first of all, and above all, to know. And it was the study of the bible that opened their eyes to truths which bore upon every possible relation of life, and upon every duty. There they

learned to look upon all men as children of the same heavenly Father, as redeemed by the same Saviour, as going to the same bar of judgment; before which all must stand stript of the factitious distinctions of this world.   They saw no reason, therefore, why one man should lord it over another, since all "are of one flesh," and if Christians, brethren in Christ.   And they learned from the bible that obedience is due to rulers, not because they are different in blood or rank from other men, but because government is "an ordinance of God."   Obedience to God secured their obedience to civil rulers.   As God cannot command what is wrong, no ruler can be justified in doing so, nor can expect obedience if he does.   And whilst they learned from the bible what were their duties, so they learned there also what were their rights.   This led them at once to do their duty and to demand their rights.

6. The great majority of them had suffered much oppression and persecution, and in that severe but effectual school had learned lessons not to be acquired in any other.   It led them to question many things to which otherwise their thoughts might never have been directed, and it gave them irresistible powers of argument in favour of the rights of the human mind to freedom of thought.   Indeed, it is remarkable how large a proportion of the early colonists of the United States were driven from Europe by oppression.   Although Virginia and the Carolinas were not expressly established as asylums for the wronged, yet during the commonwealth in England, they afforded a refuge to the "cavalier" and the "churchman," as they did afterwards to the Huguenot and German Protestant.   Georgia was colonised as an asylum for the imprisoned and "persecuted Protestants;" Maryland as the home of persecuted Roman Catholics; and the colony of Gustavus Adolphus was to be a general blessing to the "whole Protestant world," by offering a shelter to all who stood in want of one.   Even New York, though founded by Dutch merchants, with an eye to trade alone, opened its arms to the persecuted Bohemian, and inhabitant of the Italian valleys.   So that, in fact, all these colonies were originally peopled more or less, and some of them exclusively, by the victims of oppression and persecution; hence the remark of one of our historians is no less just than eloquent, that "tyranny and injustice peopled

America with men nurtured in suffering and adversity.   The history of our colonisation is the history of the crimes of Europe."[1]

7. Though incapable as yet of emancipating themselves from all the prejudices and errors of past ages, with respect to the rights of conscience, they were at least in advance of the rest of the world on these points, and founded a State in which religious liberty is at this day more perfectly enjoyed than any where else—in short, is in every respect perfect.

8. Lastly, of the greater number of the early colonists it may be said, that they expatriated themselves from the old world, not merely to find liberty of conscience in the forests of the new, but that they might extend the kingdom of Christ, by founding States where the truth should not be impeded by the hindrances that opposed its progress elsewhere.   This was remarkably the case with the Puritans of New England, but a like spirit animated the pious men who settled in other parts of the country. They looked to futurity and caught glimpses of the glorious progress that the gospel was to make among their children and children's children.   This comforted them in sorrow and sustained them under trials.   They lived by faith, and their hope was not disappointed.

CHAPTER XVII.

RELATIONS BETWEEN THE CHURCHES AND THE CIVIL POWER IN THE COLONIES OF AMERICA.—1. IN NEW ENGLAND.

IN treating of the religious character of the early Anglo-American colonies, I have spoken incidentally only respecting their forms of church government, and even now, proceed to consider these, only in so far as is required for a right understanding of the established relations between their churches and the civil government.   I shall elsewhere treat of the various religious communions in the United States, or rather of the diverse forms

---

[1] Bancroft's "History of the United States," vol. ii. p. 251.

in which the church presents itself to the world, and the doctrines peculiar to each. We have here to do only with the relations which the State bore in the different colonies to the church, and where these two bodies were united, we shall see what were the nature and extent of that union.

Many persons whom I have met with in Europe seem to have been altogether unaware of the existence of any such union, in any part of the United States, and still more have had no correct idea of what the nature of that union was, in the different parts of the country where it was to be found. To both these classes I would now give all the information they require.

If we consider for a moment what was the state of the Christian world when these colonies were first planted in the early part of the seventeenth century, we must see that the mass of the colonists would be very little disposed to have the church completely separated from the state in their infant settlements, and the former deriving no support from the latter. The church and the state were at that time intimately united in all the countries of Europe, and the opinion was almost universally entertained that the one could not safely exist without the direct countenance of the other. It is not even certain that England, or any other country, would have granted charters for the founding of permanent colonies, unless upon the condition expressed, or well understood, that religion was to receive the public sanction and support. Assuredly, James I., at least, was not likely to consent to any thing else.

Be that as it may, the first colonists themselves had no idea of abolishing the connection which they saw everywhere established between the civil powers and the church of Christ. To begin with New England, nothing can be more certain than that its Puritan colonists, whether we look to their declaration or their actings, never contemplated the founding of communities in which the church should have no alliance with the state. Their object, and it was one that was dearer to them than life itself, was to found such civil communities as should be most favourable to the cause of pure religion. They had left England in order to escape from a government which in their view hindered the progress of divine truth, oppressed the conscience, and was inexpressibly injurious to the immortal interests of

men's souls. "They had seen in their native country the entire
subjection of the church to the supreme civil power; reformation
beginning and ending according to the caprices of the hereditary
sovereign; the church neither purified from superstition, ignorance, and scandal, nor permitted to purify itself; ambitious,
time-serving, tyrannical men, the minions of the court, appointed
to the high places of prelacy; and faithful, skilful, and laborious
preachers of the word of God, silenced, imprisoned, and deprived
of all means of subsistence, according to the interests and aims
of him or her who by the law of inheritance happened to be at
the head of the kingdom.   All this seemed to them not only
preposterous but intolerable; and, therefore, to escape from such
a state of things, and to be where they could freely practise
'Church Reformation,' they emigrated." [1]

In the formation, likewise, of their civil institutions in the
new world, they determined that whatever else might be sacrificed, the purity and liberty of their churches should be inviolate. Bearing this in mind, they founded commonwealths in
which the churches were not to be subordinate to the state.
Not that they were "Fifth monarchy men;" they had no wish
that the church should engross to itself the powers of the state,
and so rule in civil as well as in ecclesiastical matters.   But
they thought it better that the state should be accommodated
to the church than the church to the state.   "It is better," said
Mr. Cotton, "that the commonwealth be fashioned to the setting
forth of God's house, which is his church, than to accommodate
the church frame to the civil state." [2]

With this in view they sought to avail themselves of all the
lights furnished by the experience of ancient as well as modern
states, and looking especially to the constitution of England as
it then stood, they framed civil governments in which, as they
hoped, not only the temporal, but still more the spiritual interests
of mankind, might best be promoted. They considered that they
had a right to do so; and held opinions on this point directly at
variance with those of the age in which they lived.   The fashion
then was to deduce all authority from the divine right of kings,

1 Bacon's "Historical Discourses on the completion of 200 years from the
beginning of the first Church in New Haven," pp. 17, 18.
2 Cotton's "Letter to Lord Say and Seal in Hutchinson's History of New
England," vol. i., p. 497.

and the theory of civil power was that of uninterrupted hereditary succession.   But the Puritan founders of New England
thought that "they were free to cast themselves into that mould
and form of commonwealth which appeared best for them," in
reference to their grand purpose; nor did they doubt that a
government thus originating in voluntary compact, would have
equal right to the exercise of civil authority with that of any
earthly potentate whatever.

Whatever were the details of their policy, and whatever the
results of some parts of it, it is most certain that they intended
that the church should in no sense be subject to the state.
They held the great and glorious doctrine that CHRIST IS THE
ONLY HEAD AND RULER OF THE CHURCH, and that no human
legislation has a right to interfere with HIS.   It has been said
that they took the Hebrew commonwealth for their model in
civil politics, and this is so far true.   But it holds as to their
penal code more than with respect to the forms of their civil
governments.   With the exception of the first few years of the
Massachusetts Bay and New Haven colonies, there was no such
blending of civil and religious authority as existed in the Jewish republic.   There was much, however, in the Hebrew commonwealth and laws that seemed adapted to the circumstances
of men who had just exchanged what they considered a worse
than Egyptian bondage, for a Canaan inhabited by the "heathen,"
whom they were soon to be compelled "to drive out."   The two
cases were more alike than at first strikes a superficial observer.[1]

---

[1] " The laws of Moses were given to a community emigrating from their
native country, to a land which they were to acquire and occupy for the great
purpose of maintaining in simplicity and purity the worship of one true God.
The founders of this colony came hither for the self-same purpose.   Their
emigration from their native country was a religious emigration.   Every other
interest of their community was held subordinate to the purity of their religious
faith and practice.   So far then as this point of comparison is concerned, the
laws which were given to Israel in the wilderness may have been suited to the
wants of a religious colony planting itself in America.

" The laws of Moses were given to a people who were to live not only surrounded by heathen tribes on every frontier save the sea-board, but also with
the heathen inhabitants, worshippers of the devil, intermixed among them, not
fellow-citizens, but men of another and barbarous race : and the laws were
therefore framed with a special reference to the corrupting influence of such
neighbourhood and intercourse.   Similar to this was the condition of our
fathers.   The Canaanite was in the land, with his barbarian vices, with his
heathenish and hideous superstitions ; and their servants and children were to
be guarded against the contamination of intercourse with beings so degraded.

" The laws of the Hebrews were designed for a free people.   Under those

There were parts of the Mosaic law, excluding, of course, all that was typical, ceremonial, and local, which the colonists thought they might do well to adopt, until, in the course of time, they should find reasons for changing to something better. Had it been the laws of Solon, Lycurgus, Numa, or Alfred that they adopted, some who now ridicule would perhaps have applauded them, as if Moses were inferior to any of those lawgivers. There are men who know more of the laws of Solon, and even of Minos, than about Moses, and who, in their ignorance, talk of the Jews of the days of Moses as if almost, if not altogether, savages; not knowing that they were quite as much civilised as any of their cotemporaries, and had their institutions prescribed to them by the Supreme Ruler and Lawgiver.

It is remarkable that with the exception of the Plymouth settlers, all the first New England colonists—all who founded Massachusetts Bay, New Hampshire, Maine, Connecticut, New Haven, Providence, and Rhode island, up to their leaving England, were members of the established church there. The Plymouth people alone were Independents,[1] had had their church organised on that principle for years, and were such even before they went to Holland. If any of the other original colonists of New England had been thrust out from the established church of the mother-country, they had not organised themselves on any other principle; and, however opposed to the spirit of its rulers and to some of its ceremonies and usages, that they were attached to the church itself, as well as to many of those whom they had left within its pale, is manifest from the letter addressed

laws, so unlike all the institutions of oriental despotism, there was no absolute power, and, with the exception of the hereditary priesthood, whose privileges, as a class, were well balanced by their labours and disabilities, no privileged classes. The aim of those laws was ' equal and exact justice;' and equal and exact justice is the only freedom. Equal and exact justice, in the laws and in the administration of the laws, infuses freedom into the being of a people, secures the widest and most useful distribution of the means of enjoyment, and affords scope for the activity and healthful stimulus to the affections of every individual. The people whose habits and sentiments are formed under such an administration of justice will be a free people."—(Bacon's " Historical Discourses," pp. 30, 31.

1 They were not, properly speaking, *Separatists*, in the distinctive sense in which that word was used at that epoch, viz. those who not only refused to have any sort of communion with the established church, but denounced all who did. The Separatists were exceedingly bitter in their hostility to every thing which bore the name of the established church of England. The farewell address of John Robinson, to the pilgrims who left Leyden to plant the colony at Plymouth, breathed a very different spirit.

to it by Governor Winthrop and his associates, just after embarking for America.

But on arriving there, they immediately proceeded to the founding of an ecclesiastical economy upon the Independent plan, having for its essential principles: " That, according to the scriptures, every church ought to be confined within the limits of a single congregation, and that the government should be democratical; that churches should be constituted by such as desired to be members, making a confession of their faith in the presence of each other, and signing a covenant; that the whole power of admitting and excluding members, with the deciding of all controversies, was in the brotherhood; that church-officers, for preaching the word and taking care of the poor, were to be chosen by the free suffrages of the brethren; that in church censures, there should be an entire separation of the ecclesiastical from the civil sword; that Christ is the Head of the church; that a liturgy is not necessary; and that all ceremonies not prescribed by the scriptures are to be rejected."

But how are we to account for a change in their views so sudden and so great? Even when Winthrop left England in 1630, neither the Presbyterian nor the Independent doctrines as to church government had made that progress in public opinion which they had made when the Long Parliament, and Cromwell and his army, began to play their parts. It is quite possible, or rather all but certain, that several of the ministers in the Massachusetts Bay colony were low Episcopalians, and friends of Archbishop Usher's scheme; but if all of the leading colonists were as much inclined to Presbyterianism, as has been thought by some, it is hard to imagine why they did not establish that form of government. It is difficult to make out, on the other hand, why they diverged so widely, and at once, from the Episcopal economy, as to adopt Independency, which is almost antipodal.

This, it appears to me, may be referred to two or three causes. First, it is natural that on quitting England, where they had suffered so much from Prelacy, they should renounce an ecclesiastical system that conferred upon any men powers so capable of being abused; nor can it be thought surprising that in such circumstances they should run to the opposite extreme, and prefer an ecclesiastical government of the most democratical sort.   Another reason for their rejecting Episcopacy would be, that they might escape the jurisdiction of the bishops, which would otherwise unquestionably have followed them.   And, lastly, there can be no question that they were much influenced by what they saw and heard of the Plymouth colony.   It will be remembered that the first division of the Massachusetts Bay settlers, under Endicott, reached Salem in 1628, and that the main body, under Winthrop, followed in 1630, and founded Boston.   It would seem that the Rev. Mr. Higginson, the leading minister in Endicott's colony, led the way in effecting the change, he having upon his arrival at Salem, or soon afterwards, introduced the Independent plan among his people, though not without much difficulty, being opposed by the two Brownes, John and Samuel, who, in consequence of this opposition, had to return to England.   Mr. Higginson was disposed to receive very favourably the accounts transmitted from Plymouth colony on the other side of the bay.   It is true that Edward Winslow in his "Brief Narrative," as well as Cotton in his "Way, &c." undertake to prove that Plymouth did not exert the influence that has been ascribed to it, and which has even by Gorton and his accomplices been charged against it as a crime.   But I think it clear that they admit the substance of the assertion or charge.[1]

The church, then, that was established in all the New England colonies, with the exception of Providence and Rhode

[1] Winslow says: "It is true, I confess, that some of the chief of them (referring to the colony of Massachusetts Bay,) advised with us how they should do to fall upon a right platform of worship, and desired to that end, since God had honoured us to lay the foundation of a commonwealth, and to settle a church in it, to show them whereupon our practice was grounded; and if they found upon due search it was built upon the word of God, they would be willing to take up what was from God." He then goes on to say that they of Plymouth showed them the warrant for their government in the Acts of the Apostles, the Epistles, and the Gospels; and that their friends, the other colonists, were well pleased therewith, and also agreed to walk in the same way, so far as God should reveal his will to them from time to time in his word.   As for Cotton, he says : "The dissuader is much mistaken when he saith, 'The congregation of Plymouth did incontinently leaven all the vicinity;' seeing for many years there was no vicinity to be leavened. And Salem itself, that was gathered into church order seven or eight years after them, was above forty miles distant from them.   And though it be very likely that some of the first comers (meaning Endicot and Higginson,) might help their theory by hearing and discerning their practice at Plymouth, yet therein is the scripture fulfilled, "The kingdom of heaven is like unto leaven, which a woman took and hid in three measures of meal till all was leavened.' "

island,[1] was what is termed in the United States, Congregational, and in England, Independent—though there is some difference between the Congregational churches in the former of
these countries and the Independent in the latter, as I shall
show in another part of this work.   I speak here of the form of
its government.   As for its doctrines they were essentially those
of the thirty-nine articles of the church of England, in other
words, Calvinistic.

Let us now see what were the relations between the churches
and the state, or "commonwealth," in New England.   In every
colony there, except the two above mentioned, the object of one
of the first acts of civil legislation, was to provide for the
support of public worship, and other laws followed from time to
time to the same effect, as circumstances required.   Without
going into unnecessary details, suffice it to say, that parishes or
towns of a convenient size, were ordered to be laid out, and the
people were directed to levy taxes by the proper authorities of
their respective towns, for erecting and keeping in due repair a
suitable "meeting-house," for the maintenance of a pastor or
minister, and for all other necessary expenses connected with
public worship.   I am not aware of any exemption from this
law being allowed for long after the colonies were founded.   Such
was the fundamental union of church and state in the colonies
that now form the States of Massachusetts, Connecticut, New
Hampshire, and Maine.

The next law adopted in Massachusetts bay colony, dates
from 1631, the year after the arrival of Winthrop and his company, and as we shall yet see, it was pregnant at once with
evil and with good.   It ran thus: "To the end that the body of
the commons may be preserved of honest and good men, it was
ordered and agreed, that for the time to come, no man shall be
admitted to the freedom of this body politic, but such as are
members of some of the churches within the limits of the same." [2]
In other words, no one was to vote at elections, or could be
chosen to any office in the commonwealth, without being a member of one of the churches.   This law was long in force in Mas-

---

[1] And they too may be called Congregational, for they were founded by Baptists, whose churches are essentially Independent in form of government; and
congregational, but not connected with the state.

[2] Bancroft's " History of the United States," vol. i. p. 360.

sachusetts and in Maine, which until 1820 was a part of that State, but it never prevailed, I believe, in New Hampshire, and was unknown of course in Rhode island.   But a like law existed from the first in New Haven, and when that colony was united in 1662 with Connecticut, where this had not been the case, it became, I believe, part of the legislation of the united colony.

Thus we find two fundamental laws on this subject prevailing in New England—the one universal, with the exception of Rhode island, the other confined to Massachusetts, Connecticut, and Maine.   In confining the exercise of political power to men, who as members of the church, were presumed to be loyal to the grand principle of the colony to which they belonged, namely, the maintenance of purity of doctrine and liberty of worship, as the first consideration, and of free political government as necessary to it, the authors of that law doubtless contemplated rather the protection of their colonists from apprehended dangers, than the direct promotion of piety.

This principle, in fact, down to the founding of these colonies, seems to have been adopted substantially by all nations, Popish and Protestant, Mahomedan and heathen, so much so that Davenport said: "These very Indians that worship the devil" acted on the same principle, so that in his judgment "it seemed to be a principle imprinted in the minds and hearts of all men in the equity of it."[1]   We need hardly remind the reader that this allegiance to the Christian faith was, until very lately, indispensable to the holding of any office under the crown in England, and that receiving the sacrament in the established church was the legal test of a man's possessing it.

In conclusion I ought to state, that in the New England colonies the ministers of the gospel had no part as such in the civil government. They were confined to their proper office and work.   Yet no men had more influence, even in affairs of state. As a body of enlightened patriots, whose opinions it was important to obtain, they were consulted by the political authorities in every hour of difficulty; and although cases might be found in which the leading men among them, at least, did not advise their fellow-citizens wisely, it was much otherwise in the great

[1] "Discourse about Civil Government," p. 24, as quoted in Bacon's "Historical Discourses."

majority of instances.   Such was the state of things throughout
the whole colonial age, and to this day, in no other country is
the legitimate influence of the clergy in public affairs—an influence derived from their intelligence, united with religion, virtue, and public spirit, more manifest, or more salutary, than in
New England.   If these colonies might be compared, in their
earlier periods, to the Hebrew commonwealth, it is certain, that
wherever there was a Moses, there was also an Aaron; and
the influence of Winthrop, and Haynes, and Bradford, and
Eaton, was not greater or happier than that of their compeers
and coadjutors, the Rev. Messrs. Cotton, and Hooker, and
Brewster, and Davenport.

CHAPTER XVIII.

RELATIONS BETWEEN THE CHURCH AND THE CIVIL POWER IN THE COLONIES.—2. THE
SOUTHERN AND MIDDLE PROVINCES.

Virginia, too, like New England, was first colonised by members of the Church of England; but there was a wide difference
between the views of the admirers of the English Prelacy of
that time, and those of the Puritans.   The established church
was then composed, in fact, of two great divisions, which, in
spirit at least, have more or less existed ever since, and were
represented in America by the High-churchmen and Cavaliers
of the south on the one hand, and the Puritans of the north on
the other.   While the latter left England in order to escape
from the oppressions inflicted on them by Prelacy abetted by
the crown, the former had no complaint against either, but
carried out with them a cordial attachment to both.

In the original charter of James I. to Virginia, it was specially enjoined that religion should be established according to
the doctrines and rites of the Church of England; every emigrant
was bound to allegiance to the king, and to conformity with the
royal creed.[1]   Still, it does not appear that any provision was

---

[1] Bancroft's " History of the United States," vol. i. p. 123.

made for the clergy until 1619, that is, twelve years after the commencement of the colony. A legislative assembly, elected by the colonists, met that year for the first time, and passed laws for the formation of parishes and the regular maintenance of the clergy; accordingly, the establishment of the Episcopal church dates formally, if not really, from that year.

Previous to this, however, and during the governorship of Sir Thomas Dale, the London company sent over to Virginia a set of "laws, divine, moral, and martial," being apparently the first fruits of Sir Thomas Smith's legislation; and by their Draconian character, they give us some idea of the notions entertained in those times of the ways whereby religion might be promoted by the civil power. They were so bad, it is true, as to be little if at all enforced. In short, they soon fell into complete desuetude, and were disclaimed at length by the Company, without whose sanction they seem to have been prepared and sent. Yet there is ample evidence to prove that they breathed very much the spirit of the times that produced them, and of the party in the Church of England to which their author belonged—a spirit which, thank God! has long since ceased to exist in that or any other part of the church of Christ in that country.

The first of those laws that bears upon religion, enjoins officers of the colony, of every description, to have a care that "the Almightie God bee duly and daily served," that the people "heare sermons," that they themselves set a good example therein, and that they punish such as shall be often and wilfully absent, "according to martial law in the case provided."

The second law forbids, upon pain of death, speaking against the sacred Trinity, or any person of the same, or against the known articles of the Christian faith.

The third law forbids blasphemy of God's holy name upon pain of death; and the use of all unlawful oaths, upon severe punishment for the first offence, the boring of the tongue with a bodkin for the second, and death for the third.

The fourth law forbids speaking disrespectfully of the word of God upon pain of death, as well as the treating of ministers of the gospel with disrespect; and enjoins the "holding of them in all reverent regard and dutifull intreatie," under penalty of being whipt three times, and of "asking public forgiveness in the assembly of the congregation three severall Saboth daies."

The fifth law enjoins upon all to attend morning and evening, every week-day, in the church for service, upon the tolling of the bell, upon pain of losing their daily allowance[1] for the first omission, to be whipt for the second, sent to the galleys for six months for the third. It also forbids all violation of the Sabbath by gaming, and commands the people to prepare themselves by private prayer for the proper attendance upon the public worship, forenoon and afternoon, upon pain of losing their week's allowance for the first omission, the same and a whipping for the second, and death for the third.

The sixth law enjoins upon every minister within the colony to preach every Sabbath morning, and catechise in the afternoon; to have a service morning and evening every day, and preach on Wednesday; "to chuse unto him foure of the most religious and better disposed" to maintain a sort of spiritual police, and to see that the church be kept in a good and decent state, and that he keep a register of births, deaths, baptisms, &c. "upon the burthen of a neglectfull conscience, and upon paine of losing their entertainment."

The seventh law commands " all who were then in the colony, or who shall thenceforth arrive, to repair to the minister, that he may know, by conference had, their religious knowledge; and if any be deficient, they are enjoined to go to him, at times which he shall appoint, to receive farther instruction, which if they refuse to do, the governor, upon representation of the fact, shall order the delinquent to be whipt once for the first omission, twice for the second, and every day till acknowledgment be made and forgiveness asked for the third; and also commands every man to answer when catechised respecting his faith and knowledge, upon the Sabbath, upon pain of the same peril." [2]

Such was Sir Thomas Smith's code, and truly may it be said

[1] For some time after the colony of Virginia was planted, all provisions were served out to all from the common store-house. It was not long, however, before this plan of having all things in common gave place to the "individual principle " of each having what he could gain by his personal exertions.

[2] These laws must be considered far more intolerant and abhorrent to the spirit of Christianity, than any of the statutes taken by the New England Puritans from those of the Hebrew commonwealth.

to promote religion with a vengeance. To the credit of the governor and council, it seems never to have been enforced.

Previous to the dissolution of the Company in 1624, the colonial legislature passed a number of laws relating to the church, three of the most important of which were as follows:

1. That in every plantation, where the people were wont to meet for the worship of God, there should be a house or room set apart for that purpose, and not converted to any temporal use whatsoever; and that a place should be empaled and sequestered only for the burial of the dead.

2. That whosoever should absent himself from divine service any Sunday, without an allowable excuse, should forfeit a pound of tobacco; and that he who absented himself a month, should forfeit fifty pounds of tobacco.[1]

3. That there should be a uniformity in the church as near as might be, both in substance and circumstance, to the canons of the Church of England; and that all persons should yield a ready obedience to them upon pain of censure.[2]

Upon the Company being dissolved, the colony fell under the immediate government of the crown, which thenceforth appointed the governors, as well as decided, in the last instance, upon all laws passed by the assembly, the council, and the governor. And from about the year 1629, the laws requiring conformity to the established church were strictly enforced, and infractions of them visited with severe penalties.

During the period of the "Grand Rebellion" in England and the commonwealth, Virginia sympathised strongly with the cause of the tottering, and eventually fallen throne and altar, and many of the friends of both found refuge there during Cromwell's protectorate. It may be remarked, however, that the colony did not meet with such a recompense from the restored royal house as its loyalty justly merited.

In 1662, in obedience to instructions from the crown, the Virginia legislature enacted several laws for the more effectual

---

[1] Tobacco was the chief article of traffic which the country produced at that time, and was often used as a substitute for a monetary circulating medium.

[2] It will be seen from these laws that the actual legislation of the more liberal "Cavaliers" of the south was not a whit more tolerant than that of the bigotted "Roundheads" of New England. So it ever is; the religion of the world, with all its vaunted liberality, is found to be more intolerant wherever it has a chance, than serious, earnest, evangelical piety.

support of the established church, together with the education of youth generally, and of candidates for the ministry in particular. But it was long before the "college" contemplated by those laws was actually established.

Early in the eighteenth century, if not even sooner, the laws of Virginia, requiring strict conformity to the established church, must either have been modified, or had begun to fall into neglect, there being positive evidence that Presbyterian meetings were held for public worship in 1722. From that period until the Revolution, avowed dissenters increased steadily and rapidly, and previous to 1775 there were many Baptist, Presbyterian, Lutheran, and Quaker churches within the colony. Still, the Episcopal predominated, and it alone was supported by law.

Maryland, founded by Roman Catholics, had no union of church and state, no legal provision for any religious sect, until 1692,[1] when Protestant Episcopacy was established by law, the country divided into parishes, and the clergy, as in Virginia, supported by a tax upon the inhabitants. This was one of the results of the revolution of 1688 in England, and of the widespread abhorrence of Popery which prevailed at that time, and long afterwards, both in the mother-country and her colonies. Gradually, and not without encountering many obstacles, the Episcopal church advanced in the number of its parishes and clergy until the American revolution, and though all other sects had ever been tolerated, was the only one supported by the state. Of the good and bad effects of that establishment we shall have to speak hereafter.

In South Carolina, all sects were at first protected by the proprietaries. In 1704, however, the friends of the Episcopal church having, by the arts of Nathaniel Moore, obtained a majority of one in the representative assembly of a colony, two-thirds of whose inhabitants were dissenters, abruptly disfranchised all but themselves, and gave the Church of England a

---

[1] Strictly speaking, it might be said that this statement is not quite exact. For when Cromwell's commissioners came into possession of the colony in 1654, the legislature, which was wholly subservient to Clayborne, a tool of the Protector, passed a law suppressing public worship among Roman Catholics and Episcopalians. And four years afterwards, Fendall, acting as governor, at first in the name of the proprietaries, and afterwards by his own usurpation, undertook to persecute the Quakers. But both these exceptions were of short duration.

monopoly of political power. But the dissenters having appealed
to the House of Lords in England, the acts complained of were
annulled by the crown, and consequently repealed by the colonial assembly two years afterwards.   Nevertheless, although
the dissenters were tolerated, and admitted to a share in the
civil government, the Church of England remained the established church of the province until the Revolution.[1]

In the same year, 1704, influenced by zeal or bigotry, the
proprietaries forced a church establishment upon the people of
North Carolina, though presenting at that time an assemblage
of almost all religious denominations—Quakers, Lutherans,
Presbyterians, Independents, &c. But, according to the royal-
ists, the majority were " Quakers, Atheists, Deists, and other
evil-disposed persons." From that time glebes and a clergy
began to be spoken of, and churches were ordered to be erected
at the public cost. But we shall yet see that the established
church made slow progress in North Carolina.

As long as New York was under the Dutch government, the
churches of that colony supported their pastors by voluntary
contributions, and there was no union of church and state. [2]
But on its falling into the hands of the English, as the royal
governors and other officers sent over to administer public affairs
were all admirers of the established church of England, they
very naturally wished to see it supersede the Dutch church,
while, at the same time, the English tongue supplanted the
Dutch as the language of the colony.   Governor Fletcher,
accordingly, in 1693, prevailed on the legislature to pass an act
for the establishment of certain churches and ministers, reserving the right of presentation to the vestrymen and church-
wardens. This act was so construed two years after, that Episcopal ministers alone received the benefit of it, although this
does not appear to have been the expectation or the intention of
the legislature.   From that period till the Revolution, the

[1] Bancroft's " History of the United States," vol. iii., pp. 18, 19.
[2] It cannot be said, I fear, that the early Dutch colonists, or rather their
colonial governors, were very tolerant.   Though there was no union of the
state and church, they were very jealous of allowing any other than the
Reformed Dutch church to exist among them. A little band of Lutherans,
therefore, which joined the colony almost at its commencement, were not
allowed to hold their worship publicly until the country passed into the hands
of the English.—Professor Schmucker's " Retrospect of Lutheranism in the
United States," p. 6.

Episcopal was the established church, although at the time of its becoming so, it was reckoned that nine-tenths of the population belonged to other communions.

East and West New Jersey, united into one province, and placed under the administration of the crown in 1702, had its future government laid down in the commission and instructions to Lord Cornbury. Toleration being allowed by these to all but Papists, and special favour invoked for the Church of England, that church was so far established there, seventy-three years before the American revolution. In Pennsylvania there never was any union of church and state, nor, so far as I know, any attempt to bring it about. Delaware was separated from Pennsylvania in 1691, and from that time had its own governors, under the immediate control of the crown. But in Delaware, as well as in New Jersey, and in Georgia, the colony of the good cavalier, James Oglethorpe, who loved " the king and the church," there can hardly be said to have been an establishment, as the "favour" shown to the Episcopal church secured a maintenance for a very small number of ministers only, and that more for the benefit and gratification of the officers connected with the government, and their families, than with the view of reaching the bulk of the people who preferred other modes of worship.

In fine, as the colonial period drew to a close there were only two colonies in which the civil power did not employ its influence in supporting one or other of two communions or churches. In New England it gave its support to Congregationalism, or, as it is called in Britain, Independency; that being established in all the colonies of that province, with the single small exception of Rhode island. In the colonies to the south of these, from New York to Georgia, with the exception of Pennsylvania, Episcopacy was the favoured form. Even in these last, however, there were material differences in the extent to which the principle of a church establishment was carried out. In New Jersey, Delaware, North Carolina, and Georgia, that establishment was quite inconsiderable, whereas in Virginia, Maryland, New York, and South Carolina, it may be regarded as having been widely and powerfully influential.

Were we to select two colonies from each of these divisions, as examples of the two favoured types of church government, so diverse, yet about equally favoured by legal enactments and a public provision, we should take Massachusetts and Connecticut, in the North, and Virginia and Maryland, in the South. In these we may compare and contrast the nature and influence of Independency, or the most popular form of church organisation, with Episcopacy; or Puritanism and High-Churchism, among the descendants of the Anglo-Saxons and the Normans of the New World.

CHAPTER XIX.

THE INFLUENCES OF THE UNION OF CHURCH AND STATE AS IT FORMERLY EXISTED IN AMERICA.—1. IN NEW ENGLAND.

In entering upon this part of my work, I should like my readers to understand that I wish simply to state the results, good or evil, of the union of church and state in America, in so far as these were the proper fruits of the particular sort of union existing in one or other, respectively, of the two important sections of the country above mentioned; and that I have no intention of discussing the advantages or disadvantages of a union of church and state in the abstract. We have to do, therefore, with the results in America, not with what they might have been in other circumstances, real or hypothetical. And as the union between church and state in the northern section, differed in some important respects from that which prevailed in the south, I shall give a separate consideration to each, and begin with New England.

Let us first consider what were the advantages resulting from this union.

1. It is not to be denied that it proved beneficial, by securing the ministrations of the gospel to the colonial settlements as fast as these were formed. The law provided that the country occupied should be divided into "towns," or parishes, with well defined boundaries, and that as soon as a certain number of families

should be found residing within these boundaries, a meeting should be called by the proper local officers, and steps taken for the establishment of public worship. The expense of building such a church as the majority of the inhabitants, or legal voters, might choose to erect, was, like other taxes, to be levied on the people of the township, according to their properties and polls, and the pastor's stipend was, in like manner, to be fixed by the decision of the majority at a like meeting of legal voters, and raised by a general yearly tax.

Thus it will be seen that the township was left to decide what sort of building should be erected, how much should be expended upon it, and the amount of the pastor's stipend. As the pastor was chosen by the people without any interference on the part of the civil authorities, or any other person, individual or corporate, the evils of patronage were unknown. In the choice of a pastor, however, be it observed, that it was the invariable rule from the first, that he should be called by the "church," that is, by the body of believers or actual members of the church— the communicants, and afterwards by the "town," that is, by the legal voters; the vote of a majority of them being requisite to the validity of a call. This plan, so eminently democratical, seemed calculated to give all parties their rights. In case of the "church" and the town disagreeing as to the choice of a pastor, some means were almost always found for bringing about unanimity. Such, in brief, was the plan pursued for above 150 years in Massachusetts, and, if I am not mistaken, in all the other New England States, where the civil power was in union with the church.

Such a law as this, it must be admitted, must have made the establishment of public worship keep pace with the increase of the population, wherever that became numerous enough, in any given direction, for the building of churches, and also must have secured to ministers of the gospel a steadier, and possibly too, an ampler support than otherwise. But it may be questioned whether the New England Puritans, with the dispositions and the objects they had on coming to the new world, would not have accomplished of their own accord, and on what is called the voluntary plan, very nearly the same results, as we see is now done in Maine and elsewhere, since the union between

church and state has ceased.   I am willing, however, to allow
that the system I have described was in this respect decidedly
beneficial.   The mere support of ¡public worship was certainly
never provided for in a more popular or less exceptionable man_
ner.   I speak of the law as it stood at the outset, and for a long
while thereafter.   We shall see presently what evils flowed
from it.

2. I have already stated that in Massachusetts, and if not in
all Connecticut, at least in New Haven, political trust and
power were confined to members of the churches of the colony.
It were absurd to suppose that this law was adopted as a means
of promoting religion; its authors were too well acquainted with
human nature to have any such expectation.   Their grand object was to confine the exercise of political power to persons in
whom they could confide.   As they have been severely censured
for their intolerance in this respect, very much from ignorance,
I conceive, of their peculiar position, I may be allowed to
dwell for a moment on the subject.   They had made a long
voyage to establish a colony in the wilderness, where they and
their children might enjoy liberty of conscience, and worship
God in purity.   Being all of one mind on the subject of religion,
as well as other great points, they thought that they were fully
authorised to establish such a colony, and certainly it would be
hard to prove that they were not.   In these circumstances,
what more natural than their endeavouring to prevent persons
from coming in among them, to defeat their object.   Desiring
above all things that their institutions should continue to be
pervaded in all time coming with the spirit in which they had
been commenced, they determined, in order to secure this, that
none but the members of their churches should enjoy the rights
and privileges of citizens, and by this they hoped to guard
against both internal and external enemies.   Dreading interference on the part of England, alarmed lest the partisans of
the prelacy from which they had just escaped, should come
amongst them and overthrow their institutions, both civil and
religious, their object was to put an impassable gulph between
themselves and persons who had no sympathy with their views
and feelings.   And this object they certainly accomplished.
They rescued their institutions from the clutches of Charles I.

and archbishop Laud.[1]   But in doing so they exposed' themselves to the greatest of evils—evils which in their disastrous
influence on truth, have not ceased to be felt down to this day.

3. Whilst the above law, no doubt, had the effect of keeping
out of the government of the colony, all influences that in those
trying times might militate against its best interests; it is no
less certain that it kept away men of a troublesome character.
Many, in fact, who made the experiment, speedily became weary
of a colony where their restless spirits found little or no scope for
interference, and accordingly soon left it, either for some other
colony or for England.

Such, I consider, were the most important advantages resulting from the union of church and state in Massachusetts, and
some other of the New England colonies; and I am not disposed
to deny, that these advantages were of no small moment in the
circumstances in which the colonists were placed.   I have next
to point out some of the evils resulting from it.

1. It gave rise to internal difficulties of the gravest nature,
with such of the colonists as were not disposed to agree to all
the measures by which it was carried out, and led to the adoption of the harshest proceedings against those persons.   One of
the first cases of this kind was that of Roger Williams, in
1633-35, and it shook the colony to its centre.   That remarkable
man had been educated for the English bar, under the patronage

---

[1] It is well known that Winthrop and his company were scarcely settled
three years in Massachusetts, before king Charles began to repent that he had
consented to the charter.   The success of the Puritans in America awakened
the jealousy of Laud and all the High Church party among the clergy.   Proof
was produced of marriages having been performed in the colony by civil magistrates; and it was discovered that the whole colonial system of church government was at variance with the laws of England.   A most formidable conspiracy
was formed against New England, and never were colonies in greater danger.
Even the letters patent were ordered by the royal council to be produced in
England; and nothing but the greatest adroitness on the part of the colonists
postponed a compliance with the measure, for the primate archbishop Laud and
his associates actually received full power over the American plantations, to
establish the government, dictate laws, govern the church, &c., &c.   Every
thing seemed to threaten ruin.   In the meanwhile the colonists remonstrated,
defended themselves in their letters as well as they could, and raised money to
fortify Boston.   They had great need, truly, to be vigilant in respect to the
admission of persons to authority among them.   As it was, nothing saved them,
probably, but the breaking out of the civil war in Great Britain, which gave
Charles I. enough to do at home.   For the details of these matters the reader
is referred to the writings of Winthrop, Savage, Hubbard, Hutchinson, Hazzard, and the excellent statement in Bancroft's "History of the United States,"
vol. i. pp. 405—414.

of Sir Edward Coke, but influenced by the conviction that he
was called to the ministry, he took orders in the established
church. Expelled from that by the bishops on account of his
Puritanical principles, he came to Boston in 1631.

Taught by persecution to examine how far human governments are authorised to legislate for the human mind, and to
bind its faculties by their decisions, Williams soon perceived a
course pursued in America which he could not but condemn as
repugnant to the rights of conscience. Regarding all intolerance as sinful, he maintained that " the doctrine of persecution
for cause of conscience is most evidently and lamentably contrary to the doctrine of Jesus Christ." The law required the
attendance of every man at public worship; Williams pronounced
this to be wrong, for to drag the unwilling to public worship
looked like requiring hypocrisy. Not less did he oppose the
law that taxed all men for the support of a system of religious
worship which some might dislike and conscientiously disapprove. " What!" exclaimed his antagonists, " is not the
labourer worthy of his hire?" " Yes," he replied, " from them
that hire him." Public functionaries were to be taken only
from among members of the church; Williams argued that,
with like propriety, " a doctor of physic, or a pilot," might be
selected according to his skill in theology and his standing in
the church.[1] In the end, Roger Williams was banished from
the colony, and having retired to Narragansett Bay, there he
became a Baptist, and founded what is now the State called
Rhode island. Absolute religious liberty was established there
from the first.

The next case occurred in 1637, and ended in the expulsion of
Wheelwright, Anne Hutchinson, and Aspinwall, who, although
they held some very extravagant notions on certain points,
would have been harmless persons had the only weapon employed against them been truth.

Testimony to the like effect is borne by the history of the
colony in subsequent years. " Since a particular form of worship had become a part of the civil establishment, irreligion was
now to be punished as a civil offence. The state was a model

1 Bancroft's " History of the United States," vol. i. p. 370.

of Christ's kingdom on earth; treason against the civil government was treason against Christ; and reciprocally, as the gospel had the right paramount, blasphemy, or whatever a jury
should call blasphemy, was the highest offence in the catalogue
of crimes. To deny any book of the Old or New Testament to
be the written and infallible word of God, was punishable by
fine or by stripes, and in case of obstinacy, by exile or death.
Absence from the ministry of the word was punished by fine." [1]
Everything indicated that this union between church and state
was operating in such a manner as rapidly to undermine the
rights and principles of both. The Anabaptists were treated in
some cases with great harshness, and when, in 1651, the
Quakers made an attempt to establish themselves in the colony,
they were expelled, and prohibited from returning upon pain of
death; a penalty actually inflicted on four of them who returned
in contravention of this enactment.

These Quakers, it is true, behaved in the most fanatical and
outrageous manner. They attacked the magistrates with the
grossest insults, and interrupted public worship with their riot-
ous proceedings. Even women among them, forgetting the
proprieties and decencies of their sex, and claiming divine direction for their absurd and abominable caprices, smeared their
faces and ran naked through the streets! It were absurd to
compare them with the peaceable and excellent people who bear
that name in our day. They gave no evidence whatever of
knowing what true religion means. Still, their punishment
ought not to have been so extreme, and should have been
inflicted for violating the decorum of society, not for their supposed heretical opinions.[2] Now, measures so disgraceful and

---

[1] Bancroft's "History of the United States," vol. i. p. 450.

[2] Penalties involving mutilation, such as boring the tongue with a hot iron,
and cutting off the ears, were enacted against the Quakers in 1657, and thus
found a place in the statute book of Massachusetts, but were soon repealed,
from the colony being ashamed of them. The fact was, as Mr. Bancroft says,
vol. i., p. 451, " the creation of a national and uncompromising church led the
Congregationalists of Massachusetts to the indulgence of the passions which
had disgraced their English persecutors; and Laud was justified by the men
whom he wronged."

But before the reader pronounces sentence without mitigation upon the
Puritans of Massachusetts, he should refresh his remembrance of what was
going on in England about the year 1633. There was William Prynne. Esq.,
barrister-at-law, who was condemned for writing a constructive libel on the
queen, by attacking the theatre, to be excluded from his profession, to lose both
his ears, stand in the pillory, pay a fine of £5000, and to suffer imprisonment for

injurious to the colony, and so contrary to what one would expect from men of such excellence in other respects, would never have been adopted had it not been for laws unhappily dictated by the colonial union between church and state.

Forty years later twenty persons were put to death for witchcraft! Now it is obvious that so absurd a spectacle would never have taken place among so enlightened a people as the colonists of Massachusetts, within the bounds of which all these executions took place, had not the union of the church and the state led the government so often to act on grounds purely religious, and to take cognisance of subjects which no political government is capable of deciding upon.[1] At all events the embarrassment created by Roger Williams, the "Antinomian controversy," as the contest with Wheelwright, Anne Hutchinson, and Aspinwall, was called, and the persecution of the Anabaptists and Quakers, unquestionably arose from the enforcement of the laws, passed in favour of the theocratic institutions of the colony, and were the legitimate results of the established union between church and state. They had a special reference to the law compelling every man to attend the public worship of the colony.

Much more disastrous were the consequences flowing from

the rest of his life! Dr. Bastwick, a physician, about the same time was condemned by the High Commission to be excluded from his profession, excommunicated, fined £1000, and imprisoned till he should recant, for having published a book in which he denied that bishops are superior to presbyters! And then there was Dr. Alexander Leighton, a Scotch divine, the father of the celebrated Archbishop Leighton, who was condemned in 1630, if I mistake not, to pay a fine of £10,000, to be whipped at the pillory at Westminster, to have one of his ears cut off, and one side of his nose slit; then be taken to the prison for a few days; then brought to the pillory at Cheapside to be whipped, have the other ear cut off, and the other side of his nose slit, and be shut up in prison the rest of his days! These are unquestionable facts. And what shall we say of the wholesale massacres of the Protestants in France, in Belgium, and Bohemia, and Moravia? To say nothing of scenes in Scotland in the days of the last two Stuarts? Verily, religious liberty was but ill understood in those days! and is it well understood even now in most countries of Europe?

[1] The putting of witches to death in Massachusetts was a legitimate result of the attempt to build up a sort of theocracy, having for its basis the civil institutions of the Jewish commonwealth. But were witches no where put to death in those days save in New England? Let the reader search and see.

I ought to add, that the rulers of Massachusetts put the Quakers to death, and banished the "Antinomians" and "Anabaptists," not because of their religious tenets, but because of their violations of the civil laws. This is the justification which they pleaded, and it was the best they could make. Miserable excuse! But just so it is; wherever there is such a union of church and state, heresy, and heretical practices are apt to become violations of the civil code, and are punished no longer as errors in religion, but infractions of the laws of the land. So the defenders of the inquisition have always spoken and written in justification of that awful and most iniquitous tribunal.

another and still more fundamental law, passed by the conscript fathers of Massachusetts and Connecticut, that of making church membership requisite to the enjoyment of the rights and privileges of citizenship. Nor was it long before these consequences appeared. Not only did many persons find admission into the colonies as settlers, who were not members of any church in the sense almost invariably attached to the term in America—that is, communicants, or as they are sometimes called, "full members," but which the worthy founders seem not to have anticipated, some of their own children grew up manifestly "unconverted," and consequently did not become communicants; the churches planted by the New England fathers having maintained at first the strictest discipline, and allowed none to become communicants until they had satisfied the proper church authorities that they were converted persons, and had the religious knowledge without which they could not fitly come to the Lord's supper. Persons who had not these requisites, as might be expected, thought it very hard to be excluded from the privileges of citizenship, although, as was generally the case, their lives were perfectly regular and moral. They therefore complained, and their complaints were felt to be reasonable, and such as parental love, even in the breast of a Brutus, could not long resist.

In these circumstances what was the course pursued by the colonial legislators, after taking counsel with their spiritual guides? Instead of abolishing the law, they decided that all baptised persons should be regarded as members of the church, —thus directly interfering with matters wholly beyond the sphere of civil legislation, and contravening likewise a former decision of the church; for although there is a sense in which all persons baptised in infancy are in their youth members of the church, it is only as pupils or wards, and must not be confounded with the membership of persons who have made a profession of their faith, after conversion, and at an age that qualifies them for taking such a step. Such at least is, I apprehend, the opinion of all churches that maintain a strict discipline. The New England fathers felt this difficulty, and accordingly it was not to all baptised persons that they gave the rights of citizens, but to baptised persons of good moral deportment, who came publicly forward and owned in the church the covenant made

for them by their parents at baptism.   I give the substance, if
not the exact words of the law.   This compromise settled the
matter for a time, by providing for the case of their own young
men when made citizens.

As respected the state, this law was not so hurtful in its
consequences as it was to religion.   The churches were filled
with baptised persons who " owned the covenant," and with the
lapse of time the number of " full members," or communicants,
diminished.   Many now enjoyed civil privileges in virtue of a
less intimate connection with the church; this was all that they
desired, and with this they were too apt to be content.   But
the evil went far beyond this.   To escape from a state of things
in which the churches, though filled with baptised people, had
comparatively few " communicants," many of the pastors were
led into the dangerous, I may say the fatal error, of considering
the Lord's supper as a means of grace, in the same sense that
the preaching of the word is such, and that all well-disposed
persons may be admitted to it as a means of conversion to the
unconverted, as well as of edification to " believers," and consequently converted persons.

Not that this was enjoined on the churches as a law of the
state.   But it was the natural and almost inevitable, though
indirect, consequence of the law adjudging all baptised persons
who " renewed the covenant," to be considered members of the
church, and entitled to the civil privileges attached to that relation.   It is easy to see what would follow.   The former measure filled the churches with baptised people who owned the
covenant; the latter practice filled the churches with unconverted communicants.   In the course of a few generations the
standard of religious truth and practice fell lower and lower.
This decline necessarily bore upon the character of the pastors,
for upon the occurrence of a vacancy, the church, that is, the
body of the communicants, almost invariably decided "the
town" or "parish," that is, the body of legal voters taxed for
the support of public worship, and who, as I have stated, gave
a concurrent call, and thus the choice, in too many cases, was
sure to fall upon a pastor equally low in point of religious character with the parties by whom he was chosen.   Such a state
of things opened the way effectually for the admission of false

doctrine, and the more so, inasmuch as there was no effectual control beyond and above what was to be found in each individual church. But this subject I may dismiss for the present, as I shall have occasion to recur to it when we come to consider the rise and progress of Unitarianism in the United States. So much for the ill consequences flowing from two of the measures by which the New England fathers endeavoured to carry into operation their ideas on the subject of the union that should subsist between the church and the state; let us now look at the mischief produced by a third such measure—that, namely, requiring each "town" to maintain public worship by levying a tax on all the inhabitants.

As the people were invested by law with an absolute control over the application of the money so raised, no great evil seems, at first sight, likely to have arisen from such a mode of supporting the church; and it may readily be supposed that at the outset, when the colonists formed a homogeneous society, and were all either members of the established churches, or cordial friends and admirers of their system of doctrine and church polity, this assessment for their support would be submitted to without reluctance. But in process of time, when, whether from the accession of fresh emigrants, or from the growing up into manhood of the children of the original colonists, there happened to be found in any particular town, a considerable number of inhabitants who either disliked the services of the parish church, or were indifferent to religion altogether, it is clear that such a law would be considered as burthensome and unjust. Men can never be made to feel that they can with equity be required to pay taxes, in any shape, to support a church which they dislike, and to which they may have conscientious objections. Hence serious difficulties, aggravated afterwards when the legislature was compelled, by the progress of true principles of legislation, to extend the rights of citizenship, and permission to have a worship of their own, to persons of all sects. It seemed unjust that these, while supporting their own churches, should be compelled, in addition, to contribute towards the maintenance of the parish, or town churches, which for long they were called upon to do.

A law, however, was passed at length, not exempting those

who did not attend the parish church, from all taxation, but allowing them to appropriate their proportion to the support of public worship according to their own fashion.   Fair as this seemed, it proved most disastrous in its consequences to the interests of true religion.   The haters of evangelical Christianity could now say: "Well, since we must be taxed in support of religion, we will have what suits us," and in many places societies, for it would be improper to call them churches, of Universalists[1] and Unitarians began to be formed, and false preachers found support where, but for this law, and on the voluntary principle, no such societies or preachers would ever have existed. It is impossible to describe the mischiefs that have flowed from this unfortunate measure, not only and particularly in Massachusetts, but likewise in Connecticut, Maine, and, I believe, in New Hampshire also.   With the aid of such a law, thousands who are now indifferent to truth or error, might easily be driven into Universalism, or some other dangerous heresy, in any part of the United States, or rather in any part of the world where religious opinion is unrestrained.

Only one farther measure was required in order to make this law for the support of public worship, as fatal as possible to the interests of true religion in Massachusetts.   This was a decision of the supreme court of that State, pronounced some twenty or twenty-five years ago, by which the distinction which had previously existed between the "church" and the "town" or "parish," was destroyed in the view of the law; and the "town," that is, the body of the people who were taxed for the support of the parish church, was allowed to exercise a control in the calling of a pastor, and in every thing else.   There then ensued great distress in not a few parishes.   In every instance in which the majority of the "town" were opposed to evangelical religion, they had it in their power by stopping his salary, to turn away a faithful pastor, and to choose a Universalist or Unitarian in his place.[2]   This actually took place in numerous in-

[1] By Universalists I mean those professed Christians in America who with many shades of difference on the subject, all agree in holding that eventually all men will be saved.   I shall have to speak of them more at large in another place.

[2] In many cases there was no great difficulty in getting such a majority, by persuading the Universalists and others, who might have ceased for years to allow themselves to be considered to belong to the parish, or congregation, or

stances, and the church, or at least the faithful part of it, which was often the majority, was compelled to abandon the church in which their fathers had worshipped, with whatever endowments it might have, and to build for themselves a new place of worship, call a pastor, and support him on the voluntary plan. The evil, however, which might have gone to still greater lengths, was arrested in Massachusetts in 1833, by the final dissolution of the union between church and state in a way hereafter to be described.

Such is a simple, brief, and, I trust, comprehensible view of the chief consequences resulting in New England from the union of church and state, as long maintained in that part of America. The reader will draw his own conclusions from this exhibition of facts, in all essential points unquestionably correct. That some of these consequences were beneficial, none will deny, but that these were more than counterbalanced by others of an opposite tendency is, I think, no less manifest.[1]

CHAPTER XX.

THE INFLUENCES OF THE UNION OF CHURCH AND STATE.—2. IN THE SOUTHERN AND MIDDLE STATES.

HAVING seen what a church establishment did for Congregationalism in New England, we have now to see what it did for Episcopacy in other provinces, and particularly in the south. In the case of the latter, as in the former, the nature of the connection between church and state, and the kind of church establishment, were very different in different colonies. That connection was closest, and the support given to religion most effective, in Virginia; next to it in these respects comes Maryland, and New York occupies the third place.

---

society, worshipping at the parish church, to return at least for a year or so, since by so doing, and paying again the assessment for the parish church, they could vote at its meetings.

[1] The reader will find in the " Spirit of the Pilgrims," vol. i., (a work published in Boston in 1825—1832,) the fullest details on this subject that have appeared as yet in any one publication.

In Virginia we find that the three main laws, connecting the church and the state, were substantially the same as those of Massachusetts at a later date. 1. The country was divided into parishes, the inhabitants of which were required to build, furnish, and uphold churches, and maintain a pastor, by an assessment proportioned to their respective means, these being estimated by the quantity of tobacco that they raised, that being the chief article of their commerce and of their wealth. 2. The people were required to attend the established churches, which were for long the only ones that existed, or that were permitted to exist in the colony. 3. The rights of citizenship were confined to members of the Episcopal church.

Now, it is beyond dispute that the division of the country into parishes, the erection of churches, and the providing of glebes for the rectors and ministers, was useful both in Virginia and Maryland. The picture presented by Dr. Hawks, in his interesting and valuable sketches of the Episcopal church in those colonies, is delightful as far as relates to these outward and material matters. Besides, there was a special necessity for some such legislation in Episcopalian colonies of the High Church party, if I may so designate them, as was the case with Virginia; for although it would be unfair to tax them with a total, or almost total, want of true living piety, they certainly had not the fervent zeal, the devoted enthusiasm in the cause of religion, which mingled with all the proceedings of the Puritans. If, in fact, in any part of America, the union of church and state was beneficial, or even indispensable in securing the formation of parishes and the building of churches, it was in the southern colonies, planted as these were by the friends of Prelacy *par excellence,* men afraid of fanaticism in religion, whatever they might think of it in some other things. These advantages were, in process of time, secured at intervals along the banks of the noble rivers of Virginia, until, at the commencement of the Revolution, that colony could boast of ninety-seven parishes, more than that number of churches, if we include chapels of ease, and above a hundred ministers.

This is the chief, or rather the only benefit, conferred on Virginia by the connection of the church with the state, for the maintenance of the clergy, as Dr. Hawks remarks, can hardly be reckoned one, inasmuch as that was nearly, if not altogether, voluntary on the part of the parishioners, and was by no means enforced as the law contemplated. During a large part of the colonial period, too, the want of ministers greatly diminished the advantages that might have accrued from having parishes marked out, and churches built in them. Thus, in 1619, there were eleven parishes but only five ministers, and in 1661, the parishes in Virginia were about fifty, the ministers only about a fifth of that number.[1]

But granting that the support secured by law to Episcopacy was ample, which in Virginia it was not, let us notice some of the evils attending on this union of church and state, and see whether they did not counterbalance all the admitted good. The first of these, and it was no trifling one, was the antipathy which such compulsory measures created towards the favoured church. Men were displeased, and felt angry at being taxed for the support of a church whose services they did not frequent, but to which they might otherwise have felt no hostility, nay, to which they might by a different course have been won. This was particularly the case in those colonies where the favour shown to the Episcopal church did not exclude the toleration of other religious bodies, that is, in all in which Episcopacy was established except Virginia. Episcopacy, in fact, became influential and powerful, in most cases long after the colonies were founded, and owed its pre-eminence purely to the favour of the State, as we have seen in the colonies of Maryland, the Carolinas, New York, New Jersey, &c. In all these, taxes for the support of a dominant church, representing in some instances but a mere fraction of the population, were extremely offensive to the members of other churches or of none, and proved hurtful in the end to the Episcopal church itself. It attached a stigma to it which it took long to efface, the more as when the Revolution was drawing on, it began to be viewed as the favoured church of the mother country, with which the colonists were about to enter into a war for what they deemed to be their rights. Thus the cause of that church became identified so far with that of the enemies of the country, as they were called. This two-

---

[1] Dr. Hawks' "History of the Episcopal Church in Virginia," p. 64.

fold animosity long prevailed in the very States where the Episcopal church was once predominant, and no doubt contributed to retard its progress in later times, so that any former favours received from the State may be regarded as having been very dearly purchased.

2. As respects Virginia at least, the interests of true religion and of the Episcopal church were seriously injured by the compulsory attendance upon the services of the churches, &c., noticed in a former chapter. In the justness of the following remarks every well informed man must heartily concur: "To coerce men into the *outward* exercise of religious acts by penal laws is indeed possible; but to make them love either the religion which is thus enforced, or those who enforce it, is beyond the reach of human power. There is an inherent principle of resistance to oppression seated in the very constitution of most men, which disposes them to rebel against the arbitrary exercise of violence seeking to give direction to opinions; and it is not, therefore, to be wondered at, that one sanguinary law to compel men to live piously should beget the necessity for more."[1]

3. Another evil resulting from the union between church and state in the southern colonies, and particularly in Virginia and Maryland, is to be found in the almost incessant disputes that long prevailed between the colonial governors and the parish vestries, respecting the right of presentation, which was claimed by both parties. In this contest the Virginia vestries were upon the whole successful; still, as the governor claimed the right of *inducting*, there were often serious collisions. In order to evade the force of that principle in English law, which gives a minister, when once installed as pastor, a sort of freehold interest in the parish, and renders his ejectment almost impossible, unless by deposition from the sacred office altogether, in consequence of his being found guilty of some flagrant enormity, instead of presenting a minister, the vestries often preferred employing him from year to year, so as to have it in their power to dismiss him when they thought fit; and this refusal to present, involved, of course, an inability on the governor's part to induct. In Maryland the governors long insisted on exercising the right of pre-

1 Dr. Hawks' "History of the Episcopal Church in Virginia," p. 49

sentation, a right that put it into their power to thrust very unworthy pastors into the church. But the case was often not much better when left to the vestries, these being often composed of men by no means fit to decide upon the qualifications of a pastor. In no case does it appear that the church itself, that is, the body of the communicants, possessed the privilege of choosing a pastor for themselves.

4. A fourth evil resulting from the union of church and state in the colonies where the Episcopal church was established, lay in this, that the ministers required from time to time by the churches behoved to come from England, or if Americans by birth, to receive ordination from some bishop in England, generally the bishop of London, to whose superintendence and government the Episcopal church in America seems to have been entrusted. As there was no bishop in America during the whole colonial period, this disadvantage continued down to the Revolution.

No doubt, many worthy men, endued with the true spirit of their calling and office, were sent over by the bishops who successively occupied the see of London, some of whom took a deep interest in the colonial church. Still, it is no less true that many of a very different stamp were sent over, or came of themselves, and these, after their being once inducted into a parish, it was found almost impossible to remove. At a distance from England, and beyond the immediate inspection of the only bishop that seemed to have any authority over them, they generally contrived to secure impunity, not only for the neglect of their duties, but even for flagrant crimes. Some cases of the most shocking delinquency and open sin occurred both in Virginia and Maryland, without the possibility, it would seem, of their being reached and punished. All that could be done by persons commissioned by the bishop of London to act for him, under the name of commissaries, was done by such men as Drs. Blair and Bray, and their successors, but the evil was too deep to be effectually extirpated by any thing short of the exercise of full Episcopal authority on the spot. Besides traditional evidence of the immoralities of some of the established clergy in Virginia and Maryland, we learn their existence and character from indubitable histories written by

Episcopalians themselves, and they were such as even to call for the interference of the colonial legislatures. The General Assembly of Virginia, in 1631, enacted that " Mynisters shall not give themselves to excesse in drinkinge or riott, spendinge theire tyme idellye by day or night, etc." [1] The fact is, that worthless and incapable men in every profession were wont to leave the mother-country for the colonies, where they thought they might succeed better than in England; and such of them as belonged to the clerical profession very naturally supposed that they might find comfortable berths in those colonies, where their own church was established, and where they heard that there was so great a deficiency of clergymen.[2]

5. And last, one of the greatest evils of the establishment we are speaking of, is to be found in the shameful acts of intolerance and oppression to which it led. Although the Quakers were in no instance put to death in Virginia, yet they were subjected to much persecution and annoyance, and were glad in many cases to escape into North Carolina. The Puritans, too, were much disliked, and severe laws were past " to prevent the infection from reaching the country." [3] Archbishop Laud's authority stood as high in Virginia as in England. An offender against that authority, of the name of Reek, was, in 1642, pilloried for two hours, with a label on his back setting forth his offence, then fined £50, and imprisoned during the pleasure of the governor.[4]

It would appear, however, either that all this vigilance could not keep out the Puritans, or else that some of the Virginians themselves had become so disgusted with their own as to wish for Puritan preachers. Be that as it may, certain it is that in

---

[1] Hening's " Laws of Virginia," 7th Car. i.—At a much later period Sir William Berkeley, governor of Virginia, in reply to this inquiry from the Lords of Plantations : " What provision is there made for the paying of your ministers ? " stated, " We have forty-eight parishes, and our ministers are well paid. But as of all other commodities, so of this, *the worst are sent to us.*"—See " Appendix to Hening's Collection."

[2] Even so late as in 1751, the bishop of London, in a letter to the well-known Dr. Doddridge, says upon this subject : " Of those who are sent from hence, a great part are of the Scotch-Irish, who can get no employment at home, and enter into the service more out of necessity than choice. Some others are willing to go abroad to retrieve either lost fortunes or lost character."—See " Biblical Repertory and Princetown Review for April, 1840."

[3] Hening's " Virginia Statutes," 223.

[4] Ibid. 552.

1642 there was transmitted from certain persons in Virginia to Boston an application for preachers, and that two actually went from Massachusetts and one from Connecticut, but were dismissed by the governor. Governor Winthrop, speaking of this affair in his Journal, says, that though the state did silence the ministers, because they would not conform to the order of England, yet the people resorted to them in private houses to hear them.[1]

In fact, it was not until the lapse of a century from those times that toleration was established in Virginia, through the persevering efforts of the Presbyterians and other non-established denominations, whose friends and partisans had by that time greatly increased, partly in consequence of this very intolerance on the part of the government, but chiefly by emigration, so as far to out-number the Episcopalians of the province when the war of the Revolution commenced.

As for Maryland, although the Quakers were greatly harassed in that colony for some time, and Roman Catholics were treated with grievous injustice, yet there never was the same intolerance manifested towards those who were called dissenters, as had been shown in Virginia. The Protestant Episcopal church was established there by law in 1692, but not in fact until 1702.

But in no colony, in which Episcopacy became established by law, was there more intolerance displayed than in New York. That establishment was effected in 1693 by Governor Fletcher, who soundly rated the legislature because not disposed to comply with all his wishes. But in zeal for Episcopacy he was outdone by one of his successors, a descendant of Lord Clarendon, Lord Cornbury, who would fain have deprived the Dutch of their privileges, and forced them into the Episcopal church. He had orders from the government at home " to give all countenance and encouragement to the exercise of the ecclesiastical jurisdiction of the Bishop of London, as far as conveniently might be in the province—that no schoolmaster be henceforward permitted to come from this kingdom, and keep a school in that our said province, without the licence of our said Lord Bishop of London."[2]

1 Savage's Winthrop, p. 92 ; Hubbard's " History of New England," p. 411.
2 " History of the Evangelical Churches of New York."

In what has been said of the intolerance manifested in several of the colonies in which the Protestant Episcopal church was established, I would not be understood as charging such intolerance upon that church in those colonies. No doubt, men of an intolerant spirit were to be found in it, but, alas! true religious liberty, and an enlarged spirit of toleration, were far from being general in those days; but it had members also of a most catholic spirit, who neither could nor did approve of such acts as the above. The intolerance was rather that of the colonial governments, and to them properly belongs the credit or discredit attached to it.

In conclusion, I cannot but think that the union of the Episcopal church with the state in some colonies, and of the Congregational church with the civil power in others, was upon the whole far more mischievous than beneficial,—an opinion, in which I feel persuaded, that the great body alike of Episcopal and Congregational ministers concur. Had the founders of the Episcopal church in Virginia and Maryland, excellent men as I believe they were, gone to work in reliance on the blessing of God, and upon their own efforts, and endeavoured to raise up a faithful native ministry, trusting to the willingness of the people to provide for their support, I doubt not that they would have succeeded far better in building up the Episcopal church, than they did with all the advantages of the state alliance which they enjoyed. They would doubtless have had to encounter many difficulties, but they would have laid a surer foundation also for ultimate success. Dr. Hawks gives a painfully interesting narrative of the struggles which the established clergy of Virginia and Maryland had to sustain with their parishioners about their salaries; the one party striving to obtain what the law assigned to them, the other, aided even at times by legislative enactments, availing themselves of every stratagem in order to evade the legal claims of the clergy. The time and anxiety, the wearying out of mind and body, which these disputes cost faithful ministers, not to mention the sacrifice of influence, would have been laid out better and more pleasantly in the unembarrassed work of their calling; nor were they likely to have been worse off in respect of this world's blessings than the faithful among them really were.

Assuredly the Episcopal church in the United States at the present day, furnishes decisive proof that Episcopacy can exist and flourish without aid from the civil government. Dr. Hawks thinks, that it has even peculiar advantages for self-sustentation, proved, as he conceives, by the experience of the Episcopal church in Scotland, and that of the Syrian churches in India, as well as in the United States. Without expressing an opinion on that point, I hesitate not to say that the Episcopal church, with all the advantage of having the colonists enlisted on her side in several of the colonies at outset, and sustained as she was by the *prestige* of the national church of the mother country, would have done far better had she relied on her own resources under God, in the faithful ministration of his word, and of the ordinances of his house, than in trusting to the arm of the state in the colonies in which she endeavoured to plant herself.

CHAPTER XXI.

STATE OF RELIGION DURING THE COLONIAL ERA.

BEFORE taking leave of the colonial era in the history of the United States, let us take a general view of the state of religion throughout all the colonies during the period of 168 years, from 1607 to the commencement of the Revolutionary war in 1775.

As communities, the Anglo-American colonies, from their earliest days, were pervaded by a religious influence, not equally powerful, yet real and salutary in all. This was especially true of New England, whose first settlers openly declared to the world that they left their native land, not so much to promote individual religion as to form Christian societies. They could have maintained silent, personal, individual communion with their heavenly Father in Lincolnshire and Yorkshire, or in Holland, as did some recluses in the monastic institutions of the earlier and middle ages. But they had no such purpose. Their Christianity was of a diffusive kind, their hearts yearned for opportunities of extending it.   Religion with them was not only a concern between man and God, but one in which society at large had a deep interest.   Hence some fruits of this high and holy principle might be expected in the communities which they founded, and we not unreasonably desire to know how far the results corresponded to such excellent intentions.   It were unfair, however, to expect much in this way, considering the circumstances of the colonists, settling in a remote wilderness, amid fierce and cruel savages, who involved them in long and disastrous hostilities, and exposed to all the fatigues and sick-nesses incident to such a settlement, and to the anxieties and difficulties attending the organisation of their governments, colli-sions with the mother country, and participation in all that country's wars.

The colonial era may, for the sake of convenience, be divided into four periods.   The first of these, extending from the earliest settlement of Virginia in 1607 to 1660, was one in which reli-gion greatly flourished, notwithstanding the trials incident to settlements amid the forests, and the troubles attending the establishment of the colonial governments.   Peace with the aborigines suffered few interruptions, the only wars worth men-tioning being that with the Pequods in Connecticut, in 1637; that between the Dutch and the Algonquins in 1643; and those that broke out in Virginia in 1622 and 1644, which were at once the first and the last, and by far the most disastrous of that period.   But these wars were soon over, and a few years sufficed to repair whatever loss they might occasion to the colonists.

This was the period in which those excellent men who either came over with the first colonies, or soon afterwards joined them, laboured long, and very successfully, for the salvation of souls.   Among these were Wilson, and Cotton, and Shepard, and Mather (Richard), and Philips, and Higginson, and Skel-ton, in the colony of Massachusetts bay; Brewster in Ply-mouth; Hooker in Connecticut; Davenport in New Haven; and Hunt and Whitaker in Virginia.   Several of the contemporary magistrates, also, were distinguished for their piety and zeal; such as the governors Winthrop of Massachusetts, Bradford and Winslow of Plymouth, Haynes of Connecticut, and Eaton of New Haven. To these we must add Roger Williams, who was pastor, and, for a time, governor in Providence.

This was the golden age of the colonial cycle. God poured out his Spirit in many places. Precious seasons were enjoyed by the churches at Boston, at Salem, at Plymouth, at Hartford, and at New Haven. Nor were the labours of faithful men in Virginia without a rich blessing. Days of fasting and prayer were frequently and faithfully observed. God was entreated to dwell among the people. Religion was felt to be the most important of blessings, both for the individual man and for the state. Revivals were highly prized, and earnestly sought; nor were they sought in vain. The journals of Governor Winthrop, and other good men of that day, present most interesting details in proof of this. America has seen more extensive, but never more unequivocal works of grace, or more indubitable operations of the Spirit.

Nor were the aboriginal heathen around the colonies forgotten in those days. Elliot and others laboured with great success among the Indians in the vicinity of Boston. Several thousand souls were converted. The Bible was translated into their tongue. Nor was it in Massachusetts alone that men cared for the souls of the " Salvages," as they were called. In Virginia, an Indian princess, Pocahontas, received the gospel, was baptised, and became a consistent member of a Christian church. Another convert, Chanco, was the instrument, under God, of saving the colony from entire extirpation.

The commencement of the colonisation of America was certainly auspicious for the cause of true religion, whatever its fortunes might be in subsequent times.

The second period is that of sixty years, from 1660 to 1720.

This might be called the brazen age of the colonies. Almost all of them experienced times of trouble. Massachusetts suffered in 1675 from a most disastrous war with " King Philip," the chief of the Pokanokets, and with other tribes which afterwards joined in a general endeavour to expel or exterminate the colonists. Violent disputes arose with the government of England respecting the rights of the colony, and to these were added internal dissensions about witchcraft, and other exciting subjects, chiefly of a local nature.   In Virginia, in 1675-76, there was a serious Indian war, and a "Grand Rebellion" which threatened ruin to the colony.   And in the Carolinas a desolating war with the Tuscaroras broke out in 1711-12.

Besides these greater causes of trouble and excitement, there were others which it is not necessary to indicate.   The influence of growing prosperity may, however, be mentioned.   The colonies had now taken permanent root.   They might be shaken, but could not be eradicated or overthrown by the rude blasts of misfortune.   Their wealth was increasing; their commerce was already considerable, and attracted many youth to the seas.   Every war which England had with France or Spain agitated her colonies also.

These causes concurring with the disastrous consequences of the union of church and state already described, led to a great decline of vital Christianity, and although partial revivals took place, the all-pervading piety that characterised the first generation suffered a great diminution.   The light of holiness grew faint and dim, and morality, in general, degenerated in a like degree.   The fathers had gone to the tomb, and were succeeded upon the whole by inferior men.   The second governor, Winthrop, it is true, showed himself, in the administration of the united colonies of Connecticut, to be a great and good man, and a father alike to the church and the state.   Among the ministers, too, there was a considerable number of distinguished men, but their labours were not equally blessed with those of the fathers.   Among the best known were the Mathers, Cotton and Increase, father and son, the latter more distinguished for the extent and variety of his acquirements than for soundness of judgment;·[1] Norton and others in Massachusetts; Pierpont in Connecticut; Dr. Blair, who for long was the bishop of London's commissary in Virginia; Dr. Bray, who held the same office in Maryland,

---

[1] Cotton Mather's acquirements were really prodigious, considering the age and the circumstances in which he lived.   His publications amounted to no fewer than 382, several of which, such as his "Magnalia, or the Ecclesiastical History of New England," were large works.   He displayed, however, such a mixture of credulity, pedantry, and bad taste, that he was not appreciated as he deserved.   The part which he took in the affair of the witches, though greatly misrepresented by some writers, did him vast injury.   He was singularly given to believe all sorts of marvels.

two persons to whom the Episcopal church in these colonies was much indebted for its prosperity.

The faithful pastors in New England received an accession to their number in the early part of this period, by the arrival from England of some of the two thousand ministers who were ejected there for non-conformity, soon after the accession of Charles I.

The third period, comprehending the thirty years from 1720 to 1750, was distinguished by extensive revivals of religion, and this, notwithstanding the agitation produced in the colonies, by the share they had in the war between France and England toward the close of that period, and other unfavourable circumstances besides. The Great Awakening,[1] as it has been called, infused a new life into the churches, more especially in New England, in certain parts of New York, New Jersey, Pennsylvania, and some other colonies, and its effects were visible long afterwards in many places. It is true that fanatical teachers did much mischief in several quarters by associating themselves with the work of God, and introducing their own unwarrantable measures, so as to rob it in the end of much of the glorious character that distinguished it at first. Yet it cannot be denied that it was a great blessing to the churches. Some important, though painful lessons, were learned, in regard to the economy of the Spirit, which have not been wholly forgotten to this day.

This was the period in which Edwards and Prince, Freylinghausen, Dickenson, Finlay, and the Tennents, laboured in the northern and the middle States; Davies, and others of kindred spirit, in Virginia; the Wesleys for a while in Georgia; whilst Whitfield, like the angel symbolised in the apocalypse as flying through the heavens, having the everlasting gospel to preach to the nations, traversed colony after colony in his repeated visits to the new world, and was made an instrument of blessing to many multitudes.

---

[1] For a full and able account of this great work of grace, as well as of other revivals of religion, of unusual power and extent in America, see a work published at Boston in 1842, intituled the " Great Awakening," by the Rev. Joseph Tracy. It is by far the fullest account of the early revivals in America that has yet appeared, and being derived from authentic sources is worthy of entire credence.

The fourth and concluding period of the colonial era, compre-hends the twenty-five years from 1750 to 1775, and was one of great public agitation. In the early part of it the colonies aided England with all their might, in another war against France, ending in the conquest of the Canadas, which were secured to the conquerors by the treaty of Paris in 1763. In the latter part of it men's minds became universally engrossed with the disputes between the colonies and the mother country, and when all prospect of having these brought to an amicable settlement seemed desperate, preparation began to be made for that dreadful alternative—war. Such a state of things could not fail to have an untoward influence on religion. Yet most of those distinguished men whom I have spoken of as labouring in the latter part of the immediately preceding period, were spared to continue their work in the beginning of this. Whit-field renewed from time to time his angel visits, and the Spirit was not grieved quite away from the churches by the commo-tions of the people. Still no such glorious scenes were beheld during this period as had been witnessed in the last; on the con-trary, that declension in spiritual life, and spiritual effort, which war ever occasions, was now every where visible, even before hostilities had actually commenced.

Such is the very cursory and imperfect review which the limits of this work permit us to take of the religious vicissitudes of the United States during their colonial days. That period of 168 years was, comparatively speaking, one of decline, and even deadness, in the greater part of Protestant Europe; indeed, the latter part may be regarded as having been so universally. Yet during the same period, I feel very certain, that a minute examination of the history of the American Protestant churches would show that in no other part of Christendom, in proportion to the population, was there a greater amount of true know-ledge of the gospel, and of practical godliness among both min-isters and their flocks. No doubt, there were long intervals of coldness, or rather of deadness, as to spiritual things, during which both pastors and people became too much engrossed with the "cares of life." But, blessed be God, he did not abandon us for ever. Though he visited our transgressions with a rod, and chastised us for our sins, yet he remembered the covenant which he made with our fathers, and the word of his promise wherein he had caused them to trust. And though our unworthiness and our unprofitableness had been great, he did not cast us away from his sight, but deigned to hear us when we called upon him in the dark and gloomy hour, and saved us with a great salvation. And this he did " because his mercy endureth for ever."

BOOK III.

CHAPTER I.

FROM the colonial we now proceed to the national period in the history of the United States. The first twenty-five years of the national existence of the States were fraught with evil to the cause of religion. First came the war of the Revolution, which literally engrossed all men's minds. The population of the country at its commencement, scarcely, if at all, exceeded 3,500,000; and for a people so few and so scattered, divided into thirteen colonies, quite independent at the outset of each other, having no national treasury, no central government or power, nothing, in short, to unite them but one common feeling of patriotism; it was a gigantic undertaking. The war was followed by a long period of prostration. Connection with England having been dissolved, the colonies had to assume the form of States, their government had to be re-organised, and a general, or federal government instituted. The infant nation, now severed from the mother country, had to begin an existence of its own, at the cost of years of anxiety and agitation. Dangers threatened it on every side, and scarcely had the general government been organised, and the States learned to know their places a little in the federal economy, when the French revolution burst forth like a volcano, and threatened to sweep the United States into

its fiery stream. In the end it led them to declare war with
France for their national honour, or rather for their national
existence. That war was happily brought to an end by Napo-
leon on his becoming first consul, and thus was the infant
country allowed to enjoy a little longer repose, as far as depended
on foreign nations.

Unfavourable to the promotion of religion as were the whole
twenty-five years from 1775 to 1800, the first eight, spent in
hostilities with England, were pre-eminently so. The effects
of war on the churches of all communions were extensively and
variously disastrous. To say nothing of the distraction of the
mind from the subject of salvation, its more palpable influences
were seen and felt everywhere. Young men were called away
from the seclusion and protection of the paternal roof, and from
the vicinity of the oracle of God, to the demoralising atmosphere
of a camp; congregations were sometimes entirely broken up;
churches were burnt, or converted into barracks or hospitals,
by one or other of the belligerent armies; often by both successively; in more than one instance pastors were murdered;
the usual ministerial intercourse was interrupted; efforts for
the dissemination of the gospel were, in a great measure, suspended; colleges and other seminaries of learning were closed
for want of students and professors; and the public morals in
various respects, and in almost all possible ways, deteriorated.
Christianity is a religion of peace, and the tempest of war never
fails to blast and scatter the leaves of the tree which was planted
for the healing of the nations.

Allow me, with a single passage from a letter written by a
distinguished and most excellent German clergyman,[1] to give
the reader some idea of the state of things during that war. It
was written not long after its commencement. The perusal of
it cannot fail to impress the mind of every Christian with the
duty of praying that the peace which now so happily reigns
among the nations, may evermore continue:—

"Throughout the whole country great preparations are
making for the war, and almost every person is under arms.

[1] The Rev. Dr. Helmuth, formerly pastor at Philadelphia. The letter from
which the extract given in the text is taken, is found in the "Hallische Nach-
richten," pp. 1367-68.

The ardour manifested in these melancholy circumstances is indescribable. If a hundred men are required, many more immediately offer, and are dissatisfied when they are not accepted. I know of no similar case in history. Neighbourhoods, concerning which it would have been expected that years would be requisite to induce them voluntarily to take up arms, became strongly inclined for war as soon as the battle of Lexington was known. Quakers and Mennonists take part in the military exercises, and in great numbers renounce their former religious principles. The hoarse din of war is hourly heard in our streets. The present disturbances inflict no small injury on religion. Every body is constantly on the alert, anxious, like the ancient Athenians, to hear the news, and amid the mass of news, the hearts of men are, alas! closed against the good word of God. The Lord is chastising the people, but they do not feel it. Those who appear to be distant from danger are unconcerned; and those whom calamity has overtaken are enraged and meditating vengeance. In the American army there are many clergymen, who serve both as chaplains and as officers. I myself know two, one of whom is a colonel, and the other a captain. The whole country is in perfect enthusiasm for liberty. The whole population, from New England to Georgia, is of one mind, and determined to risk life and all things in defence of liberty. The few who think differently are not permitted to utter their sentiments. In Philadelphia the English and German students are formed into military companies, wear uniform, and are exercised like regular troops. Would to God that men would become as zealous and unanimous in asserting their spiritual liberty, as they are in vindicating their political freedom."

It required some time for the churches to recover from the demoralising effects of a war which had drawn the whole nation into its circle, and lasted for eight long years. But the times immediately following the Revolution were, as I have remarked, far from favourable to the resuscitation of true religion, and to the restoration of the churches, even to the condition, unsatisfactory as it was, in which they stood previous to the contest. Through God's blessing, however, they not only shared in the returning tranquillity of the country, but from that time to this, with some short periods of interruption, have steadily grown with its growth and strengthened with its strength.

It is not easy to discover what was the exact number of ministers and churches in the United States when these became severed from England, but the following estimate cannot be very wide of the truth. The Episcopal clergymen may be reckoned at about 250 at most; the churches at about 300.[1] In 1788, the Presbyterians had exactly 177 ministers, and 419 congregations.[2] As the Lutherans had eleven ministers in 1748, and forty churches three years after, the former could hardly have exceeded twenty-five and the latter sixty, at the commencement of the Revolution—judging by the statistics of the directory for worship (Kirchenagende) published in 1786.[3] The German Reformed churches were not more numerous. The Dutch Reformed churches had thirty ministers and eighty-two congregations in 1784.[4] In 1776 the Associate church had thirteen ministers and perhaps twenty churches. The Moravians had probably twelve ministers and six or eight churches. The New England Congregationalists could not, at the commencement of the Revolution, have had above 600 churches and 500 pastors. The Baptists, in 1784, had 424 ministers and 471 churches or congregations.[5] The Methodists, at the time of the Revolution, did not exist as a distinct body from the established Episcopal church, and had no ordained ministers. As for the Roman Catholics, according to Bishop England's estimate, their priests did not exceed twenty-six in number when the revolutionary war commenced, but their congregations were at least twice as numerous.[6]

These statements, though far from precise, are from the best sources, and suffice to give a tolerably correct view of the numbers of the clergy and churches at the commencement of the

[1] The number of the clergy and churches in the Episcopal church given in the text, has been estimated from various historical sketches and documents.

[2] "History of the Presbyterian church in the United States," by Dr. Hodge, part ii. p. 504.

[3] Dr. Schmuker's "Retrospect of Lutheranism in the United States."

[4] See the historical sketch of the Reformed Dutch church in another part of this work.

[5] View of the Baptist churches in America, given in the "American Quarterly Register," vols. xiii. and xiv.

[6] Letter from my Lord England of Charlestown to the Central Council of the Society for the Propagation of the Faith at Lyons, published in the "Annales de la Propagation de la Foi," for the month of May, 1838, vol. x.

national existence of the country, and for the first ten years after the breaking out of hostilities with England.

From the best estimate I can make it seems very certain that, in 1775, the total number of ministers of the gospel in the United States did not exceed 1400, nor the congregations 1850. Indeed, I am convinced that this is rather too large an estimate. [1] The population of the thirteen colonies at that epoch did not exceed 3,500,000, of whom about 500,000 were slaves.

If we assume the number of ministers to have been 1400, and and the population 3,500,000 in 1775, then we have one minister of the gospel, on an average, for every 2500 souls, which, I apprehend, is not far from the exact truth.

At that epoch there was no bishop in either the Protestant, Episcopal, or Roman Catholic church. There were at that time nine colleges and two medical schools, but no schools of law or theology.

The changes that took place in the general and local government of the thirteen original colonies, on their achieving their independence, have been already noticed. Religion, as well as every other interest, shared in the change of relations that ensued. Henceforth it was with congress and the State legislatures, or rather with the national and State governments, that the churches had to do, so far as they had any political relations to sustain at all.

It will be my object in this book to point out the changes that took place in the relations of the churches to the civil power, and to show their actual position with regard to it at the present moment. This I will try to do with all the brevity consistent with a full and lucid treatment of the subject. We

[1] The most exact approximation which I make is as follows :—

	MINISTERS.	CHURCHES.
Episcopalians,	250	300
Baptists,	350	380
Congregationalists,	500	600
Presbyterians,	140	300
Lutherans,	25	60
German Reformed,	25	60
Reformed Dutch,	25	60
Associate,	13	20
Moravians,	12	8
Roman Catholics,	26	52
	1366	1840

have now to see by what means that union of church and state, which connected the Congregational church in the north, and the Episcopalian church in the middle and south, with the civil government, was dissolved; what were the results of that dissolution, and what the position in which the churches now stand to the civil power, whether as represented by the general government, or the individual States.

CHAPTER II.

THE DISSOLUTION OF THE UNION OF CHURCH AND STATE NOT EFFECTED BY THE GENERAL GOVERNMENT, NOR DID IT TAKE PLACE IMMEDIATELY.

More than one erroneous idea prevails, I apprehend, in Europe, with respect to the dissolution of the union of church and state in the United States. First, many seem to think that it was a natural and inevitable result of the separation of the colonies from the mother country, and of the independent position which they had assumed. But that union connected the established churches of America, not with the mother country, but with the colonial governments, so that when the colonies became States, the alliance that had subsisted between certain churches and them was not necessarily affected. These churches, in fact, remained, as before, part and parcel of the States, and upon these they continued to be as dependent as ever. They never had any ties with England, beyond falling incidentally, as did the colonies themselves, under the operation of English laws.

Again, many imagine that this union of church and state in America was dissolved by an act of congress; that is, by an act of the general government. But this was not the case. An article of the constitution, it is true, restrains congress from establishing any particular religion, but this restriction is not in the original draft of the constitution; it forms one of certain amendments adopted soon after, and runs as follows: "Congress shall make no laws respecting an establishment of religion, or prohibiting the free exercise thereof." That is to say, the general government shall not make any law for the support of any particular church, or of all the churches. But neither this, nor any other article in the constitution of the United States, prohibits individual States from making such laws. The constitution simply declares what shall be the powers of the general government, leaving to the State governments such powers as it does not give to the general government. This, in reference to the subject in hand, is manifest from the fact that "the establishment of religion," as we shall presently see, survived for many years, in some States, their adhesion to the constitution of the United States.

Lastly, many persons in Europe seem to be under the impression that the union of church and state was annihilated at the Revolution, or, at all events, ceased upon the organisation of the State governments being completed. This, however, was not so in all cases. The connection between the civil power, and all the States in which Episcopacy had been established in the colonial period, was dissolved very soon after the Revolution by acts of their respective legislatures. But the Congregational church in New England continued to be united with the state, and to be supported by it long after the Revolution. Indeed, it was not until 1833 that the last tie that bound the church to the State in Massachusetts was severed.

CHAPTER III.

DISSOLUTION OF THE UNION OF CHURCH AND STATE IN AMERICA—WHEN AND HOW EFFECTED.

The first State that dissolved its connection with the church was Virginia, a circumstance that seems surprising at first sight, inasmuch as its early colonists were all sincere friends of its established Episcopal church, and for a long period were joined by few persons of different sentiments. Indeed, for more than a century, dissent was scarcely, if at all, allowed to exist within the commonwealth, even in the most secret manner.

Two causes, however, concurred in producing an alteration of these feelings towards the established church. First, many whose attachment to it had been owing to their birth, education, and early prepossessions, became disgusted with the irreligious lives of many of the clergy, and the greed with which, notwithstanding that most of their time was spent in fox-hunting and other sports, in company with the most dissolute of their parishioners, they were ready to contend for the last pound of tobacco allowed them as their legal salary. Such, indeed, was the character of those clergymen, that any one who makes himself minutely acquainted with their doings, must feel amazed that the church which they dishonoured should have retained its hold upon the respect of the Virginian colonists so long as it did. What attachment to it remained, must be ascribed to its having at all times had some faithful and excellent ministers who mourned over these scandals, and by their personal worth redeemed in some measure the body to which they belonged, from the infamy brought upon it by their reprobate fellow-clergymen, or parsons, as they were oftener called. These exceptions, however, did not prevent multitudes from abandoning the church of their fathers, around which their earliest and tenderest associations still clustered. "Had the doctrines of the gospel," says one who became an honoured instrument of much good in Virginia, and probably the most eloquent preacher of his day in America, "been solemnly and faithfully preached in the Established church, I am persuaded there would have been but few dissenters in these parts of Virginia; for their first objections were not against the peculiar rites and ceremonies of that church, much less against her excellent articles, but against the general strain of the doctrines delivered from the pulpit, in which those articles were opposed, or (which was more common,) not mentioned at all; so that, at first, they were not properly dissenters from the original constitution of the Church of England, but the most strict adherents of it, and only dissented from those who had forsaken it." [1]

Prior to 1740, there was only one Presbyterian congregation, it is believed, in Eastern Virginia, though the Scotch and Irish

[1] The Rev. Samuel Davies, in his " Narrative on the State of Religion among Dissenters in Virginia."

emigrants from Pennsylvania must have introduced several into the valley.[1] There were also a few Quaker societies, some small German congregations, and a considerable number of Baptist churches, which, though small and scattered, embraced perhaps a larger number of persons upon the whole than all the other dissenting bodies put together.

It was about this time that a Mr. Samuel Morris, a layman, who had been brought to the knowledge of salvation by the reading of the scriptures, and by the perusal of Flavel's works, and Luther on the Galatians, began to invite his neighbours, who, like himself, had been living in great ignorance of the gospel, to come to his house on the Sabbath, and hear him read his favourite authors. Such were the crowds that attended, that a house had soon to be built of size sufficient to contain them. To Flavel and Luther there was added a volume of Whitfield's sermons, as furnishing spiritual food for these hungry souls. They were visited in 1743 by the Rev. Mr. Robinson, a Presbyterian sent from New Jersey on a missionary tour to the south. His preaching was greatly blessed to " the Readers." [2] He taught them to conduct their worship in the Presbyterian way, and was followed by other ministers of the same denomination. Though they were often fined for not attending the services of the established church, these simple-hearted and excellent people continued their meetings. In 1747, the Rev. Mr. Davies, mentioned above, was sent to them by the presbytery of Newcastle in Delaware; and with the exception of some months spent on a visit to England, he laboured among them until 1759, when he was chosen president of the college of New Jersey. He succeeded in building up seven churches, and from that time Presbyterianism made very considerable progress in Eastern Virginia; so that when the war

[1] The " Valley of Virginia " is a fine district of country which lies west of the first ridge of the Alleghany mountains, and between that ridge and others which lie still further to the west. It reaches quite across the State, from north-east to south-west, and is considered the best part of that province for fertility of soil. It is a part of the same valley which extends across Maryland into Pennsylvania. In the latter State it is called Cumberland Valley.

[2] A counterpart to these worthy inquirers after divine knowledge is found at the present day in the northern parts of Sweden and in Norway, where groups of persons meet on the Sabbath after church service, which in too many cases furnishes but poor nourishment to their hungry souls, to read God's word and other good books.

of the Revolution began, the presbytery of Hanover in that colony was a numerous body, and comprehended some very able and eloquent ministers. The Scotch and Irish Presbyterians were at the same time increasing in the western part of the province. The Baptist congregations increased even more rapidly. Still, it was not always easy to avoid suffering from the interference of the civil authorities. The Act of Toleration, passed in England on 28th June, 1687, extended unquestionably to the colonies, yet not a few obstacles continued to be thrown in the way of dissenters almost down to the opening scenes of the revolutionary drama.

When the Revolution came at last, the Baptists and Presbyterians were almost to a man in its favour; and many of these, but especially of the former, whose preachers had suffered by far the most from the civil authorities in the earlier part of the century, at the instigation, as they believed, whether justly or unjustly, of the clergy of the established church, were not a little influenced in the course they then adopted by the hope of seeing the success of the Revolution lead to the overthrow of an establishment which they regarded with feelings of repugnance and even of hostility. In these circumstances, it was to be expected that before the Revolution had made much progress, an assault would be made on the established church, and such an assault was made not without success.

As the history of this matter is not a little interesting, and almost quite unknown in Europe, I may enter upon it at some length.

A very general impression prevails in England, and perhaps elsewhere, that the entire separation of church and state in America was the work of Mr. Jefferson, the third president of the United States, who took a distinguished part in the struggle, and who, upon being charged with drawing up the Declaration of Independence, executed the task so much to the satisfaction of his fellow-citizens. Now, none of Mr. Jefferson's admirers will consider it slanderous to assert that he was a very bitter enemy to Christianity, and we may even assume that he wished to see not only the Episcopal church separated from the state in Virginia, but the utter overthrow of everything in the shape of a church throughout the country. Still, it was not Jefferson that induced the State of Virginia to pass the act of separation. That must be ascribed to the petitions and other efforts of the Presbyterians and Baptists.

No sooner was war declared than the Synod of New York and Philadelphia, the highest ecclesiastical body among the Presbyterians of America at that time, addressed to their churches a very judicious and patriotic letter, which, while it displayed a firm spirit of loyalty towards the government of England, evidently and naturally sympathised with the contest then begun—a contest which it was thought could not be abandoned without the sacrifice of their dearest rights. Few persons supposed at the time that the struggle was to end in a separation from the mother country. But when, in the following year, the congress issued its Declaration of Independence, the whole face of matters was changed, and ministers of the gospel had to make their election,—whether they would recognise and obey the act of the congress, or still adhere to the sovereignty of the mother country. Then it was that the first body of clergy of any denomination in America that openly recognised that act, and thereby identified themselves with the cause of freedom and independence, was the comparatively numerous and very influential Presbyterians of Hanover in Virginia. At its first meeting after the appearance of the Declaration, that body addressed the Virginia house of assembly in a memorial, recommending the separation of church and state, and the leaving of the support of the gospel to the voluntary efforts of its friends. The memorial runs as follows:

"To the honourable the general assembly of Virginia. The memorial of the presbytery of Hanover humbly represents: That your memorialists are governed by the same sentiments which have inspired the United States of America, and are determined that nothing in our power and influence shall be wanting to give success to their common cause. We would also represent that dissenters from the Church of England in this country, have ever been desirous to conduct themselves as peaceable members of the civil government, for which reason they have hitherto submitted to various ecclesiastical burdens and restrictions that are inconsistent with equal liberty. But now, when the many and grievous oppressions of our mother country have laid this continent under the necessity of casting off the yoke of tyranny, and of forming independent governments upon equitable and liberal foundations, we flatter ourselves that we shall be freed from all the incumbrances which a spirit of domination, prejudice, or bigotry, has interwoven with most other political systems. This we are the more strongly encouraged to expect by the Declaration of Rights, so universally applauded for that dignity, firmness, and precision, with which it delineates and asserts the privileges of society, and the prerogatives of human nature; and which we embrace as the Magna Charta of our commonwealth, that can never be violated without endangering the grand superstructure it was designed to sustain. Therefore, we rely upon this declaration, as well as the justice of our honourable legislature, to secure us the free exercise of religion according to the dictates of our consciences; and we should fall short in our duty to ourselves, and the many and numerous congregations under our care, were we, upon this occasion, to neglect laying before you a statement of the religious grievances under which we have hitherto laboured, that they may no longer be continued in our present form of government.

"It is well known that in the frontier counties, which are justly supposed to contain a fifth part of the inhabitants of Virginia, the dissenters have borne the heavy burthens of purchasing glebes, building churches, and supporting the established clergy, where there are very few Episcopalians, either to assist in bearing the expense, or to reap the advantage; and that throughout the other parts of the country, there are also many thousands of zealous friends and defenders of our State, who besides the invidious and disadvantageous restrictions to which they have been subjected, annually pay large taxes to support an establishment, from which their consciences and principles oblige them to dissent; all which are confessedly so many violations of their natural rights, and in their consequences a restraint upon freedom of inquiry and private judgment.

"In this enlightened age, and in a land where all of every denomination are united in the most strenuous efforts to be free, we hope and expect that our representatives will cheerfully concur in removing every species of religious as well as civil bondage. Certain it is, that every argument for civil liberty gains additional strength when applied to liberty in the concerns of religion; and there is no argument in favour of establishing the Christian religion, but may be pleaded, with equal propriety, for establishing the tenets of Mohammed by those who believe the Alcoran; or if this be not true, it is at least impossible for the magistrate to adjudge the right of preference among the various sects that profess the Christian faith, without erecting a claim to infallibility, which would lead us back to the church of Rome.

" We beg leave, further, to represent that religious establishments are highly injurious to the temporal interests of any community. Without insisting upon the ambition and the arbitrary practices of those who are favoured by government, or the intriguing seditious spirit which is commonly excited by this, as well as by every other kind of oppression; such establishments greatly retard population, and consequently the progress of arts, sciences, and manufactures; witness the rapid growth and improvements of the northern provinces compared with this. No one can deny that the more early settlement, and the many superior advantages of our country, would have invited multitudes of artificers, mechanics, and other useful members of society, to fix their habitation among us, who have either remained in their place of nativity, or preferred worse civil governments, and a more barren soil, where they might enjoy the rights of conscience more fully than they had a prospect of doing in this. From which we infer that Virginia might have now been the capital of America, and a match for the British arms without depending on others for the necessaries of war, had it not been prevented by her religious establishment.

" Neither can it be made to appear that the gospel needs any such civil aid. We rather conceive that, when our blessed Saviour declares his kingdom is not of this world, he renounces all dependence upon state power; and as his weapons are spiritual, and were only designed to have influence on the judgment and heart of man, we are persuaded that, if mankind were left in the quiet possession of their inalienable religious privileges, Christianity, as in the days of the apostles, would continue to prevail and flourish in the greatest purity, by its own native excellencies, and under the all-disposing providence of God.

"We would also humbly represent, that the only proper objects of civil government are the happiness and protection of men in the present state of existence; the security of the life, liberty, and property of the citizens; and to restrain the vicious and encourage the virtuous by wholesome laws, equally extending to every individual. But that the duty which we owe to our Creator, and the manner of discharging it, can only be directed by reason and conviction, and is no where cognisable but at the tribunal of the universal Judge.

"Therefore we ask no ecclesiastical establishments for ourselves; neither can we approve of them when granted to others. This, indeed, would be giving exclusive or separate emoluments or privileges to one set of men, without any special public services, to the common reproach and injury of every other denomination. And, for the reasons recited, we are induced earnestly to entreat that all laws now in force in this commonwealth, which countenance religious domination, may be speedily repealed; that all, of every religious sect, may be protected in the full exercise of their mutual modes of worship; exempted from all taxes for the support of any church whatsoever, further than what may be agreeable to their own private choice, or voluntary obligation. This being done, all partial and invidious distinctions will be abolished, to the great honour and interest of the state; and every one be left to stand or fall according to his merit, which can never be the case so long as any one denomination is established in preference to others.

"That the great Sovereign of the universe may inspire you with unanimity, wisdom, and resolution; and bring you to a just determination on all the important concerns before you, is the fervent prayer of your memorialists."

Besides this petition from the presbytery of Hanover, there were others from the Baptists and Quakers. The Baptists had suffered more than any other class of dissenters, and the remembrance of their wrongs, now that their day of power had come, stimulated them to an uninterrupted opposition of seven and twenty years to the established church. Indeed, they now took the lead in opposing its claims. In 1775, they presented to the general assembly an address, composed by members who had spontaneously convened, in which they petitioned, " that they might be allowed to worship God in their own way, without interruption; to maintain their own minister, separate from others; and to be married, buried, &c., without paying the clergy of other denominations." [1] To this the assembly returned a complimentary answer, and an order was made that the sectarian clergy should have the privilege of performing divine service to their respective adherents in the army, equally with the regular chaplains of the established church.[2]

The above memorials from the Presbyterians, and petitions from the Baptists, Quakers, and others opposed to the established church, were met by counter-memorials from the Episcopalians and Methodists, appealing on behalf of the establishment to the principles of justice, wisdom, and policy. Public faith, it was said, required that the state should abide by its engagements; and that a system of such old standing, and which involved so many interests on the part of persons who had staked their all upon its continued existence, possessed the nature of a vested right, and ought to be maintained inviolate. The wisdom of this course was argued from the past experience of all Christian lands,[3] and from the influence of religious establishments in giving stability to virtue and the public happiness. Policy required it, for it was insisted that were there to be no establishment, the peace of the community would be destroyed by the jealousies and contentions of rival sects. And, finally, the memorialists prayed that the matter might be referred, in the last resort, to the people at large, as they had the best of reasons for believing that a majority of the citizens would be in favour of continuing the establishment.

From this it would seem that, in the conviction of these memorialists, a majority of the population of Virginia were Episcopalians; yet it was confidently maintained in other quarters that two-thirds of the people were at that time dissenters. I am inclined to think that the greater part professed or leant

<hr>

[1] Semple's " History of the Baptists in Virginia," pp. 25—27, 62.
[2] Burk's " History of Virginia," p. 59.
[3] This was not difficult, for church establishments had existed throughout Christendom since the days of Constantine.

to Episcopacy, but that a decided majority was opposed to its civil establishment. The memorials led to a long and earnest discussion. The church had for her champions Messrs. Pendleton and R. C. Nicolas, and for her great opponent Mr. Jefferson, who speaks of the contest as the severest in which he was ever engaged.[1] After discussing the subject for nearly two months, the assembly repealed all the colonial laws attaching criminality to the profession of any particular religious opinions, requiring attendance at the parish churches, and forbidding attendance elsewhere, with the penalties attached thereto. Dissenters were to be exempted in future from compulsory contributions in support of the Episcopal church. The clergy, however, were to have their stipends continued until the first day in the ensuing year, and had all arrears secured to them. The churches, chapels and glebes, books, plate, &c., belonging to the Episcopal church, were to remain in its possession.[2] This law was passed on the 5th of December, 1776. The question of having a general assessment for the support of religion, was, at the same time, so far discussed, but the determination of it was put off to a future day.

In the course of 1777 and 1778, petitions and counter-petitions continued to be addressed to the legislature on the subject of religion. Some of the petitions prayed for the preservation of all that remained of the establishment; others advocated a general assessment for the support of all denominations; others opposed that suggestion. Some, again, called for the suppression by law of the irregularities of the "sectaries," such as their holding meetings by night, and craved that none but "licensed preachers" should be allowed to conduct the public worship of God. Among the memorials was one from the presbytery of Hanover, opposing the plan of a general assessment. After reverting to the principles laid down in their first petition, and insisting that the only proper objects of civil governments are the happiness and protection of men in their present state of existence; the security of the life, liberty, and property of the citizens; the restraint of the vicious, and the encouragement of the virtuous by wholesome laws, equally extending to every individual; and that the

[1] Jefferson's Works, vol. i., p. 32.
[2] Hening's " Statutes of Virginia," p. 34.

duty which men owe to their Creator, and the manner of discharging it, can only be directed by reason and conviction, and is no where cognisable but at the tribunal of the universal Judge, the presbytery express themselves as follows:

"To illustrate and confirm these assertions, we beg leave to observe, that to judge for ourselves, and to engage in the exercise of religion agreeably to the dictates of our own consciences, is an inalienable right, which upon the principles on which the gospel was first propagated, and the reformation from Popery carried on, can never be transferred to another. Neither does the church of Christ stand in need of a general assessment for its support; and most certain we are, that it would be of no advantage but an injury to the society to which we belong; and as every good Christian believes that Christ has ordained a complete system of laws for the government of his kingdom, so we are persuaded that by his providence he will support it to its final consummation. In the fixed belief of this principle, that the kingdom of Christ and the concerns of religion are beyond the limits of civil control, we should act a dishonest, inconsistent part, were we to receive any emoluments from human establishments for the support of the gospel.

"These things being considered, we hope that we shall be excused for remonstrating against a general assessment for any religious purpose. As the maxims have long been approved, that every servant is to obey his master, and that the hireling is accountable for his conduct to him from whom he receives his wages; in like manner, if the legislature has any rightful authority over the ministers of the gospel in the exercise of their sacred office, and if it is their duty to levy a maintenance for them as such, then it will follow that they may revive the old establishment in its former extent, or ordain a new one for any sect that they may think proper; they are invested with a power not only to determine, but it is incumbent on them to declare who shall preach, what they shall preach, to whom, when, and in what places they shall preach; or to impose any regulations and restrictions upon religious societies that they may judge expedient. These consequences are so plain as not to be denied, and they are so entirely subversive of religious liberty, that if they should take place in Virginia, we should be reduced to the melancholy necessity of saying with the apostles in like cases, "Judge ye whether it is best to obey God or men," and also of acting as they acted.

"Therefore, as it is contrary to our principles and interest, and as we think, subversive of religious liberty, we do again most earnestly entreat, that our legislature would never extend any assessment for religious purposes to us or to the congregations under our care."

This memorial, and probably still more, the strenuous efforts of the Baptists, led in 1779, to the abandonment of the proposed general assessment, after a bill to that effect had been ordered a third reading. With the return of peace, the legislature of Virginia resumed the subject of legislating in behalf of religion; and in the two sessions of 1784 two important matters were much debated. One was to provide by law for the incorporation of "all societies of the Christian religion, which may apply for the same;" the other was the old project of a general assessment for the support of religion. The celebrated Patrick Henry [1]

[1] This gentlemen, one of the most eloquent men that America has ever produced, was for many years a member of the legislature of Virginia, and governor, also, for several terms. He distinguished himself in opposing the taxation of the the colonies by England without their consent, and in the course of a very animated speech on that subject in the legislature of Virginia, said in his emphatic manner : "Cæsar had a Brutus, Charles I. had a Cromwell, and George III."— here he was interrupted by cries of " Treason ! Treason ! "—" and George III." he repeated, "should profit by their example ; if this be treason, Gentlemen, you may make the most of it."

It has been said that in his younger days Mr. Henry was inclined to infidelity. But he was ever a firm believer in Christianity, and for many years before his death a devout Christian. " He ever had a great abhorrence of infidelity," says a private letter from a member of Mr. Henry's family, given in Dr. Hawks' " Ecclesiastical History of the Episcopal Church in Virginia," pp. 160, 161, "and actually wrote an answer to ' Paine's Age of Reason,' but destroyed it before his death. He received the communion as often as an opportunity offered ; and on such occasions always fasted until after he had received the sacrament, and spent the day in the greatest retirement. This he did both while he was governor and afterwards."

The following affecting anecdote is related of him. When very old he was induced to be a candidate for the house of delegates, in a time of great political excitement. " On the day of his election," says Wirt in his Life of Patrick Henry, p. 408, " as soon as he appeared on the ground, he was surrounded by the admiring and adoring crowd, and whithersoever he moved the concourse followed him. A preacher of the Baptist church, whose piety was wounded by this homage paid to a mortal, asked the people aloud, Why they thus followed Mr. Henry ? ' Mr. Henry,' said he, ' is not a god; ' ' No !' said Mr. Henry, deeply affected, both by the scene and the remark, ' No, indeed, my friend, I am a poor worm of the dust, as fleeting and as unsubstantial as the shadow of the cloud that flies over your fields, and is remembered no more.' " The tone with which this was uttered, and the look which accompanied, affected every heart, and silenced every voice.

was the great advocate of both measures. The Hanover presbytery soon re-appeared upon the field, and opposed the latter
of these proposals, although it would have proved as favourable
to the Presbyterian church as any other. But on this occasion
there was an evident wavering on the part of the presbytery,
probably owing to an expectation that the measure would be
sure to be adopted, and from their desire to secure the least
injurious plan of giving it effect. It has also been alleged as
one cause of the temporary abatement of their zeal, that Mr.
Henry had won over to his opinions the Rev. Dr. John B.
Smith, one of the ablest members of the presbytery. Certain it
is, that an act to incorporate the churches passed by a large
vote, and a bill in favour of a general assessment passed two
readings, was ordered to be read a third time, and was then sent
forth to be submitted to the people for their opinion before being
passed into a law. On the same day, likewise, on which an act
was passed for the incorporation of such churches as might apply
for the same, leave was granted to introduce a bill for the incorporation of the Protestant Episcopal church. Mr. Henry introduced the bill. It had for its object the securing to that church
all the property that it had ever had, both in those parishes which
had churches in use, and in the still greater number which had
no ministers, and not even vestries, and where the church had
become dilapidated during the war of the Revolution. This bill
was approved by the legislature, and promised permanent peace
and protection to the Episcopal church. But the prospect was
not of long continuance. The incorporation of the Episcopal
clergy was strongly opposed in a memorial from the presbytery
of Hanover, under the influence of which the legislature delayed
further proceedings, in order that public opinion might have
time to express itself. Meanwhile petitions against the measure
were sent in from all parts of Virginia, signed by no fewer than
10,000 persons. Still, as the legislature seemed disposed to
pass the bill in question, the Presbyterian churches held a convention, at which another memorial was drawn up, and the Rev.
John B. Smith, who had now become more confirmed in his
opposition to the contemplated measure, was appointed to accompany the presentation of the memorial with his personal advo-
cacy at the bar of the assembly, and was heard there for three

successive days.   This decided the matter;   the whole scheme
was abandoned.

Thus, it was mainly owing to the exertions of the Presbyterians, Baptists, and Quakers, that the union of church and state
in Virginia was dissolved, and the scheme of having a general assessment for the support of all Protestant denominations defeated.[1]
Mr. Jefferson, it is true, when a member of Assembly in 1776,
rendered all the aid in his power, and would have been very
well pleased to have had such parties to co-operate with him
in some other schemes, if he could.   But they, not he, began
the movement in this case, and they persevered in their endeavours to render the churches altogether independent of the civil
power, and to have all placed precisely on the same footing, as
respected the civil government.

Mr. Jefferson's grand achievement, in the line of legislating
about religious rights, was the famous act "for establishing
religious freedom," drawn up by him, and adopted by the legislature of Virginia in 1785.[2]   That act in itself, however, con-

---

[1] The success of a general assessment bill would have done infinite mischief.
It never could have been confined to the Evangelical churches, and would have
ended in building up Unitarianism, Universalism, &c., in Virginia, just as a
similar measure did afterwards in New England.

[2] As the reader may wish to see this famous ordinance, which Mr. Jefferson
challenged so much credit to himself for having written and advocated, we give
it in this note :—" Whereas Almighty God hath created the mind free : that
all attempts to influence it by temporal punishments or burdens, or by civil
incapacitations, tends only to beget habits of hypocrisy and meanness, and are
a departure from the plan of the holy Author of our religion ; who being Lord
both of body and mind, yet chose not to propagate it by coercions on either, as
was in his almighty power to do : that the impious presumption of legislators
and rulers, civil as well as ecclesiastical, who being themselves but fallible and
uninspired men, have assumed dominion over the faith of others, setting up
their own opinions and modes of thinking as the only true and infallible, and
as such endeavouring to impose them on others, hath established or maintained
false religions over the greatest part of the world, and through all time : that
to compel a man to furnish contributions of money for the propagation of
opinions which he disbelieves, is sinful and tyrannical : that even the forcing
him to support this or that preacher of his own religious persuasion, is depriving him of the comfortable liberty of giving his contributions to the particular pastor whose morals he would make his pattern, and whose powers he
feels most persuasive to righteousness, and is withdrawing from the ministry
those temporal rewards, which, proceeding from an approbation of their personal conduct, are an additional incitement to earnest and unremitting labours
for the instruction of mankind : that our civil rights have no dependence on our
religious opinions, any more than on our opinions in physic and geometry : that
therefore the proscribing any citizen as unworthy of the public confidence, by
laying upon him an incapacity of being called to offices of trust and emolument,
unless he profess or renounce this or that religious opinion, is depriving him
injuriously of those privileges and advantages to which, in common with his
fellow-citizens, he has a natural right : that it tends only to corrupt the prin-

tains nothing to which a friend of full and equal liberty of conscience would perhaps object; but it gave its author great satisfaction, not because it embodied the principles of eternal justice,
but because by putting all religious sects on an equality, it
seemed to degrade Christianity, and " to comprehend," to use
his own words, " within the mantle of protection the Jew and
the Gentile, the Christian and the Mahommedan, the Hindoo
and infidel of every denomination." It was this that made the
arch-infidel chuckle with satisfaction—not, we repeat, that the
great principles embodied in the measure were right.

I have now gone through the history of the dissolution of the
union of church and state in Virginia[1]—a dissolution effected,

ciples of that religion it is meant to encourage, by bribing with a monopoly of
worldly honours and emoluments those who will externally profess or conform
to it : that though indeed those are criminal who do not withstand such temptation, yet neither are those innocent who lay the bait in their way : that to
suffer the civil magistrate to intrude his powers into the field of opinion, and to
restrain the profession or propagation of principles on suspicion of their ill-
tendency, is a dangerous fallacy, which at once destroys all religious liberty ;
because, he being, of course, judge of that tendency, will make his opinions the
rule of judgment, and approve or condemn the sentiments of others only as they
shall square with or differ from his own : that it is time enough for the rightful
purposes of civil government, for its officers to interfere when principles break
out into overt acts against peace and good order : and, finally, that truth is
great, and will prevail if left to herself, that she is the proper and sufficient
antagonist to error, and has nothing to fear from the conflict, unless by human
interposition disarmed of her natural weapons—free argument and debate—
errors ceasing to be dangerous when it is permitted freely to contradict them.

" Be it therefore enacted by the General Assembly, that no man shall be
compelled to frequent or support any religious worship, place, or ministry
whatsoever ; nor shall be enforced, restrained, molested, or burdened in his
body or goods, nor shall otherwise suffer on account of his religious opinions or
belief ; but that all men shall be free to profess, and by argument to maintain,
their opinions in matters of religion, and that the same shall in nowise diminish, enlarge, or affect their civil capacities.

" And though we well know that this Assembly, elected by the people for
the ordinary purposes of legislation only, have no power to restrain the acts of
succeeding Assemblies, constituted with powers equal to our own, and that
therefore to declare this act irrevocable would be of no effect in law; yet we are
free to declare, and do declare, that the rights hereby asserted are of the
natural right of mankind, and that if any act shall be hereafter passed to
repeal the present, or narrow its operation, such act will be an infringement of
natural right."

It has been well observed that there is a striking inconsistency between the
last clause of this act, and the doctrine taught in the preceding portion of it,
for it is of the nature of an incidental attempt to maintain certain doctrines,
by legislation, as the only orthodox and worthy of belief.

[1] I might have gone into an ampler detail of the measures pursued by the
opponents of the Episcopal church in Virginia, to annul the law incorporating
the clergy of that church, and those, also, which were followed up in 1802 by
the sale of the glebes. But such details have no proper connection with the
subject in hand.   The law ordaining the sale of the glebes was, I think, uncon-
stitutional, and would have been pronounced to be so had it been brought to a
fair and full decision before the proper tribunal. The opposition to the Episcopal church towards the end was marked by a cruelty which admits of no apology.

in reality, by the act of 6th December, 1776, which repealed all former acts relating to that union. What followed had no necessary connection with that act, but bore only upon certain measures, designed to guard against what was deemed by the majority to be an injurious legislation for promoting the interests of religion.

This early discussion of the propriety of dissolving the union of church and state in Virginia, after the revolutionary war had broken out, had some effect, probably, on other States placed in similar circumstances. Such, at least, is the prevailing impression in the absence of authentic documentary proof. After the Declaration of Independence, measures to the same effect were very promptly taken in Maryland. On the 3d of November, 1776, the legislature of that State put forth a Declaration of Rights, similar to that made by Virginia in the early part of that same year, and embodying principles directly subversive of the union of church and state. The Episcopal church, nevertheless, was secured in the possession of the glebes and all other church property, and it was decided that the stipends of all the incumbents who should remain at their posts should be paid up to the first day of the month in which said Declaration was made. This righteous decision was not departed from, and Maryland, accordingly, was spared those tedious and wretched disputes about the property of the church that had once been established; disputes that did much harm to religion in Virginia, and were little reputable to the authors of them.

In that Maryland "Declaration of Rights," it was declared "that as it is the duty of every man to worship God in such a manner as he thinks most acceptable to him, all persons professing the Christian religion are equally entitled to protection in their religious liberty; wherefore no person ought by any law to be molested in his person or estate on account of his religious persuasion or profession, or for his religious practice, unless, under colour of religion, any man shall disturb the good order, peace, or safety of the state, or shall infringe the laws of morality, or injure others in their natural, civil, or religious rights." It was further declared that no one ought to be compelled to frequent or maintain the religious worship of any denomination, save that which he chose; but, at the same time, it was affirmed that the legislature might, in its discretion, impose a common and equal tax for the support of the Christian religion in general; in such case, however, every individual paying the tax was held to possess the right of designating the religious denomination to the support of which it was to be applied; or he might resolve this legislative support of Christianity in general into mere almsgiving, and direct his tax to be applied to the maintenance of the poor.[1]

The union of church and state was dissolved in like manner, by acts of their respective legislatures, in New York, South Carolina, and all the other colonies in which the Protestant Episcopal church was predominant. But it is unnecessary to trace the steps by which this dissolution was accomplished in all cases. There was nothing particularly important, in so far as I am aware, in these details. Enough to know that the dissolution did take place at no distant periods after the Revolution.

Let us now turn to New England, where the principle of religious establishments was most firmly rooted, and the most difficult to be eradicated.

It was not until about forty years subsequent to the separation of church and state in Virginia, that the example was followed by Connecticut. It will be recollected that in the latter State the established church was the Congregational. In 1816, shortly after the close of the last war between the United States and Great Britain, all parties that differed from it—Episcopalians, Baptists, Methodists, Universalists, &c., combined to effect its overthrow. These various parties having succeeded in gaining a majority in the legislature, proceeded to abolish the legal assessment for the parish churches, and by a new law left it optional to the rate-payers to support either the parish church, or any other, as each thought fit. The same system was adopted by New Hampshire and Maine. Vermont, I believe, has at all times had essentially the voluntary scheme; that is, the people of each township have supported such churches within their respective boundaries, and in such a measure as they have thought proper. Of all the States in which there had ever been any connection between the church and the

---

[1] See Dr. Hawks' "History of the Episcopal Church in Maryland," p. 288.

civil power, Massachusetts was the last to come under the operation of the voluntary principle. The fathers of that colony, in the indulgence of their theocratic principles and ideas, had ever prided themselves in the union made by the vine of the Lord's planting and the state. They had with great satisfaction reposed under the shadow of both, and discoursed of the happy fruits of such an union. Cotton Mather, for example, in a style peculiarly his own, talks not only of the advantage, but of the honour, likewise, of a religious establishment. "Ministers of the gospel," says he, " would have a poor time of it, if they must rely on *a free contribution of the people* for their maintenance." And again: " The laws of the province (of Massachusetts) having had the royal approbation to ratify them, they are the king's laws. By these laws it is enacted that there shall be a public worship of God in every plantation; that the person elected by the majority of the inhabitants to be so, shall be looked upon as the minister of the place; and that the salary for him, which they shall agree upon, shall be levied by a rate upon all the inhabitants. In consequence of this, the minister thus chosen by the people, is (not only Christ's, but also) in reality, *the king's minister;* and the salary raised for him, is raised *in the king's name,* and is the king's allowance unto him." [1]

Before the Revolution took place, the Episcopalians had been relieved, by a special act of the legislature, from contributing to the support of the parish churches, and their congregations had been erected into incorporated societies, or poll-parishes; that is, parishes comprising only individuals, and not marked by geographical limits. But though the constitution of 1780, which maintained the old assessment for religious worship, allowed every person to appropriate his taxes to whatever society he pleased, it was still held by the courts of that State, until the year 1811, that a member of a territorial parish (which is a corporation) could not divert the taxes imposed on him for the support of religious worship to the maintenance of a teacher of an unincorporated society.[2] By the statute of 1811, amended

---

[1] " Ratio Disciplinæ; or, Faithful Account of the Discipline professed and practised in the Churches of New England," p. 20.

[2] For a brief and clear view of the laws of Massachusetts on this subject,

in 1823, a duly attested certificate of membership in any other religious society, whether incorporated or not, sufficed to relieve the holder of it from all taxes for the support of the parish church; but it was still the law and practice of Massachusetts to regard all persons, in any town or parish, who belonged to no religious society whatever, as regular members of the parish or congregational church, and taxable for the support of its clergy.

I have elsewhere spoken of the accumulated evils which grew out of the connection between the church and the state in Massachusetts. Those evils became so great that the friends of evangelical religion, in other words, of the orthodox faith of every name, resolved to unite in urging an amendment of the constitution of the State, by which some better results might be obtained. Their efforts were crowned with success. The amendment having been voted by the legislature in three successive sessions, 1831-33, became part of the organic law of the State, and the union of church and state was brought to a close.

CHAPTER IV.

EFFECTS OF THE DISSOLUTION OF THE UNION OF CHURCH AND STATE IN THE SEVERAL STATES IN WHICH IT ONCE SUBSISTED.

It will readily be believed that the union of church and state, in any country where it has once subsisted, cannot be dissolved without some attendant inconvenience. If such has been the nature of the connection that the church has been wholly dependent on the state for its support, for the keeping of its places of worship in repair, the maintenance of its pastors, and the incidental expences of public worship, very serious embarrassments must inevitably attend a sudden dissolution of such a union. Such was unquestionably the case in some of the States of

the reader is referred to a sermon of the Rev. William Cogswell, D.D., on religious liberty, preached on the day of the annual fast in Massachusetts, April 3d, 1828, and published in Boston.

America. In others, again, in which the connection had been one of no long duration, had never been very close, and had not been carried out to a great extent, that result was attended with little and not very lasting evil.

No where were the ill consequences of the disestablishment of the church felt more seriously than in Virginia, and this may be ascribed to several causes. The worthless character of many of the clergymen sent over from England, had bred in many places, from the very first, great indifference to the church and its services. The people had become tired of compulsory payments for the support of a form of worship which they had ceased to love or respect. Thus many became indifferent to religious worship of every kind, and others went off to the "dissenters" —the Presbyterians, Baptists, &c., when there were churches of these denominations in their neighbourhoods. However deplorable it might be that the venerable edifices in which their fathers had worshipped, should be almost deserted from such a cause, it was nevertheless inevitable. Not that this representation applies to every parish; in many cases the faithful and consistent lives of the pastors kept their flocks, under God, in a state of prosperity.

In the second place, a large majority, some say rather more than two-thirds of the Episcopal clergy[1] in Virginia were opposed to the Revolution, and most of these returned to England. Nor are they to be blamed without mercy for so doing. Many of them, it must be remembered, were Englishmen by birth, and England was the land of all their early associations. They had never suffered oppression, but had ever been of the party in favour with the monarch. Thus nothing could be more natural than that even good men among them should be *Tories*. Others there were, doubtless, who saw that the independence of the country would be likely so to alter the state of things, as to make it impossible for them to continue their delinquencies with the impunity which they had enjoyed when responsible only to a bishop 3000 miles off. But this loyalty to the British crown was not likely to find much forbearance among a people, so many of whom were republican in sentiment, and hostile for the time

[1] Dr. Hawks' "History of the Episcopal church in Virginia," p. 136.

to the mother country; and the Episcopal church could not fail to suffer from the sympathy shown by many of its clergy for those who were considered the country's enemies.   This was, no doubt, counteracted so far by there being in the minority of the clergy such staunch republicans and avowed partizans of the colonies as the Rev. Dr. Madison, afterwards bishop of the state, Drs. Griffith and Bracken, Messrs. Buchanan, Jarratt, Davies, and others;[1] while as regards the laity, no men in all the colonies entered more warmly into the Revolution than did the Episcopalians of Virginia.[2]

In the third place, Virginia was the immediate theatre of no small part of the war, and was repeatedly overrun by the armies of both sides.   Now, without attributing too much to wantonness, though much, no doubt, was owing to that, it may readily be supposed that the Episcopal churches, the best in the colony, would be sure to be used as barracks, store houses, hospitals, &c., thus losing at once their sacred character, and suffering much in their furnishings.   Partly, indeed, from accident, partly, it is believed, from design, not a few were destroyed by fire and other causes.

In the fourth place, so engrossed were all men's minds with the war, that the time was very unfavourable for doing good. Many of the ministers who remained in the province found great difficulty in collecting the people together, or obtaining for themselves the means of subsistence.   Some betook themselves to teaching schools, but even to that the times were unfavourable. Many mere boys shouldered the musket and went to the war, returning no more to their homes until hostilities had ceased, if death did not prevent them from returning at all.

[1] In one instance, an Episcopal clergyman of Virginia, the Rev. Mr. Muhlenburg, relinquished his charge, accepted a commission as colonel in the American army, raised his regiment among his own parishioners, served through the whole war, and retired from the service at its close with the rank of a brigadier-general.   The last sermon that he ever preached to his people before he left for the camp, was delivered in military dress.   Thatcher's "Military Journal," p. 152.   The Rev. Mr. Thurston, of Frederick county, in the same State, also bore arms as a colonel in the service of the country.

[2] Such as general Washington, Patrick Henry, (of whom we have spoken in the last chapter,) Richard Henry Lee, the mover of the Declaration of Independence, his brother, Francis Lightfoot Lee, one of the signers, George Mason, Edmund Pendleton, Peter Lyons, Paul Carrington, William Fleming, William Grayson, with the families of the Nelsons, Meades, Mercers, Harrisons, Randolphs, and hundreds of other names deservedly dear to Virginia.   Dr. Hawks' "History of the Episcopal Church in Virginia," p. 137.

Bearing these things in mind, the state of the Episcopal churches[1] in Virginia may be supposed to have been deplorable enough on the return of peace, and that they little needed the aggravation of being thrown for their support entirely upon their own members, when these were impoverished by the length of the war, and rendered by it incapable of doing much for the church, however much disposed to make sacrifices in her cause. But an extract from the distinguished author to whom I have so often had occasion to refer, will give a clearer idea of the state of things than I can:

"On the 19th of April, 1783, precisely eight years after the first effusion of blood at Lexington, peace was proclaimed to the American army by order of the commander in chief. Time was now afforded to men to direct their attention to the permanent establishment of such institutions, civil and religious, as might comport with their desires or views of duty. Much was to be done; and rejoicing with thankfulness as now we may, in the present prosperity of the church in Virginia, it is well to look back on its condition as it emerged from the Revolution, and by a contemplation of the difficulties which stood in the way of its resuscitation be moved to the exercise of gratitude. When the colonies first resorted to arms, Virginia in her sixty-one counties contained ninety-five parishes, 164 churches and chapels, and ninety-one clergymen. When the contest was over, she came out of the war with a large number of her churches destroyed or injured irreparably, with twenty-three of her ninety-five parishes extinct or forsaken, and of the remaining seventy-two, thirty-four were destitute of ministerial services; whilst of her ninety-one clergymen twenty-eight only remained, who had lived through the storm, and these, with eight others who came into the State soon after the struggle terminated, supplied thirty-six of the parishes. Of these twenty-eight, fifteen only had been enabled to continue in the churches which they supplied prior to the commencement of hostilities; and thirteen had been driven from their cures by violence or want, to seek safety or comfort in some one of the many vacant parishes, where they might

---

1 Not that the damage done by the war to other denominations was inconsiderable. The Presbyterians probably suffered more in their church edifices, from being far more obnoxious to the resentment of the enemy, as the English were considered to be at the time.

hope to find, for a time at least, exemption from the extremity of suffering."[1]

This is a dark enough picture, but it must be borne in mind that the evils it represents were almost wholly owing to the revolutionary war and its consequences, and could not have been much alleviated had the church establishment instead of being arrested in 1776, been continued until 1783.   But in the gloomy years that followed the Revolution, the Episcopal church continued prostrate, and felt the loss of her establishment most severely.   Then did it seem as if nothing short of her utter ruin would satisfy the resentment of her enemies.   She had, indeed, in the day of her power been exclusive, domineering, and persecuting; her own sins had brought upon her this severe visitation.   From her case, as well as from all past experience, persecuting churches should learn that a church that oppresses, will one day be herself oppressed, and most likely by those on whose neck she had placed her foot.

But let us turn to a brighter page.   "The Lord after he hath afflicted delighteth to heal."   So it was with the Episcopal church in Virginia.   He had some good thing in reserve for her, and had been preparing her for it by the discipline of his rod.   She gradually emerged from her difficulties.   Her people learned by degrees to trust in themselves, or rather in God, and began to look to their own exertions rather than to a tobacco tax for the support of their churches and pastors.   Faithful ministers multiplied; an excellent bishop was elected and consecrated; benevolent societies began to spring up; a theological school was planted within her borders; where many youths of talent and piety have been trained under excellent professors to preach the unsearchable riches of Christ.   And although the ministers and parishes are not now so numerous as we have stated them to have been at the commencement of the war of the Revolution, yet their number is considerable and constantly increasing. There are seventy-five ministers, and there must be above eighty churches.   But above all, I do not think it possible to find a body of ministers of equal number, in any denomination, who in point of theological education, prudent zeal, simple and effective

[1] Dr. Hawks' "History of the Episcopal Church in Virginia," pp. 153, 154.

eloquence, general usefulness, and the esteem in which they are held by the people, can be regarded as superior to the Episcopal clergy of the present·day in Virginia.[1] What a change! How wonderfully has all been overruled by God for good! Instead of perpetual wrangling with their parishioners and the law officers about the taxes on tobacco levied for their support, as was formerly the case, they are supported in a way hereafter to be detailed; I do not say extravantly or abundantly, but in general comfortably, by the contributions of their congregations. And instead of being disliked, to use no harsher term, I have reason to believe that they are universally respected, and even beloved, by the members of other churches.

In Maryland as well as Virginia, though in a much less degree, the dissolution of the union of church and state produced serious embarrassment and long-continued difficulty. In none of the colonies had the established clergy received such an ample maintenance as in Maryland. Their stipends were in many cases most liberal and ample for those days, so that to throw them at once on the voluntary support of their parishioners was a hazardous step, and for the time led to many cases of hardship. When the Revolution broke out there were twenty parishes on the eastern shore of the province, and twenty-four on the western; in all forty-four. Each of these had an incumbent, "though not always of the purest character,"[2] and at the close of the war in 1783, there were about eighteen or twenty remaining.[3] But if this diminution were owing at all to the dissolution of the union of church and state, it was so in but a small degree. The fact is, that about two-thirds of the established clergy were opposed to the war from its commencement, and refused to take the oath of allegiance to the new government, so that the greater part of them left the country. On the return

---

[1] This eulogy will not be thought extravagant by any one that has had opportunities of knowing them. I have had the privilege as well as the happiness of making the acquaintance of many of them, and have known many more by character through sources worthy of entire confidence. The late excellent bishop Moore was beloved by all who knew him. The present bishop, Dr. Meade, enjoys the confidence and esteem both of Christians and the world, in a higher degree than perhaps any other minister of the gospel in America. The professors in the diocesan Theological Seminary—the Rev. Drs. Keith, Lippitt, and Sparrow, are widely known and highly esteemed by all who know them.

[2] Dr. Hawks' "History of the Episcopal Church in Maryland."

[3] Ibid, p. 301.

of peace the Episcopal church gradually recovered from its depression, and ever since it has made pretty steady progress and been decidedly prosperous.   The late Dr. Clagget was appointed its first bishop in 1792, its convention was organised, and canons established, by which proper discipline was secured.   The clergy were for long less numerous than before the Revolution; not, however, for want of the means of supporting them, but for want of suitable men.   Some ministers did, indeed, leave their parishes, and the State itself, just after the war of the Revolution, and even so late as 1822, for want of support; but this was either before the churches had been sufficiently trained to the work of raising a maintenance for their ministers, or it arose from the churches being really too weak for the burden.   Maryland had fifty Episcopal clergymen in 1827; this number had risen to seventy-two in 1838, and a considerable proportion of the churches were still without ministers.   At no period of its establishment by the state was the Episcopal church of Maryland so prosperous as for some years back.   Not that in all cases the clergy are supported as they ought to be, or as they were during the union of church and state; but in point of talents and sound learning, combined with piety and other ministerial gifts, they are immeasurably superior to their predecessors before the Revolution.

In North and South Carolina, and in New York, though the disestablishment of the Episcopal churches, produced, as in other cases, a kind of syncope for a time,—from this they ere long recovered, and their prosperity is now incomparably greater than it ever was when they were supported by the state.   That in the State of New York may be said to have entered on its present career of extraordinary prosperity, with the election and consecration of the late Rev. Dr. John Henry Hobart, as bishop of the diocese, previous to which its churches and ministers were few in number compared with the present time.   Seldom has a church owed more to the energy and perseverance of one man.

But in no part of the United States was the proposal to disestablish the church received with more serious apprehension than in New England.   The language in which the celebrated Dr. Dwight, president of Yale college, and author of a very valuable system of theology, as well as other distinguished men of that State deprecated the measure, is still extant in pamphlets and in journals, and these have often been quoted in England by the friends, in opposition to the opponents of the church establishment there. But it ought to be known that not a single survivor at this day, of all who once wrote against the separation of church and state in Connecticut, has not long since seen that he was mistaken, and has not now found to be a blessing what he once regarded as a calamity, and had not Dr. Dwight died just as the change came into operation, no doubt, he, too, would have changed his opinion.[1] Twenty-five years have now elapsed since that time, and although I have been much in Connecticut during the last fifteen years, know many of the clergy, and have conversed much with them on the subject, out of the 200 or 300 once established ministers of that State, I am not aware of there being more than one Congregational minister in the State who would like to see the union of church and state restored in it. Indeed, the exception referred to, is probably the only one in the United States, among the Protestant ministers at least. Any others are most likely foreigners, who have not yet entered largely into the spirit of our institutions and our people. On no one point, I am confident, are the evangelical clergy of the United States, of all churches, more fully agreed than in holding that an union of church and state would prove one of the greatest calamities that could be inflicted on us, whatever it might prove in other countries. This is the very language I have heard a thousand times from our best and ablest men in speaking on the subject.

In Massachusetts, which was the last of the States to abolish the union of church and civil power, the change was adopted from a conviction of the evils, on the one side, resulting from the union in that State, and of the advantages, on the other side, that accrued more and more from its dissolution—a conviction that led all the evangelical denominations to combine

---

[1] The author has often conversed on this subject with the Rev. Lyman Beecher, D.D., who, when the change took place, was pastor of a church in Connecticut, but is now divinity professor in a theological seminary at Cincinnati, Ohio. Dr. Beecher was as much opposed to the dissolution as Dr. Dwight was, and both preached and wrote against it. But with characteristic candour he hesitates not now to confess that his apprehensions were quite unfounded. Few men rank higher in the United States than Dr. Beecher, whether as a preacher or as a writer.

for its overthrow. In fine, after ten years experience of the change, I apprehend not a single person of influence in all their ranks will be found to regret it.

And now, throughout the whole of the United States, truth stands on its own immutable vantage ground. So far as the civil power is concerned, there is not the slightest interference with the rights of conscience or with the religious worship of any one. Religious liberty, fettered by no state enactment, is as perfect as it can be. Nor is any sect or denomination of Christians favoured more than another. All depend, under God, for their support on the willing hearts and active hands of their friends, whilst the civil government, relieved from the ten thousand difficulties and embarrassments which a union of church and state would involve, has only to mete out justice with even scales to all the citizens, whatever may be their religious opinions and preferences.

CHAPTER V.

WHETHER THE GENERAL GOVERNMENT OF THE UNITED STATES HAS THE POWER TO PROMOTE RELIGION.

IT seems to be inferred by some that because the constitution declares that "congress shall make no law respecting an establishment of religion, or prohibiting the free exercise thereof;" [1] the general government can do nothing whatever to promote religion. This is certainly a mistake.

A great variety of opinions has been expressed by writers on public and political law on the question, How far any government has a right to interfere in religious matters; but that such a right exists to a certain extent is admitted by all of them. Nor can it be otherwise so long as religion shall be thought necessary to the well-being of society, and to the stability of government itself. It is essential to the interests of men, even

---

[1] First of the amendments to the Constitution.

in this world, that they should be neither ignorant of, nor indifferent to the existence, attributes, and providence, of one Almighty God, the Ruler of the universe; and, above all, a people that believe in Christianity can never consent that the government they live under should be indifferent to its promotion, since public as well as private virtue are connected indissolubly with a proper knowledge of its nature and its claims; and as the everlasting happiness of men depend upon its cordial reception.

On this subject it may be interesting to know the opinions of one of the most distinguished jurists in the United States, Mr. Justice Story, one of the judges of the supreme court:—

"The real difficulty lies in ascertaining the limits to which government may rightfully go in fostering and encouraging religion. Three cases may easily be supposed. One, where a government affords aid to a particular religion, leaving all persons free to adopt any other; another, where it creates an ecclesiastical establishment for the propagation of the doctrines of a particular sect of that religion, leaving a like freedom to all others; and a third, where it creates such an establishment, and excludes all persons not belonging to it, either wholly or in part, from any participation in the public honours, trusts, emoluments, privileges, and immunities, of the state. For instance, a government may simply declare that the Christian religion shall be the religion of the state, and shall be aided and encouraged in all the varieties of sects belonging to it; or it may declare, that the Catholic or Protestant religion shall be the religion of the state, leaving every man to the free enjoyment of his own religious opinions; or it may establish the doctrines of a particular sect, as of Episcopalians, as the religion of the state, with a like freedom; or it may establish the doctrines of a particular sect, as exclusively the religion of the state, tolerating others to a limited extent, or excluding all not belonging to it, from all public honours, trusts, emoluments, privileges, and immunities.

"Now, there will probably be found few persons in this, or any other Christian country, who would deliberately contend that it was unreasonable or unjust to foster and encourage the Christian religion generally as a matter of sound policy, as well as of revealed truth. In fact, every American colony, from its foundation down to the Revolution, with the exception of Rhode island, (if indeed, that State be an exception,) did openly, by the whole course of its laws and institutions, support and sustain, in some form, the Christian religion; and almost invariably gave a peculiar sanction to some of its fundamental doctrines. And this has continued to be the case in some States down to the present period, without the slightest suspicion that it was against the principles of public law or republican liberty.[1] Indeed, in a republic, there would seem to be a peculiar propriety in viewing the Christian religion as the great basis on which it must rest for its support and permanence, if it be, what it has ever been deemed by its truest friends to be, the religion of liberty. Montesquieu has remarked, that the Christian religion is a stranger to mere despotic power. The mildness so frequently recommended in the gospel, is incompatible with the despotic rage with which a prince punishes his subjects, and exercises himself in cruelty.[2] He has gone even further and affirmed, that the Protestant religion is far more congenial with the spirit of political freedom than the Catholic. "When," says he, "the Christian religion, two centuries ago, became unhappily divided into Catholic and Protestant, the people of the north embraced the Protestant, and those of the south still adhered to the Catholic. The reason is plain. The people of the north have, and ever will have, a spirit of liberty and independence which the people of the south have not. And therefore, a religion which has no visible head is more agreeable to the independency of climate than that which has one." [3] Without stopping to inquire whether this remark be well founded, it is certainly true that the parent country has acted upon it with a severe and vigilant zeal; and in most of the colonies the same rigid jealousy has been maintained almost down to our own times. Massachusetts, while she has promulgated in her BILL OF RIGHTS, the importance and necessity of the public support of religion, and the worship of God, has authorised the legislature to require it only for Protestantism. The language of that Bill of Rights is remarkable for its pointed affirmation

1 Kent's "Commentaries," sect. 34, pp. 35—37; Rawle " On the Constitution," chap. 10, pp. 121, 122.
2 Montesquieu, "Spirit of Laws," book 24, chap. 3.
3 Ibid. chap. 5.

of the duty of government to support Christianity, and the reasons for it. 'As,' says the third article, 'the happiness of a people, and the good order and preservation of civil government, essentially depend upon piety, religion, and morality; and as these cannot be generally diffused through the community but by the institution of the public worship of God, and of public instructions in piety, religion, and morality; therefore, to promote their happiness, and to secure the good order and preservation of their government, the people of this commonwealth have a right to invest their legislature with power to authorise, and require, and the legislature shall from time to time authorise and require the several towns, parishes, &c., &c., to make suitable provision at their own expense for the institution of the public worship of God, and for the support and maintenance of public *Protestant* teachers of piety, religion, and morality, in all cases where such provision shall not be made voluntarily.' Afterwards there follow provisions prohibiting any superiority of one sect over another, and securing to all citizens the free exercise of religion.

"Probably at the time of the adoption of the constitution, and of the amendment to it now under consideration, the general, if not the universal, sentiment in America was, that Christianity ought to receive encouragement from the state, so far as was not incompatible with the private rights of conscience and the freedom of religious worship. An attempt to level all religions, and to make it a matter of state policy to hold all in utter indifference, would have created universal disapprobation, if not universal indignation.

"It yet remains a problem to be solved in human affairs, whether any free government can be permanent where the public worship of God, and the support of religion, constitute no part of the policy or duty of the state in any assignable shape. The future experience of Christendom, and chiefly of the American States, must settle this problem, as yet new in the history of the world, abundant as it has been in experiments in the theory of government.

"But the duty of supporting religion, and especially the Christian religion, is very different from the right to force the consciences of other men, or to punish them for worshipping

God in the manner which they believe their accountability to him requires. It has been truly said, that 'religion, or the duty we owe to our Creator, and the manner of discharging it, can be dictated only by reason and conviction, not by force or violence.' [1] Mr. Locke himself, who did not doubt the right of government to interfere in matters of religion, and especially to encourage Christianity, at the same time has expressed his opinion of the right of private judgment, and liberty of conscience, in a manner becoming his character as a sincere friend of civil and religious liberty. ' No man, or society of men,' says he, ' have any authority to impose their opinions or interpretations on any other, the meanest Christian; since, in matters of religion, every man must know, and believe, and give an account, of himself.' [2] The rights of conscience are, indeed, beyond the just reach of any human power. They are given by God, and cannot be encroached upon by human authority, without a criminal disobedience of the precepts of natural as well as of revealed religion.

" The real object of this amendment was not to countenance, much less to advance Mahomedanism, or Judaism, or infidelity, by prostrating Christianity; but to exclude all rivalry among Christian sects, and to prevent any national ecclesiastical establishment which should give to an hierarchy the exclusive patronage of the national government. It thus cuts off the means of religious persecution (the vice and pest of former ages), and of the subversion of the rights of conscience in matters of religion, which had been trampled upon almost from the days of the apostles to the present age.[3] The history of the parent country had afforded the most solemn warnings and melancholy instructions on this head; [4] and even New England, the land of the persecuted Puritans, as well as other colonies where the Church of England had maintained its superiority, would furnish out a chapter as full of the darkest bigotry and intolerance as any which could be found to disgrace the pages of foreign annals. Apostacy, heresy, and nonconformity, had been stand-

1 Virginia Bill of Rights; 1 Tucker's Blackstone's Commentaries, Appendix, p. 296.
2 Lord King's " Life of John Locke," p. 373.
3 2 Lloyd's Debates, p. 195.
4 4 Blackstone's Commentaries, p. 41—59.

ard crimes for public appeals, to kindle the flames of persecution, and apologise for the most atrocious triumphs over innocence and virtue.

" It was under a solemn consciousness of the dangers from ecclesiastical ambition, the bigotry of spiritual pride, and the intolerance of sects, thus exemplified in our domestic as well as in foreign annals, that it was deemed advisable to exclude from the national government all power to act upon the subject. [1] The situation, too, of different States equally proclaimed the policy, as well as the necessity of such an exclusion. In some of the States, Episcopalians constituted the predominant sect; in others, Presbyterians; in others, Congregationalists; in others, Quakers; and in others, again, there was a close numerical rivalry among contending sects. It was impossible that there should not arise perpetual strife and perpetual jealousy on the subject of ecclesiastical ascendancy, if the national government were left free to create a religious establishment. The only security was in extirpating the power. But this alone would have been an imperfect security, if it had not been followed up by a declaration of the right of the free exercise of religion, and a prohibition (as we have seen) of all religious tests. Thus, the whole power over the subject of religion is left exclusively to the State governments, to be acted upon according to their own sense of justice and the State constitutions; and the Catholic and the Protestant, the Calvinist and the Armenian, the Jew and the infidel, may sit down at the common table of the national councils, without any inquisition into their faith or mode of worship." [2]

The preceding extracts from the learned commentator on the constitution of the United States, are sufficient to show that the general government is not restrained from promoting religion, though not allowed to make any religious establishment, or to do any thing for the purpose of aggrandising one denomination of Christians more than another.

There is also a manifest difference between legislating directly

[1] 2 Lloyd's Debates, p. 195—197.—" The sectarian spirit," said the late Dr. Corrie, " is uniformly selfish, proud, and unfeeling."—Edinburgh Review, April, 1832, p. 135.

[2] See Kent's Commentaries, lecture 24; Rawle on the Constitution, chap. 10, pp. 121, 122; 2 Lloyd's Debates, p. 195.

for religion as an end of jurisdiction, and keeping it respectfully in view whilst legislating for other ends, the legitimacy of which is not questioned; so that if we admit that the States alone could do the former, the general government might at least be competent to the latter, and in this way the harmony of the whole might be preserved.

But this restricted view of the case is not necessary. All that the constitution does is to restrain congress from making any law " respecting an establishment of religion, or prohibiting the free exercise of the same." Every thing that has no tendency to bring about an establishment of religion, or to interfere with the free exercise of religion, congress may do. And we shall see, hereafter, that this is the view of the subject taken by the proper authorities of the country.

CHAPTER VI.

WHETHER THE GOVERNMENT OF THE UNITED STATES MAY JUSTLY BE CALLED INFIDEL OR ATHEISTICAL.

Because no mention of the Supreme Being, or of the Christian religion, is to be found in the constitution of the United States, some have pronounced it infidel, others atheistical. But that neither opinion is correct will appear from a moment's consideration of the case.

Most certainly, the convention which framed the constitution in 1787, under the presidency of the immortal Washington, was of neither an infidel nor atheistical character. All the leading men in it were believers in Christianity, and Washington, as all the world knows, was a Christian. Several of the more prominent members were well known to be members of churches, and to live consistently with their profession. Even Franklin, who never avowed his religious sentiments, and cannot be said with certainty to have been an infidel, proposed at a time of great difficulty in the course of their proceedings, that a minister of the gospel should be invited to open their proceedings with prayer. Many members of the convention had been members also of the continental congress, which carried on the national government from the commencement of the Revolution until the new constitution went into effect. Now, the religious views of that congress we shall presently see from their acts.

The framers of that constitution seem, in fact, to have felt the necessity of leaving the subject of religion, as they left many things besides, to the governments of the several States composing the union. It was a subject on which these States had legislated from the very first. In many of them the Christian religion had been, and in some it still continued to be supported by law; in all it had been the acknowledged basis of their liberty and well-being, and its institutions had been protected by legal enactments. Nothing, accordingly, could be more natural in the convention than to deem the introduction of the subject unnecessary. There is yet another view of the subject.

"On this head," says an able writer, "as on others, the federal constitution was a compromise. Religion could not well be introduced into it for any purpose of positive regulation. There was no choice but to tolerate all Christian denominations, and to forbear entering into the particular views of any. Religion was likely to fare best in this way. Men, who loved it better than we do now-a-days, felt bound in prudence to leave it at once unaided and unencumbered by constitutional provisions, save one or two of a negative character. And they acted thus, not that it might be trodden under foot, the pearl among swine; but to the very end of its greater ultimate prevalence, its more lasting sway among the people." [1]

There is truth unquestionably in these remarks; still I am of opinion that the convention, whilst sensible that it were unwise to make religion a subject of legislation for the general government, thought that this, or even any mention of the thing at all, was unnecessary. The constitution was not intended for a people that had no religion, or that needed any legislation on the subject from the proposed general or national government; it was to be for a people already Christian, and

[1] "An Inquiry into the Moral and Religious Character of the American Government," p. 72.

whose existing laws, emanating from the most appropriate, or to say the least, the most convenient sources, gave ample evidence of their being favourable to religion. Their doing nothing positive on the subject seems, accordingly, to speak more loudly than if they had expressed themselves in the most solemn formulas on the existence of the Deity and the truth of Christianity. These were clearly assumed, being, as it were, so well known and fully acknowledged, as to need no specification in an instrument of a general nature, and designed for general objects. The Bible does not begin with an argument to prove the existence of God, but assumes the fact, as one the truth of which it needs no attempt to establish.

This view is confirmed by what is to be found in the constitution itself. From the reference to the Sabbath in article I., section 7, it is manifest that the framers of it believed that they were drawing up a constitution for a Christian people,—a people who valued and cherished a day associated, if I may so speak, with so large a portion of Christianity. Regarding the subject in connection with the circumstances that belong to it, I do not think that the government of the United States can justly be called either infidel or atheistical, on account of its federal constitution. The authors of that constitution never dreamt that they were to be regarded as treating Christianity with contempt, because they did not formally mention it as the law of the land, which it was already; much less that it should be excluded from the government. If the latter was intended, we shall presently see that their acts, from the very organisation of the government, belied any such intention.

Should any one, after all, regret that the constitution does not contain something more explicit on the subject, I cannot but say that I participate in that regret. Sure I am that had the excellent men who framed the constitution foreseen the inferences that have been drawn from the omission, they would have recognised in a proper formula the existence of God, and the truth and the importance of the Christian religion.

I conclude this chapter in the language of one who has ably treated this question. "Consistent with themselves, the people of 1787 meant by the federal arrangement nothing but a new and larger organisation of government on principles already

familiar to the country. The State governments were not
broad enough for national purposes, and the old confederation
was deficient in central power. It was only to remedy these
two defects, not of principle but of distributive adjustment, that
the public mind addressed itself: innovation, to any other end,
was never thought of; least of all, in reference to religion, a
thing utterly apart from the whole design. So that admitting
that the constitution framed on that occasion does not in terms
proclaim itself a Christian document, what then? Does it proclaim itself unchristian? For if it is merely silent in the matter, law and reason both tell us that its religious character is to
be looked for by interpretation among the people that fashioned
it; a people, Christian by profession and by genealogy; what
is more, by deeds of fundamental legislation that cannot deceive."[1]

CHAPTER VII.

THE GOVERNMENT OF THE UNITED STATES SHOWN TO BE CHRISTIAN BY ITS ACTS.

ANY doubts that the constitution of the United States may
suggest as to the Christian[2] character of the national government will be dissipated by a statement of facts.

In the first place, in transacting the affairs of the government, the sabbath is recognised, and respect for it enjoined; not
only so, but it is observed to a degree rarely witnessed in other
countries. All public business is suspended, unless in cases of
extreme necessity. Congress adjourns over the sabbath;[3] the

[1] " An Inquiry into the Moral and Religious Character of the American
Government," pp. 84, 85.
[2] When I speak of the Christian character of the government of the United
States, I mean that it is so far regulated by the Christian religion as to partake
of its spirit, and that is not infidel or opposed to Christianity—Christian as
those of England and other parts of Christendom are Christian—not that every
act of the government is truly conformable to the requirement of Christianity.
Alas! where shall we find a government whose acts are fully conformed to these?
[3] When the day for the adjournment of congress falls on Saturday, it sometimes happens, that on account of the accumulation of business the session is
protracted through the night into the early morning of the sabbath; for doing
which they fail not to be severely censured, as they deserve, by the religious,
and even by some of the secular journals.

courts do not sit; the custom houses, and all other public offices are shut, not only for a few hours, or a part of it, but during the whole day.

In the second place, the Christian character of the government is seen in the proclamations that have been made from time to time, calling on the people to observe days of fasting and prayer in times of national distress, and of thanksgiving for national or general mercies. Not a year passed during the war of the Revolution without the observance of such days. At the commencement of that war, the congress, in one of these proclamations, expressed its desire "to have the people of all ranks and degrees duly impressed with a solemn sense of God's superintending providence, and of their duty to rely in all their lawful enterprises on his aid and direction." The objects of a general fast are set forth: "that they may with united hearts confess and bewail their manifold sins and transgressions, and by a sincere repentance and amendment of life appease his righteous displeasure, and through the merits and mediation of Jesus Christ, obtain his pardon and forgiveness." A few months later we find the following language: "The congress do also in the most earnest manner, recommend to all the members of the United States, and particularly the officers, civil and military, under them, the exercise of repentance and reformation; and further require of them the strict observance of the articles which forbid profane swearing and all immoralities." And in 1777, the congress calls upon the nation "that with one heart and voice the good people may express the grateful feelings of their hearts, and consecrate themselves to the service of their divine Benefactor; and that together with their sincere acknowledgments and offerings, they may join the penitent confession of their manifold sins, whereby they have forfeited every favour, and their earnest supplication that it may please God, through the merits of Jesus Christ, mercifully to forgive and blot them out of remembrance; that it may please him graciously to afford his blessing on the governments of these states respectively, and prosper the public council of the whole; to inspire our commanders both by land and by sea, and all under them, with that wisdom and fortitude which may render them fit instruments, under the government of Almighty God, to secure to these United States the greatest of all blessings—independence and peace; that it may please him to prosper the trade and manufactures of the people, and the labour of the husbandman, that our land may yield its increase; to take schools and seminaries of education, so necessary for cultivating the principles of true liberty, virtue, and piety, under his nurturing hand; and to prosper the means of religion for the promotion and enlargement of that kingdom which consisteth in righteousness, peace, and joy in the Holy Ghost." In 1779, among other objects for which they call on the people to pray, we find the following: "that God would grant to his church the plentiful effusions of divine grace, and pour out his Holy Spirit on all ministers of the gospel; that he would bless and prosper the means of education, and spread the light of Christian knowledge through the remotest corners of the earth."

Similar language is found in the proclamations of 1780, 1781, and 1782. Such was the spirit which actuated the councils of the nation in the Revolution. And after the constitution had gone into effect, we find in the earlier period of its reign, that days of fasting and prayer for similar blessings were observed upon the invitation of congress. In 1812, when the last war with England broke out, we find congress using the following language: "It being a duty peculiarly incumbent in a time of public calamity and war, humbly and devoutly to acknowledge our dependence on Almighty God, and to implore his aid and protection, therefore resolved, that a joint committee of both houses wait on the president, and request him to recommend a day of public humiliation and prayer, to be observed by the people of the United States with religious solemnity, and the offering of fervent supplications to Almighty God for the safety of these States, and the speedy restoration of peace." And when the peace arrived, the same branch of the government called, in like manner, for a day of thanksgiving, which President Madison did not hesitate to recommend. And though President Jackson, I regret to say, had, as Mr. Jefferson had, scruples as to how far he was empowered by the constitution to appoint, or rather to recommend such days of fasting and prayer, and refused accordingly to do so at a time when it was most loudly called for by the circumstances of the nation, the present president, Mr. Tyler, hesitated not for a moment to call upon the people to observe such a day upon the death of the lamented President Harrison. And seldom has such a day been so remarkably observed in any country, the people flocking to their respective churches, and listening with profound attention to discourses suited to the affecting occasion. It was marked, in short, with the solemnity of a Sabbath. The nation felt that God, who had stricken down the man whom they had elevated so lately, and with such enthusiasm, to the presidency, was loudly calling upon them not to trust in " man whose breath is in his nostrils." The appointment of that fast was manifestly most acceptable to the nation at large.

In the third place, the general government has authorised the employment of chaplains in the army and navy, and at this moment there are such in all larger vessels of war.[1] If there are none in the army, it is because of the vicinity of most of the forts and garrisons to our churches, and the opportunities the men enjoy of hearing the gospel in them, or because the appointment of chaplains by a secretary of war is not likely to secure much good, and has not therefore been urged upon the government since the last war. There is always a chaplain, however, at the government military school at West Point, for the training of young officers. Moreover, the congress testifies

[1] I cannot avoid remarking, however, that the appointment of some ten or twelve chaplains in the navy, who, with the chaplain at the national military academy at West Point, are the only ministers of the gospel employed, as such, by the general government, very strikingly illustrates the incompetency of the civil power to manage spiritual matters. Most of the chaplains in the United States navy, with the exception of a few comparatively recent appointments, have been little qualified for labouring for the salvation of from 400 to 1200 men on board a ship of war. A secretary of the navy is seldom fitted to make the best selection for such a post. It would be better done if committed to some of the missionary societies, or to them in conjunction with the secretary. There have been no chaplains in the army, I believe, for twenty years, and I am inclined to think that the ministers in the vicinity of our forts and garrisons, and the missionary societies, have attended better to the spiritual interests of our officers and men than any department of the government could or would have done. The officers and men of a regiment have in some cases raised a sufficient sum among themselves for the employment of a missionary, for the greater part, or the whole of his time, to preach the gospel to them. Our forts and garrisons are often visited by ministers who volunteer to preach at certain stated times to the military stationed in them. Thus is the word of life made known to men who have devoted themselves to their country's service. It must be borne in mind that the national army has seldom numbered more than 6000 or 8000 men, until within the last four or five years, and that its present force of 14,000 is about to be reduced. It is an interesting fact that a very consider-able proportion of the officers are pious men, and do much good by holding reli-gious meetings in their respective regiments and companies.

to its interest in the Christian religion, and to its sense of its importance, by employing two chaplains, one for the senate and the other for the house of representatives, to open the sittings of these bodies every day with prayer, and who preach every Sabbath alternately, to the two houses convened in the hall of representatives, at twelve o'clock.

In the fourth place, the policy of the general government may be considered as Christian, inasmuch as it is directed, in a large measure, by a Christian spirit. As a people we have preferred peace to war; we have endeavoured to act with simple integrity and good faith to foreign nations. With few exceptions, the general government has acted fairly to the Indians on our borders, and in the instances in which it has been blamed, it is not easy to see how it could have acted otherwise. To avoid a civil war it has once or twice, perhaps, failed to act with sufficient promptitude in protecting them from their ruthless white invaders. But, generally speaking, its conduct towards the Indians has been mild and benevolent. From the times of Washington it has ever willingly lent its aid in promoting the introduction among them of the arts of civilised life; it has expended much money in doing so; and at this moment it is co-operating with our missionary societies, by giving them indirect but effectual aid in that quarter. But I shall have occasion to speak elsewhere of the conduct of the general government with respect to the Indians and slavery.

In the fifth place, the same spirit appears in what takes place in judicial affairs. As, first, the rejection of the oath of an atheist; second, the requiring of a belief in a future state of rewards and punishments, in order to the validity of a man's testimony; and, lastly, the administering of oaths on the Bible.

In the sixth place, this appears from the readiness shown by congress in making large grants of valuable public lands for the support of seminaries of learning, asylums for the deaf and dumb, and for hospitals, although aware that the institutions thus endowed were under the direction of decided Christians, who would give a prominent place in them to their religious views. This I could show by many facts, were it necessary.

But I have said enough, I trust, to prove that though the promotion of religion does not directly belong to the general government, but to the States, the former is neither hostile nor indifferent to the religious interests of the country. This, indeed, is not likely to be the case, so long at least as a large proportion of our public men entertain the respect they now show for religion. Such respect is the more interesting, as it can only flow from the spontaneous feelings of the heart. They are not tempted by any religious establishment to become the partisans of religion. Religion stands on its own basis, and seeks, not ineffectually, to win the respect and affections of all men by its own simple merits. Many of the national legislators are either members of the churches, or their warm supporters, whilst few among them are not believers in Christianity, or do not attend any sanctuary of the Most High on the Sabbath.

CHAPTER VIII.

THE GOVERNMENTS OF THE INDIVIDUAL STATES ORGANISED ON THE BASIS OF CHRISTIANITY.

AFTER considering the claims of the general government to be regarded as Christian in character, let us inquire how far the individual States, and particularly the original thirteen, are entitled to the same distinction, confining ourselves in this chapter to the evidence supplied by their earliest constitutions or fundamental laws, which were mostly made during, or shortly after, the Revolution.

Virginia was unquestionably a Christian State, but her constitution is silent on the subject. It was drawn up under the eye of one of the greatest enemies that Christianity has ever had to contend with in America; but although he had influence enough to prevent the religion which he hated from being mentioned in the constitution of Virginia, he could not obliterate all traces of it from her laws.

Connecticut and Rhode island had adopted no constitutions of their own when that of the United States was framed. The latter of these two States has been governed to this day by the charter granted by Charles II. Both States were of Puritan origin, and the charters of both were based on Christian principles. The first constitution of New York dates from 1777. It strongly guarded the rights of conscience and religious worship. It excluded the clergy from public offices of a secular nature, on the express ground that "by their profession they were dedicated to the service of God and to the cure of souls," and "ought not to be diverted from the great duties of their functions."

The constitution of New Jersey, as originally framed in 1776, besides guaranteeing to every one the "inestimable privilege of worshipping Almighty God in a manner agreeable to the dictates of his own conscience," declared that "all persons professing a belief in the faith of any Protestant sect, and who should demean themselves peaceably under the government, should be capable of being members of either branch of the legislature, and should fully and freely enjoy every privilege and immunity enjoyed by others, their fellow-citizens." Whatever may be thought of the style of this instrument, it cannot be denied that it favoured the professors of Protestant Christianity.

The constitution of New Hampshire, after laying it down that "every individual has a natural and inalienable right to worship God according to the dictates of his conscience and his reason," says, "that morality and piety, rightly grounded on evangelical principles, would give the best and greatest security to government, and would lay in the hearts of men the strongest obligations to due subjection;" and again, "that the knowledge of these was most likely to be propagated by the institution of the public worship of the Deity, and public instruction in morality and religion;" therefore to promote these important purposes, the "towns" are empowered to adopt measures for the support and maintenance of "public Protestant teachers of piety, religion, and morality." Although the towns are still authorised to take measures for the support of public worship, that is no longer accomplished by a general assessment.

The first constitution of Massachusetts was framed in 1780. In it we find the following language: "That as the happiness of a people, and the good order and preservation of civil government, essentially depend upon piety, religion, and morality; and as these cannot be generally diffused through a community but by the institution of the public worship of God, and of public instruction in piety, religion, and morality: therefore, to promote their happiness, and to secure the good order and pre- servation of their government, the people of this commonwealth have a right to invest their legislature with power to authorise and require, and the legislature shall from time to time author- ise and require the several towns, parishes, precincts, and other bodies politic, or religious societies, to make suitable provision, at their own expense, for the institution of the public worship of God, and for the support and maintenance of public Protes- tant teachers of piety, religion, and morality, in all cases where such provision shall not be made voluntarily: and the people of this commonwealth have also a right to, and do, invest their legislature with authority to enjoin upon all the subjects an attendance upon the instructions of the public teachers, as afore- said, at stated times and seasons, if there be any one whose instructions they can conscientiously attend." It was also ordained, that "because a frequent recurrence to the funda- mental principles of the constitution, and a constant adherence to those of piety, justice, moderation, temperance, industry, and frugality, are absolutely necessary to preserve the advantages of liberty, and to maintain a free government, the people ought consequently to have a particular regard to all those principles in the choice of their officers and representatives; and they have a right to require of their lawgivers and magistrates an exact and constant observance of them in the formation and execution of all laws necessary for the good administration of the commonwealth." And, lastly, it was prescribed that every person " chosen governor, lieutenant-governor, senator, or repre- sentative, and accepting the trust," shall subscribe a solemn profession " that he believes the Christian religion, and has a firm persuasion of its truth."

The constitution of Maryland, made in 1776, empowers the legislature "to lay a general tax for the support of the Christian religion," and declares "that all persons professing the Christian religion are equally entitled to protection in their religious liberty."   All tests are disallowed, excepting these: an oath of office; an oath of allegiance; "and a declaration of a belief in the Christian religion."

The first constitution of Pennsylvania, made in the same year, requires that every member of the legislature shall make this solemn declaration: "I do believe in one God, the Creator and Governor of the universe, the rewarder of the good and the punisher of the wicked; and I do acknowledge the scriptures of the Old and New Testaments to be given by divine inspiration."

The constitution of Delaware, made at the same period, premises: "that all men have a natural and inalienable right to worship God according to the dictates of their own consciences and understandings;" and declares, "that all persons professing the Christian religion, ought for ever to enjoy equal rights and privileges." In relation to the members of the legislature, it enjoins, that every citizen, who shall be chosen a member of either houses of the legislature, or appointed to any other public office, shall be required to subscribe the following declaration: "I do profess faith in God the Father, and in Jesus Christ his only Son, and the Holy Ghost, one God, blessed for evermore; and I do acknowledge the holy scriptures of the Old and New Testament to be given by divine inspiration."

The constitution of North Carolina, made about the same period, declares expressly, "that no person who should deny the being of God, or the truth of the Protestant religion, or the divine authority of either the Old or New Testament, or who should hold religious principles incompatible with the freedom and safety of the State, should be capable of holding any office or place of trust in the civil government of the State."

But the constitution of South Carolina, made in 1778, was the most remarkable of all. It directs the legislature at its regular meeting, to "choose by ballot from among themselves, or from the people at large, a governor and commander-in-chief. a lieutenant-governor and privy council, all of the Protestant religion." It prescribes that no man shall be eligible to either the senate or house of representatives, "unless he be of the Protestant religion." And in a word, it ordains "that the Christian religion be deemed, and is hereby constituted and declared to be, the established religion of the land."

Provision was also made for the incorporation, maintenance,

and government of such "societies of Christian Protestants" as choose to avail themselves of laws for the purpose, and required that every such society should first agree to, and subscribe in a book the five following articles:—

"First, That there is one eternal God, and a future state of rewards and punishments.

"Second, That God is publicly to be worshipped.

"Third, That the Christian religion is the true religion.

Fourth, That the holy scriptures of the Old and New Testament are of divine inspiration, and are the rule of faith and practice.

Fifth, That it is lawful, and the duty of every man, being thereunto called by those who govern, to bear witness to the truth."

Even more than this; the conscript fathers who made the constitution of South Carolina, went on to declare: "that to give the state sufficient security for the discharge of the pastoral office, no person shall officiate as a minister of any established church, who shall not have been chosen by a majority of the society to which he shall minister, nor until he shall have made and subscribed the following declaration, over and above the aforesaid five articles; viz. "That he is determined by God's grace, out of the holy scriptures to instruct the people committed to his charge, and to teach nothing as required of necessity to eternal salvation, but that which he shall be persuaded may be concluded and proved from the scriptures; that he will use both public and private admonitions, as well to the sick as to the whole within his cure, as need shall require and occasion be given; that he will be diligent in prayers and in reading of the holy scriptures, and in such studies as help to the knowledge of the same; that he will be diligent to frame and fashion his own self and his family according to the doctrine of Christ, and to make both himself and them, as much as in him lay, wholesome examples and patterns of the flock of Christ; that he will maintain and set forward, as much as he can, quietness, peace, and love, among all people, and especially among those committed to his charge."

Who does not recognise in this constitution the spirit of the old Huguenot confessions of faith, and of the synods of France which those who had been persecuted in the Gallican kingdom had carried with them to the new world?

The constitution of Georgia, made in 1777, says: "Every officer of the State shall be liable to be called to account by the house of assembly," and that all the members of that house "shall be of the Protestant religion."

Such was the character of the state constitutions in the opening scenes of our national existence. Of all the thirteen original States, the organic laws of one alone did not expressly enjoin the Christian religion, and almost without exception, the Protestant form of Christianity. But even Virginia was, in fact, as much Christian as any of them. From all this the reader will see how the nation set out on its career. It was, in every proper sense of the word, a Christian nation. And though the constitutions of the old States have since been deprived of what was exclusive in regard to religion, and the political privileges of the Protestants are extended to the Roman Catholics without any exception that I am aware of, yet the legislative action of those States, as well as that of the new, is still founded on Christianity, and is as favourable as ever to the promotion of the Christian religion. I am not sure whether the Jew has equal privileges with the professor of Christianity in every State, but these he certainly has in most of them, and he has everywhere the right to worship God publicly, according to the rites of his religion. In some States he holds offices of trust and influence, the law opening to him as well as others access to such offices. Thus in the city of New York, at this moment, a descendant of Abraham, who was formerly sheriff of that city, is a judge of one of the courts, and discharges its duties faithfully and acceptably. Jews form but a small body in America, and as they hold what may be called the basis of the Christian religion, worship God according to the Old Testament, and believe in a future state of rewards and punishments, such a modification of the laws as should place them on the same footing with Christians, as respects political privileges, was not deemed too latitudinarian or unsafe. They surely have as good a claim to be considered fit to become members of a government founded on the religion of the Bible, as Unitarians can pretend to, and hold safer principles than the Universalists.

I conclude by saying, in a few words, that the State governments were founded on Christianity, and almost without exception, on Protestant Christianity.   In the progress of opinion on the subject of religious liberty, every thing that looked like an interference with the rights of conscience in any sect was laid aside, and all men whose religious principles were not thought subversive of the great moral principles of Christianity, were admitted to a full participation in civil privileges and immunities.   This is the present position of the governments of the several States in the American union.   Their legislation, while it avoids oppressing the conscience of any sect of religionists, is still decidedly favourable, in general, to the interests of Christianity; the unchristian element, if I may so term it, is too insignificant, taking the country as a whole, to exert an influence of any importance on the national legislation.

CHAPTER IX.

THE LEGISLATION OF THE STATES SHOWN TO BE IN FAVOUR OF CHRISTIANITY.

We have said that the organic laws of the State governments have been so far modified, as to extend political rights to citizens of all shades of religious opinions; that in every State the rights of conscience are guaranteed to all men; and in these respects the whole twenty-six States and three Territories composing the American union, are at one.   But we must not be understood as meaning thereby, that irreligion and licentiousness are also guaranteed by the organic laws, or by any laws whatever. This would be absurd.   Rights of conscience are religious rights, that is, rights to entertain and utter religious opinions, and to enjoy public religious worship.   Now this expression even in its widest acceptation, cannot include irreligion; opinions contrary to the nature of religion, subversive of the reverence, love, and service due to God, of virtue, morality, and good manners.   What rights of conscience can atheism, irreligion, or licentiousness, pretend to?   It may not be prudent to disturb them in their private

s

haunts and secret retirements.   There let them remain and hold
their peace.   But they have no right by any law in the United
States, that I am aware of, to come to propagate opinions, and
proselytise.   Such attempts, on the contrary, are everywhere
opposed by the laws, and if, at times, these laws are evaded, or
their enforcement intentionally intermitted, this does not proceed from any question of their being just, but from a conviction
that, in some circumstances, it is the least of two evils not to
enforce them.   It is sometimes the best way to silence a noisy
brainless lecturer on atheism, to let him alone, and the immoral
conduct of some preachers of unrighteousness is the best refu-
tation of their impious doctrines.   At times, however, another
course must be pursued.   The publication of licentious books
and pictures, profane swearing, blasphemy, obscenity, the interruption of public worship, and such like offences, are punishable
by the laws of every State in the American union.   Now, whence
had these laws their origin, or where do we find their sanction?
Take the laws against profane swearing.   Where did men learn
that that is an offence against which the laws should level its
denunciations?   Surely from the Bible and no where else

Not more than one State, if even one, is supposed to have no
laws for the due observance of the sabbath.   But whence came
such regulations?   From the light of nature?   From the conclusions of human wisdom?   Has philosophy ever discovered
that one day in seven should be consecrated to God?   I am
aware that experience, and a right knowledge of the animal economy, show that the law setting apart one day in seven is good,
favourable to human happiness, and merciful to the beasts of
burden.   But the sabbath is of God, and putting aside some dim
traditions and customs among nations near the spot where the
divine command respecting it was first given to Moses, or of the
people in whose code it afterwards held a permanent place—we
find it only in the Bible.

But it is not only by the statute law of the United States
that such offences are forbidden; they are punishable likewise
under the common law which has force in those States as well
as in England.   Of this admirable part of the civil economy,
Christianity is not merely an inherent, it is a constituent part.
This, though denied by Mr. Jefferson, Dr. Cooper, and others,

has been so decided by many of the ablest judges in the land. For it has been held, that whilst the abolition of religious establishments in the United States, necessarily abolishes that part of the common law which attaches to them in England, it does nothing more, and thus many offences still remain obnoxious to it on the ground of their being contrary to the Christian religion.

A person was indicted at New York, in 1811, for aspersing the character of Jesus Christ, and denying the legitimacy of his birth. He was tried, condemned, fined, and imprisoned. On that trial chief Justice Kent, still living, and thought second to none in the country in point of legal knowledge, expressed himself as follows:—

" The people of this State, in common with the people of this country, profess the general doctrines of Christianity as the rule of their faith and practice; and to scandalise the Author of these doctrines is not only, in a religious point of view, extremely impious, but, even in respect to the obligations due to society, is a gross violation of decency and good order. Nothing could be more offensive to the virtuous part of the community, or more injurious to the tender morals of the young, than to declare such profanity lawful. It would go to confound all distinction between things sacred and profane." " No government," he maintained, " among any of the polished nations of antiquity, and none of the institutions of modern Europe (a single monitory case excepted), ever hazarded such a bold experiment upon the solidity of the public morals, as to permit with impunity, and under the sanction of their tribunals, the general religion of the community to be openly insulted and defamed." " True," he adds, " the constitution has discarded religious establishments. It does not forbid judicial cognisance of those offences against religion and morality which have no reference to any such establishment, or to any particular form of government, but are punishable because they strike at the root of moral obligation, and weaken the security of the social ties. To construe it as breaking down the common-law barriers against licentious, wanton, and impious attacks upon Christianity itself, would be an enormous perversion of its meaning." [1]

[1] Dr. Johnson's " Reports," p. 290.

These just opinions were fully sustained by the decision pronounced in Pennsylvania, at the trial of a man indicted for blasphemy, not against God directly, but against the Bible; the design charged upon him being that of "contriving and intending to scandalise and bring into disrepute and vilify the Christian religion and the scriptures of truth." On that occasion the late Judge Duncan said, that "even if Christianity were not a part of the law of the land, it is the popular religion of the country; an insult to which would be indictable as tending to disturb the public peace;" and added, "that no society can tolerate a wilful and despiteful attempt to subvert its religion." [1]

The application of the common law, by the courts of Pennsylvania, to the protection of clergymen living in the discharge of their official duties, confirms all that has been said respecting the light in which Christianity is regarded by the State governments.

Further, every State has laws for the protection of all religious meetings from disturbance, and these are enforced when occasion requires. Indeed, I am not aware of any offence that is more promptly punished by the police than interfering with religious worship, whether held in a church, in a private house, or even in the forest.

All the States have laws for the regulation of church property, and of that devoted to religious uses. In some States every religious body, immediately on being organised, is pronounced *de facto* incorporated; and in none, generally, is there any difficulty in procuring an act of incorporation, either for churches or benevolent societies.

No State allows the oath of an atheist to be received in a court of justice, and in one only, in so far as I am aware, is that of a disbeliever in a *future* state of rewards and punishments received as evidence. That State is New York, where the law requires simply the belief in a state of rewards and punishments; in other words, if a man believes that there is a God who punishes men for evil actions, and rewards them for their good ones, whether in this world or in that which is to come, his oath

[1] 11 Sergeant and Rawle's Reports, p. 394.

will be received in a court of justice. Of course, the man who believes neither in the existence of God, nor in any sort of divine punishment, cannot be sworn, nor his testimony be allowed, in a court in that State.

CHAPTER X.

THE LEGISLATION OF THE STATES OFTEN BEARS INCIDENTALLY ON THE CAUSE OF RELIGION.

IF there be no established church in any of the States at the present time, it is not, as we have shown, from any want of power in the States to create such an establishment, but because it has been found inexpedient to attempt promoting religion in that way. Experience has shown that with us all such establishments are, upon the whole, more injurious than beneficial. They have been renounced because, from the nature of the case, they could never be made to operate in such a way as not to do some injustice to one portion or other of the citizens.

To this general conviction we must ascribe what appears at first sight to be an anomaly; the power to aid religion by legal enactment expressly conferred, in the constitutions of some of the States,[1] and yet that power suffered to lie dormant, nor is there the least prospect of its ever being exercised again. But although the States have thought it best for the interests of religion itself, as well as most equitable to all classes of the inhabitants, to relinquish all attempts to promote religion by what is called an establishment, yet they have deemed it neither unwise nor unjust, to pursue the same end indirectly. Several instances of this kind have been stated already; we may notice a few more.

The States do much to promote education in all its stages, though in doing so, they often assist the cause of religion, in what might be considered almost the most direct manner possible.

---

[1] Maryland, New Hampshire, and South Carolina.

For instance, they aid colleges directed by religious men, and that, too, without stipulating for the slightest control over these institutions. On this we shall yet have occasion to speak more at large, and we introduce it here merely to indicate what the States are thus doing for Christianity in the way of concurrence with other bodies. Some States have given considerable sums to endow colleges at the outset. Others contribute annually to their support, and this while well aware that the colleges aided by such grants are under a decided religious influence. So is it also with the academies, of which there are several even in the smallest States, and many in the largest. Young men are instructed in the classics and mathematics at these, preparatory to being sent to college, and as many of them are conducted by ministers of the gospel and other religious men, they are nurseries of vast importance for both the church and the state.

Again, by promoting primary schools, the States co-operate in promoting religion; for mere intellectual knowledge, although not religion, greatly facilitates its diffusion by means of books. In the six New England States, it is long since provision was first made by law for the good education of every child whose parents choose to avail themselves of it; and, accordingly, hardly is there an adult native of those States to be found who cannot read. Some uneducated persons there are, especially in Maine, New Hampshire, and Rhode island, but they are few compared with what may be found in other lands. In all the six States, except Connecticut, each " town" is required to assess itself for as many schools as it may need. Connecticut has a school fund of above 2,000,000 dollars, yielding an annual revenue of above 112,000 dollars, and this maintains schools in every school district of the State. In New York, Pennsylvania, and Ohio, there are efficient primary school systems in operation, supported by law, and capable of supplying all the youth with education. The State support consists partly of the interest of permanent State funds set apart for the purpose, partly of money raised on each of the townships by assessment. The systems pursued in New Jersey and Delaware, though less efficient, are highly useful. Efforts are making in several of the western States to introduce a like provision, and a good deal is done in the southern States to educate the children of the poor, by means of funds set apart for the purpose.

The instruction given in the primary schools of the United States depends for its character upon the teachers. Where these are pious, they find no difficulty in giving a great deal of religious instruction; where they are not so, but little instruction is given that can be called religious. The Bible is read in most of the schools.

Several of the States have liberally contributed to the establishment of asylums for the deaf and dumb, and for the blind, almost all of which institutions are under a decidedly religious influence. The governments of several States containing large cities, have done much in aid of the efforts of philanthropic individuals and associations, for establishing retreats or houses of refuge, where young offenders and others who have not gone hopelessly astray, may be placed for reformation. These institutions have been greatly blessed.

Before concluding my remarks on the indirect bearing of the state legislation in America upon religion, I have a few words to say on one or two subjects connected with religion, but different from those already mentioned. One is marriage, which, with us, is in a great degree a civil institution, regulated by the laws of each State, prescribing how it should be performed. In so far as it is a contract between the parties, under proper circumstances of age, consent of friends, sufficient number of witnesses, &c., it has, with us, no necessary connection with religion. In all of the States it may take place, if the parties choose, before a regularly ordained minister of the gospel, and be accompanied with religious services. The civil power decides within what degrees of consanguinity and affinity it may take place. On this point, and this mainly, can any collision take place between the ecclesiastical and civil authorities. For instance, the general assembly of the Presbyterian church has lately decided, or rather repeated a decision given indirectly some years ago, that a man may not marry his deceased wife's sister, and pronounced all such marriages to be contrary to the scripture and incestuous. Such marriages, on the other hand, are expressly allowed by the laws of Connecticut, and probably are not forbidden by those of any other State. In all cases of this kind, a man must make his election which he will obey—the church or the state. As condemnation by the former subjects a man to no civil penalties, all that he can suffer is excommunication.

As for divorces, they are wholly regulated by the civil government, and fall within the jurisdiction of the States. In some, they are allowed for very few causes; much more looseness of practice prevails in others. In South Carolina, I understand that no divorce has been granted since it became a State. In some States it belongs to the legislatures to grant divorces, and in others to the courts of law.

What are called mixed marriages, or marriages betwixt Protestants and Roman Catholics, which have given rise to so much trouble of late in some countries of Europe, occasion no difficulty with us. Marriage, by our laws, being a civil contract held valid at common law, whenever the consent of the parties, supposing there is no legal impediment, is expressed in a way that admits of proof. The refusal of a priest to grant his nuptial benediction, or the sacrament of marriage, except upon conditions to which the parties might not be willing to agree, would be of little consequence. They have only to go to the civil magistrate, and they will be married without the slightest difficulty. No Roman Catholic priest, or Protestant minister, in the United States, would dare to refuse to perform the ceremony of marriage, unless for most justifiable reasons; for if he did, he would soon hear of it through the press, which is with us an instrument for correcting any little instances of tyranny or injustice, with which any man, no matter who, may think fit to annoy persons placed in any sense under his authority.

CHAPTER XI.

IN WHAT CASES THE ACTION OF THE CIVIL AUTHORITY MAY BE DIRECTED IN REFERENCE
TO RELIGION.

BESIDES the incidental bearing which the legislation of the individual States has upon religion, and which sometimes comes not
a little to its help, there are cases in which the civil authority
intervenes more directly, not in settling points of doctrine, but
in determining questions of property; and these are by no means
of rare occurrence where there are conflicting claims in individual churches. This indeed has happened twice at least, in
reference to property held by large religious denominations.
The first of these cases occurred in New Jersey, and on that
occasion the courts decided upon the claims to certain property,
urged by the Orthodox and the Hicksites, two bodies into which
the Society of Friends, or Quakers, have been divided throughout
the United States. And although the trial took place in a local
cause, or rather for a local claim, yet the principle upon which
it was decided, affected all the property held by Quaker societies
in the State.

The second case occurred recently in Pennsylvania, where
the supreme court had to decide upon the claims of the old and
new school, to certain property belonging to the general assembly of the Presbyterian church, on its being divided into two
separate bodies, each of which assumed the name of the Presbyterian church. Here the court had of necessity to decide which
of the two ought by law to be considered the true representative
and successor of the Presbyterian church before its division.
The decision, however, did not rest on doctrinal grounds, but
wholly on the acts of the bodies themselves, the court refusing
to take up the question of doctrines at all, as not being within
their province. Not so in the case of the Quakers just referred
to. There the court considered the question of doctrine, in
order to determine which body was the true Society of Friends.

I apprehend that I have now said enough to place the nature

of the mutual relations between church and state in America fairly before the reader, and will dismiss the subject by giving some extracts from a communication which the Hon. Henry Wheaton, ambassador from the United States to the court of Berlin, has had the goodness to address to me, and which presents, in some respects, a résumé, or summary of what may be said on this subject:—

"In answer to your first query, I should say that the state does not view the Christian church as a rival or an enemy; but rather as an assistant or co-worker in the religious and moral instruction of the people, which is one of the most important duties of civil government.

"It is not true that the church is treated as a *stranger* by the state.

"There are ample laws in all the States of the American union for the observance of the sabbath, the securing of church property, and the undisturbed tranquillity of public worship by every variety of Christian sects. The law makes no distinction among these sects, and gives to no one the predominance over the others. It protects all equally, and gives no political privileges to the adherent of one over those of another sect.

"The laws of the several States authorise the acquisition and holding of church property, under certain limitations as to value, either by making a special corporation for that purpose, or through the agency of trustees empowered under general regulations for that purpose. Without going into detail on this subject, it is enough to say, that they proceed upon the principle of allowing the church to hold a sufficient amount of real and personal property to enable it to perform its appropriate functions, and at the same time to guard against abuse, by allowing too great an amount of wealth to be perpetually locked up in *mortmain* by grants and testamentary dispositions *ad pios usus*. In some of the States of the union the English statute of mortmain has been introduced, by which religious corporations are disabled from acquiring real property unless by special licence of the government. In others, the capacity to acquire it is regulated and limited by the special acts of legislation incorporating religious societies. The ecclesiastical corporations existing before the Revolution, which separated the United States from the parent country, continue to enjoy the rights and property which they had previously held under acts of parliament, or of the provincial legislatures.

"Blasphemy is punished as a criminal offence by the laws of the several States.

"Perjury is, in like manner, punished as a crime; the *form* of administering the oath being accommodated to the conscientious views of different religious sects. The Quakers are allowed to *affirm* solemnly; the Jews swear upon the scriptures of the Old Testament only; and certain. Christian sects with the uplifted hand.

"There has been much discussion among our jurists as to how the oath of infidels ought to be considered in courts of justice. But, so far as I recollect, the general result is to reject the oath of such persons only as deny the being of God, or a future state of rewards and punishments, without absolutely requiring a belief in revealed religion.

"The laws regulating marriage with us are founded on the precepts of Christianity; hence polygamy is absolutely forbidden, and punished as a crime under the denomination of bigamy. Marriages between relations by blood in the ascending or descending lines, and between collaterals in the first degree, are absolutely forbidden in all the States; and in some, all marriages within the Levitical degrees are also forbidden.

"The common law of England, which requires consent merely, without any particular form of solemnization, to render a marriage legally valid, is adopted in those States of the American union which have not enacted special legislative statutes on the subject. In some of the States marriage is required to be solemnized in the presence of a clergyman or magistrate.

"All our distinguished men, so far as I know, are Christians of one denomination or other. A great reaction has taken place within the last thirty years against the torrent of infidelity, let in by the superficial philosophy of the eighteenth century.

"I believe the separation of church and state is, with us, considered almost, if not universally, as a blessing."

With these extracts which give the views of one of the most distinguished statesmen and diplomatists of America, and which confirm the positions we have advanced on all the points to which they refer, we close our remarks on the existing relations between the church and state in that country.

————

CHAPTER XII.

WE have now arrived at the close of the third book of this work.

We have traced the religious character of the early colonists who settled in America; the religious establishments which they planted; the happy and the unhappy influences of those establishments; their overthrow and its consequences; and, finally, the relations which have subsisted betwixt the churches and the civil governments since the Revolution. We are now about to enter upon the consideration of the resources which the churches have developed, since they have been compelled to look, in dependence upon God's blessing, to their own exertions instead of relying on the arm of the state.

A review of the ground which we have gone over may be given almost in the very words of an able author, to whom we have been repeatedly indebted.

1. The first settlers of the United States went to it as Christians, and with strong intent to occupy the country in that character.

2. The lives they lived there, and the institutions they set up, were signalised by the spirit and doctrine of the religion they professed.

3. The same doctrine and spirit, descending upon the patriots of the federal era, entered largely into the primary State constitutions of the republic, and, if analogy can be trusted, into the constructive meaning of the federal charter itself.

4. Christianity is still the popular religion of the country.

5. And, finally, notwithstanding some untoward acts of individual rulers, it is to this day, though without establish-

ments, and with equal liberty to men's consciences, the religion of the laws and of the government. If records tell the truth; if annals and documents can outweigh the flippant rhetoric of licentious debate; our public institutions carry still the stamp of their origin: the memory of better times is come down to us in solid remains; the monuments of the fathers are yet standing; and, blessed be God, the national edifice continues visibly to rest upon them.[1]

[1] " An Inquiry into the Moral and Religious Character of the American Government," pp. 139, 140.

BOOK IV.

CHAPTER I.

THE VOLUNTARY PRINCIPLE THE GREAT ALTERNATIVE.—THE NATURE AND VASTNESS OF
ITS MISSION.

THE reader has remarked the progress of religious liberty in the United States, from the first colonisation of the country until the present time; and traced the effects of its successive developements in modifying the relations between the churches and the state.

He has seen that when that country began to be settled by European emigrants in the beginning of the seventeenth century, freedom of conscience and the rights of the immortal mind, were but little understood in the old world. Those even who fled to the new world to enjoy this greatest of all earthly blessings, had but an imperfect apprehension of the subject and of its bearings. That which they so highly prized for themselves, and for the attainment of which they had made such sacrifices, they were unwilling to accord to others.

Not that men were not allowed in every colony to entertain whatever opinions they chose on the subject of religion, if they did not endeavour to propagate them when contrary to those of the established church, where one existed. In the colonies where the greatest intolerance existed, men were compelled to attend the national church, but they were not required, in order to be allowed a residence, to make a profession of the established faith. This was the lowest amount possible of religious liberty.

Low as it is, however, it is not yet enjoyed by the native inhabitants of Italy, and some other Roman Catholic countries.

But it was not long before a step in advance was made by Virginia and Massachusetts, of all the colonies the most rigid in their views of the requirements of a church establishment. Private meetings of dissenters for the enjoyment of their own modes of worship began to be tolerated.

A second step was to grant to such dissenters express permission to hold public meetings for worship, without releasing them, however, from their share of the taxes to support the established church.

The third step which religious freedom made, consisted in relieving dissenters from the established church—from the burden of contributing in any way to its support.

And finally, the fourth and great step was to abolish altogether the support of any church by the state, and place all of every name on the same footing before the law, leaving each church to support itself by its own proper exertions.

Such is the state of things at present, and such it will remain. In every state liberty of conscience and liberty of worship is complete. The government extends protection to all. Any set of men who wish to have a church or place of worship of their own, can have it if they choose to erect or hire a building at their own charges. Nothing is required but to comply with the terms which the law prescribes in relation to holding property for public uses. The proper civil authorities have nothing to do with the creed of those who open such a place of worship. They cannot offer the smallest obstruction to the opening of a place of worship any where, if those who choose to undertake it comply with the simple terms of the law in relation to such property.

Nor can the police authorities interfere to break up a meeting, unless it can be proved to be a nuisance to the neighbourhood by the disturbance which it occasions, or on account of the immoral practices which may be committed — not on account of the particular religious faith which may be there taught. All improper meddling with a religious meeting, no matter whether it is held in a church or in a private house, would not be tolerated.

On the other hand, as we have shown, neither the general government nor that of the States does any thing directly for the maintenance of public worship. Religion is protected and indirectly aided, as has been proved, by both; but no where does the civil power defray the expenses of the churches, or pay the salaries of ministers of the gospel, excepting in the case of a few chaplains connected with the public service.

Upon what then must religion rely? Only, under God, upon the efforts of its friends, acting from their own free will, influenced by that variety of considerations which are ordinarily comprehended under the title of a desire to do good. This, in America, is the grand and only alternative. To this principle must the country look for all those efforts which must be made for its religious instruction. To the consideration of its action, and the developement of its resources, the Book upon which we now enter is devoted.

Let us look for a moment at the work which, under God's blessing, has to be accomplished by this instrumentality.

The population of the United States in 1840, was, by the census, ascertained to be 17,068,666 souls. At present, (November 1842,) it is not far short of 18,000,000; say that it is 17,500,000. Upon the voluntary principle alone depends the religious instruction of this entire population, embracing the thousands of churches and ministers of the gospel, colleges, theological seminaries, sunday schools, missionary societies, and all the other instrumentalities that are employed to promote the knowledge of the gospel from one end of the country to the other. Upon the mere unconstrained good will of the people, and especially of those among them who love the Saviour and profess his name, does this vast superstructure rest. Those may tremble for the result who do not know what the human mind is capable of doing when left to its own energies, moved and sustained by the grace and the love of God.

Still more; not only must all the good that is now doing in that vast country, and amid more than 17,000,000 of souls, be continued by the voluntary principle, but the increasing demands of a population augmenting in a ratio to which the history of the world furnishes no parallel, must be met and supplied. And what this will require may be conceived when we state the fact that the annual increase of the population during the decade from 1840 to 1850 cannot be short of 500,000 upon an average! From 1790 to 1800, the annual increase of the inhabitants of the country was 137,609; from 1800 to 1810 it was 193,388; from 1810 to 1820 it was 239,831; from 1820 to 1830 it was 322,878; from 1830 to 1840 it was 420,174. At this rate the annual increase from 1840 to 1850 will, upon an average of the years, exceed 500,000. And the whole increase of the ten years will exceed 5,000,000 of souls. To augment the number of ministers of the gospel, churches, &c., so as adequately to meet this annual demand will require great exertion.

At the first sight of this statistical view of the case, some of my readers will be ready to exclaim that the prospect is hopeless. Others will say, Woe to the cause of religion if the government does not put its shoulders to the wheel! But I answer, not only in my own name, but dare to do it in that of every well-informed American Christian: "No! we want no more aid from the government than what we receive, and what it so cheerfully gives. The prospect is not desperate so long as Christians do their duty in humble and heart-felt reliance upon God." If we allow that 80,000 of this 500,000 of the annual increase of the population are under five years of age, and therefore need not be taken into account in calculating the required increase of church accommodation which must be annually made, as being too young to be taken to the sanctuary, we have 420,000 persons to provide for. This would require annually the building or opening of 420 churches, holding 1000 persons each, and an increase of 420 ministers of the gospel. Or, what would be much more probable, 840 churches, each holding on an average 500 persons; and a sufficient number of preachers to occupy them. That that number should be 840 would certainly be desirable. And yet a smaller number could do; for in many cases one minister must, in order to find his support, preach to two or more congregations. So if 840 churches be not built every year, something equal to this in point of accommodation must be either built or found in some way or other. Sometimes school-houses answer the purpose in the new settlements; sometimes private houses, or some public building, can make up for the want of a church.

T

Now we shall see in the sequel to what extent facts show that provision is actually made to meet this vast demand.   For the present all that I contemplate in giving this statistical view of the subject is, to enable the reader to form some idea of the work to be accomplished on the voluntary principle in America, if religion is to keep progress with the increase of the population.

CHAPTER II.

FOUNDATION OF THE VOLUNTARY PRINCIPLE TO BE SOUGHT FOR IN THE CHARACTER AND HABITS OF THE PEOPLE OF THE UNITED STATES.

Some minuteness of detail will be found necessary in order to give the reader a proper idea of the manifestations of what has been called the voluntary principle in the United States, and to trace it throughout all its many ramifications there.   But, before this, I would fain give him a right conception of the character of the people as being that to which the principle referred to mainly owes its success.

Enough has been said in former parts of this work to show, that whether we look to the earlier or later emigrations to America, no small energy of character must have been required in the emigrants before venturing on such a step; and with re-gard to the first settlers in particular, that nothing but the force of religious principle could have nerved them to encounter the difficulties of all kinds that beset them.   But if great energy, self-reliance, and enterprise, be the natural attributes of the ori-ginal emigrant, as he quits all the endearments of home, and the comforts and luxuries of states far advanced in civilisation for a life in the woods, amid wild beasts, and sometimes wilder men, pestilential marshes, and privations innumerable; the same qualities are very much called forth by colonial life, after the first obstacles have been overcome.   It accustoms men to disre-gard trifling difficulties, to surmount by their own efforts obsta-cles which, in other states of society, would repel all such attempts, and themselves to do many things which, in different circumstances, they would expect others to do for them.

Moreover, the colonies were thrown very much on their own resources from the first. England expended almost nothing upon them. Beyond maintaining a few regiments from time to time, in scattered companies, at widely separated points, and supplying some cannon and small arms, she did almost nothing even for the defence of the country. In almost every war with the Indians, the colonial troops alone carried on the contest. Instead of England helping them, they actually helped her incomparably more in her wars against the French, in the Canadas, and in the provinces of New Brunswick and Cape Breton, when they not only furnished men, but bore almost the whole charge of maintaining them. Then came the war of the Revolution, which, in calling forth all the nation's energies during eight long years, went far to cherish that vigour and independence of character which had so remarkably distinguished the first colonists.

And although in some of the colonies the church and state were united from the first, the law did little more than prescribe how the churches were to be maintained. It made some men give grudgingly, who would otherwise have given little or nothing; whilst at the same time it limited others to a certain fixed amount, who, if left to themselves, would perhaps have given more.

With the exception of a few thousand pounds for building some of the earliest colleges, and a few more, chiefly from Scotland, for the support of missionaries, most of whom laboured among the Indians, I am not aware of any aid received from the mother country, or from any other part of Europe, for religious purposes in our colonial days. I do not state this by way of reproach, but as a simple fact. The Christians not only of Great Britain, but of Holland and Germany also, were ever willing to aid the cause of religion in the colonies; they did what they could, or rather what the case seemed to require, and the monuments of their piety and liberality remain to this day. Still, the colonists, as was their duty, depended mainly on their own efforts. In several of the colonies there was from the first no church establishment; in two of those which professed to have one, the state never did any thing worth mention for the support of the churches; and in all cases the dissenters had to rely on their own exertions. In process of time, as we have seen, the union of church and state came gradually to an end throughout the whole country, and all religious bodies were left to their own resources.

Thus have the Americans been trained to exercise the same energy, self-reliance, and enterprise in the cause of religion which they exhibit in other affairs. Thus, as we shall see, when a new church is called for, the people first inquire whether they cannot build it at their own cost, and ask help from others only after having done all they think practicable among them-selves;—a course which often leads them to find that they can accomplish by their own efforts what, at first, they hardly dared to hope for.

Besides, there has grown up among the truly American part of the population a feeling that religion is necessary even to the temporal well-being of society, so that many contribute to its promotion, though not themselves members of any of the churches. This sentiment may be found in all parts of the United States, and especially among the descendants of the first Puritan colonists of New England. I shall have occasion hereafter to give an illustration of it.

These remarks point the reader to the true secret of the success of the voluntary plan in America. The people feel that they can help themselves, and that it is at once a duty and a privilege to do so. Should a church steeple come to the ground, or the roof be blown away, or any other such accident happen, instead of looking to some government official for the means of needful repair, a few of them put their hands into their pockets, and supply these themselves, without delay or the risk of vexatious refusals from public functionaries.

CHAPTER III.

HOW CHURCH EDIFICES ARE BUILT IN THE CITIES AND LARGE TOWNS.

THE question has often been proposed to me during my residence in Europe: " How do you build your churches in America since the government gives no aid?"

Different measures are pursued in different places. I shall speak first of those commonly adopted in the cities and large towns. There a new church is built by what is called " colonising." That is, the pastor and other officers of a large church which cannot accommodate all its members, or others who wish to join it with their families, after much conference, on being satisfied that a new church is called for, propose that a commencement be made by certain families going out as a colony, to carry the enterprise into effect, and engage to assist them with their prayers and counsels, and, if need be, also with their purses. Upon this, such as are willing to engage in the undertaking, go to work. Sometimes individuals or families, from two or more churches of the same denomination, coalesce in the design.

Or a few gentlemen, interested in religion, whether all or any of them are members of a church or not, after conferring on the importance of having another church in some part of the city where an increase of the population seems to require it, resolve that one shall be built. Each then subscribes what he thinks he can afford, and subscriptions may afterwards be solicited from gentlemen of property and liberality in the place, likely to aid such an undertaking. Enough may thus be obtained to justify a commencement; a committee is appointed to purchase a site for the building, and to superintend its erection. When finished, it is opened for public worship, a pastor is called, and then the pews, which are generally large enough to accommodate a family each, are disposed of at a sort of auction to the highest bidder. In this way the sum which may be required, in addition to the original subscriptions, is at once made up. The total cost, indeed, is sometimes met by the sums received for the pews, but much depends upon the situation and comfort of the building, and the popularity of the preacher.

The pews are always sold under the condition of punctual payment of the sums to be levied upon them annually, for the pastor's support and other expenses; failing which, after allowing a reasonable time, they are resold to other persons. But if all the required conditions be fulfilled, they become absolutely the purchaser's, and may be bequeathed or sold like any other property.

Instead of being sold in fee simple, the pews are sometimes merely rented from year to year. This prevails more in large towns and villages than in cities, and in such cases the churches must be built solely by "subscription," as it is called, that is, by sums contributed for that special object. Should these prove in the first instance insufficient, a second, and perhaps a third subscription follows after a longer or shorter interval.

The seats in some churches, even of our largest cities, are free to all. Such is the case with all the Quaker, and most of the Methodist meeting-houses; these are occupied on what is called the "free-seat" plan, and have the advantage of being attended with less restraint, especially by strangers or persons who may not have the means to pay for seats. But there are disadvantages also in this plan. Families who regularly attend, and who may bear the expense of the church, have no certain place where all may sit together, and in case of being delayed a little longer than usual, may find it difficult to get seats at all. The Methodist churches, accordingly, are coming more and more into the other plan in our large cities. Where they have not done so, and also in the Quaker meeting-houses, the males occupy one-half of the house, the females the other;—a rule, however, observed more constantly in the latter than in the former body. Church edifices, or meeting-houses, on the free-seat plan, must of course be built by subscription alone.

A more common practice in forming new congregations, with new church edifices, is this. The families who engage in the undertaking first obtain some place for temporary service—the lecture-room attached to some other church, a court-house, school-room, or some other such building [1] —and there they commence their regular Sabbath services at the usual hours. After announcing their intention by public advertisement, they proceed to organise a church, that is, a body of believers, according to the rules of the communion to which they belong. If Presbyterians, the presbytery appoints a committee to organise the church according to the book of discipline, by the appointment and consecration to office of ruling elders, after which it falls under the care of the presbytery. A pastor is next called and regularly inducted. Meanwhile, the congregation may be supposed to be increasing, until strong enough to exchange their temporary for a permanent place of worship. In this way new swarms are every year leaving the old hives, if I may so speak, in our large cities, and new church edifices are rising in various localities where the population is extending.

The church edifices in the chief towns and cities are, generally speaking, large and substantial buildings, especially in the more densely-settled districts. Those in the suburbs are often smaller, and not expected to be more than temporary, as they often give place to larger and better structures in a few years. In the cities and larger towns, whether on the Atlantic slope or in the valley of the Mississippi, they are in nine cases out of ten built of brick; a few are of stone; and in the New England cities and towns of second and third-rate size, they are often built of wood.

As for the cost of church edifices, it is difficult to speak precisely where the country is so extensive. In the suburbs of our large cities on the sea-board, from Portland in Maine to

---

1 In Philadelphia there is a building called the Academy, built for Mr. Whitfield's meetings; the upper part of which is now divided into two rooms, each capable of containing 400 or 500 people, and both constantly used as places of worship; one permanently by the Methodists. The other has been occupied temporarily by colonies, which have grown into churches, and then gone off to houses which they have built for themselves. In this way that one room, as I have often been told, has been the birth-place, as it were, of more than twenty different churches. It is rented to those who wish to occupy it by the corporation, to whom it belongs. In the lower storey there are schools held throughout the week.

The chapel of the university of New York is used for the same purpose. And the court-houses throughout all the land, and even some of the State houses, being those in which the legislatures of the several States assemble, are allowed to be used as places of worship on the Sabbath in a case of exigency.

New Orleans, some may not have cost more than from 5000 to 10,000 dollars; but in the older and more densely-peopled parts of those cities, they generally cost 20,000 dollars and upwards. Some have cost 60,000 or 80,000, and yet are comparatively plain, though very chaste and substantial buildings. A few have cost above 100,000,[1] without including such as Trinity church at New York, belonging to the Episcopalians, or the Roman Catholic cathedral at Baltimore, for these very elegant and expensive buildings have cost at least 300,000 dollars, if not more.[2] There may have been in some cases a useless expenditure of money on interior decorations, but in general, the churches, even in our largest cities, are neat and rather plain buildings externally, and exceedingly comfortable within.

The village churches of New England are for the most part constructed of wood; that is, of beams framed together and covered with boards, and being almost universally painted white and surmounted with steeples—they have a beautiful appear- ance. The church-going bell every Sabbath sends its notes far and wide amid the hills and dales of that interesting country. In other parts of the Atlantic States, though often of wood, like those of New England, they are still oftener of brick or stone, or of unpainted frames and boards, which is especially the case in the south.

Any one may be satisfied by careful inquiry, that even our cities and large towns, as respects churches, may well bear a comparison with the best supplied in any part of Europe. Boston, for instance, in 1840, had fifty-eight churches, many of which could accommodate from 1000 to 1500 persons, and that for a population of about 88,000 souls. New York had that year 159 churches for about 310,000 inhabitants; namely, forty-one Presbyterian, of all shades; fourteen Reformed Dutch;

[1] The church in which the late eloquent Dr. Mason was last settled as a minister in New York, cost, I believe, rather more than 100,000 dollars. It is an excellent, large, tasteful, substantial, brick building. Yet it, and some others in the lower parts of the city, whence business is driving the people to the upper part, are now to be torn down, and their sites to be covered with shops and counting-rooms. The congregations have mainly emigrated to about a mile and a half, or two miles, northward. So matters go in *our London*.

[2] Trinity church is not yet finished. When I was last in America the walls had just begun to appear, but I am told that it is a remarkably fine specimen of Gothic architecture. I have not heard what the cost will be, but including the value of the ground, I should think it cannot be less than 300,000 dollars, and may amount to 500,000.

twenty-seven Episcopal; eighteen Methodist; eighteen Baptist; eight Roman Catholic; nine African, (Methodist, Episcopal, Baptist, and Presbyterian); five Friends' meeting-houses; three Lutheran; three Moravian; three synagogues, (there are now five or six) two Unitarian; three Universalist; four Welsh and smaller denominations; and two Mariners' churches. This is from a published statement which may be depended upon as rather within the truth. The church accommodation of the Protestant population is in much higher proportion to their numbers than that of the Roman Catholics to theirs, partly owing, no doubt, to the liturgical services of the latter requiring less church accommodation than the sermon-preaching of the former.

Philadelphia is better supplied with churches than New York. Those of all the leading denominations there have greatly increased during the last few years. The Methodists, I learn from their best informed ministers in Philadelphia, have, in the course of the last fifteen years, built in the city and suburbs above twenty churches, most of which are capacious buildings; and the Episcopalians and Presbyterians have increased the number of theirs nearly in the same proportion. But our second and third rate cities and large towns, are far better supplied than either of those two places. Salem in Massachusetts, for a population of 16,000 souls, has fifteen churches; Newhaven, for about 14,000 souls, has thirteen, many of which are of large size; Poughkeepsie, on the Hudson, has 9000 inhabitants and twelve churches; Troy had in 1840 a population of 25,000 souls, and fifteen churches, and several of these very large. Newark in New Jersey, has about 30,000 inhabitants, and seventeen churches; Rochester 22,000 inhabitants, and twenty-two churches.

On this head the reader is referred to the works of Drs. Reid and Mathieson, and to that of Dr. Lang, as containing much accurate information with respect to church accommodation in the United States.

·CHAPTER IV.

HOW CHURCHES ARE BUILT IN THE NEW SETTLEMENTS.

But it is in the building of places of worship in the new settlements of the western States, and in the villages that are springing up in the more recently peopled parts of those bordering on the Atlantic that we see the most remarkable development of the voluntary principle. Let me illustrate by a particular case what is daily occurring in both these divisions of the country.

Let us suppose a settlement commenced in the forest, in the northern part of Indiana, and that in the course of three or four years a considerable number of emigrants have established themselves within a mile or two of each other in the woods. Each clears away by degrees a part of the surrounding forest, and fences in his new fields where the deadened trees still stand very thick. By little and little the country shows signs of occupation by civilised man.

In the centre of the settlement a little village begins to form around a tavern and a blacksmith's shop. A carpenter places himself there as a convenient centre. So do the tailor, the shoemaker, the waggon-maker, and the hatter. Nor is the son of Æsculapius wanting; perhaps he is most of all needed; and it will be well if two or three of his brethren do not soon join him. The merchant of course opens his magazine there. And if there be any prospect of the rising city, though the deadened trees stand quite in the vicinity of the streets, becoming the seat of justice for a new county, there will soon be half a dozen young expounders of the law, to increase the population, and offer their services to those who have suffered or committed some injustice.

Things will hardly have reached this point before some one amid this heterogeneous population come from different points of the older States, intermixed with wanderers from Europe,—Irish, Scotch, or German,—proposes that they should think of having a church, or at least, some place of worship. It is ten chances to one if there be not one or more pious women, or some pious ' man with his family, who sigh for the privileges of the sanctuary as once enjoyed by them in the distant east.   What is to be done? Some one proposes that they should build a good large school-house, which may serve also for holding religious meetings, and this is scarcely sooner proposed than accomplished. Though possibly made of mere logs and very plain, it will answer the purpose for a few years.   Being intended for the meetings of all denominations of Christians, and open to all preachers who may be passing, word is sent to the nearest in the neighbourhood. . Ere long some Baptist preacher in passing preaches in the evening, and is followed by a Presbyterian and a Methodist.   By and bye the last of these arranges his circuit labours so as to preach there once in the fortnight, and then the minister of some Presbyterian congregation, ten or fifteen miles off, agrees to come and preach once a month.

Meanwhile, from the increase of the inhabitants, the congregations, on the Sabbath particularly, become too large for the school-house.   A church is then built of framed beams and boards, forming no mean ornament to the village, and capable of accommodating some 200 or 300 people.   Erected for the public good, it is used by all the sects in the place, and by others besides.   For were a Swedenborgian minister to come and have notice given that he would preach, he might be sure of finding a congregation, though as the sect is small in America, and by many hardly so much as heard of, he might not have a single hearer that assented to his views.   But it will not be long before the Presbyterians, Methodists, or Baptists feel that they must have a minister on whose services they can count with more certainty, and hence a church also for themselves.   And, at last, the house, which was a joint-stock affair at first, falls into the hands of some one of the denominations, and is abandoned by the others who have mostly provided each one for itself.   Or, it may remain for the occasional service of some passing Roman Catholic priest, or Universalist preacher.[1]

[1] In some places in the south-western States, the primitive and temporary churches built for all denominations in the new villages or settlements are called "Republican churches;" that is, churches for the accommodation of the *public*, rather than for any one sect.   Large school-houses, also, erected for the double purpose of teaching and preaching, are called Republican meeting-houses.

Such is the process continually going on in the west, and indeed something of a like kind is taking place every year in hundreds of instances throughout all the States. Settlers of one denomination are sometimes sufficiently numerous in one place to build a church for themselves at the outset, but in most cases they hold their first meetings for worship in school-rooms or private houses.

The rapid increase of the population in some of the new villages and towns of the west, when favourably situated for trade, is astonishing, and strikes one particularly in its early stages. Thus, when in the State of Alabama, in February, 1831, I visited the town of Montgomery, in company with a worthy Baptist minister, in the course of an extensive tour through the western States, in behalf of one of our benevolent societies. It was then hardly more than a large village, and on the night of the second of the two days we spent in it, we preached in a large school-house, which, if I remember rightly, was the only place for holding religious meetings existing there at the time. We had a good congregation, though a circus was held hard by. Just three years after, when repeating the same tour, I spent a Sabbath and one or two days more at the same spot, but under amazingly different circumstances. In the morning I preached in a Presbyterian church built of frames and covered with boards, and every way comfortable, to at least 600 persons. The church, which reckoned 100 members, had got a young man as pastor, to whom they gave a yearly stipend of 1000 dollars. At night I preached in a Baptist church, built of brick, but not quite finished, which could hold 300 persons at least. Besides these, there were one Methodist Episcopal and one Protestant Methodist church, each, in so far as I can recollect, as large as the Baptist church. Then there was an Episcopal church, not less in size, though probably with a smaller congregation, than the Baptist church. And withal there was a Roman Catholic church, though not a large one, I believe. All this after an interval of only three years! Eventful years they had been. A revival of religion, which took place during one of them, had brought many souls to the knowledge of salvation.

This was, it is true, an extraordinary case, yet something

very similar in kind, although not in degree, is going on at a
great many points in the West.   I know not what reverses
the town of Montgomery may have since undergone, but what
I have stated occurred, I know, between the years 1831
and 1834.

On the Genessee river, a few miles from its entering Lake
Ontario, in the State of New York, stands a town, incorporated
as a city, called Rochester.   The place is famous for the vast
quantity of flour made at its mills.   Twenty-five years ago it
could show but a few houses scattered here and there, where
now there is a well built and flourishing city, containing, when
I was there about a year ago, 22,000 inhabitants, and twenty-
two churches, many of which were large and fine buildings,
capable of accommodating congregations of from 1000 to 1200
persons each.   Among these churches there were two for Germans, and another, I learnt, was soon to be erected for French
and Swiss.

Churches and church property of every description are held,
in the United States, by trustees chosen by the congregation
to which they belong.   The laws of almost every state provide
for this.   These trustees, who may be two, three, or more in
number, are authorised to act for the congregation, to whom
they report, from time to time, the state of the common funds.
They are charged, in most cases, with the collection of the pastor's salary, as well as with the general collection and outlay
of money for the congregation.   Without their consent the
church edifice cannot be given to any other than the ordinary
religious services of the church to which it belongs.

In some cases several, if not all of the churches in a city,
belonging to a particular communion, are held by a common
board of trustees.   All the Methodist Episcopal churches of
New York are so held.   One corporation has the proprietorship of four of the Reformed Dutch churches in that city, and
another holds Trinity church and some others belonging to the
Protestant Episcopal denomination.   In all denominations,
according to general practice, each particular church and congregation has its own trustees, and manages its own "temporal" affairs, being such as relate to the church edifice, the
ground on which it stands, and any other property or stocks

belonging to it; and it is only on questions of right to property that the civil courts, or even the State legislatures, or congress itself, can ever meddle with the affairs of the churches.

CHAPTER V.

THE VOLUNTARY PRINCIPLE DEVELOPED—HOW THE SALARIES OF THE PASTORS ARE RAISED.

UNDER this head we find different measures adopted by different churches, and in different parts of the country.

Universally where the seats and pews are the property of individuals or families, and generally where they are rented by the year, the salaries of the pastors, and sometimes all the incidental expenses, are raised by a certain yearly, half-yearly, or quarterly rate upon each pew. The proportion for each pew is fixed by the trustees, or by the elders, or by a committee appointed for that special purpose, but in most cases by the trustees, where there are such. Where the seats are free, as is the case with very many churches of all denominations in the interior of the country, the minister's salary is raised by yearly subscription. In the Methodist Episcopal churches, with few exceptions, the ministers are supported by collections among the members, quarterly public collections, &c. Sometimes, also, recourse is partially had to subscriptions, especially where there are " stationed " or non-itinerating ministers.

Among the Protestant denominations, the amount of the pastor's salary is determined, in most cases, by the churches themselves. In the Methodist churches, the amount is fixed by the general conference, in doing which much depends, in general, upon the number of the minister's family. In ordinary cases he receives so much for himself, a like sum for his wife, and so much for each of his children, according to their ages, with certain perquisites besides, such as a family dwelling-house, a horse, &c., making up altogether a comfortable maintenance for himself and his household. The collections of each "circuit" are expected, generally speaking, to suffice for the salaries of the ministers who occupy them, any deficiency being made up from funds which the conference may have in hand for meeting such contingencies. The clergy of all evangelical denominations, with two exceptions, receive fixed salaries from their people, and are expected to devote themselves to their proper vocation, and to "live by the altar." The exceptions are a part of the ministers of the Baptist church, and all the Quaker preachers. These support themselves by their labour, or from other sources, and preach on the Sabbath.

The Baptists agree with the Methodists in not considering a college education, or an acquaintance with the Greek, Latin, and Hebrew tongues, or the natural and moral sciences, indispensable for a preacher of the gospel; hence by far the greater number of them have had only an English education, together with such theological knowledge, derived from English sources, as has qualified them, in the opinion of the authorities in their churches, for undertaking the preaching of the gospel. In both these denominations, however, there are not a few truly learned men, who have passed through the curriculum of some college, and have diligently added to the acquirements of their preparatory course. The regular itinerating ministers of the Methodist churches receive salaries, and devote themselves wholly to their ministerial calling, whereas very many of the Baptist ministers, especially in the southern and western, and to a certain extent in the middle States, receive no salaries at all, or none of any consequence, so that they must support themselves in some other way.

The preachers among the Friends, who, as the reader is probably aware, may be women as well as men, receive no regular salaries; but those of them who, under the belief that they have a call from the Spirit to give themselves wholly to the work, travel through the country, visiting the Friends' "meetings," and preaching in other places, generally, nay always, if their own means are not abundant, receive considerable presents.

It is not easy to give any very satisfactory answer to the question, Whether the ministers of the gospel are well supported in the United States? Using that phrase in the sense which many attach to it, I should say, in giving a general reply to the question, that they are not. That is to say, few, if any, of them receive salaries that would enable them to live in the style in which the wealthiest of their parishioners live. Their incomes are not equal to those of the greater number of lawyers and physicians, though these are men of no better education or higher talents than great numbers of the clergy possess. None of the ministers of the gospel in the United States derive such revenues from their official stations as many of the parochial clergy of England have, to say nothing of the higher dignitaries of the church in that country. There are few, if any, of them who, with economy, can do more than live upon their salaries; to grow rich upon them is out of the question.[1]

Yet, on the other hand, the greater number of the salaried ministers in the United States are able, with economy, to live comfortably and respectably. This holds true especially as respects the pastors of the Atlantic, and even of the older parts of the western States. In New England, if we except Boston, the salaries of the Congregational, Episcopalian, and Baptist pastors, are in the largest towns, such as Providence, Portland, Salem, Hartford, Newhaven, &c., from 800 to 1200 dollars; in the villages and country churches they vary from 300 or 400 to 700 or 800, besides which the minister sometimes has a "parsonage" and "glebe," that is, a house and a few acres of land, and in addition to all, he receives a good many presents. His marriage fees are of some amount. In other parts of the country, and especially in the West, the clergy are not so well provided for. The practice in New England of giving them presents, whether casually or regularly, and at some set time, does not prevail elsewhere to the same degree.

The salaries of the clergy in the largest and wealthiest churches of the principal cities are handsome, though generally

---

[1] The statements made by foreigners, in writing about the United States, are sometimes sufficiently ludicrous. For instance, M. Beaumont, in his " Marie, ou Esclavage aux Etats Unis," accounts for the great number of churches there by the great number of ministers of the gospel. He says that the ministry is not only very honourable but very lucrative also; that most of the preachers make a fortune in a few years, and then retire from the ministry, which is the cause of there being so few old men in the pulpits of that country. Any thing more absurd on such a subject I cannot imagine, But I will do M. Beaumont the justice to say that I do not blame him so much as the stupid men who gave him such information. The gay Frenchman probably did not set his foot in more than half a dozen churches when in America, and of these not one probably was Protestant.

no more than adequate.[1] Fifteen hundred dollars, 1800, 2000,
2500, are the sums commonly given, and in a few cases, 3000,
3500, and even 4000. The Presbyterian church in New Orleans gives its pastor 5000, and the highest of all is that of one
of the bishops in the Episcopal church, which, I have been
told, is 6000.[2]

Some churches have permanent funds, which go far towards
the pastor's support. The corporation of the collegiate churches
of the Reformed Dutch church in New York, four in number
at present, has enough from this source to pay the salaries of
the four pastors. The corporation of Trinity church (Episcopal) possesses vast funds, the income from which has enabled
the trustees to contribute largely towards the building of churches
in the State of New York. Three of the Presbyterian churches
in Newark, New Jersey, which is nine miles from New York,
and contains 20,000 inhabitants, have permanent funds sufficient for the support of their public services.

But, generally speaking, a permanent fund is found to be
rather injurious than beneficial to the churches in the United
States. If out of debt, that is, if they owe nothing for their
church edifices, lecture-rooms, vestry-rooms, &c., they need no
endowment; the hearts of the people will do the rest. I speak
of the churches in the older parts of the country. The measures we take for churches in the new settlements, and which
are weak as yet, I shall show hereafter.

It often happens that ministers are not so amply or punctually provided for, through their own fault, and that of the
ecclesiastical body to which they belong. Were the duty of
supporting the ministry well, preached as often and as plainly
as it should be, they would be better provided for. As it is,

[1] The clergy are expected to be examples of hospitality and benevolence.
They entertain a great deal of company at their houses. Nothing is more
common than for ministers of the gospel, when visiting any place, whether in
town or country, to stay with their brethren : and no men among us give so
much, in proportion to their means, to all the religious and philanthropic enterprises, as our pastors of every denomination.

[2] I refer to the bishop of New York, who if he has to pay for a suffragan to
take his place as pastor of a church, or co-pastor with others in two or three
churches, as well as bear his travelling expenses when visiting his diocese, will
not have more than is necessary to support a large family in so expensive a
city as New York.

As for New Orleans, it is the most expensive for supporting a family in the
whole Union, and 5000 dollars there would in that respect be not more than
half the sum in Philadelphia.

they are enabled to live, with great economy, in comfort, and a faithful pastor will no where be allowed to starve. It is a great matter, too, that in no country in the world are ministers of the gospel more respected by the people. A great many of them are well educated men, and, with few exceptions, possess agreeable manners. Many of them belong to families of the first rank in the country;[1] and as they can at least give their families a good education, with the advantages of such an education, as well as of a good character, and the good name of their fathers, their children are almost invariably prosperous, and often form alliances with the wealthiest and most distinguished families in the country.

CHAPTER VI.

HOW MINISTERS OF THE GOSPEL ARE BROUGHT FORWARD, AND HOW THEY BECOME SETTLED PASTORS.

ALL denominations of evangelical Christians in the United States hold it to be of the highest and most solemn importance, that no man should enter the holy ministry without well-founded scriptural evidence to his own mind and conscience, that he is called of the Holy Ghost to take that office upon him; nor is he admitted to it until he has satisfied the proper authorities of the church to which he belongs, of the manifestation of that call, and of his possessing, in addition to an unblemished character, the talents and acquirements necessary to his being a competent expounder of God's word.

For a man to take upon him this sacred and responsible

[1] I could mention, were it proper, many instances of this. One or two I may state without violating the rules of propriety. No man stood higher in American society than the late General van Renselaer of Albany. One of his sons is labouring as a faithful minister in New Jersey. The late Hon. Samuel L. Southard of New Jersey was a man of distinguished talents, who had raised himself to the highest offices in the government of his native State, as well as in that of the Union, and died vice-president of the same. One of his sons is a most worthy rector of an Episcopal church in New Jersey. Mr. Southard, I judge from the name, which is common in France, was of Huguenot origin.

office, merely that he may obtain an honourable place in society, or gain a decent livelihood, would be held in the highest degree wrong, dangerous to the man's own soul, and ruinous to the spiritual interests of all who might be committed to his charge. Evangelical Christians may differ as to the evidences of conversion, but all agree as to the necessity of having a truly regenerated ministry; it being obvious, that none should preach the gospel who have not tasted its power, and submitted their hearts and lives to its transforming influence.   How shall a man who does not possess "repentance towards God and faith towards our Lord Jesus Christ," explain the nature of these to his fellowmen?   And how can he who has not been made to exclaim: "Woe unto me if I preach not the gospel!" discharge the office of a preacher with that vehement desire for the glory of God his Saviour, and for the eternal welfare of men, which alone can be approved in heaven, or be successful on earth?   A regenerated and devoted ministry must be the first of all earthly blessings to a church, and it is the only instrument that can effectually secure the morals of a community, and the stability of a government.   In these sentiments I feel assured every evangelical Christian in the United States would concur.   No greater curse could, in their opinion, befal a church next to the abandonment of the true gospel, than to have an unconverted ministry thrust upon it, and indeed the latter evil would soon be followed by the former.

Pious youths are brought forward to the ministry in various ways.   Such persons are sometimes found in the situation of apprentices to mechanical trades, or of clerks, or shopmen, or following the plough on their father's farm.   The pastor, or some member of the church to which they belong, having discovered their talents, may think these might be employed to advantage in the ministry, instead of being buried in such engagements.   But their own desires should first be ascertained, and should they be found longing to proclaim a crucified Saviour to the world, they ought to be encouraged while cherishing this feeling, to put themselves into a position for finding and following the will of God.

It is probably at the prayer-meeting, the Sabbath-school, or the Bible-class, of which I shall have to speak at large hereafter, that the character and abilities of such young persons oftenest show themselves; and from these nurseries of the church have come forth great numbers of men who are now engaged in the ministry throughout the United States. Many young men, also, who have entered our colleges with other views, become converted there, and are called to preach the gospel.

When a pious youth of promising talents, and with a strong bent to the ministry, is found without the requisite education, or the means of obtaining it, he is recommended to the education societies, which have proved a great blessing to our churches; and when approved of, he is carried through the course of instruction which the church to which he belongs requires in all who would enter the ranks of its ministers.

The process is much shorter in those churches which, without exacting a course of classical and scientific education at college, or the regular divinity course of a theological school, require only a well-grounded knowledge of the scriptures in the English tongue, and of the doctrines which they contain. After a suitable examination on the part of the proper church authorities, the candidate is permitted to exercise his gifts for a season, in order to test how far he is likely to prove an acceptable and useful preacher; and if the result be favourable, he receives full ordination from the proper quarter.

Among the Methodists, the preachers spring from the *classes*, as they are called. At the meetings of these companies of professed believers and inquirers, the graces and gifts of pious young men are most commonly discovered. In due time they are brought forward to the quarterly meeting of all the classes of the district. They are there recommended to the notice of the presiding elder, and by him are authorised to teach and preach for a time, but not to administer the ordinances of baptism and the Lord's supper. Afterwards they receive ordination from the hands of the bishop, first as deacons, and subsequently as presbyters or priests, and are employed to preach the gospel, either as travelling or *stationed* ministers. In the Congregational churches young men are consecrated to the ministry by a council of ministers commonly called a "consociation;" among the Presbyterians by a presbytery; among the Episcopalians by a bishop.

In all the churches of the United States, except the Methodists and Roman Catholics, the pastors are chosen by the people to whom they preach. Among the Methodists they are appointed by the annual conference, at which a bishop presides, regard being had to the wishes which may be expressed by the people in favour of certain ministers, as peculiarly fitted, in point of character and talents, for specific localities. The appointment of the priests to their respective churches among Roman Catholics rests wholly with the bishops.

When a church belonging to any of the other denominations loses its pastor, by his death or removal to some other place, inquiry is first made for some one not yet settled, or who, if settled, would not object to change his charge, and who, it is thought, would prove acceptable to the flock. The person fixed upon is invited to preach a few times, and should he give satisfaction, the congregation agree to call him to be their pastor, in doing which they must proceed according to the established rules of the religious body to which they belong. Thus in the Presbyterian church, no call to become pastor of a vacant church can be presented to any one without the consent of the presbytery within whose bounds the vacancy has taken place; nor can it be accepted without the consent of the Presbytery to which the minister who has received it belongs.

In the Congregational churches of New England, the practice in calling a pastor has been for the church or body of the communicants to make out a call, and for this to be followed by another from the whole congregation, or rather from the males who contribute towards the support of public worship, the amount of the proffered salary being stated in the latter call. In the Presbyterian and most other churches, each pew holder, or each head of a family who subscribes towards the pastor's salary for himself and household, and others who subscribe only for themselves, are allowed a voice in the call. Such is the more common practice, and yet there are Presbyterian churches in which none but members that are communicants can vote in calling a pastor. If the people are to be allowed a voice in calling their pastors, it will be found difficult to withhold that right from those who, though not communicants, contribute as much, and perhaps more, than those who are. Nor in a church and congregation in which the people have been well instructed in the truth, and where religion prospers, does any evil of much consequence commonly result from such an extension of the right of voting on such occasions. For when men have been faithfully instructed in the gospel, it is found that even the unconverted will readily join in calling an efficient minister, even although he be not only orthodox but very zealous and faithful. Such men have sufficient discrimination to know, and often they will say it, that if ever they are to become the religious men they hope one day to be, they need a faithful pastor to secure that great blessing. Such men have sense enough to know that a light-minded, worldly, cold preacher of the gospel, is not likely to prove a blessing to them or their families. But when church and congregation have long been hearing "another gospel," have become hardened in error, and saturated with damnable heresies, it were absurd to expect the unconverted to prefer and seek for a faithful minister. Such a state of things should not be allowed to occur. And then, with respect to all denominations that have a government encompassing and controlling the churches connected with them, there is, in the last resort, a power to prevent the settlement of unworthy ministers in the churches under their care.

CHAPTER VII.

THE VOLUNTARY PRINCIPLE DEVELOPED IN HOME MISSIONS—AMERICAN HOME
MISSIONARY SOCIETY.

Thus much has the voluntary principle done for the longest-settled, and most densely-peopled, parts of the country. Let us now see what it does for new and thinly-peopled regions, where hundreds of new congregations are rising annually, without the means of maintaining the institutions of the gospel by their own efforts. Such churches are to be found not only in the new settlements of the " Far West," but also in the growing villages of the " East."

This inability to support the public preaching of the gospel often arises from the number of sects to be found in new settlements, and even in some districts of an old State. In this respect diversity of sects sometimes causes a serious though temporary evil, not to be compared with the advantage resulting from it in the long run. It is an evil, too, which generally becomes less and less every year, in any given place; the little churches, however weak at first, gradually becoming, through the increase of population, strong and independent, and what is now an evil disappearing, or rather, as I hope to prove, being converted into a blessing.

The most obvious way of aiding such feeble churches, is to form societies for this express object among the older and more flourishing churches in the eastern States. This has been done, and in this the voluntary principle has beautifully developed itself, particularly during the last fifteen years. It began with some denominations not long after the Revolution, and early in this century we find missionary societies formed among the Congregational churches of Massachusetts and Connecticut, for the purpose of sending ministers to " the West," that is, the western part of the State of New York. The " Far West" to them was the northern part of Ohio, which was then beginning to be the resort of emigrants. The faithful men sent by these societies into the wilderness were greatly blessed in their labours, and to them, under God, many of the now flourishing churches of those regions owe their existence. Missionary societies were subsequently formed in the other New England States, for supplying destitute places within their own bounds with the preaching of the gospel as well as to help in sending it to other parts of the country.

Two societies were formed, likewise, for the same object among the Presbyterians and Reformed Dutch in the city of New York, and these supported a good many missionaries, chiefly in the new and feeble churches in the State of that name. In 1826, they were united into one body, and now form the American Home Missionary Society.[1]

[1] The epithet *American*, employed by this society, and others, which do not comprise all the religious denominations, has been greatly objected to as savouring of arrogance, and as if intimating, that the whole of America belonged

This society from its very outset has advanced with great vigour, and been directed with singular zeal and energy. At its first meeting, in 1827, it reported that in the course of the year that had closed, it had employed 169 ministers, who had laboured in 196 congregations and missionary districts. Its receipts for the same period amounted to 20,031 dollars. This powerful commencement must be ascribed to its having assumed all the engagements of the Domestic Missionary Society, out of which it sprang. The Society soon drew into affiliation with it all the State Home Missionary Societies of New England, some of which, such as those of Massachusetts and Connecticut, were of long standing and well established.[1]

It would be interesting to trace the history of an institution which has been so much blessed to a vast number of new and poor churches throughout all the States and Territories of the American confederacy. We shall, therefore, present a summary of its operations at two epochs, during the sixteen years that it has been distributing blessings with a liberal hand.

In the year ending May 1st 1835, the society employed 719 agents and missionaries. Of these 481 were settled as pastors, or employed as "stated supplies," in single congregations: 185 extended their labours to two or three congregations each, and fifty were employed on larger districts. In all, 1050 congregations, missionary districts, and fields of agency, were thus supplied in whole or in part. The persons added to the churches under the care of the society's missionaries that year were estimated at 5000; namely, 1700 by letters of recommendation

to them exclusively as a field of labour. Such an idea probably never entered the minds of those who use the word in the denomination of their societies. All that they mean in employing it is, to signify that the field to which their attention is directed is not a single State, or a few States, but the whole country.—The American Home Missionary Society embraces the orthodox Congregational churches in New England and out of it, the New School Presbyterians, and to some extent, the Reformed Dutch, Lutheran, and German Reformed churches.

1 These societies, in a great degree, manage their own affairs, appoint and support the missionaries who labour in their own bounds, and pay over the surplus of their collections, if they have any, to the American Home Missionary Society. If they need help from that society at any time they receive it. In the year 1841, the Maine Missionary Society employed seventy-two missionaries, (four-fifths of all the Congregational churches in that State were planted by this society): that of New Hampshire forty-seven; that of Vermont fifty; that of Massachusetts eighty-one; that of Connecticut thirty-five; and that of Rhode Island four:—making in all 289 missionaries sustained in young and feeble churches in the six New England States.

from other churches, and, 3,700 by examination on profession
of their faith. Several of the churches were reported to have
been blessed with seasons of more than ordinary interest in
religion; in the Sunday schools attached to them there were
about 40,000 scholars, and about 12,000 persons attended the
Bible classes. The number of persons who had joined the temperance associations had reached 70,000. The expenditure
amounted to 83,394 dollars; the receipts to 88,863.

Let us now turn to what was done by the society in the year
ending 1st May, 1842. During that year it had 791 missionaries and agents, of whom 548 had been in its service the preceding year, and 243 were employed for the first time. These
men laboured in all the States and Territories of the Union; a
few, also, in Canada. The number of Presbyterian and Congregational churches in Iowa and Wisconsin had been doubled
in the course of the year by the society's means. The number
of congregations and missionary stations occupied was 987, and
the Sunday schools and Bible classes, under the direction of the
missionaries, were attended by 64,300 persons. In 288 congregations the sum of 14,476 dollars had been collected for
religious and benevolent societies, and many of the feeble
churches had contributed largely for them, in aid of missions
to the heathen. There had been revivals in 109 churches, and
3018 conversions were reported by 288 missionaries. The disbursements of the society were 107,085 dollars; the receipts
95,291.

The plan pursued by this society, and by all the other societies
and boards established for the promotion of home missions, is
never to support a missionary at its sole charges, if it can be
avoided; but to give 100, or 150, or 200 dollars, rarely more
than 100 or 120, to a young and yet feeble church, or two congregations near to each other, on condition of their making up
the deficiency in the missionary's salary. Thus they are stimulated and encouraged to help themselves, and as soon as they
can walk alone, if I may use the expression, the society leaves
them for others which have been just organised, and which need
assistance. In this way hundreds of congregations have been
built up, and hundreds are at this moment emerging from the
weakness of childhood into the vigour of youth and manhood.

In no case, however, does the society do any thing towards the erection of church edifices. The people must find these for themselves, and this they willingly do. The cheapness of materials in the new settlements, and in the villages of the interior, renders it easy to erect such houses as will suffice until the flock gathers strength, and can do something more.

The society engages, in some cases, men of talent and experience to travel over a given district, and to ascertain at what points the people attached to one or other of the denominations which it represents might, with proper efforts, be formed into congregations. The labours of such agents are of the utmost importance, and they necessarily receive their whole salaries from the society.

It is a beautiful feature in such institutions for home missions, that while encouraging and stimulating new and feeble congregations to do their utmost to secure for themselves the regular enjoyment of gospel ordinances, they cultivate the kindly feelings of churches in the older parts of the country, and more favourably situated. Many of the latter support one missionary, and some of them several each, in the new and destitute settlements, through the agency of the American Home Mission society. Nay, there are juvenile societies in the Sunday schools that support each of them one, and some even two or three missionaries, if not more. Individuals are to be found in the Atlantic States, who support a missionary each, and thus preach the gospel, as they say, "by proxy." Still more, there are persons in New York and other cities, who have each paid the entire salary and travelling expenses of an agent labouring in a large district. One of these, with whom I have long been acquainted, a hatter, of by no means great fortune, who works with his hands at the trade, gave 600 dollars for years to support one such labourer in Illinois. Beautiful as this is, it is perhaps a finer sight still to see churches and congregations, which were aided by the society in their day, now in their turn bearing a part, if not the whole expense of a missionary labouring in a congregation not yet emerged from the feeble state that they once were in themselves. And there are now many such throughout the United States.

This notice of the American Home Missionary society we

may conclude by giving the following extract from its fourteenth annual report:—

"The results, indeed, of that mysterious and wonder-working influence which a God of grace exerts through the ministry of reconciliation, and which he connects with the missionary enterprise, all surpass finite comprehension. While the missionaries are preaching Christ and him crucified to the living, they are laying broad and deep the foundations of many generations; they are setting in motion trains of moral influences, which will not cease when they are dead; they are kindling up lights in Zion, which will shine brighter and brighter unto the perfect day. Churches, that were near unto death, are quickened, and become able of themselves to sustain the gospel, and to hand down its blessings to those who shall come after them. New churches are organised, to throw open their portals to the fathers, and the children, and the children's children, through many generations, and to send out their influences to the ends of the world. The organisation, or resuscitation of a church —Heaven's own institution—that may stand through all coming time, and bring its multitudes of redeemed ones to glory, is a great event. And to plant such churches, wherever there are souls to be gathered into them, our country over, and nurture them till they no longer need our aid, but become our most efficient fellow-labourers in hastening forward the universal reign of the Son of God, is surely a GREAT WORK! And yet, this is the work in which infinite condescension and mercy permits us, as friends of home missions, to engage, and some of which it is our privilege here to record."

CHAPTER VIII.

PRESBYTERIAN BOARD OF DOMESTIC MISSIONS, UNDER THE DIRECTION OF THE GENERAL ASSEMBLY.

PRESBYTERIANISM owes its foundation in the United States chiefly to persons who had been exiled from Scotland on account of their religious principles, and to Presbyterian emigrants from the north of Ireland. These were joined in many places by settlers from New England, who had no objections to unite with them in forming congregations on Presbyterian principles. Presbyterians of Scottish and Irish origin coalesced in other places with Huguenots from France, and colonists originally of the Dutch, or German Reformed churches. Thus did Presbyterian congregations begin to be formed towards the close of the seventeenth century. The first preachers were from Scotland, Ireland, and New England. They were few in number at first, and were often invited to preach in neighbourhoods where a few resident Presbyterians might desire to hear the gospel preached by men of the same religious principles with themselves.

The first presbytery was constituted in 1704, and the first synod in 1716. After that the work of home missions began to acquire greater consistency. Ministers were sent out on preaching tours among the small Presbyterian flocks, or rather scattered groups of Presbyterian families, particularly in the middle and southern provinces. In 1741, the synod was divided into two bodies, one retaining the old name of synod of Philadelphia, the other calling itself the synod of New York. The former soon after being constituted had its attention drawn, "not only to the wants of the people within their immediate bounds, but to those also of the emigrants who were rapidly extending themselves through Virginia and North Carolina." They wrote, accordingly, to the general assembly of the Church of Scotland, asking for ministers to preach in these colonies, and for assistance in establishing a seminary for the education of suitable young men for the ministry. A letter was also addressed to the deputies of the synods of North and South Holland, in which they expressed their willingness to unite with the Calvinistic Dutch churches in promoting the common interests of religion.

At the first meeting of the synod of New York in 1745, the circumstances of the people of Virginia were brought before them, and the opinion unanimously expressed that Mr. Robinson[1] was the proper person to visit that colony." He visited it

[1] This Mr. Robinson was a remarkable man. His manners were plain, his eloquence simple, animated, and attractive. He had but one eye, and was from that circumstance called "one-eyed Robinson." The Rev. Dr. Alexander,

accordingly, and on that, as well as on a former visit, was the instrument of doing much good.   He was followed by the Rev. Samuel Davies, formerly mentioned.

In 1758, the two synods were merged in the one synod of New York and Philadelphia, and from that time domestic missions began to receive considerable attention, and collections for that object were ordered to be made in the churches.   In 1767, or 1768, the synod had an overture, or proposal, sent from the presbytery of New York: "that there should be an annual collection in every congregation; that every presbytery should appoint a treasurer to receive and transmit the funds thus obtained; that the synod should appoint a general treasurer to whom all these presbyterial collections should be sent; and that every year a full account of the receipts and disbursements should be printed and sent down to the churches."   This was the germ of the present board of missions.   In the same year petitions for "supplies" were received from twenty-one places in Virginia, North Carolina, and Georgia.

Collections were thenceforward made in the churches.   In 1772, it was ordered that part of these moneys should be appropriated to the purchase and distribution of useful religious books, and to the promotion of the gospel among the Indians.   Two years afterwards, it was seriously contemplated to send missionaries to Africa; but on the war of the Revolution breaking out in the following year the project fell to the ground.   Even during the war there was a considerable demand for ministers from destitute congregations, and to meet this many faithful ministers made missionary tours, at no small personal hazard from the dangers of war.   Measures were taken in 1788, for forming the general assembly, which was organised in 1789, and at its very first meeting much attention was paid to the subject of missions.

"It is believed," says one of the most distinguished living ministers of the Presbyterian church, "that at this time (1789) there was not in the United States another religious denomination besides the Presbyterian, that prosecuted any domestic

Professor in the theological seminary at Princetown, New Jersey, says, that it was no uncommon thing for people to go twenty, thirty, and even forty miles, to hear him preach a single sermon.

missionary enterprise, except that then, as since, the Methodists
sent forth their circuit-preachers in all directions."[1]

In the year 1800, the Rev. Mr. Chapman was appointed a
stated missionary in the western part of the State of New York,
and to his labours we must so far ascribe the great diffusion of
Presbyterianism in that important section of the country. In
1802, the general assembly appointed a "standing committee,"
to attend to the greatly increased interests of the missionary
cause,—a measure which led to a farther extension of the work.
A correspondence was commenced with all the known missionary
societies of Europe. The committee gave much of its attention
to the coloured population, a class among whom the late John
Holt Rice, D.D., one of the most distinguished ministers that
the United States' Presbyterian church has ever produced, laboured as a missionary during seven years.

In 1816, the general assembly enlarged the powers of the
standing committee and gave it the title of "the board of missions, acting under the authority of the general assembly."
Many missionaries went forth under its auspices, to labour
among the destitute Presbyterian congregations that were continually forming in the southern and western States. Meanwhile many local societies under the direction of synods, presbyteries, and other such bodies, had sprung up, and were separately prosecuting the same objects to a considerable extent.

The general assembly again took up the subject of missions
in 1828, and farther enlarged the powers of the board, fully
authorising it to establish missions, not only in destitute parts
of the United States, but among the heathen abroad. Such,
however, was the demand for labourers at home, especially
in the western States and Territories, that nothing of importance could be done for foreign lands. It was found, besides,
that home and foreign missions could not well be united under
one board, so that in the course of a few years, the latter were
committed to the charge of another board, appointed for that
purpose by the assembly. Of its operations we shall have
occasion to speak elsewhere. The cause of domestic missions
in the Presbyterian church now went on with fresh vigour, and

---

[1] " History of the Missions of the Presbyterian church," by the Rev. Ashbel
Green, D.D.

by the synodical and presbyterial societies becoming either merged in the assembly's board, or affiliated with it, the whole assumed a more consolidated form and greater consistency. From 1838 to 1841, the missionaries increased from thirty-one to 272, according to the report for 1841, which is the latest I have seen. It presents a summary for that year of 272 missionaries employed; 500 Sunday schools attended by at least 25,000 scholars, connected with the churches under their care; 3100 members added to the churches, of whom 1800 upon examination of their faith, and 1300 upon letters of recommendation from other churches; 22,000 persons gathered into temperance societies; 35,455 dollars of receipts. The average expense of each missionary was 130 dollars. The board pursues the wise course of simply *helping* congregations, that as yet are unable to maintain pastors, by granting them so much on their undertaking to make up the deficiency.

Such is a brief notice of the operations of the home missions board of the general assembly, of that branch of the Presbyterian church commonly called the old school, to distinguish it from another branch called the new school. This board has been instrumental, under God, in giving a permanent existence to some hundreds of churches. The divine blessing has been remarkably vouchsafed to its efforts. Its affairs are managed with great wisdom and energy, and the church is much indebted to the Rev. Ashbel Green, D.D., for the deep interest which, during a long life, he has felt in this cause, and for the devotedness with which he has laboured to promote it. Nor can it fail to be a great consolation to him in his declining days, to see his love and zeal for this enterprise crowned with abundant success.

CHAPTER IX.

A SOCIETY was formed in the Protestant Episcopal church of the United States, for the promotion of home and foreign missions, in the year 1822. During the first thirteen years of its existence, that is, up to 1835, it had employed fifty-nine labourers in its home missions, occupying stations in various parts of the Union, but chiefly in the West. The society was re-organised in 1835, and as now constituted, is under the direction of a board of thirty members, appointed by the general convention of the church. The bishops, together with such persons as had become patrons of the society previous to the meeting of the convention in 1829, are members of the board, and to it is committed the whole subject of missions. But the better to expedite the business entrusted to it, the home and foreign departments are handed over respectively to two committees, each consisting of four clergymen and four laymen, under the presidency of the bishop of the diocese in which the committee resides, and both committees are *ex officio* members of the board.

It is only since 1835 that the home missions of the society have been prosecuted with much vigour, but every year now bears witness to the increasing interest felt by the Episcopal churches of the United States, in the work of building up churches in the new settlements, and other places where none of that communion had ever before existed.

During the year ending 1st June, 1841, the board had employed ninety-five missionaries, and that they did not labour without effecting much good, is apparent even from the imperfect statements of the report. At least 600 persons are estimated to have been added to the churches in 100 out of the 236 places to which the missionaries had extended their labours; and the children under catechetical instruction, in only forty stations, amounted to 1291. The income for the home missions, collected throughout the twenty-nine dioceses into which the country is divided, was 28,316 dollars. From 1822 to 1841, 186 stations had been adopted as fields of special, permanent, and, as far as practicable, regular labour. During the same period eighty church edifices had been erected in those stations, and the number of these, once aided, but no longer requiring assistance, was forty-four.

From this it will be seen that this society has not laboured in vain, but that it, likewise, is a channel by which churches that have long been favoured with the gospel, and highly prize it, are enabled to assist others until they, too, have grown up into a vigorous independence of foreign aid. " Freely ye have received; freely give;" this admonition and command should never be forgotten. It is the true basis of the whole voluntary system.

We shall only add that the missionaries employed by the board of the Episcopal church are chiefly confined to the western States and Territories; viz. two in Iowa, five in Wisconsin, eight in Michigan, eight in Indiana, seven in Missouri, nine in Illinois, five in Mississippi, three in Arkansas, one in Louisiana, five in Alabama, four in Florida, &c.

The American Baptist Home Missionary society was instituted in 1832, and has been eminently useful since in building up churches of that denomination, both in the West and in many of the Atlantic States, where the assistance of such an institution was required, as well as in establishing Sunday schools and Bible classes. Its great field of labour, however, like that of all the other societies and boards for domestic missions, has been the " Valley of the Mississippi." It has numerous branches and auxiliaries in all parts of the United States, and during the year ending in May, 1842, had ninety-seven agents and missionaries in its own immediate service, and 270 in that of its auxiliaries, making a total of 367, all of whom were ministers of the gospel, and believed to be faithful and capable labourers. They preached statedly at 661 stations, and had travelled 172,065 miles! They reported 4,222 conversions and baptisms, the organisation of thirty-six churches, and the ordination of sixteen ministers. By their instrumentality 3,131

x

persons had been induced to join the Temperance societies; 4,654 young persons had been gathered into Sunday schools and Bible classes, taught by 689 teachers. The receipts of the parent society and its auxiliaries amounted to 57,154 dollars.

The general synod of the Reformed Dutch church has a board of domestic missions which is now prosecuting, with zeal and wisdom, the work of gathering together new congregations, and fostering them during their infancy, wherever it can find openings for so doing. For several years past it has been extending its operations, and during that ending in June, 1841, it had aided thirty-three new or feeble churches. Eight of these were in the western States, and in these seven missionaries were occupied in preaching the gospel. The receipts for that period amounted to 5,889 dollars.

If the truth is to be carried into every hamlet and neighbourhood of the United States, it can only be by all denominations of evangelical Christians taking part in the enterprise; and it is delightful to trace the proofs of this conviction being widely and deeply felt.

CHAPTER X.

HOME MISSIONS OF THE METHODIST EPISCOPAL CHURCH.

It has been said with much truth that the Methodist church is in its very structure emphatically missionary, and it is an inexpressible blessing that it is so, as the United States strikingly prove. The whole country is embraced by one general conference; it again is subdivided into twenty annual conferences, each including a large extent of country, and divided into districts. Each district comprehends several circuits, and within each circuit there are from five or six to above twenty preaching places.

Ordinarily as often as once in the fortnight, a circuit-preacher conducts a regular service at each of these preaching places, whether it be a church, school-room, or in a dwelling house. In the largest towns and villages such services are held on the

Sabbath, and on a week-day or evening in other places, and thus the gospel is carried into a thousand remote spots, in which it never would be preached by the plan of having a permanent clergy, planted in particular districts and parishes.

It was a remark, I believe, of the celebrated Dr. Witherspoon, that "he needed no other evidence that the Rev. John Wesley was a great man, than what the system of itinerating preaching presented to his mind, and of which that wonderful man was the author." The observation was a just one. It is a system of vast importance in every point of view; but that from which we are at present to contemplate it is, its filling up a void which must else remain empty. Of its other advantages we shall have to speak in another place.

But, capable as the system is of being made to send its ramifications into almost every nook and corner of the country, and to carry the glad tidings of salvation into the most remote and secluded settlements, as well as to the more accessible and populous towns and neighbourhoods, many places were found, particularly in the south and west, so situated as to be beyond the reach of adequate supply from itinerant labourers,—a fact which led to the formation of the missionary society of the Methodist Episcopal church in 1819.

This society, like that of the Protestant Episcopal church, was formed for the double object of promoting missions at home and abroad. Reserving the latter for future notice, I turn at present to the former. According to the twenty-second annual report, being that for 1841, I find that it employed 216 missionaries within the limits of the United States, exclusive of those labouring among the Indians, whether within, or immediately beyond those limits. The churches enjoying the services of these missionaries, comprised above 40,000 members, and many of them had flourishing Bible classes and Sunday schools. The report for 1842, states, that among the members of the society's missionary churches, there were not fewer than 13,722 coloured people.

Perhaps of all the fields cultivated by this society, the two most interesting, and in some respects, most important, are those presented by the slaves in the extreme southern states, and by the German emigrants found in great numbers in our

x 2

chief cities. The missions among the former were commenced in 1828,[1] and originated in a proposal made to the Hon. Charles C. Pinckney, a distinguished Christian layman of the Episcopal church in South Carolina, and which has been carried into effect with much success; the slaveholders themselves, in many places, if not all, being pleased to have the missionaries preach the gospel to their people.

The following paragraph from the report for 1841, will give the reader some idea of the hazardous nature of this work: "In the southern and south-western conferences, it will be seen, under the head of domestic missions, that with commendable zeal and devotion our missionaries are still labouring in the service of the slaves upon the rice-fields, sugar, and cotton plantations, multitudes of whom, though destined to toil and bondage during their earthly pilgrimage, have by their instrumentality been brought to enjoy the liberty of the gospel, and are happily rejoicing in the blessings of God's salvation. In no portion of our work are our missionaries called to endure greater privations, or make greater sacrifices of health and life, than in these missions among the slaves, many of which are located in sections of the southern country which are proverbially sickly, and under the fatal influence of a climate which few white men are capable of enduring, even for a single year. And yet, notwithstanding so many valuable missionaries have fallen martyrs to their toils in these missions, year after year there are found others to take their places, who fall likewise in their work, 'ceasing at once to work and to live.' Nor have our superintendents any difficulty in finding missionaries ready to fill up the ranks which death has thinned in these sections of the work; for the love of Christ, and the love of the souls of these poor Africans in bonds, constrain our brethren in the itinerant work of the southern conferences to exclaim: 'Here are we, send us!' The Lord be praised for the zeal and success of our brethren in this self-denying, and self-sacrificing work."

Not less interesting are the society's missions among the Ger-

---

[1] I speak here of missions technically so called, for in their ordinary labours, the Methodists, from the first, have had much to do with the slaves in the south, as well as with the free negroes of the north. In fact, no other body of Christians has done so much good to the unfortunate children of Africa in the United States as the followers of John Wesley.

mans resident in the chief towns and cities of the valley of the Mississippi. Beginning at Pittsburg and Alleghany town, on the right bank of the Alleghany, opposite Pittsburg, it has missionaries among these foreigners in many of the chief towns on the Ohio, such as Wheeling, Marietta, Portsmouth, Maysville, Cincinnati, Lawrenceburg, New Albany, Louisburg, &c., as well as in towns remote from the river, such as Dayton and Chillicothe. It has a mission, also, at St. Louis, on the upper Mississippi. The churches gathered by the society's missionaries from among the Germans in those places, had no fewer than 824 members in 1841, and of these 200 had been Roman Catholics. Yet this work had commenced only a few years before. Fourteen missionaries were engaged in it, and several of these were men of considerable talent and learning, as well as zeal. One of them, the Rev. Mr. Nast, at Cincinnati, conducts a religious paper, with a circulation of above 1500 copies, and which seems to be doing good.

The society has a mission, likewise, among the Germans, reckoned at 30,000 at least, in the city of New York, and another among the French there. In fine, the income of this excellent and efficient society, for the year ending May 1st, 1842, amounted to 105,281 dollars, of which 90,000 dollars were expended on home missions.

Here I close these brief notices of the home missions of the chief evangelical churches in the United States. They will give the reader some idea of the mode in which new and feeble congregations are aided by the older and stronger, until able to maintain the institutions of religion themselves. The societies which we have passed under review in these four chapters, support, in all, above·1600 ministers of the gospel, in new, and as yet, feeble churches and flocks. Year after year many of these cease to require assistance, and then others are taken up in their turn. Be it remembered that the work has been systematically prosecuted for no long course of time. Twenty years ago, in fact, the most powerful and extensive of these societies did not exist; others were but commencing their operations. It is an enterprise with respect to which the churches have as yet but partially developed their energies and resources; still, they have accomplished enough to demonstrate how much may be done by the voluntary principle towards the calling into existence of churches and congregations in the settlements rapidly forming, whether in the new or the old States.

CHAPTER XI.

THE VOLUNTARY PRINCIPLE DEVELOPED—INFLUENCE OF THE VOLUNTARY PRINCIPLE
ON EDUCATION—OF PRIMARY SCHOOLS.

WE have seen how the voluntary principle operates in America in relation to the building of churches, and also the support of ministers of the gospel in the new settlements forming every year, more or less, in all quarters. We now come to consider its influence on education. Hundreds of ministers, it will be perceived, are required to meet the demands of the rapidly augmenting population. Where are these to come from? Besides, in a country where the right of suffrage is almost universal, and where so much of the order, peace, and happiness, that are the true objects of all good government, depend on officers chosen in the directest manner from among themselves, these must be instructed before they can become intelligent, virtuous, and capable citizens. Ignorance is incompatible with the acquisition or preservation of any freedom worth possessing; and, above all, such a republic as that of the United States must depend for its very existence on the wide diffusion of sound knowledge and religious principles among all classes of the people. Let us, therefore, trace the bearings of the voluntary principle upon education, in all its forms, among the various ranks of society in the United States. We shall begin with primary schools.

It may well be imagined that emigrants to the new world, who fled from the old with the hope of enjoying that religious freedom which they so much desired, would not be indifferent to the education of their children. Especially, might we expect to find that the Protestant colonists, who had forsaken all for this boon, would not fail to make early provision for the instruction of their children, in order that they might be able to read that book which is the "religion of Protestants." And such we find to have been the fact. Scarcely had the Puritans been settled half a dozen years in the colony of Massachusetts; nay, before, they began to make provision for public primary schools, to be supported by a tax assessed upon all the inhabitants. [1] And such provision was actually made, not only in Massachusetts, but in every New England colony. And such provision exists to this day in all the six New England States. Schools are maintained in every school district, during the whole or a part of every year, by law.

With the exception of the State of Connecticut, where all the public schools are maintained upon the interest of a large school fund, primary instruction is provided for by an annual assessment,—a school being taught, in every school district, by a master for the elder youth during winter, and by a mistress for the little children during summer. Wherever we find the descendants of the Puritans in America, we find a people who value education as the first of all earthly blessings; and when a colony from New England plants itself, whether amid the forests of Ohio, or on the *prairies* of Illinois, two things are ever considered as indispensable alike to temporal and to spiritual and eternal welfare,—a church and a school-house.

Nor was this thirst for education confined to the New England Puritans; it prevailed to no small degree among the Scotch and Irish Presbyterians, the Huguenots, the early German emigrants, all, in fact, who had fled from Europe for the sake of their religion. It is owing to this that primary education has been diffused so widely throughout the United States, and that no less effective legal provision has been made at length for the support of common schools in New York, Pennsylvania, and

---

[1] The small colony of Plymouth, as soon as it was in some measure settled, set about providing schools for the children, and this was several years before the colony of Massachusetts bay was planted.

But if the New England Puritans were zealous in the cause of education and learning, the Virginia colonists seem not to have any such spirit, for their governor, Sir William Berkeley, in 1670, in replying to one of the inquiries addressed to him by the Lords of Plantations, says: "I thank God, *there are no free schools, nor printing*, and I hope we shall not have them these hundred years; for learning has brought *disobedience*, and *heresy*, and *sects* into the world, and printing has divulged them, and libels against the best government. God keep us from both!"—Hening's Laws of Virginia, Appendix.

Ohio, than in the New England States, and to a considerable extent, also, in New Jersey and Delaware, whilst in all the others it has led to the adoption of measures for the education of the children of the poor, and to the creation of school funds which, taken together with other means, promise one day to be available for the education of all classes.

The white population of the United States amounted in 1840 to 14,189,218, of which number it was ascertained that 549,693 persons, above twenty years of age, could neither read nor write. A large proportion of these must have been foreigners,—Irish, Germans, Swiss, and French,—as is evident from 13,041 of them being found in the six New England States, where education is nearly as universal as can well be imagined. That a native of either sex, in short, above the age of twenty, may be found in Connecticut or Massachusetts is not denied; but that there should be 526 such persons in the former of these States, and 4448 in the latter, cannot be believed by any one who knows the condition of the people there. The greater number were not native Americans, and even of those that remained the majority were idiots.

By the census of 1840, it appears that the number of primary and common schools amounted to 47,209, attended by 1,845,245 scholars; of whom 468,264 were taught at the public charge, the remainder at that of their parents and friends. From this it will be seen that education in America depends very much on the voluntary principle; but though primary schools were in all parts of the country originated and sustained at first, as in most of the States it continues to be, by the people themselves, or rather by the friends of education, State after State is beginning to be induced by the efforts of these friends of education to make a legal provision, to a certain extent at least, for the instruction of all who may choose to avail themselves of it, for in this they do not see that they violate any rights of conscience.

The right of giving instruction is, in the United States, universal. Even where there is an all-pervading system of public schools, any number of families may join together, and employ any teacher for their children that they may prefer. Nor has that teacher to procure any licence or "brevet of instruction" before entering on the duties of his office. His employers are the sole judges of his capacity, and should he prove inefficient the remedy is in their own hands. The teachers employed by the State pass an examination before a proper committee. In all the States where there is a legal provision for primary schools, there is a yearly report from each to a committee of the township, from which again there is a report to a county committee, and that, in its turn, sends a report to the secretary or school commissioner of the State.

In most cases, a pious and judicious teacher, if he will only confine himself to the great doctrines and precepts of the gospel, in which all who hold the fundamental truths of the Bible are agreed, can easily give as much religious instruction as he chooses. Where the teacher himself is not decidedly religious, much religious instruction cannot be expected; nor should any but religious teachers attempt to give anything more than general moral instruction, and make the scholars read portions of the scriptures, and of other good books.

The Bible is very generally used as a reading book in our primary schools, though in some places, as at St. Louis, the Roman Catholics have succeeded in excluding it, and they have been struggling to do the same in New York, where they will, probably, sooner or later succeed. In so far as relates to public schools, I see no other course but that of leaving it to the people themselves; the majority deciding and leaving the minority the alternative of supporting a school of their own. This will generally be done by Christians rather than give up the Bible.

In most parts of the United States, it has been found extremely difficult to procure good teachers, few men being willing to devote their lives to that occupation in a country so full of openings in more lucrative and inviting professions and employments. Hence very incompetent teachers—not a few from Ireland and other parts of the British dominions—or none at all. This is particularly the case in the middle, southern, and western States. But it is an evil which diminishes with the increase of population, and besides, much attention has of late been paid to the training of teachers. A very laudable effort is now making in New England, and also in New York, and some other States, to attach a library of suitable books to each school. The plan is excellent and promises much good.

Primary instruction in the United States owes almost everything to religion, as the most efficient of all the principles that prompts to its promotion. Not that the Protestants of that country interest themselves in the primary schools for the purpose of proselytising children to their views, but rather that at these schools the youth of the nation may be qualified for receiving religious instruction effectually elsewhere, and for the due discharge of their future duties as citizens. And, however much they may wish to see religious instruction given at the common schools, they will not for a moment give into the opinion that all is lost where this cannot be accomplished. Primary instruction, even when not accompanied with any religious instruction, is better than none; and in such cases, they that love the gospel have other resources,—in the pulpit, the family altar, the Bible class, and the Sabbath school.

CHAPTER XII.

GRAMMAR SCHOOLS AND ACADEMIES.

But if primary schools in the United States owe much to religion, grammar schools and academies, which may be called secondary institutions, owe still more.

In 1647, not many years after the settlement of the Puritans in New England, we find the colony of Massachusetts bay making a legal provision, not only for primary, but for secondary schools also. "It being one chief project of Satan," says the statute, "to keep men from the knowledge of the scriptures by dissuading from the use of tongues; and to the end that learning may not be buried in the graves of our forefathers in church and commonwealth, the Lord assisting our endeavours; therefore be it enacted, that every township, after the Lord hath increased them to the number of fifty householders, shall appoint one to teach all children to write and read; and where any town shall increase to the number of 100 families, they shall set up a grammar school; the masters thereof being able to instruct youth so far as they may be fitted for the university." Such was the origin of the grammar schools of New England, and now they are so numerous that not only has almost every county one, but many of the more populous and wealthy possess several.

Not only so; all the other States have incorporated academies and grammar schools in very considerable numbers. Some, by a single act, have made an appropriation for the establishment of one such institution in every county within their jurisdiction. Thus in Pennsylvania, many years ago, 2000 dollars were granted for the erection of a building for a grammar school, at the seat of justice for each county, and a board of trustees, with power to fill up vacancies as they might occur in their numbers, was appointed for each. These buildings are now occupied by masters who teach the higher branches of an English education, and in most cases, also, the Latin and Greek languages, besides such instruction in the mathematics, and other studies, as may qualify the pupils for going to college. Like provisions have been made by other States, and even the newest of them in the "far west" are continually encouraging learning by passing such acts. In no case, however, does a State endow such an institution. A grant is made at the outset for the edifice that may be required; in most cases this is all that is done by the state, after which the institution has to depend upon the fees paid by the scholars for the support of the master or masters employed. In some instances, as in that of the State of New York, the grammar school has a yearly subsidy from the state, in which case there is usually some condition attached to the grant, such as gratis instruction to a certain number of poor lads, or of youths intending to become teachers of primary schools. But in most, even of the cases in which they have been aided by the state, these institutions have not only been privately commenced and carried to a certain point, previous to such assistance, but owe much more afterwards to the spontaneous support of their friends. Indeed, in all parts of the country, grammar schools, and some of these the very best, may be found which owe their existence purely to individual or associated efforts. Such is the "Burr Seminary," in the town of Manchester, and State of Vermont, which originated in a legacy of 10,000 dollars, left by a gentleman of the name of Joseph Burr,[1] for the education of poor and pious young men for the ministry. By the terms of his will, in case of an equal sum being raised by the citizens of the place for the erection of a suitable building, the purchase of apparatus, library, &c., then his legacy of 10,000 dollars might be invested as a permanent fund, the interest of which was to be applied to paying for the education of such young men as he should designate. This was done even beyond the extent required by the testator. A large and commodious edifice was erected, containing rooms for the recitation of lessons, lectures, library, philosophical apparatus, &c. The school was opened on the 15th of May, 1833, and the number of scholars for the first term was 146; many of whom were pious youths, devoting themselves to study with a view to the ministry. The institution still flourishes under the instructions of excellent men, and being situated in a secluded and moral village in the midst of the Green mountains, where living is cheap, it is attended by choice youths, some thirty or forty of whom are educated gratuitously. Such, again, is "Philips' Academy," at Andover in Massachusetts, about twenty miles north of Boston. Founded in 1778, by the joint liberality of two brothers, the Hon. Samuel Philips, of Andover, and the Hon. John Philips, of Exeter, New Hampshire; it, two years afterwards, received a charter of incorporation from the state. The fund supplied by these two brothers was afterwards augmented by the bequest of a third, the Hon. William Philips, of Boston.

This academy, which is one of the best endowed in the United States, has been truly a blessing to the cause of religion and learning. By the terms prescribed by its pious founders, it is open to all youth of good character, but they have placed it under the control of Protestants, and the religious instruction given must be orthodox in the true sense of the word. Instruc-

---

[1] Mr. Burr had been for many years a resident at Manchester, in Vermont. By patient industry and upright dealings he acquired a fortune estimated at 150,000 dollars at the time of his death. A large part of this sum he bequeathed to the American Bible Society, Board of Commissioners for foreign missions, Home Missionary Society, and Education Society, besides endowing a professorship in one college, and contributing largely to the same object in another. And in addition to all this, by the above bequest of 10,000 dollars he founded the seminary that bears his name.

tions are required to be given in the English, Latin, and Greek languages; in writing, arithmetic, and music; in the art of speaking; also in practical geometry, logic; and any other of the liberal arts, sciences, or languages, as opportunity and ability may from time to time admit, and the trustees shall direct. As the education of suitable young men for the ministry, was a leading consideration with the founders, so has the institution been in this respect abundantly blessed. Many such youths have here pursued their preparatory studies, and in 1808, availing themselves of a provision contained in the plan marked out by the founders, the trustees engrafted on the institution, or rather established in the same village, and under the same direction, a theological seminary, which has become one of the most distinguished of the kind in the United States, and will call for more ample notice hereafter.

A large proportion of the grammar schools and academies in the United States, whether incorporated or not, are under the direction and instruction of ministers of the gospel, of different evangelical denominations. These ministers, in some cases, devote their whole time to the work of academical instruction; in other cases they have, also, the charge of a church or congregation, and as they have to perform the double duties of pastor and head of a grammar school, they have usually an assistant teacher in the latter. The teachers in these academies are often pious young men, of small pecuniary resources, who, after completing their studies at college, betake themselves to this employment for a few years, in order to find the means of supporting themselves while attending a theological school. But whether ministers of the gospel, or graduates fresh from college, such teachers generally communicate instruction of a decidedly religious character. The scriptures are daily read; the school is usually opened and closed with prayer; and in many cases, a Bible class, comprising all the pupils, meets on the Sabbath afternoon, or morning, for the study of the scriptures. Thus, by the favour of God resting on these institutions, and making them effectual to the converting of many of the youths that attend them, they prove blessings to the church of Christ, as well as to the state.

Let me add, that within the last ten or twenty years, a great many excellent institutions for the education of young women have sprung up in different parts of the United States, through associated or individual efforts. The course of instruction at these is excellent and extensive, embracing all branches of valuable knowledge proper for young ladies. Upon many of these, also, God has caused his blessing to descend, and has brought not a few of the young persons attending them to the knowledge of Himself. They are generally conducted by ladies, but the teachers in some cases are gentlemen, clergymen especially, assisted by pious ladies in giving instruction. In few countries, probably, has the higher education of young ladies made greater progress than in the United States during the last few years. The Christian community there begins to feel that mothers have in a great measure the formation of the national character in their hands.

According to the census of 1840, the grammar schools and academies for both sexes in the United States, amounted to 3242, attended by 164,159 pupils.

CHAPTER XIII.

COLLEGES AND UNIVERSITIES.

In the census of the United States for 1840, the number of universities and colleges is put down at 173, and that of students at 16,233. This, however, includes not only the theological, medical, and law schools, but several other institutions improperly called colleges. A more accurate list makes the colleges amount to 103, and the students to 9,607. But even this estimate includes several institutions, which though incorporated as colleges, are scarcely so far organised as to be entitled to the name. In some cases, too, the students in the preparatory departments are reckoned along with the under-graduates, properly so called, that is, the students in the four regular classes of seniors, juniors, sophomores, and freshmen, into which the students of our colleges are divided. If we assume that 9,000 students, in all, attend the colleges, properly so called, in the United States, we come very near the truth.

It would be absurd to compare the colleges of America with the great universities of Europe. The course of studies is widely different. For while sufficiently comprehensive in almost all the colleges that deserve that name, it is not to be compared, in general, as respects depth and extent of investigation in particular branches with that of the older universities of Europe. But, upon the whole, the education to be had at one of our colleges, better capacitates a man for the work that is likely to await him in America, than would that which the universities of Europe could give him,—if one may be allowed to judge from experience.

In almost all instances, the colleges in the United States have been founded by religious men. The common course in establishing them is as follows. A company is organised, a subscription list opened, and certain men of influence in the neighbourhood consent to act as trustees. A charter is then asked from the legislature of the State within which the projected institution is to be placed, and a grant in aid of the funds at the same time solicited. The charter is obtained, and with it a few thousand dollars perhaps, by way of assistance. What else is required for the purchase of a site, erecting buildings, providing a library, apparatus, &c., &c., must be made up by those interested in the project. Thus have vast sums been raised, particularly during the last twenty years, for founding colleges in all parts of the country, but particularly in the west. A great proportion of these sums have been subscribed by persons in the neighbourhood, and more directly interested in the success of the undertakings subscribed for; but in many cases, money to a large amount has been obtained from the churches along the Atlantic coast.

Sixty-one of the 103 colleges in the United States have been opened within the last twenty-five years. Many of these are, of course, in their infancy, and not very well organised. Without reckoning grants made by the States, it would be difficult to find one that has not cost its founders above 10,000 dollars, and many have cost them twice that sum. Several[1] have cost even

[1] For instance, Pennsylvania college at Gettysburg, Pennsylvania : Centre

50,000 dollars, if not more, while at the same time, several of the older colleges, such as Yale, New Jersey, Rutgers, Williams, Hamilton, &c., have raised large sums by voluntary effort among their respective friends, for the purpose of augmenting the advantages they offer to the students that attend them. Upon the whole, I consider that it were not too much to say, that from 1,500,000 to 2,000,000 dollars, have been raised by voluntary subscriptions and donations for the erection and endowment of colleges, since the year 1816.

I have said that the state gives some aid to many such enterprises. But, excepting the universities of Virginia, Alabama, Michigan, and those of Ohio and Miami, both in the State of Ohio, and Jefferson college in Mississippi and Jefferson college in Louisiana, I am not aware of any college in the country that can be said to have been wholly endowed by the government of any State. The universities of North Carolina and Georgia, and Columbia college in South Carolina, may possibly be so far aided by the States in which they are respectively situated, as to have something like an endowment, but the aid so rendered, I apprehend, is far from sufficient. So also, Congress has aided from time to time the "Columbia college," situated near Washington city, and within the district of Columbia,[1] but the aid so received has never been at all adequate to the purposes for which it was required.

There are not above six or seven colleges, or universities, in the United States, over which the civil or political governments can exercise any direct control. It is well that it is so. A state legislation, or congress itself, would be found very unfit to direct the affairs of a college or university. Wherever, in fact, they have reserved such power to themselves in the charters they have granted, they have sooner or later, nearly, if not altogether, ruined the institutions on which they have laid their unhallowed hands. A college or university is no place for party politics, and so well is this understood, that the legislatures of

college at Danville, Kentucky; Illinois college at Jacksonville, Illinois; Western Reserve college, Ohio; to say nothing of some of the Roman Catholic colleges, which have not cost much less, from first to last, than 50,000 dollars; Amherst college in Massachusetts, has cost more than that sum probably; whilst the university of New York has cost twice, if not three times that amount.

[1] This college comes properly within the sphere of the legislation of congress, and is the only one that does so. All the others come under the jurisdiction of the several States within whose territories they stand.

the several States hesitate not to grant a college charter to a body of respectable citizens, and to appoint at once the persons recommended as trustees or directors, with power to fill up the vacancies that may occur; after which these office-bearers, having sworn to do nothing in that capacity contrary to the laws and constitution, national or local, of the country, are empowered to manage and govern the proposed college according to their own best judgment; and the regulations they may lay down to that effect. While acting within the limits prescribed by the charter and their oath, that charter must remain inviolate. So it has been determined by the supreme court of the United States.

I have said that almost every college existing in the country may be traced to religious motives, and how true this is will appear from the fact, that of the 103 colleges now in operation, twelve are under the influence of the Protestant Episcopal church, eleven under that of the Methodists, twelve under that of the Baptists, forty-one under that of the Presbyterians and Congregationalists; one is Lutheran, one German Reformed, two Dutch Reformed, two Cumberland Presbyterian; eleven are Roman Catholic, one Universalist, one Unitarian, and the religious character of seven of them I do not know. In this calculation I place each institution under the church to which the president belongs. This rule is the best that I know, and although it does not hold in every case, the exceptions are few; and without any exception, it indicates the general faith by which the institution is influenced.

Thus we see that of these 102 universities and colleges, *eighty-two* are under decided evangelical and orthodox influences. Their presidents, and I may add, many of their professors, are known to be religious men, and sound in the faith; all, with three or four exceptions, are ministers of the gospel, and many of them men of great eminence in the church. The seven colleges whose religious character I do not know, are probably under evangelical influence; six of the seven, I have reason to believe, are Protestant. I need not say how much cause for gratitude to God we have, that so many young men of the first families, and possessing fine talents, should be educated in colleges that are under the influence of evangelical principles. In many of them the Bible is studied by the students every Sabbath, under the guidance of their teachers. In all they receive a great deal of religious instruction, and are daily assembled for prayers. God has often visited some of them with the outpourings of his Spirit. Not that this religious instruction is intended to proselytise from one Protestant and evangelical church to another. In that respect, a Presbyterian father might with all safety commit his son to an Episcopalian, Methodist, or Lutheran college. Here I speak from facts that I myself have known. Several of the most distinguished dignitaries of the Episcopal church were educated at Princetown college, New Jersey, a Presbyterian institution, and founded by Presbyterians. Some of them received their first religious convictions there, and yet, I believe, they can testify that no office-bearer of that college ever attempted to bring them over to the Presbyterian church. Any advice of that kind, on the contrary, would be that they should join the church in which they were born, that is, the Episcopal.[1]

As none of the universities but that of Harvard, situated at the town of Cambridge, not far from Boston, have all the four faculties of literature, law, medicine, and theology, with that exception they ought rather to be called colleges. The theology at Harvard is Unitarian. Several of the other universities have faculties of medicine attached to them. On the other hand, Yale college at New Haven, in Connecticut, ought rather to be called a university, for it has all the four faculties, and is attended by far more students than go to Harvard.

I may add that Harvard university was the first literary institution established in the United States. It was founded in 1638, eight years after Massachusetts bay, and eighteen after Plymouth was first colonised; so that there were not many more than 5000 settlers at the time in all New England. Hardly had the forests been cleared away for the streets of their settlements, when they began to project a college or university. And yet these were the Puritans now so much vilified and slandered!

[1] The Rev. Dr. M'Ilvaine, the distinguished bishop of Ohio, and the no less excellent, though perhaps less known assistant bishop of Virginia, the Rev. Dr. Johns, were both educated and converted at Princetown college. The late bishop Hobart of New York, was educated, and was for some time a tutor there.

Great were the efforts made by those exiles to attain their object. The general court granted for the erection of a proper edifice a sum equal to a year's rate of the whole colony. John Harvard, who had come to the new world only to die, bequeathed to the college half his estate, and all his library. Plymouth and Connecticut often sent their little offerings, as did the eastern towns within the boundaries of the present State of Maine. The rent of a ferry was made over to it. All the families in the Puritan settlements each gave once a donation of at least twelve pence, or a peck of corn, or its value in Wampumpeag,[1] while larger gifts were made by the magistrates and wealthier citizens. It was for long the only college in New England, and in its halls the great men of the country were educated. For a century and a half it was a precious fountain of living waters for the church of God. But, alas! for the last half century, or nearly so, it has been in the hands of men who hold "another gospel" than that held by its pious founders.[2]

The second college founded in the United States was that of William and Mary at Williamsburg, in Virginia, in 1693. The third was Yale college above mentioned, founded in 1700. The fourth was Princetown college, New Jersey, founded in 1746. The university of Pennsylvania dates from 1755; Columbia college, in New York, from 1754; Brown university from 1764; Rutgers and Dartmouth colleges from 1770. These were all that were founded previous to the Revolution.

[1] Shells, or strings of shells, used by the American Indians as a medium of commerce.

[2] A voluminous and interesting history of this university, by the present president, Josiah Quincy, LL.D., has lately been published.

CHAPTER XIV

ONE of the most efficient, as well as the simplest means of doing good, is the Sunday school—an institution, the history of which is too well known to require any detail in this work. Mr. Robert Raikes, of Gloucester, in England, towards the close of the last century, established the first that was ever conducted upon anything like the plan now generally pursued, and the excellence of which has been proved by long experience.

The first attempt to introduce Sunday schools into the United States was made by the Methodists in 1790, but from some cause or other it failed. A society was soon after formed at Philadelphia, with the late Bishop White at its head, and a few schools were established for the benefit of the poor, taught by persons who received a certain compensation for their trouble. Early in the present century, schools began to be established in various places under voluntary and gratuitous teachers, and gradually becoming better known and appreciated, the number was found very considerable in 1816. Associations for promoting them more extensively began then to be formed in Philadelphia, New York, and other cities, and the publication of spelling and hymn-books, scriptural catechisms, &c. for the children was commenced. Some persons also did much to advance this good work individually.[1]

Measures were taken in 1823 for the forming of a national society which should extend the benefit of Sunday schools to all parts of the country; and, accordingly, the American Sunday School Union was instituted—an association composed of excellent men of all evangelical denominations, and in which therefore no particular denomination is represented as such.

---

[1] Among whom may be mentioned the late Divie Bethune, Esq., who published at his own expence a number of little books for the instruction of youth in Sunday schools.

It has now been diffusing its blessings for above eighteen years. The board of managers is composed of intelligent and zealous laymen of the various evangelical denominations, the greater part residing in Philadelphia and its vicinity, as that is the centre of the society's operations.

Its grand object is twofold;—to promote the establishment of Sunday schools where required, and to prepare and publish suitable books, some to be employed as manuals in the schools, and others for libraries intended to furnish the children with suitable reading at home. In both departments much good has been done. In the former, Sunday school missionaries, commonly ministers of the gospel and sometimes capable laymen, have been employed in visiting almost all parts of the country. They hold public meetings in every district or neighbourhood where they have any prospect of success, endeavour to interest the people in the subject, and to establish a school. Time and care are required for such a work. The nature of a Sunday school must be well explained; fit persons must be engaged as teachers, these must have their duties pointed out to them, and the motives that ought to prompt them to undertake the office presented and enforced; and money must be collected for the purchase of books.

In 1830, the society resolved to establish a Sunday school in every neighbourhood that was without any, throughout the western States or valley of the Mississippi, wherever practicable. Three years thereafter it adopted a like resolution with respect to the southern States. Both, but particularly the former of these resolutions, called forth much effort. Large sums were collected, and a great many schools were established. Every year since its commencement the society has employed many of the above missionaries; in some years as many as twenty, thirty, forty, and even fifty such. These traverse the country throughout its vast extent, resuscitate decaying schools, establish new ones, and encourage all.

In its other department the society has rendered great services to the cause of religion, and, I may add, to that of literature also. Exclusive of the scriptures, spelling-books, primers, catechisms, maps, cards for infant schools, &c., it has published 430 volumes of books for libraries, a complete set of which, well

bound, costs about seventy-five dollars. It has published, likewise, a selection from these as a library for common schools.
Among its publications may be mentioned its admirable manuals
or aids for studying the Bible; namely, a Geography of the
Bible, Natural History of the Bible, Dictionary of the Bible,
Antiquities of the Bible, Scriptural Biographies, Maps of the
Holy Land, and Books of Questions, in several volumes, on
almost all parts of the Bible, for the use of children and teachers. Whilst all these publications are thoroughly Protestant
in their character, they contain nothing repugnant to the doctrines of any of the evangelical denominations, so that there is
nothing to forbid their being used in the Sunday schools of any
of the Protestant churches. This is a great advantage, and
enables the society to establish hundreds of schools in places
where various religious bodies intermingle, and where none of
them is strong enough to support a school by itself. The society
publishes also a very valuable journal once in the fortnight. It
is replete with interesting and instructive matter, and adapted
alike to scholars, teachers, and parents.

But besides this great society, which stands ready to promote the cause anywhere, and on the most catholic principles,
there are other Sunday school societies, not less efficient in
their respective spheres. The Episcopalians have theirs, the
Baptists theirs, the Episcopal Methodists theirs, the Lutherans
theirs, and so forth. The Presbyterians, strictly speaking,
have no Sunday school society of their own, but by their publication board they publish books for Sunday school libraries.
Indeed, all the denominational Sunday school societies publish
books for their own schools, and in these they set forth and
defend the peculiar views they hold respectively, on points of
doctrine or discipline, to such an extent as they deem proper.
This is not unnatural, for each school is mainly attended by
the children of parents attached to churches of the same denomination with that of the society that supports the school. Not
that all the publications of a denominational Sunday school
society are of what may be termed a sectarian character. This
is by no means the case, and, besides, these more limited
societies buy from the Sunday school union whatever books
upon its list they may think proper to add to their own.

It is impossible to calculate the extent to which the Sunday school libraries, composed as they are of most interesting books on almost all subjects of a moral and religious character, are fostering a taste for reading among the rising youth, and the adult population, also, of the country. The scholars receive from them one or two volumes each, according to the size, every Sabbath, to read in the course of the week, and return on the Sabbath following, and these volumes thus pass into the hands of older brothers and sisters, parents, and other members of the household. The proceeds of the sales of books by the American Sunday school union amounted last year (1841) to 55,506 dollars. If we add to this the value of those sold by the denominational Sunday school societies, we should find it rise to at least 100,000 dollars. And if we further add the cost of Sunday school books purchased from the booksellers, we shall have a total far exceeding the last amount, as the value of books bought in one year for the use of Sunday schools, and mainly for the libraries attached to them.

Besides the series of 430 volumes published by the American Sunday school society, fully as many more probably have been published by the denominational societies, without including volumes published by any two of them, or by any one of them, and the American Sunday school union.[1] This would make a series of above 850 volumes of juvenile reading, much of an excellent character. Neither pains nor money have been spared in the preparation, improvement, and publication of these volumes; and, in this respect, I am inclined to think that the American Sunday school union has outstripped every other country. Much, notwithstanding, remains to be done in order to render these Sunday school books all that they ought to be. It is no easy task to write books for children well. Much talent has been bestowed upon it of late years in the United States, and such has been the demand for children's books created by the Sunday schools, that the booksellers have found it for their advantage to publish such books for those schools. Many of these are good, but many, too, worthless enough, as may readily be supposed where there is no intelligent committee

[1] The series published by the Methodist " Book Concern " exceeded 240 in 1841.

rigorously to examine them previous to publication, and to determine what should go forth to the public and what should not.

Sunday schools are held in various places; sometimes in churches, or in the lecture rooms attached to many of our large churches, or in rooms fitted up expressly for the purpose in the basement storey of many of our city churches; sometimes in the school-houses, which are very numerous, and, especially in the new settlements, in private houses. In summer they sometimes meet in barns, and I once superintended a Sunday school myself, which met for many months in a large kitchen attached to a farm-house, and that in the State of New Jersey.

The hours of meeting are very various. In the cities and large towns they commonly meet twice in the day; at 8 or 9 o'clock in the morning, according to the season, and at 2 o'clock in the afternoon, for about an hour and a half each time. In the villages and country churches they usually meet for two hours, once a day, immediately before or immediately after the public services. In some cases I have known a pastor, with a parish extending many miles in all directions from the church, meet, during an hour before his public service, with nearly all the adult part of his flock in a Bible class, and go over with them the portion of scripture given out to his Sunday schools for that day; and then, instead of having service in the afternoon, he would in the latter part of the day visit one or other, in their order, of the ten or twelve schools held by his people in as many different neighbourhoods. On these occasions he would address not only the children and teachers, but also the parents and others, who would crowd to hear him. And how could a pastor instruct his people more effectually? [1]

A word or two may not be amiss on the manner of conducting our Sunday schools. Each is under a superintendent,—a gentleman where there are scholars of both sexes, but usually a lady where there are only girls. The scholars are divided into classes according to their age and capacity. All the reading classes learn the same part of scripture, going through a certain book in order. Suppose, for instance, the fifteenth chapter of Luke, from the eleventh verse to the end. It is the parable of the

---

[1] In some of the large cities, Sunday schools are held by night, especially for the benefit of the coloured people.

prodigal son. As soon as the school is opened the scholars take their places. The service begins with prayer, by the superintendent or some other person. Each class—composed usually of six or eight persons—has its teacher, to whom the scholars repeat the lesson in the scriptures for the day. When that is done, the teacher takes the book of Bible questions, (a copy of which each scholar should have,) and asks the questions in it, relating to the passage which the class in common with the others has learned. The answers to these questions the pupils must find out through their own efforts, or with help from their parents, during the week. The teacher asks, also, such other questions as he may think useful, and calculated to lead to a more perfect understanding of the subject. An hour, perhaps, is spent in this exercise. After that the scholars return the books which they had obtained from the librarian on the preceding Sabbath, and obtain others. Then the superintendant, or pastor if he be present, addresses a few words to the whole school on the passage which they have learned, and endeavours to impress upon their minds the importance of the truths which it teaches. A hymn is sung, and a prayer offered up, and the school closes.

If there be any children that cannot read they are arranged in classes by themselves, and taught that important acquirement. In many of the schools there is a considerable number of such, and persons beyond the years of childhood who have had no opportunities of learning to read before, sometimes make the attainment in the course of a few months at a Sunday school.

In all the free States, and in such of the slave holding ones as permit the slaves to be taught, there are Sunday schools for the coloured people.[1] In these schools thousands and tens of thousands of them have learned to read the sacred scriptures, and have made much progress in divine knowledge.

The superintendents of the Sunday schools are sometimes

[1] There are Sunday schools held by some pious slave-holders in Georgia, South Carolina, and perhaps some other States, in which portions of scripture are often repeated to the assembled slaves, and remarked upon until they have committed much of them to memory. Prayer and singing are added to these exercises. Such schools no laws can well hinder, no more than they can the preaching of the gospel to the slaves. These schools have only been commenced within a few years, and are spreading in several places.

elders and deacons of the churches; sometimes they are pious lawyers, and other intelligent gentlemen; and in the vicinity of our colleges and theological seminaries they are often students of religious character, and who may be prosecuting their studies with a view to the ministry. The teachers are for the most part young people of both sexes, belonging to the churches and congregations. Wherever truly pious persons can be found willing to be thus employed they are preferred; but where this is not the case, seriously disposed and moral persons, who desire to be engaged in this benevolent work, are taken, and almost invariably it happens, that in teaching others they themselves become instructed out of the "law of God." It is to be regretted that most of the ladies after they become wives and mothers, have too many domestic cares and duties to allow them to continue as teachers in the Sabbath school. Some, however, there are who persevere in this blessed employment, their zeal triumphing over every obstacle.

As to gentlemen, many more of them may continue in the work after they have become heads of families. Hence we often find men of age and experience among Sunday school teachers, encouraging and aiding them in their toils. And it is not uncommon to find some of those who hold the very highest offices in the state, or general government, spending a portion of their Sabbaths in giving instruction to a class of young persons in a Sunday school. I have known several governors and their ladies, members of congress, and of the legislatures of the States, judges, eminent lawyers, mayors of cities, &c., who were, and who are at the present time, Sabbath school teachers, and who have felt it no degradation to be thus employed. The present distinguished chancellor of the university of New York, was the superintendent of a Sunday school, even when he held the office of attorney-general of his native State, and afterwards when he was a senator in the congress of the United States; he is a Sabbath school teacher still, and delights to associate himself with the simplest youths engaged in that heavenly employment.

The late Hon. Benjamin F. Butler was a Sabbath school teacher, even while holding the distinguished office of attorney-general to the United States. The late chief justice Marshall, and the late judge Washington, both of the supreme court of the

United States, and the former of whom was admitted to be the most distinguished jurist the country had ever produced, were warm friends and patrons of Sunday schools. Both were in their day vice-presidents of the American Sabbath School Union. Within five years of his death I saw chief justice Marshall march through the city of Richmond in Virginia, where he resided, at the head of the Sunday schools on the occasion of a celebration. And finally, the late president Harrison, who in his youth had been a rough, and far from religious soldier, but towards the close of life became interested in the things that concerned his everlasting peace, taught for several years a class of young women in a humble Sunday school on the banks of the Ohio. And the Sabbath before he left his home for Washington, there to become his country's chief magistrate; and alas! within a month thereafter to die;—he met, as usual, his Bible class.

I have dwelt the longer on this subject because of its great importance. A Sabbath school is so simple an affair that it may be begun wherever two or three persons are found disposed to undertake it. I have known even a single man keep one himself, and spend several hours every Sabbath in instructing some dozen or twenty poor youths, who came around him to learn to read and understand the word of God. I have known a lady, who, as her health did not permit her to go to a Sunday school, received a class of young ladies in her parlour every Sabbath for years. Why, then, should not Sabbath schools be established in every city, town, hamlet, and neighbourhood, where there are even two or three persons with hearts to love the kingdom of God, and hands to promote it? Were such a spirit to prevail in all lands professedly Christian, how soon would they show a very different aspect from what they do at present?

It is impossible to state with accuracy the present number of Sunday schools in the United States. They were reckoned seven years ago at 16,000; the teachers at 130,000, or 140,000; and the scholars comprising, it was supposed, 100,000 adults, at 1,000,000! These numbers must be much greater now. Who can estimate the amount of good resulting from 1,000,000 of minds being brought into contact every Sabbath with the word of Him who hath said that his "word shall not return unto him void." Thousands and tens of thousands, both teachers and scholars, are known to have become enlightened and saved, by means of the lessons given and received at Sunday Schools. But a whole volume would not suffice to unfold all the benefits conferred by this blessed institution, to which may be emphatically applied the words of the celebrated Adam Smith, in speaking of popular education in general, that it is "the cheap defence of nations."

CHAPTER XV.

BIBLE CLASSES.

AKIN to Sunday schools are Bible classes. Indeed, the former, conducted as at present in America, are little more than an assemblage of the latter.

What are commonly called Bible classes, are composed of a comparatively large number of persons, all taught by the pastor of the church, or some one other individual whom he engages to act for him. To preside over a Bible class of from twenty to some hundreds of persons, the greater number, if not all, of whom are adults, and some of them, perhaps, remarkably intelligent and well-informed, requires far higher qualifications than simply to teach a small class in a Sunday school.

These Bible classes are generally conducted by the pastors, and so highly are they valued as a means and occasion of good, that few settled pastors have not one or more among their flocks. In some cases, one for each sex is held once in the week,—that for gentlemen in the evening, that for ladies during the day. They meet according to circumstances, in the church, lecture-room, vestry-room, school-room, or in some private house. The pastor sometimes devotes his Sabbath nights to a Biblical service for the benefit of all who can attend, a practice feasible only where the population is compact, and the flock within an easy distance of the place of meeting. In country churches, these classes often hold their meetings in church before the regular service commences, or in the interval between the morning and afternoon services. This is convenient, but is apt to produce fatigue.

I have known pastors in country churches who had no fewer than 500 persons in one Bible class, if I can call it so, which met in the afternoon instead of the regular service; and others, whose Bible classes included the whole adult part of their flocks, and met previous to the forenoon service, or in the interval between that and the afternoon service.

In conducting these classes the common method is to go through some particular book of the sacred volume in course, and some system of Bible questions is generally pursued. Upon this plan all who have time and inclination for the task prepare themselves, by reading and study, for answering the questions to be found in the book of questions that is used.[1] But it is not the practice of any well-informed pastor to confine himself to the questions contained in the book. These he employs as he sees fit; by the questions he puts he assists in sustaining the attention of the people; and he takes occasion to give a great amount of scriptural instruction.

To conduct a Bible class in a manner at once interesting and profitable, requires no little preparation; and when well done, few methods of instruction are more edifying, either to the people or to the minister himself. The divine blessing has rested most remarkably upon it. Nor could we expect that it should be otherwise. What more likely to secure the divine benediction than to bring the mind to the study of that which God himself hath spoken? "The entrance of thy word giveth light; it giveth understanding to the simple." "Sanctify them by thy truth; thy word is truth."

[1] Several distinguished clergymen of the United States have written systems of Bible questions, among whom may be mentioned the Rev. Drs. M'Douell, Tyng, and Barnes. The Bible questions published by the American Sunday School Union are good, as are, also, several of those printed by the Denominational Sunday School Societies.

CHAPTER XVI.

I MUST not omit, among the means which there is reason to believe that God has greatly blessed to the advancing of his kingdom in the United States, the Maternal Societies—institutions that have not been of many years standing among us, but which have existed long enough to produce much good.

These societies are composed of pious mothers, who meet in parties, not inconveniently numerous, once in the week, fortnight, or month, for the purpose of conversing on the bringing up of their children for the Lord, listening to the reading of valuable remarks or hints on the best means of discharging this great duty, and mingling their prayers before a throne of grace in behalf of themselves and their beloved offspring. These little meetings prove very precious seasons to many an anxious, perplexed, and disheartened mother, by communicating grace, and strength, and support, and light, for enabling her to fulfil her awfully responsible part. God has greatly blessed them. For the benefit of mothers, some excellent periodicals have been published in the United States during some years past. Among these let me mention " the Mother's Magazine," published in New York, and for several years past republished in London. Mrs. A. G. Whittelsey is the editor. It appears once a month, is neatly printed, and costs only a dollar a year. The gifted editor was for above nine years assisted in it by her excellent husband, the late Rev. Samuel Whittelsey, and many judicious and able correspondents still support it with their contributions. It has a very extensive circulation, and furnishes much admirable matter for reading at the maternal societies' meetings, as well as in the family circle. Another valuable periodical is published at Utica, in the central part of the State of New York, and is read in several thousands of families. It is conducted by Mrs. Allen, the wife of a Baptist minister.

On the other hand, several publications appear once a month, or once in two months, for the benefit of fathers and of entire families. Two such are published in the city of New York; the one is intituled "the Patriarch," the other, "the Christian Family Magazine, or Parents' and Children's Journal." Both are very valuable, and have an extensive circulation. Other journals of like character, and having the same object, are published in other parts of the country. Moreover, almost all the religious newspapers, now very numerous, and some one or more of which are read in almost every Christian family, contain much that bears upon the religious education of children, and the whole economy of a Christian household.

The subject is one of vast moment. The world has never yet seen the full results of the Christian education of children. Parents have much to learn in this respect, and need all the helps and appliances possible, to enable them rightly to discharge their important duties. Were all fathers and mothers in a nation such as they ought to be, how mighty would be the influence of the gospel upon it! Were the fathers and mothers in the church of Christ to be such as they ought to be, how different would it soon become from what we see it now! A praying, devoted, holy mother! What an interesting being! Such was the mother of Samuel, of Timothy, and of thousands besides, who have been eminently useful in the world.

I have known Christian fathers who met once a week for years to pray together for their children, and their meetings have been eminently useful and happy. I have seen another kind of meeting which I wish were more common—a quarterly prayer-meeting specially for parents and children. It was affecting to see parents, the unconverted as well as the converted, bringing with them their children, dear to them as life itself, into the sanctuary on such occasions, that they might share in the earnestly-sought blessing.

CHAPTER XVII.

EDUCATION SOCIETIES.

ONE of the most interesting developments of the voluntary principle in promoting religion in the United States, is seen in the education societies,—institutions of comparatively recent date, and having for their object the granting of assistance to pious youths of promising talents but small means, in preparing for the ministry.

One of the first of these was the American Education Society, formed at Boston in 1816. Hence it has been in existence for twenty-six years, and rarely has any society been the instrument of more good.[1]

In all denominations of evangelical Christians in the United States, there are to be found among those classes of society whose means are too limited to give their sons a college education, young men of talent, to whom God has been pleased to impart the knowledge of his grace, and in whose hearts he implants a longing to preach the gospel. Now, before the education societies appeared upon the field, such youths used to find it very difficult, and sometimes even impossible, to obtain such an education as was required by the rules of the church in whose ministry they wished to place themselves. Some, indeed, might succeed by their own exertions; by dint of industry and economy they might lay up enough to enable them to secure a course of study at college to begin with. By interrupting their college studies occasionally, in order to recruit their finances by teaching a school, they might, after long delays, be able to complete the requisite course at last; and then, by similar efforts, carry

[1] This society has published, since the year 1827, a valuable periodical intituled "The American Quarterly Register." It was originated by the late Rev. Dr. Cornelius and the Rev. B. B. Edwards, the secretaries of the society at that epoch, and has been continued by the latter gentleman to this time, aided for several years by the Rev. Dr. Cogswell, successor of Dr. Cornelius; and at present by the Rev. Mr. Riddel, who has taken the place of Dr. Cogswell. Mr. Edwards is a professor in the theological seminary at Andover.

themselves through the required theological course at a seminary. Others, more fortunate, might be so far assisted by a church or some wealthy and benevolent patron or friend.[1] But the greater number, in despair of success, were apt to renounce all expectation of being able to preach the gospel, and to resign themselves to the necessity of spending their lives in the ordinary pursuits of business—not in making known the "unsearchable riches" of Christ to their fellow-men.

These remarks, it will be perceived, apply to such youths only as conscientiously cleave to those churches which require a college education, as preliminary to a theological one, in all aspirants to the sacred ministry. This is the rule, except in very extraordinary cases, with the whole of the Presbyterian churches but that called the Cumberland Presbyterians; with the Episcopalians; and with the Congregationalists. The Baptists and the Methodists, as we have seen, are less strict, and can be satisfied with a common English education, and a competent knowledge of theology. But even among these, great and laudable efforts are now put forth in order to give a higher education to as many of their candidates for the ministry as possible; and it is on this account, as well as for more general objects, that they have established so many colleges within the last few years. God is granting his rich blessing to their efforts in this great cause, and of this every year furnishes cheering evidence.

To meet the demands of the churches for a vastly augmented number of ministers of the gospel, and to help those young men who desire to respond to this demand, the American Education Society was formed on the broad basis of rendering its aid to all pious young men, of suitable talents, who appear to be called to preach Christ, and who belong to any of the evangelical denominations. The only conditions imposed upon the recipients of its bounty are an engagement; 1. To go through a full course

[1] Several of the colleges possess funds bequeathed to them for the express purpose of educating poor and pious young men for the ministry. The Rev. Dr. Green, in his historical notices of the college of New Jersey, relates, that more than half a century since, a pious young man of the name of Leslie was educated at that institution for the ministry of the gospel. But fearing to assume the responsibility of that office he devoted himself to teaching a school of a high order, in which employment he was eminently successful. At his death he bequeathed to the college the sum of 15,000 dollars, the interest of which was to be devoted to the education of poor young men for the ministry; and has already educated a large number of excellent ministers.

of collegiate and theological education in some approved college and seminary; and, 2. To refund the sums advanced to aid them, should the providence of God, in after life, give them the means of doing so.

Such are, in few words, its principles. A rigid supervision is maintained over those who accept its patronage. And setting out in its admirable career with a few young men, it has gone on, under the favour of God, diffusing its blessings far and wide. It has rendered aid to young men belonging to eight different evangelical churches. At one period, some three or four years ago, the number of persons whom it was aiding exceeded 1100 ! During the year ending May 1st, 1841, which is the date of the latest official statement of the society that I have seen, the number aided was 810. These were pursuing their education at institutions in different parts of the country; some in academies and grammar schools, some in colleges, and the rest in theological schools. And the whole number of those who had been aided, up to that time, was 3389. The receipts for that year were 63,113 dollars, and the expenditure 56,049. The amount refunded that year by beneficiaries who had completed their course of education was 6633 dollars. And the earnings of the young men who were then under the patronage of the society during the year,—chiefly from teaching schools during their vacations,—amounted to no less a sum than 21,739 dollars.

The sums granted by this society, to those who are admitted to its benefits, vary from forty-eight to seventy-five dollars a year, the latter sum being rarely exceeded. Its funds have been liberally augmented by bequests from devoted Christian friends who loved it during life, and remembered it in death. Its first president gave it 1000 dollars during his lifetime, and left it a legacy of 5000. Mr. Burr, whom we have already had occasion to speak of, also left it a handsome legacy. The late Dr. Porter, for many years a distinguished professor in the theological seminary at Andover, though far from being a man of much wealth, bequeathed to it 15,000 dollars. Many of its still living friends have given proof of large and enlightened views by the patronage they have given it. It has assisted a great number of most valuable ministers of the gospel in the course of their education, and to these we have to add no fewer than sixty of the missionaries supported in foreign lands by the American board of commissioners for foreign missions, one of the largest and oldest foreign missionary societies in the United States.

Of late years, however, the number of young men assisted by this society has greatly diminished; partly owing to the very difficult times through which the country has passed; partly because of higher requirements in the department of preliminary studies; and partly from most of the evangelical communions having now education societies of their own. Thus the " old school" Presbyterians have a board of education under the direction of their general assembly, which prosecutes its work most wisely and efficiently. It had 300 beneficiaries during the year ending 1st May, 1842, and had assisted 1740 young men in all. Its receipts for last year amounted to 26,628 dollars; its expenditure to 23,725.[1]

A number of devoted clergymen and laymen of the Protestant Episcopal church, having met at Georgetown in the district of Columbia, for the purpose of laying the foundation stone of an Episcopal church, were providentially led to talk of the importance of having a plan for aiding pious but indigent youths, of suitable talents, in preparing for the ministry. The result was the formation, in 1818, of the Protestant Episcopal Education Society. It has proved a great blessing to the church and to the world. It may be said to have originated the Episcopal theological school near Alexandria, in the district of Columbia, and nearly a tenth of the clergy of the church to which it belongs have been more or less assisted by it. A sixth of the present clergy in Ohio, an eighth of those in Pennsylvania, a fifth of those in Maryland, and a large proportion of

[1] The American churches have long been impressed with the importance of having a competent and sufficiently numerous ministry. The friends of the American Education Society observe the last Thursday of February yearly as a day of special prayer for colleges, academies, and other institutions of learning, that God may be pleased to pour out his Spirit upon them, bring many of the students to a saving knowledge of his gospel, and incline their hearts to preach it. The general assembly of the "old school" Presbyterian church recommended last year, to all the churches under their care, to observe the first Sabbath of November of that year as a day of special prayer to the Lord of the harvest, "that he would send more labourers into his harvest." They recommended the subject also to the daily intercessions of Christians in view of the vast demand for ministers of the gospel.

those in Virginia, have been aided from its funds; and it is now assisting a seventh of all the students in the several theological schools of that church in the United States.[1] I do not know the precise number of its present beneficiaries, but believe it exceeds eighty.

There are also several education societies among the Baptists, which have aided a large number of young men.[2] That of the Reformed Dutch church supported twenty-four last year. A Methodist education society has also been formed at Boston.

These statements will give the reader some idea of the education societies. Though of recent origin, they are exercising an immense influence in training up a more thoroughly educated ministry. In the absence of precise information, the young men now receiving assistance from them, may be moderately estimated at 1600 in all, and of these at least 200 annually finish their studies, and enter on the work of preaching the gospel.

CHAPTER XVIII.

THEOLOGICAL SEMINARIES.

I HAVE spoken of the various literary institutions, in their several gradations, through which our youth may pass in preparing for the professional course with which they usually close their studies. I have noticed also the education societies for assisting poor but pious young men, of suitable capacity, in their preparation for the ministry. And I now come to speak of the theological schools, in which a very large number of our candidates for the ministry complete their preparations for the sacred office.

Formerly the young men who sought to enter the ministry among the denominations which require, in those who occupy

---

[1] Dr. Hawks' "History of the Episcopal Church in Virginia," p. 261.

[2] In particular, "The Northern Baptist Education Society," and "The Baptist Education Society of New York." The former of these was instituted in 1814, and has its chief operations in Boston. During the eight years from 1831 to 1839 it had aided 279 young men in preparing for the ministry, and supported 134 in 1840. It was mainly from its efforts that the Baptist Theological Seminary at Newton was founded in 1827. The latter society was founded in 1817, and has maintained many students at the Hamilton Literary and Theological Institution, founded in 1820.

their pulpits, a college and theological education—I use the term in a technical sense, and mean nothing invidious—were compelled to study theology, more or less immediately under some individual pastor, and it was common for six or eight of them to place themselves under this, and a few under that other distinguished divine. They often resided in the house of their spiritual teacher; sometimes they boarded in families near his house; they availed themselves of his library, and were directed by him in their studies.

But this was obviously a very imperfect method. Few pastors could afford time to do their pupils justice; fewer still possessed such a range of learning as to fit them for communicating to others the acquisitions, in various branches of knowledge, required in order to a competent preparation for the ministry.

To the late Rev. Dr. John Mason of New York, one of the most eminent divines that America has ever produced, we owe the first attempt to establish any thing that could be called a theological school. He collected in Europe an extensive and valuable theological library, and commenced a course of instruction in various branches of theological study about the beginning of the present century. For years he carried it on almost single-handed, and many young men heard at his feet the masterly instructions that he was so capable of giving them.

The theological seminary at Andover was founded in 1808, and being the first, on a complete plan, founded in the United States, and the most celebrated, I shall notice it more amply than the rest.

The college buildings are beautifully situate on elevated ground near the village of Andover, about twenty miles to the north of Boston. · They consist of two large edifices for the residence of the students, and a large central building in which are the chapel, the library, lecture-rooms, &c. At a due distance behind these stand the refectory and steward's house. The grounds in front are tastefully laid out, and their walks and avenues adorned with various sorts of forest trees. Facing the seminary buildings, and forming one side of a street which borders the grounds in front, stands a row of houses where many of the professors reside. The grounds are very ample, the situation salubrious, and the buildings remarkably convenient.

This seminary forms a branch, as we have elsewhere stated, of Phillips's academy, which stands in the immediate vicinity, though the two institutions are no farther connected than by being both under the same board of trustees. The history of the Andover seminary may be given in a few words. It originated in a growing conviction of the need there was for an increased standard of qualification in the clergy, and in the obvious necessity of having something to take the place of the university of Harvard on its defection from the faith, many not only of the young men of New England generally, but also of the ministers of Boston and the adjacent towns, having pursued their studies there. Further, the good providence of God was manifested in the undertaking, by his giving both the necessary means and the heart to four or five enterprising merchants to lay the foundation.

One of these was the aged Samuel Abbot of Andover, who had already executed a will bequeathing funds to a large amount, for the support of professors and indigent students of theology in Harvard university. But having lived to witness the new movements there, and to be convinced of the danger of trusting a legacy to an institution which, in his view, had perverted the funds left by Mr. Hollis,[1] for the support of an orthodox professor of divinity, he was led to unite with Mrs. Phillips, widow of the late Hon. Samuel Phillips, one of the founders of Phillips's academy, and her son, in a plan for connecting with that academy the erection of buildings, and the appropriation of certain funds for the support of a theological professor, and of indigent students of theology.

Meanwhile, a similar plan for another seminary was formed by the late Rev. Samuel Spring, D.D. of Newburyport, and the Rev. Leonard Woods, D.D. of West Newbury, now a professor in the seminary at Andover, and funds were pledged for its endowment by Mr. Bartlett and Mr. Brown, two parishioners of Dr. Spring's, and by Mr. Norris of Salem,—all at the solicitation of Dr. Spring, who was the author of this scheme. Dr. Woods, in whose parish the institution was to be placed, was

---

[1] Thomas Hollis, Esq., a highly esteemed Christian merchant, was born in England in 1659, and died in 1731. He founded the professorships of theology and mathematics in Harvard university, and presented to it a philosophical apparatus and many books.

to be professor, and a colleague was to be appointed to assist him in his pastoral duties.

Thus far had the parties proceeded, not only without concert, but although living within the compass of twenty miles, and several of them having friendly intercourse with each other, without being cognisant of one another's plans. This seems to indicate the intervention of a kind omniscient providence, and may have been a link in the chain of causes which cordially united, in the end, the two parties into which the orthodox Congregationalists of New England were then divided, and to the adoption of a better creed for the seminary than it might have had otherwise.

These parties were, on the one hand, the so-called moderate Calvinists, moderate both in action and speculation, and, on the other hand, the Hopkinsians, the keen-sighted, active, fervid, pungent, and perhaps rather ultra men of their time. Now, to have continued and widened the separation of these parties by their having contiguous and rival seminaries, would have been no less disastrous, than their union was desirable, both for the nearer approximation of both to exact truth, and for its common defence against the advance of Unitarianism; and nothing could well have been imagined more likely to produce prompt and effectual union, as their being led to co-operate in establishing a common seminary. But it seems very doubtful how far they would ever have thus combined their efforts, had not certain members of each been led, in the providence of God, by ways that they knew not, and for a high end which they never contemplated, each to advance thus far in their projects. The evil sure to result from there being two such seminaries was obvious; the benefits to be derived from their being united in one were appreciated at least to a certain extent; yet this union of the two institutions, and the adjustment of principles common to both, cost nearly two years of anxious and incessant labour, during which the negociations were more than once well-nigh broken off, and at one time quite abandoned. "No one," says the Rev. Dr. Woods, "who did not himself act a leading part in these interesting transactions, can ever have an adequate conception of the unnumbered difficulties which the principal agents had to encounter, or of the amount of solicitude, and of effort, which fell to their lot; or of the variety of dangers to which the great object was from time to time exposed." [1]

The greatest difficulty in the way of the union was the adjustment of a common creed, to be subscribed by the professors of the seminary. The founders of Phillips's academy had already adopted the Westminster Assembly's Shorter Catechism. To this Dr. Spring, with the advice and support of his friend, the Rev. Dr. Emmons, strenuously objected, because some parts of it were widely understood to imply what he did not believe, and, partly, because he thought that more definite and extended statements on several points of doctrine were desirable. He and his friends also wished for additional barriers against heresy, and particularly for a board of visitors, professing the same creed, and with ample powers for the correction of errors. These difficulties were adjusted at last by the institution of such a board, and by the adoption of a new creed, drawn up by a committee from both parties, and couched very much in the language of the catechism, but with some omissions and some additions. And this creed is to be solemnly repeated and subscribed in the presence of the trustees of the academy, by every professor and every visitor on his induction into office; and the same is to be repeated, in like manner, by each of them, once every five years, during his continuance in office.

In this adjustment the Hopkinsians gained their main object, but at the same time, sacrificed some favourite points which they would gladly have introduced into a seminary of more sectarian character. Some, indeed, a few of whom are still to be found, persisted in their objections to the seminary on this account; but nearly the whole orthodox community of New England have cordially acquiesced in it, so that the arrangement has most happily, though silently, become a virtual bond of union amongst them. Foreign missions, and other great benevolent enterprises, to which the seminary soon gave birth, hastened and confirmed this coalescence by bringing the two parties more frequently to pray, sympathise, and act together. These results are matters of devout astonishment to many a beholder of what God has wrought amid the movements of those times.

---

[1] Manuscript History of the Theological Seminary at Andover, from which much of the information here given was derived.

The opposition, in various forms, to orthodoxy was considerable, but was of little avail in retarding its progress.   Fears were
at one time entertained lest a majority of the trustees of Phillips's
academy, under whose guardianship the seminary is placed,
should ultimately be found men of lax opinions; but as most of
the suspected parties either died or resigned their seats within
a few years, those fears gradually subsided on the vacancies
being filled up by others who were unquestionably sound in the
faith.[1] Solicitude on this head led to the greater solicitude about
creating a board of visitors, and the quinquennial renewal of
subscription by the professors and visitors, though this could
not be extended to the trustees, no provision to that effect having been made at the institution of that board.

With all these guards, and looking to the present character
of the boards, the friends of the institution consider that there
is none in the country more completely guarded against perversion.   At the same time, the most perfect freedom of inquiry is
allowed, and even encouraged among the students, in order that
their faith may rest on conviction, not on human authority or
constraint.   No subscription to a creed is required of them; nor
can any one who gives to the professors satisfactory evidence of
Christian character be debarred from entering the seminary, or
dismissed from it on the ground of his belief.   This condition
was required by the state legislature on their enlarging the
powers of the trustees, so as to enable them to hold the additional funds required for the establishment of the seminary.
And, although its expediency has by some been doubted, it seems
as yet to have had no bad consequences.   It has been thought
unreasonable to require a minute profession of faith from students who go to the institution for the very purpose of learning
what is truth, as well as how to teach it.

The seminary was opened in the autumn of 1808.   For
several years there were only three professors, but now there are
five, and also a president, who, however, has no department of
instruction, and whose duties used to be discharged by one of

---

[1] It must be kept in mind that Phillips's academy was founded in 1778, when
Unitarianism had not yet developed itself in the United States, though the
errors which led to it were to be found in Boston and its neighbourhood. When
it did develope itself, it was not strange that the board of Phillips's academy
should have been infected with them.

the professors. Each member of the faculty has a salary of
1500 dollars per annum, together with the use of a family
dwelling-house, and is debarred from receiving any compensation
for preaching abroad.

The departments of the professors are: sacred literature, including the Greek and Hebrew scriptures,—chiefly during the
first year; Christian theology,—chiefly during the second year;
and sacred rhetoric, ecclesiastical history, and pastoral theology,
—during the third year. The instruction is given partly by
written lectures and partly by the use of text-books, which are
recited in substance by the students, and accompanied with
remarks by the professors.

The students are not allowed to preach, nor are they required
to write sermons till their senior or last year. Each may then
be called on to preach in the chapel, and is also allowed to preach
abroad for six Sabbaths in his last term, within certain limits as
to distance, so as to avoid being absent from any of the lectures.
The remainder of the preaching in the chapel is chiefly performed by the president and professors in rotation.

Most of the students are graduates of colleges, and all are
admitted on examination in regard to their attainments, evidence
of piety, &c. During the first year they attend two lectures
a-day; afterwards usually but one.

Great attention is required of the professors in the cultivation
of piety among the students; which has ever been regarded by
them, as well as by the founders and guardians, as a grand object
of the institution. For this purpose they meet the students for
a devotional exercise every Wednesday evening. The students,
also, hold many conferences and prayer-meetings by themselves.

Indigent students, of whom there are many, receive half the
price of their board in commons gratuitously. No charge is in
any case made for tuition, and but a small one for the use of the
library, and for rooms and furniture.

As the design of the seminary is to furnish an able as well as
a pious clergy, and as its privileges are, to a great extent, gratuitous, each student is required at his matriculation, to promise
to complete a regular three years course of study, "unless prevented by some unforeseen and unavoidable necessity," which is
to be judged of by the faculty. This is a much longer course

than had commonly been pursued under the guidance of private pastors, and it has been found very difficult thus far to elevate the views of the community, and fully to reconcile the feelings of the students to this requisition. Indeed, the rule itself was not made for a considerable number of the first years.

As this is the oldest theological seminary in the country, it has had to make its own way unaided by previous experience; and very many are the changes, mostly for the better, it is believed, which have been made from time to time in its arrangements.

There were not many students for some years. at first, but they have gradually increased from about thirty to about 150, which has been not far from the number on the list for many years. Any farther increase has been prevented by the multiplication of kindred seminaries since its reaching that number. The whole that have been admitted from the first, amount to about 1440, though, partly from deaths, partly from many having failed to complete their course, or gone to other institutions, not 900 of these have graduated. Nearly 100 have devoted themselves to foreign, and many more to domestic missions. The American board of commissioners for foreign missions were indebted to this seminary for all their missionaries but one, for the first ten years, and many of its students have lived to become presidents and professors of colleges and theological schools, and secretaries and agents of benevolent societies.

It possesses peculiar advantages for the training of missionaries. The "society of inquiry on missions," of which almost all the students are members, is nearly coeval with it. It has a valuable library and museum, and exerts a very salutary influence on the spirit and piety of the institution. The doctrine is taught at this, as at most of the other United States' theological seminaries, that every pastor should be a missionary at heart, and that every student should be willing to go whithersoever God may call him. There are great facilities at Andover for having early intelligence from the American missionaries, by constant correspondence, by visits of returned members, and by intercourse with the office-bearers of the American boards.

The "Porter Rhetorical society," so named from its founder,

the late Rev. Dr. Porter, the first president of the seminary, has an excellent library, and exercises much influence.

The theological library of the seminary itself is thought to be one of the best in the country. It was selected for the purpose, contains 14,000 volumes, and has a fund to provide for its constant augmentation. Some of the large number of German books contained in it being of a neological character, it was at one time feared by many that these might do mischief, but such apprehensions have now yielded, in the minds of most who felt them, to the consideration of the importance of having such books in an institution where men are to be trained to face an enemy, not to flee from him.

The institution is under strict discipline. Monitor's bills are kept; all are required to attend to their studies, and to be present at the professor's lectures, at morning and evening chapel prayers, and at divine service on the Sabbath. There are instances of students being dismissed for irregularity of conduct; and one professor has been deposed, after a regular trial, for neglecting his official duties.

The total sums that have been given for the erection of the seminary buildings, the endowing of professorships, the support of indigent students, the library, &c., cannot be precisely ascertained, but they probably exceed 400,000 dollars. Mr. Bartlett, the most munificent of the donors, is supposed to have given 100,000 dollars, besides a legacy of 50,000 dollars. He is said never to have told any one how much some of the buildings which were erected at his instance cost him. Mr. Abbot gave about 120,000 dollars. Mr. Brown and Mr. Norris, also, gave large sums, though not nearly so much as the above. No general solicitation has ever been made in behalf of the institution, though it has received from individuals many benefactions, of from 500 to 5,000 dollars.

Connected with the seminary is a printing establishment, known as the Codman press, from its having a fount of oriental types presented to it by the Rev. Dr. Codman of Dorchester.

Few institutions have ever been more blessed than the Andover theological seminary. It has been intimately associated with the origin and progress of the foreign missions, and had much influence in originating the Bible, Colonisation, Tract, and Temperance societies, through the exertions of the lamented Mills[1] and his coadjutors, who were students at it. I have spoken of it more in detail, not only because of its being the oldest, the most richly endowed, and the most frequented, but also, because it has been, in some sense, a model for the rest.[2]

The general assembly of the Presbyterian church established a theological seminary at Princetown, in New Jersey, in 1812, being the second of the kind in the United States. Although, far from being richly endowed like that of Andover, it has often been greatly embarrassed for want of adequate pecuniary support, it has attained a great and well-merited celebrity by the distinguished talents of its professors, as well as the excellent course of its studies. It has for several years had an annual attendance of from 125 to 140 students, and has educated in all above 1200. The missionary spirit has prevailed in it to a gratifying degree almost from its first establishment, and a large number of its *alumni* have gone to carry the gospel to heathen lands. There is a flourishing "society of inquiry on missions," with a valuable collection of books relating to that subject.

The Princetown course comprises for the first year, Hebrew, the exegesis of the original language of the New Testament, sacred geography, sacred chronology, Jewish antiquities, and the connection of sacred and profane history; for the second year, biblical criticism, church history, and didactic theology; for the third year, polemic theology, church history, church government, pastoral theology, the composition and delivery of

[1] The Rev. Samuel J. Mills, a very zealous and able young man, who took a leading part in the formation of several of the great benevolent societies of America, and died on the coast of Africa when looking for a place where he might found a colony of negroes.
[2] The Andover faculty at the commencement of 1842, consisted of the Rev. Justin Edwards, D.D., President; the Rev. Drs. Woods and Emerson, and Messrs. Stuart, B.B. Edwards, and Park, professors:
Professor Stuart is well known for his commentaries on the epistles to the Romans and Hebrews, as well as for his Hebrew grammar and other writings. Dr. Edwards is well known and honoured as the founder of the temperance societies, but has published nothing beyond some able reports whilst engaged in that cause, and several excellent sermons. Dr. Woods has published some valuable small works on baptism, inspiration of the scriptures, &c. Dr. Emerson has not yet published much. Mr. B. B. Edwards has written much and ably for periodical publication, and is the author, besides, of several valuable works relating to missions; among these is a missionary gazetteer. He published the life of Dr. Cornelius; and in 1839 took a joint part with professor Park in giving to the world an interesting volume of translated selections from German authors.

sermons. Instruction is given both by lectures and text-books; and the entire course requires the study of many authors. The students must read essays of their own composition at least once every four weeks, and are expected, also, to deliver short addresses before the professors and their fellow-students, at least once in the month. One evening in the week is devoted to the discussion of important theological questions. Every Sabbath forenoon a sermon is delivered in the chapel by one of the professors. In the afternoon, the students assemble for a "conference" on some subject in casuistical divinity, their professors presiding and closing the discussion with their remarks, and the services commencing and concluding with singing and prayer. Questions such as the following are discussed: What constitutes a call to the ministry and the evidences of it? What is proper preparation for the Lord's supper? What is repentance? What is faith? What is true preparation for death?

These, and a hundred such questions, are seriously and faithfully discussed, and none of the other exercises, probably, is so instructive or so important to the students. It is there that the deep knowledge in spiritual things of their venerated and excellent professors most fully comes out. God has greatly blessed these heart-searching services to the students, and much is it to be wished that such exercises, and such fidelity on the part of the professors who conduct them, were to be found in every theological seminary, and theological department of an university, in the world.

It is matter for devout thanksgiving that the venerable professors[1] appointed to the Princetown seminary in its earliest years, are still spared to labour for its good. Both they and their younger colleagues rank high among the American divines, and have great weight in the church to which they belong.

The general convention of the Protestant Episcopal church

---

[1] The Rev. Drs. Alexander and Miller, both of whom have earned an extensive reputation by their public lectures as well as by their writings. The younger professors are the Rev. Dr. Hodge and the Rev. J. A. Alexander; the former well known in Europe for his excellent work on the epistle to the Romans, and the latter author of many articles in the Biblical Repository and Princetown Review, an able quarterly publication which has been conducted for nearly twenty years by the professors of the seminary, and of the college of New Jersey, both in the village of Princetown.

opened a theological institution at New York, in 1817, which though removed next year to New Haven, was soon after re-established at New York. It originated in the efforts of the late John Hobart, long bishop of the diocese of New York, and has five professors, who are eminent and influential men, both in their own church and in the community at large. Its prosperity has been almost uninterrupted. The number of students is usually about seventy-five or eighty. In 1822, the dioceses of Virginia and Maryland established another Episcopal seminary in Fairfax county, Virginia, a few miles from the city of Alexandria, in the district of Columbia. This seminary has four valuable professors, and from forty to fifty students. It has been a great blessing to the Episcopal church and to the country.

A Baptist theological seminary, established at Newton, a town about six miles from Boston, in 1825, has been a source of much good, and has sent forth a considerable number of excellent preachers. It has three able professors, and usually from thirty to forty students. The Baptists, also, established a literary and theological institute at Hamilton, in the State of New York, in 1820. It has above 150 students in all, and in the theological department from twenty to thirty, under four professors, who give instructions in the other department also.

A Lutheran theological seminary was established in 1826, at Gettysburg, in Pennsylvania, very much through the exertions of the Rev. S. S. Schmucker, D. D., who is its professor of theology. It has three professors with from thirty to forty students in all, and has proved a rich blessing to the Lutheran church. Dr. Schmucker is well known in the churches of the United States by his various writings, and his praiseworthy endeavours to bring about an union of feeling and action among the several branches of the Protestant denominations.

The Reformed Dutch church has an able theological faculty in its college at New Brunswick, in the State of New Jersey. The foundation dates from 1784, but it was for long unoccupied. It now has three professors and about forty students.

Such are the utmost details that the limits of this work will permit. Let me simply add that since the opening of the Rev. Dr. Mason's theological school, about the beginning of the cen-

tury, these institutions have amazingly increased. Most of
them, like those at Andover and Princetown, are quite distinct
from any college or university; some, under the title of *theological departments*, are connected with literary institutions, but
have their own professors, and in reality are very distinct. The
following table, presenting a summary of the whole, will probably
be found interesting.

Denominations.	Name and locality of the institution.	State in which it is situated.	Year when founded, when known.	Number of Professors.	Number of Students, 1 when known
Congregationalists.	1. Andover.	Massachusetts.	1808	5 & 1 Pres.	153
	2. Bangor.	Maine.	1820	3 ——	44
	3. Gilmanton.	New Hampshire.	1835	3 ——	26
	4. Theological department of Yale college.	Connecticut.	1822	4 ——	72
	5. Theological institute of Connecticut, at East Windsor.	Ditto.	1833	3 ——	29
	6. Theological department at the Oberlin institute.	Ohio.		4 ——	54
Old School Presbyterians.	1. Theological Seminary at Princetown.	New Jersey.	1812	4 ——	110
	2. Western theological seminary at Alleghany city, near Pittsburg.	Pennsylvania.	1828	3 ——	29
	3. Union theological seminary.	Virginia.	1812	3 ——	20
	4. Southern theological seminary at Columbia.	South Carolina.	1832	3 ——	18
	5. Indiana theological seminary at New Albany.	Indiana.	1829	2 ——	10
	6. Theological department of Marion college.	Missouri.		1 ——	unknown.

1 I give the number of students for 1840, from the American Quarterly Register for that year. The list is understated, the number being that at a given
epoch in the year, not that of all who attended during the course of it. For
instance, were the number of students in the Princetown seminary taken in the
winter of 1839-40, it might have been 120, yet by adding the students who joined
in the summer session, the number for the academic year might be 130.

Denominations.	Name and locality of the institution.	State in which it is situated.	Year when founded, when known.	Number of Professors.	Number of Students, when known.
New School Presbyterians.	1. New York theological seminary, in New York city.	New York.	1836	4 & 1 Pres.	90
	2. Theological seminary at Auburn.	Ditto.	1821	4 ———	69
	3. Theological department of Western Reserve college.	Ohio.		3 ———	14
	4. Lane seminary at Cincinnati.	Ditto comm.	1832	3 ———	31
	5. South-western theological seminary at Maryville.	Tennessee.		2 ———	24
	6. Carlinville theological seminary at Carlinville.	Illinois, opened	1838		
Episcopalians.	1. General theological seminary of the Episcopal church, New York.	New York, estab.	1817	5 ———	74
	2. Theological seminary, Fairfax county.	Virginia.		3 ———	43
	3. Theological seminary of the diocese of Ohio, at Gambia.	Ohio, opened.	1828	3 ———	10
Baptists.	1. Thomaston theological institute.	Maine, founded	1837	2 ———	23
	2. Theological institution at Newton.	Massachusetts.	1825	3 ———	33
	3. Hamilton literary and theological institute, at Hamilton.	New York.	1820	4 ———	27
	4. Virginia Baptist seminary, at Richmond.	Virginia.	1832	3 ———	67
	5. Furman theological seminary, at High Hills.	South Carolina.	1838	2 ———	30
	6. Literary and theological seminary at Eaton.	Georgia.	1834	2 ———	10
	7. Theological department in Granville college.	Ohio.	1832	2 ———	8
	8. Alton theological seminary.	Illinois.			

Denominations.	Name and Locality of Institution.	State in which it is situated.	Year when founded, when known.	Number of Professors.	Number of Students, when known.
Reformed Dutch.	Theological department in Rutger's college, New Brunswick.	New Jersey.		3 & 1 Pres.	36
Lutherans.	1. Hartwick seminary.	New York.		2 ———	15
	2. Theological seminary at Gettysburg.	Pennsylvania.	1826	3 ———	26
	3. Ditto at Lexington.	South Carolina.	1835	2 ———	10
	4. Ditto at Columbus.	Ohio.		1 ———	about 10
Associate German Reformed Church.	Theological seminary at York.	Pennsylvania.	1825	2 ———	20
	Theological department in Jefferson college.	Ditto.		2 ———	22
Asso. Refo. Church.	1. Theological seminary at Newburgh.	New York.	1836	3 ———	11
	2. Ditto at Pittsburg.	Pennsylvania.	1828	1 ———	19

The Reformed Presbyterians (Covenanters) have a theological school or class at Philadelphia, and the Moravians have one at Nazareth, in Pennsylvania, but I am not aware how many students they have, probably not more than six or eight each.

The above enumeration comprises the orthodox evangelical denominations of Protestants only. The Unitarians have a theological department at Harvard university, which had two professors and twenty-seven sudents in 1840.

The Roman Catholic theological seminaries, according to the Catholic Almanac, stood as follows in 1840:—

That at Philadelphia had ....22 students.
           Baltimore ....16 ———
           Emmetsburg.................................20 ———
           Frederick ....20 ———
           Charleston, South Carolina,............ 6 ———
           Parish of Assumption in Louisiana ... 9 ———
           Bardstown and St. Rose in Kentucky..
           Cincinnati ....
           Vincennes.................................... 9 ———
           Barrens.......................................12 ———
           Missouri ....
           St. Louis ....

In all twelve institutions and 114 students. But this list was probably incomplete, as we learn from the same authority that at the beginning of 1842 there were twenty-one ecclesiastical institutions, and 180 clerical students.

I shall conclude by stating that the entire number of theological schools and faculties belonging to the orthodox Protestant churches is thirty-eight,[1] with about 105 professors, and nearly 1500 students. The greater number of these institutions are in their infancy. Where they are connected with colleges, the theological professor generally gives lectures in the literary department, also on moral philosophy, metaphysics, logic, &c. Many of the professors in the new and smaller seminaries are pastors of churches in the neighbourhood, and all that are not preach much in vacant churches, or on extraordinary occasions, such as before benevolent or literary societies and bodies, ecclesiastical assemblies, &c. Many of them, too, are expected to employ their leisure moments in instructing the people through the press. Though the number of professors seems large when compared with that of the students, I can assure the reader that few men have more to do, or, in point of fact, do more for the cause of Christ. There are to be found among them many of the very first ministers of the churches to which they respectively belong. If not quite equal in point of science to some of the great professors in the old world, they are all, God be praised, believed to be converted, and are devoted, faithful men. Their grand object is to train up a pious as well as a learned ministry. I am not aware that there is one of them that does not open every meeting of his class with earnest prayer, in which he is joined by his pupils—a striking contrast to what one sees, alas! at too many of the theological lectures in the universities of Europe.

[1] At the Wesleyan university at Middletown, Connecticut, theological lectures are given to a class in divinity, and possibly this is done also in some of the other Methodist colleges.

CHAPTER XIX.

EFFORTS TO DIFFUSE THE SACRED SCRIPTURES.

Much has been done in the United States to place the sacred scriptures in the hands of all who can read them, and in this endeavour there is a delightful co-operation of good men of every name. Even statesmen, though they may not be decidedly religious, or, by outward profession, members of any church, lend their aid in this endeavour; and it is not uncommon to hear men of the first rank in the political circles, some occupying high places in the council of the nation, advocate at Bible society anniversaries the claims of the word of God. The impression prevails among our statesmen that the Bible is emphatically the foundation of our hopes as a people. Nothing but tne Bible can make men the willing subjects of law; they must first acquiesce with submission in the government of God, before they can yield a willing obedience to the requirements of human governments, however just these may be. It is the religion of the Bible only that can render the population of any country honest, industrious, peaceable, quiet, contented, happy.

It is twenty-six years since the American Bible Society was instituted, and it now has branches in all parts of the country. It has sent out, in all, 3,052,765 copies of the Bible, or of the New Testament, from its depository.[1] Last year alone 257,167 copies went forth to bless the nation. In the years 1829 and 1830, great and systematic efforts were made to place a Bible in every family that was without one throughout the whole land. Much was accomplished, yet so rapid is the increase of

[1] As some Bible societies are not auxiliary to the American Bible Society—such as until lately the Philadelphia Bible Society, and such as at present the American and Foreign Bible Society—we must not suppose that the number of copies of the scriptures mentioned as having left the depository of the American Bible Society includes the whole which have been circulated by societies in the United States. Besides, the American Sunday School Union, and the Methodist Book Concern, for a time published the Bible.

the population that these efforts must be repeated from year to year; and the work can only be done by dividing the country into small districts, and engaging active and zealous persons to visit every house from time to time, ascertain what families are destitute of the scriptures, and supply them by selling or giving away copies, according to circumstances. Great efforts are also made at New York, and other sea-ports, to supply foreign emigrants as they arrive on our shores.

It is a remarkable fact that what has been done by Bible societies seems not to have interfered with the business of the booksellers; for these sell more copies of the holy scriptures than they did before the Bible societies existed. The more the Bible is known, the more it is appreciated; in many a family the entrance of a single copy begets a desire to possess several; besides which, the Bible society distributions greatly augment the demand for biblical commentaries and expositions, and thus augment the trade of the booksellers, who publish and put into circulation immense editions of such works. There is a great demand for the scriptures, also, both in week-day and Sabbath schools, and great numbers of these are furnished by the book-trade.

Nor does the American Bible Society confine its efforts to the United States. It has for many years associated itself with those societies which, by prosecuting the same work in foreign lands, are labouring to hasten the coming of that day when "the knowledge of the Lord shall fill the earth." The receipts of the society for last year amounted to 134,357 dollars, of which 20,619 were appropriated to the work abroad.

The society has published the New Testament and some parts of the Old in " raised characters," for the use of the blind, and is now engaged in printing the remainder for that unfortunate class of the population.

In the year 1837, a Bible society was formed among the members of the Baptist churches, intitled the " American and Foreign Bible Society." It was formed with special reference to the circulating of translations in the course of being made by that body of Christians. Some, at least, of these translations the American Bible Society thought it could not, consistently with its constitution, aid in publishing, because the original words *baptise* and *baptism*, have been translated into words equivalent to *immerse* and *immersion*. However much it may be regretted that these words, about the meaning of which there has been so much philological disputation, are not permitted to remain untranslated, so that all denominations might be put upon the same footing, and be enabled to continue *united* in the work of Bible circulation, the issue will likely prove that in this, as in so many similar cases, God is about to make an apparent obstacle mightily subserve the advancement of his kingdom. The new society has taken up the work of foreign publication with great zeal, and doubtless it will serve to develope the energies of the large and powerful body of Christians who sustain it, to an extent to which they never would have gone but for its formation. The receipts last year, being the fourth of its existence, were 26,304 dollars; the expenditure 31,892 dollars. Meanwhile, the resources of the American Bible Society have greatly increased instead of having diminished.

CHAPTER XX.

ASSOCIATIONS FOR THE CIRCULATION AND PUBLICATION OF RELIGIOUS TRACTS AND BOOKS.

No branch of religious enterprise has been more vigorously prosecuted in the United States than that of preparing, publishing, and circulating moral and religious writings in various forms. The wide diffusion of education, at least among the white part of the population, makes it obvious what powerful advantage may be taken of the press in promoting the truth.

Associations of various kinds are engaged in this good work. We have seen that the Sunday school societies are doing much for supplying the youth of the country with moral and religious reading; we have now to speak of other societies which aim at benefitting adults, not, however, to the exclusion of the young.

First among these associations may be ranked the American Tract Society, which, like most others of a general and national character, has its seat in the city of New York. It was instituted in 1825, and hence has been eighteen years in existence. It is based on the broad principle of uniting in its support Christians of all evangelical denominations of Protestants, so far as they may be disposed to co-operate in its objects; its publications-committee is composed of clerical and lay members of the different orthodox communions; and the publications themselves convey those great truths and doctrines in which all of these communions can agree.

The operations of no society in America seem to have been prosecuted with greater vigour or more wisdom. Its report for 1842 states that, since its commencement, it has sent forth 1016 different publications, of which 131 form volumes of various sizes by themselves, and the remainder are, with few exceptions, what are called tracts, each consisting of four pages and upwards, but requiring more than one to make a volume. It has published some broad-sheets and hand-bills for posting up in public places or otherwise. And besides these 1016 publications at home, it has aided in the publication of 1634 in foreign lands. The copies of its publications thrown off last year amounted to 4,812,000, of which 245,000 were volumes. During the same period 4,478,799, including 185,152 volumes, actually issued from its depository. Among the volumes were 2786 sets of the Evangelical Family Library, of fifteen volumes each, and 524 sets of the Christian Library, of forty-five volumes each. Above 8000 separate volumes, also, of these sets were sold, and 91,000 copies of the Christian Almanac for the United States. From 100 to 150,000 of some of the smaller tracts were distributed, and the total sent into circulation during seventeen years has been 1,220,090,921 pages, or about 123,000,000 of tracts and volumes. The receipts for last year amounted to 34,941 dollars from donations, and 56,214 from sales; in all 91,155 dollars. Fifteen thousand dollars were sent to foreign countries in aid of the tract cause abroad.

The society is assisted by auxiliary associations in all parts of the United States, both in the collection of funds, and in disseminating its publications. Some of these local societies, such as those at New York, Boston, and Philadelphia, are large and efficient.

The society is zealously prosecuting two grand measures, into which I shall enter the more fully, inasmuch as they are of the utmost importance to the religious well-being of the country, and also more or less practicable in other lands. The first of these is the publication of volumes of approved excellence, such as Bunyan's Pilgrim's Progress, and Doddridge's Rise and Progress of Religion in the Soul, and their distribution throughout the country. It proposes to place not only one volume at least, as was resolved some years ago, but even a whole copy of its Evangelical Family Library, of fifteen volumes, or its Christian Library, of forty-five volumes, in as many households as are willing to buy them; and in seeking to accomplish this end, it employs able men, ministers of the gospel generally, as agents. These visit towns and cities, preach in the churches, raise funds to supply the poor with books, organise committees who are to visit all the families in their respective districts, and engage all who are able to buy one book or more, and to supply such as are too poor to purchase. Another set of agents consists of plain, but sensible, pious, and zealous *colporteurs*, or hawkers, who are sent into the " Far West" to carry books and tracts to the frontier people, engaged in felling the forests on their ever onward course toward the setting sun.

Though in operation for but a few years, this enterprise has already placed 1,800,000 volumes in the hands of families, comprising at least 4,000,000 of souls. Who can calculate the amount of good which such a work must, with God's blessing, accomplish?

I ought to add that not only is care taken that both books and tracts shall be printed with good type, and on excellent paper, but that the books are substantially bound, and the tracts covered, for the most part, with handsome paper coverings. In these respects they form a marked contrast with the publications of some societies of the same kind on the continent of Europe. It is rightly thought to be a false economy which, for the sake of saving a few hundred dollars, would fail to render attractive in appearance, as well as readable and durable, publications which are intended to interest, instruct, and save men, many of whom are wholly indifferent to religion, and might be repelled from reading them were they to appear in a mean and shabby dress.

Besides its publications in English, the society has sent out a considerable number of tracts in French, German, and other languages, for the various emigrants that arrive in the United States.

The other measure referred to is the systematic periodical distribution of tracts in cities, towns, villages, and even rural districts, though this cannot be done directly by the society, so much as by the numerous auxiliaries which it endeavours heartily to engage in carrying it through. The object is to place a tract, at least once in the month, in every family willing to receive one, and, where practicable, to accompany it with religious conversation, especially where ignorance of the gospel or family affliction renders it peculiarly called for. In pursuing this design, the city, town, or village is divided into small geographical districts, each containing a certain number of families, and having a sufficiency of zealous, intelligent, and prudent Christians to make monthly visits to every family, and leave the tract selected for the month. Some will require more than one visit, particularly the sick and the destitute; but houses where the inmates persist in refusing tracts, in spite of every effort to overcome their reluctance, are passed by.

This plan, wherever justice has been done to it in practice, has been found eminently beneficial. Cases of poverty and disease are discovered and made known to associations and individuals likely to attend to them. Many persons, living in the constant neglect of public worship, are induced to go and attend the preaching of the gospel. The churches in the neighbourhood are pointed out to them, and they are exhorted to go to such as they may prefer.

Such is the procedure in many places throughout the United States. In the city of New York it has been in operation for five or six years, and with abundance of blessed results. According to municipal regulations the city, which has above 320,000 inhabitants, is divided into wards, and to each of these, when practicable, there is appointed what is called a superintendent, generally a minister of the gospel, a young man who

devotes himself wholly to the work. The superintendents
divide their wards into districts, find a distributor of either sex
for each, hold frequent meetings with their distributors, provide
them with tracts for distribution, receive their reports, draw up
a general one for the monthly meeting of the city tract society,
under whose auspices the work proceeds, and read their reports
at those meetings. Withal they hold prayer meetings in their
respective wards almost every night in the week, and engage
competent persons to hold others which they cannot themselves
attend. The distributors labour gratuitously. The superintendents are paid usually 600 dollars each as salaries. How
matters may now be I cannot say, but I know that a few years
ago sixteen superintendents were paid by the same number of
liberal Christian merchants and mechanics in that city, who
rejoiced to be instrumental in maintaining this good work.

I shall now conclude by giving the summary of what was
accomplished in New York during the six months preceding the
20th of June, 1842, as presented at the regular monthly public
meeting, held in one of the churches in the evening of that day,
and published in one of the religious papers of that city.[1]

> 1047 average number of visitors (or distributors).
> 309,871 tracts distributed.
> 604 bibles and 505 testaments received from the New York Bible
> Society, and supplied to the destitute.
> 2096 volumes lent from the ward libraries.
> 1079 children gathered into sabbath schools.
> 335 children gathered into public schools.
> 131 persons gathered into bible classes.
> 622 persons induced to attend church.
> 835 temperance pledges obtained.
> 633 district prayer-meetings held.
> 15 backsliders reclaimed.
> 218 persons hopefully converted.
> 155 converts united with evangelical churches.

Such is the tabular view presented by six months' labour in
the field of tract distribution in one city.

Besides the American Tract Society, which may be regarded
as a vast reservoir of common truth—of doctrines about which
all evangelical Protestants are agreed—there are other societies
that publish religious tracts and books, and among these I may
mention, as distinguished for the energy of its management and

---

[1] The New York Observer of July 2d, 1842.

the extent of its operations, the " Book Concern" of the Methodist Episcopal church. This institution is situate in New York, under the general conference which, every four years, appoints a general committee to direct its operations. Two able agents are intrusted with the management, and are required to make full returns to the bishops and to the general conference. It must not be thought that all its numerous publications are stamped with the peculiarities of Methodist doctrine; not a few of them are the same in character with those published by the American Tract Society—such, for instance, as the " Saints' Rest." The sales are not confined to the main depository at New York, and the branches established at some other great centres of trade; its publications are retailed by all the travelling ministers of that extensive body, and thus find their way into the most remote log cabins of the West. And who can calculate the good that may result from reading the biographical and didactic volumes thus put into circulation? Who can tell what triumphs over sin, what penitential tears, what hopes made to spring up in despairing hearts, what holy resolutions, owe their existence, under God, to these books?

The old school Presbyterians have also a board of publication, which has put forth not only a considerable number of doctrinal tracts in which the distinctive views of that body are ably maintained, but many books also of solid worth, which are gaining an extensive circulation among its own members, and the professors of the Calvinistic system generally.

The Baptists, too, have their tract and book society earnestly engaged in the good work of supplying their people with publications addressed both to the converted and the unconverted. The Episcopalians, the Quakers or Friends, the Lutherans, and the Protestant Methodists, have all their own tract societies; the two last have their " publication committees," and their book establishments. Other denominations, also, may possibly have theirs. The amount of evangelical tracts and books put into circulation by all these "societies," "boards," and "committees," put together, cannot be exactly ascertained. Their value in money, I mean for what they are sold, must annually far exceed 150,000 dollars. They all help to swell the great stream of truth, as it rolls its health-giving waves through the land. May

God grant that these efforts may go on continually increasing from year to year, until every family shall be blessed with a well-stored library of sound religious books.

CHAPTER XXI.

THE RELIGIOUS LITERATURE OF THE UNITED STATES.

Whilst it would be very foreign to the object of this work to enter upon any discussion as to the value and extent of the general literature of the United States, it is not out of place to say something of that part of it which falls under the head of religion.

And first, let me advert to that which, without reference to to its origin, includes all the literature of a religious kind now circulating through the country. In this sense our religious literature is by far the most extensive in the world, with the single exception of Great Britain. We have a population of more than 17,000,000; and even including the African race amongst us, and regarding the inhabitants as a whole, we have a larger proportion of readers than can be found in most other countries. Indeed, I am not aware of any whole kingdom or nation that has more. Deducting the slave population we have 14,000,000 of people who, whatever may have been their origin, are very Anglo-American in character, and to a great extent, speak and read the English language. Not only so, but of these a very large proportion are religious in their characters and habits, as we shall show in another place. And of the rest there is a widely prevalent respect for Christianity, and disposition to make themselves acquainted with it.

To meet the demand created by so large a body of religious and serious readers, we have a vast number of publications in every department of Christian theology, and these are derived from various sources. Many have been translated from German and French; many from the Latin of more or less ancient times; some from the Greek; whilst many of our learned men, and particularly of our divines, read some or all these languages, and would think their libraries very deficient in the literature with which they ought to be familiar, did they not contain a good stock of such books imported from distant Europe.

Again, we have either republished or imported a great many of the best English religious works, both of the present times and of one or two centuries back. Such as seem adapted for popular use, and as many of a more learned cast as seem likely to justify their republication, are reprinted, while not a few copies of many more are ordered from Europe through the booksellers.

Some United States's reprints of English religious works, particularly of works of a practical character, have had an immense circulation. The commentaries of Scott, Henry, Doddridge, Adam Clarke, and Gill, have been extensively sold, and some booksellers owe a large part of their fortune to the success of the American editions. All the sterling English writers on religious subjects of the seventeenth century, as well as of later times, are familiar to our Christian readers, and the smaller practical treatises of Flavel, Baxter, Boston, Doddridge, and others, have been most widely disseminated. Bates, Charnock, Flavel, Howe, the Henrys, &c., are well known among us, as are also Jeremy Taylor, Barrow, Bishops Hall and Wilson, (of Sodor and Man,) and many more whom I need not name. As for more modern times, the names of Thomas Scott and Adam Clarke are household words, and Chalmers is known to hundreds of thousands who shall never see his face in this world. There are many others in Scotland with whose names we have been familiar since our youth. In English systematic theology no names are more known or esteemed than the late Andrew Fuller and Thomas Watson. Although it cannot be said that every good religious work that appears in Great Britain is republished in the United States, a large proportion of the best certainly are, especially such as are of a catholic nature, and many of them, I am assured, have a wider circulation in the United States than in England itself.

The United States have sometimes been reproached by foreigners as a country without any literature of native growth.

M. de Toqueville, arguing from general principles, and as he supposes, philosophically, seems to think that from the nature of things, the country, because a republic, never can have much literature of its own. He forgets that even the purest demo-cratical government that the world has ever seen, that of Athens, produced in its day more distinguished poets, orators, historians, philosophers, as well as painters and sculptors, than any other city or country of the same population upon record. He full well knows, also, that the government of the United States is not an unmixed democracy, and that in everything that bears upon the higher branches of learning, our institutions are as much above the control of a democracy as those of any other country. The grand disadvantage, according to M. de Toque-ville, under which our literature labours is, that authors are not encouraged by pensions from the government. But are these so absolutely indispensable? Have such encouragements accom-plished all that has been expected from them? Are they not often shamefully abused, and merely made to gratify the per-sonal predilections of ministers of state? Besides, it is notorious that in England at least, where the government professes, I understand, to patronize literature, the most distinguished au-thors, in all its various departments, owe nothing to that source. As for the patronage of associations and wealthy individuals, it may exist just as well in the United States as any where else, and in fact is not unknown there.

But our literature, it is said, is not known beyond the country itself; and this is so far true. But how few, comparatively, even of the distinguished authors of any country, are known beyond them, as might easily be shown in the case of France, Germany, Holland, Denmark, and Italy. With the exception of the *corps* of literary men, even the well-informed among the English are little acquainted with the literature of those countries, and but for what they learn through the medium of the reviews, would hardly know so much as the names of some of their most dis-tinguished authors. No doubt, every civilised nation's litera-ture greatly influences that of all others; not, however, by its having a general circulation in those countries, but because of the master minds who first familiarise themselves with it, and then transfer all of it that is most valuable into their own, just as Milton appropriates the beauties of Virgil and Tasso.

The United States have unquestionably produced a considerable number of authors in every branch of literature, who, to say the least, are at least respectable in point of eminence. [1] Their being unknown to those who make use of the fact as a reproach to the country, may possibly be owing to something else than the want of real merit; and if, upon the whole, they present only what appears to foreigners nothing beyond a respectable mediocrity, this may readily be accounted for by other causes besides any hopeless peculiarity alleged to exist in the people or their government.

The country is still comparatively new. Much has yet to be done in felling the forest and clearing it for the habitations of civilised man. But a small part of our territories bears evidence of having been long setled. Our people have passed through exciting scenes that left but little leisure for writing. Few families combine a literary taste with the possession of wealth. The greater number of our institutions of learning are of recent origin. None of them have such ancient foundations as are to be found in many European universities; our colleges have no fellowships; our professors have their time much occupied in giving instruction; our pastors, lawyers, and physicians, find but little leisure amid their professional labours for the cultivation of literature. We have no sinecures—no pensions—for learned men. There is too much public life and excitement to

---

[1] It would not be difficult to make out a tolerably long list of authors, who must be pronounced by those who know any of them to be such as would be a disgrace to no country; and many of them are not unknown in Europe. Among living writers on law in its various branches, we have Kent, Story, Webster, Wheaton : in medicine, Mott, Warren, Jackson, and many others ; in theology and biblical science, Stuart, Miller, Woods, the Alexanders, Hodge, Wayland, Robinson, Barnes, Stowe, Becher, Schmucker, Hawkes, the Abbots, &c.; in belles lettres and history, Irving, Prescott, Channing,* Bancroft, Walsh, Cooper, Paulding ; in science, Silliman, Hitchcock, Davies ; and political economy, Carey, Vethake, Biddle, Raymond. These are but a few, selected chiefly with reference to their being known to some extent, at any rate in Europe. Among the distinguished dead, we have Marshall, Livingston, Madison, Jefferson, Jay ; Rush, Dorsey, Wistar, Dewees, Godman ; the Edwards, Davis, Dwight, Mason, Emmons, Griffin, Rice ; Wirt, Ramsay ; Franklin, Ewing, and Hamilton. In the fine arts, we have had a West, and have now a Greenough ; whilst in the useful arts, as they are called, we have not been without men of some renown. as the names of Fulton, Whitney, and some others attest.

* Since the above was written Dr. Channing has been numbered with the dead.

allow the rich to find pleasure in Sybaritic enjoyments; and they
have other sources of happiness than the extensive possession of
paintings and statues, though even for these the taste is gaining
ground.

But to return to our proper subject—the religious literature
of the United States; the number of our religious authors is by
no means small. Many valuable works, the productions of native minds, issue year after year from the press, a very large
proportion of which are of a practical kind, and unquestionably
exert a most salutary influence. They meet with an extensive
sale, for the taste for such reading is widely diffused, fostered as
it is by the establishment of Sunday schools and the libraries
attached to them.[1]

To the religious literature of books must be added that of
periodical works—newspapers, magazines, reviews—and no
where else, perhaps, is this literature so extensive or so efficient. Nearly sixty evangelical religious newspapers are published once a week. The Methodists publish eight, including
one in the German tongue, and all under the direction of their
conference. The Episcopalians have twelve; the Baptists nine
or ten; the Presbyterians of all classes, including the Congregationalists, Dutch and German Reformed, Lutherans, &c.,
about thirty more. This estimate includes evangelical Protestant papers only. In all, they cannot have fewer than 250,000
subscribers. The Christian Advocate (Methodist), published
at New York, has about 26,000; a few years ago it had 30,000,
but the number fell in consequence of the establishment of other
Methodist papers. The New York Observer has 16,000 subscribers, and several of the rest have a circulation of from 5000
to 10,000 each. They comprise a vast amount of religious
intelligence, as well as valuable selections from pamphlets and
books; and though it may be the case that religious newspapers
prevent more substantial reading, yet it must be confessed, I
think, that they are doing very much good, and are perused by
many who would otherwise read little or nothing religious at
all. Besides these newspapers, there is a considerable number

[1] I need not repeat here what has been said of the immense circulation of
books by the Sunday school and the Tract and Book societies, including the
" Book Concern " of the Methodists.

of religious monthly magazines, and several quarterly reviews, in which valuable essays on subjects of importance may be found from time to time.[1]

The political papers[2] in the United States, though often extremely violent in party politics, are in many instances auxiliary to the cause of religion. Whilst the editors of some, happily not many, are opposed to every thing that savours of religion, and even allow it to be outraged in their columns, an overwhelming majority often give excellent articles, and publish a considerable amount of religious intelligence. In this respect there has evidently been an amazing improvement within the last twenty years. Many of the political journals have rendered immense service in the temperance cause, as well as in every other involving the alleviation of human suffering.

Some of the literary and political reviews of native origin are very respectable works of the kind; the North American Review, in particular, which has now existed for a quarter of a century. The New York Review, the Democratical Review, the Boston Review, are all, likewise, quarterly. There are also several valuable monthly reviews. Besides these, the leading

[1] Two of these quarterlies are published under the auspices of the Presbyterians of the old and new schools; the " Biblical Repertory and Princetown Review," at Princetown, New Jersey, which is the organ of the former, and the " American Biblical Repository," at New York. The " Methodist Magazine and Quarterly Review," and the " Christian Review," conducted by the Baptists, are both valuable periodicals; and all four contain able reviews and essays.

[2] In the year 1839, according to the statistics furnished by the post-master general, the number of " newspapers and other periodical journals in the United States" was 1555, of which 116 were published daily (the Sabbath excepted), fourteen three times a week, thirty-nine twice a week, and 991 once a week. The remainder, which were issued twice a month, monthly, or quarterly, were principally magazines and reviews. Of the newspapers, thirty-eight were in the German language, four in French, one in the Spanish, and the rest in English. Several of the New Orleans papers are published both in French and English. The circulation of these newspapers and other periodicals is immense. Of the newspapers alone the subscriptions are at least 1,000,000. And though the number is too great by one-half or three-fourths, and though many are conducted by men who are but poorly qualified for the responsible and difficult task of an editor, yet there is no denying that even the poorest of them carry a vast amount of information to readers in the most secluded and distant settlements, as well as to the inhabitants of the most populous districts. And if we take the editors in the mass, it must be acknowledged that they are very ready to lend their columns to the publication of religious articles, of a suitable character and length, when requested by good men. And did Christians feel as they ought on this subject, and do what they might, the " press" would be far more useful to the cause of religion than it is.

reviews published in Britain, the Edinburgh, the London, Quarterly, Westminster, Foreign, Dublin, &c., are all republished among us.

CHAPTER XXII.

EFFORTS TO PROMOTE THE RELIGIOUS AND TEMPORAL INTERESTS OF SEAMEN.

WE have spoken of the endeavours made to send the gospel to the destitute settlements of the United States, both in the West and in the East, but we must not forget that the population of that country includes 100,000 men whose home is on the deep, and "who do business on the great waters,"—a number which must be doubled if we include those who navigate the rivers and lakes in steamboats, sailing vessels, and other craft.

The first systematic efforts made on a large scale, in the United States, for the salvation of seamen, commenced in 1812 at Boston. Since then a considerable interest in the subject has been awakened at almost every port along the sea-board; and within the last few years a good deal has been done for boatmen and sailors on the rivers and lakes.

The American Seaman's Friend Society was instituted at New York in 1827, and is now the chief association engaged in this benevolent enterprise. It serves, in some sense, as a central point to local societies formed in the other leading sea-ports, as well as to those on the western rivers, though they are not in general connected with it officially.[1] By a monthly publication, called the Seaman's Magazine, it communicates to pious seamen of all grades much interesting information regarding the progress of truth among that class of men, with details of its own proceedings, and those of other associations of the same kind.

Chapels have now been opened for seamen, and public wor-

---

[1] There are no fewer than fifty of these local associations for the promotion of the spiritual and temporal welfare of seamen and rivermen in the United States.

ship maintained on their account in almost all the principal
sea-ports from the north-east to the south-west, chaplains being
engaged for the purpose, and supported chiefly by local societies.
Those in the service of the central society are, with few excep-
tions, stationed at foreign ports, such as Hâvre, Canton, Sydney,
New South Wales, Honolulu in the Sandwich islands, and
Cronstadt in Russia. It had chaplains at one time, also, at Rio
Janeiro, Marseilles, and some other places.

Besides promoting the establishment of public worship under
chaplains at sea-ports, the society has strongly and successfully
recommended the opening of good boarding houses and reading
rooms for seamen when on shore, and the promotion of their
temporal comfort in every way possible.

These efforts of the different associations for seamen have
been greatly blessed. Last year, in particular, was marked by
special mercies. In no fewer than ten or twelve ports there
were manifest outpourings of the Holy Spirit on the meetings
for religious instruction. A hundred and fifty sailors were
reported by one of the chaplains at Philadelphia as having been
converted under his ministry, and among these was an old man,
ninety-nine years of age, who had been, from time to time, a
drunkard for more than seventy years.

There are supposed to be 600 pious captains in the United
States mercantile navy. There are also several decidedly religious officers in the national marine, who exercise a happy
influence on the service. The pious seamen belonging to the
United States are now reckoned at about 6000, a most gratifying contrast to the state of things twenty-five years ago, when
a pious seaman, of any class, was rarely to be met with.

The income of the society for last year was 20,861 dollars,
without including the receipts of the local associations, which
must have been considerable.

CHAPTER XXIII.

We have contemplated the voluntary principle as the main support of religion and its institutions in the United States. We have now to consider its powers of correcting, or rather overcoming, some of the evils that prevail in society. And first, let us see how it has contended with intemperance, one of the greatest evils that has ever afflicted the human race.

It is not easy to depict in a few words the ravages of drunkenness in the United States. The early wars of the colonial age, the long war of the Revolution, and finally, that of 1812-15 with England, all contributed to promote this tremendous evil. The very abundance of God's gifts became, by their perversion, a means of augmenting it. The country being fertile, nearly through its whole extent, and producing immense quantities of wheat, rye, and corn,[1] the two last of which were devoted to the manufacture of whiskey, there seemed no feasible check, or conceivable limit to the over-growing evil, especially as the government had no such pressure on its finances as might justify the laying on of a tax as would prevent or diminish the manufacture of ardent spirits. Moreover, the idea had become almost universally prevalent that the use of such stimulants, at least in moderate quantities, was not only beneficial but almost indispensable for health, as well as for enabling men to bear up under toil and fatigue.

The mischief spread from year to year. It pervaded all classes of society. The courts of justice, the administration of government, the very pulpit itself, felt its direful influence. The intellect of the physician, and the hand of the surgeon, were too often paralysed by it; and it might be said, that what some

[1] The word *corn* is almost invariably employed in America to designate the grain commonly called Indian corn, or maize in England, and *blé de Turquei* in France.

thought to be ordained unto life, was found to produce death. Poverty, disease, crime, punishment, misery, were its natural fruits, which it brought forth abundantly. Society was afflicted in almost all its ranks; almost every family throughout the country beheld the plague in one or more of its members. Yet, for long, whilst all saw and lamented the evil, none stood up against it. But there were those that mourned, and wept, and prayed over the subject; and the God of our fathers who had been with them on the ocean, and amid the howling wilderness, to watch over them and to protect them, heard those prayers.

In the year 1812, a considerable effort was made to arouse the attention of Christians to the growing evils of intemperance, and a day of fasting and of prayer was observed by some religious bodies. In the following year, the Massachusetts society for the suppression of intemperance was formed, and its labours were manifestly useful. Still, "the plague was not stayed." The subject, however, was not allowed to drop. It was seen that the society had not gone far enough, and that it would not do to admit of ardent spirits being taken, even in moderation. The evil of wide-spread drunkenness never could be exterminated by such half way measures.

It was proposed, accordingly, in 1826, to proceed upon the principle of entire abstinence from the use of ardent or distilled spirits as a beverage, and that same year saw the formation at Boston of the American Temperance society. The press was soon set in motion to make its objects known, and able agents were employed in advocating its principles. Great was the success that followed. In the course of a few years societies were to be found in all·parts of the country, and were joined, not by thousands only, but by hundreds of thousands. People of all classes and ages entered zealously into so noble an undertaking. Ministers of the gospel, lawyers, and judges, legislators, physicians, took a prominent part in urging it on.

What need is there of multiplying words? The cause continues advancing to this day. To reach the poor as well as to remove temptation from the rich, the rules of the temperance societies within the last six or seven years have included "all intoxicating drinks." Upon this principle wines of all descriptions have generally been abandoned, both on account of their being generally impure with us—being imported, and all more or less intoxicating, and because they are not found necessary to persons in health, but on the contrary, injurious; besides which, it was of consequence that an example of self-denial should be given by those who could afford to buy wine to the poor who could not.

But, in the progress of the temperance reformation little was done to reclaim men who had already become drunkards. And yet at the lowest estimate there were 300,000 such in the United States; many have even reckoned them at 500,000 at the commencement of the temperance movement. No hope seemed to be entertained with respect to these. To prevent such as had not yet become confirmed drunkards from acquiring that fatal habit, was the utmost that any one dared to expect. A few drunkards, indeed, were here and there reclaimed; but the mass remained unaffected by all the cogent arguments and affecting appeals that were resounding through the country.

At length God in his wonderful providence revealed the way by which these miserable persons might be reached. And how simple! A few hard drinkers in the city of Baltimore, who were in the habit of meeting in a low tavern for the purpose of revelry, and had been drunkards for years, met one night as usual. All happened to be sober. Apparently by accident the conversation fell upon the subject of the miseries of their life. One after another recounted his wretched history. All were deeply affected with the pictures of their own degradation thus held up to their minds. Some one proposed that they should stop in their career of folly and wickedness, and form themselves into a temperance association. They did so. Rules were written and signed on the spot. They met again the next night, related their histories, wept together over their past delusions, and strengthened each other's resolutions. They continued to meet almost every night—not however at a tavern. They invited their companions in sin to join them. These were affected and won. The fire was kindled, and soon it spread. In a few weeks four hundred such persons joined the society. In a few months no fewer than 2000 drunkards in the city of Baltimore were reclaimed. Then the movement came to light. The newspapers spread the wonderful news. The whole country was astounded. Christians lifted up their hearts in thankfulness to God and took courage. Benevolent men rallied around these reformed persons, and encouraged them to perseverance.

The society of reclaimed drunkards in Baltimore was invited to send delegates to other cities; and soon the "apostles of temperance," as these men were called, went forth to every city in the land. Great was their success. Hundreds and thousands were reclaimed in New York, Philadelphia, Boston, Albany, Pittsburg, Cincinnati, and from these cities, as from great centres, other delegations of reformed drunkards went forth into almost every village and district in the country.

This movement commenced on the 6th of April, 1840. And it is now estimated that 75,000 drunkards have already been reclaimed. But it may be said that they will relapse. No doubt some will. Hitherto, however, but few have done so. And the secret of this is to be found in the immense support which the *esprit du corps* gives them. There is everywhere a considerable band of such. They meet often to encourage each other. Good men are everywhere ready to encourage and befriend them. Never has the world seen any thing like it. What an encouragement to every good effort! What confidence does it not inspire in the influence of well concerted action in behalf of virtue and religion! God has smiled wonderfully on this movement. Already many who have been thus reclaimed from intemperance, and led to frequent the house of God, have been converted by the Spirit of the Lord, and are now "sitting at the feet of Jesus, clothed, and in their right mind."

To go further into detail would not consist with the nature of this work. A large proportion of the population of the United States are now under the happy influence of total abstinence from all intoxicating drinks. In 1826, when the temperance reform commenced, it was estimated that at least 60,000,000 gallons of whiskey were manufactured and consumed annually in the United States, without including the imported brandies, rum, &c. This estimate was unquestionably a very low one. In 1840, that is fourteen years afterwards, the census stated that the number of gallons distilled during that year was 36,343,336, showing a falling off of more than 23,000,000; and yet, within the same period, the population had augmented more than 5,000,000 ! And all this reformation had been brought about solely through the operation of voluntary associations, without the slightest direct aid from the government, with the exception of its having abolished the daily ration of whiskey formerly given to the officers and men in the army. Could any thing in the world show more conclusively the resources which right principles possess in themselves for overcoming, under God's blessing, the evils which are in the world, and even those which derive most power from the depraved appetites of man? The receipts of the American Temperance Union were 10,347 dollars in the year 1841.

CHAPTER XXIV.

PRISON DISCIPLINE SOCIETY.

THE Prison Discipline Society was instituted in 1824. It had for its object an investigation into the best methods of treatment for convicts and other prisoners, with a view to their health, a proper degree of comfort, and, above all, their moral and religious reformation.

Previous to the establishment of this society, the prisons in the United States were all conducted according to the old practice of herding the prisoners together in large numbers, without any due regard to their health, and with the inevitable certainty of their corrupting one another. In most cases, there was little regular religious instruction; in some, none at all. The prisoners were generally left idle, so that their maintenance, instead of being so far defrayed by the proceeds of their work, fell entirely on the States, and involved a heavy expense.

But a great reformation has now been effected. The society's able, enlightened, and devoted secretary, the only agent, I believe, in its service, has devoted nearly his whole time and energies to the subject for seventeen years. During that period he has examined the prisons in all parts of the country, has studied whatever was defective or wrong in each, has devised improvements in the construction of prison buildings, has visited the legislatures of the several States, and delivered lectures to them on the subject, besides giving to the world, in the seven-teen reports that have come from his pen, such a mass of well-digested information upon it as is probably no where else to be found in any language. The results have been wonderful. New penitentiaries, upon the most approved plans, have been erected in almost every State by the State governments, and in many cases at a great expence. These institutions are very generally under the direction of decidedly religious men. Judi-cious and faithful preachers have been appointed in many, and in the others, neighbouring pastors have been invited to preach the gospel, and visit the inmates as often as they can. Bible classes and Sunday schools have been established in several instances, and in all pains are taken to teach prisoners to read where they have yet to learn, so that they may be able to peruse the word of God.

A great blessing has rested upon these efforts. In many pri-sons very hopeful reformations have taken place; and in many cases, it is believed, after long and careful examination and trial, that convicts, who were hardened in their sins, have submitted their hearts to that adorable Saviour who died to save the very chief of sinners. Taken as a whole, in no other country in the world, probably, are the penitentiaries and prisons brought under a better moral and religious discipline. This great result has been brought about, first, by the erection of new and more con-venient buildings, and, secondly, by giving the direction so gen-erally to decided and zealous Christians. This has brought pure Christianity into contact with the minds of convicts to an extent unknown in former times in America, and still too little known in many other lands.[1]

---

[1] It may not be generally known that two different systems of discipline are to be found in the prisons of the United States, each having its ardent admirers. There is, first, the Philadelphia system, according to which the prisoners are entirely separated day and night, so that they are unknown to each other, and live in separate chambers or cells. And there is the Auburn system, so called because adopted in the prison for the State of New York, at Auburn, a town in the central part of that State. According to it, the prisoners are separated from each other at night but work together in companies during the day, under the eye of overseers and guards, but are not allowed to speak to each other. They are assembled, also, morning and evening, for prayers; and on the Sabbath

Besides effecting this great reformation in the State penitentiaries and prisons, the society has directed much of its attention
to the asylums for the insane, and to county or district prisons
for persons committed for trial, for convicts sentenced to short
terms of imprisonment, and for debtors, in States where the law
still allows imprisonment for debt. In all these various establishments the prison discipline society is exerting much influence, and gradually effecting the most important ameliorations.
It has also discussed in a very able manner many questions in
criminal legislation; such as those of imprisonment for debt,
capital punishments, &c., and its labours in this department
have not been in vain. Yet the society has but one agent—its
excellent secretary, who devotes, as I have said, nearly all his
time and energies to the cause, and its whole receipts scarcely
exceed 3000 dollars. With these limited means, notwithstanding, it has accomplished an immense amount of good. I know
nothing that more fully demonstrates how favourably disposed
our government is to religion, and to all good objects, than the
fact, that the legislatures of so many of our States, as well as
congress itself, have been so ready to second every feasible plan
for ameliorating the condition of mankind by moral and religious
means, as far as they can do so consistently with their constitutional powers. Indeed, they are ever ready to adopt measures
suggested by good and judicious men, as likely to benefit the

they meet in the chapel for public worship, conducted by a chaplain or some
other minister of the gospel. Each system has its advantages and disadvantages.
For health, facility in communicating religious instruction, and the saving of
expense arising from the labour of the prisoners, the latter, in my opinion, has
evidently the advantage. The former furnishes greater security, enables the
prisoners to remain unknown to their fellows on leaving the prison, and more
effectually breaks down the spirit of the most hardened criminals. But the
difference in point of expense is immense : nor are the moral results of the more
expensive plan so decidedly superior as to compensate for this disadvantage.
It is a singular fact, that the Auburn system has been decidedly preferred by
the prison discipline society, and by our citizens generally, for it has been
adopted by all but four of the penitentiaries in the country, whereas the Philadelphia plan has been preferred by the commissioners sent from France, England, and Prussia, to examine our prisons. For myself, I apprehend that sufficient time has not been allowed for a due estimate of their comparative merits.
After paying considerable attention to the subject, and as far as I am able to
judge, I should say that with the right sort of men to manage a prison—religious men of great judgment and self-control—the Auburn plan is the best.
But if such men cannot be had the Philadelphia system is safer. The former
demands extraordinary qualities in the keepers, and especially in the superintendent, whose powers, as they must be great, are capable, also, of being sadly
abused. Much, indeed, depends on the keepers under either system.

public interests and to promote religion, provided they fall within their sphere of action.

I may conclude this chapter by referring to the encouraging fact, stated by the secretary in his last yearly report, presented at the public meeting in May, 1842, that crime has been for some years decreasing in the country, at the rate of from two to three per cent *per annum.* This statement, from one whose position and means of information make him the highest authority on the subject, is the more encouraging when we consider how many difficulties have to be encountered in a new·country, and what a mighty stream of emigration from foreign lands is continually bringing over new settlers who have had little proper moral culture, and not a few of whom are consummate villains. Nor is it the least gratifying to think that this occurs at a time when brute force is superseded to such an extent in the repression of vice and crime by means essentially moral.

CHAPTER XXV.

SUNDRY OTHER ASSOCIATIONS.

I SHALL now include in one chapter a notice of two or three other instances, in which the variety and energy of action possessed by the voluntary principle are remarkably illustrated.

Societies for the promotion of a better observance of the Sabbath. Although the Sabbath is recognised, and its observance enjoined by the laws of every State in the union; and although that sacred day is observed in the United States in a manner that strikingly contrasts with its observance in Europe, and particularly on the continent, yet in certain quarters, and especially in places that are in some sense thoroughfares, the violation of it is distressing, nay, alarming to a Christian mind. Hence the formation of societies for the better observance of the Sabbath.

These are sometimes of a local and limited nature; sometimes they embrace a wider sphere of operation. By publishing and circulating well written addresses and tracts; still more by the

powerful appeals of the pulpit, they succeed in greatly diminishing the evil, if not in removing it altogether. By such measures
they strengthen the hands of the officers of justice, and give a
sounder tone and better direction to public opinion, greatly to
the diminution, if not to the entire removal, of the evil sought
to be cured. What is best; this result is obtained most commonly by the moral influence of truth—by kindly remonstrance
and arguments drawn from the word of God and right reason.
I may state that I have myself seen the happiest influence
exerted by these associations.

Anti-slavery societies. And so with respect to slavery, an
evil which afflicted all the thirteen original colonies at the
epoch of their declaration of independence, and which still
exists in half of the twenty-six States, as well as in the District of Columbia and the Territory of Florida, though no
longer to be found in the six New England States, or in New
York, New Jersey, Pennsylvania, Ohio, Indiana, Illinois,
Michigan, and the Territories of Wisconsin and Iowa. With
a view to its extirpation in the States to which it still adheres,
many of the inhabitants of the northern or non-slave-holding
States have associated themselves in what are called anti-slavery
societies, and have been endeavouring, for several years past, to
awaken the public to a sense of the enormity and danger of
slavery, and to the disgrace which it entails on the whole country. By means of the press, by tracts and books, and by the
voice of living agents, they aim at the destruction of this—the
greatest of all the evils that lie heavy on our institutions. I
say nothing at present of the wisdom of their plans, or of the
spirit in which these plans have been prosecuted. I only mention these societies as a further proof of the wide application of
the voluntary principle, and of the manner in which it leads to
associated efforts for the correction of existing evils.[1]

Peace societies. And so in relation to the evils of war, and
for the purpose of preserving good men especially, and all men

---

[1] The receipts of the American Anti-slavery society for last year were about
10,000 dollars; those of the American and Foreign Anti-slavery society were
probably greater, but I have not seen the amount stated. A few years ago,
before the division took place in the American Anti-slavery society which led
to the formation of the American and Foreign anti-slavery society, its income
was 40,000 dollars, and the number of its agents was forty or fifty.

if possible, from thinking lightly of them, peace societies began to be formed as early as the year 1816, and a national society was organised in 1827. The object must be admitted to be humane and Christian. By the diffusion of well-written tracts, by the offering handsome premiums for essays on the subject, and their subsequent publication, and, above all, by short and pointed articles in the newspapers, a great deal has been done to cause the prayer to ascend with more fervency from the heart of many a Christian, " Give peace in our time, O Lord," and to inspire a just dread of the awful curse of war. To many such efforts may appear ridiculous; but not so to the man who can estimate the value of even one just principle when once established in the heart of any individual, however humble. Who can tell how much such efforts in the United States, and other countries, may have contributed, in God's holy providence, which often avails itself of the humblest means for the accomplishment of the greatest purposes, to prolong that happy general peace which has held Europe and all the civilised world in its embrace during more than a quarter of a century.

The American Peace Society employed four agents last year, and issued 5000 copies of its periodical. Its receipts were 3000 dollars.[1]

---

[1] The late William Ladd, Esq., of the State of Maine, was the founder of the American Peace Society, and for many years its worthy president. He was an excellent Christian. His heart was absorbed in the objects of the society over which he presided. Through his exertions a prize of 1000 dollars was offered for the best essay on the subject of *A Congress of Nations*, for the termination of national disputes. Four or five excellent dissertations were presented, and the premium was divided among the authors by the judges appointed to make the award; one of whom was the Hon. John Quincy Adams, formerly president of the United States. The evils of war can hardly be exaggerated. " In peace," said Crœsus to Cyrus, " children bury their fathers ; but in war fathers bury their children." " War makes thieves," says Machiavelli, " and peace brings them to the gallows." " May we never see another war," said Franklin in a letter which he addressed to a friend, just after signing the treaty of peace at the close of the American Revolution, " for in my opinion there never was a *good war* or a *bad peace*."

CHAPTER XXVI.

NOR is the voluntary principle less operative in the formation
and support of beneficent institutions than of associations for
attacking and vanquishing existing evils. But these present
too wide a field to be fully gone over in this work, besides that
they do not come properly within its scope. I shall therefore
glance only at a few points, showing how the voluntary principle operates in this direction for the furtherance of the
gospel.

In efforts to relieve the temporal wants and sufferings of
mankind, as well as in all other good undertakings, Christians,
and those, too, with few exceptions, evangelical Christians,
almost invariably take the lead. Whenever there is a call for
the vigorous exercise of benevolence, proceeding from whatever
cause, Christians immediately go to work, and endeavour to
meet the exigency by their own exertions if possible; but
should the nature and extent of the relief required properly
demand co-operation on the part of municipal and state authorities, they bring the case before these authorities, and invoke
their aid. It naturally follows that when this is given, it
should be applied through the hands of those who were the first
to stir in the matter; and this wisely too, since who can be
supposed so fit to administer the charities of the civil government as those who have first had the heart to make sacrifices
for the same object themselves? Such alone are likely to have
the experience that in such affairs is necessary.

All this I might illustrate by adducing many instances were
it necessary. In this chapter, however, I shall notice a few,
and take these collectively.

There is not a city or large town, I may say, hardly a village,
in all the country, which has not its voluntary associations of

good men and women for the relief of poverty, especially where its sufferings are aggravated by disease. These efforts, in countless instances, may not be extensive, only because there is no extensive call for their being made. Created by circumstances —when these disappear, the associations also cease to exist. But where the sufferings to be relieved are perpetually recurring, as well as too extensive to be overtaken by individual effort, these benevolent associations become permanent. Their objects are accomplished, in most instances, by the unaided exertions of the benevolent who voluntarily associate for the purpose; but if these prove insufficient, municipal or state assistance is sought, and never sought in vain. Accordingly, the stranger who visits the United States will find hospitals for the sick, alms-houses for the poor, and dispensaries for furnishing the indigent with medicines gratuitously, in all the large cities where they are required.[1] There is a legal provision in all the States for the poor, not such, however, as to do away with the necessity of individual or associated effort to meet extraordinary cases of want, especially when it comes on suddenly, and in the train of disease. The rapid and wide-spreading attacks of epidemics may demand, and will assuredly find benevolent individuals ready to associate themselves for meeting such exigencies, before the measures provided by law can be brought to bear upon them.[2]

[1] The manner of providing for the poor differs greatly in different States. In the west, where there is but little extreme poverty, the inhabitants of each township look after their poor in such a way as best suits them. Money is raised, and by a "commissioner of the poor" appropriated to the support of such as need it. Those who have families live in houses hired for them; single persons board with others who are willing to take them for the stipulated sum. In the Atlantic States, where there are more poor who need assistance, the same course is pursued in many cases. In others, "poor-houses" are erected in such counties as choose to have such establishments, and to these the townships send their quota of paupers, and pay for their board, clothing, &c. In the cities on the sea-board, the municipal authorities make abundant provision for the poor who need aid; and a great proportion of whom are foreigners.

[2] There were many illustrations of the expensive nature of individual and associated charity during the prevalence of the cholera. In all our large cities, associations, comprising the very best Christians in them, were formed with the utmost promptitude, and zealously sustained as long as needed. I saw myself, having often attended their meetings, an association of Christian ladies formed in Philadelphia, as soon as the pestilence commenced its ravages in that city. They took a house, converted it into an hospital, gathered into it all the children whom the plague had orphanised, both white and black, whom they could find, and day after day, and week after week, washed, dressed, and took care of those children with their own hands, and defrayed all the expenses of the establishment. Two of the children died of the cholera in their arms! These ladies

It is with great pleasure that I have to state that the gospel finds admittance into the establishments for the relief of poverty and disease, which have been created and maintained by the municipal and state authorities; and that I have never heard of any case in which the directors have opposed obstacles to the endeavour, of judicious Christians to make known to the inmates the blessings of religion. Prudent and zealous Christians, both ministers and laymen, are allowed to visit, and ministers to preach to the occupants of such establishments; and in several of our cities, one or more excellent ministers of the gospel are employed to preach in them as well as in the prisons. With rare exceptions they are in the hands of Protestants, though Romish priests are no where forbidden to enter and teach all who desire their ministrations.

Of all the beneficent institutions of our large cities, there is none more interesting than those intended for the benefit of *children*. Orphan asylums, well established and properly conducted, are to be found in every city of any consideration throughout the Union. Nor are these asylums for white children only, they are also for the coloured. Indeed, it cannot be said with truth that the poor and the sick of the African race, in our cities and large towns, are less cared for than those of the white race. Nor are those children only who have lost both parents thus provided for. In some of our cities, asylums are in the course of being provided for what are called *half-orphans*—that is, who have still one parent or both, but are not supported by them. I may state it, however, as a fact of which I am perfectly certain, that there is not a single foundling hospital in the United States.

In some of our cities we have admirable institutions, called *houses of refuge*, for neglected children, and such as are encouraged by their parents to live a vagabond life, or are disposed of themselves to lead such a life. In these establishments they not only receive the elements of a good English education, but are instructed also in the mechanical arts; and with these religious instruction is faithfully and successfully combined. All of these institutions were commenced, and are carried on

belonged, many of them, to some of the first families in that city in point of respectability.

by the voluntary efforts of Christians, though they have been greatly assisted by appropriations in their favour, in the shape of endowments or annuities from the State governments.[1]

Nor are the aged poor neglected. Asylums for widows are to be met with in all our large towns, where they are in fact most needed; and old and infirm men are also provided for.

At the same time, that charity which seeketh not her own, but the good of all others, no matter what may have been their character or what their crimes, has not forgotten those unfortunate females who have been the victims of the faithlessness of men. Magdalene asylums have been founded in all our chief cities, especially on the sea-board, where they are most needed, and have been the means of doing much good. It is only to be regretted that this branch of Christian kindness and effort has not been far more extensively prosecuted. Nevertheless, there are many hearts that are interested in it; and in the institutions which they have erected, the glorious gospel of him who said to the penitent woman in Simon's house, " Thy faith hath saved thee; go in peace," is not only preached, but also received into hearts which the Spirit of God has touched and broken.

---

[1] One of the best conducted of these establishments is at Philadelphia. It stands a little out of the city, occupies a beautiful site, and has a number of acres of ground attached to it. There are here usually between 100 and 200 youth of both sexes, who occupy different apartments, and are under the care of excellent teachers. The magistrates of the city have the power to send vagrant, idle, and neglected children to it. Very many youth have left this institution greatly benefitted by their residence in it. It has fallen to the lot of the writer to preach often to its inmates, and never has he seen a more affecting sight. If a man wishes to learn the value of the parental relation, and the blessings which flow from a faithful fulfilment of its duties, let him visit such an institution, and inquire into the history of each youth whom it contains. The " Farm Schools " for orphans and for neglected children, in the neighbourhoods of Boston and New York, are excellent, and have been the means of doing much good.

CHAPTER XXVII.

INFLUENCE OF THE VOLUNTARY PRINCIPLE ON THE BENEFICENT INSTITUTIONS OF THE
COUNTRY—ASYLUMS FOR THE INSANE.

THE utmost attention is now paid in the United States to a class of the unfortunate, which of all others presents the strongest claims on our sympathy,—I allude to the insane. For these very much has been done in the course of the last twenty years, by the establishment of suitable places for their reception, instead of being confined, as formerly, in the common prisons of the country. In this the prison discipline society has exerted a most extensive and happy influence, never having ceased, in its yearly reports, to urge upon the governments of the States the duty of providing proper receptacles, to which persons discovered to be insane may be conveyed as promptly as possible, with a view to their proper treatment. The society showed this to be an imperative dnty on the part of the States, and its voice has not been heard in vain.

There are now twelve asylums supported by the States, and some of these are on a large scale. That near Utica will consist, when completed, of four buildings, each 446 feet long by 48 wide, and placed one on each side of a beautiful quadrilateral area, which assumes an octagonal form by the intersection of its corners, with verandahs of open lattice work. It is intended for the insane poor of the State of New York, which State is at the sole expense of its erection, and the cost upon the completion of the whole will amount, it is supposed, to about 1,000,000 of dollars. It is calculated to receive 1000 patients.

Besides the twelve State asylums, there are two belonging to cities, namely, those at Boston and New York; six to incorporated bodies; and one is the property of an individual [1]— making in all twenty-one. One or more state asylums may

---

[1] Dr. White's at Hudson, in the State of New York.

possibly have been opened since the publication of the interesting work to which I am indebted for my information on the subject.[1]

Almost all of these asylums are constructed on the most approved plans. Nearly all are beautifully situated, have a light and cheerful aspect, and are surrounded with ample grounds, tastefully laid out in fields and meadows, pleasant gardens, and delightful walks. After visiting many such institutions in Europe I have seen none more pleasantly situated, or better kept, than the Massachusetts State asylum at Worcester, the Retreat at Hartford in Connecticut, and the asylum on Blackwell's island near New York. Indeed they are, with very few exceptions, admirably situated and well conducted.

I would particularly call attention to the fact that religious worship is kept up in all of these twenty-one institutions but four. Some have regular chaplains attached to them; in others, divine worship is conducted for the inmates by clergymen or laymen in the neighbourhood, who volunteer their services in performing this important and interesting duty. In almost every case it is done by men of evangelical sentiments. Nor is their labour in vain, it being demonstrated by ample experience that such services when performed by judicious, calm, and truly spiritual men, exert a highly beneficial influence on the insane. The gospel, when presented in the spirit of its blessed Author, is indeed admirably fitted to soothe the mental excitement of the poor deranged lunatic.

"Regular religious teaching," says Dr. Woodward, the superintendent of the asylum for the insane at Worcester, Massachusetts, "is as necessary and beneficial to the insane as to the rational mind: in a large proportion of the cases it will have equal influence. They as well know their imperfections, if they will not admit their delusions; and they feel the importance of good conduct to secure the confidence and esteem of those whose good opinion they value."

According to Dr. Earle's statements, the deaths in the European institutions for the insane vary from *thirteen* to *forty* per

---

[1] "A visit to Thirteen Asylums for the Insane in Europe, &c., to which is subjoined a brief notice of similar institutions in the United States," by Pliny Earle, M.D. Published at Philadelphia in 1841.

cent; whilst in the American asylums none exceed *ten* per cent.[1]

While the State governments have been doing so much for the establishment of hospitals and asylums for the insane, much has also been done by individual munificence. Even some of the state institutions have been assisted by donations from private citizens. Thus two in the State of Maine have given 10,000 dollars each, towards founding the asylum for that State.

CHAPTER XXVIII.

INFLUENCE OF THE VOLUNTARY PRINCIPLE ON THE BENEFICENT INSTITUTIONS OF THE COUNTRY—ASYLUMS FOR THE DEAF AND DUMB.

OUR asylums for the deaf and dumb owe their existence to a series of efforts on the part of a few Christian friends.

The late Dr. Cogswell, a pious and excellent physician in the city of Hartford, Connecticut, had a beloved daughter who was deaf and dumb. For her sake he proposed to a devoted young minister of the gospel, the Rev. Mr. Gallaudet, to go to Europe, and there to learn, at the best institutions, the most approved methods of teaching this unfortunate class of people. The mission was cheerfully undertaken. Mr. Gallaudet returned in 1816, after having spent above a year in Paris, where he studied the methods of instruction pursued at the Royal Institution for the education of the deaf and dumb, under the Abbé Sicard, the pupil and friend of the Abbé L'Epée. Thereupon an effort was immediately made to have an institution founded at Hartford. An act of incorporation was obtained in 1816, a large sum was contributed by the people of Hartford for the erection of the requisite buildings, and congress granted a township from the national lands, consisting of 23,040 acres, towards the endow-

---

[1] The number of the insane in the asylums in the United States is about 2500; in 1840 the number of the insane of all ages and conditions was, according to the census, 17,434, being about one to every 979 inhabitants. Of these 17,434 insane persons, 5162 were maintained at the public expense. and 12,272 at that of their friends.

ment of the institution. It was opened ere long for the reception of pupils, and from that time to this has been going on most prosperously. It is the oldest establishment for the purpose in the United States, and is called the American Asylum for the education and instruction of the deaf and dumb. So far, indeed, it is a national institution. It was endowed to a considerable amount by congress; it is open to pupils from all the States, and it does, in fact, receive them from the south as well as from the north. It is peculiarly, however, the deaf and dumb institution of New England, five of the States of which support within its walls, at the expense of their treasuries, a certain number of pupils every year. The number at the asylum is usually between 140 and 150. The course of study lasts four years. Mechanical arts are taught to the young men at certain hours daily, while the young women learn such as become their sex and situation in life.

Since 1816 five other institutions for the deaf and dumb have been established in the United States, all on the model of that at Hartford. They are as follows:—

1. That at New York. It has about 150 pupils, and is mainly supported by the State legislature.

2. The Pennsylvania institution, at Philadelphia. It has from 100 to 120 pupils, most of whom are maintained there at the expense of that and the neighbouring States.

3. The Ohio asylum at Columbus, a prosperous institution, with about seventy pupils, and mainly supported by the State legislature of Ohio.

4. The asylum for Kentucky, at Danville, which is chiefly, if not entirely, supported by funds arising from the sale of lands granted to it by the congress of the United States. It has perhaps twenty-five or thirty pupils, but has not been very prosperous.

5. The Virginia asylum at Staunton, an institution of very recent date. It has about twenty-five pupils, and is mainly dependent upon that State for its support.

These five, as well as that at Hartford, receive paying pupils from families who have the means of defraying the expense of educating their own children. But the number of such pupils probably does not exceed one-sixth of the whole.

The number of pupils in these six asylums runs from 510 to 545, and as the fifteen or sixteen States by which they are supported have both the means and the disposition to do so, they will doubtless furnish instruction to the deaf and dumb of the other States, which have resolved to send them thither until they can have asylums of their own. There will, indeed, be but a partial provision for some time for the indigent deaf and dumb of the new States; yet the known enterprise and benevolence of their inhabitants warrant us to believe that as soon as their population shall have become sufficiently numerous, and they shall have established those more general and important institutions that lie at the basis of an enlightened society, the whole of the confederated States will be found ready to make provision for conducting their deaf and dumb, by means of a suitable education, to usefulness and happiness. For this it is not requisite that each should have an asylum for itself— it would be found enough that two or more should unite, as at present, in having one in common.

The number of deaf and dumb persons throughout the United States in 1840 was 7659, or about one to every 2227 of the entire population; but the proportion of proper age for being placed in an asylum, to receive the usual instruction there, is hardly above a fourth of the entire number.

It is delightful to contemplate how much has been done for this interesting part of the community within the last few years, and especially delightful to the Christian to know that all the six asylums above mentioned are under the direction of decidedly religious men, and that the course of instruction pursued in them is entirely evangelical. The Bible is made the text book of their religious studies. Every morning and evening they are assembled for prayers, and then a portion of scripture is written on a large slate, about ten feet by four. Some pertinent remarks are addressed to them, followed by prayer, both the remarks and the prayer being performed, by the principal or one of the professors of the institution, by signs. In the same way, upon the Sabbath, a sermon is preached and other religious services held. God has greatly blessed these instructions. Many of the pupils throughout the asylums have become, as their lives attest, truly pious persons; and in some instances the deaf and dumb institutions have richly shared in the revivals that have occurred in the places where they are established.

CHAPTER XXIX.

INFLUENCE OF THE VOLUNTARY PRINCIPLE ON THE BENEFICENT INSTITUTIONS OF THE COUNTRY—ASYLUMS FOR THE BLIND.

In the year 1832 the Perkins institution and Massachusetts asylum for the blind was founded, as follows:—

Thomas H. Perkins, Esq., of the city of Boston, gave his valuable house and grounds, with out-buildings thereon, estimated as worth 50,000 dollars, for an asylum for the blind, provided the sum required for founding one should be raised in New England. Fifty thousand dollars having been speedily collected, and the Massachusetts legislature having voted a large annual grant to give permanency to the projected institution, the corporation entered vigorously upon the work, and opened a school for the blind, which has now been for ten years in successful operation. As the property so munificently given by Mr. Perkins, was found not in all respects suitable, it was exchanged in 1839 for Mount Washington house and grounds, in South Boston, beautifully situated near the bay which spreads out to the east of the city, and in every way adapted for the purpose. The institution is under the direction of Dr. Samuel G. Howe, a man of remarkable qualification for the post. The number of pupils for 1841, was sixty-seven, and they were reported to be making excellent progress and remarkably happy.

There are four other institutions for the blind in the United States. New York has one, which had last year about sixty-five pupils; Philadelphia one, which had sixty-two pupils; Columbus, in Ohio, one, which had fifty pupils; and in the same establishment with the asylum for the deaf and dumb at Staunton, in Virginia, there is a department for the blind with about five and twenty pupils. All these four have sprung up since the establishment of that at Boston in 1832, and they are all flourishing. The number of pupils in the whole five was, last year, about 270. The whole number of the blind in the United States in 1840, was 6916.

A few years ago, a Mr. Mill of Philadelphia bequeathed a sum to be laid out in an hospital for the blind, but I rather think that the institution that has arisen out of this bequest is not a school but a retreat, where the aged and infirm blind may pass their remaining days in comfort.

Although all these institutions are aided by the legislatures of the States within which they are established, most of them, nevertheless, may be traced to the benevolence of Christian citizens, acting individually or together. Few establishments can be contemplated by the eye of Christian sympathy with greater interest than these quiet retreats. There the blind not only learn the elements of a common education,[1] and such an expertness in some of the mechanical arts as enables them, even while under tuition, to contribute towards their own support, but cultivate music also, by which many an hour sweetly passes away, and for which many of them show so much aptitude as to qualify themselves to become teachers of it.

Nor is our literature for the blind inconsiderable, when it is borne in mind that it is not ten years since printing in "raised" characters for their use was first introduced amongst us. Above thirty volumes have been published at Boston, and about half that number at Philadelphia, comprising several of the most interesting religious works in the English language, and the perusal of which has already proved a blessing to many of the blind.[2] It is gratifying to think that these institutions have all

[1] Joseph B. Smith, a pupil of the Perkins institution and Massachusetts asylum for the blind, pursued the study of Latin, Greek, and the other branches of a preparatory course with success, and entered Harvard university in the autumn of 1839, where he has made respectable progress. He gets his lessons by the help of his companion, who carefully reads them over to him, and seeks out in the lexicon the meaning of words he does not understand. In geometry, when the diagram is too complicated for him to retain a clear conception of it, he causes it to be "embossed" upon thick paper, that he may examine it with his fingers.

[2] The books published by the institution at Boston are: the New Testament; Parts of the Old Testament; Lardner's Universal History; Selections from Old English Authors; Selections from Modern English Authors; Howe's Geography for the Blind; Howe's General Atlas; Howe's Atlas of the United States; Blind Child's First Book; Blind Child's Second Book; the Dairyman's Daughter; the Harvey Boys; Blind Child's Spelling Book; Blind Child's Eng-

along been, to a great extent, in the hands of good men, so that this benevolent enterprise has taken a happy direction from the first.

The report of the Boston institution for 1841, gives us the history of a child who had been four years a pupil there, and whose case is more interesting, probably, than any that has ever yet been known. Laura Bridgman, born in 1829, had lost, when twenty months old, the faculties of sight, hearing, and speech, and partially that of smell. At the age of nine she was placed at the institution. There she has learned to read and write, and has made very considerable progress in knowledge. The details of the manner in which she acquired these arts are exceedingly curious, but to give them does not fall within the scope of this work.

CHAPTER XXX.

CONCLUDING REMARKS ON THE DEVELOPMENTS OF THE VOLUNTARY SYSTEM.

WE here close our notice of the developments of the voluntary principle in the United States; the results will appear more appropriately in another part of my work. If it is thought that I have dealt too much in details, I can only say that these seemed necessary for obvious reasons. There being no longer a union of church and state in any part of the country, so that religion must depend, under God, for its temporal support wholly upon the voluntary principle, it seemed of consequence to show how vigorously, and how extensively, that principle has brought gospel influences to bear in every direction upon the objects within its legitimate sphere. In doing this, I have

lish Grammar; the Pilgrim's Progress; Baxter's Call; Sixpenny Glass of Wine; Life of Melancthon; Book of Sacred Hymns; Viri Romæ; Pierce's Geometry, with Diagrams; Book of Diagrams, illustrative of Natural Philosophy; Political Class Book; Blind Child's Manual.

The Pennsylvania institute, besides printing portions of the Old Testament, has published a Guide to Spelling; Select Library; Student's Magazine; French Verbs; a Grammar; and two or three books in the German language.

aimed at answering a multitude of questions proposed to me during my residence in Europe.

Thus I have shown how, and by what means, funds are raised for the erection of church edifices, for the support of pastors, and for providing destitute places with the preaching of the gospel—this last involving the whole subject of our home missionary efforts. And as ministers must be provided for the settlements forming apace in the West, as well as for the constantly increasing population to be found in the villages, towns, and cities of the East, I entered somewhat at length into the subject of education, from the primary schools up to the theological seminaries and faculties.

It was next of importance to show how the press is made subservient to the cause of the gospel and the extension of the kingdom of God—then, how the voluntary principle can grapple with existing evils in society, such as intemperance, Sabbath breaking, slavery, and war, by means of diverse associations formed for their repression or removal. And, finally, I have reviewed my country's beneficent and humane institutions, and shown how much the voluntary principle has had to do with their origin and progress.

The reader who has had the patience to follow me thus far, must have been struck with the vast versatility, if I may so speak, of this great principle. Not an exigency occurs in which its application is called for, but forthwith those who have the heart, the hand, and the purse to meet the case, combine their efforts. Thus the principle seems to extend itself in every direction with an all-powerful influence. Adapting itself to every variety of circumstances, it acts wherever the gospel is to be preached, wherever vice is to be attacked, and wherever suffering humanity has to be relieved.[1]

[1] There is one field on which the voluntary principle is accomplishing perhaps greater triumphs, and diffusing as happy an influence as on any other, but which I have not yet noticed. I refer to that presented by the numerous manufacturing establishments which have been springing up during the last five and twenty years in the middle and northern States. Large factories in the old world are proverbial for ignorance and vice. But if a man would like to see religion flourishing in manufacturing towns and among "operatives," let him visit some of those towns in New England in which cotton, woollen, or other factories have grown up, and where hundreds, in some instances thousands, of men and women are collected together under circumstances in which they are apt to exercise a most corrupting influence on one another. Let him there observe the pains taken by bands of devoted Christians, pastors, and

Nor is this principle less beneficial to those whom it enlists in the various enterprises of Christian philanthropy, than to those who are the express objects of these enterprises. The very activity, energy, and self-reliance which it calls forth, is a great blessing to the individual who exercises these qualities, as well as to those for whose behoof they are put forth, and to the community at large. Men are so constituted as to derive happiness from the cultivation of an independent, energetic, and benevolent spirit, in being " co-workers for God " in promoting his glory, and the true welfare of their fellow-men.

We now take leave of this part of our work, to enter on that for which all that has hitherto been said must be considered as preparatory—I mean the direct work of bringing men to the knowledge and possession of SALVATION.

members of their flocks, to gather these into Bible classes and Sunday schools, to induce them to attend church, to provide libraries of good books for them, to open public lectures on scientific and general as well as religious subjects; above all, let him mark the earnestness with which faithful ministers preach the gospel to them, and the assiduity with which they watch for their souls, and he will perceive how much may be done, even under very unfavourable circumstances, for saving men's souls from ruin. I have never visited more virtuous communities than I have seen in some of those villages, or any in which the gospel triumphed more signally over all obstacles.

No manufacturing town in the United States has grown up more rapidly than Lowell, near the Merrimac river, about thirty miles north-west of Boston. It was but a small village not many years ago, and in 1827 had only 3500 inhabitants. But in 1840 these had increased to 20,000. As it derives great advantages for cotton, woollen, and other factories, from the vast water power it possesses, several companies have built large mills, and employ a great number of people, mostly young women above fifteen years of age, who have been led to leave other parts of New England by the inducement of higher wages than they could command at home. This is an object with some, in order that they may help their poor parents ; with others, that they may prosecute their education, and with a third and numerous class, who being betrothed to young men in their native districts, come to earn for themselves a little " outfit " for the married life. Let us see what opportunities of religious instruction are presented to these young persons.

In 1840 there were fifteen or sixteen churches in Lowell, in the Sunday schools attached to ten of which there were 4936 scholars and forty-three teachers, in all 5369. About three-fourths of the scholars are girls, a large proportion of whom are above fifteen years of age. More than 500 became hopefully pious in 1839, yet that year was not more remarkable than others in regard to religion. Including the Sunday schools attached to the other five or six churches, the number of scholars and teachers for 1840 considerably exceeded 6000, and nearly equalled a third of the population. Nearly 1000 of the factory girls had funds in the savings banks, amounting in all to 100,000 dollars. A decided taste for reading prevails amongst them. When in Lowell in the summer of 1841, I found that two monthly magazines of handsome appearance were publishing there. One of these was the " Operatives' Magazine," and the other the " Lowell Offering." Both were of 8vo form, the one containing sixteen pages, the other thirty-two. Both displayed very considerable talent, and the Offering was filled with original articles, written solely by the female operatives.

BOOK V.

THE CHURCH AND THE PULPIT IN AMERICA.

CHAPTER I.

IMPORTANCE OF THIS PART OF THE SUBJECT.

WE now come to that part of our subject which more immediately bears upon the salvation of men's souls, and the importance of which will be readily owned, therefore, by all who
rightly appreciate the nature and value of that salvation.

It is interesting to mark the influence of Christian institutions
on society—the repose of the Sabbath—the civilising effect of
the people assembling in their churches—and the great amount
of knowledge communicated in the numerous discourses of a well
instructed ministry. Apart from higher considerations, the
benefits indirectly conferred upon a community by an evangelical
ministry, are well worth all that it costs. It softens and refines
manners, promotes health by promoting attention to cleanliness
and the frequent change of apparel; it diffuses information, and
rouses minds that might otherwise remain ignorant, inert, and
stupid. But what is this compared with the preparation of the
immortal spirit for its everlasting destiny? This world, after
all, is but the place of our education for a better; of how much
moment, then, that the period of our pupilage should be rightly
spent!

The church, with its institutions, is of divine ordination. It was appointed by its great Author to be the depository of the economy of salvation as far as human co-operation is concerned, and is designed to combine all the human agencies which God, in infinite wisdom, has resolved to employ in the accomplishment of that salvation. How important, then, that the church should meet the design of its divine Founder, not only as regards its proper character, but also, in the development and right employment of the influences which it was constituted to put forth for the salvation of the world.

As the church on earth is but preparatory to the church in heaven, it was obviously intended to bear some resemblance to the celestial state. As the depository to which God has committed the custody of his revealed truth, and as his chosen instrument for its diffusion among mankind, it ought obviously to be kept as pure as is possible for an institution placed in the hands of imperfect creatures at the best, from everything which would impede the discharge of its high functions.

But we must not misapprehend the church's office. She has received no power of original legislation. She is nothing but an agent. Christ is the Lawgiver and the Head of the church. He has given her the revelation of his will, and clearly defined her sphere of action. Nor can she justly expect his blessing if she goes beyond the boundaries of her duty.

By a holy life on the part of her members; by a conversation such as becometh saints; by well-directed efforts to make known the gospel to dying men everywhere, whether by the faithful proclamation of it on the part of the ministry whom God hath appointed, or by more familiar instruction in the Sunday school and the Bible class, or around the family altar, or by the distribution of the scriptures and other religious books, united with constant, fervent, and believing prayer, that the Holy Spirit may render all these means successful, the church is required to exert her influence in saving the world. It is thus that she becomes "the light of the world;" it is thus that she proves herself to be "the salt of the earth." But in order to fulfil this high mission she ought to be as nearly as possible what the Saviour of men intended her to be—a company of saints redeemed by his blood, renewed by his Spirit, and devoted to his service—ever bearing the cross that she may wear the crown, and preparing for that day when she shall be presented to her Lord, "not having spot or wrinkle, or any such thing," but "holy and without blemish," for she is "his body."

CHAPTER II.

THE EVANGELICAL CHURCHES IN THE UNITED STATES MAINTAIN DISCIPLINE.

This is a point of inexpressible importance to the prosperity of a church, and I rejoice to say that such is the light in which it is viewed by Christians of all the evangelical denominations in the United States, almost without exception.

I do not suppose there is a single evangelical church in the country that does not keep a record of its members; I mean of those whom it has received according to some regular form or other *as members*, and who, as such, are entitled to come to the Lord's supper. As this whole subject is not only important, but by some readers may not be easily comprehended, I may venture upon some detail.

1. There is no evangelical church in the United States, that is, no organised body of believers worshipping in one place, that does not hold a creed comprehending the following points, at least: the existence of one God, in three persons, Father, Son, and Holy Ghost, of the same substance, and equal in all the attributes of their nature; the depravity, guilt, condemnation, and misery of all mankind; an all-sufficient and only atonement by the Son of God, who assumed human nature, and thus became both God and man in one person; and by his obedience, suffering, death, and intercession, has procured salvation for men; regeneration by the Holy Ghost, by which repentance and faith are made to spring up in the soul; the final judgment of all men; and a state of everlasting misery for the wicked, and of blessedness for the righteous. On these doctrines, in their substantial and real meaning, there is no difference among the evangelical churches in the United States.

2. Neither is there any evangelical church in America that does not hold the necessity of a moral life—of a life against which no charge inconsistent with a Christian profession can be brought—in order to a man's being a proper member of a church of Jesus Christ; or which would not promptly exclude an immoral person, on being sufficiently proved to be such, from its membership. No doubt there are immoral persons among the members of the churches. They are persons whose guilt cannot always be established by such proof as the laws of Christ's house requires, and their number, it is believed, is comparatively small.

3. There are few, if any, evangelical churches, in which the profession of a mere general or "historical belief," as it is called, in the great doctrines above stated, accompanied even by an outwardly moral life, would be considered sufficient to render a man fit to be admitted to the Lord's supper. Nineteen-twentieths of all the evangelical churches in that country believe that there is such a thing as "being born again," "born of the Spirit." And very few, indeed, admit the doctrine that a man who is not "converted," that is, "renewed by the Spirit," may come without sin to that holy ordinance.

There may be difference of opinion among truly evangelical Christians respecting the amount of evidence of conversion necessary in the case. But I may unhesitatingly affirm that, with few exceptions, all expect some evidence in every candidate for admission to the church and participation in its most precious privileges, and such evidence, too, as induces the belief that, as the scriptures express it, he has "passed from death unto life." The belief is almost universal that the sacrament of the Lord's supper was appointed for the converted or regenerated, and should, as far as possible, be administered only to such. The number of those who hold a different opinion is small. Accordingly, it would be found upon inquiry that all the pastors of our evangelical churches are very careful to explain with what dispositions of the heart and will, as well as with what views of the understanding, one should come to the Lord's supper, and that these are truly such as no unregenerate person can possess. This holy sacrament is rarely dispensed in our churches without being preceded by a discourse on the nature of the preparation required in order to a right "communicating," or receiving of this ordinance; and all irreligious persons—in fact all persons, be their lives outwardly what they may—who have not the testimony of their consciences that they possess, so far as they honestly perceive the state of their hearts, the qualifications described, are solemnly warned of the sin, and consequent danger to their souls, incurred by unworthy partaking of that holy supper.

It is, indeed, too true that, with all their care, unworthy persons do sometimes come to the Lord's table. Many, no doubt, gain admission to the churches who are, after all, not converted. To say that many do so from base, hypocritical motives would imply a very mistaken view of the case, for with us there is no visible inducement to such a course. No civil privilege hangs on a man's being a member of the church and receiving the sacrament, as is the case in some countries in Europe, nor is it reckoned dishonourable for a man not to belong to some church. None of us presumes for a moment that a man must have committed a crime and on that account excluded, if he be not seen going twice or thrice a year at least —on the great festivals for instance—to the sacrament of the Lord's supper.[1] No such idea is known in the United States. Our pastors and other church officers, whose duty it is to govern the churches, do not profess to be infallible. They cannot know the heart. They can only judge according to the evidence presented to them. They very naturally lean to the side of charity; and with every desire on their part to do their duty, there are many doubtless admitted in every church without being truly converted, and when once admitted remain members, unless they withdraw of their own choice, or go to some other part of the country, or are excluded on account of some open immorality.

But while we cannot hope that even in the evangelical churches which are most rigorously strict in their admission to membership, and to the communion of the supper, all the members are converted persons, yet the number of such as are of

---

[1] In Sweden, for instance, a man cannot give his testimony in a court of justice who has not taken the sacrament of the Lord's supper within the year immediately preceding!

scandalous lives is small. Nor are such persons suffered long
to continue when their characters become known. On this
subject our churches form a very striking contrast with some
which I have seen in other parts of the world. Nor have we
many persons who come in crowds to the Lord's supper on some
great festival, such as Easter or Christmas, and stay away from
it during the rest of the year. Still less will there be seen,
what I was told sometimes occurs in Protestant churches which
I have visited in other lands, a few persons waiting outside the
church, on such occasions, until the communion service commences, then making their way in, approaching the communion
table or altar, receiving the emblems of the Saviour's body and
blood, and as soon as possible hastening out and departing!
As if there were any virtue in such horrible mockery and pro-
faneness! I bless God that we have nothing that even approaches to this in point of impiety; and yet we have to mourn
over the fact that many of the members of our churches do not
manifest that spirituality, devotion, and zeal which they ought
to possess. But were there no discipline in our churches, and
were all the world, whatever might be their character, permitted to come to the Lord's supper, the state of things would be
in every respect worse. We do make an effort to separate the
church from the world, and to make it manifest that there is
a difference, and that not a small one, between those who belong
to the former, and those who seek their happiness in this world,
and have their desires bounded by it.

CHAPTER III.

THE WAY IN WHICH MEMBERSHIP IN OUR CHURCHES IS OBTAINED.

OFTEN has the question been addressed to me, " How do people
become members of your churches in America?" This has
been said to me particularly on the continent, where, in too
many countries, discipline seems to be almost unknown, and
where, I have been assured, there are many churches in which

2 D

all who choose may come to the Lord's supper, and that this alone is requisite in order to a man's membership of a church. This, too, it is said, often takes place without saying a word to the pastor, or any other officer of the church. Widely different is the practice which obtains in the evangelical churches of the United States. I will describe it in few words.

Every faithful pastor, who preaches regularly in any particular place for a year or two, is supposed to become pretty well acquainted with the people of his charge. In most cases, he not only comes to know the families that compose his flock, but also, more or less, of nearly every individual, especially of the adult population. This is almost certain to be the case where the flock is not very numerous. This general acquaintance gives him some knowledge of the character of almost every individual. With most, if not all, he endeavours to have some conversation, more or less directly, on the subject of salvation, and the hopes of eternal life which he may be entertaining.

In addition to this, his Bible classes and Sunday schools bring him into frequent contact with the more juvenile part of the people over whom the Holy Ghost has made him overseer. He finds frequent opportunities of speaking with them about their souls. Besides, he is not alone. The elders, deacons, or other officers of his church, assist him much with their co-operation. Through these, as well as through zealous, judicious, and faithful private members of his church, he learns continually the state of mind of most, if not of all the people in his congregation. This knowledge is of the greatest consequence when persons come to converse with him respecting their salvation. In our revivals, as will appear presently, it is common for the pastor to appoint a time for meeting at his house, or at some other convenient place, those who are awakened to a sense of the importance of religion. On these occasions he converses with each individual; if it be possible, gives such directions as they may need, and prays with the whole. When they are too many for him to speak to all of them, he makes use of the assistance of some of the most experienced of the officers of his church. Sometimes a neighbouring minister will come and help him. I have seen twenty, fifty, a hundred, and even as many as three hundred persons, all, with few exceptions, adults, come together in deep distress of soul, on such occasions.

In such little meetings the pastor learns the progress of religion in the souls of his people. But when there is no special "seriousness," as we say, or uncommon attention to religion among his people, then it may be that the number of those who come from time to time to speak to him respecting their salvation will be small. And if he ceases to be faithful in preaching the gospel, and his church gets cold in its zeal, in its faith, and in its prayers, then it may happen that for a while he may not have any.

In many of our churches the sacrament of the Lord's supper is administered once in three months, in many once in two, and in others once a month. Some time before, the pastor gives notice that he will meet at a certain time and place all such as wish to join the church on that occasion, and to receive the communion for the first time. He meets with them, and converses with them, and learns the state of their minds, as far as it is possible for man to judge. In many cases the persons come to him repeatedly to lay open their hearts, and receive his counsel. If he believes that they have met with the change of heart of which the Saviour speaks in his interview with Nicodemus, he encourages them in the resolution to join the church. If he thinks that they are not prepared for this important step, he advises them to defer it for a season, that they become so. In some cases, as in that of the Presbyterians universally, the pastor reports the matter to the session of the church, and the candidates have generally to appear before that body, which consists of the pastor and the elders, who may be from two to twelve in number. In the Congregational and Baptist churches, it is the "church," that is, the body of the members of the church, who hear the candidates state the history of the work of grace in their hearts, and give their reasons for believing that they have become "new creatures in Christ Jesus." If the person who applies to be received as a member of the church is a stranger, or one of whose deep seriousness the pastor and the brethren of the church had been ignorant, then he is examined more fully upon his "experience," or the work of God in his soul. He is asked to tell when and how he became concerned

2 D 2

for his salvation, the nature and depth of his repentance, his views of sin, his faith in Christ, his hopes of eternal life, &c., &c. These examinations are sometimes long, and in the highest degree interesting. Solemn, and yet to the faithful pastor, joyful work, to deal with souls in these interesting seasons. But the faithful pastor is always engaged in guiding the souls of his people in the way that leads to life.

The day arrives for administering the Lord's supper; the preparatory services, including a sermon, are gone through; the moment comes for commencing those which relate to this sacred ordinance. Before he commences them, the pastor, in many churches, calls upon all those who are now about to join the church to come forward and take their places before the pulpit. He reads their names aloud, and in Pædobaptist churches baptises those of them who have not been baptised before, together with the infant children of parents who have such to present. He then puts certain questions to the adults, embodying the chief articles of the church's creed, and to these they answer in the affirmative. This is sometimes followed by his reading out the form of a covenant, which they must give their assent to and engage to keep.[1] The forms in which all this is done vary in

----

[1] As the reader may be desirous of seeing one of these summaries of faith and covenant, I here give the following one, selected from among the many which I have seen. The pastor addresses the candidates standing in the midst of the church in the following language :—

FAITH.

"In the presence of God and this assembly you do now appear, desiring publicly and solemnly to enter into covenant with Him and his church according to the gospel; professing your full assent to the following summary of faith :

"Art. 1. You solemnly and publicly profess your belief in one God, the Almighty Maker of heaven and earth, who upholds all things, and orders all events according to his own pleasure, and for his own glory.

"Art. 2. You believe that this glorious Being exists in three persons; God the Father, God the Son, and God the Holy Ghost, and that these three are one, being the same in substance, equal in power and glory.

"Art. 3. You believe that the scriptures of the Old and New Testaments were given by inspiration of God, and are our only rule of faith and practice.

"Art. 4. You believe that God at first created man upright, and in his own image ; that our first parents fell from their original uprightness, and involved themselves and their posterity in a state of sin and misery.

"Art. 5. You believe that all men since the fall are by nature depraved, having no conformity of heart to God, and being destitute of all moral excellence.

"Art. 6. You believe that Jesus Christ is the Saviour of sinners, and the only Mediator between God and man.

"Art. 7. You believe in the necessity of the renewing and sanctifying operations of the Holy Spirit, and that to be happy you must be holy.

different churches and denominations, but the substance is the same, and it takes place most commonly, I believe, at the public services on Saturday preparatory to the celebration of the communion on the Sabbath following.

I may add that many, particularly of the Presbyterian churches in the interior, still retain the old practice of the communicants taking their seats for a short time at a long table in the principal aisle of the church, the bread and wine being handed round, accompanied with prayer and a brief exhortation. In the cities and large towns the communicants occupy certain pews assigned to them, either in the middle of the church, or in the end next to the pulpit. In the Episcopal church the communicants receive the sacrament kneeling round the altar. Though the administration of this sacrament most commonly takes place immediately after the forenoon sermon,

"Art. 8. You believe that sinners are justified by faith alone, through the atoning sacrifice of Jesus Christ.

"Art. 9. You believe that the saints will be kept by the Almighty power of God from the dominion of sin, and from final condemnation, and that at the last day they will be raised incorruptible, and be for ever happy.

"Art. 10. You believe that the finally impenitent will be punished 'with everlasting destruction from the presence of the Lord, and from the glory of his power.'

" Thus you believe in your hearts, and thus you confess before men.

COVENANT.

" You do now, under this belief of the Christian religion as held in this church, publicly and solemnly avouch the eternal Jehovah, Father, Son, and Holy Ghost, to be your God and the God of yours, engaging to devote yourselves to his fear and service, to walk in his ways, and to keep his commandments. With a humble reliance on his Spirit, you engage to live answerable to the profession you now make, submitting yourselves to the laws of Christ's kingdom, and to that discipline which he has appointed to be administered in his church. That you may obtain the assistance you need, you engage diligently to attend, and carefully to improve all the ordinances he has instituted.

" Thus you covenant, promise, and engage, in the fear of God, and by the help of his Spirit.

" In consequence of these professions and promises, we affectionately recognise you as members of this church, and in the name of Christ declare you entitled to all its visible privileges. We welcome you to this fellowship with us in the blessings of the gospel, and on our part engage to watch over you, and to seek your edification as long as you shall continue among us.

" May the Lord support and guide you through a transitory life, and after this warfare is accomplished, receive you to His blessed church above, where our love shall be for ever perfect, and our joy for ever full. Amen."

In some churches the *summary of faith* used on these occasions, and the *covenant*, accompanied by a short and pertinent address to the members of the church, is printed in a little book, which also contains a list of all their names, and their residences if in a city, a copy of which is possessed by each member. It is a convenient manual, as well as a solemn remembrancer, which it is profitable to consult frequently.

it is now celebrated in many churches in the afternoon, preceded by a short sermon or address. In a Presbyterian church in Washington city, it used, a few years ago, to be celebrated at night, and may be so still. The effect was solemn and not unpleasing, and it had the advantage in the eyes of those who attach importance to such matters, of coinciding with the hour of its first institution. But a more important advantage, in my opinion, lay in its admitting of the communicants being joined by many from other churches, on an occasion so well calculated to unite the hearts of all in Christian sympathy and love.

Let me further add, that in almost all our churches those who are not members usually remain and witness the solemn ceremony—a most proper and profitable custom, for the very occasion speaks in most affecting language to the unconverted heart, and affords an admirable opportunity for the faithful and skilful messenger of God, to appeal to such on behalf of him whose sorrows are so touchingly set forth in an ordinance which may truly be called an epitome of the gospel.

CHAPTER IV.

THE RELATIONS WHICH UNCONVERTED MEN HOLD TO THE CHURCH.

I have known many persons in different parts of Europe, who, after listening to statements such as the above, seemed at a loss to comprehend the position held with respect to the church by those who are not its members, and they have asked again and again for explanations on the subject. I have told them in reply, that such of those persons as are the children of pious parents, hold towards the church a very interesting relation, which though invisible, if I may so speak, is real, and that such of them as have been baptised in infancy, in my opinion, maintain an important relation to it, which ought to be made much more of than is usual among the Pædobaptist branches of the Protestant church. We are very faulty on this point in the United States, but not more so, I apprehend, than are our Protestant brethren in other lands. Very affecting appeals, nevertheless, are often made by our faithful ministers to such of their hearers as are not yet converted, yet who have knelt by the side of a devout mother, have felt her hand resting on their youthful heads, and who, when in the arms of a pious parent, received the symbol of that "washing of regeneration," without which none can serve God acceptably, either on earth or in heaven. Nor are such appeals in vain.[1]

But the question has often been proposed to me: "Are men who are not allowed to come to the Lord's supper, willing to attend your churches?" Most certainly they are. They are too well instructed in religion not to be aware that admission to that ordinance would do them anything but good as long as they remain unreconciled to God through Jesus Christ.[2] Many of them, indeed, would recoil with horror were a minister to propose such a thing. Yet they value the privilege of going to the sanctuary. They have been taught from their childhood that the preaching of the gospel is the great instrumentality appointed by God for the salvation of men. They go in the hope of one day finding that which they know to be essential to their happiness even in this life. Others may be influenced by the force of education, or by that of habit, by fashion, by the desire of seeing others and being seen, by the charms of the preacher's

---

[1] Some most interesting investigations have been made in the churches in New England, the portion of the United States where the gospel has been longest, most extensively, and most faithfully preached, taken as a whole, which have shown in the most decisive manner that the "children of the church," that is, the children of believers, who have been dedicated to God in baptism, have shared most largely in the blessing of God's grace; and that nothing can be more completely unfounded than the reproach that "the children of Christians, and especially those of ministers and deacons, do worse than those of other people." The very reverse has been demonstrated by a widely-extended and carefully prosecuted inquiry. Indeed, what other result could a man who believes God have expected?

[2] Foreigners sometimes commit great mistakes from not being aware of our customs in this respect. A Spanish gentleman once called on the late Rev. Sylvester Larned, of New Orleans, one of the most eloquent pulpit orators of his day, to say that he wished to join his church, and to receive the sacrament of the supper there, "for," said he with an oath, "you are the most eloquent man I have ever heard! Mr. Larned spent an hour with him in explaining what was required in order to his becoming a member of his church; in other words, what it is to be a true Christian, and the Spaniard went away with a heavy heart to reflect on a subject which had never been presented to his mind in the same light before.

eloquence, and so forth. In no other part of the world, perhaps, do the inhabitants attend church in a larger proportion than in the United States, and certainly no part of the continent of Europe can compare with them in that respect. The contrast between the two must strike any one who, after having travelled much in the one comes to see any of the cities of the other, with the single exception of New Orleans, which is hardly as yet an American city, and even it in point of church attendance, is far better than Paris, Rome, Vienna, Hamburg, or Copenhagen.

Not only do persons who have not yet become members by formal admission as such attend our churches; they form a very large part of our congregations. In many cases they constitute two-thirds, three-fourths, or even more, this depending much on the length of the period during which the congregation has been organised, and hardly ever less than a half, even in the most highly favoured churches. Nor do they attend only; they are liberal supporters of the public worship, and are often found as liberal in contributing of their substance for the promotion of good objects as the members of the church themselves, with whom they are often ultimately connected by the ordinary business of life, and by family ties. Multitudes of them are like the young man whom Jesus loved, but who "still lacked one thing." They attend from year to year as did the impotent man at the pool of Bethesda, nor do they attend in vain.[1] It pleases God to make the faithful preaching of his word instrumental to the salvation now of one, now of another; and sometimes by a special outpouring of his Spirit he brings many at the same time into his kingdom.

The non-professing hearers of the word, then, are to be con-

---

[1] In the State of Connecticut, a series of most interesting inquiries have been prosecuted, during the last few years, under the auspices, I believe, of the general association of the Congregational churches; one of which relates to the influence which the faithful preaching of the gospel, in a community—a parish for instance—exerts upon the mass who hear it for a long period of time. The results are most striking, and clearly demonstrate the blessing of having the stated and regular use of the means of grace. It has been found that of those who habitually attend churches where the gospel is faithfully preached, the number who, sooner or later, are made to experience its saving power is surprisingly great; and, on the contrary, the number of those who die without giving any evidence of possessing true piety is small. The investigation has been made in all parts of the State, and has everywhere conducted to the same important and delightful conclusion. I know not whether this inquiry has ever been prosecuted so thoroughly and extensively in any other part of the world.

sidered as simply what we call them, members of the congregation, not of the church. We can look, as I have said, for their assistance in many, if not all good undertakings, as well as in the ordinary support of the gospel. Many, in the character of trustees, are faithful guardians of the property of the church and congregation. Many teach in our Sunday schools, and find instruction themselves in their endeavours to instruct others.

One great advantage in this is that unconverted men, who know themselves to be such, occupy their proper place. No law, no false custom, compels them to be members of the church. Hence their position is less dangerous in several respects. They are less tempted to indulge self-delusion, and are more open to the direct unimpeded shafts of the truth. Their position, too, tends to give them a remarkable simplicity and frankness of character. The term " Christian," generally signifying with us not a mere believer in Christianity, but one who professes to be a disciple of Christ, and is known as such. Nine persons out of ten of those who make no profession of religion would, in many places, on being asked, " Are you a Christian?" promptly reply, " No, I am sorry to say I am not,"— meaning thereby that he was sorry to say that he did not believe himself to be a truly religious man, or what the word *Christian* ought to signify, and is with us so often employed to express. This is obviously better for unconverted persons— better for their own consciences—than to be involved in a church relation, and yet be without religion. It is every way better, also, for the pastor and the church; and the prospect of the word of God gaining an entrance into the heart of the unrenewed is many times more encouraging than if they were members of the church, and " had a name to live" while in reality " dead in trespasses and sins."

CHAPTER V.

I HAVE been often been asked in Europe, What measures are adopted by our churches in enforcing discipline—how unworthy persons, for instance, are prevented from coming to the Lord's table? The very question indicates familiarity with a state of things very different from what prevails in the United States— with a state of things in which the decisions of the ecclesiastical authority are enforced by the civil.

Church discipline with us, though wholly moral, is thought quite sufficient. The case must be rare, indeed, of any one, not the member of some recognised church, coming forward to receive the sacrament in an evangelical church. He hears the qualifications necessary to a worthy participation in the ordinance; he knows that none but Christians of good repute in other evangelical churches are invited to join the members of that particular church on the solemn occasion, and if he belongs to neither of these categories, he is not likely to unite himself to the Lord's people. But if he should, he does so on his own responsibility before God; the church is not to be blamed for his conduct. Even were a person who had been excommunicated for open immorality, and universally known to be so, to take his seat among the members of the church, its office-bearers in carrying round the symbols of the Saviour's body and blood, would probably pass him by, or if that could not be done, they would rather allow the matter to take its course than risk confusion at so solemn a moment, in the conviction that the church having done her previous duty to the unhappy man, she is not to blame for his unauthorised intrusion. I know of one solitary occasion, on which one of the office-bearers whispered in the ear of a person who ought not to have been among the communicants, that it would be better for his own soul, as well as due to the church, that he should retire, and he did so. But this was unobserved by most of those immediately around, or, if observed, they did not know the cause of his retiring. I never knew or heard of a single other case.

No difficulty whatever, I repeat, can arise on this subject. Our discipline is moral, and the people are too well instructed on the subject of their duties not to know what they should do, and what to abstain from doing. We have no *gens d'armes* or other police agents, to enforce our discipline, and if such functionaries are ever seen about our churches in any character but that of worshippers, it is on extraordinary occasions, to keep order at the door; and their services are not often needed even for that purpose.

In regard to church members who subject themselves to censure for open sin, or gross neglect of duty, they are dealt with according to the established discipline of the body to which they belong; and that, in all our evangelical churches, is based upon the simple and clear directions given by our Lord and his apostles. Unworthy members after having been dealt with according to scriptural rule, are excluded until they give evidence of sincere contrition for their sin. Where the case is flagrant, and the sin persisted in, after all attempts to reclaim the offender have failed, he is openly excommunicated before the church and congregation. A less open declaration of the offence and punishment takes place in other cases. But whatever be the course pursued, unworthy men are excluded in all our evangelical churches as soon as their offence can be properly taken up by the church. I state this as a general fact. Once excluded, the world does not long remain ignorant of what has taken place, and the church thus avoids the charge of retaining persons of scandalous lives in her communion.[1] Any defect in our administration of church discipline does not lie, I conceive, generally speaking, in its being harsh and impatient; while, on the other hand, there is nothing in the institutions of the country, or in the opinions and habits of the people, to prevent its being as

---

[1] The deposition of a minister of the gospel when it occurs, which when we consider how numerous the ministry are, cannot be thought frequent, is commonly announced in the religious and other journals, in order that the churches may be duly guarded against the admission of the deposed person into their pulpits, through ignorance of his character and present position.

rigid as the legislation of the great Head of the church demands. If there be failure any where, it is chargeable to want of fidelity on the part of those who are entrusted with the exercise of discipline.

CHAPTER VI.

CHARACTER OF AMERICAN PREACHING.

In order adequately to describe American preaching, one would require to be intimately acquainted with the churches of the country throughout its vast extent, but this knowledge it falls to the lot of few to possess. Foreign writers on the subject have been either travellers, whose books betray a very limited acquaintance with the churches and their ministers, or untravelled authors, whose judgment has been formed upon such specimens as they could find in printed discourses, or hear from the lips of preachers from the United States during visits to Europe. In either case, whatever may have been the impartiality of the judges, the *data* for forming a sound opinion upon the subject have been manifestly insufficient. Few persons in Europe have read enough of American sermons to form an accurate judgment respecting the various qualities of American preaching, for few preachers in that country have published volumes of sermons, or even isolated and occasional discourses. Some of the most effective preachers have published very little, and many nothing at all. And as for those preachers from the United States who have visited Europe, not six have been able to preach in any language but the English; and the other language, with all but one or two of these, has been German. Except in Great Britain and Ireland, then, and to a very limited extent in Germany, United States preaching is unknown, except from books and the oral reports of persons who have visited the country. As for the American preachers who have visited Europe, they have been few in comparison with the whole body, and have been confined for the most part to

those of one or two denominations. Many of them have crossed
the Atlantic as invalids for the recovery of their health; others
have come with some object to accomplish which left little time
for preaching. Under such circumstances they could hardly be
expected to preach as well as at home, and yet there have been
some who, while in Europe, reflected no discredit on themselves
or their country as pulpit orators.[1]

Preaching in the United States varies exceedingly both in
manner and in *substance*, but most in manner. The clergy in
the Presbyterian, Congregational, Episcopal, Reformed Dutch,
Lutheran, German Reformed, Moravian, Reformed Presbyterian,
Associate, and Associate Reformed churches, have, with few
exceptions, passed through a regular course of education in
Latin, Greek, the natural and moral sciences, and theology,
such as is now pursued at our colleges and theological seminaries, or what was tantamount to it. Many, especially the
younger men, have some knowledge of Hebrew, though this
seldom amounts to much. As for the Baptist ministers, it
were hard to discover how many have gone through a similar
course—certainly not half, perhaps not a fourth of them. A
still smaller proportion of the Methodist preachers have had
that advantage, though, upon the whole, they are probably
as well informed as the Baptist ministers are. Ministerial
education among the Cumberland Presbyterians is much in the
same state as among the Methodists.

The clergy of certain denominations, who have not passed
through a collegiate course, are often spoken of, but very

[1] Among the American preachers whose visits are still remembered with
interest in Great Britain, (and some of them on the continent also,) but who are
no longer with us, may be mentioned the Rev. Drs. Mason, Romeyn, Bruen,
Henry, and Hobart, who were certainly no mean men. Of those who have
visited Europe within the last few years, and who are still permitted to pro-
secute their work among us, are the Rev. Drs. Spring, Humphrey, Cox,
M'Auley, Codman, Breckinridge, Patton, Rev. Mr. Kirk, and others of the
Presbyterian and Congregational churches; Dr. Bethune of the Reformed
Dutch; the Rev. Drs. Milnor, M'Ilvaine (bishop of Ohio), Hawkes, Tyng, and
Clark, of the Episcopal: the Rev. Drs. Emory, Capers, Fiske, President
Durbin, and Bishop Soule, of the Methodist; the Rev. Drs. Wayland and
M'Murray of the Baptist; and the Rev. Dr. Kurtz and the Rev. Mr. Riley of
the Lutheran and German Reformed churches, are widely known in Great
Britain, and some of them on the continent. The last named two were kindly
received in Germany, and heard with attention, both when they spoke of the
infant seminaries for which they pleaded, as well as when they proclaimed
"that name which is above every name," and which is "like ointment poured
forth."

unjustly, as "uneducated," "unlearned," "illiterate," and so forth. Very many such have, by great application, made most respectable attainments. Some have acquired a considerable knowledge of the Latin and Greek classics, and a far greater number have, by the diligent perusal of valuable works in English, stored their minds with a large amount of sound learning, which they use with much effect in preaching. Nor is this surprising. A man may acquire an immense fund of knowledge through the sole medium of the English tongue. Benjamin Franklin knew nothing of the ancient languages, and not much of any of the modern, beyond his mother tongue and French; yet few men of his day were better informed, or wrote his mother tongue with equal purity. So, also, with Washington. And who ever used the English language with greater propriety and effect than Bunyan; or where in that language shall we find a sounder or abler theological writer than Andrew Fuller? Yet neither Bunyan nor Fuller were ever at college.

It is a great, though a common mistake, to suppose that Methodist ministers when "on circuit" read nothing. There being generally two on each circuit, who alternate in their courses, the one resting while the other is on his preaching tour, each has half his time for making up his reports, carrying on his correspondence, and prosecuting his studies, and that this last is done to some good purpose is clearly shown by the preaching of the great majority. Many Baptist ministers, also, who have never attended college, are close students, and carefully prepare for the pulpit; while others, of whom so much cannot be said, give themselves much to the reading of certain favourite authors.

Nearly all the Episcopal and Congregational clergy write their sermons, and read them more or less closely when delivered. So do many of the Presbyterian and Reformed Dutch, and some, also, of the Baptist ministers. A large proportion of the Presbyterian clergy, the great majority of the Baptist, and nearly all the ministers of the Methodist, Cumberland Presbyterian, and other evangelical denominations, neither write their sermons in full, nor read any considerable part of them. Few, however, of any church commit their sermons to memory; the great majority of such as do not write out their discourses, carefully study the subjects of them, and generally note down the principal heads to be used in the pulpit, as taste or habit may incline.

The delivery of the ministers among us who read is not in general very animated; still, it is sufficiently attractive in most instances to interest hearers endued with any capacity for distinguishing between sound and sense, and who prefer a well-reasoned, well expressed, and instructive discourse to mere animated declamation, accompanied with much less commonly of these qualities. Good reading, though in all countries much more rare than good, or at least attractive and effective speaking, will generally be preferred, nevertheless, by hearers of high intellectual acquirements.

Ministers of all denominations who do not read their discourses, possess a much more animated delivery, and generally display more of what may be called "oratory" in their manner than their brethren who read. But their sermons can hardly have the same order, clearness, and freedom from repetition. Still they need not be wanting in instructiveness, and they have greatly the advantage in point of fervour, and in those direct and powerful appeals which owe their effect almost as much to look, and tone, and manner, as to the truths which the speaker expresses. Not that such appeals can be of much avail if no truth be conveyed by them, but truth may become much more effective when pressed upon the attention in an attractive and impressive manner.

Those of the clergy of the evangelical churches in the United States, who have passed through a regular classical and theological course of education, and who in point of numbers may be estimated at about 7000, taken as a whole would be pronounced less animated than the most celebrated preachers in Great Britain and Ireland, France and Germany, and I may add, Denmark and Sweden, Not a few of them, however, are not wanting in fervour, and even *fire* in their delivery. But this is not the case with those of our ministers who have had a less complete education, and have been very differently trained. Our Methodist ministers have a certain course of reading prescribed to them for the four probationary years preceding their being ordained elders or presbyters. During that time they have their circuit labours to perform; what they learn is put to instant use, and incorporated, as it were, with their very being. Now, this preparatory course has no tendency to keep down the eagerness for energetic preaching, so much felt by men who regard themselves as called by God to preach his gospel, but which is so much restrained by the precise knowledge and artificial rules of eloquence taught in colleges. Besides, as they generally preach to moderate assemblages, and these mainly composed of the poorer and simpler classes, they are far less apt to feel embarrassed than youths, who having first spent several years at a college, and then several more at a theological seminary, have acquired so nice a taste, and have become so nervously sensible to the slightest deviations from the strict rules of grammar and rhetoric, that they almost dread to speak at all lest they should offend against either. But the grand advantage possessed by the Methodist itinerant preacher, and one which, if he has any talent at all, he cannot fail to profit by, is, that he may preach in many or all of the eight, ten, or more places in his circuit, the discourse with which he sets out, and which he has been preparing during the rest afforded him while his colleague has been going his rounds. This frequent repetition of the same sermon is an inestimable means of improvement. Each repetition admits of some modification, as the discourse is not written out for preaching, and enables the preacher to improve what seemed faulty, and to supply what seemed deficient in the preceding effort. No men, accordingly, with us become readier or more effective speakers. Their diction, indeed, may not be so pure as that of men who have spent several years in the schools, yet it is surprising with what propriety vast numbers of them express themselves, while in point of forcible and effective delivery they far surpass, upon the whole, preachers who have passed through the colleges.

What has been said of the Methodists applies to the Cumberland Presbyterians, a body of Christians which we shall give some account of hereafter, and which is to be found exclusively in the west and in Texas. Like the Methodists, they have circuit or itinerant preachers, and about an equal proportion of their ministers have never pursued a course of study at college. It may be applied, also, but not to the same extent, to what is called, neither with strict propriety, nor always in kindliness of feeling, the uneducated portion of Baptist preachers. They have not the advantages of the itineracy, and many of them are too much occupied with their secular pursuits to have much time to spare for study. Still among them, also, there will be found a great deal of energetic eloquence—rather homely at times, yet often highly effective, and flowing from a mind more intent upon its conceptions than upon the language in which they are to be clothed; and more desirous of producing a certain effect on the understanding and hearts of the hearers, than of exciting admiration for the graces of a fine style and elegant delivery.

Some of the tourists from abroad that have visited the United States have affected to despise our "uneducated" and "ignorant" ministers, and have thought what they call the "ranting" of such men a fit subject of diversion for themselves and their readers. Such authors know little of the real worth and valuable labours of these humble, and in comparison with such as have studied at colleges and universities, unlettered men. Their plain preaching, in fact, is often far more likely to benefit their usual hearers,[1] than would that of a learned doctor of divinity issuing from some great university. Their language, though not refined, is intelligible to those to whom it is addressed. Their illustrations may not be classical, but they will probably be drawn either from the Bible or from the scenes amid which their hearers move, and the events with which they are familiar; nor would the critical knowledge of a Porson, or the general acquirements of a Parr, be likely to make them more successful in their work. I have often heard most solemn and edifying discourses from such men. I have met with them in all parts of the United States, and though some, doubtless, bring discredit upon the ministry, by their ignorance, their eccentricities, or their incapacity, and do more harm than good to the cause of religion, yet, taken as a whole, they are a great blessing to the country. A European who should denounce the United States as unci-

---

[1] Let me not be misunderstood. I would not for a moment convey the idea that the people who attend the preaching of the Methodist, and non-classically educated Baptist ministers, consist only of the poor and uneducated. On the contrary, in many places, and especially in the south, they have the most intelligent and respectable part of the population among their hearers. At the same time it has ever been the peculiar glory of the former, that through their instrumentality "the poor have the gospel preached to them."

2 E

vilised, and the inhabitants as wretched, because he does not everywhere find the luxuries and refinements of London and Paris, would display no more ignorance of the world and want of common sense, than were he to despise the plain preaching of a man who enters the pulpit with a mind replete with scriptural knowledge, obtained by frequent perusal of the Bible, and the assistance of valuable commentaries, besides being generally well informed, and with a heart full of love to God and concern for men's souls, even although he may never have frequented the groves of an academy, or studied the nicer graces of oratory. To the labours of such men more than 10,000 neighbourhoods in the United States are indebted for their general good order, tranquillity, and happiness, as well as for the humble but sincere piety that reigns in many a heart, and around many a fire-side. To them the country owes much of its conservative character, for no men have inculcated more effectively those doctrines which promote obedience to law, respect for magistracy, and the maintenance of civil government, and never more than within the last year or two, during which they have had to resist the anarchical principles of self-styled reformers, both religious and political. No men are more hated and reviled by these demagogues, whose projects, I rejoice to say, find comparatively but a small and decreasing number of friends and advocates. To the influence of the pulpit, and that of the religious and sound part of the political press, we owe a return of better sentiments in several States, in relation to capital punishments in the case of murder in its highest degrees, and the more frequent condemnation and execution of murderers. And in a late insurrectionary movement in Rhode island, the leading journals of that State attest, that the clergy of all denominations exerted a powerfully salutary influence.[1]

But the subject of preaching ought to be viewed in its highest and most important aspect—that of the salvation of souls.

The first characteristic of American preaching, I should say, is *simplicity*. It is simple in the form of discourse or sermon, usually adopted by the better educated classes especially of the

---

[1] "Nothing," says the Providence Journal in July 1842, "has filled the enemies of law and order with greater rage, than the high and noble stand taken by the clergy against their insurrectionary doctrines."

ministry. The most natural and obvious view of a subject is
preferred to the far-fetched, the philosophical, it may be, and the
striking. The grand aim of our preachers, taken as a body, is
to present the true meaning of a text, rather than to produce
what is called *effect*. Again, preaching in the United States is
simple in point of language, the plain and familiar being preferred to the ornate and rhetorical. Such of our preachers as
wish to be perfectly intelligible, prefer words of Saxon to those
of Latin origin, as being better understood by the people. Vigour, too, is preferred to beauty, and perspicuity to embellish-
ment. Not that we have no preachers whose composition is
ornate, and even elegant, but I speak of the mass. Lastly, our
preaching is simple in point of delivery. The manner of our
preachers, their gestures, and their intonation, must be allowed
to be extremely simple. There is little of the rhetorician's art
in it; little that is studied and theatrical. There may be animation, and in some cases even vehemence, accompanied with a
loud and powerful utterance, but the manner remains simple—
the hearer's attention is not diverted from what is said to him
that says it. Truth, accordingly, has a better chance, so to
speak, of making its way to the hearts of the audience, than
when announced with all the fascinations of a splendid address
and captivating manner. Not that eloquence is unknown or
under-valued, but that simplicity of delivery predominates over
show, and the preacher would rather carry truth home to his
hearer's hearts than extort their applause. Nor do our ministers affect a peculiar manner or intonation of voice,[1] as is the
case in some countries, but every good preacher endeavours to
take with him into the pulpit what is natural and habitual to
him in that respect.

The second grand characteristic of American preaching lies
in its being *serious* and *earnest*. Thanks be to God, the
preachers of our evangelical churches seem, in general, to be

---

[1] The Methodist, and many of the Baptist preachers, have more of what
may be called *English intonation* than those of other denominations. This
may doubtless be ascribed to the influence of some leading English preachers,
such as Bishops Coke and Asbury among the former, and the late Dr. Staugh-
ton and others among the latter. This I mention not by way of disparagement, but solely because I wish to state what appears to me to be a real
peculiarity. I have already given my opinion of the eloquence of this part of
the ministry in the United States.

2 E 2

truly converted men, and preach as if they felt the infinite moment of what they say. "We believe and therefore speak," seems to be the main-spring of all their endeavours, and to give the tone to all their preaching. They feel it to be a serious office to speak to dying men of the interests of their immortal souls, and to prepare them for death, judgment, and eternity. They would recoil from the task under an overwhelming sense of its awfulness, were it not that they believe themselves called to it by the Holy Ghost. "Woe unto me if I preach not the gospel," are words that often address themselves to their hearts, and urge them to the faithful discharge of their vows. Can we wonder that the preaching of such men is serious and earnest?

A third characteristic of American preaching is its dwelling much upon *immediate reconciliation with God*, by sincere repentance towards him, and faith towards the Lord Jesus Christ. Reconciliation with God! that is the great duty urged by the gospel, and the doing of that duty "now," "to-day," while it is "the accepted time," and "the day of salvation,"—not its postponement until to-morrow, or a "more convenient season" —is what is mainly urged by our evangelical ministers generally, so as to form a prominent characteristic of their preaching. This it is which communicates to their preaching so much of Richard Baxter's style, as exhibited in his writings. No excuse, no delay on the part of the unconverted sinner can be accepted; the solemn call to repent and seek now the salvation of his never-dying soul, is made to sound in the sinner's ear, and no peace is given until he has not only heard but obeyed it.

A fourth characteristic of American preaching lies in its being *highly doctrinal*. This is particularly the case with such of our ministers as have passed through a regular course of classical and theological studies; and, of these, those who write and read their discourses, indulge rather more perhaps than those who speak from premeditation merely, in what may be called a *dogmatic* style, using the word in its original significa- tion. Although with those who have pursued such a regular course of study, the practical and hortatory style may prevail over the doctrinal and exegetical, yet the latter has unques- tionably a very considerable place in their sermons, as all will admit who have regularly attended such preaching for a sufficient time to enable them to judge satisfactorily on the subject. Many of our pastors expound certain portions of the Bible in order, but this the most difficult, and yet when happily done, most profitable of all methods of presenting truth is not, I am sorry to say, so common as it ought to be. The Bible classes may, perhaps, be considered so far as a substitute for it, and if a substitute can be admitted at all, they are certainly the best that can be named.

A fifth characteristic of our preaching lies in its being *systematic* or *consecutive*—words which make farther explanation necessary, as neither of them expresses the idea which I wish to convey. What I mean is, that the best preaching in our evangelical churches maintains a proper connection among the discourses successively delivered from the same pulpit, instead of each presenting a separate or isolated statement of truth, a sermon one Sabbath being given on one particular subject, on the Sabbath following another sermon on a totally distinct subject, and so on throughout the year. A preacher ought, indeed, to change his topics according to the circumstances and characters of his hearers. But there is such a thing as dwelling on one subject in all its bearings, in successive discourses, so as to make it more thoroughly understood, and convey a deeper impression than could otherwise be done. And there is such a thing, also, as presenting all the subjects which should constitute the themes of a preacher's discourses, in their proper connection with and relation to one another. Preaching on isolated subjects, without any connecting link, and of which no better account can be given than that the preacher finds certain topics and texts easy to preach upon, is not likely to do much good. This is not what men do when they would produce a deep and effectual impression on any other subject. They strive, by all possible means, to present it in all its aspects and bearings, and do not quit one point until they have well established it. They make every succeeding statement and argument bear upon and strengthen that which preceded, and in this way they make it manifest that they are steadily tending to a great final result, from which nothing, not even want of systematic process in argumentation, must be allowed for a moment to divert them. " It is line upon line, line upon line

—precept upon precept, precept upon precept," with them; and as the blacksmith can expect to make an impression upon the heated iron only by directing his hammer to the same point and its immediate vicinity, in many successive blows, so the minister does not hope for success in opening the eyes of blind sinners, or rightly guiding those who are scarcely more than half awake, but by oft-repeated and faithful presentation of the same truths in all their bearings. This last can hardly be called a prevailing characteristic, for, alas! with a good deal of systematic preaching, we have still too much, even among our settled clergy, of that sort which, with more propriety of idea than accuracy of expression, has been called *scattering*.

A sixth characteristic of American preaching is the extent to which it may be called *philosophical*. By philosophical I mean, founded on a study of the faculties and powers of the human mind, and of the principles which govern its operations. Though not general, this characteristic distinguishes the evangelical clergy of New England in particular, and others who have devoted much of their time to theology as a study. Much that is true, and much, also, that is absurd has been said against introducing philosophy into religion. True philosophy in its proper place is a valuable auxiliary or handmaid, rather than an enemy to theology, but when she ceases to be a servant and assumes the mastery, undertaking that for which she is incompetent, she fails in doing the good she might otherwise have done, and becomes purely mischievous.[1]

---

[1] "I think," says M. de Toqueville,* "that in no country in the civilised world is less attention paid to philosophy than in the United States. The Americans have no philosophical school of their own; and they care but little for all the schools into which Europe is divided, the very names of which are scarcely known to them. Nevertheless, it is easy to perceive that almost all the inhabitants of the United States conduct their understanding in the same manner, and govern it by the same rules; that is to say, that without ever having taken the trouble to define the rules of a philosophical method, they are in possession of one, common to the whole people." I do not know when I ever read any thing with more unmingled astonishment than I did these opinions, which are faithfully transferred from the author's original. Certainly, one rarely finds such an acknowledgment of a widely existing effect, for which the proper and only possible cause is devised. The fact is, that in few countries in the civilised world is philosophy, in the sense in which this word is used on the continent, viz. metaphysical or psychological science, is more pursued, at least to all practical and valuable ends, than in the United States. There is scarcely a college—at least a Protestant one, and there are upwards of eighty

* "Democracy in America," part second, chapter I. (Reeves' translation) p. 1.

A seventh characteristic of American preaching is its *direct-ness*. This distinguishes our preaching so generally, that it were hard to say which of the evangelical denominations has most of it. You everywhere find it the preacher's object, first of all to be perfectly understood, and then to preach to the heart and conscience, as well as to the understanding. In doing this, great plainness of speech is used, and care taken to avoid every thing by which the barbed dart may be arrested before it reaches the heart at which it is aimed.

An eighth characteristic of American preaching is its *faith-fulness*. I know not how often I have been asked in Europe whether our ministers are not intimidated by the rich and influential in their congregations who may dislike the truth. The question has not a little surprised me, for I never dreamed that the courage of evangelical ministers in 'preaching the gospel could be doubted. Certainly no man could have such a doubt after witnessing what it has been my lot to witness in all parts of the United States. The dependence of our ministers upon their flocks for their stipends, seems not to affect in the least their faithfulness in preaching repentance towards God and faith towards our Lord Jesus Christ. The relation that subsists between pastor and people is certainly more intimate and kindly, and calls for more mutual forbearance than where the law makes the former wholly independent of the latter. But the very kindness, tenderness of feeling, and respect which it creates, are only

such—in which it is not studied with considerable care by the students in the last year of the course. In addition to reading such authors as Locke, Reid, Dugald Stewart, Brown, &c., the professor of that department gives lectures, or explanations of the text-book employed. Thus do the thousands of young collegians make considerable proficiency in this science, especially in its more popular and practical aspects. And thus do our public men, our professional men, all, in a word, who have passed through college, (and they are the men, with few exceptions, that most influence the public mind,) become acquainted with the principles that guide the operations of the human mind. There is not a country in the world, not even excepting Scotland itself, where metaphysics have so much influence upon preaching as in New England—where, indeed, they have had sometimes too much influence. We have not in the United States great professors who occupy themselves with nothing but philosophy, and who have rivalled Kant, and Hegel, and Schelling, in the nature of their speculations; nor is it likely that we ever shall have such. The nature of our Anglo-Saxon mind hardly admits of the thing. Besides, we have too much public life, and too much to engross our attention, to allow us to prosecute extensively *im-practical* (if we may use the word,) speculations. Nevertheless, we have a few men, such as Mr. Ralph W. Emerson, of Boston, who equal Mr. Carlyle himself in admiration of the German transcendentalists, and have, probably, come as near to understanding them.

additional motives to render a good minister faithful to the souls of those with whom he maintains such interesting relation, and who show him so many proofs of affection as a faithful pastor is very sure to receive amongst us. Most certainly facts do not establish the superior faithfulness of ministers who are independent of their flocks, taken as a body. On the contrary, this very independence often leads to indolence, neglect, and sometimes even to insolence, qualities which it ill becomes a minister of Christ to display, and which are utterly inconsistent with the gospel. And it may safely be affirmed, that with us, the great majority of men who have been brought up under evangelical preaching, but who have not yet been converted, would rather have a faithful than an unfaithful pastor. They know that religion, though they have it not, is of vast importance, and they know well the difference between him that preaches "smooth things," and him that faithfully declares the "counsel of the Lord." Not only does their conscience approve of the former and not the latter, but they feel that there is far more prospect of their salvation under the ministry of the one than of the other. Besides, other things being equal, a man who preaches faithfully "Christ crucified," is sure to prove in the end a more attractive preacher than he who does not. For what theme can ever be compared with that of the love of God towards sinners of mankind, and the gift of his Son to redeem them from destruction? Therefore, if a man wishes to be esteemed and supported by his people, let him be faithful; that is, in the sense in which Paul was faithful, who was also neither rash nor unfeeling, but, on the contrary, prudent and mild, and strove to commend himself "in love" to all to whom he preached the "unsearchable riches of the gospel."

The ninth characteristic of American preaching is, that it is eminently *practical*. Not only are the unconverted urged to "acquaint themselves with God, and be at peace with him, that thereby good may come to them," and believers exhorted to "grow in grace, and in the knowledge of the Lord Jesus Christ;" but the latter are also urged, from the moment of their conversion, to commence living for God, and for the salvation of men. The doctrine has of late years been more and more preached, that every Christian, be his sphere in life what it may, is under obligation to live for the salvation of others, and that by his conversation, by his holy example, as well as by personal sacrifices, he should do all that he can to promote this salvation far and near. Blessed be God, this style of preaching is not without effect. It is the cause, under God's blessing, of the annually increasing efforts made by Christians of that land, for the building up of Christ's kingdom, both at home and abroad.

The tenth and last characteristic of American preaching is, that it *speaks much of the work of the Spirit.* I know of no one idea that has been so much a *dominant* one in the American churches for the last fifty years, or rather for the last 100 years, as that of the importance of the office and work of the Holy Spirit. The need in which the world lies of the operations of this Holy Agent, the indispensableness of his co-operation with the preaching of the gospel, and the use of all other means to effect the salvation of men, together with the gracious promise of this great ascension gift of the crucified and exalted Saviour, are themes on which the ministry of the evangelical churches in America often dwells, and not in vain.

I have now said what I have deemed necessary respecting the character of American preaching. The limits of this work have not permitted me to dwell on these topics, nor is it necessary. All that I have aimed at was to give the reader what I deem some just conceptions on a subject in which I supposed he might be interested.

We come now to the consideration of the question of revivals of religion in America, a subject of the greatest importance, and at the same time attended with no ordinary difficulties in the minds, perhaps, of some into whose hands this book may fall. I would, however, most respectfully call the attention of such, and, indeed, of all who may read this volume, to the chapter which follows. Though long, it will well reward them for any attention they may bestow upon it. I know not where the whole subject has been so well presented in any language, and cannot but hope, that with God's blessing, it will prove eminently useful. It confirms the opinions respecting American preaching which I have given in the preceding pages. The distinguished friend and professor to whom I am indebted for it, and of whom I have spoken in the introduction, is better qualified by his position, and by his experience, to write such an article than any other man I know of in the United States. God grant that the day may speedily arrive when the dispensation of the Spirit will be better understood and appreciated in all parts of Christendom than it is at present; and when the abundant gift of this blessed Agent shall fill the churches with light, and life, and holiness. No where, as it seems to me, is the Holy Spirit honoured as he ought to be, and must be before the world shall be converted. This is true of even the best portions of the Protestant churches; whilst as to some of the rest, as well as for the Roman Catholics in mass, it would seem as if they had not yet "heard whether there be a Holy Spirit."

CHAPTER VII.

REVIVALS OF RELIGION.

EXTRAORDINARY seasons of religious interest, denominated revivals of religion, have existed in the American churches from a very early period of their history. The cause of this peculiarity in the dispensation of divine grace may be traced, in part, to the peculiar character and circumstances of the first settlers of the country. They were English Puritans, who had suffered the severest persecution for their principles in their native land, and who fled into the wilderness to enjoy those principles unmolested, and to carry them out in their full extent.

The leading point in controversy between our fathers and the English government was freedom of worship; the right to have the gospel preached among them, in its most searching application to the conscience and the heart, "without human mixtures or impositions." To secure this privilege they willingly "endured the loss of all things," and it was therefore natural that they should prize it highly. Accordingly, the attachment of the first settlers of New England to the ordinances of public worship, and especially the reliance they placed on "the preaching of the word" as the chief instrument, under

God, for the conversion of their children and dependents, were among the most striking traits in their character. Strict as they were, even to sternness, in family discipline; literally as they obeyed the injunction, "Thou shalt teach these things diligently unto thy children, and shalt talk of them when thou sittest in thy house, and when thou walkest in the way, and when thou liest down, and when thou risest up," they still felt that it is the truth pre-eminently, as dispensed in "the great congregation," under the combined influence of awakened sympathy and awe of the divine presence, which is made by the Holy Spirit "the power of God unto salvation." This feeling modified all their habits and institutions as a people. It made them settle in villages around their places of worship, and not, like their southern neighbours, upon scattered plantations; it led them to support two religious teachers for each of their infant churches; it founded colleges for the preparation of a ministry adequate to these high duties; it established week-day lectures, on which those who lived in the outer settlements, at the distance of six or eight miles, felt it a privilege and a duty regularly to attend; it pervaded, in short, all the arrangements of society, and gave a prominence to *preaching*, a disposition to multiply religious meetings, and a reliance upon this mode of urging truth upon the conscience, greater perhaps than has ever existed among any other people.

Another trait in the character of the first settlers of New England, in common with their brethren at home, was a strong faith and expectation of *special* answers to prayer. The English Puritans never regarded prayer as a mere means of grace, but (what it truly is) as a means of moving God, of inducing him to grant what he could not otherwise be expected to bestow. Nor did they stop here. They did not expect merely the blessing of God *in general* on the requests they made, but direct and specific answers, according to their need, in every pressing emergency. This strong faith in the efficacy of prayer, the first settlers of New England carried with them when they fled into the wilderness. It was their support and consolation under all the trials of famine, pestilence, and savage warfare. They felt that special and extraordinary answers were often vouchsafed them when they cried to God; that there were periods in their history when his arm was made bare for their deliverance, in a manner scarcely less remarkable than if he had interposed by direct miracle; and the result was, that the spirit of the early New England Christians was emphatically a spirit of *prayer;* which led them to the throne of grace, with the highest confidence of being heard, on every occasion of especial interest to themselves, their families, and the church.

To see the connection of these two traits of character with the spirit of revivals, we have only to consider the influence they would naturally exert at one of the most interesting crises which can ever happen to a minister and his church—I mean the commencement of increased thoughtfulness among the unconverted part of the congregation. Such seasons exist, at times, in every place where the gospel is faithfully preached. Some alarming providence, some general calamity which weakens for a time the fascination of worldly things, some impressive sermon, some instances of sudden conversion, may strike upon the consciences of considerable numbers at once, and awaken up that latent sense of guilt and danger, which it is impossible for the most thoughtless wholly to suppress. At such a period, how has many a pastor felt, both in Europe and America, that if he could then enjoy the hearty co-operation and fervent prayers of the whole body of his church; if he could draw the impenitent around him in more frequent meetings, and hold their minds fixed in the steady and prolonged contemplation of divine truth, while the world was shut out from view, and the seriousness of one might spread by contact till it reached the hearts of many;—how has he felt, that, by the blessing of God, this interest in religion might extend throughout the whole congregation; might rise to deep anxiety and pungent conviction; that the Holy Spirit might be present to renew the hearts of many; and that more might be done for the salvation of his people in a few weeks or months, than under ordinary circumstances in as many years. And what would this be, if his desires were realised, but a *revival of religion,* an outpouring of the Holy Spirit, as a result of the prayers and efforts of the people of God? Now, I need not say how entirely the early settlers of New England were prepared, by the traits of character described above, to enter at once on this very course of action. Prayer and preaching were the living principle of their institutions; special prayer upon special emergencies, with the confident expectation of direct and specific answers; preaching the most plain and pungent, enforcing those peculiar doctrines of grace which humble man and exalt God, and which have in every age been made powerful to the " pulling down of strongholds." There was much also in the state of their infant settlements to favour the desired result. They were a world within themselves, cut off by their distance and poverty from most of the alluring objects which seize on the hearts of the unconverted in a more advanced state of society. They were all of one faith, there was none among them to question or deny the necessity of a work of the Spirit; and the minds of their children were prepared, by their early religious training, to bow submissive under the sacred influence. In these circumstances, how natural was it to multiply the means of grace upon any appearance of increased seriousness; to press with redoubled zeal and frequency to the throne of God in prayer; to urge their children and dependents with all the fervour of Christian affection, to seize the golden opportunity, and make their "calling and election sure;" to remove, as far as possible, every obstacle of business or amusement out of the way; and to concentrate the entire interest of their little communities on the one object of the soul's salvation! How natural that these labours and prayers should be blessed of God; that the truth preached under these circumstances should be made like " the fire and the hammer, to break in pieces the flinty rock;" that extraordinary effusions of the Holy Spirit should be granted; that there should be an " awakening," as it was then called, or in modern language, a REVIVAL OF RELIGION.

That such was actually the result in numerous instances we have the fullest evidence. The celebrated Jonathan Edwards, author of the " Treatise on the Will," states that his grandfather, who preceded him as pastor of the church in Northampton, Massachusetts, was favoured during his ministry with five seasons of this kind, which he called his " harvests," occurring at various intervals during the space of forty years. His father, he also says, had four or five similar periods of " refreshing from on high " among the people of his charge: and he adds,

that such had been the case with many other of the early
ministers; that no one could tell when awakenings commenced
in New England; that they must have been very nearly co-eval
with its first settlement.

Some of the States farther south were settled, to a limited
extent, by Presbyterians from the west of Scotland and the
north of Ireland, who had also suffered persecution. Many of
these had the same general traits of character, and especially
the same absorbing interest in religion, with their New England
brethren. In addition to this, they had brought with them the
cherished tradition of several remarkable outpourings of the
Holy Spirit in their native land, at Kilsyth, at Stewarton, at
Irvine, at the kirk of Shotts, and in the county of Antrim, which
led them to pray for and expect similar dispensations of the
Spirit to their infant churches. These, at a later period, shared
largely in the influences of divine grace, and handed down the
spirit of revivals to their descendants.

The early awakenings, mentioned above, seem to have been
generally of a calm and silent character; and it rarely happened that two congregations in the same neighbourhood were
visited at the same time. In the year 1735, a remarkable
change took place in this respect. An increased power, and
wider extent, were given to the dispensation of the Spirit; a
large tract of country became in this and the following year the
seat of numerous awakenings, which about this time took the
name of revivals. As this forms an important epoch in the history of our revivals, I shall dwell upon it somewhat at large,
and then trace more briefly the progress of these works of grace
down to the present time.

The revival of 1735 commenced at Northampton, Massachusetts, under the preaching of Jonathan Edwards, mentioned
above. The town, at an earlier period, had enjoyed five awakenings; but at this time religion had suffered a very great decline,
not only in Northampton, but in New England at large. A
pernicious practice had been gradually introduced of admitting
persons to full communion in the church on the ground of a
blameless external deportment, without strict inquiry into their
religious experience, or decisive evidence of renewing grace. The
disastrous consequences were soon felt. The tone of spiritual

feeling was lowered in the churches by the admission of many who had a "name to live but were dead." Prayer and effort for the salvation of the impenitent had greatly decreased; and as a natural consequence, there had been for more than thirty years a very marked suspension of divine influence throughout New England.

The preaching of Mr. Edwards which gave rise to this revival, like all preaching which prepares the way for extensive reformations, was doctrinal in its character. He dwelt with great force of argument and closeness of application on the leading doctrines of grace, which had begun to lose their power in the prevailing declension,—justification by faith alone, the necessity of the Spirit's influences, and kindred topics.

Under such preaching, in connection with a sudden and alarming providence, in the beginning of 1735, a solemn and very soon an overwhelming interest in religious truth, pervaded the whole town. For the space of six months, the revival went on with a power and extent never before known. Hardly a family could be found in the place in which there were not one or more under conviction of sin, or rejoicing in hope. So entire was the absorption in the interests of the soul, that a report went abroad that the people of Northampton had abandoned all worldly employments, and given themselves wholly up to the pursuit of eternal life; and though this was an exaggeration, it is true that Mr. Edwards found it necessary to remind some of his flock that their secular duties were not to be neglected. The enlightened character of the population, all of whom were well educated, (all, even the poorest, being taught in the same schools at the public expense,) guarded them effectually against fanaticism; while at the same time, the strength of emotion which prevailed, the distress under a sense of sin, and the joy in giving the heart to God, were, in most cases, far greater than in the early awakenings. The work was confined to no class or age. Ten persons above ninety, and more than fifty above forty years of age; nearly thirty between ten and fourteen, and one of only four, became, in the view of Mr. Edwards, subjects of renewing grace. More than 300 were added to the church as the fruits of this revival, making the whole number of communicants about 620, being nearly the entire adult population of the town, which consisted of 200 families. I will only add, that Mr. Edwards' well known principles on the subject, led him to guard his people throughout the revival, with the most watchful care, against hasty and delusive hopes of having experienced renewing grace. He conversed with each individual separately, not only while under conviction of sin, but in repeated instances after the supposed change of heart took place, pointing out the evidences and nature of true piety; warning them against self-deception, and leading them to the strictest examination into their spiritual state. Such has been the course pursued in the New England churches generally, down to the present day; and the consequence has been, that neither in that revival, nor in most of our well conducted revivals, has there been reason to suppose, that more persons were self-deceived, than in the ordinary accessions to the church, at times of no prevailing religious concern.

The scenes presented in this work of grace were so striking and wonderful as to awaken the liveliest interest in the whole country round. Many flocked to Northampton from the impulse of curiosity, or even worse motives; not a few of whom, struck with the order, solemnity, and strength of feeling which they every where witnessed, and cut to the heart by the powerful appeals of Mr. Edwards in the meetings they attended, were themselves brought under conviction of sin. Many of these gave evidence of genuine repentance after they returned home, and did much to extend the work into the places where they belonged. Members of the neighbouring churches, also, and ministers of the gospel from parts more remote, resorted thither to witness the triumphs of redeeming grace; to catch the spirit of the revival, and bear it—a spirit of hope, and prayer, and fervent effort—to the towns where they resided. The blessing of God, in many instances, went with them; the work spread from place to place, until in less than a year, ten of the adjacent towns in Massachusetts, and seventeen in Connecticut, lying directly south of them, were favoured with an out-pouring of the Holy Spirit; and some remote places were visited in other States, where settlements had been made by emigrants from New England, or by the Scottish Presbyterians spoken of above. Many thousands gave evidence in their subsequent lives of having experienced a genuine conversion in this work of grace.

In 1740, revivals commenced anew at Northampton, Boston, and many other places, very nearly at the same time, and spread within eighteen months throughout all the English colonies. For some time, this appears to have been, to an unusual degree, a silent, powerful, and glorious work of the Spirit of God. An eye-witness states, under date of May, 1741, that from Philadelphia to the remotest settlements beyond Boston, a distance of nearly 500 miles, there was in *most* places more or less concern for the soul. "Whole colleges are under conviction, and many savingly converted. Our minister, (Mr. Pemberton of New York,) being sent for to Yale college on account of the many distressed persons there, in his going and coming preached twice a day on the road, and even children followed him to his lodgings, weeping and anxiously concerned about the salvation of their souls." At a later period, however, some were unhappily betrayed into intemperate zeal, which called forth opposition, and produced great excitement and contention. Mr. Edwards came forward with his usual ability to defend the work, and at the same time repress undue excesses. One hundred and sixty of the most respectable ministers of New England, New York, and New Jersey, joined in a public attestation to its genuineness and purity in most places, while they united with Mr. Edwards in condemning the improprieties which had occurred in too many instances. But a spirit of jealousy and strife was engendered, which is always fatal to the progress of a revival. It therefore terminated in the year 1743. Notwithstanding these unfortunate admixtures of human imperfection, the work as a whole, was most evidently shown by its results to have been of God. Those who had the best means of judging estimated the number of true converts, as proved by their subsequent lives, at 30,000 in New England alone, at a time when the whole population was but 300,000; besides many thousands more among the Presbyterians of New York, New Jersey, Pennsylvania, and the more southern settlements.

It will interest the reader to know, that about this time there was an out-pouring of the Spirit upon one of our Indian tribes, corresponding exactly in its character and effects to the widely extended work of grace among the tribes.

In June, 1745, DAVID BRAINARD, who has been so extensively

known for his piety and missionary zeal, began to labour among a small collection of Indians in New Jersey. For the first six weeks, they manifested such entire indifference and stupid unconcern that he was about to leave them in despair, when he was somewhat encouraged by the conversion of his interpreter. The interest with which this man now entered into the subject, and the warmth and unction with which he translated Mr. Brainard's discourses, struck the Indians with surprise, and arrested their attention. "On the eighth of August," says Mr. Brainard in his journal, (which I slightly abridge,) "I preached to the Indians, now about sixty-five in number. There was much visible concern among them when I discoursed publicly; but afterwards, when I spoke to one and another particularly, the power of God seemed to descend upon them like 'a mighty rushing wind.' Almost all persons of all ages were bowed down with concern together, and were scarcely able to withstand the shock. Old men and women, who had been drunken wretches for many years, and some children, appeared in distress for their souls. One who had been a murderer, a *powow* or conjuror, and a notorious drunkard, was brought to cry for mercy with many tears. A young Indian woman who, I believe, never before knew that she had a soul, had come to see what was the matter. She called on me in her way, and when I told her that I meant presently to preach to the Indians, she laughed and seemed to mock. I had not proceeded far in my public discourse when she felt *effectually* that she had a soul; and before the discourse closed was so distressed with concern for her soul's salvation, that she seemed like one pierced through with a dart." Such scenes were repeated in a number of instances during the following eight weeks. Some months after, in reviewing the events of this revival, he says: "This surprising concern was never excited by any harangues of terror, but always appeared most remarkable when I insisted on the compassion of a dying Saviour, the plentiful provisions of the gospel, and the free offer of divine grace to needy sinners. The effects have been very remarkable. I doubt not that many of these people have gained more *doctrinal* knowledge of divine truth since I visited them in June last, than could have been instilled into their minds by the most diligent use of proper and instructive means for whole years together without such a divine influence. They seem generally divorced from their drunkenness, which is 'the sin that easily besets them.' A principle of honesty and justice appears among them, and they seemed concerned to discharge their old debts, which they have neglected, and perhaps scarcely thought of for years. Love seems to reign among them, especially those who have given evidence of having passed through a saving change. Their consolations do not incline them to lightness, but on the contrary are attended with solemnity, and often with tears and apparent brokenness of heart." After some months of probation he baptised forty-seven out of less than 100 who composed the settlement. Surely we may unite with him in saying, "I think there are here all the evidences of a remarkable work of grace among the Indians which can reasonably be expected."

The fifty years that followed were years of war and civil commotion; first in a conflict of nearly twenty years between the English and French for ascendency in North America, and afterwards in a struggle of the colonies for independence, and the formation of a federal government. During this long period the country was kept in a state of perpetual agitation, under the influence of passions hostile to the progress of spiritual religion in any form, and peculiarly hostile to the prevalence of any extended work of grace. Revivals, however, did not wholly cease, as might reasonably have been expected. On the contrary, I have been struck with surprise in looking over the accounts of that wide-spread work of grace which soon after commenced, to see in how many instances they point back to some preceding season of spiritual refreshing during those fifty years of war and civil strife.

The period just referred to of increased influence from on high, commenced at the close of the last century, and has often been styled the *era of modern revivals*. Owing to its importance in this character, I shall dwell upon it somewhat more fully, and shall then turn to other topics which demand our attention. It was preceded by a spirit of fervent prayer and deep solicitude among Christians, on account of the growing tendency in our country to infidel principles. For this a preparation had been made by the crimes and vices of a long protracted war; and the breaking out of the French Revolution had given to the enemies of religion the most confident expectations of a speedy triumph. The minds of multitudes had become unsettled. Wild and vague expectations were everywhere entertained, especially among the young, of a new order of things about to commence, in which Christianity would be laid aside as an obsolete system. The people of God, under these circumstances, were driven to the throne of grace with redoubled fervour of supplication, that while "the enemy came in like a flood, the Spirit of the Lord would lift up a standard against him." Another subject of solicitude was the religious wants of our new settlements, which began at this time to spread abroad in the wilderness, to an unparalleled extent. There was every reason to fear, that if left to themselves, in the rapidity of their progress they would leave behind them the institutions of the gospel. This gave rise to a missionary spirit in the older States, which has been the salvation of that growing part of our country. Massachusetts and Connecticut, especially, from which emigrants by tens of thousands were going forth every year, entered into this cause with the liveliest interest. Large contributions were made from time to time by the churches; and as regular missionaries could not be procured in sufficient numbers, many of the settled clergy were induced, by the exigency of the case, to leave their flocks under the care of the neighbouring pastors, and perform long tours of missionary labour in the new States.

The spirit thus awakened of more fervent prayer to God and more active zeal in his service, was followed by the divine blessing. A number of churches in the interior of Connecticut and Massachusetts, were favoured, in 1797, with an outpouring of the Holy Spirit, which gradually spread into many of the neighbouring towns. The utmost care was taken to guard, from the first, against any recurrence of that spirit of intemperate zeal which had brought reproach, to some extent, on the revival of 1740. These efforts, most happily, were attended with complete success. Rarely, if ever, has there been a series of revivals in our country, more calm, more pure, more lasting and salutary in their effects. As one means of extending the work, ministers who had enjoyed the presence of God among their own people, were selected by some ecclesiastical body, and sent forth, generally two together, on preaching tours among the neighbouring

churches. The expectation of their coming drew large audiences
wherever they preached. They came with that fervour of spirit,
and that close and direct dealing with the consciences of men
which a preacher gains during the progress of a revival, and
which he rarely gains to an equal degree under any other circumstances. The churches which they visited being, in most
cases, prepared to receive them by a previous season of fasting
and prayer, and animated by their presence and labours to redoubled fervour of supplication, were, in many cases, favoured
with an immediate out-pouring of the Holy Spirit. Under these
and similar influences, the work of God spread into more than
100 towns in Massachusetts and Connecticut, and into a still
greater number of places in the new settlements of Vermont,
New Hampshire, Maine, and New York, which had but recently
formed a wide-spread field of missionary labour.

In the meantime our Presbyterian brethren, already mentioned, entered into the work with equal zeal and effect, and
carried the spirit of revivals west of the Alleghany mountains.
In Kentucky, lying in the centre of these new States of the
West, a revival commenced in the year 1801, which spread
over the whole State, and within the two following years extended to the north and south, throughout a track of country
600 miles in length. Owing to the rude state of society
in those new settlements, there occurred in these revivals
some irregularities, which threw a suspicion upon them for a
time in the views of Christians in the eastern States. Some
undoubtedly of the vast multitudes who were then awakened
were wrought upon merely by the excitement of the occasion.

But as to the character of the work in general, we have the
following testimony from one of the most enlightened Presbyterian clergymen of Virginia, who visited the scene of those
revivals, for the sake of forming for himself a deliberate judgment on the subject. " Upon the whole, I think the revival in
Kentucky among the most extraordinary that has ever visited
the church of Christ. And, all things considered, it was peculiarly adapted to the circumstances of the country into which
it came. Infidelity was triumphant, and religion on the point
of expiring. Something extraordinary seemed necessary to
arrest the attention of a giddy people, who were ready to con-

clude that Christianity was a fable, and futurity a delusion. This revival has done it. It has confounded infidelity, and brought numbers beyond calculation under serious impressions."

In the year 1802, in answer to long-continued and fervent prayer, the Holy Spirit was poured out in a remarkable manner on Yale college, then under the presidency of the Rev. Timothy Dwight, D.D. As a work of this kind, in a seat of learning, will naturally be regarded with peculiar interest, I shall here transcribe (with some slight abridgment) an account of this revival, drawn up at the request of the writer, by the Rev. Noah Porter, D.D., who was then a member of the institution. " The grace which some of the students had witnessed, and of which they were all informed, in churches abroad, they longed to see in the college. That God would pour out his Spirit upon it was an object of distinct and earnest desire, and their fervent and united prayers. For many months they were accustomed to meet weekly " in an upper room," and " with one accord," for prayer and supplication. Those meetings are still remembered by survivors who attended them, as seasons of unwonted tenderness of heart, freedom of communication, and wrestling with God. Early in the spring of 1802, indications of a gracious answer to their prayers began to appear. It soon became obvious that quite a number were especially impressed with divine truth; that a new state of things had commenced in the seminary; that God had indeed come to it in the plenitude and power of his grace. Some who, not knowing that there were any to sympathise with them, had concealed their convictions, were now encouraged to speak out, and others, anxious to share in the blessing, joined them; so that in the last ten days of the college term, not less than fifty were numbered as serious inquirers, and several, daily and almost hourly, were found apparently submitting themselves to God. These were truly memorable days. Such triumphs of grace none, whose privilege it was to witness them, had ever before seen. So sudden and so great was the change in individuals, and in the general aspect of the college, that those who had been waiting for it were filled with wonder as well as joy, and those who knew not " what it meant " were awe-struck and amazed. Wherever students were found—in their rooms, in the chapel, in the hall, in the college yard, in their walks about the city—the reigning impression was, "surely God is in this place." The salvation of the soul was the great subject of thought, of conversation, of absorbing interest. The convictions of many were pungent and overwhelming, and the peace in believing which succeeded was not less strongly marked. Yet amidst these overpowering impressions, there was no one, except a single individual, who, having resisted former convictions, yielded for a time to dangerous temptations, in whose conduct any thing of a wild or irrational character appeared. But the vacation came, and they were to be separated. This was anticipated with dread. It was to be feared that their dispersion, and the new scenes and intercourse attendant on their going home, would efface the incipient impressions of the serious, and break up the hopeful purposes of the inquiring and anxious. Such, however, was not the result. It may even be doubted whether the number of sound conversions was not greater, as well as more good done to the cause of the Redeemer generally, than would otherwise have been the case. Wherever they went, they carried the tidings of what God was doing for this venerated seat of learning; they engaged simultaneously the prayers and thanksgiving of the church in its behalf; and many of them came directly under the guidance and counsel of deeply affected parents, ministers, or other Christian acquaintances. By epistolary communications and personal visits to each other, also, as had been agreed on at their separation, special means were employed to sustain the feelings which had been excited, and to conduct them to a happy result; and it was so ordered by God, that when they again assembled, the revival immediately resumed its former interest, and proceeded with uninterrupted success. It was generally understood at the time, that out of 230 students then in college, about one-third, in the course of this revival, were hopefully converted to God."

During the forty years which have since elapsed, there have been fifteen similar works of grace in the institution, one of them more extensive, and the others less so, than the one here described. At a later period, Princetown college, which belongs to the Presbyterians, was favoured with one of the most extraordinary effusions of the Holy Spirit ever experienced by any of our seats of learning. The younger colleges have also shared richly in these visitations of divine grace. The consequence has been, that the number of pious students has been very greatly increased. In Yale college, not long before the revival of 1802, there were only four members of the church among the undergraduates; for some years past they have exceeded 200, being more than half the entire number. In other colleges there has been a correspondent increase; though in all these cases it is to be ascribed, in no small degree, to the general advance of spiritual religion in our churches.

From the period we have now reached, it is unnecessary, and indeed impossible, to trace distinctly the progress of our revivals. They have become, if I may so speak, a constituent part of the religious system of our country. Not a year has passed without numerous instances of their occurrence, though at some periods they have been more powerful and prevalent than at others. They have the entire confidence of the great body of evangelical Christians throughout our country. There exists, indeed, a diversity of opinion as to the proper means of promoting them, some regarding one set of measures, and some another, as best adapted to this end. But, while these differences exist, as to what constitutes a well conducted revival, all, or nearly all, agree that such a revival is an inestimable blessing: so that he who should oppose himself to revivals, *as such*, would be regarded by most of our evangelical Christians as *ipso facto* an enemy to spiritual religion itself.

In the foregoing sketch of the rise and progress of our revivals, I have confined myself chiefly to the Congregational and Presbyterian churches (which are substantially one), and have described these works of grace, particularly as they exist in New England. I have done so, because having their origin in those churches, it was proper to trace them forward in the line where they commenced; and because I was best acquainted with their history, and the character they assumed, in the communion to which I belong. It is of such revivals that I shall continue to speak; and without disparagement to others, I may be permitted to express my preference for that mode of conducting revivals which has generally prevailed in the Congregational churches of New England. These churches have had a longer experience on this subject than any other; they have enjoyed more revivals in proportion to their numbers; and, what I deem of the highest importance is, that they have uniformly kept them under the guidance and control of a learned ministry, whose habits and principles led them to repress all undue excitement, to check every thing extravagant, coarse, or disorderly; and to guard the supposed subjects of the work, by the severest tests, against self-deception. Nearly all the objections against revivals, which have any show of reason, have been occasioned by a want of caution in these respects. The things to which they apply are mere adjuncts and excrescences, forming no part of a genuine revival. They are passing away, just in proportion as the ministry where they exist become more thoroughly educated; which, I rejoice to say, is continually more and more the case.

The view of revivals which we have now taken, limited and imperfect as it is, suggests many interesting topics of inquiry and remark. I have time, however, to touch on only two. First, What mode of presenting truth, in these seasons of religious interest, has been found most effectual to the conviction and conversion of sinners? Secondly, What is the advantage of such seasons? What is there in the fact that many are awakened *at once*, and are pressing *together* into the kingdom of God, which is peculiarly adapted (under the divine blessing) to secure the desired result?

In entering upon the first of these subjects, I would remark that the ordinary strain of preaching in the Congregational churches of New England (where revivals have prevailed with great frequency) is, to an uncommon degree, *doctrinal* in its character. A preparation is thus made to give the gospel its full effect whenever a season of religious interest arrives. The mind is pre-occupied with clear and discriminating views of divine truth. The argument, upon every point, has been gone over again and again in its full extent. Those humbling doctrines especially, which men so love to misrepresent and abuse, are dwelt upon much, explained fully, and argued out at large; and great pains are taken so to state them, as to show their perfect consistency with the dictates of right reason, and the consciousness of every honest mind. In seasons of revival, the most effective preaching is of the same general character, though, of course, more fervid and urgent. It does not consist, to any great extent, in exhortation, in any appeals, however forcible or just, to mere excited sensibility or feeling. Its object still is to pour *truth* upon the sinner's mind; to make him see, under his new circumstances of awakened interest, the *evidence* of those doctrines which he has admitted, perhaps, in speculation all his life, and yet never once truly believed; to anticipate all his objections; to strip him of every plea and pretence for delay; to fill and occupy his whole soul with *reasons* for immediate right action, and thus shut him up to " the obedience of the truth." Such preaching, though it be plain and even homely, if it flows from a full heart and large experience, is ordinarily much blessed of God in seasons of revival.

The leading doctrine at such seasons is that of " the new birth,"—of the sinner's entire dependence, for a change of heart, on the direct interposition of God. And yet, for this very reason, the other doctrine implied above, of *duty*, of *obligation* to immediate right action, is urged with redoubled force. Without feeling this, the sinner cannot feel his guilt, for there *is* no guilt, except in the violation of duty; and where guilt is not felt, the influences of the Spirit are not given to renew the heart. And here, at this precise point, is the great difficulty in dealing with the impenitent. They do not believe that God requires them, in their present state, to become instantly holy. It is not possible, they think, that he should command them to do that very thing without the influences of his Spirit, which, if ever done, will be the result of those influences. They therefore feel that there must be, somewhere at this stage of their progress, a kind of neutral ground—a resting-place; where, having done their part in " awaking out of sleep," they are allowed to " wait God's time," (in the customary phrase,) until he has done his part, and renewed their souls. Nor are these views confined to the impenitent. They have been openly avowed by some theological writers, and have exerted a secret but most powerful influence upon far greater numbers who never maintained them in form. There has been extensively a feeling, that all which the unconverted are bound to do is diligently to use the means of grace; that if they do this, it would be hard in God to withhold the renewing influence of his Spirit; and that he has promised that influence to their prayers and exertions if sincere—meaning, of course, a kind of sincerity in which there is no true holiness. These views prevailed in New England previous to the revival of 1735, and were one cause of the great decline in religion which preceded that event. Mr. Edwards was, therefore, called upon, when that work commenced, to take his ground on this subject; and the principles which guided him in that revival, have been the great controlling principles in all our revivals ever since. They are thus stated by his biographer: "to urge repentance on every sinner as his *immediate duty;* to insist that God is under no obligation to any unrenewed man; and that a man can challenge nothing, either in absolute justice or by free *promise,* on account of any thing he does before he repents and believes." The celebrated Whitefield, when he first visited America in 1740, was much struck with the power imparted to our preaching by these principles. "How can *they* possibly stand," says he in a letter to an English friend, "who were never brought to see and heartily confess, that after they had done all, God might notwithstanding deny them mercy! It is for preaching in this manner that I like Messrs. Tennents. They wound deeply before they heal. They know there is no promise made but to him that believeth, and therefore they are careful not to comfort overmuch those that are convicted. I fear I have been too incautious in this respect, and often given comfort too soon. The Lord pardon me for what is past, and teach me more rightly to divide the word of life in future." Against this disposition to "comfort too soon,"—to allow the impenitent some resting-place short of instant submission, the following very pointed cautions were once given by Dr. Nettleton, who has had great experience in the conduct of revivals. "Now, what do you mean by this? Do you mean to encourage the sinner in his sins, and take his part against God? You are attempting to ease and soothe him while he is in rebellion against God. When the sinner is in this distress, there are two things that press heavily upon him —a sense of his obligation to repent, and a fearful apprehension that he never will repent. Now if you tell him to 'wait God's time,' and the like, you take off this obligation at once. You remove all anxiety, and most probably cause him to sink down into a state of stupidity and indifference on the subject. You take away the apprehension also, and the danger is that he will sink down into a state of stupidity, or mistake the relief he feels for a change of heart. Now, instead of quieting him in his sins by such language, you should endeavour to increase his distress as much as possible. You should *press him down*, and tell him he must submit to God, and generally he will. I know some have been brought out truly regenerated after all this flattery, but it was not in consequence, but in spite of it. Again, you say, ' Look to the promises.' Now there is no promise to the impenitent, and how can you expect him to look to the promises while he is in his sins. I distinguish between *promises* and *invitations*. Men are invited to repent, but there is no promise to them till they do repent." Such has been the uniform mode of exhibiting this subject. The promises of God are a part of his *covenant*, and the indispensable conditions of the covenant are repentance and faith.

But the impenitent, when thus pressed with the duty of at once giving their hearts to God, are extremely apt to say, (or at least to feel,) "I *cannot*, Christ has declared it to be beyond my power. It cannot, therefore, be my immediate duty; I am *authorised* to wait till power is given me from on high." Here, as in the former case, the New England clergy are guided by the principles of Edwards. They apply that familiar distinction of common life, which he made so clear and palpable in theological science, the distinction between *natural* and *moral* ability and inability. "You are not unable in the sense you claim. You have all the faculties which constitute a moral being. He who is capacitated to do wrong, must, from the nature of the case, be capacitated to do right. Your *cannot*, therefore, is only *will not*. Christ, who has spoken of the inability you plead, has explained its nature: " Ye *will not* come unto me that ye might have life." "Oh! Jerusalem, how often would I have gathered thy children together, as a hen gathereth her chickens under her wings, and ye *would* not." These views have formed the basis of New England preaching for nearly a century. Dr. Dwight, speaking of this subject, says: "The nature of this inability to obey the law of God is, in my view, completely indicated by the word *indisposition*, or the word *disinclination*. A child is equally unable to obey a parent against whom his will is as much opposed as to obey God. In both cases this inability, I apprehend, is of exactly the *same nature*. Indisposition to come to Christ, therefore, is the true and the only difficulty which lies in our way."[1] Nor are these views confined to New England. A distinguished Scottish divine, Dr. Witherspoon, afterwards president of Princetown college, speaking of the alleged impossibility, says: "Now consider, I pray, what sort of impossibility this is. It is not natural but moral. It is not want of *power*, but want of *inclination*."[2] I am far from saying that no preacher is favoured with revivals of religion, who does not thus explicitly assert man's power as a moral agent to give his heart to God. Men see their way with very different degrees of clearness and confidence, through the numerous questions that arise out of such a statement. I only say, that the views of Dwight and Witherspoon given above, prevail universally among the New England clergy, and to a great extent in the Presbyterian church; and that those who maintain them, consider these views as lying at the foundation of all their successful efforts to promote revivals. When they can go to the impenitent sinner and treat him, (after the manner of Dr. Dwight,) just as they would treat a child in rebellion against an earthly parent; and can make him *feel* that the whole difficulty in his case is a mere reluctance to duty; they find the great impediment removed out of the way. They feel an unembarrassed freedom in pressing obligation, and a power of fastening conviction of sin upon the conscience, which they never possessed before. A writer of great experience in revivals has remarked: "Whatever may be the speculative opinions of ministers with regard to the nature of depravity, inability, regeneration, &c., it is a fact, that where their ministry is successful, as it is in revivals, they preach to sinners as if they believed them to be possessed of all the powers of moral agency *capable* of turning to God, and *on this account*, (and no other,) inexcusable for not doing so. Some have seen these points more

---

[1] Theology, Sermon cxxxiii.   [2] Works, vol. ii. p. 279.

clearly, and have explained them more philosophically, and
more scripturally than others, but there has always been a substantial agreement in their mode of preaching, among those who
have been blessed in turning sinners to righteousness."[1]

But it may be said, granting (as indeed we must on *some*
ground,) the duty of the unconverted to turn instantly to God,
still they will never succeed in doing it without an influence
from on high. Why then press them so urgently to the act?
Why multiply motives as if you expected to produce the change
by the mere force of moral suasion? Is it not true, after all,
that both you and they must "wait God's time?" It would be
enough to answer, that God himself has set us the example:
"Make you a new heart and a new spirit, *for why will ye die?*"
Christ and his apostles urged to repentance by argument and
persuasion, just as they did to any of the ordinary acts of life.
The whole Bible is filled with warnings, expostulations, and en-
treaties, pressing a lost race with every motive that two worlds
can offer to immediate right action. Nor is it difficult to see,
at least, some of the reasons. First: Let the sinner really put
himself to the act of giving his heart to God, and he will learn
as he can never learn in any other way, the depth of his depravity, the utter and hopeless destitution of all spiritual sensibility within him. Nothing can so effectually crush his pride
and self-reliance. This *practical* demonstration of his entire
helplessness in himself considered, may be just the thing that
was necessary to bring him to that point where alone it would
be proper for God to grant him the renewing influences of his
grace. Secondly: The Spirit, in sanctifying, operates "through
the truth;" and the presence of that truth upon the mind as an
instrumental cause, is, therefore, just as necessary to the result,
(at least in the case of adults,) as the renewing influence itself.
While it was the uniform doctrine of the apostle Paul that the
redeemed are "begotten of God," he thought it no arrogance to
say, "*I* have begotten you through the gospel." Without
affirming that the influences of the Spirit are granted in exact
proportion to the wisdom and power with which truth is urged
upon the conscience, we may safely say, that such, to a very

[1] Views and Feelings requisite to Success in the Gospel Ministry. By W.G.
Walton.

great and prevailing extent, is the fact.   It is, at least, all that man can do; and if the doctrine of the sinner's dependence leads us to do this with one particle of diminished force, if we do not ply him with truth and motive just as earnestly as if we expected to convert him by our own efforts alone; it is a serious question whether our orthodoxy has not lost its true balance.   Is there not reason to fear that very excellent men sometimes err on this subject from the best of motives, the desire to exalt the grace of God.   "How often," says a writer quoted above, (W. G. Walton,) "do we hear the preaching of the word compared to the blowing of rams' horns around the walls of Jericho!   The man who preaches has certainly, in himself considered, no power to convert the souls of his hearers, than was possessed by the Jewish priests to demolish the bulwarks of that city.   But are the *instruments* used in the two cases equally impotent?   Are the truths of the gospel no more adapted to the conversion of the soul, than the blast of a horn to the destruction of a city."   No honour is done to the Holy Spirit by exalting his influences in conversion, at the expense of the truth which he has himself revealed.   It is the glory of that blessed Agent, that in turning the soul to God, he does it in strict accordance with the laws of our moral constitution.   "Sanctify them *through* thy truth," was the prayer of Christ himself; and I believe it will be found, that the most successful preachers are those who have the most exalted views of the power of divine truth in turning the soul to God.   Such views give a peculiar solemnity, and earnestness, and authority in preaching, by which attention is secured, and conviction wrought in the minds of the hearers."   Thirdly: The result produced by renewing grace is *right action*.   "God," says Edwards, "produces all, and we *act* all.   For that is what he produces, viz. *our own acts*."   (Efficacious Grace, sec. 64.)   Is it not, therefore, most reasonable to suppose, that this grace (if bestowed at all,) will be granted to those who are putting themselves to the act of giving their hearts to God, who "strive to enter in at the strait gate;" and not to those who remain in the attitude of mere passive recipients?   Account for it as we will, there is no fact which our revivals have taught us more fully than this, *the great success which attends the urging of sinners to turn immediately to God, as though we expected them to do it at once and upon the spot.* Among the numerous cases in point which occur at once to my mind, I will briefly mention one. A young man, soon after joining one of our colleges, called on a friend one evening, and stated that he had always been taught to regard religion as the highest interest of life, but had always shrunk from making it a personal concern; that his change of residence, separation from friends, and sense of loneliness, had made him desirous to seek salvation, and that he now wished to learn the way. A long conversation ensued, in which the object was, not so much to point out what he should do when he returned to his room, as to lead him (if such were the will of God,) to embrace the Saviour at once, even before the conversation closed. With this view, the character of God and Christ was dwelt upon at large; their treatment of him during his years of past rebellion, and his treatment of them under the continued invitations of their mercy; with examples taken from the case of those whose absence had produced this unwonted tenderness, of unwearied assiduity and kindness on their part requited with insult, ingratitude, and rebellion on his. The design was, to show him in this familiar way, the exact state of mind into which he was required to come; the ingenuous sorrow, heartfelt confidence and grateful love, whose nature and reasonableness he could so perfectly understand in respect to an earthly parent. I have thus dwelt for a moment on the instructions given, for the sake of remarking how extremely simple and elementary it has been found necessary to make them. Such is the case even with those who, like this young man, have been most religiously educated. As these views of the subject were seen to open upon his mind with continually deepening interest and solemnity, under the prolonged exhibition of divine truth, the question was at length proposed, "Can there ever be a more favourable moment than the present for attempting to put forth the feelings now described? You will not do it, indeed, without an influence from on high. That influence may justly be withheld, but it *may*, also, be granted: 'Peradventure, God may give you repentance." Will you then go with me to the throne of grace, not to gain more conviction, not to do any preparatory work, (for this will defeat the object,) but to put yourself at once, as I go before you in prayer, to the exercise of this ingenuous sorrow for sin, and grateful trust in the blood of Christ?" They knelt down together to perform this duty, and closed with a solemn dedication of the soul to God. They rose and read over the fifty-first Psalm, the fifty-fifth chapter of Isaiah, and other appropriate passages, and went again with increased solemnity to the throne of grace. Four hours were thus spent, and they separated for the night. They met in the morning, and the young man said, "I hope I have given my heart to God; I think I did it before we parted last evening." That hope he has never relinquished, and during a number of years which have since elapsed, the uniform tenor of his life as an active and devoted member of the church of Christ, has given satisfactory evidence that he was not deceived.

This, then, is the point to which all my observations are directed—the union of these two doctrines of *activity* and *dependence*, which are so commonly felt to be subversive of each other; the bringing of both to bear with undiminished force on the minds of the impenitent. Establish one of these doctrines to the exclusion or weakening of the other, and just to the same extent is the gospel robbed of its power. Inculcate dependence without pressing to the act of instantly giving up the heart to Christ, and the sinner sits down quietly to "wait God's time." Urge him to duty on the ground of his possessing all the requisite power, while (with the Pelagian) you do away his dependence, and his reluctant heart will lead him to take his *own* time, and that is *never*. Address him on the Arminian scheme of *gracious aid* which is always ready at his call, (except in cases of extreme contumacy,) and how strongly is he tempted to put off to a more "convenient season," what he feels may at any time be done! But place him under the pressure of both these doctrines—the necessity of action on his part in coming to God, the weighty obligations which urge him to it, the crushing sense of guilt every moment he delays, the momentous interests which seem to be crowded into the decision of the passing hour, the encouragement to "strive as in an agony" afforded by the gift of the Spirit's influences to others around him, (an encouragement peculiarly great in seasons of revival, and giving them so much of their power,) the feeling that God may justly withhold those influences, and that every moment of delay increases

2 G

the danger of this fearful doom—and have we not here most perfectly combined all the elements of that system of grace which is emphatically the power of God unto salvation?]

I will conclude my remarks on this part of the subject in the words of the late Rev. Dr. Griffin, formerly a professor at Andover, and afterwards president of Williams college, Massachusetts. Being requested to account for the prevalence of revivals in this country, he gave the following as the principal reason.

"It is found in the distinct apprehensions which prevail in New England about the instantaneousness of regeneration, the sinfulness of every moral exercise up to that moment, and the duty of immediate submission. Such a view of things leads the preacher to divide his audience into two classes, and to run a strong and affecting line of demarcation between them. When one feels that the moral, sober, prayerful, unregenerate part of his audience are doing pretty well, and can afford to wait a little longer before they submit, he will not be so pressing, nor fall with such a tremendous weight upon their conscience. When he feels that they cannot do much more than they do, but must wait God's time, he will not annoy and weary them, and make them sick of waiting, and compel them to come in. But when one enters the pulpit under a solemn sense that every unregenerate man before him, however awakened, is an enemy to God, is resisting with all his heart, and will continue to resist till he submits—that he must be born again before he is any better than an enemy, or has made any approaches toward holiness; when one looks round upon the unregenerate part of his audience, and sees that they are under indispensable obligations to yield at once—that they have no manner of excuse for delaying —that they deserve eternal reprobation for postponing an hour; when one feels from the bottom of his heart that there is nothing short of regeneration that can answer any purpose, and that he cannot leave his dear charge to be turned from enemies of God to friends ten years hence—delivered from condemnation ten years hence—but must see it *now*. Oh! how will he pray and preach? He will give God no rest, and he will give sinners no rest; and he will bring down their immediate, pressing, boundless obligations upon them with the weight of a world. Under such preaching sinners must either turn to God or be miserable.

There is no chance for them to remain at ease this side of infidelity itself."

We pass now to consider the second question proposed, viz. What is there in the fact that many are awakened *at once*, and are pressing *together* into the kingdom of God, which is peculiarly adapted (under the divine blessing) to secure the desired result? This question has been virtually answered in the facts stated or implied in the preceding part of this chapter. I will, however, briefly advert to them again, and present in a single view some of those influences which unite to give extraordinary power to a well-conducted revival of religion.

As far as human instrumentality is concerned, the conversion of sinners depends on two things—the clear and vivid presentation to their minds of divine truth, and importunate prayer, on the part of Christians, for the influences of the Holy Spirit to give that truth effect. I am, therefore, to show what there is in these seasons of concentrated religious interest, which is peculiarly adapted both to animate the prayers and efforts of the people of God, and to give the gospel readier access to the hearts of the impenitent, and superior efficacy in bringing them to "the obedience of the truth." In doing so, I shall point to certain original principles of our mental constitution which have confessedly very great power in moving the minds of men, and shall endeavour to show that revivals appeal to these principles or springs of human action, with a force and effect altogether greater than can ever be realised under any other circumstances. I shall thus give what may not improperly be termed *a theory of revivals*, and shall show that they are not seasons of mere excitement and fanaticism, but might reasonably be expected, from their consistency with the great laws of human action, to produce those great and lasting reformations with which they have actually blessed the American churches. In pursuing the subject, I hope I shall not be suspected of losing sight for one moment of the fact, that the Holy Spirit is the author of all the good produced in this case, both in the hearts of Christians and impenitent sinners. But it is the glory of that blessed Agent, that in dispensing his sanctifying influences, he does not set aside or destroy the established laws of human agency; and it is not therefore detracting from these influences, but rather doing them honour, to point out their perfect consistency with the great principles of our mental constitution.

1. The first of these principles to which I shall now advert, and which relates particularly to Christians, is strongly awakened *desire*.

The scenes presented in a revival are eminently adapted to create those strong spiritual desires which are only another name for fervent prayer, and are indispensable to all successful Christian effort. Let any church, in its ordinary state of feeling, hear that the Holy Spirit is poured out on a neighbouring town; let some of its members visit the spot, and bring back a report of what is passing there; that the people of God are animated with all the zeal of their first love, fervent in prayers and labours for the salvation of sinners, full of joy and hope; let them tell of the crowded assemblies, the death-like stillness, the solemnity and awe depicted on every countenance; of some who but a few days before were thoughtless and even abandoned to sin, now bowed down under a sense of guilt, and of others rejoicing in the hope of having found the Saviour, and reconciliation through his blood; let it appear that there is nothing disorderly or extravagant in this movement, nothing but the natural and appropriate effect of *divine truth* applied to the conscience by the Spirit of God,—and what is there that can appeal more strongly to all the sensibilities of a Christian heart? What more natural, under the impulse of the fervent desires thus awakened, than to "put away all their idols," to bow before God in deep self-abasement for their past backslidings, to mourn over the multitudes around them who are in danger of perishing in their sins, and to pour out the prayer of the prophet from overflowing hearts, "O Lord, revive thy work in the midst of the years, in the midst of the years make known; in wrath remember mercy." And if, through the grace of God, a similar dispensation of the Spirit is granted in answer to their prayers, how much more fervent and absorbing do those desires become as the blessing is brought home to their own doors! How do we see parents pleading for their children, wives for their husbands, friend for friend, with all the importunity of the patriarch of old, " I will not let thee go, except thou bless

me." How is all reserve laid aside—all the ordinary backwardness of Christians to speak and act openly on the side of the
Redeemer, and every feeling absorbed, amidst these triumphs of
divine grace, in the one great question, " Lord, what wilt thou
have me to do" for the advancement of thy cause? Faint and
feeble indeed, when compared with these, are the spiritual
desires which are found to prevail in any ordinary state of the
church!

2. The second of these principles, now to be mentioned, is
expectation.

If I were asked, Why revivals are so frequent in America,
and so rare in Europe, my first answer would be, that Christians expect them on one side of the Atlantic, and do not expect
them on the other. These seasons of " refreshing from on
high," are a part of the blessing that rested on our fathers; and
the events of the last forty years especially have taught us, that
if we seek their continuance in the spirit of those with whom
they commenced, we shall never seek in vain. Nor is there any
thing to confine them within our own borders. They have been
carried by our missionaries to a number of Indian tribes. Our
stations in Ceylon have been repeatedly visited with the effusions of the Holy Spirit; and the Sandwich islands, within the
last three years, have been favoured with one of the most glorious dispensations of divine grace which the world has ever witnessed. Similar periods of " refreshing from on high" existed
formerly in Scotland; and there are cheering indications in
recent events, that God may even now be ready to bring down
again the blessing of their fathers upon the churches in that
country. In all the evangelical churches of Europe, indeed,
where the gospel is preached with plainness and power, there
are seasons of more than ordinary religious interest, which, if
not revivals in our sense of the term, (and they sometimes
are,) would undoubtedly become revivals, if the same expectation of this result could only pervade those churches, which
animates their brethren of America under similar circumstances.

But leaving this more general view of the subject, it is obvious
that nothing is more calculated to fill the hearts of Christians
with courage and expectation and hope, than the feeling that God
is in the midst of them with the peculiar dispensations of the

grace. One must witness the scene, indeed, to have any just conception of the power of a revival in this respect;—of the multiplied appeals which it makes to this most essential element in all the successful efforts of men. " God is pouring out his Spirit in a neighbouring town!" In how many hundreds of instances has this thought, and the encouragement it afforded, been the starting point of those exertions, which resulted, under the divine blessing, in the commencement of one revival more. " God is *here* with the effusions of his Spirit!" Who does not feel the thrill of joy, of hope, of confidence, which pervades the heart of every spiritually-minded Christian? What can be more suited to revive the decaying graces of backsliders, and to bring the whole church to harmonious action, to fervent prayer and strenuous efforts! When the confidence thus inspired has been high and yet humble, resting on the mighty power of the Spirit, and the efficacy of divine truth, when has God ever failed to bestow a signal blessing? On the contrary, if the work of grace has not gone forward, as was hoped, how uniformly do we find that the people of God either became faint-hearted in consequence of some difficulty or delay, and did not *expect* to succeed; or that their confidence was misplaced, that they rested on some favourite instrument or system of measures, and not on the arm of the Most High! Nor is the influence of which I speak confined to Christians. It acts on the minds of the impenitent in various ways, and with great power. " God is calling some of my companions into his kingdom!" This thought strikes upon the hearts of many who have been religiously educated—who have always intended at some time to seek eternal life, and who are induced by what is passing around them to do it *now*, because they are encouraged to hope they shall succeed. " God is renewing the hearts of many others, why may he not renew mine?" This thought to the awakened sinner, writhing under conviction of sin, crushed by a sense of his utterly helpless condition in himself considered, tempted under repeated failures to give up all in despair;—this thought affords him an encouragement which is worth to him more than worlds beside; and, as I before remarked, it is an encouragement which especially abounds in a season of revival. " God is causing the stout-hearted to fall before him!" This thought often awakens in the impenitent another kind of expectation, mingled with dread, as a revival goes forward; it is *that they will be compelled to yield, that they cannot stand before it.* Sometimes it disarms opposition, and sometimes it makes men flee. An instance occurs to me, which I will briefly mention. A student in one of our colleges, during a powerful work of grace, struggled for a time to ward off conviction by argument and ridicule; and finding that he could not succeed, framed a plausible excuse and obtained liberty to return home. As he drove into his native village, at the close of the day, rejoicing at the thought of having escaped from the revival, he saw large numbers of people returning from the house of God. " What has happened? What is going on?" was his first inquiry when he alighted at his father's door. " A revival of religion has just commenced," was the reply; and one and another of his most thoughtless companions were mentioned as under conviction of sin. He felt, like one of old, that it was in vain to flee from the presence of God. All his former convictions revived at once, aggravated by a sense of his guilt in striving to suppress them. He gave himself to the pursuit of eternal life, and through the grace of God, (as he hoped,) within a few days found the Saviour from whom he had attempted to flee. He returned at once to college, called immediately on those whom he had deterred from seriousness by his influence and example, and invited them to his room that evening, telling them that he had a story to relate. When they met, he gave them a full account of the efforts he had made to resist the strivings of the Spirit, and the conclusion to which (through the grace of God) he had come; and ended with the exhortation, " Go ye and do likewise." Such are some of the ways in which revivals appeal to this powerful principle of our nature, with a force never to be expected at a period of no general interest in religion.

3. A third principle intimately connected with this subject is *sympathy.* God, in establishing public worship, has decided, that the social and sympathetic feelings of our nature ought to be enlisted in the cause of religion. It would be strange, indeed, if it were otherwise; if that powerful principle which binds man to his fellow were yielded up to Satan for the destruction of unnumbered millions who "follow a multitude to do evil;" and

were never employed by the Holy Spirit in bringing those who
act in masses on every other subject, to act, at least, sometimes
together in coming to the "obedience of the truth." That strong
tendency of our nature to be moved and excited because we see
others excited around us, is not of necessity a blind and head-
long impulse; it may be guided by reason, and made subservient
to the best ends of our intellectual and moral existence. In
respect to every subject but religion, this is conceded by all;
and he would be thought superlatively weak, who should refuse
the aid of sympathy in any other enterprise for the well-being
of man. But what is there so mysterious or unreasonable in
the fact, that when the Holy Spirit has impressed one mind
with a sense of its responsibilities and violated obligations, and
awakened within it correspondent feelings of fear, shame, and
self-condemnation; these views and feelings should spread by
contact into other minds; that this blessed Agent should make
use of sympathy as well as attention, memory, and various other
principles of our nature, in bringing men to a knowledge of
God? That he does so operate where revivals are wholly unknown, that the awakening of one individual is frequently made
the occasion of arresting the attention of a number of his associates, and fastening conviction on their minds, is matter of familiar observation in every religious community. When such
cases become numerous, and other influences unite with this to
deepen the impression of divine truth; that is, when there is a
revival, this principle operates with still greater power and much
wider extent. Hundreds are drawn to religious meetings at
first, simply because the current sets that way. When there,
they are led by the awe and solemnity which pervade the place
to listen, perhaps for the first time in their lives, with fixed
attention, and impartial self-application to the word dispensed.
Their incipient conviction of sin is heightened by the emotion
which prevails around them, and by conversation with those
who have felt longer and more deeply than themselves. They
are led to "strive as in an agony," to "enter in at the strait
gate; and thus "the kingdom of heaven suffereth violence, and
the violent take it by force." As the strong images I have
used, so perfectly descriptive of the state of things in a revival,
are borrowed from the language employed by our Saviour him-

self with evident approbation in describing similar scenes in his own day, it is certain there is nothing inconsistent with perfect soundness of mind, or the presence of the sanctifying Spirit, in a season of simultaneous and highly awakened interest on the subject of the soul's salvation. That such seasons are liable to be abused, and have, in some instances, actually degenerated, under the guidance of weak and rash men, into scenes of disorder or mere animal excitement, is no more an argument against them, than a similar abuse of any of the great powers of nature, or principles of our mental constitution, is an argument against their legitimate and well-directed use. We should remember, too, that if there is danger on one side there is danger also on the other. Men may die of palsy as well as fever. And when so many millions are sunk in the anticipated slumbers of the second death, we ought not to be too timid or fastidious as to the means employed in awakening them to the extremity of their danger. The fact, however, is (as more and more fully shown in our revivals,) there can be in very powerful operation what may be called *moral* sympathy; that is, the action of one mind upon another in sober, calm, but very deep emotion, under just views of divine truth, without any of that animal excitement or nervous agitation, which leads to strong and sometimes disorderly exhibitions of feeling. In this respect, a very important change has taken place in our New England revivals in the progress of a century. During the remarkable work of grace in 1735, persons were often so agitated under the powerful preaching of the word, as to groan and cry out in the midst of religious worship under the anguish of their spirit. The clergy did not encourage these strong expressions of feeling, but they thought them, to some extent, perhaps unavoidable, and therefore to be tolerated. In the progress of the next great revival in 1740-3, this practice became still more prevalent; and was connected, to a certain extent, with other forms of bodily excitement, such as trances, &c., which produced great contention, and created a prejudice, in the minds of many, against the entire work. This led our Congregational clergy, when revivals re-commenced on a broad scale at the close of the last century, to unite from the first to discountenance this practice; to repress mere animal excitement of every kind; to make their religious meetings, especially in the evening, short, (not generally exceeding an hour or an hour and a half,) in order to prevent exhaustion and nervous agitation; and to impress upon their people that the presence of the Holy Spirit ought to be recognised in silence and awe, not with noise and confusion. So complete was their success, that although I have been much conversant with revivals for more than thirty years, I have never, but in one instance, and that a very slight one and for a moment, witnessed any audible expression of emotion in a religious assembly. All our experience has shown that it is wholly unnecessary, and from what we see in other sects where it prevails to some extent, we are constrained to feel, that it is injurious, not only as creating prejudices against revivals, but as leading many to mistake nervous excitement for the influences of the Holy Spirit.

4. A fourth of these principles is the *spirit of inquiry* awakened among the thoughtless and prejudiced by the striking scenes of a revival.

When crowds are seen flocking to the house of God, many persons are drawn thither by the impulse of mere curiosity, and when thus brought under the power of divine truth are often taught of the Spirit; like the Athenians assembled by the same impulse around Paul on Mar's Hill, who we are told "clave unto him and believed." Others who have always doubted or denied the doctrines of grace, are led by what is going on around them, to enter into the argument for the first time with candour and attention; until struck by the blaze of evidence, not only from the word preached, but from the lives and conversation of Christians in their revived state, like the man described in the epistle to the Corinthians, they are "convinced of all, are judged of all, and so falling down on the face shall worship God, and report that God is in you of a truth." Others still, who were wholly sceptical as to the existence of any inward principle of spiritual life, when they witness the amazing change produced in the character of many around them, are compelled to exclaim, "This is indeed the finger of God." Many, too, who went to religious meetings purposely to find occasion to cavil and blaspheme, have had the scales fall from their eyes in the midst of their iniquity, and been led to cry out with the persecutor of old, "Lord, what wilt thou have me to do?" Thus the *notoriety* given to religion by the scenes of a revival, is turned with great effect to the furtherance of the gospel.

5. As a fifth of these principles, I may mention the influence of *that prolonged and exclusive attention to divine truth* which prevails in a revival.

The power of fixed and continuous attention in deepening the impressions of any subject, is one of the most familiar principles of mental science. To nothing, however, does it apply with so much force as religion, whose objects are at once so vast, so remote, and so repulsive to the natural heart. Men *must* look at their condition and ponder it deeply, before they can feel the extremity of their wretchedness and guilt. It is the first step in turning to God; and one reason, no doubt, why so many sit from year to year under the ordinary preaching of the word, moved and affected, in some degree, almost every Sabbath, and yet making no progress in divine things is, that the impressions produced are not *followed up* and deepened during the subsequent week. On the contrary, even when a person feels but slightly moved, if his mind can be held to the subject in steady and prolonged attention, while every object is excluded that can divert his thoughts, and the whole field of vision is filled with clear and vivid exhibitions of divine truth; it is surprising to see how rapid, in many cases, the progress of conviction becomes. An instance has already been mentioned (and many others might be adduced,) of a young man who appeared to be brought in this way, through divine grace, into the kingdom of God, in a conversation of a few hours. The period was still shorter in the days of the apostles; and whether it be the will of God to make it long or short, the best means certainly that a man can use is, to hold the mind fixed in the solemn contemplation of divine truth.

But the impenitent, to a great extent, are very imperfectly qualified for such a task. Their minds are so wandering, so unused to dwell on spiritual objects, so estranged from the throne of grace, so entirely in the dark as to the nature of those feelings with which they must come to God, that most of the time they give to contemplation is wasted in chaotic thought;

and they are often led to relinquish the attempt in despair. It is not, therefore, sufficient when their attention is awakened to send them to their Bibles and their closets. In addition to this, they need, at every step, the assistance of an experienced mind to *hold them to the subject*, to remove obstacles out of the way, and throw light on the path before them. Here, then, is the great principle of revivals. At certain seasons which seem peculiarly to promise a divine blessing, an extraordinary effort is made (such as cannot from its nature last many months,) to bring the impenitent completely under the power of divine truth. Religious meetings are made so frequent, as not on the one hand to weary and distract the mind, nor on the other to leave the impression made at one meeting to be effaced or much weakened before the next arrives; but to keep the impenitent constantly, as it were, in an atmosphere of divine truth, brightening continually around them, and bringing their minds more and more perfectly under "the power of the world to come." There is preaching, perhaps, an hour every evening, but the subject is not left there. At the close of the service all who are willing to be considered as serious inquirers, are invited to remain for a half hour longer, to receive more familiar and direct instruction suited to their case; while the members of the church withdraw to the vestry, or some other convenient room, to implore the influences of the Holy Spirit on the meeting to be continued under these new and more interesting circumstances. There is much to awaken deep emotion in the separation thus made; as parent and child, husband and wife, friend and friend, part from each other, the one to be prayed for and the other to pray. The great object of the meeting with inquirers, as thus continued, is to bring them at once to the point; to anticipate and remove objections; to draw them off from resting in any mere preparatory work; to set before them the great objects in view of which, if at all, they will (through divine grace,) exercise right affections, and then *call them to do it;* leading them to the throne of grace in the fervent expression of repentance for sin, faith in Christ, and deliberate consecration to the service of God. The inquirers are then invited to assemble again at some convenient hour the next day—or the next evening, if there is preaching only every other night—at what is called the meeting

for inquiry.   Here the pastor converses for a few moments with
each individual separately as to the peculiar state of his feelings,
and then addresses them collectively, as before, on the one great
subject of coming at once to Christ.   An hour is also appointed
at which he will meet those who are desirous to see him alone.
Those who entertain hopes are strictly examined, formed into
praying associations, encouraged to judicious effort for the salvation of others, and frequently assembled as a body to receive
instruction in the evidences of genuine piety.   The members of
the church, in the meantime, if they do their duty, are actively
engaged according to their ability in similar labours in their
own families and neighbourhoods.   Their efforts, if well-directed,
present religion in a new and striking form.   It is brought
home to "the business and bosoms of men," as it can never be
by mere preaching.   Thus, in a great variety of ways, divine
truth is made to bear on the impenitent during the progress of
a revival, with a directness, force, and continuity of impression,
which can never be attained under any other circumstances;
while the people of God are pleading before him to give that
truth effect, with a fervour of supplication corresponding to the
interest of the scene around them.

6. Another principle involved in revivals is, *the removal of
many causes which prevent the access of divine truth to the mind
under ordinary circumstances.*

I can barely glance at a few of these.   In a season of general
religious interest, much of that *reserve* is laid aside which ordinarily prevails in respect to close conversation on personal religion, and which forms so effectual a guard for backsliding Christians and impenitent sinners, against the intrusion of this un-
welcome subject.   Men are expected, at such times, to speak
freely; and if they do it with kindness and a little tact, they can
converse with almost any one on the state of his spiritual concerns without wounding his pride or awakening his resentment.
The *sense of shame,* the *reluctance to be singular,*—one of the
strongest impediments (especially with the young,) to entering
on a religious course,— loses at such times almost all its power.
In an extensive revival the singularity lies on the other side.

Those *changes* in business or family arrangements, which must
often be made as the result of becoming religious, are regarded

at such seasons with diminished dread and repugnance. Is a man engaged in some dishonourable or sinful employment, as for instance, the making or vending of ardent spirits? The sacrifice is less when he is only one among many who are called to make it. Has the subject of family prayer been an impediment to his entering on a religious course? Such are the habits and feelings of our churches, that no one can be recognised as a consistent Christian who refuses to lead his household statedly to the throne of grace. Has a feeling of diffidence or awkwardness as to commencing this duty been one reason for shrinking from the service of Christ? How entirely does this obstacle disappear when so many around are erecting the family altar, when, as I once knew in a single small neighbourhood, twelve plain and uneducated men in one week are seen entering on the duty of family worship.

The ordinary *amusements* of life, which interest the feelings and divert the attention, are at such periods wholly laid aside among those who are friendly to revivals.

The concerns of *business* are made to yield on such occasions to the higher interests of eternity. The people of God will find or *make* time for the numerous seasons of prayer and preaching which demand their presence; and will so arrange that their children and dependents shall enjoy every facility that is requisite to the effectual pursuit of eternal life.

Such, without dwelling farther on the subject, are some of the ways in which impediments to the progress of the gospel are removed out of the way, by extraordinary seasons of attention to religion.

7. The next principle which I shall mention is, the tendency of revivals to bring men to a *decision*, and to make them decide *right* on the subject of religion.

"Hell," says an old English writer, "is paved with good intentions,"—intentions never carried into effect, because the time for their execution never quite arrived. On these dreams of the future a revival breaks in with startling power, and calls men to instant decision, "Choose ye this day whom ye will serve." Those who believe in religion at all, believe and know that they can never enjoy a more favourable season to secure the salvation of their souls. Every thing, at such a time, presses upon them with united force to make them decide at once, and decide right. The well known shortness of such a season, to them perhaps the end of their day of grace—the uncommon clearness and pungency with which the truth is preached—the solicitude of Christian friends—the importunity of young converts who have just "tasted that the Lord is gracious"—the impulse of the mass of mind around them, moving in one direction, with all the multiplied influences that concentre in a revival, unite to impress the truth with irresistible force, " *Now* is the accepted time, *now* is the day of salvation." In the mean time, one step prepares the way for another; a decision on one point braces up the mind for further and more important decisions in the onward progress. " Shall I yield to the urgency of my friends, and regularly attend religious meetings?" The effort costs perhaps but little. " Shall I remain after the service closes, and thus acknowledge myself an inquirer?" The struggle is far greater, but if the victory is gained over his backwardness and pride, he is still more likely to go on. " Shall I attend the meeting for inquiry? " " Shall I go to my pastor, lay open my heart, and tell him of the world of iniquity which I find within?" In addition to the other happy. consequences of taking such a step, the strength of purpose gained by the effort is one security against his going back; he is now *committed*, and a sense of consistency unites with higher motives to urge him forward. Thus the multiplied exercises of a revival bring the sinner continually to the trial; press him to instantaneous decision; and prepare the way, through divine grace, for his entering into the kingdom of God.

8. Another principle involved in revivals is the tendency of that *lively joy which prevails among Christians, and especially young converts,* to render religion attractive to the unconverted.

At ordinary seasons, a life of piety too often appears to the impenitent, and especially to the young, under a forbidding aspect. Christians find but little in the state of things around them to call forth their affections, before the unconverted, in lively expressions of spiritual joy. If they do not decline in the warmth of their feelings (as they too often do) they are apt at least to retire within themselves, and to seek their chief enjoyment in secret communion with God. But in times of revival every thing is changed. Their hearts naturally flow forth in warm expressions of thankfulness and joy, as they witness again the triumphs of divine grace. They renew the fervours of their first love. In their intercourse with the unconverted, they naturally assume an unwonted tenderness of manner, as they seek to bring them by their faithful admonitions to the cross of Christ. The effect is often most striking. The impenitent look at religion under a new aspect, as they see the kindness and solicitude of so many around them for their spiritual good. A lady, during a recent revival, as she entered the shop of a tradesman of infidel principles, recollected that though she had dealt with him for some years, she had never spoken to him on the subject of religion. She alluded at once to the scenes which were then passing in the town; to the surprising changes that had taken place in some of her acquaintance; and inquired whether any of those whom he employed were interested in the work. The man was deeply affected as the conversation went on, and at last, wiping his eyes, he said with much emotion, " I know not why it is that the ladies who deal with me are so anxious for my good. A number have spoken to me on the subject before, and one or two have conversed with some of my workmen. Religion *must* be something very different from what I had supposed."

But the effect on the impenitent is still more striking, when they witness the joy which is manifested in the countenance and conversation of the new converts to religion. Every natural man bears in his bosom a testimony that he is in the wrong. He has, too, a sense of *want*, an insatiable desire of some good which he has never yet obtained; and when he sees multitudes around him who have found that good, where he knows it can alone exist, in the favour of God; how strong is the appeal to one of the deepest principles of our nature, especially in the case of those who are already somewhat convinced of sin, and of the unsatisfying nature of all worldly enjoyment! It is the very appeal so beautifully set forth in the parable of the prodigal son. It was the reflection that there was *bread enough and to spare* in his father's house, while he perished with hunger, that made him exclaim, " I will arise and go unto my father!" Some years ago, two young ladies, under deep conviction of sin, went after an evening meeting to the house of their pastor for further instruction.　As the preacher conversed with them much at large, and was urging them by motives drawn from the love of Christ instantly to accept the offered salvation, one of them was observed to rest her head upon her hand as in deep abstraction, till her face sank at last on the table in solemn and overpowering emotion.　After a few moments of entire silence, she looked up with a countenance of serene joy, dropped upon one knee before her companion, and said with the simplicity of a child, " Julia, *do* love Christ.　He is so beautiful.　Do come with me and love him!"　The effect was overwhelming.　" She has entered in while I remain out."　" One shall be taken and another left."　It was this which seemed to be the means (under God) of bringing her also to Christ before she laid her head that night upon her pillow.

9. The last of these principles to which I shall advert is, *the solemnity and awe inspired by a sense of the peculiar presence of God, the sanctifying Spirit.*

The feeling of the supernatural is one of the strongest and most subduing emotions of the human heart.　It has been used by the adversary of souls to convert unnumbered millions into bond-slaves of the most degrading superstition; and it is worthy of being employed by the Spirit of all grace as an instrument of bringing the chosen of God to that liberty wherewith Christ shall make them free.　It is the great distinctive sentiment of a revival of religion.　" How dreadful is this place: it is none other than the house of God and the gate of heaven."　Such is the feeling with which those who believe in the reality of divine influence move amidst the scenes which are hallowed by the especial presence of the sanctifying Spirit.　In the children of God, as they are employed in bearing forward the triumphs of his grace, it awakens that mingled awe and delight which, we may imagine, filled the breasts of those who bore, before the armies of Israel, the ark of the covenant, on which rested the shechinah of the Most High.　To the enemies of God it comes with a solemnity of appeal, second only to that of the bed of death, and the scenes of approaching judgment, as they see around them the striking manifestations of his presence, who " will have mercy on whom he will have mercy, and whom he

will he hardeneth." " Grieve not the Spirit," is the admonition
continually impressed upon them by the messengers of the
Most High. " Grieve not the Spirit," is the argument urged
especially by those who have recently tasted the sweetness of
his renovating grace. " Grieve not the Spirit," is the admonition which comes to them at times from those who feel that
they have wasted their day of grace. A striking instance of
this kind occurred within my own knowledge. A lady who
had passed unsubdued through more than one of these seasons
of visitation from on high, and who had deliberately stifled her
convictions, and delayed repentance, was lying on the bed of
death when another revival commenced. When intreated to
avail herself of this last period (to her) of the Spirit's influences,
she replied that it was utterly in vain; that she had deliberately resisted his grace, and now felt that the curse of abandonment was upon her. Nothing could change her views. She
went down to the grave with the admonition continually upon
her lips, to those who stood around her bedside, "Grieve not the
Spirit." They were the last words she uttered as she entered
the eternal world.

Thus have I given a brief sketch of the rise and progress
of our revivals; of the mode of presenting divine truth which
has been found most effectual at such periods; and of those
principles in our mental constitution which are appealed to
with peculiar power by these seasons of concentrated religious
interest. As the limits assigned me have already been exceeded, I must here leave the subject, commending the very
imperfect exhibition, which has now been made, to the candour
and prayers of the Christian reader.

CHAPTER VIII.

SUPPLEMENTARY REMARKS ON REVIVALS IN RELIGION.

MAY I be allowed to add a few words to the full and able discussion of the subject of religious revivals contained in the preceding chapter.

The reader will have perceived that it relates particularly to the revivals in New England, that being the part of the United States with which the author is most intimately acquainted. But as it has fallen to my lot to be conversant with the different evangelical denominations of all parts of the country, during several years devoted to religious and philanthropic enterprises before my coming to Europe, it may not be amiss that I should give the result of that experience.

I should say, then, that the same blessed influences of the Spirit which have been so signally manifested in the churches and many of the literary institutions of New England, have been experienced, and perhaps in no less a measure, in the evangelical churches of all denominations throughout the United States. I have been myself a witness to these blessed movements in almost every one of those States, at one time or another, and have ever found their effects to be, in all essential respects, the same.

It may be fairly remarked, I think, that under a permanent, well-instructed minister, revivals are usually less alloyed with unnecessary, and on the whole, injurious accompaniments, such as great physical excitement, manifesting itself in sobbing, or crying, or ineffectual efforts to retain one's composure. Still, it is not the case that a preacher has it in his power to repress all such agitation. Much depends on the kind of people he has to do with. Among the rude and uneducated who are accustomed to boisterous expressions of feeling, there will always be found more visible and irrepressible excitement than in other cases, as any one who is acquainted with the lowest classes in any

2 H 2

country will admit. Judicious preachers will certainly endeavour to suppress all undue excitement and agitation, as interrupting the services, and preventing the more composed from profiting by them.

It is not very wonderful, however, when a considerable number of persons who have been living all their lives long in rebellion against God, and in the neglect of their souls, become, as it were, suddenly awakened out of a profound sleep, that in the distress into which they are thrown by a view of the jeopardy in which they stand, they should be ready, like Saul of Tarsus, to exclaim: "Lord! what wilt thou have me to do?" No man can be more a friend of order than I am, yet I have seen times when under the preaching of the gospel, such pungent distress has been produced by pressing the truth on plain and comparatively ignorant minds, that it was impossible to maintain the calmness that might be found in a congregation of better educated and more refined persons, among whom, nevertheless, there might be quite as much real contrition of heart for sin.

That some excellent men who have been eminently useful in the ministry, are not sufficiently careful in repressing unnecessary manifestations of feeling is certain, and they are to be found in all denominations. Some even are so much wanting in prudence as rather to encourage such outbursts of feeling. But among so many ministers, widely different from each other in education, intellectual acquirements, and modes of thinking on almost every subject, entire agreement as to the best ways of conducting a revival, so far as human agency is concerned, is not to be expected.

It is delightful to think that revivals of religion have really occurred, and do every year occur, to a greater or less extent, in all our States and among all the evangelical denominations. And although they may not always be so quietly and judiciously dealt with as might be desired, in the newer parts of the country, and where the population is somewhat rude, yet they have certainly exerted a happy influence upon the churches and upon society, wherever they have occurred.

CHAPTER IX.

ALLEGED ABUSES IN REVIVALS OF RELIGION.

It was my first intention not to add any thing to what has been said in the chapter on revivals, respecting the abuses alleged to have been connected with them, but, on farther reflection, I consider that a few words more on that point would not be amiss.

No man, certainly, who is at all acquainted with human nature, should be surprised to hear that the greatest blessings bestowed on mankind are liable to be abused, and even the purest and noblest qualities to be counterfeited. Where then is there any matter of astonishment should we find that abuses mingle with religious revivals, through man's imprudence and the malignity of the great adversary, or should we even discover some revivals to deserve being called spurious.

I ought, however, to premise that whatever abuses may have at any time taken place in the revivals in America, or whatever spurious ones may have occurred, it cannot be disputed that our truly zealous, intelligent, and devoted Christians, whatever be their denomination, not only believe in the reality of revivals, but consider that when wisely dealt with, they are the greatest and most desirable blessing that can be bestowed upon the churches. There are, I admit, persons among us who oppose religious revivals, and it would be sad evidence against them if there were not. There are the openly wicked, the profane, Sabbath-breakers, enemies of pure religion in any form, and avowed or secret infidels. These form the first category, and it is not a small one. They may be found in our cities and large towns, and sometimes in our villages, and are the very persons whom strangers are most likely to meet with about our hotels and taverns. Next, there are Roman Catholics, Unitarians, Universalists, and others whose Christianity is so marred with errors and heresies, that they cannot be owned as brethren by those who hold the evangelical faith of the Reformers. These, too, almost without exception, hate revivals, nor can we wonder that they should. A third class consists of those members of our evangelical churches who conform too much to the opinions and practices of the world; are so much afraid of what they call enthusiasm and fanaticism as to do nothing, or nothing worth mention, for the promotion of the gospel, and would never be known to be Christians either by the world or by their fellow-Christians, were they not occasionally seen to take their places at the communion table. Some such there are in all our evangelical churches, and in one or two of those, whose discipline is laxer than it should be, they constitute a considerable party.

Now, it is natural that European travellers in the United States, when not decidedly religious themselves, should chiefly associate with one or all of these three classes, and that taking up their notions from them, they should have their note books and journals filled with all sorts of misrepresentations with respect to our religious revivals. Hence many, who have never visited America, owe all their ideas on that subject to writers whose own information was partial and incorrect, and who, as their very books show, know nothing of true religion, and would never have touched upon the subject, but that they wished to give piquancy to their pages by working up for the wonder and amusement of their readers every false and exaggerated statement, and foolish anecdote, that on that subject had been poured into their ears.

But serious and worthy people in Europe, and particularly in Great Britain, have been prejudiced against revivals in another way. They have too readily allowed themselves to be carried off by what has been written by excellent men among us, who, apprehending much danger to the cause of revivals from the measures taken to promote them by some zealous but, in their opinion, imprudent men, and perceiving the mischievous results of such measures, have faithfully exposed them and warned the churches to be upon their guard, and this they have done in the columns of our religious journals, in pamphlets, and in books. Their endeavours met with much success against the enemy, who, on failing to prevent, had been seeking to pervert these blessed manifestations of divine mercy, but, as was natural, the strong language which they had been prompted to indulge by the actual view of some evils, and the apprehension of worse, impressed foreigners with very exaggerated ideas of those evils. This result was perhaps unavoidable, yet is much to be deplored, for injury has thus been done to the cause abroad by men who would be the last to intend it.

It is an infelicity to which all endeavours for good are subject in this evil world, that they are liable to be marred by proffered aid from men, who, notwithstanding the fairest professions, prove at length to have been more actuated by their own miserable ambition than by a true zeal for God's glory and man's salvation. Such false friends did no small injury to the great revival of religion in 1740-43, already mentioned; and so, likewise, did the successive revivals that took place in the West in 1801-3 suffer much from the imprudence of some who desired to be leaders in the work of God. This was the case particularly in Kentucky. And within the last few years, after a blessed period marked by revivals in many parts of the country, the same adversary who, when "the sons of God come to present themselves before the Lord," seldom fails to obtrude himself among them, and who can on such occasions assume the garb, as it were, "of an angel of light," contrived for a while to do no little damage to the work. Some good men, as we still consider the greater number of them to have been, not content with the more quiet and prudent character which had hitherto marked the revivals, attempted to precipitate matters by measures deemed unwise and mischievous by many worthy and experienced persons, both ministers and laymen. The passions, instead of the judgment and the conscience, were too much appealed to; too much stress was laid on the sinner's supposed natural ability, and not enough on the needed influence of the Holy Spirit; too superficial a view was presented of the nature and evidences of conversion; in a word, the gospel was held forth in such a way as not to lead to that self-abasement which becomes a sinner saved wholly by grace.

One of the reprehended measures was the practice of earnestly pressing those who were so far awakened to a sense of their sin and danger, to come at the close of the sermon to seats immediately before the pulpit, called " anxious seats," or seats for such as were anxious to be saved, in order that they might be specially prayed for, and receive some special counsels. This, though comparatively harmless perhaps, when adopted by prudent men among certain classes of people, was much the reverse when attempted in large congregations by men not gifted with extraordinary prudence. It proved a poor substitute for the simpler and quieter method of meeting such as chose to remain after the public services were over, in order to administer such advice as their case might require, or for the good old practice of having special meetings at the pastor's house, or in the church vestry or lecture room, for such as were " inquiring the way to Zion."

Another measure, hardly deserving to be called new, for it has long existed in substance in the Presbyterian churches of the interior, and at one time, I understand, in Scotland also, that of having public services during three or four days on sacramental occasions, was found hurtful, when carried to the extent encouraged by some, at what are called "protracted meetings." These, when transferred from the West to the East, and when they began to be more frequent with us, were called " four days' meetings " or " three days' meetings," from the length of time during which they were held. But when prolonged as they were in some places—I know not how long, sometimes, I understand, for a month or forty days, the practice was regarded as an abuse, and as such it was resisted. No one, perhaps, would condemn such meetings when called for by particular circumstances, but when people seem inclined to rely more on them than on the ordinary services of the sanctuary, and to think that without them there can be no revivals and no conversions, it is time they were abolished, or at least restored to their proper use.

But what was thought worst of all was the proposal, for it hardly went farther, of having an order of revival preachers, who should go through the churches, spending a few weeks here and a few weeks there, for the sole object of promoting revivals. This was justly opposed as subversive of the regular ministry, for it is easy to see that such men, going about with a few well-prepared discourses on exciting topics, and recommended perhaps by a popular delivery, would throw the pastors on the background, give the people "itching ears," and in a few weeks do more harm than good. No one would deny that evangelists might be very useful in the new settlements, where a regular clergy cannot be at once established, and even in building up churches in the older parts of the country, or preaching to churches without pastors. Few, likewise, would deny that some zealous, able, and judicious ministers might render important services in going from church to church at the pastor's special request for his assistance. Such men should have an eminently humble, kind, and prudent spirit, and an over-ruling desire to seek the interests of their brethren rather than to promote their own, and some such we have had who were widely useful. But should it be thought that the churches require such men, they ought to be placed under the special control of the ecclesiastical bodies to which they belong, and without whose express and continued approbation they ought not to undertake or continue such engagements. Nothing could be more dangerous to the peace of the churches than that every man, who may fancy himself a revivalist, or "revival preacher," should be allowed to go wherever people desire to have him, with or without the consent of their pastors. Accordingly, the institution of any such order was opposed, and the preachers who had been thus employed were urged each to settle at some one spot, which they did; and thus the churches hear no more of revival preachers, or revival makers, as some deserved to be called.

I have said more on this subject than I intended, but not more perhaps than was required. Yet should any of my readers have been led to suppose that the abuses I have described affected our churches generally, he is mistaken. They began to manifest themselves about the year 1828, and lasted about ten years without, however, having ever prevailed widely, and in some extensive districts they have been altogether unknown. Of the twice ten thousand churches of all denominations amongst us, in which "the truth as it is in Jesus" is preached, only a few hundreds are believed to have been affected by them, and even these have now become pretty well rid both of the abuses and their consequences. During the last four years our churches have been more extensively blessed with revivals than at any

time before, and all well-informed persons, whom I have consulted, agree that those blessed seasons have never, probably, been more free from whatever could offend a judicious
Christian. For these things we are glad; they demonstrably
prove that though our sins be great, the God of our fathers hath
not forsaken us.

Before closing the subject of the abuses attending religious
revivals, although there be no special connection between them,
I may say something about camp meetings, respecting which I
have had many questions put to me in some parts of Europe.
Most foreigners owe their notions of these meetings to the same
sources from which they have taken their ideas of revivals—the
pages of tourists, who have raked up, and woven into episodes
for their travels, all the stories they have anyhow chanced to
meet with, and some of whom, possibly, have even gone to the
outskirts of one of these assemblages, and looked on with all
the wonderment natural to persons who had never entered into
the spirit of such scenes, so far as either to comprehend their
nature or ascertain their results.

Camp meetings, as they are called, originated in sheer necessity among the Presbyterians of Kentucky in the year 1801,
during that great religious revival, which after commencing in
the west part of North Carolina, had penetrated into Tennessee,
and spread over all the then settled parts of the west. It so happened, that on one occasion, in the early part of that revival, so
many people had come from a distance to the administration of
the Lord's supper at a particular church, that accommodation
could no where be found in the neighbourhood for all, during
the successive days and nights which they wished to spend at
the place. This induced as many as could to procure tents, and
form something like a military encampment where, as provisions
were easily to be had, they might stay till the meetings closed.
Such was the origin of camp meetings. They were afterwards
held at various points during that extraordinary season of religious solicitude. The country was still very thinly settled, and
as a proof of the deep and wide-spread feelings that prevailed
on the subject of religion, many persons attended from distances
of thirty, forty, and even fifty miles; nay, on one occasion, some
came from a distance of even 100 miles. It is not surprising

that the meetings should have lasted for a period of several
days, for many who attended them had few opportunities of
public worship, and hearing the gospel in the wilderness in which
they lived.

They were held, when the weather permitted, in the midst
of the noble forest. Seats were made of logs and plank, the
under rubbish having been cleared away; a pulpit was erected
in front of the rows of seats; and there, in the forenoon, afternoon, and evening, the ministers of the gospel made known the
"words of eternal life." Public prayer was also held at the
same spot early in the morning, and at the close of the services
at night. Around, at proper distances, were placed the tents,
looking to the seated area prepared for the great congregation.
Lamps were suspended at night from the boughs of the trees,
and torches blazed from stakes, some eight or ten feet high, in
front of each tent. In the rear of the tents, in the mornings
and evenings, such simple cooking operations went on as were
necessary. Each tent was occupied by one or two families,
intimate friends and neighbours sometimes sharing in one tent,
when their families were not too large. A horn or trumpet
announced the hour for the commencement of the public
services.

Such was a primitive camp meeting in the sombre forests of
Kentucky forty years ago. Solemn scenes occurred at them,
such as might well have made many who scoffed at them
tremble. Such, also, both as respects their arrangements, and
in many places, also, as respects the spirit that has predominated at them, have been the camp meetings held since. They
were confined for years to the frontier settlements as they ought
perhaps always to have been, for there they were in some measure necessary. I have attended them in such circumstances,
have been struck with the order that prevailed at them, and
seen them become the means of doing unquestionable good.
They served to bring together, to the profit of immortal souls,
a population scattered far and wide, and remaining sometimes
for years remote from any regular place of worship. The reader
must not suppose that all who come to these meetings encamp
at them. Only families from a great distance do so. Those
within a circuit even of five miles, generally go home at night

and return in the morning, bringing something to eat during the interval of public worship.

In the remote settlements of the far West the utility of camp meetings seems to be admitted by all who know any thing about them, but in densely settled neighbourhoods, and especially near cities and large towns, whether in the west or the east, they are apt to give rise to disorder. The idle rabble are sure to flock to them, especially on the Sabbath, and there they drink and create disturbance, not so much at the camp itself, for the police would prevent them, but at taverns and temporary booths for the sale of beer and ardent spirits in the neighbourhood. It is true, that since temperance societies have made such progress these evils have much diminished; and even in such more populous places good is undoubtedly done at these meetings; the thoughtless who go to them from mere curiosity being made to hear truths that they never can forget. Nor are these meetings blessed only to the lower classes, as they are called. A young man of the finest talents, once my class-fellow at college, and afterwards my intimate friend, having gone to one of them from mere curiosity, was awakened by a faithful sermon to a sense of his need of salvation; his convictions never left him until he found peace by "believing in the Son of God," and he lived to become a most popular and eloquent minister of the gospel.[1]

Camp meetings are occasionally held in the far West by the Presbyterians, especially by the Cumberland Presbyterians, as also by some of the Baptists possibly, but for long they have been nearly monopolised by the Methodists, and I understand, that many among these have the impression that except in the frontier and new settlements, they had better give place to "Protracted Meetings," which is the course, I believe, they are now taking.

Such is the account I have to give of camp meetings. Wicked men have sometimes taken advantage of them for their own wicked purposes, and such abuses have been trumpetted through the world with the view of bringing discredit on the religion of

---

[1] The late Rev. Joseph S. Christmas, sometime pastor of a Presbyterian church at Montreal in Canada, and afterwards settled in New York, where he died a few years ago. An interesting memoir of him has been published.

the country. Without having ever been a great admirer of
camp meetings, 1 must say, after having attended several, and
carefully observed the whole proceedings, that I am satisfied
that the mischiefs alleged to arise from them have been greatly
exaggerated, while there has been no proper acknowledgment of
the good that they have done.

In some parts of the West there is a practice, familiar to me
in early life, and of which I still retain very tender and pleasing
recollections. It consists in holding the public service of the
sanctuary in a forest during summer, both to accommodate a
greater number of people, and also for the sake of the refreshing
shade afforded by the trees. Seats are prepared in rows before
a temporary pulpit made of boards, and there from a temple
made by God himself, prayer and praise ascend unto him who
dwelleth not in temples made with hands, and who is ever present where contrite and believing hearts are engaged in worshipping him.

In such scenes, too, it is now common, in almost all parts of
the United States, for Sabbath schools to assemble on the Fourth
of July, if the weather be good, for the purpose of hearing appropriate addresses, far more religious than political, of uniting in
prayer for the blessing of God upon the country, and the country's
hope, the rising generation, and of praising Him from whom all
our privileges, civil and religious, have been received. Temperance meetings on the same occasion, are now held in our
beautiful forests, and something better is heard than the boast-
ful and unchristian self-adulation, to say nothing of the profane-
ness and ribaldry which too often characterised such scenes in
the "olden time," when temperance societies and Sunday schools
were unknown.

CHAPTER X.

CONCLUDING REMARKS ON THE CHURCH AND THE PULPIT IN AMERICA.

A STRANGER upon visiting extensively our evangelical churches of all denominations would be struck, I am sure, with the order that prevails in them, and this applies equally to the smaller prayer meetings to be found in every parish and congregation that has any life in it, and to the greater assemblies that meet for public worship. Foreigners seem impressed with the idea, if I may judge from what I have often heard hinted rather than expressed, that there is a great deal of disorder and lawlessness in the United States, and they infer, that there must be no less insubordination in the religious commonwealth than they ascribe to the civil. But both opinions are totally unfounded. It does not follow because of a few disturbances arising from the disgraceful opposition made in some places to the slavery abolitionists, and the resentment of an exasperated populace against gangs of gamblers in others, that the whole country is a scene of continual commotion. In no part of the world have there been so few dreadful riots attended with loss of life as in the United States during these last sixty years. There are bad men among us, and there are crimes, but after all, life is quite as safe among us as in any country I ever visited, and I have been in most of those that are considered civilised.

As for the church, a regard for law and order reigns to a degree not surpassed in any other country. There is no confusion of the respective rights of the ministry and people. The duties of both are well understood everywhere. Most of the churches, such as the Presbyterian and the Episcopalian in all their branches, possess and maintain a strong ecclesiastical government, and even the Congregational, however democratic in theory, have a government that exercises a hardly less powerful control. How seldom do we hear of disorder occurring at

the little meetings of Christians held for prayer and the reading
of the word—meetings so numerous, and almost always conducted by pious laymen!   How seldom do private church members encroach by word or deed, at meetings of any kind, on the
proper sphere of those who hold office in the churches!   Indeed,
on no one point are our churches more perfectly united in opinion than with respect to the necessity of maintaining due order
and subordination.   The ministry enjoys their full share of influence.   No one ever hears of unauthorised unlicensed persons
being allowed to speak in our meetings for public worship.
Those levelling doctrines, now spreading in other countries—
doctrines which would reduce the ministry to nothing, and encourage lay brethren to take it upon them to preach or teach in
the churches, I dare affirm, will not make much progress amongst
us.   Attempts to introduce something of this sort have often
been made but in vain.   We have, indeed, our meetings in
which debate is allowed, and there the laity may even take the
lead, but these meetings are about the temporal affairs of the
church, or the calling of a pastor, not for the public worship
of God.

Experience has also taught us the necessity of maintaining
order at meetings held during revivals,—occasions on which, in
consequence of the strong excitement of the most powerful feelings
of the human heart, there is a special call for watchfulness in this
respect.   It is a sad mistake to multiply meetings unnecessarily
during revivals, or to prolong them to unseasonable hours at
night, to the exhaustion of strength, the loss of needed repose,
and the unnatural and dangerous irritation of the nervous system.
Yet these are the points in which the inexperienced are most liable to err.   They begin a meeting, say at seven o'clock in the
evening.   The preacher feels deeply, and the people are much interested.   Instead of preaching for an hour, he is tempted, by the
manifest attention of his hearers, to go on for an hour and a half
or two hours, and instead of sending them home at half past eight
o'clock, or at nine at the farthest, so that they may have time
for meditation and secret prayer, in which, after all, the sinner
is most likely to give his heart unto God, he dismisses them at
ten or eleven o'clock, fatigued, yet excited, and altogether unfit
for the exercises of the closet.   This is sometimes done under

the idea that the people would lose their serious impressions were the work to be short. But here there is often a temptation of the adversary. No revival ever suffered by evening meetings being confined to a moderate length. Let the people be almost compelled to leave the house rather than unduly protract such meetings.

One of the most important and difficult duties of a minister in a revival is rightly to direct awakened souls. Alas! how often are even good men found to fail in this. Many ministers, whom I have known, seemed to me to excel in addressing unawakened sinners, and yet to fail when they came to give clear, intelligible, and scriptural directions to those who were awakened. Many, too, fail in judging of the evidences of conversion, and "heal the hurt of the people softly."

But on no point am I convinced, from what I have seen in America, is there a greater call for the exercise of a sound prudence than in receiving into the church persons who entertain the belief that they have "passed from death unto life." While they may possibly be kept back too long, the great error lies on the other side. The new convert naturally desires to join himself to those whom he now considers to be the children of God. He thinks that it is his duty to do so, and he may possibly be right. But the office-bearers in the church, whose duty it is to see to the admission of none but proper persons into it, are no less clearly bound to see that the candidate for membership shall give such evidences of piety as, on scriptural grounds, shall be deemed satisfactory. The one may be perfectly right in desiring to enter, and in coming to them for admission; the others may be no less justified in refusing until they have had satisfactory evidence of the applicant's piety. No harm can result from this temporary conflict of duty, if I may call it so. Both seek to do what is right, and both will soon find their way clear.

I consider hasty admissions to our churches to be the greatest of all the evils connected with revivals in some parts of the country, and among some denominations in particular. But this evil is not peculiar to revivals. It is quite as likely to occur when there is no revival as when there is. With all possible care it is difficult to keep a church pure, in a reasonable sense of that word. How absurd, then, to expect it when the doors are thrown wide open to admit hastily all that profess to be converted? Experience shows the necessity of decided views on this subject, and of firmness in enforcing them. On this point, as well as on all others relating to the discipline and government of the church, too much care cannot be taken to avoid latitudinarian practices. The church must be kept as a living body of believers—a company of persons who have come out from the world, and are determined to adorn the profession which they have made. In their organisation and action, order, which is said to be " heaven's first law," must be maintained. In this opinion I am sure Christians of all denominations in the United States sincerely and entirely concur.

BOOK VI.

THE EVANGELICAL CHURCHES IN AMERICA.

CHAPTER I.

PRELIMINARY REMARKS IN REFERENCE TO THIS SUBJECT.

THIS part of our work we propose to devote to a brief notice of the doctrines, organisation, and history of each of the evangelical denominations in the United States, nothing beyond a sketch of these being consistent with our limits. We will endeavour, of course, to confine ourselves as much as possible to what is important, omitting what we can best afford to leave out.

We begin with the five most numerous evangelical denominations in the United States. These, in the order of their rise, are the Episcopalians, the Congregationalists, the Baptists, the Presbyterians, and the Methodists, and in that order we shall proceed to notice them. We shall then consider as briefly as possible the smaller orthodox denominations, such as the Lutherans, the German Reformed, and other German sects, the Reformed Dutch church, the Cumberland Presbyterians, the Protestant or Reformed Methodists, the Reformed Presbyterians or Covenanters, the Associate Church, the Associate Reformed, the Moravians, the Quakers, &c.

Numerous as are the evangelical denominations in the United States, yet when grouped in reference to doctrine on the one hand, or church government on the other, it is surprising into how small a number they may be reduced. In doctrine we have but two great divisions,—the Calvinistic and the Arminian schools; the former, with its various peculiarities, comprehending the Presbyterians, usually so called, the evangelical Baptists, the Episcopalians, the Congregationalists, the German Reformed, the Dutch Reformed, the Covenanters, the Associate, and the Reformed Associate Churches; the latter, with its variations, comprehending the Methodists of all branches, the Lutherans, the Cumberland Presbyterians, and the United Brethren or Moravians.

Considered in reference to their forms of church government, they all range themselves in three great families. The *Episcopal;* comprehending the Protestant Episcopal Church, the Methodist Episcopal, and the Moravians: the *Presbyterian;* including the Presbyterians, usually so called, the Dutch Reformed, the German Reformed, the Lutherans, the Cumberland Presbyterians, the Covenanters, the Associate, and the Associate Reformed: the *Congregational;* (or Independent, as it is more commonly called in England,) embracing the Congregationalists and the evangelical Baptists.

But when viewed in relation to the great doctrines which are universally conceded by Protestants to be fundamental, and necessary to salvation, then they all form but one body, recognising Christ as their common head. They then resemble the different parts of a great temple, all constituting but one whole; or the various corps of an army, which though ranged in various divisions, and each division having an organisation perfect in itself, yet form but one great host, and are under the command of one chief.

This suggests the observation that on no one point are all these churches more completely united, or more firmly established, than on the doctrine of the supremacy of Christ in his church, and the unlawfulness of any interference with its doctrine, discipline, and government, on the part of the civil magistrate. There is not a single evangelical church in the United States that does not assert and maintain the glorious doctrine of the Headship of Christ in his church, and that from him alone comes all just and lawful authority in the same. On this point they hold unanimously the great doctrine which the

Church of Scotland has been so nobly contending for. If the civil power has ever referred for a moment to the doctrine and discipline of the church it has only been in courts of justice, and that solely for the purpose of determining which of two parties has a valid title to be considered as the church in question. For example: A church divides; the parties into which it is divided contend for the property that belonged to it when entire; and the court before which they come for a decision of their claims, is compelled to look to points of doctrine and discipline in order to settle this question as to property. Thus it was in the great Quaker case formerly referred to.

————

CHAPTER II.

THE PROTESTANT EPISCOPAL CHURCH.

The Protestant Episcopal Church in the United States derives its origin from the Church of England, of which it was not only an offshoot, but to which it is "indebted, under God, for a long continuance of nursing care and protection." [1] It agrees with that church in doctrine; and its ritual and formularies, with some variations introduced after the Revolution by which the colonies became independent States, are the same. Unlike the mother church, however, it is in no way connected with the state, nor do its bishops, in virtue of their office, enjoy any civil powers, immunities, or emoluments.

The chief particulars in which the service book differs from that of the Church of England are as follows: 1. A shorter form of absolution is allowed to be used instead of the English, which is however retained, and most generally used in the public service. 2. The Athanasian creed is omitted. 3. In the administration of baptism, the sign of the cross may be dispensed with, if requested. 4. The marriage service has been considerably

[1] Preface to the American Book of Common Prayer.

abridged. 5. In the funeral service some expressions, considered as liable to misconstruction, have been altered or omitted. 6. There has been a change, of course, in the prayers for rulers. The other modifications, being of less importance and chiefly verbal, need not be specified.

As in the parent church in England, there are three ranks or orders in the ministry, and these are believed by its friends to be of apostolical institution, viz. bishops, priests, and deacons. Ordination is performed solely by the bishops. The churches choose their own pastors, but their installation requires the consent of the bishop of the diocese.[1] The regulation of the temporal affairs of each church is confided to a board of churchwardens. The spiritual rule rests mainly with the pastor, or rector, as he is more commonly called.

The increase and wide diffusion of the Episcopal Church in the United States has led, I understand, to the determination that each State shall constitute a diocese, except when its extent, and the number of churches in it, may require its being divided, like that of New York, into two dioceses. In some instances, however, as in Virginia, where the State is extensive, and the churches not very numerous, and especially should the principal or senior bishop not enjoy robust health, an assistant bishop has been appointed.

Each diocese has its affairs directed by an annual convention, composed of the diocesan clergy and a lay delegate from each church, the clergy forming one house and the laity another. The bishop presides, should there be one; if not, a president is chosen in his place. A concurrent vote of both houses is necessary before any measure or law can pass.

Every three years a general convention is held; the last always appointing the place of meeting for the next after. This body is composed of clerical and lay delegates from each State or diocesan convention, who form the house of delegates; and of the bishops, who form the house of bishops. When any pro·

---

[1] When the bishop is unable to preside at the installation or institution of a minister as rector, or pastor of a church, he appoints a committee of neighbouring presbyters to act as institutors on the occasion. So also in dioceses that have no bishops, if the services of a neighbouring prelate cannot be obtained, a self-constituted committee of neighbouring presbyters may give institution.

posed act has passed one house, it is sent to the other for its concurrence; the consent of both houses being requisite to its having the force of law. The Episcopal Church, throughout the country, is governed by the canons of the general convention. These canons regulate the election of bishops, declare the qualifications necessary for obtaining the orders of deacon and priest, the studies to be previously pursued, the examinations to be undergone, and the age which candidates must have attained before they can be admitted to the three grades of the ministry. The age of twenty-one is required for deacon's orders, twenty-four for those of priest, and before a man can be ordained a bishop he must have completed his thirtieth year.

Candidates for ordination do not, as in the Church of England, subscribe the thirty-nine articles, but simply the following declaration: " I do believe the holy scriptures of the Old and New Testaments to be the word of God, and to contain all things necessary to salvation; and I do solemnly engage to conform to the doctrines and worship of the Protestant Episcopal Church in these United States." These doctrines are understood to be contained in the articles of religion, printed with the book of common prayer, and implied in the liturgy of the church. The fall of man, the Trinity of divine persons in the Godhead, the proper Deity and humanity of the Saviour, the atonement through his sufferings and death, the regenerating and sanctifying influence of the Holy Spirit, the general judgment, the everlasting reward of the righteous and punishment of the wicked,— or, in other words, what are called the doctrines of the Reformation,—are fully taught in these formularies, and are in reality professed by those who subscribe the above declaration.

The Episcopal was the first Protestant Church planted on the American continent, and the reader has seen how it was the favoured church in Virginia from the earliest settlement of that State until the Revolution; also, how it came to be established in the colonies of Maryland, New York, and the Carolinas. But notwithstanding all the aid which it received from the civil government, its prosperity was far from commensurate with its external advantages. When the Revolution commenced, it had not more than eighty clergymen in the colonies north and east of Maryland, and even these, with the exception of such as were

settled in Philadelphia, New York, Newport, Boston, and a few
other of the most important cities and towns, were supported by
the Society for the Propagation of the Gospel in Foreign Parts;
whilst in the colonies of Virginia, viz. the Carolinas and Georgia, all the clergy taken together were but few.   The number
in Virginia and Maryland, amounting to about 150, greatly
exceeded that of all the other colonies.

The causes of this ill success, during the colonial era, lay, as
we have stated, in the church being dependent upon England
altogether for Episcopal supervision, and, in a great degree, for
its ministers; in the unfitness of most that were sent over by
the bishop of London, to whose diocese the Episcopal churches
in America were then attached; and the great difficulties attending the raising up of a native clergy, and sending them to England for consecration.   We have also seen how disastrous were
the Revolution and the changes it effected on the Episcopal
Church in all the colonies, and particularly in Virginia, and
that it was many years before it could rise from the prostration
in which the return of peace in 1783 found it.

One of the first measures attempted after that event was the
formation of an ecclesiastical constitution, by a special convention of the clergy from several of the States, held in Philadelphia in 1785, for the purpose of uniting all the Episcopal
churches in one body.   Another important measure was the
ordination of American bishops.   For this purpose the above
convention, which was the first that was held, opened a correspondence with the archbishops of Canterbury and York.   This
was followed by the British parliament passing an act, authorising the English prelates to consecrate bishops for America.   The
Rev. Drs. White and Provoost, the former of Philadelphia, and
the latter of New York, were thereupon sent over to England,
and received ordination to the Episcopal office from the hands
of the archbishop of Canterbury and the archbishop of York,
the bishops of Bath and Wells, and of Peterborough, assisting.
Upon their return to America, Bishops White and Provoost
entered upon the discharge of their Episcopal duties in their
respective dioceses.

A short time before the consecration of Bishops White and
Provoost, the Rev. Samuel Seabury, D.D. had gone over to

England for consecration to the Episcopal office. But having abandoned all hope of success from that quarter, he went to Scotland, and was consecrated by three of the non-juring bishops of that kingdom. Upon his return he became bishop of Connecticut. In the convention of 1789, it being proposed to ordain another bishop, that body requested Bishops White and Provoost to unite with Bishop Seabury in performing that act, the presence of three bishops being necessary. But Bishop White having some doubts whether it was consistent with the faith understood to have been pledged to the English bishops, not to proceed to an act of consecration without having first obtained from them the number held in their church to be canonically necessary to such an act, the difficulty was terminated by sending the Rev. James Madison, D.D., of Virginia to England, and his consecration there. At the next triennial convention, held in the city of New York in 1792, the four bishops, Drs. White, Provoost, Madison, and Seabury, ordained the Rev. Dr. Thomas John Clagget to the Episcopal office in the diocese of Maryland.

About that epoch the church may be said to have passed its apogee of depression, occasioned by the Revolution and its effects. Its subsequent history has been marked by an increasing prosperity. I have not the means of knowing what was the precise number of its clergy in 1792, but I am sure that it could not have exceeded 200, and its bishops were four. Just forty years later, in 1832, according to the journal of the general convention held in New York in October of that year, the number of the bishops had increased to fifteen, and that of the clergy to 583. Ten years later still, in 1842, we find the number of bishops augmented to twenty-one, the clergy to 1000,[1] and that the churches exceed 1140.

Nor has the spiritual prosperity of this church been less remarkable than its external. It possesses a degree of life and energy throughout all its extent, and an amount of vital piety in its ministers and members such as it never had in its colonial days. It is blessed with precious revivals, and flourishes like

---

[1] This is the number stated by the Rev. Dr. Tyng of Philadelphia, at the Church Missionary Society anniversary in May last. Dr. Tyng is a distinguished minister in the United States Episcopal Church, and an authority that cannot be questioned.

a tree planted by the rivers of water.   And in no portions of the country does it possess more spiritual health than in the States of Virginia aud Maryland, where, in the anti-revolutionary era it was in a deplorable state as regards piety, both in its ministry and its laity.   Happier days have dawned upon it in those States, and indeed every where else.   Even whilst writing this chapter I have received a letter from an excellent young Episcopal minister settled in a country parish in the centre of Virginia, who informs me that the last winter and spring were seasons of remarkable blessing to the Episcopal church in that State.   He informs me that about 100 persons have been added to the church at Norfolk; nearly as many to that at Petersburg; whilst at Richmond,[1] so interesting was the state of things that the rectors of the churches there (three or four in number,) did not feel it to be their duty to leave their flocks in order to attend the convention of the diocese which had just taken place.

I have already spoken of the societies which have sprung up in the Episcopal Church for the promotion of domestic missions, Sunday schools, the education of poor and pious young men for the ministry, and the publication of religious tracts and books.

I have also taken some notice of the theological schools or seminaries connected with it: viz. One at New York; another in Fairfax county, Virginia, a few miles from Alexandria, in the district of Columbia; and a third at Gambier, Ohio, in connection with Kenyon college.   These institutions have already sent forth a large number of young men into the ministry, and some 140 or 150 are at this moment pursuing their theological studies at them, under the instruction of able professors.

The clergy of the Episcopal Church in America, like those of the Established Church in England, are divided into two classes, one called "high church" and the other "low."   Sometimes these parties are called "evangelical" and "non-evangelical," but not with accuracy, for not a few of the high churchmen, that is, men charged with carrying their preference of Episcopacy to the most extravagant length, are entirely evangelical in their doctrines and preaching.   But a part of these high churchmen are not considered evangelical,—not so much because of what they

---

[1] These three are the largest cities in the State.

do preach, as because of that they do not preach. Their sermons are of too negative a character; neither are the sinner's
sin and danger as fully and earnestly set forth as they should
be, nor is the glorious sufficiency of Christ unfolded, and salvation by faith alone fully and clearly presented. Their preaching, consequently, does not reach the hearts of their hearers as
does that of their evangelical brethren, nor does it lead the
members of their churches to renounce the "world, its pomps
and its vanities," to as great an extent as they should do. Yet
these ministers are not to be classed with the fox-hunting,
theatre-going, ball-frequenting, and card-playing clergy of some
other countries. They are an infinitely better class of men and
ministers.

I know not the comparative numbers of the evangelical and
non-evangelical clergy, but infer from the remarks of the excellent authority last referred to, that they are in the proportion of
about two thirds of the former to one third of the latter. Of
the twenty-one bishops, fourteen are considered, I believe, entirely evangelical, while seven cannot properly be placed in
that category. But all are laboriously occupied in their official
work, and I believe it would be difficult to find an Episcopal
body of equal number, in any other country, surpassing them
in talents, zeal, and piety. To be a bishop with us is quite a
different thing from holding that office where bishops live in
palaces and have princely revenues. Our bishops, to the best
of my knowledge are, without exception, parish priests also, and
can find time to visit their dioceses only by employing an assistant preacher, or rector, to fill their places when they are engaged in their visitations. Their revenues do not much exceed,
in some instances do not equal, those of many of their clergy.

As for the Puseyite or Tractarian doctrines, or whatever they
may be called, I regret to say that five out of the seven high-
church bishops, are supposed either to have *embraced* them, or
at least, to be very favourable to them, while among the clergy
of that party, it is to be feared, that this heresy has made very
considerable progress. But it is thought that among the *people*
there is little disposition to go into such semi-popish doctrines
and practices, and that this new-fangled system will never make
much way in the country at large.

The prospects of the Episcopal Church in the United States are certainly very encouraging. The friend of a learned and able ministry, to form which she has founded colleges and theological institutions; [1] she sees among her clergy not a few men of the highest distinction for talents, for learning, for eloquence, and for piety and zeal. A large number of the most respectable people in all parts of the country, are among her friends and her members. Under such circumstances, if she be true to herself and her proper interests, with God's blessing she cannot but continue to prosper and extend her borders.

CHAPTER III.

THE CONGREGATIONAL CHURCHES.

THE faith of the Congregational churches of America is that common to the evangelical churches of both hemispheres, but their organisation and discipline are, to a considerable extent, peculiar to themselves. A large and most respectable body of dissenters in Great Britain, formerly known as Independents, have of late preferred the name of Congregational; but the differences between American Congregationalism and that which bears the same name in England are, in some respects, highly important. Some of these differences, as well as the points of agreement, will appear in the statements which follow.

New England is the principal seat of the Congregational churches. This is the region which the Puritans planted in the first half of the seventeenth century; and here they have left upon the structure and institutions of society, and upon the opinions and manners of the people, the deepest impression of their peculiar character. In all these States, with the exception of Rhode

---

[1] The founding of the theological seminary of this church, at the city of New York, was greatly promoted by the princely gift of 60,000 dollars, (above £12,000,) by a Mr. Jacob Sherred. Such beneficence deserves to be most gratefully commemorated.

island, the Congregationalists are more numerous than any other
sect; and in Massachusetts and Connecticut they are probably
more numerous than all others united.

Out of New England the Congregationalists have never been
zealous to propagate their own peculiar forms and institutions.
Of the vast multitudes of emigrants from New England into
other States, the great majority have chosen to unite with
churches of the Presbyterian connection, rather than to maintain their own peculiarities at the expense of increased division
in the household of faith. In so doing they have followed the
advice, and fallen in with the arrangements of the associated
bodies of Congregational pastors in New England. Yet in the
States of New York, Ohio, Michigan, and Illinois, many congregations retain the forms of administration which have descended to them from the New England fathers, and refuse to
come into connection with any of the Presbyterian judicatories.
Since the recent division in the Presbyterian church, the number of such congregations is increasing.

The whole number of Congregational churches in the United
States is probably not far from 1500, of which more than 1000
are in New England. The number of ministers is about 1250,
and of members or communicants 160,000. This estimate does
not include those churches originally or nominally congregational, which have rejected what are called the doctrines of the
reformation. These churches are better known by their distinctive title, Unitarian. The churches of this description are
nearly all in Massachusetts; a few are in Maine, two or three in
New Hampshire, one or more in Vermont, as many in Rhode
island, and one, in a state of suspended animation, in Connecticut. Out of New England there are perhaps from six to ten
churches of the same kind, differing very little in their principles, or in their forms, from the Unitarians of England.

The " pilgrims," as they are called,—the little band of exiles
who, having fled from England into Holland, afterwards, in
1620, migrated from Holland to America, and formed at Plymouth the first settlement in New England,—were separatists
from the Church of England; and for the crime of attempting
to set up religious institutions not established by law, they were
compelled to flee from their native country, embarking by stealth

and at night as fugitives from justice, as we have related in detail elsewhere.[1] But those bodies of emigrants, far more numerous and far better prepared and furnished, who, from 1628 onward, planted Salem and Boston, Hartford, and New Haven, —the emigrating Puritans, who were the actual founders of New England, and whose character gave direction to its destiny,— were men who considered themselves as belonging to the Church of England, till their emigration into the American wilderness dissolved the tie. They were Puritans in England, it is true, but the Puritans were a party within the church moving for a purer and more thorough renovation, and not a dissenting body, with institutions of their own, out of the church. The ministers who accompanied the Puritan emigrants, or rather who led them into the wilderness, and who were the first pastors of the churches in New England, were, before their emigration, almost without exception, ministers of the Church of England, educated at the universities, episcopally ordained, regularly inducted into livings; non-conformists, it is true, as refusing to wear the white surplice, to baptise with the sign of the cross, or to use other ceremonies which seemed to them superstitious, but yet exercising their ministry as well as they could under many disabilities and annoyances. Cotton and Wilson of Boston, Hooker and Stone of Hartford, Davenport and Hooke of New Haven— not to extend the catalogue—were all beneficed clergymen before their emigration. These men having emigrated to what were then called "the ends of the earth," and supposing that their expatriation had made them free from that ecclesiastical bondage to which they had been "subjected unwillingly," set themselves to study, with their bibles in their hands, the scriptural model of church order and discipline, and to form their churches after the pattern thus discovered. The result was Congregationalism —a system which differed as much from Brownism on the one hand, as it did from Presbyterianism on the other. After the Puritans in America had set up their church order, the Puritans in England, having become a majority in parliament, attempted to reduce the established church of that nation to the Presbyterian form; and it was not till a still later period that Congre-

[1] See Book ii., chap. 1.

gationalism, or as it was more generally called there, Independency, began to make a figure under the favour of Cromwell.

Thus it appears that Congregationalism in America, instead of being an offset from that in England, is the parent stock. No Congregational church in England, it is believed, dates its existence so far back as the Act of Uniformity in 1662; but many of the New England churches have records of more than 200 years.

It may also be remarked that American Congregationalists are not "dissenters," and never were. In New England the Congregational churches were for a long time the ecclesiastical establishment of the country, as much as the Presbyterian Church is now in Scotland. The whole economy of the civil state was arranged with reference to the welfare of these churches; for the state existed, and the country had been redeemed from the wilderness, for this very purpose. At first no dissenting assembly, not even if adopting the ritual and order of the Church of England, was tolerated. Afterwards dissenters of various names were permitted to worship as they pleased, and were not only released from the obligation to contribute towards the support of the established religion, but so incorporated by law that each congregation was empowered to tax its own members for the support of its own religious ministrations. But still till the principle was adopted that the support of religion is not among the duties of civil government, the Congregationalists maintained this precedence—that every man who did not prefer to contribute to the support of public worship in some other form, was liable to be taxed as a Congregationalist. Thus, though some of the members of one denomination in New England sometimes affect to speak of the Congregationalists around them as "dissenters," those who do so only expose themselves to contempt. Every man sees that if there is such a thing as "dissent" in New England, the Episcopalians, with the Baptists and the Methodists, and all the other sects who have at different times separated themselves from the ecclesiastical order originally established on the soil, and still flourishing there, are the dissenters.

The Congregationalists differ from most other communions, in that they have no common authoritative standards of faith and order, other than the holy scriptures. Yet their system is well known among themselves, and from the beginning they have spared no reasonable pains to make it known to others. John Cotton, the first teacher of the first church in Boston, was the author of a book on "the Keys of the Kingdom of Heaven," published as early as 1644, which in its time was highly esteemed, not only as a controversial defence of Congregationalism, but also as a practical exposition of its principles. John Norton, too, teacher of the church in Ipswich, and afterwards settled in Boston, gave to the reformed churches of Europe in 1646 a full account of the ecclesiastical order of New England, in a Latin epistle to Apollonius, a Dutch minister, who, in the name of the divines of Zealand, had written to America for information on that subject. In 1648, a synod of pastors and churches, called together at Cambridge (a town near Boston) by the invitation of the civil authorities of Massachusetts, drew up a scheme of church discipline, which, from the place at which the synod met, was called the "Cambridge Platform." This platform, however, though highly approved at the time, and still quoted with great deference, was never an authoritative rule; and at this day some of its principles have become entirely obsolete. In 1708, a synod or council, representing the pastors and churches of Connecticut, was assembled at Saybrook by the invitation of the legislature of that colony. By this Connecticut synod a system was formed, differing in some respects from the Cambridge Platform, and designed to supply what was deemed the deficiencies of that older system. The Saybrook Platform was adopted by the churches of Connecticut, and was for many years in that colony a sort of standard recognised by law. Its application was gradually modified, and its stringency relaxed or increased by various local rules and usages, and by successive acts of the legislature; and at the present time the Platform alone is a very inadequate account of the ecclesiastical order of Connecticut.

The following outline, it is believed, will give the reader some idea of the system of New England Congregationalism as it is at this day.

1. The Congregational system recognises no church as an organised body politic, other than a congregation of believers stately assembling for worship and religious communion. It

falls back upon the original meaning of the Greek word ἐκκλησία, and of the Latin *cœtus*.

Popery claims that all Christians constitute one visible organised body, having its officers, its centre, and its head on earth. The first reformers seem to have supposed that each national church has its own independent existence, and is to be considered as *one* organic body, which has somewhere within itself, in the clergy, or in the people, or in the civil government of the nation, a power to regulate and govern all the parts. Congregationalism rejects both the universal church of the Papists, and the national churches which the Reformation established in England, in Scotland, in certain States of Germany and Switzerland, and attempted to establish in France.

Hence the name *Congregational*. Each congregation of believers is a church, and exists not as a subordinate part, or as under the sovereignty of a national church; nor as a part, or under the sovereignty of an organised universal church, but substantively and independently.

Other religious communions in America are organised under the form of national churches, and are named accordingly. Thus we have "the Presbyterian church in the United States," "the Protestant Episcopal Church in the United States," "the Methodist Episcopal Church in the United States,"—but no intelligent person ever speaks of the Congregational Church in the United States, or of the American Congregational Church. Congregationalists always speak of the *churches* of America, or of New England, or of Massachusetts, except when in courtesy to other denominations they use their forms of speech in speaking of them and of their affairs. In like manner the apostles speak of the *churches* of Macedonia, Galatia, or Judea, but never of *church* national or *church* provincial.

2. A church exists by the consent, expressed or implied, of its members to walk together in obedience to the principles of the gospel, and the institutions of Christ. In other words, a church does not derive its existence and rights from some charter conceded to it by another church, or by some higher ecclesiastical judicatory. When any competent number of believers meet together in the name of Christ, and agree, either expressly or by some implication, to commune together statedly in Christian

worship, and in the observance of Christ's ordinances, and to perform toward each other the mutual duties of such Christian fellowship, Christ himself is present with them, (Mat. xviii. 20,) and they receive from Him all the powers and privileges which belong to a church of Christ.

At the orderly formation of a church the neighbouring churches are ordinarily invited to be present by their pastors and delegates, as witnesses of the faith and order of those en-- gaged in the transaction, and that they may extend the "right hand of fellowship," recognising the new church as one of the sisterhood of churches.   The neglect of this, though it might be deemed a breach of courtesy and order, would not, of itself, so vitiate the proceedings as to prevent the new church from being recognised ultimately by the churches of the neighbourhood.

3. The officers of a church are of two sorts—*elders* and *deacons*. When the Congregational churches of New England were first organised two centuries ago, the plan was, that each church should have two or more elders,—one a pastor,—another charged with similar duties under the title of a teacher,—the third or- dained to his office like the other two,—a ruling elder, who, with his colleagues, presided over the discipline and order of the church, but took no part in the official and authoritative preaching of the word, or in the administration of baptism and the Lord's supper.   Thus it was intended that each church should have within itself a presbytery, or clerical body, perpetuating itself by the ordination of those who should be elected to fill successive vacancies.   This plan, however, soon fell into disuse; and now, except in the rare cases of colleagues in office, all the powers and duties of the eldership devolve upon one whose ordinary official title is *pastor*.   The office of deacons, of whom there are from two to six in each church, is to serve at the Lord's table, and to receive, keep, and apply the contributions which the church makes at each communion for the expenses of the table, and for the poor among its own members.   Originally, the dea- cons, as in the primitive churches, received on each Lord's day the contributions of the whole congregation, which were applied by them for the support of the ministers, and for all other eccle- siastical uses.   But at an early period other arrangements were adopted as more convenient.

2 K

4. Admission to membership in the church takes place as follows. The person desiring to unite himself with the church
makes known his wishes to the pastor. The pastor, (or in some
churches the pastor and deacons, or in others, the pastor and 'a
committee appointed for the purpose,) having conversed with the
candidate, and having obtained by conversation and inquiry
satisfactory evidence of his having that spiritual renovation—
that inward living piety, which is considered as the condition of
membership, he is publicly proposed in the congregation on the
Lord's day, as a candidate, so that if there be any objection in
any quarter, it may be seasonably made known. One, two,
three, or four weeks afterward, according to the particular rule
or usage of the church, a vote of the "brotherhood," (or male
members,) is taken on the question, "Shall this person be admitted to membership in the church?" After this, the candidate appears before the congregation, and gives his assent to a
formal profession of the Christian faith read to him by the pastor, and to a form of covenant, by which he engages to give himself up to God as a child and servant, and to Christ as a redeemed sinner, and binds himself to the church conscientiously
to perform all the duties of Christian communion and brotherhood.

5. The censures of the church are pronounced by the pastor
in accordance with a previous vote or determination of the brotherhood. The directions given by Christ in regard to the
treatment of an offending brother (Mat. xviii. 15—17,) are, in
most churches, literally and directly adhered to in all cases.
First, one brother alone confers with the brother offending or
supposed to offend, and this is the first admonition. Then, if
satisfaction has not been obtained, the same qrother takes with
him one or two others, and the effort is repeated,—this is the
second admonition. If this effort is ineffectual the whole case is
reported to the church, i. e. the brotherhood; and if the church
do not obtain satisfaction, in other words, if they find him guilty
of the offence alleged against him, and do not find him at the
same time penitent and ready to confess his fault, they, as a
body, admonish him, and wait for his repentance. If he refuses
to hear the church, that is, if the admonition, after due forbearance, is unsuccessful, the brethren by a vote exclude him from

their fellowship, and the pastor, as Christ's minister, pronounces a public sentence of excommunication.

In some churches a public and notorious scandal is sometimes taken up by the church as a body, without waiting for the first and second admonition in private.   Yet, in such cases, the church commonly acts by a committee, who follow the method just described; first one, and next two or more confer with the offender privately, and then they report to the church what they have done, and with what success.

Some churches have a "standing committee" who, with the pastor, prepare all business of this nature for the action of the church.   Every complaint or accusation against a brother is brought first to this committee, and an attempt is made by them to adjust the difficulty, and to remove the offence without bringing the matter to the church.   If that attempt is unsuccessful, the committee, having investigated the case, having heard the parties and the witnesses, report to the church the facts of the case, with their own opinion as to what ought to be done.   The committee are never invested with the power of inflicting any church censures.

6. The arrangements among the Congregationalists of New England for the support of public worship are in some points peculiar.   The *church*, of which we have thus far spoken exclusively, is entirely a spiritual association.   But it exists in an amicable connection with a civil corporation called the *parish*, or the *ecclesiastical society*, which includes the congregation at large, or more accurately, those adult members of the congregation who consent to be a civil society for the support of public worship. This civil corporation is the proprietor of the house of worship, of the parsonage,[1] if there be one, and sometimes of other endowments, consisting of gifts and legacies which have from time to time been made for the uses for which the society exists.   It can raise funds either by voluntary subscription, or by the sale or rent of the pews in its house of worship, or by assessing a tax upon the estates of its members, in which last case the funds raised can be applied only to the current expenses of the society. It enters into a civil contract with the pastor, and becomes bound

[1] Or manse, as it is more commonly called in Scotland.

in law to render him for his services such compensation as is agreed on between him and them.

A stranger may not easily understand the difference between the church and the society, and the relations of each to the other, without some farther explanation. The church, then, is designed to be a purely spiritual body. The society is a secular body. The church consists only of such as profess to have some experience of spiritual religion. The society consists of all who are willing to unite in the support of public worship,—it being understood only, that no person can thrust himself into its ranks, and obtain a voice in the administration of its affairs, without the express or implied consent of those who are already members. The church watches over the deportment of its members, they being all bound to help each other in the duties of the Christian life; and on proper occasions it censures or absolves from censure those under its care. The society has nothing to do with church censures. To the church belong the ordinances of baptism and the Lord's supper. The society has no concern with the administration of either ordinance. The church has no property except its records, and its sacramental vessels, and the eleemosynary contributions received and dispensed by its deacons. The society is a body incorporated by law for the purpose of holding and managing any property necessary for the support of public worship, or designated by donors for that use. The church has its pastor and deacons, and sometimes its committees, for the management of particular departments of the church business. The society has its clerk, its treasurer, and its prudential committee elected every year; and the pastor of the church is also the minister and religious teacher of the society; and every family of the congregation is considered as belonging to his charge.

The great advantage of this part of the system is, that it gives to every member of the congregation an interest in its prosperity, and a voice in the management of its affairs, while at the same time it gives to the church every desirable facility for keeping itself pure in doctrine and in practice. There is nothing to secularise the church; no temptation to admit irreligious or unconverted men as members for the sake of causing them to take an interest in the support of public worship; and no temptation inducing such men to seek admission to the church. The pastor and the place of worship are as much theirs as if they were communicants.

The pastor, it has been already remarked, is not only the president or bishop of the church, but also the religious teacher and minister of the society. Of course he is elected by a concurrent vote of the two bodies. In this the church generally takes the lead. The candidate is to some extent known to the people, for he has already preached to them on probation. His fitness for the place has been the subject of colloquial discussion in families and among neighbours. The church meets, under the presidency of a neighbouring minister, or perhaps of one of its own deacons, and decides, sometimes by ballot, and sometimes by the lifting up of hands, (χειροτονεᾳ,) to call him to the pastoral office, if the society shall concur. The society, in like manner, meet, and by a vote express their agreement with the church in calling this candidate to take the pastoral charge of the church and society. After this the society determines by vote what salary shall be offered to the candidate on the condition of his accepting the call, and to propose any other stipulations as part of the contract between the people and their pastor. Committees are appointed by the church and by the society to confer with the pastor elect, and to report his answer; and then, if his answer is favourable, to make arrangements for his public induction into office. Sometimes the society leads in the call of a pastor, and the church concurs. If either of these two bodies does not concur with the other—which very rarely happens— the election fails of course, and they wait till another candidate shall unite them.

7. The pastors of neighbouring churches form themselves into bodies for mutual advice and aid in the work of the ministry. This body is called an association. It has its stated meetings at the house of each member in rotation. At every meeting each member is called upon to report the state of his own flock, and to propose any question on which he may desire counsel from his brethren. In these meetings every question which relates to the work of the ministry, or the interest of the churches, is freely discussed. The associations of each State meet annually by their delegates in a general association.

But the most important part of the duties of the association is to examine those who desire to be introduced to the work of the ministry. This is on the principle that, as lawyers are to determine who shall be admitted to practise at the bar, and as physicians determine who shall be received into the ranks of of their profession, so ministers are the fittest judges of the qualications of candidates for the ministry. The candidate, therefore, who has passed through the usual course of studies, liberal [1] and theological, cannot begin to preach—will not be recognised by any church as a candidate—till he has received from some association a certificate of approbation, recommending him to the churches, which is his license to preach the gospel on trial. Such a certificate is not granted without his having passed a close examination, particularly in respect to his piety, his soundness in the faith, and his acquaintance with the system of Christian doctrines.

8. The fathers of the New England churches seem to have acknowledged no minister of the gospel other than the pastor or teacher of some particular church. In their zeal against a hierarchy, they found no place for any minister of Christ not elected by some organised assembly of believers to the work of ruling and teaching in that congregation. The evangelist was thought by them to be like the apostle, only for the primitive age of Christianity. Accordingly, the pastor, when dismissed from his pastoral charge, was no longer a minister of Christ, or competent to perform anywhere any function of the ministry. In connection with this view, it was also held that the power of ordination as well as of election to office resides exclusively in the church, and that if the church has no elders in office, this power of ordination may be exercised either by a committee of the brethren, or by some neighbouring elders, appointed to that function by the church, and acting in its name. But these views were very early superseded. The distinction is now recognised between a minister of the gospel having a pastoral charge, and a minister who sustains no office in any church. The man ordained to the pastoral office is of course ordained to

---

[1] By the word " liberal," as applied to education, is meant that which is obtained in making the curriculum of a college. It is synonymous with " classical."

the work of the ministry; and if circumstances occur which make it expedient for him to lay down his office of pastor, he does not of course lay down the work of the ministry to which he was set apart at his ordination. Sometimes a man, having no call from any church to take the office of a pastor, is set apart to the work of the ministry, that he may be a missionary to the heathen, or that he may labour among the destitute at home, or that he may perform some other evangelical labour for the churches at large. Such ordinations are rare, except in the case of foreign missionaries, or of missionaries to some new region of the country where churches are not yet organised.

Ministers, therefore, whether pastors or evangelists, are now ordained only by the laying on of the hands of those who are before them in the ministry; for though it belongs to the church to make a pastor, it belongs to ministers to make a minister.

9. The reader has already learned that the Congregational churches disavow the name *Independent*. From the beginning they have held and practised the communion of churches. Continually, and by various acts of affection and intercourse, they recognise each other as churches of Christ, and as bound to render to each other, on all proper occasions, an account of their doings. They receive each other's members to occasional communion in ordinances. Members of one church, removing their residence to another church, take from the one a letter of dismission and recommendation, and without that are not received to membership in the other. The principle that, in matters which concern not one church alone, but all the churches of the vicinity, no one church ought to act alone, is continually regarded in practice. The ordination or installation of a pastor, and in like manner his dismission from his office even by the mutual consent of him and his flock, never takes place without the intervention of a council of pastors and delegates from neighbouring churches. When any act of a church is grievous to a portion of its members—when any contention or difficulty has arisen within a church which cannot otherwise be adjusted—when a member excommunicated deems himself unjustly treated, a council of the neighbouring churches is called to examine the case, and to give advice; and the advice thus given is rarely if ever disregarded. If a church is deemed guilty of any gross

dereliction of the faith, or of Christian discipline, any neighbouring church may expostulate with it as one brother expostu-
lates with another, and when expostulation proves insufficient,
a council of the neighbouring churches is called to examine the
matter; and from the church which obstinately refuses to listen
to the advice given by such a council, the neighbouring churches
withdraw their communion.

In Connecticut the communion of the churches has been practised for about 130 years in " consociations," or voluntary con-
federations of from six to twenty contiguous churches, binding
themselves to call upon each other in all cases of difficulty which
require a council. Elsewhere councils of churches, though ordinarily selected from the immediate vicinity, are selected at the
discretion of the church by which the council is convened.

Under this ecclesiastical system the churches of New England have, it is believed by many, enjoyed for more than two
centuries a more continued purity of doctrine, and fidelity of
discipline, and a more constant prosperity of spiritual religion,
than has been enjoyed by any equal body of churches, for so
long a time, since the days of the apostles. No religious communion in America has done more for religion and morals among
its own people, more for the advancement of learning and general
education, or more for the diffusion of the gospel at home and
abroad. None has been more characterised by that large and
manly spirit which values the common Christianity of all who
" hold the Head," more than the peculiar forms and institutions
of its own sect.

The highest ecclesiastical bodies by which the Congregational
churches in the United States are, in a sense, united or associated, are: the general associations of Connecticut, Massachusetts, New Hampshire, and New York; the general convention
of Vermont, the general consociation of Rhode island, and the
general conference of Maine. These bodies meet annually, and
they maintain the " bond of fellowship" by sending delegates to
each other. It must not be understood that all the evangelical
Congregational churches in the States just named are " associated," that is, connected with the inferior associations, and
through them with the " general association," " general convention," " general consociation," or " general conference" of the

State in which they are situated. But the number not thus
united with their sister churches is not great. The Congregational churches in Ohio, Michigan, Illinois, and the Territories
of Wisconsin and Iowa are not yet sufficiently numerous to
render the organisation of general associations convenient, or else
other causes have prevented this measure from being adopted.

The Congregationalists in New England have eight colleges,
five theological seminaries and faculties, and about 300 students
in theology.   In the other States where they exist, they give
their aid to the Presbyterian literary and theological institutions.

CHAPTER IV.

THE REGULAR BAPTIST CHURCHES.

NEXT to the Episcopalians and the Congregationalists, the Baptists are the oldest of the various branches of the Christian
church in the United States.   And if we were to include under
this name all who hold that immersion is the true and only
scriptural mode of baptism, without reference to the orthodoxy
of their faith, we should find that they are also the largest
denomination in that country.   But if we separate from them a
portion at least of those minor bodies which, though agreeing
with them on that point, differ both as to the proper mode of baptism and its subjects, and also in church government, we shall
find that they are not equal in number to the Methodists.

In their church government the Baptists of all denominations are Independents, that is, each church is wholly independent, as respects its interior government, even of those other
churches with which it may be associated in ecclesiastical union.
Each separate church possesses and exercises the right of licen-
sing or granting permission to preach the gospel, and of ordaining elders or presbyters clothed with all the functions of the
ministerial office.   This is the old ground at first maintained
by the Independents.   The Congregationalists, spoken of in the
last chapter, seem to be Independents in theory, but in spirit

and practice they are very nearly Presbyterians, and have often been called Congregational Presbyterians.

Delegates from different Baptist churches hold public meetings for purposes of mutual counsel and improvement, but not for the general government of the whole body, all right of interference in the concerns of individual churches being disclaimed by these ecclesiastical assemblies. A very large majority of our evangelical Baptist churches are associated by their pastors in district associations and state conventions, which meet every year for promoting missions, education, and other benevolent objects. A general convention, called the Baptist General Convention of the United States, meets likewise every three years, the last always appointing the place of meeting for the next after. The general convention is restricted by its constitution to the promotion of foreign missions. It held its first meeting in 1814. But within the last ten years a home missionary society, a general tract society, and several societies for the education of poor and pious youths having talents adapted for the ministry, have sprung up in the Baptist body, and already exert a wide and happy influence.

The Baptists, like the Congregationalists, make it a fundamental principle to adopt the Bible as their only confession of faith. Yet most, if not all, of the evangelical churches that bear the name, find it convenient in practice to have a creed or summary of doctrine, and these creeds, although they may vary in expression, all agree in the main, and, with few exceptions, among the Regular and Associated Baptists are decidedly Calvinistic.

A few years ago, the Baptist convention of the State of New Hampshire adopted a declaration of faith, consisting of sixteen articles, and a form of church covenant, which they recommended to the Baptist churches of that State, and which are supposed to express, with little variation, the general sentiments of the whole body of orthodox Baptists in the United States. The subjects of these articles are: Of the scriptures; the true God; the fall of man; the way of salvation; justification; the freeness of salvation; grace in regeneration; God's purpose of grace; perseverance of saints; harmony of the law and gospel; a gospel church; baptism and the Lord's supper; the Christian sabbath; civil government; the righteous and the wicked; the world to come.

On all these subjects, excepting baptism, these articles express the doctrines held by the Calvinistic churches of all denominations. The holy Bible is pronounced to have been "written by men divinely inspired,"—"has God for its Author, salvation for its end, and truth, without any mixture of error, for its matter,"—"is the true centre of Christian union, and the supreme standard by which all human conduct, creeds, and opinions should be tried." The "true God," it is affirmed, is "revealed under the personal and relative distinctions of the Father, the Son, and the Holy Ghost; equal in every divine perfection, and executing distinct and harmonious offices in the great work of redemption." "The salvation of sinners" is taught to be "wholly of grace, through the mediatorial offices of the Son of God, who took upon him our nature, yet without sin; honoured the law by his personal obedience, and made atonement for our sins by his death; being risen from the dead, he is now enthroned in heaven; and uniting in his wonderful person the tenderest sympathies with divine perfections, is every way qualified to be a suitable, a compassionate, and an all-sufficient Saviour." "Justification," it is affirmed, "consists in the pardon of sin and the promise of eternal life," and "is bestowed not in consideration of any works of righteousness which we have done, but solely of his (Christ's) own redemption and righteousness."

On the FREENESS OF SALVATION it is taught "that the blessings of salvation are made free to all by the gospel; that it is the immediate duty of all to accept them by a cordial and obedient faith; and that nothing prevents the salvation of the greatest sinner on earth, except his own voluntary refusal to submit to the Lord Jesus Christ; which refusal will subject him to an aggravated condemnation." "Regeneration consists in giving a holy disposition to the mind, and is effected in a manner above our comprehension by the Holy Spirit, so as to secure our voluntary obedience to the gospel; and its proper evidence is found in the holy fruit which we bring forth to the glory of God."

On the subject of GOD'S PURPOSE OF GRACE it is stated: "That election is the gracious purpose of God, according to which he regenerates, sanctifies, and saves sinners"—is "consistent with the free agency of man"—"comprehends all the means in connection with the end"—"is a most gracious display of God's sovereign goodness"—"utterly excludes boasting, and promotes humility, prayer, praise, trust in God"—"encourages the use of means in the highest degree"—"is ascertained in its effects in all who believe"—"is the foundation of Christian assurance"— and that "to ascertain it with regard to ourselves, demands and deserves our utmost diligence."

On the subject of the PERSEVERANCE OF THE SAINTS it is affirmed: "That such only are real believers as endure unto the end; that their persevering attachment to Christ is the grand mark which distinguishes them from superficial professors; that a special providence watches over their welfare; and they are kept by the power of God through faith unto salvation."

According to this confession of faith, "a visible church of Christ is a congregation of baptised believers, associated by covenant in the faith and fellowship of the gospel, observing the ordinances of Christ; governed by his laws; and exercising the gifts, rights, and privileges, invested in them by his word; that its only proper officers are bishops or pastors, and deacons, whose qualifications, claims, and duties, are defined in the epistles to Timothy and Titus."—And "Christian baptism is the immersion of a believer in water, in the name of the Father, the Son, and the Holy Ghost; to show forth a solemn and beautiful emblem of our faith in a crucified, buried, and risen Saviour, with its purifying power," and "is a pre-requisite to the privileges of a church relation."

The "CHRISTIAN SABBATH is the first day of the week," and "is to be kept sacred to religious purposes;"—"civil government is of divine appointment for the interests and good order of society; and that magistrates are to be prayed for, conscientiously honoured and obeyed, except in things opposed to the will of our Lord Jesus Christ, who is the only Lord of the conscience, and Prince of the kings of the earth."

And finally, on the subject of the WORLD TO COME, it is taught: "That the end of this world is approaching; that at the last day Christ will descend from heaven, and raise the dead from the grave to final retribution; that a solemn separation will then

take place; that the wicked will be adjudged to endless punishment, and the righteous to endless joy; and that this judgment
will fix for ever the final state of men in heaven or hell on principles of righteousness."

The covenant which follows this declaration of faith expresses
in a few brief articles the determination of those who enter
it: "to walk in brotherly love"—"to exercise a mutual care, as
members one of another, to promote the growth of the whole
body in Christian knowledge, holiness, and comfort"—"to uphold the public worship of God, and the ordinances of his house"
—"not to omit closet and family religion," or the "training up
of children and those under their care"—to "walk circumspectly
in the world," and be as the "light of the world, and the salt of
the earth,"—and finally, to "exhort" and "admonish one
another."

Such, in substance, is the "Declaration of Faith and Covenant," adopted, as I have said, by the Baptist convention of New
Hampshire a few years ago, and no doubt substantially exhibiting the doctrines held by the great body of the Regular and
Associated Baptists throughout the United States. It will be
perceived that it is moderately Calvinistic, and, indeed, to one
or other shade of Calvinism all the Regular Baptists in America
adhere. Part of their body, particularly in the southern and
south-western States, are regarded as Calvinists of the highest
school. Their doctrinal views probably coincide with those of
Dr. Gill more than with those of any other writer. But a far
greater number of their ministers follow in the main the views
of Andrew Fuller,—views which, take them all in all, form one
of the best systems of theology to be found in the English
language.

Baptist churches have increased in the United States with
great rapidity, particularly within the last fifty or sixty years.
For although they date from Roger Williams, formerly mentioned,[1] who having changed his sentiments on the subject of
baptism a few years after his arrival in Massachusetts bay, was
the first Baptist preacher, and founded the first Baptist church
in America, at Providence, in 1639; it was long before his fol-

---

[1] Book ii. chap. 4.

lowers made much progress beyond Rhode island. This arose, it would appear, from their being violently opposed in most of the other colonies, both to the north and to the south. In Massachusetts they were at first "fined," "whipped," and "imprisoned," but though they afterwards obtained liberty of worship there, they had but eighteen churches at the commencement of the Revolutionary war. In Virginia, where they also met with much opposition and bitter persecution,[1] they had scarcely, at that epoch, obtained any footing at all. In fact, with the exception of Rhode island, Pennsylvania, and perhaps Delaware, they almost no where enjoyed perfect freedom from molestation until the country had achieved its independence by a struggle in which the Baptists, to say the least, in proportion to their numbers, took as prominent a part as any other religious body in the land.

But slow as was their progress before the Revolution, it has been much otherwise since. This will be seen from the following statement taken from the very complete "View of the Baptist Interest in the United States," prepared by the Rev. Rufus Babcock, junior, D.D. of Poughkeepsie, New York, and published in the American Quarterly Register, in the years 1840 and 1841. The number of Baptist ministers, churches, and members, at five different epochs, are stated there as follows:

	CHURCHES.	MINISTERS.	MEMBERS.
In 1784	471	424	35,101
1790-92	891	1150	65,345
1810-12	2164	1605	172,972
1832	5320	3618	384,920
1840	7766	5204	570,758

Dr. Babcock estimates the superannuated ministers and others who, from various causes, are not actively engaged in the ministry, at about a seventh of the number in the above table. Deducting these, and another seventh for the licentiates, who also are included, we shall have 3717 ordained ministers actually employed in 1840; which is, upon an average, less than one minister for two churches. Including the licentiates, who almost all preach more or less regularly, and many of them in vacant churches, the number of preachers for that year was 4460.

[2] It happened often in that colony that their preachers were cast into prison for preaching the gospel. And often they were to be seen preaching from the jail-windows to the people assembled outside!

Dr. Babcock makes a curious estimate of the probable proportion of the inhabitants in each State, supposed to be directly
under the influence of Baptist preaching. Without going unnecessarily into his details, we find as the result of his researches,
that in 1840 these amounted to a fifth of the population in
Massachusetts, and to a fourth in Virginia, being the two provinces in which the Baptists were most persecuted; whereas in
Rhode island which was their asylum, the proportion rises to
two-fifths or nearly a half.

In this enumeration Dr. Babcock includes some of the smaller
Baptist sects, such as those of the *six principles*, who hold as
their creed the six principles mentioned in the epistle to the
Hebrews. (chap. vi. ver. 1, 2.)   These, in 1841, had sixteen
churches, ten ministers, and 2017 members.   But the shades of
difference in doctrine are not of much consequence so far as
regards the vital interests of the truth.

Above 3,000,000 of souls, being between a fifth and a sixth
of the entire population of the United States, and embracing a
respectable share of the wealth, talent, learning, and influence of
the country, are supposed to be connected with the Regular
Baptists.   A large and important part of their churches lies in
the southern States, and includes many slaves and slave-owners.
With the exception of the Methodists they form by far the
most numerous and influential body of Christians in that section
of the country.

A strong prejudice against learning in the ministry unhappily
prevailed at one time in this body, particularly in the southern
States, and this we might ascribe to several causes.   In the
religious denomination, which in Virginia, and the other southern
colonies they considered their greatest enemy, learning was too
often associated with want of piety, and sometimes with open
irreligion.   The effects of this prejudice have been very injurious, and are felt to this day in the Baptist churches throughout the southern and south-western, and even to a considerable
extent even in the middle States.   But a brighter day has
dawned.   Great efforts have been made by zealous and devoted
men among them, to establish colleges and theological seminaries, with what success we have stated elsewhere.   I know not
how many young men are preparing for the ministry, in theo-

logical and other institutions, but ten years ago they were estimated at 300 in New England, and about twice that number in
other parts of the United States.

We have already spoken of the efforts of the Baptists in the
Bible, tract, Sunday school, and home missionary causes, and
shall have yet to speak of what they are doing in the department of foreign missions.

We shall conclude by remarking, that although not a third
perhaps of the ministers of this denomination of Christians have
been educated at colleges and theological seminaries, they comprehend, nevertheless, a body of men who, in point of talent,
learning, and eloquence, as well as devoted piety, have no supe-
riors in the country, and even among those who can make no
pretensions to profound learning, not a few are men of respectable general attainments, and much efficiency in their Master's
work.

Notices will be given of the smaller Baptist denominations in
their proper place, and they will afterwards be grouped together
when we come to arrange in families the various religious bodies
constituting the great " household of faith " in the United States.

CHAPTER V.

THE PRESBYTERIAN CHURCH.

In speaking of the Congregational churches we entered into a
full analysis of their organisation, because they comprise most
of the great features of all the churches founded on what are
called Independent principles, forming the basis of the churches
of several other denominations, particularly the Baptists.   For
a like reason in speaking of the Presbyterian Church, we shall
go into considerable detail in speaking of its principles and
church organisation, so as to save repetition when we come to
notice other churches having the same principles and essentially
the same organisation.

The Presbyterian Church is so called because it is governed

by presbyters and not by prelates. The name, therefore, applies
to any church organised and governed on that principle. Usage,
however, has confined it in America to one of several churches,
who agree in believing that the government of the church
belongs to its elders or presbyters. The Dutch Reformed
Church, the German Reformed, the Scotch Secession churches,
are as truly presbyterian as that denomination to which the
name is now, among us, almost exclusively applied.

Presbyterians believe that the apostles in organizing the
church were accustomed, in every city or place where a congregation was gathered, to appoint a number of officers for the
instruction and spiritual government of the people, and for the
care of the sick and poor. The former class of these officers
were called presbyters, the latter deacons. Of these presbyters
some laboured in word and doctrine, others in the oversight and
discipline of the flock, according to their gifts, or to their designation when ordained. As the terms bishop and presbyter were
indiscriminately used to designate the spiritual instructors and
governors of the congregation, in every church there came to
be three classes of officers, which are denominated the bishops
or pastors or teaching presbyters, the ruling presbyters, and
the deacons.

The Presbyterian churches with us are organised on this plan.
Each congregation has its bishop or pastor, its ruling elders, and
its deacons, except in cases where the duties of the last mentioned
class are assumed by the elders. The duty of the pastor is to
preach the word, to administer the sacraments, to superintend
the religious instruction of the young, and to have the general
oversight of his flock as to their spiritual concerns. He is
always chosen by the people over whom he is to exercise his
office. It will appear, however, from the following account of
the method pursued in the selection and installation of a pastor,
that the choice of the people is subject to several important limitations. When a congregation is vacant the people assemble,
after due notice, to choose a pastor. This meeting must be presided over by an ordained minister invited for that purpose, who
must endorse the minutes of their proceedings, and certify their
regularity. If a majority of the qualified members of the congregation, *i. e.* of those who contribute to the support of the

2 L

minister, agree upon a candidate, a call is made out in the following terms, viz.

"The congregation of A. B. being, on sufficient grounds, well satisfied of the ministerial qualifications of you, C. D., and having hopes, from our past experience of your labours, that your ministrations in the gospel will be profitable to our spiritual interests, do earnestly call and desire you to undertake the pastoral office in the said congregation; promising you, in the discharge of your duty, all proper support, encouragement, and obedience in the Lord. And that you may be free from worldly cares and avocations, we hereby promise and oblige ourselves to pay to you the sum of ————— in regular quarterly payments, during the time of your being and continuing the pastor of this church. In testimony whereof we have respectively subscribed our names."

This call is taken to the presbytery under whose care the congregation is placed, and the presbytery decide whether it shall be presented to the person to whom it is addressed. If, in their judgment, there exists any sufficient reason for withholding it, it is returned to the people, who must then proceed to a new election. If the person called belongs to the same presbytery to which the congregation is attached, or is a licentiate under their care, they put the call into his hands and wait for his answer to it. But if he belongs to a different presbytery, they give the congregation leave to prosecute it before that body, who have the right to decide whether it shall be presented to the candidate or not.

It thus appears that no man can become the pastor of a congregation under the care of a presbytery whom they do not deem to be a sound and competent minister of the gospel. And in order to enable them to judge intelligently on this point, before proceeding to his ordination they examine him "as to acquaintance with experimental religion, as to his knowledge of philosophy, theology, ecclesiastical history, the Greek and Hebrew languages, and such other branches of learning as to the presbytery may appear requisite; and as to his knowledge of the constitution, the rules and discipline of the church." Should the candidate be found deficient in any of these particulars, it is the right and duty of the presbytery to reject him. But if they are satisfied with his ministerial qualifications, they appoint a time for his ordination in the presence of the people. When the time appointed has arrived, and the presbytery convened, a member appointed for the purpose preaches a sermon suitable for the occasion, and then proposes to the candidate the following questions: viz.

"Do you believe the scriptures of the Old and New Testaments to be the word of God, the only infallible rule of faith and practice?

"Do you sincerely receive and adopt the Confession of Faith of this church as containing the system of doctrine taught in the holy scriptures?

"Do you approve of the government and discipline of the Presbyterian Church in these United States?

"Do you promise subjection to your brethren in the Lord?

"Have you been induced, as far as you know your own heart, to seek the office of the holy ministry from love to God, and a sincere desire to promote his glory in the gospel of his Son?

"Do you promise to be zealous and faithful in maintaining the truths of the gospel, and the purity and peace of the church, whatever persecution or opposition may arise unto you on that account?

"Do you engage to be faithful and diligent in the exercise of all private and personal duties, which become you as a Christian and as a minister of the gospel; as well as in all relative duties, and the public duties of your office; endeavouring to adorn the profession of the gospel by your conversation, and walking with exemplary piety before the flock over which God has made you overseer?

" Are you now willing to take the charge of this congregation, agreeably to your declaration at accepting their call? And do you promise to discharge the duties of a pastor to them as God shall give you strength?''

The presiding minister then puts the following questions to the congregation:

"Do you, the people of this congregation, continue to profess your readiness to receive ————— whom you have called to be your minister?

"Do you promise to receive the word of truth from his mouth

with meekness and love; and to submit to him in the due exercise of discipline?

"Do you promise to encourage him in his arduous labours, and to assist his endeavours for your instruction and spiritual edification?

"And do you engage to continue to him while he is your pastor, that competent worldly maintenance which you have promised; and whatever else you may see needful for the honour of religion and his comfort among you?"

These questions being answered in the affirmative, the presbytery proceed to ordain the candidate with prayer and the laying on of hands.

The elders are regarded as the representatives of the people, and are chosen by them for the discipline of the church in connection with the pastor. They must be made members of the church in full communion, and when elected are required to profess their faith in the scriptures as the only infallible rule of faith and practice, their adoption of the Westminster Confession as containing the system of doctrine, and their approbation of the government and discipline of the Presbyterian church; and the members of the church are called upon publicly to acknowledge and receive them as ruling elders, and to promise to yield them all that honour, encouragement, and obedience in the Lord, to which their office, according to the word of God, and the constitution of the church, entitles them. The pastor and elders constitute what is called the session, which is the governing body in each congregation. They are authorised to inquire into the knowledge and Christian conduct of the members of the church; to admit to the sacraments those whom, upon examination, they find to possess the requisite knowledge and piety; to call before them offenders, being members of their own church; to decide cases of discipline, and to suspend or excommunicate those who are judged deserving of such censure. It is their duty, also, to keep a register of marriages, of baptisms, of those admitted to the Lord's supper; and of the death or removal of church members.

All the proceedings of the session are subject to the review of the Presbytery, and may be brought before that body in several different ways. The session is required to keep a record of their official acts, and this record is laid before the presbytery, for examination, twice every year. Should any thing appear on the record which, in the judgment of the presbytery is irregular, inexpedient, or unjust, they have authority to see the matter rectified. Or, if any one feels himself aggrieved by a decision of the session, he has the right of appeal to the presbytery, where the case may be reviewed. Or, if any member or members of the inferior court, or any one affected by their decision, consider their action irregular or unjust, he or they have the right of complaint, which subjects the whole matter to a revision in the higher judicatory.

The deacons are not members of the session, and consequently have no part in the government of the church. It is their duty to take charge of the poor, to receive and appropriate the moneys collected for the support or relief of the sick or needy.

A Presbyterian church or congregation has thus a complete organisation within itself; but it is not an independent body. It is a part of an extended whole, living under the same ecclesiastical constitution, and therefore subject to the inspection and control of the presbytery, whose business it is to see that the standard of doctrine and rules of discipline are adhered to by all the separate churches under its care.

This superior body, the presbytery, consists of all the pastors or ordained ministers, and one elder from each session, within certain geographical limits. There must be at least three ministers to constitute a presbytery, but the maximum is not fixed. Hence our presbyteries vary from three to sixty or eighty members. It is the bond of union between the ministers and churches within its limits. Among its most important duties is the examination and ordination of candidates for the holy ministry. Every such candidate is required to place himself under the care of that presbytery within whose bounds he ordinarily resides. He must produce satisfactory testimonials of his good moral character, and of his being in full communion with the church. It is made the duty of the presbytery to examine him as to his experimental knowledge of religion, and as to his motives in seeking the sacred office. And it is recommended that the candidate be required to produce a diploma of the degree of bachelor or master of arts, from some college or university, or at least, authentic testimonials of his having gone through a regular course of academic instruction. The presbytery itself, however, is required to examine him as to his knowledge of the Latin, Greek, and Hebrew languages, and on the subjects embraced in the usual course of study pursued in our colleges. He must, also, present a Latin exercise on some point in theology; a critical exposition of a passage of scripture, as a test of his ability to expound the original text; a lecture or homiletic exposition of some portion of the word of God; and a popular sermon. If these exercises and examinations are past to the satisfaction of the presbytery, the candidate is required to answer affirmatively the following questions: viz.

" Do you believe the scriptures of the Old and New Testaments to be the word of God, the only infallible rule of faith and practice?

" Do you sincerely receive and adopt the Confession of Faith of this church, as containing the system of doctrine taught in the holy scriptures?

" Do you promise to study the peace, purity, and unity of the church?

" Do you promise to submit yourself, in the Lord, to the government of this presbytery, or of any other presbytery in the bounds of which you may be called?"

The presbytery then proceed to his licensure in the following words, viz., " In the name of the Lord Jesus Christ, and by that authority which he has given to his church for its edification, we do license you to preach the gospel wherever God, in his providence, may call you, and for this purpose, may the blessing of God rest upon you, and the Spirit of Christ fill your heart. Amen."

This licensure does not confer the ministerial office, or give authority either to administer the sacraments, or to take part in the government of the church. It is merely a declaration that the recipient, in the judgment of the presbytery, is qualified to preach the gospel and to become a pastor. It is from this class of probationers that the congregations select and call their ministers; and when a licentiate receives a call to a particular church, he is renewedly examined on all the subjects above specified before he is ordained.

It is by means of these examinations, and by requiring assent to the Confession of Faith, that the Presbyterian church in America has endeavoured to secure competent learning and orthodoxy in its ministry; and it is a historical fact, which ought to be gratefully acknowledged, that since the organisation of the church in that country, a century and a half ago, the great body of its ministers have been liberally educated men; and it is also a fact that no man who has avowedly rejected the Calvinistic system of doctrine, has been allowed to retain his standing as a minister of that church. Its history contains not the record of even one Arminian or Pelagian, much less Socinian, as an approved or recognised minister in its connection. Some few instances have occurred of the avowal of such sentiments, but they have uniformly been followed by the ejection from the ministry of those who entertained them. And more recently, the promulgation by a part of its ministers of doctrines at variance with its standards, though those doctrines were not considered by their advocates as involving a rejection of the Calvinistic system, was one of the principal causes of the separation of the body into two distinct organisations. So also with regard to learning, when a portion of the church in the western, and then more recently settled parts of the country, insisted on introducing into the ministry men who had not received a liberal education, they were required to separate and form a denomination of their own. From their peculiar circumstances, such separations involve no civil penalties or forfeitures. If any set of men think that the interests of religion can be better promoted by an imperfectly educated and more numerous ministry, than by a smaller body of better educated men, nothing prevents them from acting on their convictions and organising on their own principles. By so doing, however, they of necessity separate from a church which makes a liberal education a requisite for admission into the sacred office. In like manner, if any man or set of men renounce the doctrines of the Westminster Confession, they are at perfect liberty to preach what they believe to be true, but they must not expect to remain ministers of a church in which that Confession is the standard of doctrine. External union has indeed been sacrificed by acting on this principle, but spiritual fellowship has been rather promoted than violated thereby, as neither party, in such cases, have excommunicated the other. And there is no hardship or injustice in the course above indicated, since the church is in one sense a voluntary society whose terms of ministerial communion are known to the world; and those who disapprove of its doctrines need not, and in general do not, seek admission to its ministry. There are other denominations within whose pale they can minister without objection or difficulty.

It follows from what has been said, that it is the duty of the presbytery to exercise a watch and care over its own members. Every minister at his ordination promises subjection to his brethren in the Lord, that is, he promises to recognise the authority of the presbytery and the other ecclesiastical bodies, as exercised agreeably to the constitution of the church, and to submit to their decisions. He receives his office from the hands of the presbytery, and it is in the power of that body, on sufficient grounds, and after a fair trial, to suspend or depose him. It is, however, provided that no charge shall be received against a minister of the gospel, unless on the responsibility of some competent accuser, or on the ground of public scandal. When a minister is accused either of error in doctrine or immorality of conduct, he is regularly cited to answer the charge; he is informed of the witnesses who are to appear against him, and full time is allowed for the preparation of his defence. In short, all the formalities which are the safeguards of justice are scrupulously regarded so as to secure a fair trial to any accused member.

The presbytery, then, is the court of review and control over all the sessions of the several churches within its bounds. It is the supervising body, bound to see that the pastors are faithful in the discharge of their duty; having also authority to examine, license, and ordain candidates for the ministry; to instal them over the congregations to which they may be called; to exercise discipline over its own members; and, in general, to order whatever relates to the spiritual welfare of the congregations under its care.

With the presbytery the organisation of a Presbyterian church is complete. So long as the number of ministers and churches is so small that they can conveniently meet at the same time and place, there is no need of any superior body. The formation of synods and a general assembly becomes necessary only when the church is too large to be comprised under one presbytery. It is desirable that the governing body should meet, at least, twice annually. This cannot be done when the members of that body are very numerous, and scattered over a great extent of country. To remedy this inconvenience, instead of one presbytery embracing all the ministers and churches, several are formed, each exercising its functions within prescribed limits, and all meeting annually as a synod. A synod is therefore nothing but a larger presbytery. Agreeably to our system, it must be composed of at least three presbyteries. All the ministers within its bounds, and one elder from each session, have a right to act as members. From 1705 to 1716 there was but one presbytery. The number of ministers and churches had, at the latter date, so increased that three presbyteries were formed, who continued to meet as a synod until 1787, when convenience suggested the division of the body into four synods, under a representative assembly, composed of delegates from all the presbyteries. Under the present system, the synod is a body that intervenes between the presbytery and general assembly. It has power to receive and determine all appeals regularly brought up from the presbyteries; to decide all references made to them; to review the records of presbyteries, and to approve or censure them; to redress whatever has been done by the presbyteries contrary to order; to take effectual care that presbyteries observe the constitution of the church; to erect new presbyteries, and unite or divide those which were before erected; and, generally, to take such order with respect to the presbyteries, sessions, and people under their care, as may be in conformity with the word of God and the established rules, and which tend to promote the edification of the church; and, finally, to propose to the general assembly, for their adoption, such measures as may be of common advantage to the whole church.

The general assembly is the highest judicatory of the Presbyterian church, and the bond of union between its several parts. It is composed of an equal delegation of ministers and elders from each presbytery. Every presbytery sends at least one minister and one elder; if it consists of more than twenty-four members, it sends two ministers and two elders, and so on in like proportion.

The assembly has power to determine all appeals and references regularly brought before it from inferior judicatories; to review the records of the several synods; to give its advice and instructions in all cases submitted to it,—and constitutes the bond of union, peace, correspondence, and mutual confidence among all the churches under its care. To it also belongs to decide all controversies respecting doctrines and discipline; to reprove, warn, or bear testimony against error in doctrine or immorality in practice; to erect new synods; to superintend the whole church; to correspond with foreign churches; to suppress schismatical contentions and disputations; and, in general, to recommend and attempt reformation of manners, and the promotion of charity, truth, and holiness, through all the churches under its care.

So long as all the ministers of the church were united in one synod, that body had a right to make rules which had the force of constitutional regulations obligatory on all the presbyteries. This was reasonable and safe as long as the whole church met in one body, as its rules were the voluntarily imposed conditions of membership. But since the formation of the general assembly, composed not of all the ministers, but of a comparatively small delegation from each presbytery, this power no longer belongs to this highest judicatory. The assembly cannot alter the constitution of the church. Every proposition, involving such change, must first be sent down to the presbyteries, and receive the sanction of a majority of them, before it becomes obligatory on the churches.

Having given this brief exhibition of the principles of church government adopted by Presbyterians in the United States, it is necessary to advert to their doctrinal standards. The Confession of Faith and the Larger and Shorter Catechisms prepared by the assembly of divines at Westminster were, as is well known, adopted by the Church of Scotland, and the same symbols have from the beginning constituted the creed of the Presbyterian Church in this country. The formal adopting act was passed by the synod in 1729. In that act we find the following language, viz., " We do agree that all the ministers of this synod, or that shall hereafter be admitted into this synod, shall declare their agreement in, and approbation of, the Confession of Faith, with the Larger and Shorter Catechisms of the assembly of divines at Westminster, as being, in all necessary articles, good forms of sound words and systems of Christian doctrine; and do also adopt the said Confession and Catechisms as the confession of our faith." On the same page of the records is found the following minute, viz., " All the members of the synod now present, except one who declared himself not prepared, [but who at a subsequent meeting gave in his adhesion,] after proposing all the scruples that any of them had to make against any of the articles or expressions in the Confession of Faith, and Larger and Shorter Catechisms of the assembly of divines at Westminster, have unanimously agreed in the solution of those scruples, and in declaring the said Confessions and Catechisms to be the confession of their faith; except only some clauses in the twentieth and twenty-third chapters, concerning which the synod do unanimously declare that they do not receive those articles in any such sense as to suppose the civil magistrate hath a controlling power over synods, with respect to the exercise of their ministerial authority, or power to persecute any for their religion, or in any sense contrary to the Protestant succession to the throne of Great Britain. The synod observing the unanimity, peace, and unity in all their consultations and deliberations in the affair of the Confession, did unanimously agree in solemn prayer and praise."

It appears that some doubt arose whether the expression, " essential and necessary articles " in the above acts, was to be understood of articles essential to the system of doctrine contained in the Confession of Faith, or of articles essential to Christianity. To remove this ambiguity, the synod, the following year, unanimously adopted the following minute, viz., " Whereas some persons have been dissatisfied with the manner of wording our last year's agreement about the Confession, supposing some expressions not sufficiently obligatory upon intrants; overtured that the synod do now declare that they understand those clauses which respect the admission of intrants, in such a sense as to oblige them to receive and adopt the Confession and Catechisms, at their admission, in the same manner and as fully as the members of the synod as were then present;" that is, they were to adopt it without exception, save the clauses relating to the powers of civil magistrates in matters of religion.

When the general assembly was formed in 1787, the Confession of Faith and Catechisms were revised, and those parts which relate to the power of the magistrates modified, and ever since it has without alteration been the standard of doctrine in the Presbyterian Church, and every minister, as already stated, is required at his ordination to declare that he "sincerely receives and adopts the Confession of Faith of this church as containing the system of doctrines taught in the holy scriptures."

We have elsewhere stated how church property is held; how churches are erected; how the salaries of ministers are raised; and how feeble churches are aided by home missionary societies, boards of missions, &c.

We shall now proceed to give a very slight sketch of the history of the Presbyterian Church in the United States. The first presbytery, consisting of seven ministers, and representing about the same number of churches, was organised in Philadelphia in 1705; at present the number of ministers is not far from 2600, and that of the churches is about 3500. This extraordinary increase can only be explained by a reference to the settlement of the country. The New England States were settled by English Puritans, many of whom, especially those who arrived about the commencement of the civil war, as well as those who came after the Restoration, were Presbyterians; New York was settled by the Dutch, who were also Presbyterians; but these classes have retained their own separate ecclesiastical organisation, though both have contributed largely to the increase of the Presbyterian Church. The Germans, also, who settled in great numbers in Pennsylvania, and in the northern portions of Virginia, have in like manner formed extended churches of their own; yet they also have, in many cases, contributed to swell the number of American Presbyterians. The French emigrants, who came to this country towards the close of the seventeenth century, were almost all Protestants and Presbyterians. These are the collateral sources whence the Presbyterian Church in America derived the materials of its growth.

From the beginning of the last century to the Declaration of Independence, there was a constant current of emigration of Presbyterians from Scotland, and still more from the north of Ireland. These emigrants settled principally in New Jersey, Pennsylvania, in the central portions of Virginia, and in North and South Carolina. Since the commencement of the present century, the same process has been going on. The central and western portions of the State of New York, forty years ago, was a wilderness; it has now a population of more than 1,000,000 of people of European descent. The western States in the Valley of the Mississippi, then in the almost exclusive possession of the Indians, have now a like population of more than 6,000,000. The progress of the Presbyterian Church, therefore, although rapid, has not been out of proportion to the progress of the country. On the contrary, the widely-extended denominations of the Methodists and Baptists are, to a great extent, composed of persons whose ancestors belonged to Presbyterian churches.

It will easily be believed that the Presbyterian Church, in the midst of a population which doubles itself every twenty-four years, felt that her first and most urgent duty was to supply this growing population with the preaching of the gospel. It has been a missionary church from the beginning. Its first pastors, though settled over particular congregations, spent much of their time in travelling and preaching to the destitute. And as soon as their numbers began to increase, they adopted a regular system of missions. The synod, at its annual meetings, appointed missionaries to go to the destitute portions of the country, and sustained them by the contributions of the churches. Soon after the formation of the general assembly, that body appointed a standing committee of missions, whose duty it was to collect information as to the wants of the church, to appoint missionaries, to designate their field of labour, to make provision for their maintenance, and to report annually to the general assembly. In 1816, this committee was enlarged, and constituted the board of missions, and has ever since been engaged in the benevolent work of sending the gospel to the destitute parts of the church. For some years past the number of missionaries sent out by this board has ranged from 200 to 300, and its income from 20,000 to 30,000 dollars, as has been shown in another part of this work.[1]

As many members of the Presbyterian Church prefer voluntary societies to ecclesiastical boards for conducting missionary and other benevolent operations; and as they wished different evangelical denominations to unite in this work; as, moreover, there was an evident necessity of doing more than had yet been done to meet the constantly increasing demands for missionary labour, they determined to form a society to be called the American Home Missionary Society, already spoken of elsewhere. [2] This society has received the support of full one half of the Presbyterian Church, of the whole body of the Congregational churches, New England churches, (one of the most efficient bodies in the country,) and, to some extent, of the Dutch Reformed churches. It has, therefore, been extensively useful. Its income has varied of late years from 60,000 to 80,000 dollars, and its missionaries from 400 to 700.

It is in this way that the Presbyterian Church has endeavoured, in some measure, to keep pace with the demands of the country for ministerial labour. These exertions have not, indeed, been adequate to the occasion, and yet the fact, that fifty years ago, this church had less than 200 ministers, and now has nearer 3000 than 2000, shows that it has not been entirely wanting to its duty.

It is obvious, that this great demand for ministerial labour must lead the church to look anxiously around for the means of obtaining an adequate supply of educated men. In the first instance, the attention of its members was naturally directed to the mother country. The necessities of the numerous settlements were frequently urged on the presbyteries of Scotland and Ireland, and on similar bodies in England. From these sources a large proportion of our early ministers were obtained; indeed, as far as can be ascertained, all the ministers connected with the Presbyterian Church, from 1705 to 1716, with two or three exceptions, were from Great Britain or Ireland. The older provinces of New England subsequently furnished many able and faithful men, who aided efficiently in building up the Pres-

---

[1] Book iv. chap. 8.   [2] Ibid. chap. 7.

byterian church. But the supply from these sources was precarious and inadequate. From an early period, therefore, measures were adopted to secure the education of ministers at home.
About the year 1717, the Rev. William Tennent, who had been
a presbyter of the Episcopal Church in Ireland, opened a classical
academy in Pennsylvania, which was familiarly known as the
" Log college," where many of the most distinguished of the
early native ministers received their education. Similar institutions were soon after established in various other places; and in
1738, the synod, in order to secure a properly educated ministry,
passed an act to the following effect: viz. "That all the presbyteries require, that every candidate, before being taken on trial,
should be furnished with a diploma from some European or New
England college; or, in case he had not enjoyed the advantage
of a college education, he should be examined by a committe of
synod, who should give him a certificate of competent scholar-
ship when they found him to merit it."

In 1739, the synod determined to take measures to establish
a seminary of learning under their own care; but the circumstances of the country, and of the church itself, prevented any
thing being done until 1744. In that year it was agreed: 1.
That there should be a school kept open, where all persons who
pleased may send their children, and have them taught gratis,
in the languages, philosophy, and divinity. 2. In order to carry
on this design, that every congregation under the care of the
synod be applied to for yearly contributions. 3. That whatever sum of money could be spared from what was necessary to
support a master and tutor, should be devoted to the purchase
of books. This was the origin of what is now the college at
Newark, in the State of Delaware.

At this period of our history there were two synods, the old
synod of Philadelphia, and the synod of New York, which was
formed in 1745. The former, at this time, directed their efforts
to the support of the Newark academy, and of the academy in
Philadelphia, out of which has sprung the university of Pennsylvania; the latter raised and sustained the college of New
Jersey, at Princetown; and after the union of the two synods in
1758, the united body concentrated their efforts in the support
of the last mentioned institution. Though the college at Prince-

town owes its origin to the synod of New York, and sprang from the desire of furnishing a supply of educated men for the ministry of the Presbyterian Church, it has always been open to the youth of all denominations. The number of its alumni is about 2500, of whom about 500 became preachers of the gospel.

Since the establishment of the college at Princetown, more than forty similar institutions have been formed in different parts of the country, which are more or less intimately connected with the Presbyterian Church; that is, their trustees, officers, and patrons, are either exclusively or principally Presbyterians. [1] As the institution at Princetown is the oldest of these colleges, we state its organisation and course of instruction as a specimen of the rest. It received its charter from George II. in 1748, by which a board of trustees was incorporated as a college. This board supplies its own vacancies, and thus perpetuates itself; it makes the statutes of the college, holds its property, and appoints its officers. These officers, consisting of a president, seven professors, and four tutors, constitute the faculty to whom the immediate government and instruction of the students is committed.

The course of study is continued through four years. During the Freshman year the students read Livy, Xenophon's Anabasis, Roman Antiquities, Algebra, Horace, Æschines de Corona; during the Sophomore year, Horace, Demosthenes de Corona, Euclid, Plane Trigonometry, History, Cicero de officiis, etc., Homer's Iliad, Spherical Trigonometry, Mensuration, Navigation, and Nautical Astronomy; during the Junior year, Analytical Geometry and Conic sections, Descriptive Geometry, Differential Calculus, Cicero de Oratore, Euripides, Philosophy of Mind, Evidences of Christianity, Integral Calculus, Sophocles, Natural Theology, Civil Architecture; during the Senior year, Belles Lettres, Logic, Moral Philosophy, Political Economy, Natural Philosophy, Latin Rhetorical works, Greek Tragedy, Astronomy, Chemistry, Constitution of the United States. Instruction is also given in the French, Spanish, Italian, and German languages, at the option of the students, without extra charge; all the classes have Bible recitations on the Sabbath;

[1] The whole number under the influence of the Presbyterians and Congregationalists is forty-one.

during which day they prepare a portion of the Greek Testament, to be recited on Monday morning.

In other colleges substantially the same course is pursued. These institutions are sustained principally by the fees for tuition, by private endowments, and, in some instances, by grants from the state.

It will be seen that the course of instruction in these institutions is not professional; there is no faculty of law, medicine, or divinity. In some few cases one or more of these faculties have been added to the usual academical faculty. Thus in Harvard university, Cambridge, Massachusetts, and in Yale college, Connecticut, all the faculties are united, and in the university of Pennsylvania there is a faculty of medicine, and in that of Virginia of law and medicine. It has been found, in general, more expedient to have separate institutions for professional studies, especially in reference to theology, as our colleges are frequented by young men belonging to different religious denominations.

For a long time, however, after the organisation of the Presbyterian Church there was no public provision for the theological education of candidates for the sacred office. After completing their academical studies, such candidates were accustomed to place themselves under the direction of some experienced pastor, who superintended their studies, and assisted them in preparing for their examinations before the presbytery. Sometimes a pastor whose taste or acquirements peculiarly fitted him for the task, would have a class of such pupils constantly under his care. As early, however, as 1760, a proposition was introduced into the synod for the appointment and support of a regular professor of theology ; and a few years afterwards the trustees of the college of New Jersey having appointed such a professor the synod took measures to aid in sustaining him.

The general assembly, however, in 1811, determined to establish a separate institution for the theological education of candidates for the ministry; and in 1812 the institution was located at Princetown, New Jersey, and went into immediate operation. This seminary is under the immediate supervision of a board of directors, who meet semi-annually to examine the students, and superintend its affairs. This board is appointed by the general assembly, and to the latter body also it belongs to elect the pro-

2 M

fessors, determine their duties and salaries. Having already spoken of this seminary, as well as all the others which are under the control of the Presbyterians, when giving an account of the theological seminaries in the United States,[1] we say no more respecting it in this place.

In a former part of this work, when describing the development and influence of the voluntary principle, (Book iv.) we gave an account of the American Education Society, and the Board of Education of the general assembly of the Presbyterian Church—institutions which have done so much to increase the number of the ministers of the gospel in this denomination. We spoke, also, of the Board of Publication, which the assembly of one of the great divisions of the Presbyterian Church has established, and the good which it is doing. We, therefore, pass over these operations, which have so intimate a connection with the history of this church. We also say nothing at present respecting the foreign missions of this church, inasmuch as we shall have occasion to speak of these hereafter.

It has been our object in this chapter to give our readers, in the first place, a distinct idea of the organisation of the Presbyterian Church; of the manner in which its several congregations are formed and governed; what provision is made to secure the orthodoxy, learning, and fidelity of their pastors; and, in the second place, briefly to state the means adopted to extend the church, and, in general, to promote the cause of religion. There is still one general subject which should not be passed over: it is, What has been the result of this organisation, and of these means? or, What has been the character of the Presbyterian Church in the United States? Has it been a pure, enlightened, laborious, and harmonious body? Materials for an answer to this question may, in a measure, be found in the preceding pages, we shall therefore say but little in reply to it.

Purity in a church may be understood either in reference to orthodoxy, or adherence to the truth of God as revealed in his word; or in reference to the manner of life of its ministers or members. In reference to the former of these views, we think it may safely be asserted that the Presbyterian Church has, by

---

1 Book iv. Chap. 18.

the grace of God, been preserved pure to a very uncommon degree. The correctness of this statement is to be found, not so much in the early adoption of the Westminster Confession of Faith, and the requisition of an assent to that Confession on the part of all candidates for ordination; as in the fact, that there has never been any open avowal of Pelagian or Arminian doctrines in the bosom of our church. Cases have occurred of ministers being censured, or suspended from office, for teaching such doctrines, but no case has occurred of a Presbyterian minister who avowedly rejected the Calvinistic system, and yet retained his standing in the church as one of its authorised preachers. Of late years, indeed, there has been much discussion on doctrinal subjects, and many sentiments have been advanced, which many excellent men considered as virtually, if not formally implying the rejection of the Calvinistic doctrines of original sin, election, and efficacious grace. With regard to these controversies, however, there are two remarks to be made. The first is, that the advocates of these sentiments strenuously denied that they were inconsistent with the doctrines just mentioned; and the second is, that the opposition made to the exercise of discipline on account of these sentiments, was the principal cause of the division of the Presbyterian Church into two portions of nearly equal size. It therefore remains true, as stated in a preceding page, that no Presbyterian minister has avowed himself either a Pelagian or Arminian, and yet been allowed to retain his standing as one of the accredited teachers of the church. This, indeed, may be considered by many as great bigotry. But the very thing which its friends glory in is the fact, that the Presbyterian Church in America, having a Calvinistic creed, has been faithful in adhering to it.

As to the other application of the word pure, it may also be safely asserted, that although painful cases of immorality in ministers have occurred, yet we know of no case in which it has been overlooked; we know no case in which either drunkenness, licentiousness, or any similar offence, has been proved against any minister, or been notoriously true with regard to him, without leading to his suspension or deposition from office. If such instances have ever occurred they must be exceedingly rare. We do not mention this as any thing peculiar to the Presbyterian Church; the same remark, as far as we know, might be made, with equal justice, of any of the evangelical denominations in the country. As it regards the private members of the church, since much depends upon the fidelity of the several sessions, we can only say, that according to our rules of discipline, no person chargeable with immoral conduct can be properly retained in communion with the church; and that public sentiment is in accordance with these rules. The cases are certainly rare, in which any such offence as falsehood, drunkenness, fornication, or adultery, would be tolerated in any church member. Discipline is so far preserved in our churches, that it would be a matter of general reproach, if any congregation allowed the name of any man of known immoral character to remain upon its list of communicants.

In asserting the claim of the Presbyterian Church in America to the character of an enlightened body, all that is meant is, that she has successfully endeavoured to maintain as high a standard of literary qualifications in her ministry as other Christian denominations in the United States, or as the circumstances of the country rendered expedient or possible. From the beginning she insisted on the necessity of learning in those who intended to enter the sacred office, and early endeavoured to establish institutions for their suitable education. Even when the demand for ministers was so great as to present a strong temptation to relax her requisitions, she constantly refused. The proposition was more than once introduced into the old synod, that in view of the pressing necessity for ministerial labour, the presbyteries might be permitted to license men to preach the gospel who had not received a liberal education; but it was uniformly rejected. It has already been stated that the constitution of the church requires that every candidate should pass repeated examinations before he is admitted to ordination; that he must give satisfactory evidence of possessing a competent knowledge of the Latin, Greek, and Hebrew languages; of his acquaintance with the subjects usually studied in our colleges; and he must, after completing his academical studies, spend at least two years in the study of theology under some approved teacher. These requisitions have been enforced with a good degree of fidelity. For a long time, a knowledge of Hebrew was not generally insisted upon, on account of the difficulty of obtaining competent teachers; but since the establishment of theological seminaries, a knowledge of that language has become with the Presbyterian ministers (and many others also) an almost uniform attainment.

In answer to the question, Whether the Presbyterian Church has been a laborious and active body of men? it may be said that in this respect she has fallen behind some of her sister churches, but has kept in advance of others. The rapid increase of the church since its organisation in 1705, the efforts she has made to found academies, colleges, and theological seminaries; the labour and money contributed to the support of foreign and domestic missions, show that although she has come far short of her duty, she has not been entirely unmindful of her high vocation.

With regard to the last question proposed, viz., Whether the Presbyterian Church has been a harmonious body? the answer may not appear so favourable. The existence of parties seems to be an unavoidable incident of freedom. In other words, liberty gives occasion for the manifestation of that diversity of opinion, feeling, and interest, which never fails to exist in all large communities whether civil or religious. The expression of this diversity may be prevented by the hand of power, or concealed from the force of counteracting motives; but where no power exists to forbid its manifestation, or where no interests are endangered by its avowal, it will not be slow in making its existence known. In the Romish church all expression of difference of opinion, on certain subjects, is forbidden; on all others, where there is liberty, there is conflict. In richly endowed and established churches there is so much to be sacrificed by the avowal of dissent, that conformity must ever be expected to be more general than sincere.

Nothing out of the analogy of history, therefore, has happened to the Presbyterian Church in the occasional conflicts through which she has passed. As this church was composed of men sincerely attached to the doctrines of the Reformed Churches, it was not disturbed by any doctrinal controversy for more than 100 years after its organisation. Before the middle of the last century, there arose a great religious excitement both in Great

Britain and in America. In England this excitement was produced principally by the instrumentality of Wesley; and in this country by that of Whitefield, Edwards, the Tennants, Blairs, and other distinguished preachers of that day. In Scotland it either increased or occasioned the secessions from the national church which still exist in that country. In England it led to the formation of the great and independent body of the Methodists. In New England it gave rise to great controversy, and to separations from the established churches; and in the Presbyterian Church it caused a division of the synod of Philadelphia, which was its highest ecclesiastical body, into two independent bodies, which continued separate from each other from 1741 to 1758. To any one who examines this period of its history, it will appear that it was not difference of opinion as to the nature of religion, or as to its doctrines, nor as to church government, nor as to the necessity of learning in the ministry, which led to this separation, but the difference of opinion as to the revival then in progress, and to the disorders, mutual criminations, and consequent alienation of feeling which are so apt to attend seasons of great and general excitement. The terms of union adopted by the two synods in 1758 expressly recognise the harmony of the two bodies on all the points above specified, and declare their purpose to bury all remembrance of their differences respecting the revival.

From the time of the union just mentioned, in 1758, until within a few years, the Presbyterian Church in America was as harmonious and united a body of ministers and members, as could be found in that or any other country. The causes of the recent unhappy division are numerous, many of them of long standing and gradual operation; and all of them difficult of appreciation by those who are not familiarly acquainted with the history of that church.

It has already been stated that before the commencement of the present century, the Presbyterian Church was in a great measure composed of those European Presbyterians and their descendants who were settled in the middle and southern States. Since the year 1800, there has been going on a constant and very great emigration from the New England States to the central and western parts of New York, and to the north-western

States of the Union. These emigrants had, in general, been accustomed to the congregational form of church government prevalent ·in New England. As they met, however, in their new locations with many Presbyterians, and as their ministers generally preferred the Presbyterian form of government, they united with them in the formation of churches and ecclesiastical judicatories. In 1801, the general assembly and the general association of Connecticut agreed upon what was called "The plan of union between Presbyterians and Congregationalists in the new settlements." Under this plan, which purports to be a temporary expedient, a great number of churches and presbyteries, and even several synods, were formed, composed partly of Presbyterians and partly of Congregationalists. Though this plan seems to have operated beneficially for a number of years, yet, as it was extended far beyond its original intention, as it gave Congregationalists, who had never adopted the standards of doctrine of the Presbyterian Church, and who were avowedly opposed to its form of government, as much influence and authority in the government of the church as an equal number of Presbyterians, it naturally gave rise to dissatisfaction as soon as the facts of the case came to be generally known, and as soon as questions of discipline and policy arose, in the decision of which the influence of these Congregationalists was sensibly felt.

In addition to this source of uneasiness, was that which arose out of diversity of opinions in points of doctrine. Certain peculiarities of doctrine had become prevalent among the Calvinists of New England, which naturally spread into those portions of the Presbyterian Church settled by New England men. These peculiarities were not regarded, on either side, as sufficient to justify any interruption of ministerial communion, or to call for the exercise of discipline, but they were sufficient to give rise to the formation of two parties, which received the appellations of Old and New School. Within the last ten or twelve years, however, opinions have been advanced by some of the New England clergy, which all the Old School, and a large portion of the New School party in the Presbyterian Church, considered as involving a virtual denial of the doctrines of original sin, election, and efficacious grace, and which were regarded as inconsistent with ministerial standing in the body. Several attempts were made to subject the Presbyterian advocates of these opinions to ecclesiastical discipline. These attempts failed, partly on account of deficiency of proof, partly from irregularity in the mode of proceeding, and partly, no doubt, from an apprehension, on the part of the New School brethren, that if the opinions in question were made matters of discipline, their own peculiarities would not escape censure. Certain it is that the whole of that party united in frustrating the attempts made to set the seal of the church's disapprobation on the doctrines then in dispute. The failure of these attempts greatly increased the dissatisfaction of the Old School party, and awakened in them serious apprehensions for the doctrinal purity of the church.

To these sources of uneasiness was added the diversity of opinion as to the best mode of conducting certain benevolent operations. The Old School, as a party, were in favour of the church, in her ecclesiastical capacity, by means of boards of her appointment and under her own control, conducting the work of domestic and foreign missions, and the education of candidates for the ministry. The other party, as generally preferred voluntary societies, disconnected with church courts, and embracing different religious denominations for these purposes. It might seem, at first view, that this was a subject on which the members of the church might differ without inconvenience or collision. But it was soon found that these societies or boards must indirectly exert a great, if not a controlling influence on the church. The men who could direct the education of candidates for the sacred office, and the location of the hundreds of domestic missionaries, must sooner or later give character to the church. On this account this question was regarded as one of great practical importance.

It was in the midst of the differences and alienations, arising from these various sources, that the general assembly met in 1837. Both parties had come to the conclusion that a separation was desirable; but though they agreed as to the terms of the separation, they could not agree as to the mode in which it should be effected. The general assembly, therefore, resolved to put an end to the existing difficulties in another way. It first abolished the plan of union, above mentioned, formed in 1801; and then passed several acts, the purport and effect of which were to declare that no Congregational church should hereafter be represented in any Presbyterian judicatory; and that no presbytery or synod, composed partly of Presbyterians and partly of Congregationalists, should hereafter be considered as a constituent portion of the Presbyterian Church. These acts were defended on the ground that they were nothing more than the legitimate exercise of the executive authority of the general assembly, requiring that the constitution of the church should be conformed to by all its constituent parts.

Had the synods and other judicatories affected by these acts seen fit to separate from the Congregationalists, with whom they had been united, and to organise themselves as purely Presbyterian bodies, the general assembly would have been bound by its own acts to recognise them as constituent parts of the church. But those brethren having assembled in convention at Auburn, in the State of New York, unanimously resolved that they would consider the plan of union as still in force, its abrogation by the general assembly to the contrary notwithstanding; and that they would not separate from their Congregational members. Accordingly, in 1838, the delegates from the presbyteries included in these synods, attended the general assembly, and claimed their seats as members. As this was not immediately granted, (though it was not refused,) they rose, nominated a moderator and clerk, and being joined by those members who sympathised with them, they declared themselves the true general assembly, and withdrew from the house.

A suit was immediately brought by them before the supreme court of Pennsylvania to decide which assembly was to be regarded as the true one, or which had the right to appoint the professors, and administer the funds belonging to the theological seminaries under the care of " The general assembly of the Presbyterian Church in the United States of America." The decision of the judge and jury was in their favour; but when the cause was taken before the court in bank, that is, before the court with all the judges present, that decision was reversed, and the way left open for the New School assembly to renew the suit if they should think proper. There the matter now rests, leaving what is called the Old School assembly in possession of the succession, and in the management of the seminaries.

It may be remarked that this decision has given to that assembly very little more than what was admitted to be their due by the opposite party; that is, in the terms of separation, agreed upon by the two parties in 1837, but which were not acted upon, it was admitted that the seminaries and funds, having, in fact, been founded and sustained by them, should be under the control of the Old School body; and these funds constitute almost the whole sum held in trust by the general assembly.

For the preceding account, I am indebted to a very distinguished and excellent minister in one of the bodies into which the Presbyterian Church was divided in 1838. It is as impartial, I am sure, in its relation of that event as could be expected from one who viewed it from so near a point, and who was compelled, by a sense of duty, to take part in the proceedings attending it.

To one who takes no part in the question, and looks at it dispassionately, certain positions, I conceive, must appear manifestly just. In the first place, the compact between the general assembly and the general association in 1801, though made with the best intentions, was decidedly contrary to the constitution of the former body. It was a measure which can only be ascribed to the desire of its authors to accomplish a present apparent good, without taking sufficient time or pains to examine all its probable bearings. Its immediate result was the building up of a large number of churches of a mixed character, and without that bench of ruling elders which is essential to the interior organisation of a Presbyterian church. But granting this, and I do not see how it can well be denied, the dissolution of this " Plan of Union," by the assembly of 1837, seems to have been abrupt. Time should have been allowed for the churches to be affected by it to adopt the Presbyterian polity in its whole extent, if they had a mind to do so, before having recourse to so severe a measure.

It is obvious, in the second place, that the Presbyterian Church from the first, or nearly so, was composed of diverse elements which could not be easily assimilated. This diversity had been increasing every year, especially within the last half century. Look at the different races that from time to time have entered into the composition of the Presbyterian Church.

A large proportion of its ministers, on the one hand, are either from Presbyterian churches in Scotland and Ireland, or are descended from Scotch and Irish Presbyterians, and these naturally feel much attached to the Westminster Confession of Faith, and to the catechisms and form of government with which they have been familiar from their childhood. Another large proportion of its ministers are, on the other hand, from New England, where they received all their early impressions from the Congregational churches; so that however much they may have respected the Presbyterian Church on entering it, and however that respect may have increased since, they cannot, from the nature of things, feel as much attachment to all the details of its doctrines and government as others who, if I may so speak, were born Presbyterians. Hence the latter have been disposed to be satisfied with a general conformity with its doctrines and government, though in this they did not fully act up to the engagements which they took upon entering it. This led to a variation, if not in doctrines, at least in statements of doctrine, perfectly tolerable in Congregational churches, where extended creeds are unknown, and to a looseness in ecclesiastical administration, both which were incompatible with the precision of a church whose standards are so full on every point, and with a discipline, the rules of which are laid down with so much minuteness.

In the third place, the doctrinal difference lay more in philosophy than in any thing else. It originated in the attempt, not at all improper in itself, to reply to the objections which the enemies of Calvinism have ever made to its distinctive features, so repugnant to the natural heart. In these explanations of certain points, views were expressed, apparently at variance in some instances with the doctrines of man's depravity, of election, efficacious grace, &c., as they had usually been held.

Nor do I think it is to be denied, that some of these speculations were pushed too far, and expressed in a manner calculated to excite alarm. There was, in some cases, a needless departure from the usual theological phraseology, and this excited concern and suspicion, even when at bottom there was no real diversity of doctrine. On the other hand, a proper disposition was not always shown to estimate unessential shades of opinion, and even of doctrine, at their just value and consequences, even when denied on one side were too strenuously alleged on the other. Thus were differences magnified until what was philosophical in the explanation of a doctrine, and did not change the doctrine itself, was thought subversive of it, and fraught, of course, with imminent danger to the cause of truth.

In the fourth place, as to the mode of conducting the benevolent undertakings of the church, whether by boards appointed by the general assembly or through voluntary societies, as they are called, whether independent of kindred institutions or connected with them, and this, after all, was the question that helped most to produce the division, it seems clear to me, that the brethren and churches that preferred the former of these methods, ought at once to have been allowed that preference, and that it was a fatal mistake to shut them up to the support of what they did not think the safest or most scriptural modes of promoting the extension of the Messiah's kingdom at home and abroad.

Faults, in short, there were on both sides, and as happens so often in such cases there was not a little of *man*, in a matter in which nothing should have been allowed to influence a single decision but a regard for the glory of God and the interests of his church.

But the division has taken place, and whatever of strife or agitation attended it is passing away. A better spirit is unquestionably prevailing, and these two powerful bodies are engaged in the only rivalry worthy of them—that of striving which shall do most for the cause of Christ throughout the world. In this each of them is now free to adopt the method it may think best. The Old School, as they are called, have their own boards of missions, domestic and foreign, of education and of publication. The New School combine their efforts with the Congregationalists of New England, and some other and smaller denominations, in supporting the American Home Missionary Society, Board of Commissioners for foreign missions, and Education Society. Both zealously support the American Bible, Tract, and Seaman's societies, and others of a like general kind.

In fact, the unwieldly bulk to which the Presbyterian Church had grown, as well as the co-existence in it of two great elements, too dissimilar to admit of harmonious action, had long made it evident to many that it must be divided; and the division that has taken place is about as fortunate a one as well could have occurred. Although it must be referred, in a considerable degree, to sectional, doctrinal, and economical questions, yet none of these have in all cases determined the present position of the parties concerned. Thus in the New School church we find Scotch and Irish ministers, and the descendants of emigrants from Scotland and Ireland, whilst New England men may be found in the Old. In the former, there are men who hold the old views of Calvinistic doctrine; in the latter, there are some who hold the New England modifications of those views. Finally, the New School is not without adherents who prefer ecclesiastical boards for benevolent operations, whilst the Old School has some who remain attached to voluntary societies. The division, however, coincides more, if I may use the expression, with the natural line of demarcation, if I may so term it, in the last named particular than in the others, and for a reason already mentioned.

The relative proportions of the two bodies will appear from the following statement. In May last, (1842,) the Old School had under its care:

> 17 Synods,
> 101 Presbyteries,
> 2025 Churches,
> 1291 Ordained Ministers,
> 290 Licentiates,
> 237 Candidates,[1]
> 141,000 Communicants.

In the year 1840, according to their minutes, the New School had under their care:

> 16 Synods,
> 88 Presbyteries,
> 1375 Churches,
> 1260 Ministers,
> 102,060 Communicants.

The number of licentiates and candidates is not given, but probably bears the same proportion to that of the churches and pastors as those of the Old School do to theirs.[2]

---

[1] That is, students of theology who have not yet been licensed to preach.

[2] The reader will remark that the returns of the New School are of no later date than 1840, in consequence of its general assembly not having met since that year. Continued to 1842, its statistics would present a considerable increase.

Thus it appears that the two together, and in almost all
respects they may be considered as one body, have at least

3400 Churches,
2551 Ordained Ministers,
probably 800 Licentiates and Candidates,
and 243,060 Communicants.

Regarding them as one whole, it were difficult to find in any
part of Christendom a branch of the kingdom of Christ better
educated or more distinguished for general learning, zeal, enterprise, liberality, and soundness in all essential doctrine. Their
ministers present a body of 2500, almost without exception
liberally educated men, who, after all their debates, and final
separation into two, are more thoroughly sound Calvinists in
point of doctrine than any equally numerous ministry to be found
in any other country.

The question is often asked, whether they will ever unite
again? That is by no means improbable; but whether they do
or not, seems to me of little consequence. In their separate
state they will accomplish more than if united. There will soon
be the most perfect intercourse between their churches and
pastors. The energies of both find free and ample scope which
was never the case before with either, but particularly with the
Old School, who never felt at ease or assured of the future. The
New School will probably ally itself more closely than ever with
the Congregationalists, and maintaining a somewhat less rigid
economy than the Old School in regard to the organisation of
churches in regions abounding with New England Congregational emigrants, they cannot but increase rapidly, the more
especially as New England will act on the middle, the southern,
and still more, on the north-western States, chiefly through
them.

In conclusion let me add, that the general assembly of the
New School, in its session in May 1840, proposed to the presbyteries under its care certain important changes in its constitution, which have since been adopted. One is, that the general
assembly shall be held triennally instead of annually. Another
is, that all appeals from the decisions of a church session shall
not, in the case of lay-members, be carried beyond the presbytery,
or in the case of ministers beyond the synod. By these modifications they have made the business of their general assembly

much more simple and easy, and given more time to that body
to deliberate for the promotion of the best interests of the
church.

CHAPTER VI.

THE METHODIST EPISCOPAL CHURCH.

THIS large and influential body holds the doctrinal opinions of
the Wesleyan Methodists of England, and its ecclesiastical
economy is in all important points identical with theirs.   It
took its rise in 1766, when a Mr. Philip Embury, who had
been a local preacher in some of Mr. Wesley's societies in the
north of Ireland, and had come over to America with a few
other pious persons of the same connection, began to hold meetings for exhortation and prayer in his own house at New York.
A considerable society was gradually formed in that city, which
at that time, it would appear, could reckon on but a small number comparatively of living and zealous Christians among its
inhabitants.   In a few months it was found necessary to fit up
a large hired room as a place of worship, and the congregation
was farther augmented by the preaching of a Captain Webb of
the British army, who having been converted under the preaching of Mr. Wesley in England, and being now stationed at
Albany, paid frequent visits to the little flock at New York.
    Ere long similar meetings began to be held in several places
on Long island, in Philadelphia, and at other points.   In 1768,
a large place of worship was erected in New York, being the
first Methodist church ever built in the United States.   Next
year, on Mr. Wesley being requested to send over two of his
preachers, Messrs. Richard Boardman and Joseph Pillmore
came to New York, and about the same time Mr. Robert Straw-
bridge, another local preacher from Ireland, came over and settled in Frederick county, Maryland, where he held meetings at
his own house, and those of other pious persons in the neighbourhood.   This extension of the Methodists into the south was

further promoted by a visit from Mr. Pillmore into Virginia and North Carolina.

Pressing representations of the need of help having been made to Mr. Wesley, Mr. Francis Ashbury and Mr. Richard Wright were sent over from England in 1771, and under the labours, particularly of the former, the work went on increasing year after year, until the commencement of the Revolution. That event greatly retarded the progress of Methodism in some places, not only by the ever untowardly influence of present war on such undertakings, but also by the suspicions attached by the revolutionists to Mr. Ashbury, and several of his fellow-preachers, as being native Englishmen who had been too short a period in the country to have its interests truly at heart.

At length with peace came independence, and thus, greatly to the encouragement of Mr. Ashbury and his fellow-labourers, a wide and effectual door for the preaching of the gospel was opened to them. Hitherto this attempt to revive true godliness had been confined entirely to laymen of the Episcopal Church, and with it their efforts were more connected than with any other, inasmuch as none of them had at first any intention of separating from its communion. But worthy ministers of that church being hard to be found in some places, while none were to be had at all in others both before the Revolution broke out and during its progress, Mr. Wesley was urged to send over ordained ministers, who might administer the ordinances to his followers. To this he was greatly opposed at first, but when the Revolution was over, considering that from the change of circumstances he might now lawfully do what he had refused doing while the colonies were under the government of England, he sent over as superintendent of the Methodist churches in America, the Rev. Dr. Coke, a presbyter of regular standing in the established Church of England. He was accompanied by Mr. Richard Whatcoat and Mr. Thomas Vasey, whom he, Dr. Coke, and the Rev. Mr. Creighton, had ordained presbyters or priests, just before the sailing of the three from Bristol in September 1784. These brethren were the bearers of a letter from Mr. Wesley to the Methodist preachers and societies in America, stating his reasons for considering himself now at liberty to accede to their requests, and informing them, that he had appointed Dr. Coke and Mr. Ashbury to be joint superintendents of all the societies in that country founded upon his rules, and Messrs. Whatcoat and Vasey to act as elders among them, by baptising and administering the Lord's supper.

On the arrival of these delegates a conference of the preachers was immediately convened at Baltimore. It was opened on the 25th of December 1784, and was attended by sixty out of the eighty preachers then in the country. One of its first acts was the unanimous election of Dr. Coke and Mr. Ashbury as superintendents, thereby confirming Mr. Wesley's appointment. Dr. Coke, and the other two presbyters then ordained Mr. Ashbury, first a deacon, next a presbyter, and finally a superintendent. Thereupon the two superintendents, or bishops as they soon began to be called, and as their successors are styled to this day, ordained twelve of the preachers then present to the office of presbyters or elders.

Thus was the Methodist Episcopal Church in the United States organised sixty-two years ago, and the Methodist societies severed from the Episcopal Church, in the communion of which they had hitherto remained. From that epoch they formed a new and independent religious denomination, which was soon vastly to outnumber that from which they had sprung. At that their "day of small things," their ministers and lay-preachers, including Dr. Coke and his co-delegates from England, amounted to eighty-six, and the members in all to 14,986. But small as was this beginning, great and glorious has been their increase since.

The proceedings of that conference were highly important. Twenty-five articles were adopted as the confession of faith for the infant church. We will give first the titles of the whole, and then a few of them at large. The titles are as follows. Of faith in the Holy Trinity; of the Word, or Son of God, who was made very man; of the resurrection of Christ; of the Holy Ghost; of the sufficiency of the holy scriptures for salvation; of the Old Testament; of original sin; of free-will; of the justification of man; of good works; of works of supererogation; of sin after justification; of the church; of purgatory; of speaking in the congregation in such a tongue as the people understand; of the sacraments; of baptism; of the Lord's supper; of both kinds; [1] of the one oblation of Christ, finished upon the cross; of the marriage of ministers; of the rites and ceremonies of the churches; of the rulers of the United States of America; of Christian men's goods; of a Christian man's oath.

On almost all these subjects the articles express doctrines held by every enlightened Protestant. In fact, they are a selection from the thirty-nine articles of the Church of England, with some verbal changes, and the omission of some words and parts of sentences. The seventeenth article of the Church of England, (on predestination and election,) is, of course, omitted, the doctrine therein taught not being held by the Methodist Episcopal Church in America. Nor do we find that of the perseverance of saints, for neither do they hold it. But on all the great doctrines essential to salvation, nothing can be more clear, or more consistent with the word of God than the sense of these articles. For instance, on original sin,—what more scriptural than the seventh article, which says: "Original sin standeth not in following of Adam, (as the Pelagians do vainly talk,) but it is the corruption of the nature of every man; that is, naturally engendered of the offspring of Adam, whereby man is very far gone from original righteousness, and of his own nature inclined to evil and that continually."

On the subject of free will it is said that: "That the condition of man after the fall of Adam is such, that he cannot turn and prepare himself by his own natural strength and works to faith, and calling upon God; whereupon we have no power to do good works, pleasant and acceptable to God, without the grace of God by Christ preventing us, that we may have a good will, and working with us when we have that good will."

So in respect to justification by faith, good works, works of supererogation, the sacraments, and other subjects, the same doctrines are held as by the reformers of blessed memory.

Besides these twenty-five articles, the conferences have adopted a system of rules [2] in thirty-five sections, which treat of the entire economy of their church, the manner of life becoming its

---

[1] Or elements—bread and wine—both to be administered to the people.
[2] These rules, originally drawn up by Mr. Wesley, were considerably modified in America.

ministers and private members, the proper style of preaching, &c. In giving directions as to the manner of treating the doctrine of perfection, the twenty-second section runs as follows: "Let us strongly and explicitly exhort all believers to go on to perfection. That we may all speak the same thing, we ask once for all, Shall we defend this perfection, or give it up? We all agree to defend it, meaning thereby (as we did from the beginning,) salvation from all sin by the love of God and man filling the heart. The Papists say, 'This cannot be attained till we have been refined by the fire of purgatory.' Some professors say, 'Nay, it will be attained as soon as the soul and body part.' Others say, 'It may be attained before we die; a moment after is too late.' Is it not so? We are all agreed we may be saved from all sin, properly so called, before death, *i. e.* sinful tempers; but we cannot always speak, or think, or act aright, as dwelling in houses of clay. The substance then is settled; but as to the circumstances, is the change gradual or instantaneous? It is both the one and the other. 'But should we in preaching insist both on one and the other?' Certainly we should insist on the gradual change; and that earnestly and continually. And are there not reasons why we should insist on the instantaneous change? If there be such a blessed change before death, should we not encourage all believers to expect it? And the rather, because constant experience shows, the more earnestly they expect this, the more swiftly and steadily does the gradual work of God go on in their souls; the more careful are they to grow in grace; the more zealous of good works; and the more punctual in their attendance on all the ordinances of God; (whereas just the contrary effects are observed whenever this expectation ceases.) They are saved by hope,—by this hope of a total change, with a gradually increasing salvation. Destroy this hope and that salvation stands still, or rather decreases daily. Therefore, whoever will advance the gradual change in believers should strongly insist on the instantaneous."

For a more thorough acquaintance with the doctrines of the Methodist Episcopal Church, I may refer to Mr. Wesley's four volumes of Sermons, and his Notes on the New Testament, where all the peculiar views of that body are fully exhibited, and which may be regarded as its real confession of faith. Its discipline comprehends the rules above referred to, modified and enlarged from time to time by various enactments of the general conference. We shall attempt a summary of it from the very clear and succinct statements of the Rev. Dr. Bangs, in his "History of the Methodist Episcopal Church in the United States," [1] a work to which, in preparing this chapter, we have been greatly indebted on other points. We begin with the "societies" and "classes," which are the primary bodies of believers in this extensive, well adjusted, and most efficient ecclesiastical system.

1. In the first place, there is what is called the *society*, which includes all the members of the church residing in any particular place, or connected with it.

2. Every society comprises one or more *classes*, each consisting of from twelve to twenty or more individuals, who meet once a week for mutual edification. These classes are the real normal schools, if we may so speak, of the Methodist Church.

3. The minister, under whose pastoral care the classes in a society are placed, appoints a leader to each, whose duty is to see every member of his class once a week, to inquire how their souls prosper, and to receive what they are willing to give for the support of the church and the poor.

4. Stewards are appointed in each society by the quarterly conference, on the nomination of the ruling preacher. These have charge of all the moneys collected for the support of the ministry, the poor, and for sacramental occasions, and disburse it as the Discipline directs.

5. There are *trustees* who have charge of the church property, and hold it in trust for the use of the Methodist Episcopal Church. These are elected by the congregation in those States where the laws so provide; in other places they are appointed as the Discipline directs.

6. There are in most societies *exhorters*, who receive their

---

[1] Vol. i., pp. 245-250. This work, in 4 vols., by the Rev. Nathan Bangs, D.D., brings the history of the Methodist Church down to the close of the general conference held in 1840. It is an invaluable work, written in a truly calm and Christian spirit, and displays a sincere desire to present every subject which it treats in an impartial manner. It presents a very complete history of the Methodist Church in America from the very first.

license from the quarterly meeting conference, and have the privilege of holding meetings for exhortation and prayer.

7. A preacher is one who holds a license to preach, but may not administer the sacraments. He may be a travelling or a local preacher. The former devotes his whole time to the ministry, and is supported by those among whom he labours; the latter generally supports himself by some secular employment, and preaches on the Sabbath, as well as occasionally at other times, but without temporal emolument. Both receive a license, signed by a presiding elder, from a quarterly meeting conference, after being recommended each by his respective class, or by a leader's meeting. Thus the people, in those nurseries of the church—the " classes" and " leaders' meetings"—have the initiative in bringing forward those who are to preach the gospel. After this license from a quarterly meeting conference, they may be taken into the travelling service by an annual conference; after two years spent in which, and pursuing at the same time a prescribed course of reading and study, they may be ordained as deacons. Then after two years' circuit travelling as deacons, and pursuing a further course of reading and study, they may be ordained presbyters or elders. Such is the training for the ministry in the Methodist Episcopal Church, and it is much more efficient than persons not well acquainted with it would suppose.

8. A deacon holds a parchment of ordination from a bishop, and besides his duties as a preacher, he is authorised to solemnise marriages, to administer baptism, and to assist the elder or presbyter in the administration of the Lord's supper.

9. An elder, in addition to these functions, is authorised to administer all the ordinances of God's house.

10. A presiding elder has the charge of several circuits, collectively called a district. It is his duty to visit each circuit once a quarter, to preach and administer the ordinances, to convene the travelling and local preachers, exhorters, stewards, and leaders of the circuit for a quarterly conference, and in the absence of a bishop, to receive, try, suspend, or expel preachers, as the Discipline directs. He is appointed to his charge by the bishop, who may, for the time being, have a special oversight of the annual conference in which he is placed. This office arose

from the necessity of always having some one to administer the ordinances throughout the circuits, for it often happens that the travelling preachers, from their not having received ordination as elders, cannot administer the Lord's supper, nor even baptism, if they are not deacons.

11. A bishop is elected by the general conference, to which body he is amenable for his official and moral conduct. It is his duty to travel through the country, to superintend the spiritual and temporal affairs of the church, to preside in the annual and the general conference, to ordain such as are elected by an annual conference to the office of deacons and elders, and to appoint the preachers to their stations. As there are several bishops, they usually divide the country among them, each having his own field, and all meeting at the general conference. The episcopacy in this church is, however, an *office*, not an *order*.

12. A *leaders' meeting* is composed of all the class leaders in any one circuit or station, under the presidency of the preacher placed in charge of that circuit or station. Here the weekly class collections are paid into the hands of the stewards, and inquiry is made into the state of the classes, delinquents reported, and inquiries made as to the sick and poor.

13. A *quarterly meeting conference* is composed of all the travelling and local preachers, exhorters, stewards, and leaders belonging to any particular station or circuit, under the presidency of the circuit elder, or, in his absence, of the preacher who takes charge in his place. Here exhorters and local preachers are licensed, and preachers recommended to an annual conference to be received into the travelling ministry; appeals are likewise heard from any dissatisfied member against the decision of a committee of the society to which he belongs. This body performs therefore a most important part in the whole system.

14. An *annual conference* is composed of all the travelling preachers, deacons, and elders within a specified district of country. These are the executive and judicial bodies, acting under rules prescribed to them by the general conference. Here the characters and conduct of all the travelling preachers within the bounds of the conference are examined yearly; applicants for admission into the travelling ministry, if accounted worthy, are

received, continued on trial, or dropped, as the case may be; appeals from local preachers, which may be presented, are heard and decided; and persons fit for ordination, as deacons or elders, are elected. An annual conference possesses original jurisdiction over all its members, and may therefore, try, acquit, suspend, expel, or locate any of them, as the Discipline in such cases provides.

15. The *general conference* assembles once in four years, and is composed of a certain number of delegates, elected by the annual conferences. It has the power to revise any part of the Discipline, not prohibited by restrictive regulations; to elect the book agents and editors, and the bishops; to hear and determine appeals of preachers from the decision of annual conferences; to review the acts of those conferences generally; to examine into the general administration of the bishops for the four preceding years; and to try, censure, acquit, or condemn a bishop if accused. This is the highest judicatory of the church.

16. A *love-feast* is a meeting of the members of a society, held occasionally, in which they partake of a simple repast of bread and water, during an hour, at which such as are disposed relate what God has done for their souls. These meetings were instituted by Mr. Wesley, as a sort of resuscitation of the Αγαπαι (Agapæ) of the ancient church. Their object is to make the members better acquainted with each other, and promote brotherly love and mutual edification.

17. The salaries of the ministers are raised by various collections in the societies, and also in public meetings. Provision is made for aged and infirm ministers who have continued to exercise the duties of the ministry until incapable of further service. Omitting unnecessary details, I need only say that each travelling minister receives at present 100 dollars a year for himself, the same sum for his wife, if he has one, sixteen dollars a year for each child under seven years of age, and twenty-four for those above that and under fourteen years. Besides, the stewards of each circuit and station are directed to provide a "parsonage," or house of residence, for the family of each married preacher on their circuit or station, and also to grant an allowance for their fuel and table expenses. In these

respects there is no difference between the preachers, deacons, elders, presiding elders, and bishops,—all receive the same salaries; the last have an allowance, however, for their travelling expenses. The widows of all the ministers receive 100 dollars each.

The above is the provision fixed by the general conference; but, we believe, that in many circuits and States the collections, &c. do not fully meet it.

Such is an outline of the Methodist Episcopal Church in the United States, and it is as minute as a work like this could admit. Since its organisation in 1784, though not without its share of difficulties, its career upon the whole has been remarkably prosperous, and God has enabled it to overcome every hindrance with wonderful success. We have seen the numerical amount of its ministers and members fifty-eight years ago ; in 1841 it was as follows:—

> 6 Bishops, 32 annual conferences.
> 3,587 Travelling ministers, who devote themselves entirely to the ministry.
> 6,393 Local preachers, assisting the regular travelling ministers with frequent preaching.
> 852,918 Communicants.

And the probable proportion of the community under the influence of this church's ministry, that is, who attend its preaching, as stated by bishop Soule before the British Conference in August last (1842), is 5,000,000. Surely we may well exclaim: "what hath God wrought!" It covers the whole land with its net-work system of stations and circuits, and carries the gospel into thousands of the most remote as well as the most secluded and thinly peopled neighbourhoods.

This denomination has made great exertions to increase the number of its church-edifices within the last few years. But its itinerating ministers preach in thousands of places where no such buildings are yet erected, or at least none belonging to that denomination. In these cases they hold their meetings in school-houses, court-houses, and private-houses.

No American Christian who takes a comprehensive view of the work of God going on in his country, and considers how wonderfully the means and instrumentalities employed are adapted to its extent and its wants, can hesitate for a moment to bless God for having in his mercy provided them all. Nor will he

fail to recognise in the Methodist economy, as well as in the
zeal, the devoted piety, and the efficiency of its ministry, one of
the most powerful elements in the religious prosperity of the
United States, as well as one of the firmest pillars of their civil
and political institutions.

We have already spoken of the home missions, the tract,
book,[1] and Sunday school operations of this church.   In another
place we shall have occasion to say what is doing in the cause of
foreign missions.

The Methodist Episcopal Church was long reproached with
neglecting to promote learning among its ministers, and it was
charged even with having no wish that its ministry should be
learned.   There was some truth in this, for though its influential
and enlightened members were never opposed to learning, they
had a well-founded dread of a learned but unconverted ministry.
They attempted even at an early period of their church's history to found seminaries for education.   Among these there was
a college at Maryland, which flourished from 1787 to 1795, when
the building was burnt down.   A second was attempted at Baltimore, but there, too, the college building was burnt, and a
church that adjourned it shared the same fate.   These calamities,
involving a loss of about 90,000 dollars, had a discouraging
effect for a time, but for some years past the Episcopal Methodists have shown a noble desire to promote the education of young
men for the ministry, and other walks of life in which they may
advance the cause of Christ.   In order to this they have founded
no fewer than twenty-one academic institutions, besides twelve
colleges, two of which are called universities, and these fountains
of knowledge God is blessing by shedding upon them the influence
of his grace.

No fewer than four religious newspapers are published under
the auspices of the general conference, and four more under those
of annual conferences, besides others that are edited and owned
by individuals of that body.   These journals must have a vast
circulation in the aggregate.

Having concluded our notices of the five larger evangelical

---

1 The "Book Concern" of this church is established in New York, and is
carried on by agents and editors appointed by the general conference. It is
conducted with great energy.

denominations, we shall now proceed with the smaller in the same order, and thus associate them with respective families of churches to which they more properly belong.

<hr>

CHAPTER VII.

THE MORAVIAN CHURCH.

The United Brethren, or as they are more familiarly called, the Moravians, form the only one of the smaller evangelical denominations in the United States that is Episcopal, in the usual acceptation of that word. They claim descent, as is well known, from the ancient churches of Moravia and Bulgaria, founded by Methodus and Cyrillus, two Greek monks. Notwithstanding repeated persecutions from the Roman Catholics, some remains of these churches survived in Bohemia and Moravia as late as 1722, when a party of them fled for refuge from continued vexation in Moravia to the estates of Nicholas Lewis, count of Zinzendorf in Upper Lusatia, and there they founded Herrnhut. Their protector, some years after that, became one of their bishops, and laboured most zealously for more than twenty years in the cause of God, by forming societies of the United Brethren. While on a visit to America in 1741, he took part in founding a mission among the Indians, and greatly contributed to the establishment of several settlements for those of the Brethren who might choose to emigrate thither. Such was the origin of the pleasant villages of Bethlehem, Nazareth, and Litiz, in Pennsylvania, and Salem in North Carolina. Moravian families meanwhile settled, and formed societies in Philadelphia, New York, and several other places.

The peculiar economy of the United Brethren is too widely known to require any notice of it here. Their settlements in America are the same abodes of order, provident regard for the morals of the young, and for the comfort of the aged, of cheerful industry and pleasant social life, enlivened by the sweet strains of music, and withal of the interest in missions, that their settlements are in the old world. It may be said, perhaps, that too much worldly prosperity has been to them as to so many other Christians, a hindrance to their piety.

They maintain flourishing boarding schools for girls at Bethlehem, Litiz, and Salem, and one for boys at Nazareth, where, also, their young men preparing for the ministry commonly pursue their studies.

The Moravian missions among the Indians within the boundaries of the United States, are mainly supported as well as directed by their congregations in that country.[1] Their doctrines coincide, in the main, with those of the Augsburg Confession. The number of their churches, &c. in the United States is as follows:—twenty-four churches; thirty-three ministers; 5745 members, and an entire population of about 12,000 souls.

CHAPTER VIII.

SMALLER BAPTIST DENOMINATIONS.

THERE are a few Baptist denominations in the United States, not usually included with the Regular Baptists noticed in Chapter IV. They are as follows:—

1. THE SEVENTH DAY BAPTISTS—who have forty-two churches, forty-six ministers, and 4503 members. The population under their instruction and influence is reckoned at about 25,000. They are quite evangelical in the doctrines that relate to the way of salvation, and are in good repute for piety and zeal. They differ from the Regular Baptists as to the day to be observed as the Christian Sabbath, maintaining, in opposition to these, that the seventh day was not only the Sabbath originally appointed by the Creator, but that that appointment remains unrepealed.

Their churches are widely scattered throughout the States.

---

[1] An interesting historical sketch of these missions will be found in Mr. J, C. Latrobe's "Rambles in North America."

There are two or three in New Jersey,[1] several in New York, some in Ohio, one or two in Rhode island, and one in Virginia. They observe Saturday with great strictness as their Sabbath, have Sunday schools, and one religious newspaper. Altogether they are a very worthy people.

2. FREE WILL BAPTISTS. This body dates in America from 1780, when its first church was formed in New Hampshire. In doctrine they hold a general atonement, and reject election and the other Calvinistic points. On the Trinity, justification by faith alone, regeneration, and sanctification, they are, with some exceptions, sound.

Starting with the wrong principle that, dispensing with written creeds, covenants, rules of discipline, or articles of organisation, they would make the Bible serve for all these, they were soon in great danger from Arians and Socinians creep-ing in among them. But of late years they have separated from the Christ-ians, (a heretical sect we have yet to notice, and likewise opposed to creeds,) and are consequently endeavouring to regain a sound orthodox position. Some of them have come to see that creeds are unavoidable, and had better be *definitely expressed* in writing than merely *understood*. They have accord-ingly introduced creeds, and, in some instances, even written articles in the form of a constitution. This augurs well.

Their church government, like that of all the Baptists, is vested primarily in the churches, or assemblages of believers convened for worship. These send delegates to quarterly meet-ings, the quarterly meetings to the yearly meetings, and these again to the general conference. The office-bearers in their churches are elders and deacons. The former are ordained jointly by the church to which they belong, and by the quar-terly meeting acting by a 'council. Each quarterly and yearly meeting has an elders' conference, which, with the general con-

---

1 In New Jersey, and I doubt not in other States also, there are special laws in their favour. This disposition on the part of the civil power in the United States, not to coerce the consciences of any religious community, however small, strikingly contrasts with the legislation of France in a like case. In the winter of 1840-41, when the factory children's labour bill was before the chamber of deputies, it was asked whether there ought not to be a clause for the protection of Jewish children in the observance of their Sabbath if they chose. " No," said the commission upon the bill, " they are too few to make that necessary." To this M. Fould, the banker, himself a Jew, assented, saying that the Jews were only 300,000 in the kingdom.

ference, regulates the affairs of the ministry as far as the presbytery is concerned. Thus they depart from the principle of a
pure Independency. Within the last ten years they have
entered on the work of sending the gospel to the heathen, and
there can be no better sign than this. Many of their churches
have Sunday schools and various charitable institutions. A
religious paper, also, is published under their auspices at Dover,
New Hampshire.

Until a few years ago, these Arminian Baptists took but little
interest in the education of young men for the ministry; but
they now have a flourishing academy at Parsonsfield, in the
State of Maine.

They had 753 churches and 612 ministers in 1840, and in
1841 their communicants were reckoned at 47,217.[1]

3. DISCIPLES OF CHRIST, as they call themselves, or CAMPBELL-
ITES, or REFORMERS, as they are most commonly called by others.
It is with much hesitation that, by placing these in this book, I
rank them among evangelical Christians. I do so because their
creed, taken as it stands in written terms, is not heterodox.
Not only do they not deny, but in words their creed affirms the
doctrine of the Trinity, of salvation by the merits of Christ, and
the necessity of the regenerating and sanctifying influences of
the Holy Spirit. Yet I understand that there is much about
their preaching that seems to indicate that all that they consider
necessary to salvation is a cold, speculative, philosophical faith,
together with immersion as the only proper mode of baptism;
so that there is little, after all, of that "repentance towards God,"
and " faith towards our Lord Jesus Christ," which are the indispensable terms of the gospel.

The founder of this sect is a Mr. Alexander Campbell, a
Scotchman who, together with his father, left the Presbyterian
Church in 1812, and became Baptists. Soon after this change
he began to broach doctrines that can hardly be called new, for
the Christ-ians, now though not always a heretical sect, had
advanced them before his time. His views seem to be substantially as follows: " All sects and parties of the Christian
world have departed, in greater or less degrees, from the sim-

1 Dr. Babcock's Notices of the Baptist Interest in the United States, in
the American Quarterly Register for November, 1841, p. 183.

plicity of faith and manners of the first Christians." "This defection," Mr. Campbell and his followers "attribute to the great varieties of speculation, and metaphysical dogmatism of count-less creeds, formularies, liturgies, and books of discipline— adopted and inculcated as bonds of union and platforms of communion in all the parties which have sprung from the Lutheran Reformation." All this has led, as they suppose, to the displacing of the style of the living oracles, and the affix-ing to the sacred diction ideas wholly unknown to the apostles of Christ.

And what does Mr. Campbell propose to do? Simply " to ascertain from the holy scriptures, according to commonly-received and well-established rules of interpretation, the ideas attached to the leading terms and sentences found in the holy scriptures, and then use the words of the Holy Spirit in the apostolic acceptation of them!" But let us hear him further: "By thus expressing the ideas communicated by the Holy Spirit, in the terms and phrases learned from the apostles, and by avoiding the artificial and technical language of scholastic theology, they propose to restore a pure speech to the house-hold of faith." And in this way they expect to put an end to all divisions and disputes, and promote the sanctification of the faithful. And all this is proposed by those who reject all creeds for churches; excepting, indeed, that which consists in making the Bible speak theirs! However plausible it may be to talk in this way, all church history has shown that there is no more certain way of introducing all manner of heresy than by dis-pensing with all written creeds and formularies of doctrine, and allowing all who profess to believe in the Bible, though attach-ing any meaning to it they please, to become members of the church. For a while, possibly, this scheme may seem to work well. But, ere half a century, all manner of error will be found to have entered and nestled in the house of God.

"Every one who believes what the evangelists and apostles have testified concerning Jesus of Nazareth, and who is willing to obey him, is a proper subject for immersion." And this is the sum and substance of what Mr. Campbell says respecting the way in which a sinner is to attain salvation. This is all well enough if *faith* be truly explained, and the sinner really does come to Christ with that godly sorrow for sin, from which saving faith is never dissevered. But if a mere general belief in what the evangelists and apostles have said, together with immersion, be all that is required, it is not difficult to see that churches may soon be gathered in which there will be but little true religion.

It is on this account that evangelical Christians in America, Baptists as well as Pædobaptists, have many fears about Mr. Campbell and his followers. It is believed, however, that, as yet, there are not a few sincerely pious people among his congregations, who have been led away by his plausible representations respecting the evils of creeds. Time can only show the issue. Two or three religious papers are published by ministers of this denomination, and are almost entirely devoted to the propagation of the peculiar tenets of the sect. The churches in its connection are constituted purely on Independent principles. Its statistics are not well ascertained. Mr. Campbell says that it now embraces from 150,000 to 200,000 persons. As for the churches and ministers, I have never seen their numbers stated.

CHAPTER IX.

SMALLER PRESBYTERIAN CHURCHES.—THE CUMBERLAND PRESBYTERIANS.

THE Cumberland Presbyterians arose as follows. In the extensive, and, in some respects, wonderful revival of religion that took place in Kentucky during the years 1801—1803, the call for Presbyterian ministers was far beyond what could be satisfied, and in this exigency it was proposed by some of the ministers that pious laymen of promising abilities, and who seemed to have a talent for public speaking, should be encouraged to make the best preparations in their power for the ministry, and thereafter be licensed to preach.

This suggestion was carried into effect. Several such persons were licensed by the presbytery of Pennsylvania, and a new presbytery which had been formed in the southern part of the State in 1803, and was called the Cumberland Presbytery, admitted and ordained those licentiates, and took on trial others of similar characters and attainments.

These proceedings were considered disorderly by the synod of Kentucky, and a commission was therefore appointed to examine them, and to inquire what were the doctrines held by persons thus admitted into the ministry, in a way so foreign to the rules and practice of the Presbyterian Church. The upshot was, that the course pursued by the Cumberland Presbytery was condemned, and this sentence having been confirmed by the general assembly of the whole Presbyterian Church, before which it had been brought by appeal, the censured presbytery withdrew from that body, and constituted itself an independent church in 1810, ever since which it has been called the Cumberland Presbyterian Church.

Its doctrines occupy a sort of middle ground between Calvinism and Arminianism. It holds that the atonement was made for all mankind; it rejects the doctrine of eternal reprobation; holds a modified view of election; and maintains the perseverance of the saints; but on the other points is essentially Calvinistic.

In its ecclesiastical polity it is Presbyterian; the session, presbytery, synod, and general assembly are all constituted in the manner described at length in our notice of the Presbyterian church. It differs, however, in one point from all other Presbyterian churches, by having adopted the *itinerating* system of the Methodists. By that system of circuits and stations, its ministers have been able to reach almost all parts of the valley of the Mississippi; that being the great scene of their labours. But their church is not confined to the western States and Territories of the American Union—it reaches into Texas, where it has now a Presbytery and several churches. The general assembly has under its superintendence twelve synods, forty-five presbyteries, about 550 churches, and the same number of ministers, and about 70,000 communicants. Several religious newspapers are published under its auspices. For the education of its youth it has one flourishing academy at Princetown in Kentucky, and has lately opened another at Uniontown in Western Pennsylvania. Among its preachers there are several men of highly respectable talents and acquirements.

CHAPTER X.

REFORMED DUTCH CHURCH.

WE have elsewhere stated that the country embracing what are now the States of New York, New Jersey, Delaware, and Pennsylvania, was at one time claimed by the Dutch in right of discovery. A trading port was established by them in 1614, at the spot now occupied by the city of New York, but it was not until 1624 that any families from Holland settled there. A few years after, the Rev. Everardus Bogardus was sent over to preach to the colonists, and was the first Dutch pastor that settled in America.[1] He was succeeded by John and Samuel Megapolenis, the latter of whom was one of the commissioners appointed by General Stuyvesant to settle the terms on which the colony was surrendered to the English in 1664.

The colony having been planted and maintained by the Dutch West India company, to it the colonists applied from time to time for ministers, as new churches were formed or the older ones became vacant, and the seat of the company being at Amsterdam, the directors naturally applied to the Classis of that city to choose and ordain the persons that were to be sent out. Hence that classis and the synod of North Holland, with which it was connected, came, by the tacit consent of the other classes and synods of the Dutch National Church, as well as by the submission of the churches in the colonies, to have an influence over the latter, which, in the course of time, proved a source of no little trouble to the parties concerned.[2] To such an extent was it carried that

[1] This excellent man left the colony to return to Holland in 1647, and is supposed to have been lost at sea in the same vessel with Governor Kieft.
[2] The Classis of Amsterdam and the synod of North Holland retain to this day the charge of the churches in the colonies in the East Indies, and other parts of the world, belonging to the kingdom of the Netherlands.

the colonial churches were not thought entitled to take a single step towards the regulation of their own affairs.

How far the West India company aided the congregations that were gradually formed in its American colonies, is not now known, but it is supposed to have done something for their support.[1] Some of its governors were decided friends and members of the church, and certain it is that those congregations in New Netherlands were considered as branches of the established Church of Holland.

The English took possession of the colony in 1664, and guaranteed to the inhabitants all their religious rights. Nothing of any consequence to the churches took place for about thirty years, and there being but few English in the colony, they were attended by nearly the whole population. But in 1693, on Col. Samuel Fletcher becoming governor, he succeeded, as we have elsewhere noticed, by artifice and perseverance, in having the Episcopal Church established in the city of New York and four of the principal counties of the province, so that from that time all classes were taxed for the support of Episcopacy, though its partizans formed but a small minority of the colonists.

But the inconvenience of having no ecclesiastical authority in America higher than a consistory could not fail to be felt by the Dutch Reformed Church, and accordingly, in 1738, some of its ministers proposed having an association of the clergy, called a *co-etus*, but which was to have no power either to ordain pastors, or to determine ecclesiastical disputes. Innocent as well as inadequate as was this measure, the concurrence of the classis of Amsterdam could not be obtained till 1746 or 1747. But it was soon found that nothing short of having a regular classis of their own could meet the wants of the churches. Not only was there the heavy expense and delay attending getting ministers from Holland, or sending young men thither to be educated, but, worse than all, the churches had no power of choosing ministers likely to suit them. Urged by such con-

---

[1] It would seem that it was a considerable time before any church edifice of respectable appearance was erected in New Amsterdam, as New York was then called; for De Vries, in the account of his voyage to New Netherlands, relates that he remarked to Governor Kieft in 1641, "that it was a shame that the English should pass there, and see only a mean barn in which we performed our worship."

siderations, the co-etus resolved in 1754 to propose a change of its constitution to that of a regular classis, and a plan to that effect was transmitted to the congregations for their approval. But the project was opposed by a powerful party, mainly formed of those who had been sent over from Holland, and called the Conferentie. Amid the distraction and confusion caused by this opposition of parties, religion made little progress, and many influential families left the Dutch Church, and joined the Episcopal.

All difficulties were at length adjusted through the prudent mediation of the late Rev. John H. Livingstone, D.D.,[1] then a young man. Having gone to Holland for the prosecution of his studies in 1766, the synod of Holland and classis of Amsterdam were led by his representations to devise a plan, which, after Mr. Livingstone's return to America in 1770, was submitted to a meeting held in New York in October, 1771, and attended by nearly all the ministers, and by lay delegates from nearly all the congregations. After a full discussion, having been unanimously adopted, it was carried into effect the following year. The whole church was divided into five classes, three in the province of New Jersey, and two in that of New York; and a delegation of two ministers and two elders from each classis constituted the general synod, which was to meet once a year.

The prosperity of the Dutch Church, particularly in the city of New York, was retarded by another cause, namely, the long-continued opposition to preaching in English. The Dutch tongue having been gradually disappearing ever since the conquest of the colony in 1664, many of the youth had grown up almost in utter ignorance of it, and went off to the Episcopal and Presbyterian Churches, especially the former, for the latter had as yet but a merely tolerated and feeble existence. At length the Rev. Dr. Laidlie, a Scotch minister, was invited from Holland, and commenced preaching in English in 1764, from which time

1 Few men have ever lived in America more useful or respected than Dr. John H. Livingstone. For many years he was a pastor in New York city. But the latter part of his life was spent in New Brunswick, in the State of New Jersey, where he was professor of theology in the seminary of the Reformed Dutch Church. He died in the year 1825, revered by all of every denomination who knew him. He has left an abiding impression of his character upon the church of which he was so distinguished an ornament.

Dutch fell still more rapidly into disuse. The last Dutch sermon was preached in the collegiate churches in the city of New
York in 1804, though in some of the churches it was used some
years longer. But it has now been quite abandoned in the pulpit throughout the United States.

The Revolutionary war, also, proved disastrous to the Dutch
Church, particularly in the city of New York. One of the church
edifices there was used as an hospital, another as a cavalry riding
school, during the occupation of the place by a British force
from 1776 to 1783. But with the return of peace prosperity
returned to this as well as other evangelical communions, and
it has been steadily advancing ever since. In all the States it
had only eighty-two congregations and thirty ministers in 1784;
but the former have now risen to 253, and the latter to 234.
The communicants are from 26,000 to 27,000.

A college was founded by the Dutch Reformed at New Brunswick, in New Jersey, in 1770, which, after various vicissitudes,
has now been open for many years, and is firmly established and
flourishing. It is called Rutger's college. Connected with it
there is a theological seminary, with three able professors, and
between thirty and forty students.

The Dutch Church is doing much for Sunday schools, home
missions, and the education of young men for the ministry. It
has a society also for foreign missions, auxiliary to the American
Board of Commissioners for Foreign Missions, and now maintaining some six or eight missionaries with their wives at two
or three stations in Borneo.

The church is at present organised in a general synod, two
particular synods, and nineteen classes. Its standards are those
of the Reformed Church of Holland, viz., the Belgic Confession, the Heidelberg Catechism, the Canons of the Synod of
Dort, &c. Its doctrines are in all respects purely Calvinistic.
From the first it has been favoured with an able, learned, and
godly ministry. In its earlier days the labours of such men as
the Rev. Theodorus J. Freylinghuysen, Drs. Laidlie and Wes-
terlo, and others of like character, were greatly blessed. In our
own times many of its ministers stand in the first rank among
our distinguished American divines, and many of its congregations have enjoyed very precious religious revivals. For the

edification of the people, one of the most instructive and best conducted religious papers, called the Christian Intelligencer, is published weekly in the city of New York.

CHAPTER XI.

SMALLER PRESBYTERIAN CHURCHES—THE ASSOCIATE CHURCH—THE ASSOCIATE REFORMED CHURCH—AND THE REFORMED PRESBYTERIAN CHURCH.

These are often called the "Scottish Secession churches." They were originally established by emigrants from Scotland and Ireland, and are mainly composed to this day, of Scotch and Irish emigrants and their descendants. The first and last of the three were, in their origin, branches of similar churches in Scotland, and out of an unsuccessful attempt made in America to unite the two sprang the second.

In the year 1733, as is well known, the Rev. Messrs. Ebenezer Erskine, Alexander Moncrieff, William Wilson, and James Fisher, by a protest addressed to the commission of the general assembly of the Church of Scotland, seceded from the prevailing party in the judicatories of that church. The ground of this separation was not a disagreement with the doctrines, order, or discipline of that church, but dissatisfaction with what the dissenters considered to be an inadequate maintenance of those doctrines, and enforcing of that order and discipline. These seceders, joined afterwards by many others, organised the *Associate Presbytery*, and soon became a numerous and important branch of the kingdom of Christ in Scotland.

Seventeen years after this secession a number of persons, chiefly Scotch emigrants, sent a petition from Pennsylvania to the Associate (Antiburgher[1]) synod in Scotland, praying that ministers might be sent from that body to break unto them the bread of life. Two ministers, Messrs. Gellatly and Arnot, were accordingly sent over in 1753 or 1754, with power to form

---

[1] The Secession became divided into Burghers and Antiburghers, by a controversy on the lawfulness of what was called the Burgess oath.

churches, ordain elders, and constitute a presbytery. The labours of these brethren were crowned with success; several congregations were soon organised, and a presbytery formed in the eastern part of Pennsylvania; and as other ministers were sent over from Scotland from time to time, there were about eight or ten in all before the breaking out of the Revolution. But in 1782, the presbytery was reduced to the original number of two ministers, in consequence of one or two being deposed, and others joining several ministers of the Reformed Presbyterian Church, or Covenanters, in forming the Associate Reformed Church.

Notwithstanding these untoward circumstances the two ministers, with the congregations adhering to them, persevered, and their numbers being speedily recruited from Scotland, such, at last, was their success in training young men among themselves, that in 1801 they had four presbyteries, which that year, by a delegation from their ranks, formed the ASSOCIATE SYNOD of NORTH AMERICA, a body which meets annually. The presbyteries have now been quadrupled, I believe, and extend over the middle, southern, and western States. According to a recent report, they have 183 churches, eighty-seven ministers, and 16,000 communicants. This is too small an estimate, but the most correct that I have had an opportunity of seeing.

They have a theological school, with two able professors and some fifteen or twenty students, in connection with Jefferson college in the western part of Pennsylvania, eighteen miles from Pittsburg. For their organ they publish a valuable monthly journal called the "Religious Monitor." The doctrines of the Associate Church are thoroughly Calvinistic; its polity completely Presbyterian. It has enjoyed the labours of many able ministers.

ASSOCIATE REFORMED CHURCH. This body, as we have seen, owed its existence to an attempt made in 1782, to unite in one body the few Associate and Reformed Presbyterian churches then to be found in the United States. But as the success of the attempt was only partial, the coalition being refused by certain members of both churches, both survive to this day, and thus a project for merging two denominations in one, resulted in the creation of a third.

The Associate Reformed Church has rapidly increased. Starting with a small number of ministers and churches in 1782, it has now no fewer than three synods, one in the north of New York, one in the south, and one in the west, the northern being the largest. It has a theological seminary at Newburgh in the some State, with three professors, and some fifteen or twenty students. The western synod has a seminary at Pittsburg, with one professor and about twenty students.

The doctrines of this church are Calvinistic, and its polity Presbyterian; points on which it hardly at all differs from the Associate synod. The latter maintain a state of strict isolation from other communions, and in their church psalmody confine themselves exclusively to the Book of Psalms closely rendered into metre. They also strenuously continue the custom of having fast and thanksgiving days to precede and follow the administration of the sacrament of the supper. On all these points the Associate Reformed are less strict.

The churches of the Associate Reformed have lately been reported as 214, their ministers as 116, and their communicants as 12,000. This estimate is quite too low. About twenty years ago, part of this communion joined the Presbyterian Church, but the greater part preferred maintaining their independent position. They have a considerable number of able ministers. The late Dr. John M. Mason was for the greater part of his life one of their most distinguished members, but latterly he joined the Presbyterian Church. The Christian Magazine, a monthly periodical, is published under the auspices of the Associate Reformed.

The REFORMED PRESBYTERIAN CHURCH or COVENANTERS, comprise about forty churches, twenty ministers, and 35,000 communicants. Their first presbytery was constituted in Pennsylvania in 1774, but several, if not all, of its members united with ministers of the Associate Church, as we have seen, in 1782. In doctrine and polity they agree with the great body of Presbyterians, with this exception, that they attach themselves more closely to the principles of what is called in Scotland the Second Reformation, commencing with the famous assembly of 1638. Hence "the Cameronians," as they are also called in Scotland, never approved of the settlement of church affairs in that country, immediately after the Revolution of 1688. With the

Church of Scotland, and the fathers of the Secession in 1733, they maintain inviolate what may be called the church establishment principles of the Westminster Confession, only, that they carry these principles somewhat farther than either,—holding, that as Christ, in his kingly character, is the head and source of all power, civil governments are bound to own his authority, and in all their laws and actings to conform themselves to the rules of holy scripture. Some of them, accordingly, refuse to take the oath of allegiance to the government of the United States.

A theological class of young men preparing for the ministry in this church has usually existed in Philadelphia, under the care of one of its distinguished ministers. Its congregations take an interest in Sunday schools, and other benevolent enterprises. Of late they have begun to attend to foreign missions, and now support one or two missionaries in India, in connection with the board of missions of the Old School Presbyterian church.

No church in the United States, in proportion to its extent, has had a larger number of great men in its ministry. One of these, the late Alexander M'Leod, D.D., ranked in his day with Drs. Mason, Griffin, Dwight, and other distinguished preachers.

CHAPTER XII.

THE LUTHERAN CHURCH.

The first Lutherans that emigrated to America came from Holland, and settled at New York about the year 1626, that is, two years after the regular occupation of New Netherlands by the Dutch. But they were few in number, and as long as the Dutch held the country, they worshipped in private houses only. But on the colony being transferred to the English in 1664, they obtained leave to open a place of public worship, and had for their first minister Jacob Fabricius, who arrived in 1669.

Next among the Lutherans came the Swedish colony that settled on the Delaware in 1636. It flourished for a while, but receiving no new comers from Sweden, the colonists gradually fell into the use of the English tongue, and as there were no Lutheran clergymen who could preach in English, on losing their Swedish pastors, they went to the English Episcopal church for religious teachers, and became ultimately merged in that denomination. Nevertheless, by their charter they are still styled Swedish Lutheran churches.[1]

The third Lutheran emigration to the United States was that of the Germans. Their first settlements were in Pennsylvania, soon after the grant of that province to William Penn, in 1680, whence they spread by degrees, not only through Pennsylvania, but also into Maryland, Virginia, the interior of New York, and, since the Revolution, over the western States. Emigration from Germany may be said to have fairly commenced on a large scale in 1710. Its primary cause lay in the persecution of the Protestants in the Palatinate. It has continued from that time to this day adding tens of thousands almost every year to the population of the country. The western, northern, and southern parts of Germany; Wurtemberg, Bavaria, Baden, and the German parts of Switzerland and Alsace in France, have from first to last sent immense multitudes in quest of homes in America.

The first emigrants brought no pastors with them, but they had pious schoolmasters who held meetings on the Sabbath, and read the scriptures, Arndt's True Christianity, and other religious books. The Swedish ministers, too, of those early times visited the small scattered groups of faithful souls, and administered to them the ordinances of religion.

Among the first German ministers in America were the Rev. Messrs. Bolzius and Gronau, who laboured in a colony from Saltzburg in the south of Germany. These emigrants had been driven from their native country by persecution, and had settled in Georgia. Other emigrants from Germany settled about the same time in the Carolinas, where a considerable number of Lutheran churches are to be found at this day. In 1742,

---

[1] " Annals of the Swedes on the Delaware," by the Rev. J. C. Clay, pp. 3, 4, 161, &c.

the Rev. Henry Melchior Mahlenburg, an eminently learned,
zealous, and successful minister, arrived in that district, and,
during a course of fifty years, was the honoured instrument of
greatly promoting religion among the German population. He
was one of the founders, in fact, of the Lutheran Church in
America, which, by repeated arrivals of other distinguished
men from Germany, had become widely extended before the
commencement of the Revolutionary war. But it, as well as
other churches, suffered much from that war. Many of the
German colonists took up arms in defence of their adopted country. The early wars with the Indians, also, proved very pre-
judicial to the Lutheran churches on the frontiers.

The rapid progress made by this church since the Revolution,
and particularly since the constitution of its general synod in
1820, may be seen from the following succinct summary, taken
from the Lutheran Almanac for 1843, and fully to be relied on.

> The number of Ministers and Licentiates is   423
> ——   Congregations...................   1371
> ——   Communicants..................146,303

Besides one general synod, there are nineteen district synods,
twelve of which are united with the general synod. There are
four theological seminaries, one college, and four classical schools;
one orphan house; an education society, a foreign missionary
society, and a book establishment. During the year 1841, the
Lutheran ministry received an accession of fifty-eight new mem
bers; 9022 new members were added by confirmation, and 9000
by emigration; 17,776 children and adults were baptised. Three
new synods were formed in 1841, seventy-six new churches
built, and eighty-eight new congregations organised.

These results do, indeed, call for heartfelt thanks to the Giver
of all good. I know not a single more promising circumstance,
in regard to true religion in America, than its rapid progress
among the vast German population of the United States, as
exhibited in the Lutheran and German Reformed Churches.
Wonderful, indeed, has been the change during the last twenty
years.

The establishment of Pennsylvania college, near Gettysburg,
under the auspices of the general synod, has been a great blessing. This college, which has been liberally assisted by the

legislature of Pennsylvania, and receives 1000 dollars a year from that State, has a president, five able professors, and about 150 students. The general synod's theological seminary, which, also, is placed at Gettysburg, has three distinguished professors, and usually from twenty-five to thirty students. It began with one professor, the Rev. Samuel S. Schmucker, D.D., to whom, under God, it mainly owed its existence, in 1826, since which time it has educated upwards of 140 young men for the ministry. The institution is most pleasantly situated, and has a well selected library, great part of which, together with a considerable amount of funds for the founding of the seminary, was obtained in Germany through the efforts of the Rev. Benjamin Kurtz, D.D. The Lutherans have three other theological schools, one at Hartwick in New York, another at Lexington in South Carolina, and a third at Columbus, Ohio. Sixty-one young men were prosecuting their studies at these in 1841, and 115 more were engaged in preparatory studies at academies and colleges. These simple facts exhibit an extraordinary change in the state of this church from what it was twenty-five years ago.

Among its distinguished men we may mention the Rev. Messrs. Bolzius, Gronau, H. M. Muhlenburg, Kunze, Schmidt, Kurtz, Goring, another Muhlenburg, Helmuth, Melsheimer, Storch, Endross, Lochman, Schæffer, Ruthrauff, Shober, Geissenhainer, Schmucker, (the professor's father,)—all men of great influence in their day. Several of its living ministers, also, are men of acknowledged talents, learning, piety, and usefulness. Many of the earlier ministers were educated at Franke's institute at Halle, which, indeed, may be regarded as the mother of the Lutheran Church throughout a large part of the United States. [1]

The same doctrines are held as in the evangelical Lutheran churches in the various countries of Europe, with some differences which we shall presently notice. They comprehend the following points:—"That there is a trinity of persons in one Godhead;" "the proper and eternal divinity of the Lord Jesus Christ;" "the universal depravity of our race;" "the vicarious nature and

---

[1] Nor have the churches in America ceased to feel a warm interest in the *Alma Mater* of so many of their pastors. When she suffered so much from the French in 1814, collections were promptly made by them, and forwarded to the amount of 2334 dollars.

unlimited extent of the atonement;" "that men are justified gratuitously for Christ's sake, through faith;" "the word and sacraments means of grace;" "a future judgment, and the award of eternal life and happiness to the righteous, and eternal misery to the wicked." On the subject of election, predestination, &c., they are well known to be rather Arminian than Calvinistic.

The Lutheran Church in America has a short but excellent liturgy, while her ministers are at the same time allowed a discretionary power with regard to it. It observes a few of the chief festivals, such as Christmas, Good Friday, Easter Sunday, Ascension day, and Whitsunday. Like the Episcopal and the German Reformed churches, it administers the rite of confirmation to baptised persons after their arriving at years of discretion, and going through a course of catechetical and biblical instruction.

It deserves notice that the Lutheran Church in the United States, as is well known to those who are intimately acquainted with it, has become much more sound than it once was, and than some of its branches in Europe are, in regard to a few such points as the following: First, *it quite rejects the authority of the fathers in ecclesiastical controversy.* The Reformers relied too much upon them. Secondly, it no longer requires assent to the doctrine *of the real or bodily presence of the Saviour in the eucharist.* In other words, it has renounced the doctrine of consubstantiation, and holds that of our Lord's spiritual presence, as understood by other evangelical Protestants. Again, *it has rejected the remnant of private confession,* which it at first retained. Fourth, it has abolished the remains of papal superstition in the abjuration of evil spirits at baptism. Fifth, it has made a more systematic adjustment of its doctrines. Sixth, it has adopted a more regular and stricter system of church discipline. This, as respects individual churches, is essentially Presbyterian. The synods in their organisation and powers resemble presbyteries, but with fewer formalities, and their decisions are couched more in the form of recommendations, whilst the general synod is altogether advisory, and resembles the general associations of the Congregational churches of New England. Conferences of several neighbouring ministers are held for preaching and protracted meetings for the benefit of their congregations. And, lastly, its ministers are no longer bound to all the minute points of an extended human creed. All that is required of them is a belief in the Bible, and in the Ausburg Confession as a substantially correct expression of Bible doctrines. The American Lutheran Church thinks, that a written creed should be short, comprehending like that of the apostles, which was long the only creed in the primitive churches, only the doctrines necessary to salvation. So much for its doctrines, order, and discipline.[1]

I have only to add that this church is taking a deeper and deeper interest every year in the religious and benevolent undertakings of our times. Sunday schools and Bible classes are very generally to be found in her congregations. She has had an education society, with numerous branches, since 1835, which has assisted above 100 young men in preparing for the ministry. We shall speak hereafter of her Foreign Missionary Society, founded in 1837. Finally, two valuable religious papers, one in English, and the other in German, extensively diffuse among the people intelligence relating to the progress of the Redeemer's kingdom on the earth.

CHAPTER XIII.

THE GERMAN REFORMED CHURCH.

THIS offshoot from the church bearing the same name in Germany is, like it, Presbyterian in its government, and Calvinistic in its doctrinal standards.

The "Reformed" being mingled with the Lutherans in the early German emigrations, societies of the former soon appeared, particularly in Pennsylvania, and spread, ere long, to the south and west of that province. These, though long existing apart,

---

[1] In making this statement I have been greatly indebted to professor's Schmucker's "Portraiture of Lutheranism," and his "Retrospect of Lutheranism in the United States," both published at the request of the general synod of the church.

were at last united in 1746, by the Rev. Mr. Schlatter, who, having been sent from Europe for the purpose, succeeded in giving a better organisation as well as more union to their churches. Their increase since has given them an important place among American Presbyterians.

It is a singular fact, that the first missionaries to the German Reformed in America, were sent out by the *Classis* of Amsterdam in Holland, through which channel their churches continued to receive their ministerial supplies, and to which they were kept, down to the year 1792, in the same subordination as the Dutch churches in America used to be. Mr. Schlatter, the pioneer in this good cause, was soon followed by other men sent over by the said classis and synod.[1]

The dependence of the Reformed German Church in the United States on the Dutch Church in Europe, was brought to a close in 1792, in consequence of the difficulty of maintaining the previous relations of America with Holland after the conquest of the latter by the French. An independent constitution was accordingly adopted, consisting of clerical and lay delegates; but it was not until 1819 that the synod was divided into classes or presbyteries, and based upon a representation of the classes by clerical and lay delegates. The church being now left to its own resources, the training of young men for the ministry was for many years entrusted to such pastors as were willing to receive students of theology into their families; still, the want of proper institutions for that purpose was deeply felt. At length, in 1824, the synod resolved that they would have a theological seminary, and this resolution took effect the following year, by the opening of an institution at Carlisle, a pleasant town in central Pennsylvania. Dr. Mayer was appointed the first professor, and continued in the discharge of that office until 1829, when his resignation was tendered and accepted. During this period the seminary was removed from Carlisle to York, and from that to Mercersburg in the same State, about fifty miles from Carlisle, and there it is now permanently established. Marshall college was opened in connection with it in 1837, and

[1] Among these were Weiber, Steiner, Otterbein, Hendel, Helfenstein, Helfrich, Gebbard, Dallicker, Blumer, Faber, Becker, and Herman. One only of all these is still spared to the church; the rest have gone to their reward.

the Rev. Dr. Rauch, who had been president of the preparatory department of the seminary at York, was chosen president. Under that distinguished scholar and excellent minister it soon enjoyed an enviable reputation; but in the spring of 1840, the church was called to lament his premature decease. The present theological professor, Dr. Nevin, is a man of distinguished abilities and deep piety. There are about twenty-five students of theology, and the academical classes have an attendance of from eighty to 100 youths.

The German Reformed Church seems to have experienced a crisis in 1841, that year having been appointed to be celebrated as a centenary jubilee for all its congregations. A century having elapsed since its first organisation in America, such an acknowledgment of God's mercies was deemed eminently becoming, and that the occasion might be turned to the best account, it was resolved that an effort should be made to raise sufficient funds for the endowment of the seminary and college at Mercersburg. The result must have fully realised the expectations of the church's most sanguine friends, for at a late meeting of its synod upwards of 80,000 dollars were ascertained to have been subscribed, and to a large amount actually collected, while the contributions of more than half of the congregations had yet to be reported. Assurances have since been received that more than 100,000 dollars, the amount originally specified, will be obtained.

The field which this church has to occupy is very extensive. Besides the large German population in the Atlantic States, the Great West—the valley of the Mississippi—over which German emigrants are now settling in vast numbers, cries to this and to the Lutheran Church for help; and it is hoped, that in a few years a host of labourers from both will be raised up for the harvest, which is ripe for the sickle.

The German Reformed synod has now in its connection about 180 ministers, distributed thus: 112 in Pennsylvania; thirty-seven in Ohio; three in Indiana and Illinois; ten in Maryland; ten in Virginia and North Carolina; and three in New York. It is supposed to have about 600 congregations, and from 75,000 to 100,000 communicants. It may be said with truth that its congregations are rapidly increasing in the knowledge of Jesus

Christ, and from present indications we hail the period as not far distant when instead of being reckoned, as they have long been, among the least of the tribes of Israel, they will be found occupying a place in the very van of the sacramental host of the Lord. In home missionary, educational, and foreign missionary efforts, they are taking a deeper and deeper interest every year, while uniting with the Congregational, and New School Presbyterian churches, in supporting the American Home Missionary Society, the American Education Society, and the American Education Society, and the American Board of Commissioners for Foreign Missions.

CHAPTER XIV.

SMALLER GERMAN SECTS.

THERE are some smaller bodies of German Christians in the United States, which may be classed, though not, perhaps, in all cases without qualification, among the evangelical denominations. The Moravians might have been placed here, but we have put them in a separate chapter, partly because they are Episcopal, partly because they are no longer purely German either in blood or language.

First, then, there is a body called "the United Brethren," or German Methodists. From the name one might suppose them to be Moravians, but they are quite a distinct body. Their other name, German Methodists, they owe to their having almost all the peculiarities of the Episcopal Methodists, from whom they differ hardly in anything but language. Among their earlier and more distinguished ministers were the Rev. William Otterbein, originally a minister of the German Reformed Church, Henry Widener, Henry Becker, and Simon Herre. Their present numbers I do not know. The late Bishop Asbury, of the Methodist Episcopal church, in his sermon on the death of the Rev. Martin Boehm, in 1812, says: "Will it be hazarding too much to say that in Pennsylvania,

Maryland, and Virginia, there are 100 preachers, and 20,000 people in the communion of the United Brethren?" Many of these faithful men have gone to glory, and many are yet alive to preach to congregated thousands. Pre-eminent among these is William Otterbein.[1] Now, they may safely be said to be at least as numerous as they were thirty years ago, but probably they are not much more so, for the Methodist Episcopal church has now many German ministers and congregations, and the United German Brethren have never had the compact and powerful organisation necessary for enabling such a body to extend its influence and increase its numbers.

2. There are the WINEBRENNARIANS, so called from their founder being a Mr. Winebrennen, a pious and zealous German, who resides, if still alive, in eastern Pennsylvania, where his followers are chiefly found. They form several congregations, and are said to be quite evangelical in their doctrines, and, as a body, irreproachable in their lives. Their ministers, though not well informed, have the reputation of being devoted, laborious, and useful men. Winebrennen seems to have commenced his labours among the Germans very much in the spirit and with the aim of Hans Honga in Norway.

3. The MENNONISTS, consisting, it is said, of above 200 small congregations. They are an amiable and, in the main, evangelical people, yet rendered somewhat lukewarm, it is to be feared, by their worldly prosperity. They are, for the most part, descended from Mennonist emigrants from Holland and Germany. Their confession of faith, as stated by one of their ministers, Mr. Gan of Ryswick in Holland, appears to be moderate orthodoxy. They reject infant baptism, but though their founder, Simon Menno, maintained that baptism should be by immersion, they do not deem it indispensable. On the contrary they sprinkle, or rather pour water upon the head of the candidate, after which follow the imposition of hands and prayer.

The Mennonists of Holland, as is well known, claim to be descended in the main from those Waldenses who, towards the close of the twelfth century, emigrated in great numbers to that

---

[1] "History of the Methodist Episcopal Church," by the Rev. Dr. Bangs vol. ii., pp. 370, 371.

country. If this be so, then the Mennonists in America have in their veins the blood of those wonderful survivors of long ages of persecution and oppression.

CHAPTER XV.

Secessions of greater or less magnitude have detached themselves from time to time, and glided off like avalanches from the mount Zion of the Methodist Episcopal Church, not, however, so as either to diminish its grandeur, or change its physiognomy; most of them having sooner or later melted away to nothing.

The first that occurred was that of the Rev. William Hammet of Charleston, South Carolina, in 1785. His followers took the name of *Primitive Methodists*. The second was that of the Rev. James O'Kelly, in Virginia, about 1792. His followers called themselves *Republican Methodists*. This was by far the more serious of the two, but both soon and for ever disappeared from the scene.

In the year 1816, about 1000 of the people of colour in the Methodist Episcopal Church at Philadelphia, headed by a Mr. Richard Allen, seceded from the main body. Allen was a man of considerable talent, who, from having been once a slave in one of the southern States, besides procuring his freedom, had acquired a handsome property, and becoming a preacher in the Methodist connection rose to be ordained an elder. After his secession he was ordained a bishop at the first general conference of his followers, by prayer and the imposition of hands by five local elders, of whom one was a presbyter in the Protestant Episcopal Church. What the number of ministers in this small communion may be I know not. Since the death of Allen, instead of a bishop it has two superintendents.

Another secession of coloured members took place at New York in 1819, and it has now several congregations of people of colour in New Jersey, Connecticut, Rhode island, and Massachusetts.   Three years ago they had twenty-one circuits, thirty-two preachers, and 2608 communicants.   They are believed to have adhered to the doctrines and polity of the body from which they seceded, and their dissatisfaction with which arose from their preachers not being admitted into the itineracy, and consequently having no share in the government of the church, nor a right to receive salaries, being only local preachers.

There were one or two other secessions about the same time by which the Methodist Episcopal Church lost a few of its congregations, but they were not of such consequence as to call for special notice.   But it sustained a far more serious loss in 1828, when a considerable number of preachers, chiefly local, and of lay members, withdrew from it at Baltimore, and in other parts of the country.   As this secession has resulted in the formation of a new communion which promises to be permanent, it calls for further notice.

In what was said of the Methodist Episcopal Church the reader will have remarked, that its constitution lodges the supreme power, legislative, judicial, and executive, in the itinerating ministers.   They alone compose the yearly or general conference.   But to two classes of the members this has all along been felt to be oppressive.   First, to the local preachers, who, although they may be ordained ministers, can have no voice in the government of the church.   Nay, ministers who may have been for years in the itinerating service, the moment that from sickness, duty to their families, insufficient support, or any other cause, they leave that service, have no longer any voice in the affairs of that church.   Next, there were laymen who thought that the laity ought to be represented in the church courts; that is, should be admitted to the annual and general conferences.

This dissatisfaction began to assume a more decided character about the year 1820.   A journal having been established for the purpose of advocating what were called "equal rights;" this led to the sending up of numerous petitions to the general conference held in 1824.   These being unfavourably received, much excitement and discussion followed.   The party that wanted reform urged their demands with more eagerness, and even violence, and consequently, some suspensions from church privileges took place in Baltimore and elsewhere.   Such was the state of matters when the general conference met in 1828; failing in obtaining redress from which, they who thought themselves aggrieved seceded, and formed a new body under the title of the PROTESTANT METHODIST CHURCH IN THE UNITED STATES. In taking this step they have made no change in their doctrines, nor any innovations in church polity, beyond what they had unsuccessfully petitioned for—the admission of lay representatives and of the local preachers to the government of the church. They have also ceased to have bishops, all ordination among them being now confined to the imposition of hands by presbyters. Their general conference meets once in seven years, instead of once in four years like that from which they seceded.

According to a recent report of the statistics of this body, it has one general and twenty-one yearly conferences, near 400 travelling preachers, besides a large number of local preachers, and 60,000 communicants. Its general conference has instituted a board of domestic and foreign missions, as also a book concern, which from its head quarters in Baltimore has issued a great quantity of religious publications in various forms. There are four religious newspapers, also, published under its auspices. Its churches are to be found in all parts of the country, but particularly in the middle, northern, and western States.

CALVINISTIC METHODISTS,—a small Welsh communion, consisting of twenty churches and as many pastors. They are an evangelical and zealous body, and as it is only a few years since the greater part of them came to America, they still use the Welsh language in their public worship and in their families. Though found in several States, they are most numerous, I believe, in New York.

CHAPTER XVI.

THE FRIENDS OR QUAKERS.

This religious community first appeared in England towards the middle of the seventeenth century, and had an early share in the colonisation of the United States. We have seen that its reputed founder and first preacher, George Fox, visited several of the southern provinces, and announced his message, as he himself relates, to a " willing people." But the proselytes to his peaceful doctrines, especially if they attempted to propagate them, encountered violent persecution almost everywhere, and although they were from the first protected in Rhode island, and did at length obtain toleration in the south, they never made much progress until, through the influence and exertions of William Penn, they obtained an asylum first in New Jersey, and afterwards in Pennsylvania, towards the close of that century.

They are now supposed to have about 500 congregations in the United States, and are chiefly settled in the south-east of Pennsylvania, in New Jersey, New York, Rhode island, Maryland, and Virginia, though some may be found in all the States. In Philadelphia, alone, they have six or eight large congregations or " meetings."

It is far from easy to make out what were the doctrines really held by George Fox, and some of the other early Friends, or Quakers, as they are more commonly called. They spoke so much about the " light within," and the " Christ in the heart," and so little about the proper divinity of Jesus Christ, the inspiration and divine authority of the scriptures, &c., that good men of that day much doubted how far they held the saving truths of the gospel. But the subsequent writings of Penn, Barclay, and others, to whom may be added many excellent authors of the present day, make it certain that the great majority of well-informed Friends have been sound in " the faith that saves."

But within the last fifteen years a deplorable schism has taken place. Doctrines of the most dangerous character, embodying, in fact, a kind of fanatical deism, having been widely disseminated by the preaching and writings of the late Elias Hicks, of Long island, New York, who was one of their ministers, they separated into two quite distinct bodies, each maintaining that it held the doctrines of the original Quakers. [1] One party is called the Orthodox, the other the Hicksites, from the name of their leader, or rather founder. Their relative numbers are not exactly known, but the Orthodox are supposed to be fully three-fifths of the whole, or to have 300 congregations.

The peculiarities of the Friends, in respect to plainness of dress, refusing to uncover the head as a mark of respect to their fellow-men, whatever be their station, rank, or office, the use of the singular *thou* and *thee* instead of the plural *you* in all cases where custom has sanctioned the superseding of the former by the latter, their refusing to take an oath, and to bear arms, are too well known to require remark.

They have no " hireling ministry," and think it wrong to educate men for that office, maintaining that those only should be suffered to preach who are moved from time to time by the Spirit to deliver a message from God. All remain perfectly silent at their meetings, unless some one feels thus moved to speak for the edification of those present, or to pray. In almost every congregation there are members, who from being often moved to speak, are called " preachers," and they may be of either sex. Some, too, think that the Spirit moves them to travel about for the purpose of visiting and preaching. But these, before receiving authority to proceed on such missions, must first be approved by the monthly and quarterly meet-

---

[1] The highest law court in New Jersey decided a few years ago, in a suit respecting property held by one of the " Quarterly meetings" in that State, that the so-called Orthodox Quakers are the true successors of the founders of the denomination—in other words, hold the true doctrines of the people called Friends. This decision was formed after a long and very thorough investigation of the subject, conducted by a master in chancery, who was employed during several months in taking the testimony of distinguished Friends as to what were the doctrines of the society.

ings. Though they have no salaries, provision is made when
required for the support of them and their families by presents
from richer Friends. The supervision of the churches is
vested in the monthly meetings, composed of all the congregations within a convenient distance from each other; the
quarterly meetings, which comprise all within a larger circle;
and the yearly meetings, including all within one or more of
the States, and of which, we believe, there are eight.

The Friends have a tract society, a bible society, and some
Sunday schools. They have made some attempts, also, but to
no great extent, to bring the Indian tribes to the knowledge
of the gospel. The characteristic traits of this peace-loving
people are the same in the United States as in England and
elsewhere—frugality, simplicity of manners, strictness of morals,
care for the poor of their society, and abhorrence of oppression in every form. This may be emphatically said of the
Orthodox. Of the Hicksites, who, in my opinion, have departed fundamentally from the gospel, it is to be feared that
a far less favourable account will yet have to be given. The
substantial orthodoxy of William Penn, and many others of the
same school, has produced good fruits which never can be
looked for from the delusions of Elias Hicks.

Far from rapidly increasing in America, I rather think that
" the Friends" are stationary, if not positively declining, in
point of numbers, and the too frequent neglect of the religious
education of their children, together with the rejection of the
outward administration of baptism and the Lord's supper, must
ever prevent them, in my opinion, from enjoying great or continued prosperity as a church.

CHAPTER XVII.

THE SUMMARY.

WE have now completed our notices of the various evangelical churches or denominations in the United States; and to assist the reader in taking a general view of the whole, we shall place them before his eye at once in a tabular form. In doing this we shall first arrange them in the order in which we have already passed them under our review; that is, of their successive appearance in America. We shall then re-arrange them under various heads, such as Episcopal, Congregational, &c.

	Churches.	Ministers.	Commun.	Population.
I. EPISCOPAL.—				
Protestant Episcopalians.........	1,140	1,000	100,000	700,000
Moravians.............................	24	33	5,745	12,000
Total...	1,164	1,033	105,745	712,000
II. CONGREGATIONAL.—				
Orthodox churches..................	1,500	1,250	160,000	1,000,000
III. BAPTIST.—				
Regular Baptists....................	7,766	3,717[1]	570,758	⎫
Free Will do.........................	753	612	47,217	⎪
Seventh day do......................	42	46	4,503	⎬ 3,423,000
Disciples of Christ, or Campbellites............................				⎭
Total...	8,561	4,375	622,478	3,423,000
IV. PRESBYTERIAN.—				
Regular Presbyterians—Old and New Schools....................	3,400	2,551	243,000	⎫
Cumberland Presbyterians.......	550	550	70,000	⎪
Dutch Reformed Church.........	253	234	26,000	⎪
Associate Synod.....................	183	87	16,000	⎪
Associate Reformed...............	214	116	12,000	⎬ 3,312,000
Reformed Presbyterians, or Cameronians......................	40	20	3,500	⎪
Lutherans.............................	1,371	423	146,303	⎪
German Reformed..................	600	180	75,000	⎭
Winebrennarians...................				
Total...	6,611	4,161	591,803	3,312,000

[1] See remarks in chap. iv. of this Book for the grounds on which the ordained ministers in the Regular Baptist communion are estimated at 3717.

	Churches or other places of worship.	Preachers.	Commun.	Population.
V. METHODIST.—				
Methodist Episcopal Church.	25,109[1]	{3,587 T.M.[2] 6,393 L.M.[3]}	852,918	5,000,000
Protestant Methodists.........		400 T.M.	60,000	300,000
United German Brethren......		100	20,000	100,000
Welsh Calvinistic Methodists.	25	25	2,500	12,500
Total...	25,134	{4,112 T.M. 6,393 L.M.}	935,418	5,412,500

MENNONIST.............................	200	—	—	—
ORTHODOX QUAKER....................	300			

By uniting the Congregationalists with the Presbyterians, which, as they are in all important respects the same, is perfectly proper, we reduce the evangelical denominations in the United States to four great families, and, thus arranged, they present the following summary:—

	Churches.	Ministers.	Commun.	Population.
Episcopalians.......................	1,164	1,033	105,745	712,000
Presbyterians.......................	8,111	5,411	751,803	4,350,000
Baptists.............................	8,561	4,375	622,478	3,423,000
Methodists..........................	25,134	4,112[4]	935,418	5,400,000
Total...	42,970	14,931	2,415,444	13,885,000

This synopsis suggests a few observations.

1. We have left out the Campbellites, both because we have no correct information as to their statistics, and because though many of them are, no doubt, sound on all essential points, yet not knowing how many, we cannot place them with entire confidence among the evangelical denominations. Neither have we included the Mennonists, the Winebrennarians, nor some of the smaller secessions from the Methodist Episcopal Church. Had all these been included, the number of churches, ministers, and members, together with the amount of the general population

---

1 I am indebted for the above estimate of the probable number of places, including churches, school-houses, and private houses, in which the Methodist itinerant and local ministers preach, to my friend president Durbin. It has been made with much care, and, 1 doubt not, is considerably within the truth. President Durbin has a wide and accurate acquaintance with the country, as well as with the entire economy of the church to which he belongs.

2 Travelling ministers.   3 Local ministers.   4 Travelling ministers.

under the moral influence of the churches included in this category, would have been much greater.

2. It is impossible to state the number of churches or congregations, properly so called. Those of the Episcopalians, Presbyterians, and Baptists, taken together, amount to 17,836. But those belonging to the different Methodist communions it is impossible to ascertain, no return of them having been made. There can be no doubt that of the places of worship which I have given on president Durbin's authority, more than 7500 are churches properly so called. This, then, would make the entire number of the churches of the evangelical denominations, without counting the Campbellites, Mennonists, &c., exceed 25,000, and supposing these to contain upon an average 500 people each, they would accommodate more than 12,000,000 of the 17,000,000 of inhabitants. But if we take in all the places, whether churches or not, at which the gospel is preached, in most cases once a week at least, and in others once a fortnight, seldom less often, these will be found to amount to 42,970. And even to these there ought to be added a part at least of the Campbellite, Mennonist, and Winebrennarian places of worship, and those of some of the smaller Methodist sects, before we can arrive at a full enumeration of all the places, churches, and others, in which salvation by a crucified Saviour is proclaimed to sinners.

3. The summary gives 14,931 as the number of ministers who devote themselves entirely to the work. Adding the 6393 Methodist local preachers we have 21,324 as the number of actual preachers of the gospel. Even this is exclusive of those of the omitted denominations, and of the licentiates in the Baptist and Presbyterian churches, who cannot well be estimated at less than 1000, and who may fairly be set against the deduction to be made on account of ordained ministers employed as professors and missionaries. But taking the above 14,931 as the number, all things considered, of ministers that are evangelical on all the saving doctrines of the gospel, and divide the population of the United States, which in the beginning of the year 1842 was about 17,500,000, by this number, the result will be one such minister for near 1200 souls. Now, figures cannot express moral influences; such calculations are nevertheless not without their use. A country which has an evangelical preacher on an

average for every 1170 souls, may be considered as pretty well supplied, if they be well distributed and faithful. A perfect distribution, is, indeed, altogether impossible with a population rapidly diffusing itself over immense half cultivated regions, yet much is done to obviate the disadvantages of such a state of things. The aid rendered by the Methodist local preachers must be regarded as an important auxiliary to the more regular ministry. The general faithfulness of this ministry has already been fully discussed.

4. The members in full communion with the churches enumerated exceed 2,400,000 in number. Now, although it be very certain that all these do not live up to their profession, yet as they belong for the most part to churches that endeavour to maintain discipline, we may fairly presume that they comprehend, at least, as large a proportiou of consistent Christians as any equal number of professors in other parts of Christendom.

5. The last column of the summary assumes 13,885,000 of the whole population as under the influence of the evangelical denominations. Accuracy in such a calculation is hardly to be expected, but I have taken the best data I could find, and doubt not that the estimate I have made is not much wide of the truth. Including the denominations that claim to be evangelical, this estimate would exceed 14,500,000, while that of the communicants could not be stated below 2,500,000.

CHAPTER XVIII.

NUMBER OF EVANGELICAL SECTS.

Much has been said in Europe about the multiplicity of sects in the United States, and many seem of opinion that the religious liberty enjoyed there has led to the almost indefinite creation of different religious communions. This requires a little examination.

No doubt, absolute religious liberty will ever be attended

with a considerable subdivision of the religious world into sects. Men will ever differ in their views respecting doctrine and church order, and it is to be expected that such differences will result in the formation of distinct ecclesiastical communions. In the absence of religious liberty matters may be much otherwise, but how far for the better a little consideration will show. People in that case may be constrained to acquiesce, ostensibly at least, in one certain ecclesiastical organisation, and in certain modes of faith and worship sanctioned and established by law. But such acquiescence, it is well known, instead of being real and cordial, is often merely external and constrained; and, if so, its worthlessness is no less evident and palpable.

But as respects the evangelical communions in the United States, it must have struck the reader that this multiplicity has mainly arisen, not from the abuse of religious liberty by the indulgence of a capricious and sectarian spirit, but from the various quarters from which the country has been colonised. Coming in large numbers, and sometimes in compact bodies, from different parts of the old world, nothing was more natural than the desire of establishing for themselves and their posterity the same religious formularies and modes of worship, church government, and discipline, which they had cherished in the lands that had given them birth, and persecution for their adherence to which had led, in many instances, to their having emigrated at all. Hence we find, in the United States, counterparts not only to the Episcopalian, Congregational, Baptist, and Methodist churches of England, and to the Presbyterian churches of Scotland, Ireland, and Wales, but likewise to the Dutch and German Reformed churches, the German Lutheran church, the Moravians, Mennonists, &c. Indeed, there is scarcely an evangelical communion in America which is not the mere extension by emigration of a similar body in Europe. The exceptions hardly can be reckoned such, for they consist of separations from the larger bodies, not because of differences with regard to essential doctrines and forms of church government, but on points of such inferior consequence that they can scarce be regarded as new sects at all.

In fact, if we take all the evangelical communions that have fallen under review, and contemplate the confessedly funda-

mental doctrines maintained by each, it is suprising to observe
how nearly they are agreed. It may, we believe, be demonstrated that among the evangelical communions in the United
States, numerous as they are, there is as much real harmony of
doctrine, if not of church economy, as could be found in the
evangelical churches of the three first centuries.

Indeed, as we before remarked, by grouping the former in
families, according to their great distinctive features, we at once
reduce them to four, or at most five. Thus the Presbyterians,
commonly so called, of the Old and New Schools, the Congregationalists, the Dutch and German Reformed, the Scotch Secession churches, and, we may add, the Lutherans and Cumberland Presbyterians, form but one great Presbyterian family,
composed of elder and younger members, all of them essentially
Presbyterian in church polity, and very nearly coinciding, at
bottom, in their doctrinal views. Among several of these communions there subsists a most intimate fraternal intercourse,
and the ministers of one find no difficulty in entering the service
of another without being re-ordained.

Again, between the different evangelical Baptist sects there
is no really essential or important difference; and the same
may be said of the Methodists. Indeed, if we except those
opinions on certain subjects which distinguish the Episcopalians,
Baptists, and orthodox Quakers respectively, the evangelical
Christians of the United States exhibit a most remarkable coin-
cidence of view on all important points. On all doctrines necessary to salvation—the sum of which is " repentance towards
God," and " faith towards the Lord Jesus Christ," there is
really no diversity of opinion at all. Of this I may now give a
most decisive proof.

I have already spoken of the American Sunday School Union.
Among the laymen who compose its board of directors, are to
be found members of all the main branches of the evangelical
Protestant church—Episcopalians, Congregationalists, Baptist,
Presbyterians, Lutherans, Dutch and German Reformed, Methodists, Quakers, and Moravians. It publishes a great many
books for Sunday school libraries every year, none of course
being admitted the contents of which are likely to give offence
to any member of the board, or repugnant to the peculiarities of

any of the religious bodies represented at it.　In the summer of 1841 the Rev. Dr. Hodge, a professor in Princetown theological seminary was requested by its committee of publications to write a book exhibiting the great doctrines of the gospel as held by all evangelical Christians, and this the worthy professor did to the entire satisfaction, not only of the board, but I believe I may say of all evangelical Christians throughout the land that have read this work.　It is appropriately entituled, "The Way of Life;" the subjects are the scriptures; sin; justification; faith; repentance; profession of religion; and holy living; under which several heads the fundamental doctrines of the gospel are presented in an able and yet most simple and familiar manner. It is a work, in short, which none can read without surprise and delight, at observing the vast extent and fulness of the system of truth, in which all evangelical communions are agreed.

These communions, as they exist in the United States, ought to be viewed as branches of one great body, even the entire visible church of Christ in that land.　Whatever may have been the circumstances out of which they arose, they are but constituent parts of one great whole—divisions of one vast army, though each brigade, and even each regiment, may have its own banner, and its own part of the field to occupy.　And although to the inexperienced eye, such an army as it moves onward against the enemy may have a confused appearance, the different divisions of infantry being arranged separately, the artillery interspersed, and the cavalry sometimes in the front, sometimes in the rear, and sometimes between the columns, yet all are in their proper places, and to the mind of him who assigns them their places, and directs their movements, all is systematic order where the uninitiated sees nothing but confusion.　Momentary collisions, it is true, may sometimes happen,—there may be jostling and irritation occasionally,—yet they all fulfil their appointed parts and discharge their appropriate duties.　So is it with the "sacramental host of God's elect."

No doubt this multiplication of sects is attended with serious evils, especially in the new and thinly peopled settlements.　It often renders the church small and feeble.　But this is an evil that diminishes with the increase of the population.　With a zealous and capable ministry the truth gains ground, the people are gathered into churches, congregations increase in numbers and consistency, and though weak ones are occasionally dissolved, the persons who composed them either going into other evangelical churches, or emigrating to other parts of the country, such as maintain their ground become only the stronger, and it often happens, particularly in the rural districts, that the number of sects diminishes while the population increases.

Great, however, as may be the disadvantages resulting from this multiplicity of different communions, were they all reduced to one or two, we apprehend still worse evils would follow. Diversity on non-essential points among the churches and ministers of a neighbourhood, often gives opportunity to those who reside in it, to attend the services and ministrations that each finds most edifying, instead of being reduced to the sad alternative of either joining in forms of worship which they conscientiously disapprove, and of listening to a minister whom they find unedifying, or of abstaining from public worship altogether. Rather than this, surely far better to bear the expense of having two or three churches in a community, for which, looking only at the mere amount of population, one might suffice.

CHAPTER XIX.

ALLEGED WANT OF HARMONY AMONG THE EVANGELICAL CHRISTIANS OF THE
UNITED STATES.

It has been often and widely stated in Europe, on the authority of a certain class of visitants from the old world who have published their travels, tours, &c., in the new, that there is much unseemly strife among our various religious denominations. Here, I hesitate not to say, there has been much gross misrepresentation. No doubt, our evangelical churches feel the influence of mutual emulation. Placed on the same great field, coming into contact with each other at many points, and all deeply and conscientiously attached to their peculiar doctrines and ecclesiastical economy, they must naturally exercise, on the one hand, the utmost watchfulness with respect to each other, and on the other, put forth all the legitimate means in their power to augment their own numbers. The result of such mutual provocation to good works is eminently happy. There may, indeed, be temporary cases of disagreeable collision and unbrotherly jealousy, but ordinarily these are of short duration. The best of men are, after all, but men. Hence even a devoted gospel minister, after having long had some particular neighbourhood all to himself, may dread the opening of a new place of worship of a different communion in the vicinity of his own, lest some of his hearers should thereby be drawn away, and such an apprehension may, for a time, excite some not very kind feelings in his breast. But universal experience shows, that such feelings are usually groundless, and soon cease to be indulged by any but the most narrow-minded persons.

Sometimes, too, a zealous, and in most cases vain and ignorant preacher, will show himself in a neighbourhood where the churches all belong to communions different from his, and then in his self-sufficiency may begin to denounce and attempt to proselytise. Such men, however, soon create disgust rather than any other feeling, for with us most of those who join this or that church, do so after examination of its doctrines, government, and discipline, and when once satisfied on these points, above all, after finding its services edifying, they are not disposed to allow themselves to be disturbed by every bigoted and noisy brawler that may seek to gain them over to his creed and church, which, after all, may not essentially differ from their own.

Notwithstanding such cases, I hesitate not to affirm, that taking the evangelical churches in the mass, their intercourse, in all parts of the country, manifests a remarkable degree of mutual respect and fraternal affection. Whilst earnest in maintaining alike from the pulpit and in the press, their own views of truth and church order, there is rarely anything like denunciation and unchurching other orthodox communions, but every readiness, on the contrary, to offer help when needed. Thus, among all but the Episcopalians, whose peculiar views of ordination stand in the way, there is a frequent exchanging of pulpits. I have known the pulpit of an excellent Baptist minister in Philadelphia, when he was laid aside by ill health, supplied during two years by other ministers, and by those of pædobaptist churches for much of that time. During more than seven years the author of this work was engaged in benevolent efforts in America, which led him repeatedly to visit every State in the American confederacy, and while on this mission he preached in the pulpits of no less than ten evangelical communions, including all the leading ones.

This brotherly feeling widely prevails among the laity also. In all parts of the country they scruple not, when there is no service in their own places of worship, to attend others though of another communion, and indeed in our cities and large towns not a few Christians regularly attend the week-day lectures of pastors not of their own communion, when these fall on different evenings from those of their own pastors. Not only so, but as there is no bar to intercommunion, except in the case of the Baptists, whose views respecting baptism in all but a few instances prevent it, and in that of the small Scottish Covenanting churches, the members of one evangelical communion often join with those of another in receiving the Lord's supper in the same church. In this respect, a very catholic spirit happily prevails. The answer of the Rev. Mr. Johnes, pastor of the Presbyterian church in Morristown, New Jersey, to General Washington, who, on one occasion, during the war of the Revolution, desired to receive the sacrament of the Lord's supper with Mr. Johnes' congregation, but stated that he was an Episcopalian, is just what 10,000 ministers of the gospel would make in like circumstances: " Sir, it is not a Presbyterian, or an Episcopalian table, but the Lord's table, and you as well as every other Christian are welcome to it."

Numerous occasions, moreover, bring all evangelical Christians together. The Bible, temperance, colonisation, Sunday school, and tract societies, not to mention such as are formed from time to time for particular and perhaps local objects, Sabbath observance, education, and the like, all bring Christians of different denominations into better acquaintance with each other, and tend to promote mutual respect and affection.

Within the last few years, Dr. Schmucker, already mentioned, has proposed a plan of union for all the evangelical Protestant churches, which has met with much favour, so that a

society has been formed for promoting it. Dr. Schmucker, who,
I may remark, is much beloved among Christians of all denominations, as well as extensively known by his writings, does
not propose any amalgamation or *fusion* of the churches, but
the adoption merely of certain fixed principles, upon which all
the evangelical churches shall acknowledge the ecclesiastical acts
of each other, and maintain a fraternal intercommunion.

Another proposal of like tendency will, I trust, ere long be
carried into effect. It is that there should be a yearly meeting
of the friends of foreign missions, held in one or other of the
principal cities, for receiving summary statements from each of
the missionary societies of its operations and success. Such a
meeting, if well conducted, might do much substantial good both
by diffusing important information as to the progress of the
kingdom of Christ, and also by promoting brotherly love among
Christians of different churches.

Taking all the professed Christians, amounting, it has been
seen, to near 2,500,000, in our evangelical churches, I hesitate
not to say that far more mutual respect and brotherly love prevail among them than were they all coerced into one denomination. The world has already seen what sort of union and brotherhood can be produced by all being brought into one great
church that admits of no deviation from the decrees of its councils and conclaves. There may indeed be external agreement,
yet beneath this apparent unanimity there may be internal divisions and heartburnings in abundance. There may be union
against all who dare to impugn her dogmas, but who can tell
the almost infernal hatred with which her religious orders have
been found to regard each other. Compared with this, all the
temporary *attritions*, together with all the controversies and
exacerbations of feeling that accompany them, that take place
in our evangelical Protestant denominations, are as nothing.

Common civility, on the contrary, concurs with Christian
charity to make the enlightened members of one denomination
respect and esteem those of another, and to appreciate the
beautiful sentiment recently attributed by the chancellor of the
exchequer, in the British parliament, to the late Mr. Wilber-
force: " I experience," said that distinguished philanthropist,
" a feeling of triumph when I can get the better of these little

distinctions which keep Christians asunder.   I would not that
any one should sacrifice his principles; but, exercising the Protestant right of private judgment, leave each to his own conclusions.   It is delightful to see that in this way men of different
sects can unite together for the prosecution of their projects for
the amelioration of human society.   When I thus unite with
persons of a different persuasion from myself, it affords me an
augmented degree of pleasure; I rise into a higher nature, into
a purer air; I feel that fetters which before bound me are dissolved, and I delight in that blessed liberty of love which carries all other blessings with it."

Still, the question remains, Whence have foreigners, while
visiting the United States, received the impression, which, by
being promulgated in their writings, has led me to write this
chapter.   The answer is easy.   While such is the prevailing
respect and regard for each other among the members of our
evangelical churches, they all unite in opposing, on the one hand,
the errors of Rome, and, on the other, the heresy that denies
the proper divinity and atonement of Christ, together with those
other aberrations from the true gospel which that heresy involves.
Now, it is this refusal to hold fellowship with errors of vital
moment,—it is this earnest contending for saving truth—that
leads tourists in the United States, whom chance or choice has
thrown into the society of persons opposed in their religious
tenets to the evangelical churches, to charge us with uncharitableness.   *Hinc illæ lachrymæ.*

We deny not that in some of the divisions of churches that
have taken place in the United States, men have at times permitted themselves to speak and write with an acrimony unbe-
coming the gospel, and, by so doing, may have made an unfavourable impression on foreigners.   But such cases have been
local and exceptional rather than general and ordinary, and
never could justify any sweeping charge against the evangelical
denominations as a body.

BOOK VII.

UNEVANGELICAL DENOMINATIONS IN AMERICA.

CHAPTER I.

INTRODUCTORY REMARKS.

HAVING thus reviewed, as far as the compass of our work would permit, the evangelical churches or denominations in the United States of America, we come now to speak of those that are considered as *unevangelical* by orthodox Protestants; and under this head we shall, for convenience sake, range all those sects that either renounce, or fail faithfully to exhibit the fundamental and saving truths of the gospel. Here, however, let us not be misunderstood. When we put Roman Catholics in the same category with Unitarians, we would not for a moment be supposed as placing them on the same footing. The former, doubtless, as a church, hold those doctrines on which true believers in all ages have placed their hopes for eternal life, yet these have been so buried amid the rubbish of multiplied human traditions and inventions, as to remain hid from the great mass of the people. Still, as in their doctrinal formularies they have not denied "the Lord that bought them," however much they may have multiplied other "saviours," they must not be confounded with those who have openly rejected that " sure foundation which is laid in Zion." While therefore we must deplore their "holding the truth in unrighteousness," and instead of presenting through their numerous priesthood the simple and fundamental doctrines of the gospel, their supplanting these, in a great measure, by introducing "another gospel," we would not say that an enlightened mind may not find in their church the way of life, obstructed though it be by innumerable obstacles.

Neither would we be thought to put the Unitarians on the same footing with the Universalists. The moral influence of the preaching of the former, and their standing in society, make them far more valuable than the latter as a component part of the general population. Nor would we put the Jews, or even the more serious part of the Universalists, on the same level with "Socialists," "Fourierists," "Shakers," and "Mormons."

All that we mean by putting these various bodies in one category is, that they can none of them be associated with the evangelical Protestant churches,—with churches whose religion is the Bible, the whole Bible, and nothing but the Bible,—nor, indeed, do we suppose that however much they may dislike being all reviewed in one and the same section of this work, they would any of them choose to be associated with the evangelical Protestant communions, or considered as entitled to that appellation.

The doctrines and economy of the Roman Catholics being well known almost everywhere, a very general account of that church may suffice, though it is by far the most important of all the bodies that are to be noticed in this section of our work. As the appearances, and the spread of Unitarianism in "the land of the pilgrims" on the other hand, has been matter of much surprise and curiosity in Europe, as full an account of its rise, progress, and present prospects in the United States, will be given as our plan will permit. Of the other bodies that find a place here we shall give such an account, at least, as will enable the reader to form a tolerably correct idea of their true character and present condition.

CHAPTER II.

THE ROMAN CATHOLIC CHURCH.

MARYLAND, we have seen, was originally a Roman Catholic colony, founded on most liberal principles, under the auspices and through the exertions of Lord Baltimore. And although Protestant Episcopacy was established in the colony under the reign of William and Mary, the laws of England against Roman Catholics being at the same time rigorously enforced, they continued, nevertheless, to form the most numerous and influential body in the province down to the American Revolution. Even to this day, though now but a small minority of the entire population, not exceeding in fact 80,000, and inferior in point of numbers both to the Protestant Episcopalians and Methodists, they have much influence, and are perhaps the wealthiest communion in the State.

Unless in Pennsylvania and Rhode island, I am not aware that the Roman Catholics anywhere enjoyed their fair share of political rights at the commencement of the war of the Revolution, but now, I believe, they are everywhere upon the same footing with others, and enjoy all the political privileges that our constitution affords.[1]

---

[1] I have often heard Roman Catholics in Europe reproach the Protestants of the United States with intolerance, and in proof of this they have chiefly urged the burning by the populace of a convent at Charlestown, near Boston, in 1834. That, indeed, is the only case, I believe, which even they themselves can possibly urge as amounting to persecution, and as in the notoriety that it has obtained, it has been sadly misrepresented, especially by the late Bishop England in his letters to the Propaganda Society, I need make no apology for giving a more correct statement here.

The convent in question, which was of the order of *Ursuline* Sisters, and was founded in 1820, was rather a boarding school for girls than anything else. The number of nuns varied from eight to ten, and that of the pupils from twenty to sixty. The buildings, furniture, and grounds were ample and valuable. The occasion of its being destroyed was as follows: One of the nuns, a Miss Harrison, who taught music, while suffering from temporary derangement caused by excitement, left the establishment for a short time. Hence a report that she had been ill-treated, which soon spread through the adjacent borough of Charlestown, and then through Boston, which is within two miles distance. Strong suspicions having been entertained for several years, on what founda-

The acquisition of Louisiana in 1803, and of Florida in 1820, very considerably increased the Roman Catholic population of the country. To this must be added an immense emigration from Europe, but mainly from Ireland and Germany, during the last sixty, still more during the last twenty-five years. At the beginning of 1842, they were estimated by well-informed Roman Catholics at 1,300,000 souls in all. Their increase has been rapid since the Revolution, partly owing to the above territorial acquisitions, partly to conversions, but most of all to emigration. According to the Metropolitan Catholic Almanac for 1842, published at Baltimore, there were at that time in the United States—

1 Archbishop and 20 bishops.

562 Priests, of whom { 448 employed in the ministry.
{ 114 as professors of colleges, &c.

541 Churches and chapels, and 50 building.

470 Other stations for preaching where churches had yet to be built. In all 1011 places for preaching.

21 Ecclesiastical institutions.

180 Clerical students.

21 Literary institutions for young men, whereof 12 or 13 are incorporated colleges.

1712 Young men, students.

36 Female religious institutions (convents).

28 Female academies, in which there were 2963 pupils.

77 Charitable institutions.

88 Religious associations.

tion I know not, of highly improper conduct on the part of some of the nuns, Miss Harrison's case inflamed the minds of the populace, and led to a riot on the night of August 11th, 1834, ending in the entire destruction of the convent with all its furniture, the actors being for the most part young men and boys from Charlestown and Boston. This outrage was condemned in the strongest terms by all respectable people, and an able report was published a few days afterwards, and subscribed by thirty-seven Boston Protestants, all of the highest moral respectability, in which the reputation of the convent was decidedly, and I dare say justly, vindicated. Some of the rioters were identified and punished, and the better part of the public demanded that the State of Massachusetts should indemnify the Roman Catholics for the loss they had sustained. I regret that, from various causes, no indemnification has to this day been made, mainly, I should think, because it was insisted that the State should rebuild the convent—a demand opposed by many who would grant a full pecuniary compensation, but have no idea that the State, as such, should give any apparent sanction to an establishment of that kind. There is every indication that the Massachusetts legislature will fully compensate in money, leaving the Romanists to rebuild the convent or not as they please. All that will then have to be regretted is delay.

But the Romanists have little reason to complain. Let them look at the intolerance with which Protestants are treated in almost all countries, whether in the old or new world, in which their religion is the dominant one. Be it remembered, too, that the convent at Charlestown was destroyed under the conviction that it was an immoral institution, not because it was a Roman Catholic one. Indeed, I am satisfied from what I heard at Boston a few weeks after its destruction, that had it been a Protestant boarding school it would, under the same circumstances, have shared the same fate.

The Roman Catholics have, also, seven weekly papers, of which one appears in German, and three monthly, and one annual periodical.

It is clear from all this that the Romish Church has gained a firm and extensive footing in the United States. The building of fifty church edifices in one year is a large increase for a denomination believed to influence, more or less directly, 1,300,000 of the country's inhabitants. For such objects large sums are received from the Propaganda Society in France, and the Leopold Society in Austria; no less than 63,000 dollars having been sent by the former in 1839-40, after even larger sums from the same source in preceding years, but I have no means of ascertaining how much has been remitted by the latter.

The assertion has often been made by the controversial opponents of the Roman Catholics in the United States, that they never can be safe citizens of a republic, and that the predominance of their church would involve the overthrow of our political constitution. Such an opinion must rest, I should think, on the presumed hatred of the priests to republican institutions, and the impossibility of controlling the influence they possess over their people. However this may be, not a few valuable citizens and stern partriots in that country have professed, at least, to belong to the Romish church, and it remains to be seen how far it is possible for the Romish priests to obtain or exercise the same influence over their followers there that they possess in some European countries. One thing is certain; the Protestant population, and the clergy in particular, are not likely to allow their movements to pass unobserved. The last few years have witnessed a great deal of discussion in the United States on the doctrines and influence of Romanism, and much distinguished talent and deep research have been exhibited in the course of it.[1] Neither has this discussion been confined to any particular denomination of evangelical Protestants, but has extended almost to every pulpit in every branch of that body. Never was there so general a determination to give publicity to the opinions they

---

[1] Among the ablest writers on this subject may be reckoned the Rev. Drs. Brownlee and R. J. Breckinridge, and the Rev. Messrs. Boardman and Berg. To these may be added the late Rev. Drs. John Breckinridge and Nevins— men of distinguished piety and learning, and whose memory is precious to many of the churches in America.

entertain of the true character and dangerous tendency of the Roman Catholic religion, nor have its abettors been silent under these attacks.

Much curiosity is felt in Europe as to how far the increase of the Roman Catholics in the United States arises from proselytism? No doubt it may partly be ascribed to that, but much more to the emigration of Roman Catholics, and of persons of Roman Catholic origin from Europe. As for proselytism, the Protestants possibly gain as much as the Roman Catholics from that source.[1]

The Roman Catholics of the United States have done much for the establishment of schools and other institutions of learning, no doubt with the view of thereby extending their church. This is very evident, for were it done for the sake of education alone, they would never send money from France, Italy, and Spain, where so immense a proportion of the people are deplorably and confessedly ignorant of its common elements, to a country, where even in the most ignorant districts a larger proportion of the people can read than in the best educated parts of those nations.

A considerable proportion of the sums received from Europe is laid out in building churches and cathedrals, several of which are costly and splendid edifices. That at Baltimore cost 300,000 dollars; those of Cincinnati and St. Louis cost much less, yet are large and showy buildings.

A visitor from Europe would, on entering the Roman Catholic churches of the United States, be struck with the few pictures and other such ornaments that they exhibit. This may arise from time and money being required for such things. The priests, too, dress like other citizens when not engaged in their official duties. Nor will it escape a stranger from any part of

---

[1] Captain Marryatt, in his work on the United States, asserts, that the Roman Catholics are increasing rapidly in Ohio, Indiana, Illinois, and other parts of the valley of the Mississippi, and states it as his opinion, that theirs will at no distant day be the predominant religion in all that region. But his mere opinion unsupported by authentic statistical documents is really very little worth in such matters. The gallant captain is at home on the sea, but when he attempts to describe the state of things in the American confederation, he is evidently in a world of which he knows little or nothing. A man who could allow himself to be hoaxed as he was when in that country—an author who could believe and gravely relate, that the excessive modesty of the young ladies there leads them to put pantaloons on the legs of their pianos—is hardly fit for the task of carefully collecting and comparing facts, and deducing from them fair conclusions.

Roman Catholic Europe, that processions and religious services in the streets are hardly ever seen in the United States. It is not that the religion of Rome changes its nature on crossing the Atlantic, but only that it has comparatively few adherents in the States.

By the rapid multiplication of their priests in the United States the Roman Catholics have, no doubt, checked those conversions from their church to Protestantism which were frequent in former times. Bishop England, in one of his letters to the Propaganda, stated a few years ago, that "the church" had lost no fewer than 50,000 of her legitimate children in his diocese by such conversions, for want of shepherds to look after them.

CHAPTER III.

UNITARIANISM.

To understand the history of Unitarianism in New England, the reader must have a clear idea of the leading ecclesiastical usages of the Puritans, and of the principles on which they were founded.

The Puritans held that all men are by nature destitute of true piety; that they naturally grow up in the practice of sin; and that no one becomes religious except by a change in his habits of thought, feeling, and conduct, which they ascribed to the special operation of the Holy Spirit as its supernatural cause. They believe that the truly pious are ordinarily conscious of this change in the action of their own minds when it takes place, and are able to describe it; though they may not then know that the change of which they are conscious is regeneration. In some cases, they admitted, the man is not aware of any change at the time of his conversion; yet he will be conscious of exercises afterwards, such as no unregenerate man ever has, and he can describe them. Some may be regenerated in infancy, which it is lawful for us to hope is the case with all who die before they are old enough to profit by the external means of grace. If any of them live to maturity they will not be able to remember the time of their change, but they will be conscious of sensible love to God and holiness, penitence for sin, and other pious exercises, and can give an account of them. They believed, therefore, that every converted person who has arrived at the age of discretion, has a religious "experience" which he can tell, and by hearing which other pious persons may judge of his piety. The evidence thus afforded, however, was to be compared with his conduct in all the relations of life; and if this also was "such as becometh saints," he was to be accounted a pious man.

A church they held to be "a company of faithful persons," that is, persons who have saving faith, regenerate persons, agreeing and consenting "to meet constantly together in one congregation for the public worship of God and their mutual edification; which real agreement and consent they do express by their constant practice in coming together for the worship of God, and by their religious subjection," that is, by subjecting themselves voluntarily, from religious motives, "to the ordinances of God there."[1]

To become a member of a church, according to these principles, a person must voluntarily apply for admission. But if the admission were open to all applicants, bad men would come in, who neither knew their duty, nor were willing to perform it. With such members, Congregationalism would not be a safe system of church government. The applicant must, therefore, furnish evidence of his fitness for membership. He must give an account of his religious experience. This being satisfactory, he must be "propounded;" that is, his application for membership must be announced from the pulpit, and his admission must be deferred for a given time, that all the members might have opportunity to acquaint themselves with his life and conversation. These being found such as the gospel requires, he was allowed to become a member, by publicly entering into covenant with the church and with God.

It must be particularly observed, that the burden of proof rested on the applicant. Every man, the Puritans held, is born

[1] Cambridge Platform, 1648; chap. iv. sec. 4.

in sin; and if no evidence of a change appears, the presumption is, that he is still in his sins. They regarded and treated all in whom no evidence of regeneration appeared as unregenerated; as persons who must yet be converted or finally perish.

Throughout Christendom, in that age, neither Jews, Turks, pagans, infidels, or excommunicated persons, could enjoy the full privileges of citizenship. These privileges belonged only to persons who were in communion with the churches established by law. The same rule was adopted in New England. None but members of the churches could hold offices or vote at elections. Here, however, it operated as it did no where else. As the churches contained only those who were, in a judgment of charity, regenerate persons, a large portion of the people, among whom were many persons of intelligence, of good moral character, and orthodox in their creed, were excluded from valuable civil privileges.

The principles on which this system was founded, the Puritans brought with them from England; but the system was first brought to maturity here; and New England Congregationalists, when on visits to their fatherland, did much towards giving its form and character to the Congregationalism that afterwards prevailed there. The system appears to have been adopted in 1648, with a good degree of unanimity; but as the number of unconverted adults increased, both by emigration and by the growing up of children without piety, there was an increasing dissatisfaction with it. By the year 1662, such a change of opinions had been wrought that what was called the "half-way covenant" was introduced, by a recommendation of a general synod. According to this new system, persons baptised in infancy were to be considered members of the church to which their parents belonged; though they were not to be admitted to the Lord's table without evidence of regeneration. Such persons, on arriving at maturity, "understanding the doctrine of faith, and publicly professing their assent thereto, not scandalous in life, and solemnly owning the covenant before the church, wherein they give up themselves and their children to the Lord, and subject themselves to the government of Christ in the church," had a right to baptism for their children. This was an important change. It relieved the applicant for church membership from the necessity of furnishing evidence of his piety, and obliged the church, if it would exclude him, to prove that he was heretical in his opinions or scandalous in his life. This change was strenuously opposed; and as the synod had only advisory power, and many churches disapproved its decisions, it never became universal.

One step more remained to be taken. In 1704, "the venerable Stoddard" of Northampton, avowed his belief that unregenerate persons ought to partake of the Lord's supper; and in 1707, he published a sermon in defence of that doctrine. He maintained that the Lord's supper is a means of regeneration, and that unrenewed men, regarding themselves, and being regarded by the church as such, ought to partake of it as a means of procuring that desirable change in their own hearts. One of his arguments was, that it is impossible to distinguish the regenerate from the unregenerate, so as to admit the former and exclude the latter. After some controversy this doctrine gained an extensive prevalence among the churches which had adopted the "half-way covenant" system. Among these churches, the principles and rules of admission were now completely reversed. The church was now obliged to convict the applicant of a scandalous life, or of heresy, or admit him to full communion; and one reason for it was, the supposed impossibility of judging whether he was regenerate or not.

Stoddard was a decided Calvinist; but his system fostered the growth of Arminianism. It taught the impenitent that they had something to do before repentance, as a means of obtaining saving grace. The unregenerate communicant supposed himself to be obediently walking in the way which God had appointed for such persons as himself. He could not, therefore, feel much to blame for being what he was, or much afraid that God would remove him from the world without first preparing him for heaven. This, combined with the belief that the regenerate could not be distinguished from the unregenerate by their Christian experience, was enough to throw the conscience into a profound sleep.

The labours of the great Edwards, and the "revival of 1740, as it is usually called, form the next turning point in this history. Edwards was the grandson of "the venerable Stoddard,"

and his successor at Northampton. In consequence of the manifest increase of Arminianism, and the consequent habit of relying
on works done in impenitence as a means of preparing for
heaven, Edwards commenced his course of sermons on justification by faith. These discourses, and others on kindred topics,
were the means of a very powerful revival, which became fully
developed at Northampton early in 1735, and spread into many
other towns in Massachusetts and Connecticut. The converts
in this revival were generally able to give a clear account of the
exercises of their own minds in their awakening, their conviction of sin, their submission to God, and acceptance of Christ as
their all-sufficient Saviour. So many undeniable instances, in
which the regenerate could be distinguished from the unregenerate by the history of their religious exercises, gave a serious
shock to the doctrine that making such a distinction is impossible. It taught ministers to hope and labour for conversions
of which evidence could be found. It made those who had no
evidence of their own conversion afraid that they were still unregenerate. By special request, Edwards prepared a narrative of
these "Surprising Conversions," which was printed in London,
with an introduction by the Rev. Drs. Watts and Guise. It
was soon reprinted in Boston, and was extensively read, and
exerted a powerful influence on both sides of the Atlantic.

From this time there continued to be similar revivals, on a
smaller scale, in various parts of New England. In 1739, and
the beginning of 1740, they were evidently increasing. The
celebrated Whitfield, who was ordained in 1736, had already
excited much attention in England, and was preaching with
great success in the southern American colonies. To help forward this good work, he was invited to Boston, where he arrived
in October, 1740. The exciting point of his doctrine was the
necessity of a sensible change of heart in order to preparation
for heaven. Like the old Puritans, and like Edwards, he held
that every man is born in sin, and unless some evidence appears
to the contrary, is to be esteemed an heir of perdition. The
believers of this doctrine had always been numerous and powerful, both among the clergy and in the churches of New England; and by those who were not its believers, it was rather
neglected than opposed. It was now brought home to men's

hearts as they had never known it to be before. All have heard of the eloquence of Whitfield; and that of Edwards, though in a different style, was at least equally effective, and more sure to leave permanent results. These men had powerful allies in several of the pastors in Boston and other parts of New England, and especially in the Tennents, and their fellow-labourers in New Jersey and Pennsylvania.

These men assumed an established truth, and proclaimed with all possible distinctness and earnestness the doctrine that regeneration is a change accompanied with evidence by which it may be proved, and that all in whom no such evidence is found are unregenerate, and in the broad road to perdition. They preached to them accordingly, not as Christians who needed instruction, but as impenitent enemies of God and righteousness, who must be converted or perish for ever. Multitudes were awakened, convinced, converted; and in a few years, tens of thousands were added to the churches; and other multitudes, who were already in the churches, were in like manner awakened and brought to repentance.

Such an attack on men's hopes of heaven could not fail to provoke resistance. As has been shown already, the habit had been formed of hoping favourably concerning all who were not proved guilty of heresy or immorality, and of admitting all such to the communion of the churches, for this reason, among others, that perhaps they were regenerate. The promoters of the revival made unsparing war upon all such hopes, and pronounced all who had nothing else to rest upon heirs of perdition. This their opponents called " censoriousness;" and those who practised it were denounced as uncharitable, as usurpers of God's prerogative of judging the heart, as fanatics who delighted to throw orderly, quiet Christians into needless alarm. Such was the usual language of that part of the clergy who leaned strongly towards Arminianism, of their followers, and of many others. Some zealous promoters of the revival were guilty of great errors, and really deserved these reproaches; and its adversaries were not slow in seizing the advantage thus brought within their reach. They convinced many that the revival was made up of uncharitableness and fanaticism, and thus succeeded in setting limits to its progress.

In a few years after the commencement of this revival, Edwards became so fully convinced that the prevailing system of admission to the communion, introduced by his grandfather and predecessor, was wrong, that he could no longer practise it. He published his " Treatise on the Qualifications for Full Communion," in which he maintained that none ought to be admitted without such a declaration concerning the exercises of their own minds as, if true, would imply that they were regenerate persons. This change of opinion led to his dismission in 1750. His doctrine on this point, however, even then, had many advocates. It spread rapidly among the friends of the revival, and is now held by all the Congregational churches of New England that have not become Unitarian. Where the system of Stoddard and the half-way covenant have not been abolished by a formal vote, they have fallen into disuse, for none think it right to· practise according to them. The ancient doctrine of the Puritans has been restored, and evidence of piety is required of those who would become members of the church.

The principal faults charged upon the promoters of the revival by its opponents were censoriousness and undue excitement. They laboured to exclude both from their own parishes, and, as far as they could, from the country. To a considerable extent they were successful. They produced a profound calm on the subject of religion among all who were governed by their influence,—a calm which amounted to indifference. And as to censoriousness, they adhered to the practice of admitting men to the communion of the church without evidence of their piety. Their doctrine was, that every man's piety is to be taken for granted, unless some scandalous error of doctrine or practice proves him destitute of it. The most important characteristic —the fundamental element—of New England Unitarianism was now fully developed. A party was formed, the members of which condemned and avoided all solicitude concerning their own spiritual condition or that of others.

When this state of mind had been produced and confirmed, the remainder of the process was natural and easy. As in this party there was to be no strong feeling with respect to religion, except a strong unwillingness to be disturbed by the " censoriousness" of others, there could of course be no vigorous opposition to a change in doctrines, no vigilance against error. A system of doctrines, too, was wanted, containing nothing to alarm the fears or disturb the repose of the members of the party. The doctrines of man's apostacy from God, and dependence on mere grace for salvation, of the necessity of an atonement by the blood of the Son of God, and of regeneration by the special influence of the Holy Spirit, were felt to be alarming doctrines. They were the doctrines by which Edwards and others had filled their hearers with anxiety, and produced excitement. They were therefore laid aside; but silently and without controversy, for controversy might have produced feeling. Men were suffered to forget that the Son and the Spirit have anything important to do in the work of man's salvation; and then it became easy to overlook their existence. In this way the Unitarian party was formed, and furnished with all its essential attributes long before Unitarian doctrines were openly avowed, and probably long before they were distinctly embraced in theory, except by a very small number.

Unitarianism being introduced in this manner, it is evident that no distinct account of the successive steps of its progress can be given. The revivalists of 1740 asserted that "Socinianism" was even then in the land. This assertion was then repelled as a slander; but Unitarians now admit and assert that several leading opponents of the revival were Unitarians at that time, or soon after. The prevalence of Unitarianism, however, was not then extensive. The greater part of those who are now claimed as having then belonged to the "liberal" party were only Arminians, or, at the farthest, Pelagians; and some of them were decided Calvinists.

From 1744 to 1762 the colonies were engaged, almost incessantly, in the wars that secured them against the arms of France. In 1765 troubles with England began, and continued till 1783. Then came the formation of our system of government, and the anxious period of its early operations. Thus the attention of men was drawn off from religion, and fixed on other subjects for about half a century, affording a favourable opportunity for habits of indifference to become confirmed, and for error to make progress unobserved.

Yet it was not wholly unobserved. In 1768, the Rev. Dr.

Hopkins preached in Boston on the divinity of Christ, and published the sermon; assigning as a reason for the choice of his subject his belief that it was needed there. From time to time other testimonies appeared of similar character.

The first congregation that became avowedly Unitarian was that at the " King's Chapel" in Boston. It was Episcopalian. Being without a pastor, they employed Mr. Freeman, afterwards Dr. Freeman, as reader, in 1782. In 1785 he succeeded in introducing a revised liturgy, from which the doctrine of the Trinity was struck out. He applied to several American bishops for ordination, but none would ordain him. He was therefore ordained by the church-wardens in 1787. For many years he maintained a constant correspondence with the leading Unitarians in England, and was a convenient medium of communication between them and the secret adherents of the same doctrines in America.

The first Unitarian book by an American author is said to have been " Ballou on the Atonement," published in 1803. Mr. Ballou was pastor of a Universalist society in Boston. But the term *Universalist* must not be understood here as it often is in Europe. It designates the belief that all intelligent beings,—men and devils, if there are any devils—will be saved. Some Universalists hold that all men at death pass directly into heaven; others that a part of mankind will undergo a limited punishment in hell, or rather in purgatory, in proportion to the number and atrocity of their sins. The doctrine has been favoured by a few men of considerable learning and respectable morals; but its chief success has been among the ignorant, the vulgar, and the vicious, not one of whom was ever known to be reformed by it. Mr. Ballou was a man of some genius but little learning. His works have done something to diffuse Unitarian opinions among Universalists. A Mr. Sherman, in Connecticut, published in favour of Unitarianism in 1805. He was dismissed from his pastoral charge about the same time, and in a few years left the ministry and lost his character. In 1810, Thomas and Noah Worcester began to publish their modification of Arianism in New Hampshire. The same year the church in Coventry, Connecticut, became suspicious that their pastor, the Rev. Abiel Abbot, was a Unitarian. The subject was brought before the consociation to which that church belonged, and he was dismissed. He then called together a council, composed chiefly of men suspected of Unitarianism, who dismissed him a second time, and gave him a certificate of regular standing. The irregularity of this transaction called forth many expressions of disapprobation.

In and around Boston no Congregational church had yet avowed itself Unitarian. Harvard college had an orthodox president and professor of theology till after the commencement of the present century. After the death of Professor Tappan in in 1804, the Rev. Dr. Ware was elected as his successor. While the question of his election was pending, a suspicion of his Unitarianism was suggested, but it was repelled by his friends as a calumny. Even when President Kirkland was elected in 1812, it has been said, on high Unitarian authority, that he could not have been elected if he had been known as a defender of Unitarianism.

No pastor of a Congregational church in or near Boston had yet avowed himself a Unitarian, either from the pulpit or the press. Yet the style of preaching adopted by many was such as to excite suspicion; several periodicals openly advocated Unitarianism, and Unitarian books were imported and published in considerable numbers. Orthodox ministers, when attending councils for ordaining pastors, found themselves opposed and thwarted in their attempts to ascertain the theological views of the candidates. Many other circumstances indicated the presence and secret diffusion of error; but the means were wanting of fastening the charge upon individuals. There was therefore an increase of preaching and publishing against Unitarianism. In the Panoplist, a monthly magazine commenced in Boston in 1806, this subject received special attention; but all its warnings were denounced as "calumny." The facts, however, could not be much longer concealed.

In 1812, the memoir of Lindsay by Belsham was published in London. Only a few copies of the work were imported, and these were carefully kept from the sight of all but a select few for nearly three years. At length, the Rev. Dr. Morse, after months of fruitless effort, succeeded in obtaining possession of a copy. The account there given of Unitarianism in America

was extracted and published in a pamphlet. It contained letters from several leading Unitarians in Boston, especially Dr.
Freeman, of various dates, from 1796, or thereabouts, to 1812.
In these letters the spread of Unitarianism, and the means used
to promote it, were described without reserve. Concealment was
no longer possible. Unitarianism was therefore openly avowed
by those who had been detected, and by others whose character
and interests were closely identified with theirs.

The ecclesiastical results of this disclosure need to be particularly explained. Among Congregationalists each church, that
is, each congregation of covenanted believers, has full power to
manage its own ecclesiastical concerns, without subordination to
any earthly tribunal. There was no way therefore of compelling churches that had become Unitarian to part with their Unitarian pastors. On the same principle, pastors and churches
that continued orthodox were at liberty to withhold Christian
fellowship from those in whom they had no confidence. There
was no means of compelling orthodox ministers and churches to
perform any act by which a Unitarian would be virtually
acknowledged as a Christian minister, or his church as a Christian church. Orthodox ministers therefore refused to exchange
pulpit labours on the Sabbath with those whom they believed
to be Unitarians, or to sit with them in ecclesiastical councils,
or in any other way to recognise them as ministers of Christ.
This practice, however, was adopted gradually. Many orthodox
men were slow in believing that one and another of his neighbours was a Unitarian; and many undecided men contrived to
avoid for some time a declaration in favour of either party, and
to keep on good terms with both. At length, however, successive disclosures made the dividing line so visible, throughout its
whole length, that every man knew his own side of it, and the
parties are completely separated without any formal excommunication of one by the other. They meet only once in a
year in the " General Convention of Congregational ministers;"
and they continue to meet together there only on account of a
fund of about 100,000 dollars for the support of their widows.

On the publication of Mr. Belsham's disclosures, it was found
that all the Congregational churches in Boston had become Unitarian, except the Old South and Park Street, which last had

been established within a few years by some zealous Trinitarians. The whole number of Unitarian churches in various parts of New England, but mostly in the eastern part of Massachusetts, was supposed to be about seventy-five; though subsequent disclosures showed it to have been considerably larger. They had then almost entire possession of Harvard college; and by a change in its charter, deliberately planned some years before, but hurried through the legislature at a favourable moment, they secured the control of it to their party.

A considerable number of churches in Massachusetts had funds, given by the pious of former generations, for the support of the ministry and of Christian ordinances. The main object of the donors was to secure to their descendants, in perpetuity, the services of learned, pious, and orthodox pastors; and the funds were committed to the church, and not to the parish, because the church, being composed of persons of approved piety, would guard them most effectually against perversion. Such was the case with the First Church in Dedham. In 1818, a majority of the inhabitants of the parish with which that church was connected chose a Unitarian to be their pastor. The church refused to receive him as their pastor. A few of its members, however, seceded from the church, chose the Unitarian for their pastor, and commenced a lawsuit against the church for the possession of its property. In March, 1821, the supreme court of Massachusetts decided in their favour, and established the principle that, in all such cases, those who act with the majority of the parish are the church, and have a right to the funds. By this decision many churches have been deprived of their funds, their houses of worship, and even the furniture of their communion table; and many Unitarian churches owe their existence to means thus obtained.

After this decision the existence of a church, as distinct from the parish, became unimportant among Unitarians. Its secular interests were wholly in the power of the parish, and might as well be held by the parish directly. Their churches, as has been shown, were never intended to be bodies from which the unregenerate should be excluded. There was, therefore, no longer any important end to be answered by their existence. Generally, it has not been thought best to disband them; but in a considerable number of instances they have been suffered to become extinct, and there remains only the parish and the pastor, who administers the ordinances indiscriminately to all who desire it. According to some of their own writers, the result is that the ordinances become cheap in men's esteem, and few care to receive them. Church discipline, of course, has fallen into entire disuse. The discipline of the clergy appears to be also extinct. If any of their clergy become scandalously immoral, they are not formally deposed from the ministry, or visited with any ecclesiastical censure, but are allowed to continue in office till their reputation becomes such that none will employ them, and then to retire silently to private life.

In 1825 the number of Unitarian congregations was estimated at 120. Now, in 1841, they are said to amount to 230. There are several causes of this increase.

In 1825 the process of taking sides was not completed. Of the few which then remained without character, a part have doubtless become decidedly Unitarian.

Mr. Ballou's work on the atonement has already been mentioned as the first Unitarian work by an American author. That and other works of a similar character prepared the Universalists, somewhat extensively, to avow Unitarian opinions. The Unitarians have, to a great extent, and it is believed generally, embraced the doctrine of the final salvation of all men. There is therefore no doctrinal distinction between the two sects. As Unitarianism is esteemed the more genteel religion of the two, Universalists are under a strong temptation to change their name, and call themselves Unitarians. Such changes very naturally occur when a Universalist congregation becomes vacant, and a Unitarian preacher of acceptable address offers himself as a candidate. Sometimes congregations change from one of these sects to the other, and back again, as temporary convenience dictates.

Unitarianism, as has been shown, originally grew out of a dislike to the practice of requiring evidence of piety in candidates for admission to the churches. There are many, in various parts of the country, in whom this fundamental feeling of the sect is very strong, but who yet are unwilling to live without some form of religion. They are easily organised into a society which requires no creed, and subjects them to no discipline. Societies thus formed, however, often vanish as easily and suddenly as they are made.

In 1787 a "Society for propagating the gospel among the Indians and others in North America" was incorporated by the legislature of Massachusetts. It acquired permanent funds to the amount of 9000 dollars. It elects its own members; and a majority of them having proved to be Unitarian, the society has passed wholly into the hands of that sect. It expends the income of its fund in supporting two or three preachers among the remnants of Indian tribes in New England. One or two other unimportant societies, not originally formed by them, have in like manner passed under their control. They have no organisation for foreign missions. To the Bible Society they contribute something, but the amount is not known.

The "American Unitarian Association," formed in 1825, is their principal organisation for united action. Its object is declared to be "to diffuse the knowledge and promote the interests of pure Christianity throughout our country." Its sixteenth annual report gives the names of 117 clergymen who have been made life members by the payment of thirty dollars each, of whom eight are dead. The whole number of life members are stated at 374. It expended during the year ending in May 1841, the sum of 4962 dollars, which was 81 dollars 89 cents more than its receipts. The expenses of administration were, the salary of the general agent, 1800; his travelling expenses, 100; office rent, 200; total 2100 dollars; being very nearly three-sevenths of the whole.

This association has published 179 different tracts, the prices of which vary from one cent to six cents. During the year ending in May 1841, it aided sixteen destitute congregations, of which ten were in New England, three in the State of New York, and three in the western States. The lowest appropriation for this purpose was thirty dollars; and the highest 300. It also expended 570 dollars for missionary services, of which 530 was expended to the west of New England.

The smallness of the amount expended by Unitarians in the way of associated action is not to be ascribed to parsimony, but to religious indifference. A large part of the wealth of Boston,

and of the eastern part of Massachusetts, is in their hands; and
their capitalists have made many splendid donations to literary,
scientific, and humane institutions.

Their churches probably contain some truly regenerate persons, who became members of them before they were avowedly
Unitarian, and who remain there from reverence for ancient
usages, attachment to the places where their ancestors worshipped, and other similar causes. Others of them are men of
stern and almost Puritanic morality, who have had from infancy great reverence for religion in the gross, but have never
seriously studied its application to themselves in the detail of its
doctrines and duties, and who would have remained stedfast
members of the same congregations just as quietly had those
congregations remained orthodox.

In philosophy the Unitarians of New England were at first,
and for some years, followers of Locke; holding, that all our
ideas, or at least the elements of which they are formed, are
received through the senses. Very naturally, therefore, they
built their belief of Christianity wholly on evidence addressed
to the senses. They believed that miracles had been wrought,
because it appeared so extremely improbable that the apostles
were deceived concerning them, or attempted to deceive others;
or that the canonical writings ascribed to them are spurious; or
that the accounts of miracles which they contain are interpolations. Those miracles they hold to be the testimony of God,
addressed to the senses of men, proving the truth of Christianity.
Yet they did not admit the infallibility of the apostolic writings
as we have them. Many of them hold that the authors of the
several parts of the New Testament had no inspiration which
secured them against mistakes and false reasoning; and they
very generally held, that strong texts in favour of the doctrine
of the Trinity, the divinity of Christ, or the personality of the
Holy Spirit, must be interpolations or corruptions. Their religious guide, therefore, was so much of the Bible as they judged
to be true; and their religion was, in its theory, the conformity
of their hearts and lives to certain external rules, which, in all
probability, were originally given by God, and which have been
transmitted to us in a record which is not free from error. To
this individuals among them appended more or less of sentiment

and imagination, according to the prompting of their own genius. A system like this can never long continue to satisfy any community. It fails to meet certain feelings of spiritual want, which are sure to spring up in many minds. Hence there has been among the more serious, ever since the separation, a gradual going over to orthodoxy, which has retarded the growth of Unitarianism. Now, the orthodox Congregational churches in Boston are about as numerous as the Unitarian, and the worshippers much more numerous; and the result is similar in the surrounding country.

A few years since, German Transcendentalism made its appearance among the Unitarian clergy, and has spread rapidly. Its adherents, generally, are not very profound thinkers, nor very well acquainted with the philosophy which they have embraced, or with the evidence on which it rests. It promises to relieve its disciples from the necessity of building their religious faith and hopes on probabilities, however strong, and to give them an intuitive and infallible knowledge of all that is essential in religion; and it affords an unlimited range for the play of the imagination. It has charms, therefore, for the contemplative and for the enthusiastic.

The controversy on this subject became public in 1836. It was brought out by an article in the Christian Examiner; maintaining that our faith in Christianity does not rest on the evidence of miracles; that a record of miracles, however attested, can prove nothing in favour of a religion not previously seen to be true; and that, therefore, we need to see and admit the reasonableness and truth of the doctrines of Christianity, before we can believe that miracles were wrought to commend it to mankind. The "Old School" Unitarians, as they called themselves, pronounced this theory infidelity; for it struck at the foundation of the only reasoning by which they proved the truth of Christianity. The controversy was protracted, and somewhat bitter; but no attempt was made by the "Old School" to separate themselves from those whom they denounced as infidels.

The charge of Pantheism is brought against the Transcendentalists generally, by their Unitarian opponents; and, in fact, some of their publications are evidently Pantheistic, while others are ambiguous in that respect. Some of them have borrowed largely from Benjamin Constant, and maintain that all religions, from Fetichism to the most perfect form of Christianity, are essentially of the same nature, being only developements, more or less perfect, of the religious sentiment which is common to all men. According to them, all men who have any religious thoughts or feelings are so far inspired; Moses, Minos, and Numa, and a few others, had an unusual degree of inspiration; and Jesus of Nazareth most of all. They do not believe, however, that even Jesus was so inspired as to be in all cases an infallible teacher; and they declare themselves by no means sure that we shall not yet see his superior. They reject Christ as a mediator in every sense of the term, and delare, that in order to be true Christians we must hold intercourse with God as Christ himself did, without a mediator.

These impious doctrines have been promulgated in periodicals and otherwise, from time to time with increasing boldness. In the spring of the present year 1841, they were put forth without disguise and without reserve in a sermon at an ordination at South Boston. Several of the leading Unitarian clergy of the "Old School" were present and took part in the services. It is said, that some of them in performing their parts uttered sentiments at variance with those of the preacher, from which attentive hearers might infer that the sermon did not meet their approbation; but there was no explicit condemnation of the sermon either then or afterwards, till public attention was called to the subject by three evangelical clergymen who attended the ordination as hearers, and took notes of the discourse. These three witnesses, some weeks after the ordination, published extracts from the ʿsermon in several religious newspapers, and called on the members of the ordaining council to say, whether they recognised the preacher as a Christian minister. Public attention was roused. Several intelligent Unitarian laymen united in the demand. Continued silence became impracticable. A number of articles appeared in newspapers and magazines, in which individual Unitarian ministers denounced the sermon, and pronounced its doctrines deistical; but they carefully avoided the question, whether its author was recognised by them as a Christian minister. Others of them preached and wrote in his defence. His ecclesiastical relations still remain undisturbed.

Some of his Unitarian neighbours have recognised his ministerial character by exchanging pulpits with him on the Sabbath; and he has, in his turn, preached the weekly lecture maintained by the Unitarian clergy of the Boston association. It is understood, therefore, that the public avowal of doctrines like his, forms no obstacle to a regular standing in the Unitarian ministry.

Why was not this defection arrested in its progress by ecclesiastical authority? The answer is easy.

In Connecticut, where one or two ministers became Unitarian while the community remained orthodox, it was done. Those Unitarian ministers were removed from their places, and the progress of error was arrested. In Massachusetts, the defection was carried on by a different process. Men did not fall, one at a time, from orthodoxy into open Unitarianism; but almost the whole community in the eastern part of the State, sunk down gradually and together. For a long time there was no proof by which any one could be convicted of heresy; and when proof was obtained the heretics were found to be the majority in the ecclesiastical bodies to which they belonged, and of course, if any process had been commenced, would have decided all questions in their own favour.

It is evident from this history, that the Congregationalist doctrine of the independence of individual churches has been the means of saving New England from universal apostasy. Had the synod in 1662, instead of being merely advisory, possessed jurisdiction over the churches, it would have imposed the half-way covenant upon them all. As it was only advisory, a considerable number of churches rejected its advice, and adhered to the ancient practice of the pilgrims.[1] So, half a century later, had there been an ecclesiastical government to which all the churches owed obedience, Stoddard's doctrine of admitting the unregenerate to full communion would have been enforced upon all; for numbers and influence were in its favour. And when Edwards, after the great revival of 1740, re-proclaimed the

[1] Many readers, however, will be of opinion that but for the isolation of ministers and congregations under the Congregational system, error must have been much sooner discovered, and checked in its beginnings. The same remark applies to the apostacy of many *nominally* Presbyterian ministers and congregations in England, These never were Presbyterians *in fact*. Error thus had leave to work its way unchecked by the oversight either of bishop or presbytery.—ED.

ancient doctrine concerning church membership, had there been an ecclesiastical tribunal having authority over, all the churches, he and his reformation would have been put down at once, and the admission of the unregenerate to the Lord's table would have been required of all. And finally, consider the state of things in 1815, when conclusive proof was first obtained of the existence of Unitarianism among the Congregational clergy in eastern Massachusetts. The Unitarians had the majority in the ecclesiastical bodies of which they were members. Had these bodies possessed jurisdiction over all churches within their bounds, they might have established Unitarianism in them all, and might have forbidden all efforts for the revival or preservation of orthodoxy. If there had been a body representing all the churches in the State, and having authority over all, the majority would have been orthodox; but the Unitarians were numerous and powerful enough to have thrown off its jurisdiction, and to have subsisted by themselves as they now do. If the civil government had been invested with power to enforce religious uniformity, it could have prevented such a result; but it would not have done it; for the most important powers of the civil goverment were then, and with few exceptions, have been ever since, wielded by Unitarian hands.

In all these instances, the independence of the churches secured to the most orthodox the privilege of adhering to the whole truth, both in doctrine and practice, and of exerting themselves in its defence and for its diffusion. This privilege there have always been some to claim and to use. Error, therefore, has always been held in check till truth could rally its forces and regain its ascendancy.

CHAPTER IV.

THE CHRIST-IAN CONNECTION.

THE body that assumes the title of *Christians* is of purely American origin. They are more generally called in the United States *Christ-ians*, the *i* in the first syllable being pronounced long, though this pronunciation, I need hardly say, is rejected by themselves.

Dating their rise from about the year 1803, they appeared, it seems, in New England, Ohio, and Kentucky, some say also in the south, nearly about the same time. They boast of having no founder—no Luther or Calvin, no Whitfield or Wesley— that can claim any special influence among them. They are the largest *no-creed* sect in America, and had their origin in the dissatisfaction that existed in some minds with what they called the "bondage of creeds," and still more, with the bondage of discipline that prevails, as they insist, in all other churches. This may be easily accounted for. Many of the most active promoters of the new sect had been excluded from other communions because of their denial of some important doctrine, or their refusal to submit to discipline and government.

The Christ-ians, according to some of their leading authorities, had a threefold origin. The first members of their societies, or churches, in New England, were originally members of the Regular Baptist connection; in the west they had been Presbyterians, and in the south Methodists. Their churches have all along been constituted on the following principles: "The scriptures are taken to be the only rule of faith and practice, each individual being at liberty to determine for himself, in relation to these matters, what they enjoin: no member is subject to the loss of church fellowship on account of his sincere and conscientious belief, so long as he manifestly lives a pious and devout life. no member is subject to discipline and church

censure but for disorderly and immoral conduct: the name
Christian to be adopted, to be exclusive of all sectarian names,
as the most appropriate designation of the body and its members: the only condition or test of admission, as a member of a
church, is a personal profession of the Christian religion, accompanied with satisfactory evidence of sincerity and piety, and a
determination to live according to the divine rule or the gospel
of Christ: each church is considered an independent body, possessing exclusive authority to regulate and govern its own
affairs." [1]

Although their founders continued to cleave more or less
closely to some, at least, of the peculiarities of the various
bodies in which they had been brought up, a process of assimilation to each other has been gradually going on, and has at
length brought them to a considerable degree of uniformity on
most points of doctrine.   Trinitarians for the most part at the
outset, they have now almost unanimously rejected the doctrine
of the Trinity as unscriptural, and although they refuse to be
tied down to a creed, the following may be considered as a fair
outline of the doctrines that prevail among them: " There is
one living and true God, the Father almighty, who is unorigin-
ated, independent, and eternal, the Creator and Supporter of all
worlds; and that this God is one spiritual intelligence, one infinite mind, ever the same, never varying: that this God is the
moral Governor of the world, the absolute source of all the
blessings of nature, providence, and grace, in whose infinite
wisdom, goodness, mercy, benevolence, and love, have originated
all his moral dispensations to man: that all men sin and come
short of the glory of God, consequently fall under the curse of
the law: that Christ is the Son of God, the promised Messiah,
and Saviour of the world, the Mediator between God and man,
by whom God has revealed his will to mankind; by whose sufferings, death, and resurrection, a way has been provided, by
which sinners may obtain salvation—may lay hold on eternal
life; that he is appointed of God to raise the dead, and judge the
world at the last day: that the Holy Spirit is the power and
energy of God,—that holy influence of God by whose agency,

[1] See an "Account of the Christian Connection, or Christ-ians," by the Rev.
Joshua V. Himes, in the Encyclopedia of Religious Knowledge.

in the use of means, the wicked are regenerated, converted, and recovered to a virtuous and holy life, sanctified and made meet for the inheritance of the saints in light; and that, by the same Spirit, the saints, in the use of means, are comforted, strengthened, and led in the path of duty: the free forgiveness of sins, flowing from the rich mercy of God, through the labours, sufferings, and blood of our Lord Jesus Christ: the necessity of repentance towards God, and faith towards our Lord Jesus Christ: the absolute necessity of holiness of heart and rectitude of life to enjoy the favour and approbation of God: the doctrine of a future state of immortality: the doctrine of a righteous retribution, in which God will render to every man according to the deeds done in the body: the baptism of believers by immersion: and the open communion at the Lord's table of Christians of every denomination having a good standing in their respective churches."[1]

Although each church is wholly independent of all others in the management of its affairs, yet for the promotion of their mutual prosperity, they have associations called "State conferences," composed of delegates from the clergy and the churches, but with only advisory powers. In 1833, in twenty States, there were thirty-two State conferences, embracing, it was estimated, 700 ministers, 1000 churches, and 75,000 members. Their ministers are now estimated at 800, their churches at upwards of 1000, and their members at 150,000, which last is probably much too high. On the other hand, the population supposed to be under their influence, and estimated at 300,000, is manifestly too low a reckoning, though many of their congregations are small, particularly in the west.

Generally speaking, their ministers are men of little education, but a laudable desire for improvement in this respect has been showing itself. The State of Indiana granted them a charter some years ago for a college at New Albany, but whether it has taken effect I know not. They have no theological seminaries. For some years past they have had a religious journal called "The Gospel Palladium," published in the State of New York, and it has a considerable circulation. They have a book

[1] See "Account of the Christian Connection, or Christ-ians," by the Rev. Joshua V. Himes, as above.

association also.   Upon the whole, much inferior as the Christians are to the Unitarians in point of wealth, the size of any of
their churches, the learning and eloquence of their ministers,
and the rank and respectability of their members, yet being far
more numerous, and having doctrines of quite as elevated a character, their influence upon the masses, whilst kindred in nature,
is perhaps greater in extent.

CHAPTER V.

THE UNIVERSALISTS.

In our chapter on the Unitarians we expressed our views of the
moral influence of the doctrines of the Universalists.   The latter were little known as a sect in America until about the middle of the last century, when a few persons of reputation partially
or wholly embraced their doctrines.   These were afterwards
preached by the Rev. John Murray, who came from England in
1770, and were embraced by the Rev. Elhanan Winchester, a
Baptist minister of considerable talent.   Both Murray and Winchester held the doctrine of restoration, that is, that after the
resurrection and the judgment, the wicked, after suffering in
hell for a time, and in a measure proportioned to their guilt,
will eventually be recovered through the influences of the Spirit,
and saved by the atonement of Christ.   About 1790, the Rev.
Hosea Ballou appeared as a Universalist preacher, and taught
that all punishment is in this life, and consequently, that the
souls of the righteous and the wicked alike pass immediately at
death into a state of happiness,—a doctrine which being much
more acceptable to the unrenewed heart, became much more popular than that of restoration as above described.   The restora-
tionist preachers in the United States hardly exceed twelve or
fifteen in number, and their churches are even fewer, whereas
the Universalists, properly so called, have rapidly increased
there within the last forty years.   In 1801, there were but

twenty-two avowed Universalist preachers; they now state their numbers to be as follows:—above 300 preachers; about 650 churches; and 600,000 of the population under their influence. The last item we suspect is much too high.   Their congregations are mostly small, and many attend from mere curiosity.

The doctrines of the American Universalists are well expressed in three articles adopted as a "Profession of belief" by the general convention of Universalists, held in 1803.   It is said to be "perfectly satisfactory to the denomination," and runs as follows:—

1. " We believe that the holy scriptures of the Old and New Testaments contain a revelation of the character of God, and of the duty, interest, and final destination of mankind.

2. " We believe that there is one God, whose nature is love; revealed in one Lord Jesus Christ, by one Holy Spirit of grace, who will finally restore the whole world of mankind to holiness and happiness.

3. " We believe that holiness and true happiness are inseparably connected; and that believers ought to be careful to maintain order, and practise good works; for these things are good and profitable unto men."

Although their churches are all severally independent of each other, yet for consultation they have local associations, State conventions, and a general convention.   They have begun of late years to pay some attention to education, and have now what they call a university in the State of Vermont, and three or four inferior institutions.   Most of their preachers, though men of little learning, by directing all their thoughts to one point, and mustering every plausible argument in favour of their doctrines, become wonderfully skilful in wielding their sophistry, so as readily to seduce such as want to find an easier way to heaven than what can be found in the scriptures, when these are not tortured and perverted to serve some particular end.   They pretend to say that they have no fewer than from fifteen to twenty, mostly political, newspapers, advocating their doctrines in different parts of the country.

The only Universalists whose preaching seems to have any moral influence, are the handful of restorationists—the rest are heard with delight chiefly by the irreligious, the profane, Sabbath-breakers, drunkards, and all haters of evangelical religion. Their preaching positively exercises no reforming influence on the wicked, and what worse can be said of it?[1]

CHAPTER VI.

SWEDENBORGIANS AND TUNKERS.

THE *New Jerusalem Church*, or *Swedenborgians*, are not numerous in America. Their doctrines were first propagated there, I believe, by some missionaries from England. Their churches, which are small, are about eight and twenty or thirty in number, and isolated members of the sect are to be found in various parts of the country. They have about thirty-five ministers, with hardly 10,000 souls under their instruction. Their churches, in point of government, are, in the main, independent, with consultative conventions of their ministers held from time to time. Their doctrines which, the reader must be aware, are of Swedish origin, and have for their author Baron Emanuel Swedenborg, are a strange "amalgamation," as some one has justly remarked, "of Sabellianism, the errors of the Patripassions, many of the antiscriptural notions of the Socinians, and some of the most extravagant vagaries of mysticism. Their mode of interpreting scripture is totally at variance with every principle of sound philology and exegesis, and necessarily tends to unsettle the mind, and leave it a prey to the wildest whimsies that it is possible for the human mind to create or entertain." They practise both baptism and the Lord's supper.[2]

---

[1] On the opening of a Universalist place of worship in any of our cities and villages, it is flocked to chiefly by low, idle, and vicious persons. Curiosity sometimes attracts others of a better description for a time, but it is a remarkable fact, established by the testimony of Universalists on becoming converted to the truth, that few can, however desirous, ever bring themselves to believe the doctrine of universal salvation. Most are like the New England farmer who, at the close of a Universalist service, thanked the preacher for his sermon, saying, that he liked his doctrine, and would give him five dollars if he would prove it to be true!

[2] The Swedenborgians say that they are increasing faster in America than

Tunkers. The Tunkers or Dunkers are, on the other hand, a sect of German origin. They are Restorationists on the doctrine of universal salvation, and teach that men may do works of supererogation, on which latter points, as well as on some others, they show a strong leaning towards Romanism. They allow marriage, but make much account of celibacy; in baptism they hold that the dipping should be repeated thrice, and observe the seventh day as their Sabbath. Their church order is like that of the Regular Baptists, except that every brother is allowed to speak, and the most fluent is generally chosen the regular minister. Most of the men in this communion wear their beards long, and dress in long coats, or tunics, reaching to their heels, and bound at the waist with a girdle. They are but a small body in the United States, having not more than from forty to five and forty churches, and these are insignificant in point of attendance. Their ministers are supposed to be about equal in number to their churches, and the aggregate amount of their members to be about 3000.

CHAPTER VII.

THE JEWS.

WHATEVER may have been the early legislation of the Anglo-American colonies in regard to the descendants of Abraham, it is certain, that the unconverted Jew now finds an asylum, and the full enjoyment of his civil rights in all parts of the United States. Yet I know not how it happens, unless it be owing to the distance of our country from Europe, and its presenting less scope for the petty traffic which forms their chief employment in the old world, but it was only at a comparatively recent

anywhere else at present. If this be so, their increase throughout the world must be slow indeed. The late Judge Young, of Greensburg, in Pennsylvania, and a few other men of some influence, have been reckoned among their converts.

period that any considerable number of Jews found their way to our shores. So much have they increased among us during the last ten years, that there is now computed to be no fewer than 50,000 in the United States. They have about fifty synagogues and the same number of Rabbis. Five or six synagogues are now to be found in New York instead of one, as a few years ago. There is one in which the service is conducted in English, at Charlestown in South Carolina, and, no doubt, in other cities also. A few instances of conversion to Christianity have taken place, but only a few, the attention of Christians, we may truly say, not having been sufficiently turned to that object. This may have been from the fewness of the Jews, until of late years, making them to be overlooked, or from the want of suitable persons to devote themselves to the work. We are pleased to see that some interest has begun to be taken in the subject during the last year.

CHAPTER VIII.

RAPPISTS, SHAKERS, MORMONS, ETC.

THE *Rappists* are a small body of German Protestants, who came to the United States from Wurtemburg about 1803 under their pastor, a Mr. George Rapp. They settled at a place called Economy, on the Ohio, about fifteen miles below Pittsburg. From Economy part of them, headed by Mr. Rapp, went to the Wabash river in Indiana, and on its banks formed a new settlement, called Harmony, but this they afterwards sold to the well known Robert Owen, and returned to Economy in Pennsylvania. Their distinguishing principle is an entire " community of goods," upon what they suppose to have been the example of the primitive Christians. The whole scheme, however, of this small community, for it comprises but a few hundred members, seems mainly of a worldly and mere economical character, though they keep up the form of religious observances and services.

The *Shakers* are a fanatical sect of English origin. About 1747, James Wardley, originally a Quaker, imagining that he had supernatural dreams and revelations, founded a sect which, from the bodily agitations practised in some parts of their religious services, were called Shakers, or Shaking Quakers, not, however, that they are to be for a moment supposed to be connected with the respectable people called Quakers or Friends. Ann Lee, or rather Mrs. Standley, for she had married a man of that name, the daughter of a blacksmith in Manchester, England, adopted Wardley's views and the bodily exercises of his followers. From the accounts we have of her she must have become a thorough adept during nine years which she spent in convulsions, fastings, &c.; for she is said to have clenched her fists in the course of her fits so as to make the blood pass through the pores of her skin, and wasted away so that at last she had to be fed like an infant. About 1770 she discovered the wickedness of marriage, and began " testifying against it." She called herself "Ann the Word," meaning that the Word dwelt in her. And to this day her followers say that " the man who was called *Jesus*, and the woman who was called *Ann*, are verily the two first pillars of the church, the two anointed ones."

In May, 1774, Ann Lee, otherwise Mrs. Standley, together with three elders, and others of the sect, emigrated to America, and two years after formed a settlement at Niskayuna, a few miles from Albany, in the State of New York. From that, as from a centre, they put forth shoots, until at length there are now about fifteen Shaker settlements, or villages, in different parts of the United States, comprising some 6000 or 8000 souls. Their doctrines are a strange mixture of the crudest errors with some few gospel truths, but it would be a sad misnomer to call them *Christian*. They call themselves the millennial church. They hold that the millennium has begun, and that they are the only true church, and have all the apostolic gifts. They insist that baptism and the Lord's supper ceased with the apostolic age; that the wicked will be punished for a definite period only, except such as apostatise from them, and these will be punished for ever; that the judgment has already commenced; that Christ will not again appear in the world, except in the persons of his followers, that is, the Shakers; that marriage is sinful, and that "they that have wives should be as though they had none," even now, and that thus alone purity and holiness, and the consequent beatitude of the heavenly state, can be attained; that sin committed against God is committed against them, and can be pardoned only for Christ's sake through them. Such are some of their absurd tenets. The discipline of their churches rests for the most part with "their elders," who follow the instructions left by "Mother Ann Lee." In their religious worship, they range themselves at intervals in rows, and then spring upwards a few inches; sometimes, however, they become so excited in this exercise as to throw off their upper garments, and jump as if they would touch the ceiling, all, as they say, to express their joy in the Lord. After this they sit down and listen awhile to their preachers, and then, when tired of hearing, resume their dancing freaks!

They maintain the doctrine of a communion of goods. The men and women live apart. The children of proselytes to their doctrines are instantly separated, by the boys being sent into the male apartment, and the girls into the female. Of course it is only by such recruits that a community of this kind can keep up its numbers.

The Shakers have the reputation, in general, of being honest and industrious, but I have had no means of ascertaining what their interior life and conduct may be, beyond this, that no small number of their members have left them in disgust, and are far from speaking well of them. The reader will perceive their insignificance in point of numbers, yet, to believe some European travellers, there is cause to fear that the United States may one day be overrun with this ignorant and deluded sect. But the absurd importance which such writers would fain attach to the Shakers is easily accounted for; their eccentricities afford a topic sufficiently marvellous and amusing to fill a chapter or two in the "Diary" or "Note-book," whilst in the United States nobody thinks it worth while to bestow a thought upon them. So long as they respect the persons, rights, and property of others, the government suffers them to gratify their fancies undisturbed. Accordingly, they remain a small and little known community, that must in time utterly disappear instead of growing into something like importance, which would be the probable result of their being persecuted.   Were the Shakers to appear in some European countries, a very different, and, in my opinion, a far less prudent course might be followed.   Accustomed to meddle with everything, even with conscience itself, their governments would probably interfere under the plea of saving the children from being brought up in such delusion.   But we prefer letting them alone, under the conviction that, all things considered, it is better to do so, and with the hope that the light that surrounds them, and with which they must come into contact in their intercourse with the world, will in God's own time reach their souls.   To interfere with those parental ties, and that consequent responsibility which God himself has established, must always be a difficult and dangerous task even for the best and wisest of governments.

The *Mormons.*   The annals of modern times furnish few more remarkable examples of cunning in the leaders, and delusion in their dupes, than is presented by what is called Mormonism. An ignorant but ambitious person of the name of Joseph Smith, jun., residing in the west of the State of New York, pretends that an angel appeared to him in 1827, and told him where he would find a stone box, containing certain golden plates, with a revelation from heaven inscribed on them.   Four years after this, the plates having of course been found as described, the impostor set about the writing out of this revelation, and pretended, with the aid of a pair of stone spectacles found also in the box, to read it off to a man of the name of Harris, and afterwards to one called Cowdery, these acting as his amanuenses. The " prophet," as he is now called, took care, of course, that neither of them, nor any one else, should see the plates, the part of the room he occupied having been partitioned off from where they sat by a blanket.   After three years spent in concocting this new revelation, the book at last was completed, and published as a 12mo volume of 588 pages at Palmyra, in the State of New York.   It is commonly called the Mormon's Bible, but more properly *The Book of Mormon*, and is divided into fifteen books or parts, each purporting to be written by the author whose name it bears.   These profess to give the history of about a thousand years from the time of Zedekiah, king of Judah, to

A.D. 420. The whole work professes to be an abridgment by one Moroni, the last of the Nephites, of the seed of Israel, from the records of his people. Not to trouble the reader with details respecting this absurdest of all pretended revelations from heaven, we need only say that it undertakes " to trace the history of the aborigines of the American continent, in all their apostacies, pilgrimages, trials, adventures, and wars, from the time of their leaving Jerusalem, in the reign of Zedekiah, under one Lehi, down to their final disaster, near the hill Camorah, in the State of New York, where Smith found his golden plates, and in that final contest, according to the prophet Moroni, about 230,000 were slain in battle, and he alone escaped to tell the tale." [1]

But the *Book of Mormon*, which they do not consider so much in the light of a substitute for the holy scriptures, as of a supplement to them, does not contain all Joseph Smith's revelations; a 12mo volume of about 250 pages, called *the Book of Covenants and Revelations*, and filled with the silliest things imaginable, of all sorts, has been added to it by way of supplement. Thoroughly to comprehend the whole system, however, one must read Mr. Parley P. Pratt's "Voice of Warning," for he is an oracle among the Mormons, and also the newspaper which they publish as an organ for the dissemination of their doctrines. We may add, that aided by his wonderful spectacles, Smith is making a new translation of the Bible, although quite unacquainted with Hebrew and Greek!

The publication of his own Bible in 1830, may be considered as the starting point of the sect. For some years he made but few converts; but having removed to Kirtland in Ohio he was there joined by Sidney Rigdon, formerly a heterodox Baptist preacher, who had been preparing the way for Mormonism by propagating certain doctrines of his own, and being a much better informed man than Smith, it is chiefly under his plastic hand that the religious economy of the sect has been formed. From Ohio they began to remove, in 1834, to Jackson county, in Missouri, where they were to have their "mount Zion," the capital and centre of their great empire. The people of Mis

[1] Turner's " Mormonism in all Ages," published at New York, and to be had at Wiley and Putnam, booksellers, London.

souri, a few years after, compelled them to leave it, upon which they went to Illinois, and there they are now building the city of Nauvoo, on the left bank of the Mississippi, and have been flocking to the spot ever since, until their numbers amounted to 10,000. Smith and Rigdon are still their chief prophets. For a while they had many to sympathise with them on account of the severity with which they had been supposed to be treated in Missouri; but so much has lately come to light in proof of the inordinate ambition, and vile character and conduct of their leaders, who want to found a kind of empire in the West, that their speedy annihilation as a sect seems now inevitable. One dupe after another is leaving them, and exposing the abominations of the fraternity and its chiefs. Smith and some others seem now marked out as objects on which the laws of the land must soon inflict summary justice. · Their leaders are evidently atrocious impostors, who have deceived a great many weak-minded but well-meaning persons, by holding out to them promises of great temporal advantage. "Joe Smith," as he is commonly called, will soon find that America is not another Arabia, nor he another Mahomet; his hope of founding a vast empire in the western hemisphere must soon vanish.

To conclude, the Mormons are a body of ignorant dupes, collected from almost all parts of the United States, and also from the British islands. A full exposition of the wickedness of their leaders has lately been made by a John C. Bennet, formerly a major-general in the "Legion of Nauvoo," and an important man among them.

CHAPTER IX.

THESE sects can hardly be placed with propriety among religious denominations of any description, the most they pretend to being a code of morals, such as it is. The avowed Atheists are happily few in number, and are chiefly to be found among the frequenters of our remaining groggeries and rum-holes.

As for our Deists, including unbelievers in Christianity of all classes, there is a considerable number, especially in New York, and some of our other large cities and towns. A very large proportion of them, however, are foreigners. The infidelity of the present times in the United States is remarkably distinguished from what was to be found there fifty years ago, when that of France, after having diffused itself in the plausible speculations of a host of popular writers, wherever the French language was known, became at length associated with the great Revolution of that country, and obtaining credit for all that was good in a work which it only corrupted and marred, became fashionable in America as well as Europe, among the professed admirers of liberty in what are called the highest classes of society. At the head of these in the United States stood Mr. Jefferson, who was president from 1801 to 1809, and who in conversation, and by his writings, did more than any other man that ever lived, to propagate irreligion in the most influential part of the community. In the same cause, and about the same period, laboured Mr. Thomas Paine, and at a later date Mr. Thomas Cooper, who endeavoured to train to infidelity by sophistical reasoning, and still more, by contemptible sarcasms and sneers, the youth whom it was his duty to teach better things.

Now, however, it is much otherwise. When men dislike evangelical truth, they take refuge in something which under the name of Christianity makes a less demand on their conscience and their conduct. Open infidelity meanwhile has descended to the lower ranks. It now burrows in the narrow streets, and lanes, and purlieus of our large cities and towns, where it finds its proper aliment—the ignorant and the vicious, to mislead and to destroy.

Owenism, Socialism, and Fourrierism, are of foreign origin, and do not differ materially from each other. The two first are from England, the last from France, and all three are but economical or political schemes, in which infidelity seeks to embody and sustain itself. Robert Owen from Scotland, and Miss Francis Wright from England, endeavoured some years ago to form the first infidel community upon the social principle adopted by the Shakers and the Mormons, failing in which they set about endeavouring to bring over the labouring classes of New York, and other great cities, to certain agrarian schemes. But after much labour in travelling, lecturing, and forming societies for the circulation of infidel tracts and books, their efforts have proved almost fruitless. Their lectures at first attracted crowds both of Americans and foreigners, who attended them from curiosity, but ere long their audiences consisted chiefly of foreigners, and such is the state of things at present.[1] That there is a considerable amount of infidelity in America is too true, but it cannot be compared to the vast amount of true religion, much less with the much vaster amount of respect for religion and religious belief which so largely pervades the moral atmosphere of the country. Of the truly great men of the nation very few are infidels.

---

[1] At one while it was feared that vast numbers of the lower or labouring classes in New York, as well as in Philadelphia, and other cities, would be carried away by the plausible but vile discourses of Miss Francis Wright. But facts soon proved, that those fears were groundless. Even in the acmé of her popularity, a friend of mine who was present at one of her lectures told me, that she was hissed no less than two or three times for making the assertion, and repeating it, that Washington was an infidel! There are few people in the United States who would not consider it a dishonour done to the name of that great and good man, whom humanity in the entire claims as her own, to call him an *infidel*.

CHAPTER X.

GENERAL REMARKS ON THE STATE OF THEOLOGICAL OPINION IN AMERICA.

HAVING concluded these notices of the various denominations —evangelical and non-evangelical—in the United States, I would now make a few remarks on the past history and present state of theological opinion in that country. Fully and philosophically treated, this could not fail to interest sincere inquirers after truth in all countries, but it would require not a chapter but a volume, and would hardly be consistent with the nature of this work. We must leave such a discussion to another time, and probably to other hands, and shall now merely touch on a few general topics.

I. Let us first mark some of the causes and influences to which this diversity of religious doctrines may be traced. The chief of these are:

1. Difference of origin and ancestry. This we have already noticed, but must now again refer to it.

Had the whole territory of the United States been originally settled by one class of men, holding one system of religious opinions, more uniformity of doctrine might reasonably have been looked for. But what philosophical inquirer, knowing the different origins of New England, Pennsylvania, Virginia, and New York, would expect that the mere federal union of States that differ so much in their original inhabitants, could ever bring them all to complete religious uniformity? Let us but look at the number of different religious bodies—different, I mean, in their origin—to be found in these and the other States of the Union. (1.) The New England Congregational churches, formed by emigrant Puritans, and down to the epoch of the Revolution sympathising strongly with all the changes of opinion among the English dissenters. (2.) The Presbyterian Church in its larger and smaller branches, very much of Scotch and Irish origin, and still aiming at an imitation of the Church of Scotland as their pattern. (3.) The Episcopal Church, an offshoot from the Church of England, dreading, and almost scorning, to borrow ideas from any quarter save its parent church. (4.) The Dutch Reformed Church, which long received its ministers from Holland, and still glories in the Heidelberg Catechism and the Decrees of the Synod of Dort. (5.) The Lutherans, the Reformed, and other German churches who preserve their old nationality, both by being still organised as distinct communions, and by the constant emigration of ministers and people from their original fatherland. Now, why should we expect to see all these fused and amalgamated in the United States more than in Europe?

2. Mark, too, that none of their ministers can extend any such *direct* influence over other churches than their own, as might make the exercise of brotherly love pass into close intimacy and final amalgamation. Each of them has its own colleges and theological seminaries; each its own weekly, monthly, or quarterly periodicals; and some of them may almost be said to have an independent religious literature, edited and published by their own responsible agents. All this is counterbalanced only by many ministers of different denominations receiving their classical and scientific education at the same institutions, preparatory to their more strictly professional studies.

3. The freedom allowed in the United States to all sorts of inquiry and discussion, necessarily leads to a diversity of opinion, which is seen not only in there being different denominations, but different opinions also in the same denomination. Perhaps there is not a single ecclesiastical convention in which there are not two parties at least, whose different views lead sometimes to discussions keenly maintained, yet turning generally upon points which, however interesting, are confessedly not of fundamental importance. On what may be called vital or essential points there is little disputation, just because there is much harmony in all the evangelical communions. Nor could it well be otherwise, seeing that in doctrine and practice they all take the Bible as their inspired and sole authoritative guide.

4. Nor must we forget that what may be called provincial peculiarities necessarily lead so far to diversities of religious sentiment. A true eastern man from Connecticut, and a true

western man, born and brought up on the banks of the Ohio, can hardly be expected to speculate alike on dubious points in theology, any more than on many other subjects. So, also, are the inhabitants of the north and south distinguished from each other by peculiarities fully as marked as those that distinguish the northern from the southern inhabitants of Great Britain.

II. Yet it is not difficult to draw a line between the various unevangelical sects on the one hand, and those that may be classed together as evangelical denominations on the other. The chief of the former, as we have said, are the Roman Catholics, Unitarians, Christ-ians, Universalists, Hicksite Quakers, Swedenborgians, Tunkers or Dunkers, Jews, Shakers, and so on down to the Mormons, beginning with the sect that has buried the truth amid a heap of corruptions of heathenish origin, and ending with the grossest of all the delusions that Satanic malignity or human ambition ever sought to propagate. Now, it will be observed that, with the exception of the two first, these sects have few elements of stability. Their ministers are almost all men of little learning, and that little is almost all concentrated in specious endeavours to maintain their tenets, by perverting the scriptures, by appealing to the prejudices of their hearers, and by misrepresenting and ridiculing the doctrines of opponents who meet their subtle arguments with the plain declarations of scripture, as well as with unanswerable arguments drawn from sound reason. The congregations of the Universalists and Christ-ians—both which are Unitarian Baptists, and the most numerous of the unevangelical sects next to the Roman Catholics—are far from large, except in some of the largest cities and towns in New England, and they often last but a few years, disappearing almost entirely before the extension of the evangelical communions. At times a religious revival almost annihilates, in the course of a few weeks, the attempts made by some Universalist preacher to form a society of that sect, at places where the faithful herald of the gospel has lifted up a standard for truth. And as none of the unevangelical bodies, not even the Roman Catholics absolutely, can debar their members from attending the preaching of evangelical ministers when they come into their neighbourhood, they present no insurmountable barrier to the advance of truth.

A better and more intimate acquaintance with the state of society in the United States than foreigners can well possess, seems necessary to account for the number, variety, and numerical magnitude of some of our unevangelical sects, and thus to abate the surprise which these may occasion to many of our readers. Nevertheless, to a certain extent, this may be brought within the comprehension even of those who have never seen the country. First, then, be it observed that not only can a far larger proportion of the white inhabitants of the United States read than is to be found in almost any other country, but they actually *do* read and pursue the acquisition of knowledge in almost every possible way. Novelty, accordingly, has always great attractions for them. Next, with the exception perhaps of Scotland, in no other country is there so little work done on the Lord's day; not only does the law require, but the disposition of the people enforces this; and as they are not at all of a character that would incline them to spend the day at home in idleness, they naturally take advantage of the opportunities within reach of attending public meetings, and listening to what may be said there. And religion being a subject to which they attach more or less importance almost universally, it is what they most like to hear discussed on the Sabbath. Thirdly, where there is no evangelical preaching, vast numbers, particularly of such as have no decided religious convictions, will resort to a Universalist, or even to an infidel preacher, if one is announced in their neighbourhood, rather than go no where at all. No doubt, curiosity leads them thither first, and perhaps for long afterwards. Fourthly, absolute religious liberty being the principle of the government, the people may everywhere have what preaching they please, if they can find, and choose to be at the expense of maintaining it; and accordingly, they who dislike faithful evangelical preaching, often combine to form a congregation where some heterodox preacher may hold forth doctrines more acceptable to them. Congregations so formed, especially in cities and large towns, may last for years, or even become in some sense permanent, but in by far the greater number of cases they disappear, part of their members removing to some other place, and others becoming converts to the orthodox creed of the surrounding evangelical churches.

Thus it will be perceived that the unevangelical sects in the United States are mainly composed of persons who, in other countries, would remain stupidly indifferent to religion, spending their Sabbaths in employments or amusements wholly secular. Even this may be thought better by some than that they should "give heec to doctrines of devils," upon the principle that no religion is better than a false one. This may be true in many cases but hardly in all. Experience proves, I think, very decidedly in America, that persons that occupy their minds with the subject of religion, even when they doubt the truth or embrace positive error, are more accessible to the faithful preaching of the gospel, than others that are sunk in stupid indifference and infidelity. The forms of error in that country have, with one exception, no element of stability—no vigorous dogmatism or permanent fascinations to oppose to the solid orthodoxy of evangelical preaching. The one exception is Romanism, which presents a sort of *mosaic* of truth and error, so artfully combined as to exert a charm over the minds of those who have once received it, which it is almost impossible to dispute.

Next to Romanism, Unitarianism is of all forms of error that assume the title of Christian, the most stable. Its professors are chiefly to be found in the eastern parts of Massachusetts, but as those, as well as other parts of New England, are constantly sending out emigrants to the new settlements, small knots of persons with Unitarian leanings may be found in the middle, southern, and western States. Still, this dispersion of Unitarianism, and its sprouting up at various points, not in Massachusetts, has rather the appearance than the reality of increase. It may be more than doubted, whether it be not positively declining at Boston and the vicinity. Except that it by no means prevails in the same proportion, it is very much in America what Rationalism is in Protestant Europe—a disease caught by the church from the epidemic scepticism of the eighteenth century—a scepticism which is now in both hemispheres taking the form of a mystical pantheism. The career of Unitarianism, which one of its advocates calls not a "religion but a fashion,"[1] as a sect or party, is manifestly drawing to a

---

[1] The Rev Mr Bronson.

close; and such, I rather think, is the impression of its most intelligent and eminent leaders. It seems to be given up as incapable of diffusion, and the thirty years experience it has had of a separate organisation confirms to my mind this conclusion, though others may think differently. At all events, no one who is well informed with regard to the present aspect of things in America, can claim for Unitarianism much vigour or any greater positive increase than that of the natural increase of the population within its pale; and it may be doubted how far it is increasing even so much as that.

A certain amount of moral influence for good may fairly be attributed to some of the unevangelical sects, but this can hardly be said of those Universalists, and they comprise nearly the whole, who deny a future judgment and all punishment beyond this life; while as for the Atheists, Deists, and Socialists of every hue, it is hardly slander to say, that their influence upon society is positively mischievous.

As for the Shakers, Mormons, and other such agglomerations, they may be accounted for, I apprehend, on two principles. First, the blinding nature of human depravity, which makes men prefer anything, however absurd, that looks like religion, and suits their fancies, to retaining, or rather to obtaining, the true knowledge of God. Next, these bodies always hold out some temporal good—some economical advantage, which, far more than any religious consideration, tempts persons to enter them. One would suppose, for example, that a religion which, like that of the Shakers, makes the sinfulness of marriage a fundamental principle, and obliges married proselytes to live single, could never find followers. Yet as persons sometimes tire of the marriage tie, or rather of those with whom it has bound them as husband and wife, so some may be found willing, even by becoming Shakers, to rid themselves of a burden that feels grievous to them. So, also, in the separation of children from their parents, and the entire breaking up of the family relationships, weak people may always be found ready to snatch at any opportunity of ridding themselves of parental responsibility, by shifting it upon other shoulders. This despicable and unmanly selfishness may be regarded as the main foundation of Fourierism and all other forms of Socialism.

2 T

III. We have yet to consider the extent of doctrinal agreement and diversity in and among the communions classed together as evangelical—a subject already noticed, but to which it is necessary to return, in order that the reader may perceive its connection with certain other interesting and important topics.

1. They agree generally in holding the body of doctrines professed by the Reformed churches of France and Switzerland, as embodied in the Westminster Assembly's Catechisms, and in the doctrinal articles of the Church of England. In particular, they hold the supremacy of the scriptures as a rule of faith, and that whatever doctrine can be proved from holy scripture without tradition is to be received unhesitatingly, and that nothing that cannot so be proved shall be deemed an essential point of Christian belief. They hold the inspiration of the scriptures—the three persons in the divine unity—the holiness of the first human pair as created and placed upon próbation—their fall, and the involved or consequent apostasy of the whole human race—the necessity of some atonement (sufficient to vindicate the justice of God's government,) in order to the pardon of sin—the fact of such an atonement having been made by the humiliation, sufferings, and death of Jesus Christ, who is both God and man—the offer of forgiveness to all mankind, as provided for them by the mercy of God in Christ—the free justification of the believer, not for his works past, or foreseen, nor for his faith, but for Christ's sake alone—the necessity of an inward spiritual renovation in order to salvation—the fact that this spiritual renovation is the result not of human endeavours, but of the Holy Spirit operating upon the soul, and thus making the call of God in his word, and by all instrumentalities outward to the soul, an effectual call—the dependence of the believer, for his progress in holiness, on the continued communion with God by the indwelling of the Holy Spirit—the resurrection of the dead—the universal judgment—the eternal state of happiness for the saved, and of misery for the lost.

2. The Methodists and some smaller bodies reject the Calvinistic or Reformed doctrine of predestination, especially in its application to the individuals who, in the fulfilment of God's counsels, become the subjects of renewing grace. They also deny

the doctrine, that all who are once renewed to holiness are effectually and certainly kept by the power of God through faith unto salvation. But in other communions these doctrines are held as clearly taught in the scriptures, and as of great practical value.

3. A considerable proportion, perhaps a third, of the clergy and members of the Episcopal Church, agree with what is called the Oxford party in the Church of England; so far, at least, as to ascribe to sacraments and other external institutions, a certain spiritual efficacy not recognised by other Protestants.

4. The theological discussions and disputes which sometimes agitate these various communions are such, for the most part, as to make it no easy matter to convey a just idea of them to a foreigner. In many instances, indeed, the disputants themselves can hardly state the point in debate to each other's satisfaction. For instance, I could not expect to state minutely the differences between the " Old School" and " New School," in the Presbyterian churches, without giving offence to one party or the other, or perhaps to all parties.

Let it suffice then to say that, generally, the debates among theologians in America are debates about the constitution of the human mind, the analysis of responsibility and moral agency, and the old question of " fate and free will." Some hold that all mankind, individually, are literally responsible before God for the sin of their first parents; others hold only that, in consequence of Adam's sin, all his posterity are sinners. Some hold that sin consists in a propensity to sin concreated in the soul, or, at least, existing in the soul from the indivisible instant in which its existence commences, anterior to all choice, all intelligence, all desire or emotion; others hold that sin consists only in the perversion of the powers of human nature. Some hold that the " new birth" is not only figuratively and morally, but literally and physically, a new creation; that it is a change in the being itself, from which a moral renovation inevitably proceeds; that anterior to repentance, to faith, to any right movement of the soul, there is not merely an influence of the Holy Spirit upon the soul, but a subjective change within the soul, which change they call repentance. Others, on the contrary, hold that conversion, or the turning of the soul to God

2 T 2

in repentance and faith, is regeneration, and is the effect of a
divine influence upon the soul. Some hold that the renewed
man will persevere in holiness, because the power of God upon
him is such that he *cannot* fall away; others that God's promise
to keep him cannot fail, and that therefore he *will* not fall away
Some hold that God, in his works of creation, providence, and
redemption, has not constituted the best system possible to him,
and that he might have done much better than he has done;
others hold that the system of the universe, including all events,
is absolutely the best; the best which the mind of God could
conceive; better with all the sin which exists than it could have
been if all creatures had retained for ever their allegiance to
God; and others still hold that this system, including all the
evil which exists under it, is, on the whole, better than any
other system of creation and government could have been, but
not better than if all God's creatures had remained holy and
happy. Some hold that in every instance in which sin takes
place, God, on the whole, prefers that sin to holiness in its
stead; others hold that God never chooses evil rather than good,
or sin rather than holiness, yet that in every instance in which
sin actually takes place, he, for some wise reason, chooses to
permit rather than to interpose his power to prevent it. Some
hold that all the acts of voluntary agents are predestined in
such a way that the agent has no power to act otherwise than
he does act; others hold that while all the acts of moral agents
are certain beforehand in the counsels of God, nothing in that
certainty is inconsistent with the power of the voluntary agent
to act otherwise.

Such is a specimen of the controversial theology in the evangelical, and particularly in the Congregational and Presbyterian
denominations. Were I to indicate the probable direction of
religious opinion and theological science in the United States,
amid this metaphysical strife, I should little hesitate to say that
it is tending, on the whole, towards a higher appreciation of the
simplest and most scriptural Christianity, that is, of the gospel
as "glad tidings" to all men, tidings of forgiveness for guilt
through the expiation made by the Son of God, and tidings of
the gift of the Holy Spirit to lead sinners to repentance, and to
carry on a work of sanctification in the hearts of the believing.

The demand is everywhere for a Christianity that can be *preached*, and that, being preached, will commend itself to every man's conscience in the sight of God. Under such a demand, wire-drawn speculations about Christianity—remote from any application to the conscience, to the sinner's fears, and to the hopes and devout affections of the believer—are felt to be impertinent. Thus the gospel is preached less and less as a matter of traditionary dogmatism and speculation, and more and more as *gospel*, the message of God's mercy to needy and guilty man, to be received by every hearer as suited to his wants, and to be hailed with faith and joy as life from the dead. Against this general tendency there is, and there will be, occasional, local, and party resistance; the surface may be ruffled from time to time by some wind of doctrine or speculation rather, and the current may seem to be setting in the opposite direction. But I am fully persuaded that, on the whole, if not from year to year, at least from one period of change to another, the progress of religious opinion will be found to be towards the simplest and most scriptural views of the gospel as God's gracious message, which every man may embrace, and should embrace immediately, and away from those philosophical and traditionary expositions of Christianity which it only embarrasses the preacher to deliver, and the hearer to receive.

The increased attention which the theologians of America are giving to the accurate and learned investigation of the holy scriptures, may be regarded as an indication of the tendency of theological science in that country. That the scriptures are the only authority in matters of faith is not only universally acknowledged in theory, but more and more practically acted upon. Thus the science and art of interpretation are more and more appreciated. The best theologian must be he who best understands, and who can best explain the Bible. The questions, What did Edwards hold? What did the Puritans hold? What did the Reformers hold? What did Augustine, Jerome, or the earlier Fathers hold?—though admitted to be important in their place, are regarded as of small importance in comparison with the questions, What saith the scripture? What did Christ and the apostles teach? Under this influence the tendency of theological science, as well as of the popular exposition

of Christianity from the pulpit, is towards the primitive simplicity of Christian truth.

The great achievement of American theology is that it has
placed the doctrine of the atonement for sin in the clearest
light, by illustrations drawn from the nature of a moral government. No where is the distinction between the work of Christ
as the propitiation for the sins of men, and that of the Holy
Spirit in renewing and sanctifying the sinner, more clearly
drawn,—no where is the necessity of each to the salvation of
the soul more constantly and forcibly exhibited. The tendency
of our theology, under the impulse of the Edwardean exposition
of the doctrine of the atonement, is to avoid the habit—so common to philosophers and philosophising theologians—of contemplating God exclusively as the First Cause of all beings and
all events, and to fix attention upon him as a moral governor of
beings made for responsible action. Here it is that the God of
the Bible differs from the God of philosophy. The latter is
simply a first cause—a reason why things are—sometimes, if
not always, a mere hypothesis to account for the existence of
the universe, another name for nature or for fate. The former
is a moral governor, that is, a lawgiver, a judge, a dispenser of
rewards and penalties. God's law is given to the universe of
moral beings for the one great end of promoting the happiness of
that vast empire. As a law, it is a true and earnest expression
of the will of the lawgiver respecting the actions of his creatures. As a law, it must be sanctioned by penalties adequate
to express God's estimation of the value of the interests trampled on by disobedience. As the law is not arbitrary, but the
necessary means of accomplishing the greatest good, it may not
be arbitrarily set aside. Therefore, when man had become
apostate, and the whole human race was under condemnation,
God sent his Son into the world, in human nature, "to be made
a sin-offering for us;" and thus, by his voluntary sufferings
magnifying the law, "to declare the righteousness of God, that
God may be just, and the justifier of him who believeth." Thus
it is that God, as a moral governor, is glorified in the forgiveness
of sinners; that He calls all men to repent, with a true and
intense desire for their salvation; that He sends into a world of
rebellion the infinite gift of his Spirit, to impart life to those who

are dead in sin; that in a world of sinners, who, if left to them-selves, would all reject the offered pardon, He saves those whom He has chosen out of the world; that He uses the co-operation of redeemed and renewed men in advancing the work of saving their fellow-men. Men are saved from sin and condemnation, not by mere power, but by means that harmonise with the nature, and conduce to the ends of God's moral government. This method of illustrating the gospel, carries the preacher and the theologian back from the Platonic dreams and dry dogmatising of the schools, to the Bible. It sets the theologian upon studying, and the preacher upon imitating, the freedom, simplicity, and directness, with which the apostles addressed the understandings and sensibilities of men. And thus it may be regarded as coin-ciding with other indications of the tendency of religious opinion in the various evangelical bodies of America.

I would remark, in conclusion, that few things in the history of the gospel more strikingly prove its inherent life and divinity, than the extent to which it has secured and retains a hold upon the American people. Their Christianity is not the dead for-malism of ecclesiastical institutions—upheld by law, tradition, or the force of fashion.[1] It is not a body of superstitions, lying with oppressive weight upon the common mind, and giving sup-port to a domineering priesthood. It is not that Rationalism, which retaining little of Christianity but the name, has had a brief ascendancy in some parts of Protestant Europe. It is evangelical Christianity,—the Christianity of the New Testa-ment. Wherever the stranger sees a place of worship in our cities, or in the country, the presumption is—the probability is,

---

[1] Much has been said in Europe about the *tyranny of public opinion* in the United States, but, I confess, I never have been able to comprehend what this expression means. M. de Toqueville employs it but without giving any clear idea upon the subject, as has been well remarked by the Hon. John C. Spencer, in his Notes to the American edition of M. de T's. work. If public opinion be strong and decided in America, it is because the character of the people makes it so. When they form an opinion, more especially on any matter in which the judgment or the conscience is concerned, (and what subject of a practical kind does not involve one or other of these?) they are not willing to change it but for good reasons. And in all matters of religion, and morals especially, the Pro-testant faith, which has so much influence with a large proportion of the popu-lation, concurs with the earnestness and steadiness of tne Anglo-Saxon char-acter, to make public opinion, not only strong but right, on all points on which it has been sufficiently informed. Mr. Laing, in his excellent work on Sweden, has some judicious remarks on this subject, proving that he takes a truly philo-sophic view of it.

with few exceptions, ten to one—that there God is worshipped in the name of the one Mediator, with faith and penitence; that there pardon is offered to the guilty, freely through Christ the Lamb of God; and that there the Holy Spirit is looked for, and is given to renew the heart of the sinner, and to fill the believing soul with joy and peace. The worship may, in many instances, be such as would offend the sensibilities of cultivated minds— most unlike the choral pomp of old cathedrals—still, rude as it may be, it is often that only acceptable worship which is offered in spirit and in truth. The gospel may be preached there igno- rantly, and with many imperfections, still, it is the gospel, and often does it become "the wisdom of God, and the power of God unto salvation."

BOOK. VIII.

EFFORTS OF THE AMERICAN CHURCHES FOR THE CONVERSION OF THE WORLD.

CHAPTER I.

WE cannot well close our view of the religious condition of the United States without a brief notice of what the churches there are doing for the propagation of the gospel in other lands. This forms a natural sequel to what has been said of their endeavours to plant and to sustain the institutions of the gospel on their own soil.

Some readers, indeed, may be surprised to learn that our churches are doing anything at all for the spiritual welfare of other countries, while they have so much to do in their own. When they hear that our population is increasing at the rate of 500,000 of souls in the year, so that nothing short of the most gigantic efforts can effect a proportionate increase of ministers and congregations; when they read of no fewer than 60,000 emigrants arriving from Europe, the greater number of whom are ignorant of the true gospel, and many of them uneducated, poor, and vicious, they may be astonished that the American churches, unaided by the government in any way, receiving no tithes, taxes, or public pecuniary grants of any kind, even for the support of religion at home, do nevertheless raise large sums for sending the gospel to the heathen. Such, however, is not the feeling of enlightened and zealous Christians in America itself. They feel that while called upon to do their utmost for religion at home, it is at once a duty and a privilege to assist in promoting it abroad. They feel assured that he that " watereth shall himself be refreshed," and that in complying so far as they can with their Saviour's command to " preach the gospel to every creature," they are most likely to secure the blessing of that Saviour upon their country. And facts abundantly prove that they are right.

Moreover, our churches have a special reason for the interest they take in foreign missions. No churches owe so much to the spirit of missions as they do. Much of the country was colonised by men who came to it not only as a refuge for their faith when persecuted elsewhere, but as a field of missionary enterprise; and their descendants would be most unfaithful to the high trust that has been bequeathed to them, did they not strenuously endeavour to carry out the principles of their fore-fathers. Alas, we have to mourn that we have done so little to impart the glorious gospel, to which our country owes so much, to nations still ignorant of it! Still, we have done something, and the candid reader will perhaps admit that we have not been altogether wanting to our duty, nor greatly behind the churches of other countries in this enterprise.

CHAPTER II.

EARLIER EFFORTS TO CONVERT THE ABORIGINES.

Notwithstanding the common mistake at the present day, of those who conceive that religious liberty, and to some extent, also, the enjoyment of political rights, were the sole inducements that led to the original colonisation of the United States, we have seen that both Virginia and New England were designed to conduce to the spread of Christianity by the conversion of the aborigines, as is proved both by the royal charters establishing those early colonies, and by the expressed sentiments of the Massachusetts settlers.

The royal charter granted to the Plymouth company having referred to the depopulation of the country by pestilence and war, and its lying unclaimed by any other Christian power, goes on to say: "In contemplation and serious consideration whereof, we have thought it fit, according to our kingly duty, so much as in us lieth, to second and follow God's sacred will, rendering reverend thanks to his divine Majesty for his gracious favour in laying open and revealing the same unto us before any other Christian prince or state; by which means without offence, and as we trust to his glory, we may with boldness go on to the settling of so hopeful a work, which tendeth to the reducing and conversion of such savages as remain wandering in desolation and distress, to civil society and Christian religion." And in this, the charter professes to favour the "worthy disposition" of the petitioners to whom it was granted. Nothing could be more natural, therefore, than that John Robinson, pastor of that part of the church which remained at Leyden, in Holland, should exclaim in his letter to the governor of the colony at Plymouth, "O that you had converted some before you killed any!" But in fact, the Plymouth colonists applied themselves to the conversion of the natives from the very first. They endeavoured to communicate the knowledge of the gospel to the scattered Indians around them, and took pains to establish schools for their instruction. The result was, that several gave satisfactory evidence, living and dying, of real conversion to God. A poor small colony, struggling for its very existence with all manner of hardships, could not be expected to do much in this way, yet in 1636, we find that it made a legal provision for the preaching of the gospel among the Indians, and for the establishment of courts to punish trespasses committed against them.

The Massachusetts charter sets forth that "to win and incite the natives of that country to the knowledge and obedience of the only true God and Saviour of mankind, and the Christian faith, in our royal intention, and the adventurer's free profession, is the principal end of the plantation." The seal of the colony had for its device the figure of an Indian, with the words of the Macedonian entreaty, "Come over and help us." And here, as at Plymouth, some not altogether abortive attempts were made to convert the natives from the very first.

Thus, these two colonies might be regarded as self-supporting missions, and rank among the earliest Protestant missionary enterprises. The Swedes had in the preceding century done something for their benighted countrymen in the northern part of that kingdom. French Huguenots, too, as we have seen, made an attempt so early as 1556, under the auspices of the brave and good Coligny, to carry the gospel to America, by founding a settlement in Brazil. Calvin furnished several pastors for it from his school at Geneva. But Villagagnon, who took the lead, having relapsed to Romanism, put three of the Genevan pastors to death; whereupon some of the colonists returned to Europe, and the remainder were massacred by the Portuguese. A subsequent attempt made under the same auspices, to plant a Protestant colony in Florida, also failed. Thus, even assuming, which is not very certain, that these attempts were of a missionary character, certain it is, that the New England colonies may be regarded as the first *successful* enterprises of the kind.

In 1646, the Massachusetts legislature passed an act for the encouragement of Christian missions among the Indians, and that same year the celebrated John Eliot began his labours at Nonantum, now forming part of the township of Newton, about six miles from Boston. Great success attended this good man's preaching, and other modes of instruction. Nor were his labours confined to the Indians near Boston. From Cape Cod to Worcester, a tract of country near 100 miles long, he made repeated journeys, preaching to the native tribes, whose language he had thoroughly mastered, and had translated the scriptures and other Christian books into it. Both editions of his Indian Bible, the one of 1500 copies in 1663, the other of 2000 copies in 1685, were printed at Cambridge, near Boston, and were the only Bibles printed in America until long after. Eliot, who has ever since been called the "Apostle of the Indians, died in 1690, at the age of eighty-five. "Welcome joy," was one of his last expressions. His labours, and those of others whom he engaged in the same great work, were blessed to the conversion of many souls, and many settlements of "praying Indians" were formed in the country round Boston.

But Eliot was not the first who preached the gospel with success to the Indians in New England. Thomas Mayhew began his labours among them on the island called Martha's Vineyard, in 1643. In 1646 he sailed for England to solicit aid; but the ship was lost at sea. His father, Thomas Mayhew, the proprietor of the island, though seventy years of age, then undertook the task, and continued it till 1681, when he died at the age of ninety-three. His grandson succeeded; and for five generations, till the death of Zachariah Mayhew in 1803, aged eighty-seven years, that family supplied pastors to the Indians living on Martha's Vineyard.

In Plymouth colony we find honourable mention made, among those who laboured to evangelise the Indians during Eliot's lifetime, of Messrs. Treat, Tupper, and Cotton; while in Massachusetts, besides Eliot, there were Messrs. Goskin, Thatcher, and Rawson; and in Connecticut, Messrs. Hitch and Person. The result of their united labours was seen in 1675, in fourteen settlements of "praying Indians, twenty-four congregations, and twenty-four Indian preachers." Besides religious instruction, the Indians were taught agriculture, and the other most necessary arts of civilised life.

But that very year (1675), King Philip, the chief of the Pokanoket tribe, instigated by his hatred of Christianity, and still more probably by jealousy of the growing power of the English settlers, made an unprovoked war upon the colonies. It ended in the annihilation of his party, not, however, without vast injury to the "praying settlements." Still, though the gospel experienced a check, it soon began again to make progress, so that in 1696 there were thirty Indian churches in Massachusetts colony, and two years later 3000 reputed "converts."

In Rhode island, Connecticut, and Long island, which belonged to the province of New York, though its eastern part was colonised by emigrants from New England, missionary efforts were less successful. Still, the gospel was not wholly without effect, and portions of the Narragansett, Pequod, Nantick, Mohegan, and Montauk tribes were converted to Christianity, and long formed "Christian settlements," some remnants of which exist to this day.

The news respecting the progress of the gospel among the

Indians in New England, excited so much interest in the mother country from the first, that " The Society for propagating the Gospel in New England" was incorporated in England so early as 1649, and though its charter was annulled at the Restoration in 1660, a new one was granted the following year, re-organising the society under the title of " The Society for propagating the Gospel among the heathen nations of New England and the parts adjacent in America." The celebrated Robert Boyle took a great interest in it, and was its "governor" or president for thirty years. The good Baxter was its friend. In 1698, "The Society for promoting Christian knowledge" was founded by members of the established church in England; and in 1701 " The Society for propagating the Gospel in foreign parts" was instituted. This last joined with the first in aiding the American missions, as did also, at a later day, " The Society for propagating Christian knowledge," which was founded in Scotland. A considerable portion of the funds expended by these societies, in the missions among the Indians, was contributed by the churches in America; for, before the Revolution, they had no independent missionary organisations of their own, owing to their dependent condition as colonies. In 1762, the Massachusetts legislature incorporated a society formed at Boston, " for promoting Christian knowledge among the Indians in North America," but the ratification of this act by the crown being refused, the missions had still to be conducted on behalf of the societies in Great Britain, through American committees formed at Boston and New York.

In 1734, Mr. John Sergeant began to labour among some Mohegans whom he had gathered round him at Stockbridge in Massachusetts, whence the name given them ever after of " Stockbridge Indians." That good man, whose labours were greatly blessed, died in 1749, whereupon these Indians passed under the care of the great Jonathan Edwards, who had been settled at Northampton. It was while labouring as a humble missionary at Stockbridge that he wrote his celebrated treatises on the " Freedom of the Will" and " Original Sin." Having spent six years at Stockbridge, he was called to be president of Princetown college, New Jersey. After the Revolution, the Stockbridge Indians, many of them being Christians, removed to the central part of the State of New York, thence to Indiana, thence to Green Bay, and at last to their present settlement on the east of Lake Winnebago, where they have a church and a missionary.

Contemporaneously with the commencement of Mr. Sergeant's labours at Stockbridge the Moravians began a mission in Georgia, whence they were compelled by supervening difficulties to remove soon after to Pennsylvania. In compliance with applications transmitted by them to Hernhut in Germany, the society sent over several missionaries, and these worthy men began in 1740 to labour very successfully among the Mohegans on the borders of the States of Connecticut and New York. But the opposition of wicked white men compelled them at length to remove, with as many of the Indians as would accompany them, to the neighbourhood of Bethlehem in Pennsylvania, and there they remained for several years, but suffered much in consequence of the hostilities betwixt France and Britain in 1755-63. From that they went first to the banks of the Upper Susquehanna, and afterwards to beyond the western borders of Pennsylvania, where they joined some Indian converts of the excellent David Leisberger from the Alleghany river. These quarters they exchanged in 1772 for others on the Muskingum river, in Ohio, where they enjoyed great spiritual prosperity for a season. From that they moved afterwards to the Sandusky river in the same State. After many calamities and much suffering during the Revolutionary war, in which the Indians generally took part against the Americans, and after several changes of quarters subsequent to the return of peace, they finally settled on the river Thames in Upper Canada, where they built the town of Fairfield, at which they now reside.

David Brainerd commenced his short but useful career in 1743 among the Indians between Albany and Stockbridge, near what is now called New Lebanon. He preached afterwards to the Indians at the Forks of the Delaware, in Pennsylvania, the site of the present town of Easton. And, finally, he laboured for a short time, but with amazing success, among the New Jersey Indians at Crossweeksung. On the termination of his labours by death, at the age of thirty, his brother John continued them, and was much blessed in the attempt. Upon

John's death in 1783, his Indian flock had the ministrations of
the Word continued chiefly by the pastors in the neighbourhood
until 1802, when it joined the Stockbridge Indians at their settlement in New York.

A school for the Indian youth was opened at Lebanon in
Connecticut in 1748, under the Rev. Eleazer Wheelock, and
there the well known Indian preacher, Mr. Occam, and the
celebrated Mohawk chief, Brant, were educated. It was afterwards removed to Hanover, in New Hampshire, where it is
still to be found, and is nominally connected, I understand,
with Dartmouth college. Its proper title is " Moor's Charity
School."

One of the most useful of the more recent missionaries among
the Indians was the Rev. Samuel Kirkland, who began his
labours with the Oneidas in the State of New York in 1764,
and died in 1808, having preached the gospel to the Indians,
with some short interruptions, for more than forty years.

We have elsewhere referred to something being done in the
way of Indian missions in Virginia, but in none of the southern
colonies was there anything of this kind accomplished deserving
particular mention. The wars between the aborigines and the
emigrants, that broke out soon after the arrival of the latter,
and were repeatedly renewed afterwards, extinguished any little
zeal they may have ever felt in such a cause.

These notices will, no doubt, surprise such of our readers as
have been under the impression that the colonists never did
anything for the conversion of the Indians to the gospel. Still,
who can but regret that more was not done to bring the original
occupants of the soil to that knowledge both of Christianity, and
the arts of civilised life, by which alone the gradual extinction
of so many of their tribes could have been arrested? The efforts
of the colonists, however, encountered many obstacles. The
wars between France, when mistress of the Canadas, and the
British empire, of which the United States were then a part,
invariably drew their respective colonies, together with the
intervening Indian tribes, into hostilities. These were protracted, bloody, and cruel, so as to leave deep traces of exaspera-
tion in the minds of all who did not possess a large share of the
spirit of the gospel. All war is dreadful, but Indian warfare is

horrible to a degree altogether beyond the conception of those who have only heard of it at a distance, and it ultimately begot such a spirit of hatred and revenge among the colonists as proved exceedingly unfavourable to missions.   I stop not here to inquire who was wrong in the first instance.   Only let me remark in passing, that they are egregiously mistaken who assume that the colonists were always in the wrong.

Again, the churches in the colonies were neither numerous nor rich, so that upon the whole, those in New England, and perhaps those, also, in New York and New Jersey, did as much, probably, in proportion to their ability then as they do now.

At length came the long war of the Revolution, and the still longer period that followed of distraction, confusion, and spiritual desolation.   Small, indeed, was the prospect then of sufficient attention being paid to missions among the Indians, many of whose tribes were far from being peaceably disposed to the United States' government.   And no sooner did the country and the government begin to recover from this state of moral syncope, than they fell into fresh troubles in consequence of the wars between the British and French following upon the French revolution—troubles which ultimately brought on the war of 1812-1815, between the United States and Britain.   Thus, it was not until the peace of 1815, and the general restoration of good will between the Indian tribes and the United States, that a favourable opening for missions among the former was again presented.   Blessed be God, our churches have ever since been more and more interested every year in this good cause, as will appear from the operations of our societies for foreign missions.

It is no easy task, indeed, to Christianise and civilise savages who from times unknown have been devoted to hunting and to war; and when not thus occupied, lounge like their dogs about their miserable hovels and tents, clad in skins, and leaving to their women, or squaws, the drudgery of cultivating a little patch of maize, making the fires, and even dressing the animals that have been slain in the chase, as well as all other domestic cares.   Their aversion to the methodical labour required for the arts of civilised life is such, as none can conceive without a personal knowledge of them.   Not a single noble aspiration seems ever to enter their souls, but all they care about seems to be,

that they may pass away life as their fathers did, and then die
amid the vague and shadowy visions of the unknown future.
In short, as long as their forests last, and game can be found,
they seem not to have a thought of adopting the habits of
civilised life.

Some persons are for ever indulging mawkish lamentations
over the disappearance of the aboriginal tribes of North America,
and if one may interpret their sentimental distress on this subject, would rather see that vast continent occupied by a few
hundred thousand savages, roaming the forests, and continually
at war with each other, than covered with a civilised and Christian population; either forgetting, or else never having known,
that a state of savageism is not only wretched but necessarily
tends to annihilation.

But how civilised men are to share the same continent with
uncivilised, without the latter being supplanted and made to
disappear, is a question by no means of easy solution. On a
continent of great natural resources, and possessing every thing
calculated to invite civilised men to its shores, becoming known, it
is easy to see, that the time cannot be distant when civilised men,
by natural increase and immigration, will crowd upon and displace
the uncivilised. To save the latter from extinction, under such
circumstances, one or other of two courses must be pursued:
either we must amalgamate the two races, which is next to impossible whilst one remains uncivilised, and can only be done by
reducing one of them to a species of slavery, and thus bringing
them into the bosom of civilised society, as was very much the
course pursued by the Spaniards in Mexico and South America;
or to allow them to preserve their natural or tribial existence in
some distinct territory. The plan pursued by the Spaniards
was revolting to the feelings of the English colonists, and they
adopted, accordingly, that of letting the Indians continue a
separate existence.

But even this, easy as it may seem at first sight, is attended
with many difficulties. It would be very practicable if all men
were what they ought to be; for then after the emigrants had
purchased the territory they required, the Indians would have
been left in undisturbed possession of what they chose to reserve
to themselves, and the two races would live in each other's pre-

sence, respecting each other's rights, and each contented with its own possessions. But this, alas! is not a likely result among fallen men whom even Christianity has only partially restored. As the civilised increased in numbers, they desired more and more territory, which the Indians did not hesitate to sell, as long as their own domain seemed almost boundless, and so the white men went on pushing the red farther and farther towards the west. Meanwhile the latter disappointed the expectations of those who had looked forward to their adopting the manners and customs of civilised life. Living in close proximity to the white men's settlements, these they often visited with the skins of animals or blankets thrown over their shoulders, and their extremities exposed in the coldest weather; and then, after lounging about the houses of the colonists, and taking such presents as might be offered, they returned to their comfortless wigwams without having acquired the slightest desire to exchange their wretched mode of living for the conveniences and comforts they had just witnessed. They were too fond of the habits in which they had been nurtured, and too averse to every thing like steady industry.

Nor were the colonists wanting in efforts to induce their savage neighbours to adopt civilised usages. Provision was made in almost every treaty that they should be supplied with articles of comfort, and agricultural and other useful implements. But brandy, alas! was included at times, that being thought, in those days of ignorance, one of the first requisites of life,—equally necessary to the civilised and uncivilised man. Addresses without number were presented to "chiefs" and "councils" by the colonial governors in favour of civilisation, but these were all in vain. The little that was done must be ascribed to the missionaries sent to them, chiefly by the churches in the colonies. These succeeded, in several instances, in so far civilising the Indians among whom they laboured, and to them the still extant remnants of tribes may be said to owe their surviving to this day, inasmuch, as those in which Christianity never gained any footing, and in which agriculture and the mechanical arts never made any progress, almost wholly disappeared, either by becoming extinct or by being merged in other uncivilised and heathen tribes.

2 u 2

The result would, doubtless, have been much more favourable had the missionary spirit of the earliest colonists continued to distinguish their followers. But, alas! mere cupidity tempted many to those shores for the sole object of enriching themselves by all practicable means, however unjustifiable, and often by over-reaching the poor ignorant savage. Nay, even good men suffered themselves to be too much influenced by the horrid massacres often committed by the Indians upon the frontier settlements in their wars with the colonists. These atrocities could hardly fail to cool the zeal for promoting the best interests of their barbarous neighbours, which such men had previously felt.

Add to other untoward influences that of the phraseology of the royal charters, where what were called "rights" to certain lands were granted without the slightest reference being made to the previous "rights" of the uncivilised occupants of the soil. This seems to have suggested almost all the subsequent efforts made to obtain *per fas aut nefas*, the territories marked out by those charters. Thus the poor Indians had no certain resting place. A few reservations which certain remnants of partially Christianised and civilised tribes have retained in some parts of New England and New York, are now the only Indian settlements to be found in all the Atlantic States. Had the wise, though much vilified, plan pursued for some years past by the United States' government been sooner adopted—had the tribes whose lands were included in the royal charters been all collected on one territory, beyond the boundaries of any charter, and ample enough for their support by hunting in the first instance, and afterwards by tillage, even the limited attempts that were made to civilise them might have taken effect. But, alas! where was there a territory ample enough to be found over which no charter could extend its claims? At last, by the acquisition of Louisiana, this desideratum was supplied, and men as benevolent as America has ever seen soon comprehended the important use that might be made of it, and pressed it upon the attention of the government. Accordingly, the country lying between the present State of Arkansas and the great American desert which stretches as far west as the Oregon mountains, was set apart for the purpose, being sufficiently large, and containing much good land, and to it the government has succeeded in removing above twenty tribes, or remnants of tribes, from its own organised States and Territories.   Soon all that remain will follow, so that there will be an Indian population of above 100,000 souls on a compact territory stretching about 500 or 600 miles from north to south, and about 200 from east to west. Thither, also, have the missionaries, who had been labouring among those tribes, gone; and though the removal of the several tribes from their ancient homes, and from the graves of their forefathers, has been followed by some years of that hardship and suffering which all removals from ancient settlements, whether more or less civilised, to the denser forests must occasion, yet they are surmounting these, and gradually establishing themselves in their new homes.   In process of time, they will have their little farms and lots of ground cleared, comfortable houses erected, mills built, and the more necessary arts of civilised life introduced among them.   Great progress is already making, and the time, I trust, will come when the inhabitants of this Indian territory will accept the offer made by congress to the Cherokees, shortly after the Revolution, to receive a delegation from them to the national congress, and thus admit them as a constituent portion of the United States, and subject to its laws.

As this removal of the Indian tribes to a territory west of the Mississippi has subjected the general government to great misrepresentation, and, in my opinion, to most unjust censure, I may say a few words further respecting it.   What has been most censured is the removal of the Cherokees, a tribe of Indians formerly situated chiefly in the State of Georgia, and by far the most advanced in civilisation of all the aboriginal race.

By the charter granted to Oglethorpe and his friends, Georgia claimed an extensive territory to the west of her present limits, out of which the States of Alabama and Mississippi have since been formed.   This territory she agreed to cede to the United States, provided the general government should buy out the claims of the Indians residing within her present limits, and remove them elsewhere.   The general government accordingly removed the Creek Indians, after buying up their claims, from the south-western part of the State to the west of the Mississippi.   But the Cherokees, whose lands lay in the north-western corner, refused to sell them, although the general government for years tried every method that it deemed proper to induce them to do so. Georgia at length resolved to survey those lands, and to extend her jurisdiction over both their Indian occupants, and all who lived among them, upon which the missionaries retired, with the exception of two, who refused to take the oath of allegiance to the State, on the ground that Georgia had no right of jurisdiction over the Cherokee territory. Being arrested and thrown into prison for this, they appealed to the supreme court of the confederation, which gave judgment in their favour, and ordered them to be set at liberty. This was demanded accordingly by the marshal of the United States for the State of Georgia. The governor of Georgia refused compliance. This was reported by the marshal to the supreme court. Its next yearly meeting was now drawing on, and the constitution then required that the chief justice should call upon the president to enforce compliance, which by his oath of office the latter was obliged to do. At this crisis, the governor of Georgia, well aware that the president would do his duty, first offered pardon to the imprisoned missionaries, and as they refused to accept this, as a last resort he convened the legislature, and it, on some trivial ostensible pretext, abolished the penitentiary or state prison, and so turned the missionaries out of doors. So the affair ended. The cause of the Indians was, in fact, sustained by the general government, and though they received much trouble from their Georgian neighbours, they remained several years longer on their lands, and then sold them to the United States for a great price,[1] and removed west of the Mississippi, where they are now settled. Although their removal was attended with much hardship, and a good deal of sickness, they are represented as doing well in their new territory, where they are placed beside the Choctas, Chickasas, Creeks, and other tribes.

It is hard to see wherein the general government was to blame in all this. It was in favour of removing the Indians, believing that it would be best for them to leave a territory where they

[1] Five millions of dollars, besides the expenses of their removal, and a year's support in their new homes. All this was in addition to the lands which they received in exchange for their former country.

could never live in tranquillity, and place themselves in another which, being the absolute property of the United States, could not, under any pretext, be claimed by any single State. There, if any where, they can, and I have no doubt, will be protected.

So also the course pursued by the general government in relation to the Seminole Indians in Florida has been held out as cruel and unjust in the highest degree, as designed to uphold slavery, &c. &c. Now, though far from thinking that in this matter the government has acted wisely, I think it obvious that the situation of the long narrow peninsula in question, although nineteen-twentieths of it are quite unfit for any species of culture, might make the possession of it desirable. A large sum accordingly was offered for it to the 3000 or 4000 Indians who roamed over it, and whose depredations on the white inhabitants of the country adjoining had long been exceedingly vexatious. A treaty was made, as the government thought, with chiefs having full authority to that effect. But this the Indians refused to keep; hence hostilities broke out, and after having lasted for years are only now about to terminate. That the government was deceived by its agents is very probable, but I do not believe that its intentions were unjust.

Upon the whole, I think that the national government in its transactions with the Indians has sincerely aimed at doing them justice. Its influence is happily exercised in promoting peace among the tribes of the west, the disputes constantly arising among which its officers and agents do their best to terminate in a peaceful way, and by the influence of persuasion alone. It has often, indeed, to bear the blame due only to unfaithful agents, by whom it is sometimes both deceived and committed.

The general government has been blamed because rum and other ardent spirits are carried by unprincipled men to the Indians on the borders, yet no government could well do more to prevent this. It has not only forbidden, but has taken measures to prevent all such traffic; and these have not been wholly in vain. But what government on earth could effectually guard such an immense frontier of almost boundless forests as that of the United States? England and France find it impossible to guard effectually a few hundred miles of coast against smuggling; how much more difficult the task which the United

States are blamed for not accomplishing? But the formation of temperance societies among the Indians, and the passing of severe laws among themselves against every villain, white or red, who may be found engaged in such commerce, will be a more effectual remedy.

In conclusion, I would state that the United States' government has done much incidentally, during the last twenty-five years, to promote missions among the Indian tribes, by a yearly grant of 10,000 dollars for the establishment of schools, blacksmith's shops, and other trades. This sum is generally expended through the several missionary societies, and of course by the missionaries, as the persons most competent for the task; many, if not all, of them being well acquainted with the various handicrafts most necessary to the partially civilised people among whom they live. The present secretary of war, the Hon. John C. Spencer, has spoken in the highest terms of the judicious manner in which this money has been applied, and of the good which has been accomplished. A similar testimony has recently been rendered by a committee of congress, to which the same subject had been referred. It is pleasant to state a fact which shows the favourable disposition of the government towards the benevolent enterprise of Christianising and civilising the tribes on our borders, to whom we are far from having done our duty. Many of the tribes, it may be added, appropriate large sums from the yearly pensions they receive from the United States' government to the establishment of schools and the promotion of the arts.[1]

We now proceed to give some notice of the various missionary societies in the United States, and in doing so shall have occasion to speak of what has been done since 1815 to introduce Christianity among the Indians.

[1] The United States' government has done much to procure a favourable reception for the missionaries among the Indians, and to induce the latter to set apart large sums from the price paid for their lands by the United States, and which is generally done in the shape of *annuities,* for the promotion of education and religion, as well as the useful arts. These annuities now exceed 1,000,000 of dollars. Many of the tribes which have removed to the territory assigned to them west of the Arkansas, appropriate very considerable sums annually to the support of schools for the education of their children. To preserve these tribes, or rather all the tribes to which it can find access, from the ravages of the small-pox, the United States' government sends fit persons from time to time to vaccinate them.

CHAPTER III.

THE American Board of Commissioners for Foreign Missions is the oldest society for foreign missions in the United States. It has also the greatest number of missions and missionaries, and the largest amount of receipts. Several religious sects, agreeing substantially in their views of the gospel, and in their ecclesiastical organisations, unite in sustaining it. These are the Congregational, numbering about 1200 churches, about the same number of Presbyterian churches, and the Reformed Dutch and German Reformed, numbering together about 700 churches; though but a small number of the German Reformed churches yet take an interest in foreign missions. The great body of the Congregational churches are in the New England States. The others, so far as this missionary institution is concerned, are almost entirely in what are called the middle and western States. The number of congregations which are professedly connected with it and operate through it on the heathen world, is about 3000, in which there may be 2,000,000 of souls.

ITS ORIGIN AND CONSTITUTION. The board had its origin in the following manner. Several young men, graduates of New England colleges, and preparing for the gospel ministry at the theological seminary at Andover, in the State of Massachusetts, agreed, in the year 1809, to unite their efforts in establishing a mission among the heathen in some foreign land. In this they were encouraged by the faculty of the seminary. As the general association of Congregational ministers in Massachusetts were to hold their annual meeting in June 1810, these young men were advised to submit their case to that body. This was done by

---

Within the territory claimed by the United States, there are now above fifty missionary stations, about fifty missionaries, above forty assistant missionaries, American and native, and not much under 5000 communicants or members of churches. There is also a very considerable number of schools and scholars.

four of their number—Mills, Judson, Newell, and Nott, in the
following paper:—

"The undersigned, members of the Divinity college, respectfully request the attention of their reverend fathers, convened
in the general association at Bradford, to the following *statement* and *inquiries*.

"They beg leave to *state*, that their minds have been long
impressed with the duty and importance of personally attempting a mission to the heathen; that the impressions on their
minds have induced a serious, and they trust, a prayerful
consideration of the subject in its various attitudes, particularly in relation to the probable success, and the difficulties
attending such an attempt; and that, after examining all the
information which they can obtain, they consider themselves
as devoted to this work for life, whenever God, in his providence, shall open the way.

"They now offer the following *inquiries,* on which they solicit
the opinion and advice of this association.   Whether with their
present views and feelings they ought to renounce the object of
missions as either visionary or impracticable; if not, whether
they ought to direct their attention to the eastern or western
world: whether they may expect patronage and support from a
missionary society in this country, or must commit themselves
to the direction of a European society; and what preparatory
measures they ought to take previous to actual engagement.

"The undersigned feeling their youth and inexperience, look
up to their fathers in the church, and respectfully solicit their
advice, direction, and prayers."

On the 29th of June, the association elected a Board of Commissioners for Foreign Missions, consisting of nine persons.
The board, at its first meeting, held in the following September,
adopted the name of the *American Board of Commissioners for
Foreign Missions*, thus recognising its high calling to act for all
in every part of the nation, who might choose to employ its
agency in the work of missions among the heathen.   The transaction of its ordinary business, however, was delegated to an
executive committee called the *prudential committee*, the members
of which reside at or near Boston, where is the seat of its operations.   Subsequently it was found necessary to obtain an act of

incorporation from the legislature of Massachusetts, in order that the board might the better manage its financial concerns. This act, being respected by the legal tribunals of all the other States in the republic, has been found of great use, especially in the recovery of bequests contested wrongfully by heirs at law. It requires one third of the members to be laymen, and one third clergymen; the remaining third may be either clergymen or laymen. Members are elected by ballot. The object of the board is expressly recognised in the act to be "the propagation of the gospel in heathen lands, by supporting missionaries and diffusing a knowledge of the holy scriptures;" and full power is granted to hold an amount of permanently invested funds sufficient for the purposes of credit in the commercial world, and also to receive and expend annually, in pursuance of its object, any amount of contributions its patrons may think proper to place at its disposal.

The number of corporate members is about 130, residing in nineteen of the States, religious men, having in general a high standing in their respective professions. These form the body corporate, the *trustees* in respect to the financial concerns of the institution. But with these are associated a large body of honorary members, amounting at present to 3500, who are made such by the payment of 100 dollars if laymen, or fifty dollars if clergymen; and who share equally in the deliberations of the annual meetings, but do not vote, as that would interfere with the charter. A third class of members are called corresponding members; they are foreign members and are elected by ballot. In addition to the usual office-bearers for presiding at the annual meetings, and recording the proceedings at these meetings, there are three corresponding secretaries and a treasurer, whose time is fully occupied with the business.

Its History. The proceedings of the board, and the results of its experience and operations for the thirty years past of its existence, must necessarily be stated in the most comprehensive and summary manner.

It is among the remarkable facts in the history of this institution, and in the ecclesiastical history of the country, that, at the outset, neither the board nor its prudential committee, nor indeed any of the leading minds in the American churches at that time, could see the way clear for raising funds enough to support the four young men who were then waiting to be sent forth to the heathen world. One of them was accordingly sent to England by the prudential committee, mainly to see whether an arrangement could not be made with the London Missionary Society, by which a part of their support could be received from that society, and they yet remain under the direction of the board. That society wisely declined such an arrangement, and at the same time encouraged their American brethren to hope for ample contributions from their own churches as soon as the facts should be generally known. From this time no further thought was entertained of looking abroad for pecuniary aid. Indeed, the largest legacy the board has yet received was bequeathed to it by a benevolent lady in Salem, Massachusetts, in the early part of the year 1811. The first ordination of American missionaries to the heathen in foreign lands, was in that place on the 6th of February, 1812. These were Samuel Newell, Adoniram Judson, Gordon Hall, Samuel Nott, and Luther Rice, all from the little missionary band in the theological seminary at Andover. They proceeded forthwith to Calcutta, in the East Indies, but without being designated to any specific field by the Committee. There was not then the hundredth part of the knowledge of the heathen world in the American churches that there is now. The prudential committee seem to have been unable to point to any one country, and tell their missionaries decidedly to occupy that in preference to other contiguous countries. The comparative claims of the different benighted portions of the unevangelical world was a subject then but little understood. The missionaries were left to decide what field to occupy after their arrival in India.

Messrs. Judson and Rice had not been long with the Baptist missionaries at Serampore, near Calcutta, when they declared themselves converts to the peculiar views of those missionaries in relation to baptism. Their consequent separation from the society which sent them forth, gave rise to the formation of a Baptist Board for Foreign Missions in the United States. Messrs. Hall, Newell, and Nott, after much painful voyaging from place to place, occasioned by the reluctance of the East India Company to tolerate missionaries, and especially American missionaries in India, (the United States and Great Britain being then unhappily at war,) at length, in 1813, found a resting place and field of labour at Bombay, in Western India. This was the commencement of the mission to the Mahrattas.

The Mahrattas possess strong traits of character as a people, compared with other nations of India, as is evident in their history for ages past. The American missionaries were the first to go in among them, and they entered as the husbandman would into an unbroken forest. No preparatory work had been done, except merely that of conquest by a Christian power, and it must be confessed that few tangible results have yet been witnessed in that mission. But there is no doubt that the Mahrattan people now stand differently related to the Christian religion from what they did in 1813. Much unavoidable preliminary ground has been gone over; the truth stands nearer to the native intellect and heart; the spiritual conquest of the country is far easier than it was then.

Among the Tamul people, found in the northern district of Ceylon and in southern India, there was some degree of preparation when the mission to that people was commenced in 1816; in Ceylon, by means of the Portuguese and the Dutch; and on the Continent, by means of the celebrated missionary Schwartz and his associates. Hence, through the blessing of God, the obvious results have been greater there than among the Mahrattas. The systematic measures which were early adopted by the Ceylon mission for training a native agency, and the success attending them, did much to give an early maturity to the plans of the board for raising up a native ministry in connection with all its other missions, of which more will be said in the sequel. The most efficient seminary for educating heathen youths for helpers in the work of the gospel, is believed to be the one connected with the mission in Ceylon. The number of pupils is 160, all of whom are boarding scholars, and about 100 of them are regarded as truly pious. There is also a female seminary, containing more than 100 boarding scholars, where the educated native helpers of the mission may obtain pious educated wives; and there are free schools containing 3000 pupils, which are a nursery for the seminaries, and among the most effective means of securing congregations to hear the preached gospel. In 1834, a branch of this mission was formed at Madura, on the continent, and in 1836 another at Madras, with the special object of printing books in the Tamul language on a large scale.

The first mission sent by the board to eastern Asia was to China in 1830. A pious merchant in New York city furnished many of the facts and arguments which justified its commencement, and then he gave two missionaries their passage to Canton, and their support for a year. One of these missionaries subsequently visited Siam, and opened the way for a mission to that country; as he did also to Singapore, and to Netherlands India. The mission to Singapore has not answered the expectations of the board, and is about being discontinued. The operations in Netherlands India, have been much embarrassed hitherto by the restrictive policy of the Dutch colonial government. The mission in Siam has had a prosperous commencement; but its prospects have not that cheering certainty which animates the labour of missionaries under such a government as now rules in British India.

Turning our attention to western Asia, we find a number of interesting missions under the care of this board. The Greek mission, commenced in the year 1829, grew out of the sympathy which was felt for the Greek people throughout the Christian world, in their struggle for independence from the Turkish yoke. Dr. King, who commenced it, had previously been connected with the Palestine mission. It was to the Holy Land, in fact, that the first mission in the series was sent, in the year 1821. Messrs. Fiske and Parsons were the pioneers in the enterprise. In 1828, after their decease, war and the hostilities of the Maronites towards the mission, compelled the surviving missionaries to retire from Syria for a season; and it is to this occurrence, in the developements of providence, we trace the establishment of the mission among the Armenians of Constantinople and Asia Minor, which has been so signally useful to that people. Two missionaries of the board had indeed gone to Asia Minor as early as 1826, but their mission was to the Greeks. In the year 1830, Messrs. Smith and Dwight were sent on an exploring tour into Armenia, and were instructed to visit the Nestorians in the Persian province of Aderbaijan. This visit brought that remnant of the most noted missionary church of ancient times to light, and induced the board to send a mission to restore the blessings of the gospel to that people. The mission was commenced on the plain of Ooroomiah, and has recently been extended to the independent Nestorian tribes among the Koordish mountains. The leading object of the mission is to educate the clergy, and by reviving among them, through the blessing of God, the spirit of the gospel, to induce them to resume the preaching of it with more than their ancient zeal. The press has been introduced. More than 400 Nestorians are in free schools, supported by the mission, and taught by eighteen priests and sixteen deacons; and upwards of sixty are boarding-scholars in seminaries. There is also a class of about a dozen in theology, instructed by the missionaries. We already begin to witness the gradual reviving of preaching among the ecclesiastics. The great thing wanting among this people is spiritual life. They number about 100,000 souls.

The Syrian mission has, for some years past, been cultivating an acquaintance with the Druzes of Mount Lebanon. These are about as numerous as the Nestorians, and resemble them in the mountaineer traits of courage and enterprise. The Druzes are a sort of heretical Mahommedans. Recently those inhabiting the mountains of Lebanon have, as a community, placed themselves under the religious instruction of the missionaries. Their motive may be the improvement of their civil condition by becoming Protestant Christians, but the fact of their permitting the mission to open a seminary at the seat of their government, and to preach the gospel, and introduce schools freely among them, should be acknowledged with gratitude to God.

The Armenian church has proved to be scarcely less interesting as a field for missionary labours than the Nestorian. It has even afforded more abundant spiritual fruit. An evangelical influence is strongly developed among the Armenian clergy; and in many instances where they have had no personal communication with members of the mission, but only with the holy scriptures, or with some of the books published by the mission, there are hundreds of Armenians, it is thought, whose minds, rejecting the corruptions and superstitions of their church, have come under the salutary influence of a gospel that looks for justification only through faith in Christ. In short, the grand principles by

means of which the Spirit of grace wrought out the Reformation
in Europe, are seen to be operating in western Asia, and their
progress ought to engage the prayerful interest of all Christians.

A mission was sent to South Africa in 1836, and high hopes
were entertained of a prosperous issue. But these hopes have
been in great measure blasted by the singular emigration of the
Dutch boërs from the English colony, and their consequent
wars upon the Zulus. The mission to western Africa, though
commenced in 1834, has not yet advanced beyond Cape Palmas,
where it has a very interesting seminary for Grebo youth; but
its ultimate destination, as soon as the way is opened up the
Niger, is to the populous and healthful countries of the interior.
Along the coast, however, eastward of Cape Palmas, there is
work for many missionaries.

The results of the mission of the board in the Sandwich
islands, a group of islands in the north Pacific ocean, constitute
one of the great moral wonders of the age. The first missionaries landed on those islands in the year 1820. At that time
the natives were savage and pagan, without letters, without a
ray of gospel light; though they had just before strangely burnt
their idols—a fact unknown in the United States when the
missionaries embarked on their errand of mercy. In 1840,
after the lapse of only twenty years, this same people might
properly have claimed the title of a Christian people. Though
necessarily destitute in great measure, owing to their poverty,
of the more imposing insignia of civilisation, they then had the
elements and basis of it in Christian institutions, schools, a
written language, the press, and books, and in the extensive
prevalence of pious dispositions and habits. Within this space
of time the language had been reduced to writing, and about
100,000,000 of pages had been printed by the mission in the
native language. As the alphabet contains but twelve letters,
and each letter has but a single sound, it is easy learning to
read. One-third of the population can read. The children of
the chiefs are educated by a member of the mission in a boarding
school designed for them alone, which the chiefs support: this
is at Honolulu, in the island of Oahu. At Lahainaluna, on
the island of Maui, there is a seminary, for which a large stone
edifice has been erected, containing nearly 100 boarding pupils;

and at Wailuku, on the same island, there is a corresponding female institution, containing about fifty.   At Waialua, on Oahu, there is a manual labour or self-supporting school.   Two other boarding schools are at Hilo, on the island of Hawaii, which are supported chiefly by the natives.   The free schools number about 14,000 pupils.   Laws have been passed by the government defining and securing the rights of property to the people, and taking the power of imposing taxes from the individual chiefs and vesting it exclusively in the national council, which is to assemble annually.   But the most remarkable fact of all is the extraordinary outpouring of the Holy Spirit in the years 1838 and 1839, in consequence of which many thousands of the natives were hopefully converted to God.   The number of church members (who are admitted to that relation only after a credible profession of real piety) increased in that space of time from 5000 to more than 18,000.   The natives have erected many houses for public worship, and a still greater number of school houses, and on the Sabbath-day, which is generally observed by abstaining from labour and amusements, the sound of the church-going bell is heard in not a few of their valleys.

The board has very properly spent a portion of its funds in missions to the more important and influential tribes of the North American Indians.   It began with the Cherokees and Choctaws in 1816-18, who then inhabited a tract of country within the chartered limits of some of the south-western States.   These two missions, for more than ten years, had great success.   The poor Indians were then driven almost to desperation by those who wished for their lands, and were bent on inducing them to remove beyond the Mississippi river.   These efforts had a cruel success.   The missionaries have followed the two tribes above-mentioned in their exile.   Missions were also instituted at different times among the Creeks and Chickasaws, eastward of the Mississippi, and among the Osages westward; but they have been discontinued.   Subsequent to the year 1830, missionaries were sent to the savage, wandering Ojibwas, Sioux, and Pawnees, in the vast territory north-west of the United States; and in 1835 they were sent across the continent, beyond the Rocky Mountains, to the Indians in the Oregon territory. There are several missions among the feeble remnants of the

2 x

once powerful Six Nations, found on the borders of Lake Erie, in the State of New York.

The following table will give a view, at a single glance, of the times when the several missions were commenced, their number and the number of their respective stations in the year 1841, the number of the missionaries who have been sent forth from the beginning, and the number now in the several fields:—

MISSIONS.	Time of commencement.	No. of stations.	Whole No. of ordained missionaries sent.	Present No. of ordained missionaries.	Whole No. of laymen sent.	Present No. of laymen.	Whole No. of females sent.	Present No. of females.	Whole No. of labourers sent.	Present No. of labourers.
Africa.										
Zulus, South Africa,	1836	2	5	3	1	1	7	4	13	8
Grebos, West Africa.	1834	2	3	2	1	1	4	3	8	6
Europe.										
Greece.	1829	2	6	4			6	3	12	7
Asia.										
Turkey,	1826	6	19	16	1		18	15	38	31
Syria,	1821	4	15	10	3	2	15	11	33	23
Persian Nestorians,	1834	1	5	5	2	1	5	5	12	11
Independent Nestorians,	1839	1	2	2	1	1	2	2	5	5
Persian Mohammedans,	1835	1	1	1			1	1	2	2
Mahrattas,	1813	4	18	7	5	2	21	10	44	19
Tamulians, Madras,	1836	3	2	2	1	1	4	3	7	6
Do. Madura,	1834	5	11	8	1	1	13	9	25	18
Do. Ceylon,	1816	7	16	10	2	2	20	14	38	26
Siam,	1831	2	9	7	1		12	9	22	16
China.	1830	1	4	3	2	1	1	1	7	5
Indian Archipelago.	1833		3				3		6	
Singapore,	1834	1	9	7	1		12	9	22	16
Borneo.	1838	3	8	7			9	8	17	15
North Pacific.										
Sandwich Islands.	1820	17	32	25	25	14	64	40	121	79
North American Indians.										
Cherokees,	1816	5	11	4	27	3	50	14	88	21
Choctaws,	1818	5	9	4	25	1	42	7	76	12
Pawnees,	1834	1	1	1	3	2	4	3	8	6
Oregon,	1835	4	5	5	4	4	8	8	17	17
Sioux,	1834	2	4	3	3	2	8	6	15	11
Ojibwas,	1831	2	3	3	6	4	12	9	21	16
Stockbridge,	1828	1	2	1	2		4	1	8	2
New York Indians,	1826	4	8	4	3	1	21	10	32	15
Abenaquis.	1835	1	1	1			1	1	2	2
Discontinued Missions.										
South America,	1823-25	2							2	
North American Indians,										
Chickasaws,	1827-35	4					6		10	
Creeks,	1832-37	1			2		2		5	
Osages,	1826-37	5			6		15		26	
Machinaw,	1826-37	1			7		9		17	
Maumee.	1826-35	1			1		4		6	
32—6=26		87	226	145	136	44	403	206	765	395

The number of missions, therefore, now existing under the care of this board is twenty-six; and these embrace eighty-seven stations, 145 ordained missionaries, forty-four lay helpers, (that is, physicians, printers, teachers, &c.,) and female helpers, (chiefly wives of missionaries,) enough to swell the number to 395. It appears, also, that the board since it commenced operations, has sent forth 226 ordained missionaries, 136 lay helpers, and 403 females; making a total of 765. To these about 150 native helpers are to be added, who have been trained on the ground, and are supported by the funds of the board; and these swell the number of present labourers to about 560; and the grand total to more than 900. Most of the ordained missionaries, after graduating at some college, spent three years in a theological seminary before receiving ordination. The annual expenditure for these missions is near 300,000 dollars.

A tabular view of the educational operations of the several missions, and also of the extent to which the press has been employed:—

MISSIONS.	EDUCATION.						PRINTING.				
	Seminaries.	Pupils.	Boarding Schools.	Pupils.	Whole No. of Boarding Scholars.	Free Schools.	Pupils in the Free Schools.	Printing Establishments.	Presses.	Type Foundries.	Founts of Type,	Number of pages printed from the beginning.
Zulus,						1	45	1	1		2	7,180
Grebos,	1	54			54	4	105	1	1		1	1,875,132
Greece,						2	125					4,709,500
Turkey,			2	10	10	4	90	1	2	1	9	44,408,260
Syria,	1	44	1	16	60	7	200	1	1	1	1	2,451,000
Nestorians,	1	39	1	23	62	17	414	1	1		1	
Mahrattas,	1	60	4	82	142	23	704	1	3	1	8	28,025,687
Madras,						16	485	1	8	1	10	33,750,000
Madura,			6	109	109	100	3207					
Ceylon,	1	162	3	150	312	85	3084	1	4		6	51,640,800
Siam,			1	4	4			1	1		1	3,222,960
China,								1	1		1	
Singapore,	1	57	1	10	67			1	1	1	3	14,071,168
Borneo,						1	25					
Sandwich Isl.,	1	84	5	152	236	200	14,000	2	3		5	99,196,673
Cherokees,			2	60		5	200	1	1		1	2,203,200
Choctaws,			1	15		7	157					3,048,150
Pawnees,												37,000
Oregon,						3	130	1	1		1	51,600
Sioux,						1	75					173,000
Ojibwas,						3	80					707,000
Stockbridge,												
N. Y. Indians,						10	250					192,000
Abenaquis,						1	20					63,000
Total...	7	500	27	631	1056	490	23,396	15	29	5	50	228,833,310

2 x 2

Of the 24,400 youth in the mission schools of this board, somewhat more than 1000 are boarding scholars, in schools where the leading object is to train up a native ministry. Five hundred are in seminaries designed exclusively for males, where the course of study is as extensive as it can be, while the languages of the several countries where they exist are no better furnished with works of sound literature and science. In general, the text-books for all the schools have to be prepared by the missionaries, and a very great progress, on the whole, has been made in this department, especially in geography, arithmetic, geometry, sacred history, and the first principles of religion and morals.

About 290,000,000 of pages have been printed at the fifteen printing establishments connected with the missions of this board. These establishments have printed books and tracts in thirty-one different languages, spoken by more than 450,000,000, exclusive of the English. These languages are the Zulu, Grebo, Italian, Greek, Armenian, Turkish (in the Armenian character), Arabic, Mahratta, Portuguese, Goojurattee, Hindosthanee, Latin, Tamul, Teloogoo, Siamese, Chinese, Japanese, Malay, Bugis, Hawaiian, Cherokee, Choctaw, Seneca, Abenaquis, Ojibwa, Ottawa, Creek, Osage, Sioux, Pawnee, and Nez Perces; thirteen of which were first reduced to writing by missionaries of the board.

About sixty churches have been gathered among the heathen, and formed as nearly on the Congregational or Presbyterian model for such ecclesiastical organisations, as the nature of the case would permit. None but converts who have been received as members of the church, after giving credible evidence of piety, are allowed to partake of the Lord's supper. The whole number of church members is about 20,000. The spiritual fruits of the missions to the oriental churches are, of course, not included in this number, such not having been gathered into distinct and separate churches; the effort there having been to infuse the spirit of the gospel into those religious communities as they now are.

THEORY OF THE MISSIONS OF THE BOARD. The board does not regard any of its missions as being permanent institutions. Their object is, through the grace of God, to impart the spirit and plant the institutions of the gospel where they do not exist, and then to leave them to the conservative influences that shall have been gathered about them. This is true theoretically, and it will come out in fact as soon as the means are furnished for prosecuting the work with becoming vigour. The missionary is emphatically, in the essential principle of his calling, a sojourner, pilgrim, stranger, having no continuing city.

The leading object of its missions, therefore, is the training and employment of a native ministry, as the only way in which the gospel can soon become indigenous to the soil, and the gospel institutions acquire a self-supporting, self-propagating energy. And the fact is important to be noted, that the elders, or pastors, whom the apostles ordained over the churches they gathered among the heathen, were generally, if not always, *natives of the country*. While the apostles had not the facilities of the present day for training men for this office by education, they had not the necessity for so doing. Among their converts at Ephesus, Berea, Corinth, Rome, and elsewhere, they had no difficulty in finding men who only required some instruction in theology, and scarcely that when endowed with miraculous gifts, to be prepared for the pastoral office. How they did, or would have done, beyond the Roman empire and the bounds of civilisation, we are not informed; but in the use they made of a native ministry we recognise one of the grand principles of their missions, and also the true theory of missions—simple, economical, practical, scriptural, mighty through God.

The manner in which the board is endeavouring to carry out this theory in practice has perhaps been sufficiently indicated. But the subject is one of so much importance that it will be worth while to quote part of an article upon it, which was submitted by the prudential committee to the board, at the annual meeting in the year 1841.

I. *On the manner of raising up a native ministry.*

" 1. This must be by means of seminaries, schools of the prophets, such as, in some form or other, the church has always found necessary. There should be one such seminary in each considerable mission. It is an essential feature of the plan that the pupils be taken young, board in the mission, be kept separate from heathenism, under Christian superintendence night and day. In general, the course of study should embrace a period of from eight to ten or twelve years, and even a longer time in special cases. Pupils can be obtained for such a course of education in most of the missions; but, as a nursery for them, it is expedient to have a certain number of free schools, which also greatly aid in getting audiences for the preachers.

" 2. There will be but partial success in rearing a native ministry, unless the seminary be in the midst of a select and strong body of missionaries, whose holy lives, conversation, and preaching shall cause the light of the gospel to blaze intensely and constantly upon and around the institution. Experience shows that in such circumstances we are warranted to expect a considerable proportion of the students to become pious.

" 3. The student, while in the seminary, should be trained practically to habits of usefulness. But this requires caution, and must not be attempted too soon. Those set apart for the sacred ministry might remain as a class in theology at the seminary, after completing the regular course of study; or, according to the old fashion in this country, which has some special advantages, they might pursue their theological studies with individual missionaries, and under such superintendence exercise their gifts before much responsibility is thrown upon them.

" 4. The contemporaneous establishment of female boarding schools, where the native ministers and other educated helpers in the mission may obtain pious and intelligent partners for life, is an essential feature in this system. A native pastor, with an ignorant, heathen wife, would be greatly embarassed and hindered in his work. In this manner Christian families are formed, and at length Christian communities, and there is a race of children with Christian ideas and associations, from among whom we may select our future pupils and candidates for the ministry."

II. *On the employment of this native ministry.*

" The pupils in the seminaries will have different gifts, and the same gifts in very different degrees. All the pious students will not do for preachers. Some may be retained as tutors in the seminary, others may be employed as school teachers, others as printers, bookbinders, etc. Those set apart for the ministry, while they are taught the way of the Lord more perfectly, can

be employed as catechists, tract distributors, readers, or superintendents of schools, and thus gain experience and try their
characters.   In due time they may be licensed to preach, and
after proper trial, receive ordination as evangelists or pastors.

" While care should be taken to lay hands suddenly on no
man, there is believed to be danger of requiring too much of
native converts before we are willing to intrust them with the
ministry of the word.   Generations must pass before a community, emerging from the depths of heathenism, can be expected
to furnish a body of ministers equal to that in our country.

" Could the present native church members at the Sandwich
islands be divided into companies of 180 each, 100 churches
would be constituted.   Native pastors should be in training
for these churches, and evangelists for the numerous districts
where churches are not yet formed, and where the people are
consequently exposed to the inroads of the enemy.   In the
other missions the chief employment, at present, must be that
of evangelists.   In the Tamul missions, hundreds might find
ample employment; and in the Oriental churches, our leading
object should be to bring forward an able evangelical native ministry with the least possible delay."

III. *On the power and economy of the plan.*

"In most of our missions we are opposed by three formidable
obstacles, namely, *distance, expense,* and *climate.*   England was
opposed by the same obstacles in her conquest of India.   And
how did she overcome them?   By employing native troops; and
it is chiefly by means of them she now holds that great populous
country in subjection.   We too must have native troops in our
spiritual warfare.   Why not have an army of them?   Why not
have as numerous a body of native evangelists as can be directed
and employed?

"Such a measure would effect a great saving of *time.*   Indeed,
we can never leave our fields of labours till this is done.   Our
mission-churches must have native pastors, and pastors of some
experience, who can stand alone, before we can leave them.   Besides, we should make far greater progress than we do had we
more of such helpers.

"And what economy of *money* there would be in the operation
of this plan!   The cost of a ten years' course of education for

five natives of India would not be more than the outfit and passage of one married missionary to that country. And when a company of missionaries is upon the ground, it costs at least five times as much to support them as it would to support the same number of native preachers. The former could not live, like the latter, upon rice alone, with a piece of cotton cloth wrapped about their bodies for clothing; and a mud-walled, grass-covered cottage, without furniture, for a dwelling; nor could they travel on foot under a tropical sun. They could not do this and at the same time preserve health and life.

"The cost of educating 1000 youth in India, from whom preachers might be obtained, and afterwards of supporting 200 native preachers and their families, would be only about 25,000 dollars; which is but little more than the average expense in that country of twenty-five missionaries and families. Now, if the preaching of two well-educated native preachers, labouring under judicious superintendence, may be expected to do as much good as that of one missionary, we have in these 200 native preachers the equivalent, in instrumental preaching power, for 100 missionaries, and at an expenditure less by nearly 75,000 dollars a year. And then, too, the native preacher is at home in the country and climate, not subject to a premature breaking down of his constitution, not compelled to resort for health to the United States, or to send his children thither for education. Besides, the native churches and converts might gradually be brought to assume a part or the whole of the support of the native ministry; while it is very doubtful whether it will ever be expedient for the missionary to receive his support from that quarter.

"One hundred thousand dollars a year would board and educate 4000 native youth. That sum would support 500 or 600 native ministers with their families; and if the value of this amount of native preaching talent equalled that of only 200 missionaries, the annual saving of expense would be at least 125,000 dollars. But it would in the end be worth much more; so that we see, in this view, how our effective force among the heathen may, in a few years, be rendered manifold greater than it is at present, without even doubling our annual expenditure. Some progress has even now been made towards this result. We already have 500 male youth in our seven seminaries; and a still greater number, male and female, in our other twenty-seven boarding schools. But the scheme, however promising and indispensable, cannot be carried into effect without a large addition of first rate men to the company of our missionaries."

It is interesting to observe how the attention of Protestant missionaries from Europe, as well as the United States, has been drawn of late to the importance of a native ministry, as a means of carrying on the work of missions among the heathen. There can, however, be no doubt, that this board has taken the lead of all other missionary societies in giving that subject the prominence practically, which it deserves in the great system of missionary operations.

The Annual Meetings of the board. The annual meetings of the board must receive a brief notice. They are held in the month of September, in some one of the more important cities of the eastern or middle States, and occupy three days. The session is for deliberation and business. The annual meeting for the year 1841 is a fair specimen of the usual attendance of members. There were fifty-six corporate, and 102 honorary members present. Of the corporate members five were heads of colleges, (there are thrice that number belonging to the corporation;) thirty-one were pastors of churches, or otherwise employed in the Christian ministry; ten were civilians; and the remaining ten engaged in mercantile or medical pursuits.

The first day of the session is employed in bringing forward the business of the meeting, so far as the prudential committee is concerned, which is done in writing. This, including the different parts of the annual report, is usually referred to some fifteen or more committees, who report during the session. Their reports often give rise to friendly discussions, which are always interesting, and often eloquent. All the meetings are open to the public, and are usually held in a church, that there may be room for those friends and patrons who wish to attend. In the evening of the first day a sermon is preached before the board by a member appointed to the service at the previous meeting, and the members unite in celebrating the Lord's supper during the session. A meeting for popular addresses is held in the evening of the second or third day. The last day of the session is generally the great day of the feast in point of interest; and it may truly be said that the annual meeting of this board, as a whole, has for several years past exerted a great and good influence on the community, its proceedings being more extensively and carefully reported in the religious newspapers than those of any other religious or charitable institution in the country.

PUBLICATIONS. The publications issued by the board directly are: 1. The "Missionary Herald," published monthly in about 24,000 copies; 2. The "Day Spring," a monthly publication just commenced in the form of a small newspaper; 3. The "Annual Report," a document of about 200 pages, of which 4000 or 5000 copies are issued annually; and, 4. The "Annual Sermon," and occasional missionary papers of various descriptions.

Among the numerous works which have been occasioned more or less directly by its missions, though not published by it or at its expense, the following may be mentioned:—

Memoir of Mrs. Harriet Newell; by Rev. Leonard Woods, D.D., 1815.—Memoir of the Rev. Levi Parsons; by Rev. Daniel O. Morton, 1824.—Memoir of the Rev. Pliny Fisk; by Rev. Aloan Bond, 1828.—Memoir of Catherine Brown, a Christian Indian of the Cherokee nation; by Rev. Rufus Anderson, 1824.—Memoir of Rev. Gordon Hall; by Rev. Horatio Bardwell, 1834.—Memoir of Mrs. Harriet L. Winslow; by Rev. Miron Winslow, 1835.—Memoir of Mrs. Myra W. Allen; by Rev. Cyrus Mann, 1834.—The Little Osage Captive; by Rev. Elias Cornelius, 1822.—Memoir of Mrs. Sarah Lanman Smith; by Rev. Edward W. Hooker, D.D., 1839, Syrian Mission.—Memoir of Mrs. Elisabeth D. Dwight and Mrs. Judith S. Grant, 1840. —The Christian Brahmin, or Memoirs of the Life, Writings, and Character of the converted Brahmin, Babajee; by Rev. Hollis Read, 2 vols., 1836.—Memoirs of American Missionaries, formerly connected with the Society of Inquiry respecting Missions in the Andover Theological Seminary, 1832.—Tour around Hawaii, (one of the Sandwich islands;) by Rev. William Ellis, 1826.—A Residence in the Sandwich Islands; by Rev. Charles Samuel Stewart, 1828.—History of the Sandwich Islands' Mission; by Rev. Sheldon Dibble, 1839.—Observations on the Peloponnesus and Greek Islands; by Rev. Rufus Anderson, 1830.—Researches in Armenia; by Rev. E. Smith and

Rev. H. G. O. Dwight, 1833.—Residence at Constantinople; by Rev. Josiah Brewer, 1830.—The Nestorians, or the Lost Tribes; by Asahel Grant, M.D., 1841.—Missionary Sermons and Addresses; by Rev. Eli Smith, 1833.—Journal of a Missionary Tour in India; by Rev. William Ramsey, 1836.— Journal of a Residence in China and the Neighbouring Countries; by Rev. David Abeel, 1834.—The Missionary Convention at Jerusalem, or an Exhibition of the Claims of the World to the Gospel; by Rev. David Abeel, 1838.—Journal of an Exploring Tour beyond the Rocky Mountains; by Rev. Samuel Parker, 1838.—Essays on the Present Crisis in the Condition of the American Indians, first published in the National Intelligencer under the signature of William Penn, 1829; by Jeremiah Evarts.—Speeches on the Passage of the Bill for the Removal of the Indians, delivered in the Congress of the United States, 1830.—History of the American Board of Commissioners for Foreign Missions; by Rev. Joseph Tracy, 1840.

CHAPTER IV.

BOARD OF FOREIGN MISSIONS OF THE PRESBYTERIAN CHURCH.

WE have gone into considerable detail in the preceding chapter in order to exhibit, once for all, the grand principles of our American missions—the establishment of schools for the Christian instruction of youth, and especially for raising a native ministry among the heathen themselves, and the employment of that most important auxiliary, the press. The views of the American Board of Commissioners for Foreign Missions on these points are held, I believe, without exception, by all our other missionary associations, so that we may dispense with going into the reconsideration of them in the notices that are to follow.

We turn next to the Presbyterian Church's Board for Foreign Missions, not because next in point of date or extent of operations, but simply because it derives its support from a member of the same great Presbyterian family of churches, of certain other branches of which the American Board of Commissioners for Foreign Missions is the great missionary organ. The two societies, in fact, comprise all that is now done for the conversion of heathens, Mohammedans, and Jews, by Presbyterians of all shades in the United States.

The board of which we have now to speak was constituted only in 1837, the congregations which it represents having before that combined with others in supporting the American board, and many of them, indeed, with a truly liberal spirit, now support both. The latter of the two boards arose from a conviction which had long been gaining ground, that the Presbyterians as a church, and by the medium of their supreme ecclesiastical judicature, ought, like the Church of Scotland, to undertake foreign as well as domestic missions.

As the Old School Presbyterian Church which appointed and supports this board, numbers 1291 pastors and 2025 churches, and as nearly all these have it in their power to aid the cause, there is every prospect of its becoming in a few years a very efficient association. Its receipts for the year ending May 1st, 1842, were 60,324 dollars, and it had expended about 800 dollars more than this. Besides its regular receipts, it received 2000 dollars from the American Bible Society for the printing and circulation of the scriptures, and a like sum from the American Tract Society for the publication of tracts. It has the following missions:—

Iowa, or Sac Indians in the Indian territory westward of the Missouri. Here it employs a minister, a teacher, and a farmer, and their wives, with an encouraging prospect of good being done by preaching, and still more by schools. Intemperance is found the greatest bar to the progress of the gospel among the Indians.

Chippewa and Ottawa tribes. Two missionaries and their wives are labouring with considerable and encouraging success among these two tribes, which are still in the western part of Michigan, not having been yet removed to the west of the Mississippi.

Creek Indians. These form a powerful tribe of above 21,000

souls, in the Indian territory to the west of the States of Arkansas and Missouri.   Until of late they have been averse to receiving missionaries, but the board has now taken measures, with the consent of their chiefs, for establishing a mission among them.

TEXAS. One missionary and his wife have been stationed on the western border of Texas, but as this mission is intended for the benefit of Mexico, they remain where they are only until the door is opened for their admission into the latter country.

WESTERN AFRICA. The board has two missionaries, with their wives and one coloured female teacher, sent from the United States, and two male native teachers, at Cape Palmas, the site of a colony of coloured people from America. The mission bids fair to be eminently useful.

THE CHINESE. This mission is established for the present at Singapore. Two missionaries, one of whom is married, and a physician and his wife, are employed in preaching and in the education of youth among the Chinese, who either permanently reside at that port or occasionally visit it.

SIAM. In this kingdom the board maintains one missionary and his wife, who are preparing themselves for their future work by acquiring the language of the country, and making themselves useful in the meantime by an abundant distribution of portions of the holy scriptures and tracts.

NORTHERN INDIA. Here it is that the board has its most extensive missions, having at its different stations at Lodiana, Sabathu, Saharunpur, Allahabad, and Futtehgurh, no fewer than seventeen ordained missionaries, most of whom are married, one printer, three teachers, and one catechist, all Americans, besides two native catechists, and one native assistant. This mission has been remarkably successful, considering how lately it was commenced. Schools have been established at the different stations, and a considerable number of publications, including parts of the Bible, have been issued in the Hindustani, Persian, Panjabi or Gurmukhi, and Hindi languages. To this, preaching in the native languages at the different stations is now added, and in English, also, at one or more of these, for the benefit of the British officers and other residents, some of whom, we rejoice to say, have shown much kindness to the missionaries, and have liberally contributed to the support of the schools.

The missionaries in this quarter have lately formed themselves into three presbyteries, and these have been organised as the *Synod of Northern India* by the general assembly in America, to which it is subordinate.

The board takes a deep interest in China, and looks forward to the day when the truth may find an effectual entrance into that populous empire. It has, at a great expense, had 3326 matrices made in Paris for the casting of as many different types, which, by their combinations, can produce above 14,000 different characters,—a number, according to the report for 1841, amply sufficient for missionary purposes. Hence it would seem that the question how far the Chinese language may be printed with moveable type is about to be resolved by this board; and it is a striking fact, that solely to its liberality the ingenious French printer, M. Marcellin-Legrand, under the direction of M. Ponthieu, who discovered this method of printing Chinese, and of Walter Lowrie, secretary to the board, and himself an excellent Chinese scholar, owes his having been enabled to make so much progress in preparing a complete fount of type in that important but difficult tongue.

The board is annually appointed by the general assembly, and to that body it makes its report. The business, however, is mainly conducted by a very efficient committee subject to its supervision, and through this committee as its organ it issues a monthly publication, called *The Foreign Missionary Chronicle*, presenting not only full accounts of its own missions, but summaries also of what is done by other missionary societies. From 5000 to 6000 copies of this valuable periodical are circulated through the churches.

The board has now under its direction, sent out by the church that appoints it, sixty-five labourers at foreign stations, of whom twenty-eight are ministers of the gospel. It has, besides, eight native assistants, some of whom are learned persons, and all of them hopefully pious, and in different stages of trial and preparation for labouring among their benighted fellow-countrymen. Through the stations occupied by these missionaries, the Presbyterian Church is brought into contact with five different heathen nations, estimated to comprise two-thirds of the whole human race.

CHAPTER V.

MISSIONS OF THE BAPTIST CHURCHES.

The operations of this board now extend over twenty-eight years. It was first constituted in 1814, by the Baptist General Convention for Foreign Missions, which meets triennially, and is in fact a missionary society. To it the board makes a regular report of its proceedings.

This association has from small beginnings advanced from year to year in resources and efficiency until, through God's blessing, it embraces all the four great continents within the sphere of its operations. These have been conducted with singular wisdom, zeal, and perseverance, and have been crowned with remarkable success.

Its history shows how wonderfully God, in his providence, orders and over-rules events while enlisting new agencies for the accomplishment of his purposes. In 1812, the American Board of Commissioners for Foreign Missions, a Pædobaptist society, sent several missionaries to Bengal. On their voyage thither, two of these, the Rev. Messrs. Judson and Rice and their wives, changed their views and became Baptists; an event that not only gave much distress to other members of the mission, but produced, perhaps, other feelings besides chagrin in the minds of the members of the board that had sent them out. On their arrival they found that the British East India Company would not permit them to labour within its territories; so that after a few weeks stay they had to leave Calcutta. Messrs. Judson and Rice, however, with their wives, were received with great kindness by the excellent Dr. Carey and his associates, Baptist missionaries from England settled at Serampore, a small Danish possession not many miles above Calcutta. There was no Baptist foreign missionary society at that time in the United States, but as Messrs. Judson and Rice had become Baptists, were now in India, and wished to remain and preach the gospel there to the heathen, their case drew the attention of the Baptist churches in America, and a society was organised for their support. Meanwhile, Mr. Judson withdrew into the Burmese territory, and there commenced a mission which has been signally blessed. The society, which they were the means of originating, is now a great institution, with no fewer than twenty missions in various parts of the world. How wonderful are the ways of God! bringing good from what seems to man, for a time at least, to be evil. Had not the two missionaries become Baptists, where would have been the blessed mission to Burmah, and how many years might have elapsed before the American Baptists entered on the pursuit of foreign missions? And had not the governor-general of India excluded American missionaries from Bengal, where would have been the promising American missions in Ceylon, in the southern part of Hindostan, and on the western side of the Indian peninsula?

Such was the origin of the Baptist Board of Foreign Missions; let us now glance at its various enterprises as reported by the board for 1841.

MISSIONS IN NORTH AMERICA. These are eight in number, and embrace the following tribes: the Ojibwas, Ottawas, Oneidas, and Tuscaroras, Otoes, Shawanoes, and others, Cherokees, Creeks, and Choctaws, the three last residing on the Indian territory. Among these various tribes the board has thirteen stations, one out-station, three regular preachers, eight teachers, one printer, who also preaches, two female teachers, twelve female assistants; in all twenty-eight American missionaries and assistants, eleven Indian assistants, twelve churches, comprehending 798 members, and six schools attended by 159 scholars.

IN EUROPE. In France, the board has eight stations, and six out-stations, one missionary and his wife, six native preachers, and three native assistants. In Germany and Denmark it has five stations, six native preachers, and three native assistants. In Greece, two stations, two preachers, three female assistants, one native assistant, and 414 members.

In WEST AFRICA, the board has three stations, three preachers, one teacher, who is also a preacher, two female assistants, one native assistant, and fifteen churches among the Bassas, a native tribe near the colony of Liberia.

In ASIA, the board has missions among the Karens on the borders of Burmah, in Siam, in China, in Arracan, in Assam, and at Madras and Nellore in British India. These, forming eight distinct missions, comprehended in 1841 forty-one stations and out-stations, fifty-six missionaries and assistant missionaries, seventy-one native assistants, thirty churches, 1600 church members, thirty-five schools, and 635 scholars.

The total numbers, including all the missions, were, according to the same report, as follows:—

    20 Missions.
    80 Stations and out-stations.
    97 Missionaries and assistant missionaries, (Americans.)
  102 Native preachers and assistants.
   68 Churches, comprehending more than 2000 members.
  487 Baptisms in the course of the year reported on.
   44 Schools, and 872 scholars.

The receipts for that year had amounted to 56,948 dollars, and the disbursements to 61,860 dollars. In addition to its regular receipts the board had received 15,000 dollars from the American and Foreign Bible Society, for the publication of the scriptures; 4,700 dollars from the American Tract Society for the publication of Tracts; and 4400 dollars from the United States government towards the support of schools among the Indians.

This brief notice will give the reader some idea of this excellent society's operations, and of the good that it is doing. A detailed account of its missions, particularly of those among the Burmans and the Karens, would be interesting, but would far exceed the limits of this work. It is delightful to see how much interest in the cause of missions has sprung up in this numerous and important branch of the church in the United States. May God grant that it and every other may soon come up to the full measure of its ability and duty in this great work.

Let me add in conclusion, that the Missionary Magazine, an able and interesting monthly publication, has long been the organ of the society, and has a wide circulation among the Baptist denomination.

CHAPTER VI.

THE Missionary Society of the Methodist Episcopal Church was formed in 1819, under the auspices of the general conference, but for many years its efforts were chiefly directed to domestic missions, including those to the slaves in the southern States, and to the aboriginal tribes within, or adjacent to, the western frontier of the United States. It afterwards directed its attention to the colonies of free coloured Americans on the west coast of Africa, and, at a still later period, it established missions on the territory to the west of the Oregon mountains, and at some important points in South America. The German emigrants, found swarming in our principal cities, at the same time engaged much of its attention. Its efforts in behalf of these and of the slaves, as properly falling under the head of home missions, we have already noticed, and will now give some account of what are, properly speaking, its foreign missions.

NORTH AMERICAN INDIANS. The society in 1841 had twenty-five missionaries labouring within or beyond the western frontier of the United States among the following tribes, or remnants of tribes, the Wyandots, Oneidas, Shawnees, Delawares, Kickapoos, Pottawottamies, Chippewas, Choctaws, Cherokees, &c., &c. The report for that year states the Indian members of the mission churches gathered from these tribes to have amounted to 2341.

TEXAS MISSION. The society had no fewer than eighteen missionaries stationed in the republic of Texas in 1841; these had laboured with much success; and they now form a yearly conference, which, by conducting its own affairs, will probably do away with the necessity of having any independent mission in that country. This conference comprehends three presiding elders' districts, eighteen travelling ministers, twenty-five local preachers, and 1853 members.   A college, also, has been established under its auspices.

LIBERIA MISSION, at and in the vicinity of the American colony on the west coast of Africa, was commenced in 1833 by the late Rev. Melville B. Cox, an excellent man, who fell a victim to the climate a few months after his arrival.   With his dying breath he exclaimed: "Though a thousand fall, Africa must not be given up." He was succeeded by others, and they, too, sank under a climate so fatal to white men.   At length the Rev. John Seys was sent out, and he, through God's blessing, has been preserved to this day.   He has been greatly blessed in putting the affairs of the mission in order, and superintending the labours of coloured preachers from the United States, the society having to depend chiefly on these.   Nevertheless, it sent out two white missionaries in January last.   The mission now includes a yearly conference, consisting of seventeen preachers, all coloured, with the exception of Mr. Seys the superintendent, and the two brethren lately sent out.

Of the church members, about 1000 in all, 150 are native Africans, who within the last two years were worshipping gods of wood, stone, leather, anything, in short, that their imagination could fashion into a god!

SOUTH AMERICAN MISSION.   In 1841, the society had five missionaries at Rio Janeiro, Monte Video, and Buenos Ayres, labouring not unsuccessfully to introduce the gospel to those cities, now so ignorant of the truth.   These worthy men, however, I grieve to say, the pressure of the times has obliged the society to recall, at least for the present.   The unsettled state of affairs, indeed, at Monte Video and Buenos Ayres, rendered it almost impossible to make any progress at those places.

OREGON MISSION.   Both in its origin and its success this has been one of the most remarkable of all the missions of the American churches.   About the year 1828, the tribe of Indians called Flat Heads, living to the west of the Oregon mountains, prompted probably by what they had seen and heard of the Christian religion among the trappers of the American and Hudson's Bay Fur Companies, sent some of their chiefs into the United States to inquire as to the various forms of religious worship observed there, and to decide upon which to recommend.

After a long and painful journey they reached St. Louis, and stated the object of their coming to the late General Clarke, [1] then government agent for Indian affairs in that district, by whom it was communicated to the ministers of the gospel in the place. A great sensation was naturally produced. The Methodist Missionary Society was the first that took the matter up, and, desiring to act with prudence, sent two judicious and experienced persons across the Oregon mountains to visit the Indians, ascertain their present position, and choose a proper situation for a mission. On their arrival they found the way wonderfully prepared by the Lord's providential dispensations, so that after their return a mission on a large scale left New York for the Oregon country. After a journey of some months it reached the place of its destination, and was welcomed by the Indians and the agents of the Hudson's Bay Company stationed in that region.

This mission, which from the first has been remarkably blessed, consisted in 1841 of no fewer than sixty-eight persons, including teachers, farmers, mechanics of all kinds, women and children, all, of course, connected with the society. It is designed, in fact, to be in a great measure a self-supporting mission. Its object partly is by exhibiting the advantages of civilisation, to induce the Indians to engage in tillage, and to adopt the other arts and usages of civilised life, in all which the mission has succeeded much beyond expectation. Its spiritual success has been still more remarkable, for the Indian converts amounted two years ago to no fewer than 1000. The mission, upon the whole, is an experiment of the most interesting kind.

The total number of this society's ordained missionaries amounted in 1841 to eighty-five. Its total income for that year was 121,850 dollars; its disbursements 124,879 dollars, of which 90,000 were for home, and 34,879 for foreign missions.

---

[1] The name of this gentleman is well known in connection with that of the late Governor Lewis, from the exploring tour they made in company across the Oregon mountains to the Pacific ocean, during Mr. Jefferson's presidency.

CHAPTER VII.

BOARD OF MISSIONS OF THE PROTESTANT EPISCOPAL CHURCH.

This board was constituted in 1835. Its domestic operations we have noticed in another place, and have now to speak of its foreign missions which extend to various parts of the world.

WESTERN AFRICA. It has a very flourishing mission at Cape Palmas, and at two or three stations a few miles distant in the interior. In 1841, it comprised four ordained ministers, together with two white and eight coloured teachers. The place has been well chosen, for Cape Palmas is one of the healthiest spots on that notoriously unhealthy coast. Several American ladies have resided there in the enjoyment of good health for some years. Attached to the mission there are several schools, partly for the colonists, partly for the natives, and attended by above 100 scholars, youths and adults. The preaching of the missionaries is well attended and has been blessed to the salvation of souls.

CHINA. It has a missionary and his wife in the east, formerly at Batavia, from which they removed to Singapore, and are preparing for China. They are probably now at Macao.

GREECE. The board has a very prosperous mission at Athens. There the Rev. Mr. Hill is stationed with Mrs. Hill, who is a remarkably efficient person, and several American ladies as teachers, besides whom there are about twelve native teachers. Mr. Hill has been very successful in raising and supporting schools for infants, for boys and for girls, attended by about 800 scholars. He preaches, also, on the Sabbath and other occasions, in Greek, to a congregation of young and old. Yet, owing to the perpetual jealousy of the Greek clergy, and their influence with the government, the missionaries find themselves exposed to many difficulties.

CRETE. In this island, also, there is a thriving mission, conducted by one ordained missionary, assisted by his wife and two other American ladies, besides two natives engaged as teachers.

CONSTANTINOPLE and MARDIN.   The Rev. Dr. Robertson and his wife are at the former, and the Rev. Mr. Southgate and his wife at the latter of these places.   Dr. R. labours chiefly among the Greeks.   Mr. S. who has travelled much in Asia Minor, and the adjacent parts of the east, has given the results of his observations in his interesting journals.

TEXAS.   In this republic, the board last year employed three missionaries, who were labouring with some success at Houston, Matagorda, and Galveston.

It hence appears, that the whole of the board's ordained missionaries amounted in 1841, to twelve, labouring in seven distinct missions, besides whom there were fifteen American ladies chiefly engaged in teaching, and no fewer than twenty native teachers.   All these missions, with the exception of that to China, which the war between the Chinese and British empires would hardly allow to be organised, has met with encouraging success.   The receipts, exclusive of grants from the American Tract Society, and one or two Bible associations, amounted to 22,980 dollars, and the disbursements to 30,514 dollars.   This was for the foreign missions alone.   The board issues an interesting publication, entituled, "the Spirit of Missions," for the diffusion of missionary intelligence among the churches.

CHAPTER VIII.

FOREIGN MISSIONS OF OTHER DENOMINATIONS.

MISSIONS OF THE FREE-WILL BAPTIST CHURCHES.   The Free-will Baptist Foreign Missionary Society was organised in 1833, and originated in the correspondence of the Rev. Mr. Sutton, of the English General Baptist Mission, with Elder Buzzel, a Free-will Baptist minister in the United States.   Mr. Sutton wrote in 1831, representing the deplorable state of the heathen in India, and calling on his American brethren to come up to the help of the Lord against the mighty.   Returning to England in 1833,

Mr. Sutton went from that to America, there spent several months preaching to the churches; then, after another short visit to his native land, he made an extensive tour in 1834 through the Free-will Baptist churches in the United States, preaching on missions, and acting as the corresponding secretary of a missionary society which had been formed the preceding year.   Having succeeded in rousing these churches to a sense of their duty, he sailed in 1835 for India with the Rev. Messrs. Noyes and Phillips and their wives, being the first missionaries from the new society.   On their arrival they went with Mr. Sutton to Orissa, a province lying on the western shore of the bay of Bengal, some hundred miles south-west from Calcutta.   They have been labouring chiefly at Balasore with much faithfulness and success.   More missionaries were to be sent out in 1839, and although we are not aware of the present number in the field, there cannot be fewer than six or eight, including female assistants.   The society owes much, we understand, to subscriptions and collections at monthly prayer meetings.   The Rev. Luther Palmer of Norwalk, Ohio, a Free-will Baptist pastor, some time ago gave himself and all his property, valued at 5000 dollars, to the society, wishing the latter to be applied to the support of the press in India.   Such liberality reminds us of Pentecostal days.   The yearly receipts of the society are not much short, we believe, of 5000 dollars.

FOREIGN MISSIONARY SOCIETY OF THE LUTHERAN CHURCH IN THE UNITED STATES.   This society, which dates from 1837, originated in an appeal from the German missionaries in India, Mr. Rhenuis and his associates, to their brethren in the United States, for the assistance they required in consequence of their separation from the Church Missionary Society of England, on account of certain of its views and measures which they disapproved, after having laboured for several years in its service.   In answer to their appeal, a convention of Lutheran ministers and lay members was held at Hagerstown, in Maryland, and the society was organised.   From its commencement until May 1st, 1841, it had received 3682 dollars, and had disbursed, chiefly in remittances to the missionaries, 3000 dollars.   But these missionaries having renewed their connection with the English Church Missionary Society, the American Lutherans have resolved to send out missionaries from their own churches, as soon as fit persons can be found.

FOREIGN MISSIONS OF THE MORAVIANS OR UNITED BRETHREN. The Moravian Brethren in the United States formed a society for propagating the gospel among the heathen in 1787; an act for incorporating it was passed by the State of Pennsylvania; and it has been actively employed ever since in promoting missions. As its operations, however, are merged in those of the society, or "Unity," at Herrnhut in Germany, I am unable to give a definite account of them. The general society has missionaries among the Cherokees, now removed to the Indian territory, and at Fairfield in Upper Canada, as well as in other parts of America, but I cannot say how many of the missionaries are from the United States, though, I believe, there are not many. Neither do I know precisely what are the receipts of the United States' society, but believe they do not exceed 3000 dollars. Some years ago it received a handsome legacy from a gentleman at Philadelphia. It has a monthly missionary magazine.

Such are the societies in the United States which have been expressly formed for propagation of the gospel in pagan countries, although some of them have missions in countries nominally Christian.

Let me add that the American Bible Society, and the American and Foreign Bible Society, supported by the Baptists, have been making large yearly donations towards the circulation of the holy scriptures in foreign, and especially pagan lands. Some, also, of the State and other local Bible societies, such as those of Massachusetts and Philadelphia, have done something in this way. The American Tract Society has likewise made yearly grants of from 10,000 to 40,000 dollars for the publication and distribution of religious tracts in foreign, and chiefly in heathen lands. The American Sunday School Union, too, has granted both books and money for promoting its objects abroad. I am unable to state the yearly amount of these donations with perfect accuracy, but believe that, taking the average of the last ten years, they have exceeded 50,000 dollars.

CHAPTER IX.

AMERICAN SOCIETY FOR AMELIORATING THE CONDITION OF THE JEWS.

THIS society was formed in 1820, for the purpose of providing an asylum, and the means of earning a comfortable livelihood in America, for Jews whose conversion to Christianity exposed them to persecution and the loss of the means of living. A farm, accordingly, of about 500 acres was purchased, on which it was proposed to have a colony of converted Jews, who, by tillage and other useful arts, might support themselves and their families. Somehow or other this project did not answer the expectations of its projectors, and so much did the society lose the confidence of the Christian public, that for a while it seemed quite lost sight of. A year or two ago, however, the impulse given to the conversion of the Jews in Scotland and other European countries, led some of the old friends of the American society to think of reviving it, and directing its efforts to the employment of missionaries among the Jews, either in America or elsewhere. As the society is incorporated, and has property to the amount, I believe, of from 15,000 to 20,000 dollars, it may commence its operations immediately among the Jewish people, of whom there are said to be about 50,000 in the United States, whose conversion has never, it must be confessed, called forth the interest and the efforts that it ought to have done.

CHAPTER X.

THIS, which is the latest in its origin of all the foreign missionary societies, was formed in 1839, for promoting evangelical
religion in all nominally Christian countries, and was suggested
by the growing conviction of many persons in the United States,
that until pure Christianity be restored in nominal Christendom,
the conversion of the heathen world can hardly be looked for.
There are millions of Protestants, and ten millions of Romanists,
so manifestly ignorant of the great doctrines of the gospel, as to
prove by their lives that they are little better than baptised
heathen.   Ten thousands professing Christianity may be found
in some countries who have actually never read a page of the
book which God intended should be emphatically the people's
book, but which those who put themselves forward as their
guides have kept from them, either from ignorance of its value,
or from a dread of its influence when read.

Now, while many societies seek to promote true religion in
the United States, and many also to send the gospel to the heathen, the Foreign Evangelical Society makes it its peculiar
province to cultivate that great intermediate field, presented by
professedly Christian countries in which, whatever may be their
civilisation, the gospel is almost as little really known as it is
to the very heathen,—some being beset with the darkness of
Romanism, and others with the still worse darkness of Rationalism.   In many such countries God, in his holy providence,
has been evidently opening the way for the admission of the
long excluded light. Vast revolutions have in the course of the
last fifty years shaken, for a time at least, the spiritual despotism that had reigned so long over a great part of Christendom,
both in Europe and America; and the bitter fruits of infidelity
in all its forms have disposed many, in countries where it had

sapped the foundations of faith, to return to the simple truths of the gospel, unperverted by human speculation and "philosophy falsely so called." The last revolutions in France and Belgium, in particular, seemed to lay those countries more open to evangelical effort; and it was hoped that, at no distant day, Spain and Portugal also would be found accessible to the word of God.

After much inquiry, partly conducted by an agent sent expressly to France and other countries of Europe, an association was formed in 1836, which, three years after, took the form of a regular society, not, however, for sending missionaries from America to Europe, but for assisting the friends of evangelical religion in France, Belgium, and other countries similarly circumstanced. It has accordingly aided the evangelical societies of France and Geneva, and, though not to the same extent, some other and more local associations. Gradually extending the range of its efforts, it has also promoted the same cause by the distribution of tracts in Germany, and has even aided the friends of the truth in Sweden in what they are doing to communicate the blessings of the gospel more effectually to the Laplanders. As the society's executive committee is not restricted to any particular method of effecting its objects, it has turned its attention to a variety of ways of procedure.

While making these efforts in Europe, the society has found among the Roman Catholic population of Lower Canada, which is almost wholly of French origin, a most important and providentially prepared field, now occupied by a very prosperous mission. As this mission originated with some friends of the gospel in Switzerland, it is supported to a certain extent by an association at Lausanne. Attached to it there is a large mission house, in which above twenty Canadian converts are preparing for future labours as teachers, *colporteurs*, evangelists, preachers, &c. There are no fewer than eight or nine missionaries, all but two of whom are natives of France or Switzerland; all have been accustomed to the French tongue from childhood, and several speaking no other. No one can foresee what may be the results of this auspicious commencement among a people with whom all previous attempts of a like kind had failed.

The society contemplates at the same time commencing operations at several points of South America, as soon as persons fitted for the work can be found.

CHAPTER XI.

FINALLY, we propose to say a few words respecting the American Colonisation Society, because of its connection with missions in western Africa, and its bearings upon the general interests of humanity, though not a missionary society itself.

Though originating in sincere desires to promote the benefit of the African race, on the part of some of the best men that America has ever seen, this society has for many years past been much decried in America, and misrepresented to some extent in Europe. The three persons who may be regarded as its founders, have all passed from the present scene to their reward above. These were the late Rev. Dr. Finlay of New Jersey, the Rev. Samuel J. Mills of Connecticut, and the Hon. Elias B. Caldwell of Washington city, clerk to the supreme court of the United States. The society was organised in 1817, and its objects are expressed as follows, in the second article of its constitution: "to promote and execute a plan of colonising (with their consent,) the free people of colour residing in our country, in Africa, or such other place as Congress shall deem most expedient." The primary motive of its founders was to place the coloured man in circumstances in which he might acquire that real independence of station and character, and consequently, that equality in social life which they supposed that he cannot reach in the midst of a white population.

Soon after the society was constituted, the Rev. Messrs. Mills and Burgess were sent as commissioners to explore the west coast of Africa, and select a site for the proposed colony. The first expedition was sent over in 1820, under the Rev. Samuel Bacon, who was appointed governor, but he and many of the colonists were cut off by the fever of the country, in attempting to form a settlement at Sherbro, which consequently failed. Another attempt followed a year or two afterwards, and though the site was not so good as might have been found, it proved far better than the former, and is now called Liberia, lying between the 8th and 11th degrees of north latitude. No great extent of country was bought at first, but other parcels have been added since, and the society hopes ere long to obtain the entire coast from Cape Mount on the north to Cape Palmas on the south, and extending to about 300 miles in length. Its chief possessions at present are about Cape Messurado in the north, and Cape Palmas in the south; a large part of the intervening coast is now in the possession of native chieftains, and on purchasing it, which the society hopes soon to be able to do, it proposes to plant colonies at different points, for the double purpose of extending the present settlements and of abolishing the slave trade, still vigorously prosecuted at two or three points on this part of the coast.

Monrovia, the chief town in the northern cluster of colonies, has a convenient port, and is of considerable extent. There the governor of Liberia resides. There are eight or ten villages, also, to the north and south, and in the interior, settlements having been made on the Stockton and St. Paul's rivers, as well as at other points to the distance of eight or ten miles from Monrovia. A colony planted at Cape Palmas by the Maryland Auxiliary Colonisation Society, consists of about 550 or 600 colonists from America.[1] Many natives, however, live both there and in Liberia on lands of their own, but within the limits of the colony, and subject to its laws; in fact, they form an integral part of the population.

These colonies have been of slow growth, for the society, unaided by the general government, has been unable to conduct the enterprise on a large scale. Inexperience, too, has led to several blunders in the first years, to which must be added want of union and energy on the part of the National Society, and the loss of the confidence of part of the public, particularly of

[1] It is an interesting fact, that the governor at Cape Palmas, Mr. Rushworm, is a gentlemen of colour, brought up in America as a printer, and who ably conducted, for several years, the *Liberia Herald*, a newspaper of respectable character, established at Monrovia about ten or twelve years ago.

the members of the Anti-slavery and Abolition societies. Not-withstanding all this the society has been gradually advancing. Its yearly income has for some time past been about 50,000 dollars,[1] and its colonies, now supposed to number about 4000 emigrants, are in a thriving state. Fatal as the climate of Liberia is to white men, the coloured find it so much otherwise, that the mortality amongst them has not been greater than was to be expected,—not more than what was experienced by the first settlers in Virginia and Massachusetts. Cape Palmas, from its elevated position, has been found remarkably healthy, and not oppressive even to the missionaries, though whites.

It has been well ascertained that at the distance of from fifteen to twenty miles the country rises in the interior, and at no great distance farther becomes even mountainous. Hence it is inferred, that the climate there is salubrious. A few more years of suc-cess will enable the colonists to purchase the lands east of the "back settlements," and to open a way to the hilly country. Already, in fact, they are making a road from Monrovia into the interior, so as to have a highway for trade in cam-wood and other productions of the country. The soil is almost everywhere fertile, and vegetation luxuriant, so that a large population might be abundantly provided for. Instead of a single crop in the year, as in colder climates, two may be had of many vegetable productions. The sweet potatoe, rice, sugar cane, the coffee plant, and other tropical produce, can be raised with ease. The grand difficulty in agriculture lies in the want of good fences, and the destruction of posts and rails by insects. This must be overcome by making hedges of the sour orange, or by employ-ing shepherds, herdsmen, and boys.

Many of the colonists have now their little farms. Others, and perhaps too many, are more occupied in trading with the natives. They keep a quantity of small craft for trading along the coast, and carry on a brisk barter with numerous vessels, American, British, &c., &c., touching from time to time at Monrovia.

---

[1] In 1841, it amounted to 66,536 dollars. But this is exclusive of that of some State societies which manage their own affairs, like that of Maryland, to which the State of that name granted 200,000 dollars, payable in ten yearly instalments. The colony established by that society, it will be seen, is at Cape Palmas.

It appears from the testimony of impartial men, with good opportunities of information, that these colonies have had a beneficial influence on that coast, and have tended to repress the slave trade. Such was that of Captains Bell and Paine of the United States navy, who were there in 1840, and who both vindicate the colonies from many charges equally false and absurd,—among others, that of conniving at that infamous trade. That plantations mainly composed of liberated slaves should be altogether immaculate, no man of sense would expect or require. But that they are, as communities, thriving remarkably well, and that they are also exerting a happy influence on the natives, is what I for one must believe, from the abundant testimony of credible witnesses,—among others, of several excellent missionaries, with whom I have been long and intimately acquainted.[1]

I have remarked that the society has been much opposed, especially by the friends of the anti-slavery societies in the United States. This opposition I consider somewhat unreasonable—although no small amount of it has arisen from the manner in which the society has been advocated. Its friends have been apt to recommend it as presenting the *sole* method of ridding the United States of slavery. This is absurd. It has diverted the minds of slave-holders in the south from the duty of universally emancipating their slaves, whether they shall remain in the country or not; and, in so far, has done mischief. Its friends have said too much, also, about the impossibility of the coloured population rising to respectability and political equality in the United States. The difficulties are indeed great, but good men should never lend their aid in fostering the unreasonable prejudices against the coloured race, entertained by too large a part of our people.

Notwithstanding these and some other errors which might be mentioned, I cannot but feel the deepest interest in the cause of African colonisation; first, because even before slave-holders, it may be advocated in such a way as to favour emancipation, a thing which cannot be done at present by the agents of our

---

[1] This applies chiefly to Liberia. I regret to say, that very recent information makes me fear that the Maryland colony at Cape Palmas, is not acting so favourably on the mission there as it ought to do. It is to be hoped that the society at home will see the necessity of directing it to alter its policy.

"Abolition" and "Anti-slavery societies;" secondly, because it provides slave-holders who wish to emancipate their slaves, and who by certain State laws are obliged to remove their slaves out of the State when so emancipated, with an opportunity of sending them to a country which *does* afford the prospect of their rising to independence and comfort; thirdly, because the colonisation of Africa in one way or other, presents the sole effectual method of breaking up the slave-trade; and lastly, because it is the surest way of introducing civilisation into Africa, and also furnishes a *point d'appui* for the prosecution of Christian missions. Such is the opinion of the Rev. Dr. Philip, the distinguished and judicious superintendent of the London Missionary Society's missions in South Africa, as ably maintained in a letter addressed by him eight years ago, to the students at the theological seminary, at Princetown, New Jersey.

The Presbyterians, Baptists, Episcopalians, and Methodists, have all, as we have seen, flourishing missions in these colonies. [1] The numbers of evangelical preachers, of all denominations, is no less than forty. God has greatly blessed his word in these communities which, considering the recent servitude and ignorance of most of the colonists, are said to exhibit an extraordinary prevalence of morality.

I know not how any person can read without interest the following statement of the report of the Methodist Missionary Society, read at the annual meeting in May, 1842. I give them as reported in one of the New York papers.

"The Liberia mission includes an annual conference of seventeen preachers, all coloured, except the superintendent and the two brethren lately sent out. It has a membership of nearly one thousand individuals, of whom 150 are natives, who, until the last two years were worshipping gods of wood, and stone, and clay.

"There are thirteen day schools within the bounds of the mission, in which from 550 to 600 children receive daily instruction; fourteen churches, some of which are very neat; and one built of stone, in size forty by sixty feet. There are also eight

---

[1] The Roman Catholics have, also, commenced a mission at Cape Palmas, and will doubtless do the same ere long at Liberia. The Right Rev. Dr. Barron and Patrick Kelly, priests, were sent last summer (1842,) to Cape Palmas.

mission houses, or parsonages, four school houses, one of which (the academy,) is a stone building, twenty by forty feet; and a large printing office, also of stone, with an excellent press.   In the schools there are upwards of forty native children and youth, who are preparing for future usefulness.   Many of them read the scriptures and write well, and are burning with zeal to carry the gospel to regions yet beyond them.

"Tribes at a distance have sent for missionaries, and the board is anxious to push the victories of the cross still further into the interior.   If means can be furnished, the board expect a vast amount of native agency will be called into operation.   If the society were able to thrust forth but a few scores of such young men of Africa as Simon Peter, who recently visited this country, the Liberia mission of the Methodist Episcopal Church would be rendered a blessing to thousands of the African race yet unborn.   In view of the success which has attended this mission, the report exhorted the church to adhere to the motto of the dying and lamented Cox: 'Though a thousand fall, Africa must not be given up.' "

The chairman introduced the Rev. John Seys, superintendent of the African mission, who rose and spoke substantially as follows:

"Mr. Chairman, I hold in my hand a resolution given to me for presentation to the society, with a request that I would make some remarks in sustaining it."

He then read the following resolution:—"*Resolved*, That the Liberia mission, including as it does a portion of the interior of western Africa, constitutes one of the most promising fields for missionary enterprise; and that the touching appeals from the half awakened natives of different tribes which have reached us through our missionaries, while they proclaim the ripeness of the harvest, imperatively call upon the church for the requisite supply of efficient labourers.

"I presume this resolution was assigned to me on account of my connection with the Liberian mission.   I can say it affords me much pleasure to present such a resolution.   Years have now elapsed since I stood among you—since I was sent by you as an almoner of the gospel to poor, long neglected Africa.

"The resolution speaks of Africa as one of the most promising

2 z

fields of missionary enterprise. Is it so? Yes, sir, it is so. And
if the missionary sickle be but applied, the field will yield a rich
and noble harvest to the church.   Out of 1000 church members,
150 are native converts.   But two years ago I found them bow-
ing down to images of wood, and clay, and stone, and leather,
and everything which their fancy could make into a god.   These
idols they placed about their persons, put them in their houses,
and carried about with them wherever they went.

"Soon after a number of them had been converted, they appointed a day for meeting, when they were admitted to the
church.   And what a scene!   Bonfires were kindled in the
town of Heddington, and the praises of Immanuel ascended with
the smoke of the burning idols.   At the same time the hearts
of these young converts were burning with desire to carry the
gospel to the tribes beyond them.

"Western Africa is a most promising field, because her native
converts are eager to carry the gospel to the country in the interior.   The boys at the love feasts tell the tale of their conversion.   Pray God to keep them good—to make them grow up
men—and be missionaries to '*the tother people.*'   The natives
will prove themselves doubly qualified for the missionary work,
as they have less fear of the peculiar diseases of the country, can
be supported with less means, and understand the languages of
the country."

Nor is the interest which the converted colonists and natives
feel in missions unfruitful, if we may judge from the fact
mentioned in the "Luminary," the valuable and well-conducted journal of the colony, that the sum of 208 dollars was
collected at a late meeting of the missionary society of the
conference.

CHAPTER XII.

THE SUMMARY.

Thus it will be perceived that almost every evangelical church in the United States is doing more or less for the propagation of the gospel in foreign, and especially in heathen lands. I know not, indeed, that there is a single exception, unless it be among some of the smaller German denominations, or some branches of the Methodist and Presbyterian churches. Even these, however, seem almost all to contribute towards this great object through societies or boards, either belonging to other denominations, or common to several. Thus the Covenanters support a missionary in the East Indies in connection, I believe, with the Presbyterian Church's board of missions; the Associate Reformed churches so far aid the same board; and some of the German Reformed churches aid the American Board of Commissioners for Foreign Missions, as do, also, some of the Cumberland Presbyterian churches.

This is a gratifying fact, whether we regard it as a sign of life, or an earnest of its still further increase in the churches. Not that these have done all that their glorious Lord may justly look for at their hands, but that what they have hitherto done is but the promise of much greater things for the future, we may reasonably infer from the comparatively recent period that either domestic or foreign missions began seriously to interest the Christian public of the United States. Previous to 1812, there was not a single foreign missionary society in the country, with the exception of that of the Moravian Brethren, and not till long after did the churches do anything worth mention in that field. The last twenty years, or rather the last ten years, have witnessed much improvement in this respect, and we pray that it may go on in a far greater ratio until every church shall have come up to the full demands of its duty.

It is difficult to present at one view the statistics of all these missionary efforts with perfect accuracy, at least if we would include all the particulars upon which the reader may think information desirable. On the main points we may obtain pretty accurate results. Including the missions of the evangelical churches alone, and those of the others are hardly of sufficient importance to call for notice, the receipts from all sources for propagating the gospel in foreign, and chiefly heathen lands, for the year ending August 1st, 1842, may safely be reckoned at 572,198 dollars.[1] This is exclusive, also, of the income of the colonisation societies, amounting say to 60,000 dollars, these not being missionary societies.

The number of distinct missions prosecuted by the United States' churches is at least sixty-five; that of stations and out-stations exceeds 200. These employed in 1841-42 at least 375 preaching American missionaries, who, with few exceptions, were ordained ministers, and above seventy American laymen —chiefly physicians, printers, teachers, and catechists. The American females, chiefly wives of missionaries and teachers, amounted to 420, making a total of 875 persons from the United States connected with these missions, and all labouring, in one way or another, to promote the gospel among the heathen. The natives who assist as ministers, evangelists, teachers, distributors of tracts, &c., &c., amounted at least to 375.

[1] The following table gives the details on this point :—

DOLLARS.

The American Board of Commissioners for Foreign Missions,	318,396
Board of Foreign Missions of the Presbyterian Church,	60,324
Board of Foreign Missions of the Baptist Churches,	56,948
Foreign Missions of the Methodist Episcopal Church,	34,879
Foreign Missions of the Protestant Episcopal Church,	22,918
Foreign Missionary Society of the Free-will Baptists, (about)	5,000
Foreign Missionary Society of the Lutheran Church, (about)	2,000
Foreign Missionary Society of the UnitedBrethren, (about)	3,000
Foreign Evangelical Society,	18,733
Grants from American Bible Society, the American and Foreign Bible Society, and the American Tract Society, estimated to be at least	50,000

Total......572,198

Nor does this statement include the annual grant of the general government of 10,000 dollars for the support of schools among the Indian tribes, which is laid out through the missionary societies. I have not been able to obtain the exact amount raised by three of the societies ; but the supposed sums cannot be far from the truth.

CONCLUSION.

In the foregoing pages I proposed to treat of the origin, history, economy, action, and influence of religion in the United States of America; and in the execution of this task I have endeavoured to omit nothing that seemed requisite to a full elucidation of the subject. The extent of ground necessarily traversed, has rendered it indispensable that I should lay before the reader very numerous details, but these, I trust, he has found at once pertinent and interesting. Here the work properly ends, yet had the volume not already exceeded the ordinary bulk, I would fain have added what, previous to going to press, I had taken some pains to prepare, a body of remarks by way of answer to various attacks that have been made on the religious character of my country. Thus we are charged with allowing our population hopelessly to outgrow the provision made for their spiritual wants—with making a very inadequate provision for the Christian ministry, and for the erection of church edifices—with individual covetousness and niggardliness in promoting religious and benevolent institutions at home and abroad—with social insubordination—immorality—bad faith in dealings with public and private creditors—and, above all, with the legalisation in some States, and an unchristian toleration in all, of slavery. The facts which I have sought to lay before the reader historically, simply, clearly, and faithfully, will already have answered some of these charges. To expose the misrepresentations and calumnies that have been mixed up with all of them, would require a separate publication. Meanwhile, in the few remaining pages of Appendices, I have added some calculations and biographical notices falling more immediately within the scope of this volume.

APPENDIX, NO. I.

ALLEGED CHURCH DESTITUTION IN THE UNITED STATES.

FROM 1837 to 1840, for an annual increase of the population to the extent of about 450,000 souls, that of the evangelical ministry of all denominations seems to have considerably exceeded 650, and the number of church edifices, without including all the places used for public worship, erected in 1841 alone, appears to have been 880. This would give about one minister to every 690 souls, and one church to every 500 souls, of the above increase of inhabitants. Although it will be seen from the tables in the summary of evangelical churches, ministers, communicants, and population, that partly from the very scattered condition of the inhabitants, covering so vast a territory, partly from the presence of several denominations at one spot, often leading to a plurality of churches and ministers where one might suffice, this increase of ministers and churches is not so adequate to the wants of the country as might at first sight appear; still, it is so inconsistent with what many of our readers may have heard of the "moral wastes" in the United States, as to require some explanation.

First, then, be it remembered that at the Revolution the number of ministers was only one for every 2500 souls; and that the war of independence itself, and many other circumstances, concurred to prevent much being done to overtake this great and accumulating arrear in the religious institutions of the country. The destitution in 1775 continued to increase from that period till 1815, so that notwithstanding the more recent extension of the churches and of institutions for the training of ministers, and for assisting feeble congregations, no wonder that a great deal has yet to be done in recovering what may be called *moral wastes.*

Second. Churches and ministers not being provided beforehand for the new settlements, and a certain amount of population within a given district being required before means can well be taken for forming a church and obtaining a minister, some time must elapse during which "moral wastes" may be found in newly settled districts. The same remark applies to the mountainous district embracing the Alleghany range and its skirts. From the interior of Pennsylvania, down through Virginia, the eastern parts of Kentucky, and Tennessee, and the western parts of North Carolina, there is an immense tract of country where the population is thinly scattered through narrow valleys, and in some places, particularly in Virginia, Kentucky, and North Carolina, there is considerable destitution of the regular ministrations of the gospel. From such places the cry of the man of Macedonia, "Come over and help us," is continually sounded in the ears of the churches in more favoured districts, nor is it heard in vain. Much has been done for them by our Home Missionary societies, and by the boards of the different churches, and much, no doubt, will yet be done.

In the Third place, the representations made on this subject by some of our societies, are often calculated, though undesignedly, to mislead a stranger. That there is much real destitution to warrant strong appeals is, no doubt, true; but one is apt to forget that there is much that is *hypothetical* in what is said of the danger that threatens if this destitution be not supplied. This danger is imminent; still, it is as yet but a contingency. If the required efforts be not made, error and irreligion will overspread the country—if the Protestants be not on the alert, Romanism will conquer it for itself. But it is precisely to prevent such results that these appeals are made.

Lastly ; it is not to be denied that the agents and missionaries of our home mission societies, have unintentionally and unwittingly promoted erroneous impressions respecting the religious destitution of the country. When these societies were formed some ten or fifteen years ago, the first missionaries and agents sent into the west found many districts, and even whole counties, deplorably destitute ; and in published reports and letters they gave most affecting accounts of the want of shepherds to collect the sheep scattered over these moral wildernesses. Sometimes they thought that like Elijah of old they were "left alone;" not being aware, or if aware, not rightly estimating the fact, that men of other denominations were labouring in the same regions, as itinerating, if not as settled ministers. Such unintentional misrepresentations led the Methodist and Baptist churches to publish statements, proving that the alleged destitution had been greatly exaggerated. Hence of late years, it has been usual to give the names of places requiring ministers and churches of the denomination to which the writer belongs, acknowledging at the same time, the services of ministers of other denominations where they are to be found. Exaggerated statements may often be traced, also, to the warm feelings of extempore speakers at public meetings, leading them to commit themselves to expressions that have not been duly weighed, and to these finding their way, often with additional exaggerations, into newspapers. Within the last fortnight, I have read in one of the best religious newspapers in the United States, the notes of a minister from the east as he passed through Pennsylvania to the " far West." The writer did not see a single church in any but a few of the numerous towns and villages through which he passed from Philadelphia to Pittsburg! Yet, I who have been along the same route no fewer than twelve or more times, and who know every town and village upon it, having travelled it, not only as he did, in stages, but by railroad, in private carriages, on horseback, and even on foot, hesitate not to say, that there is no town, or even village of any considerable size, that has not at least one church belonging to some communion or other. These, however, are not the prominent buildings, steeple-houses, as Quakers would call them, to be seen in the eastern States. Many are plain humble buildings, standing in some retired street, and if visible at all to the writer as he whirled along, hardly to be distinguished from a warehouse or respectable barn. And if such mistatements are honestly made at times by our own countrymen, how much more apt must foreigners be to make equally hasty and erroneous conclusions ?

APPENDIX, No. II.

SUPPORT OF THE MINISTRY—ERECTION OF CHURCH EDIFICES, ETC.

THE total amount of money raised in the United States for the support of the ministry in the evangelical denominations, may be calculated as follows:—

I. Episcopalian ministers, as stated in summary of Book VII....1033
Deduct for missionaries and professors, say........................ 48
                                                                 ———
                                                                 985
Total salaries of 985 ministers, say at an average of 400
dollars each... 394,000

II. Ministers of the Presbyterian family of churches, including
Congregationalists, Lutherans, &c., as in summary..............5411
Deduct foreign missionaries......................................171
Deduct professors in 47 colleges.............................141—312
                                                                 ———
                                                                 5099
Averaging the salaries of these 5099 at 400 dollars each, gives......2,039,600

III. The Baptist ministers, according to the summary, amount to 4375
Deduct for missionaries and professors, say....................... 133
                                                                 ———
                                                                 4242
As a considerable number of the Baptist ministers receive
small salaries, and some none at all, we can allow 200
dollars only as the average of their salaries. This gives........... 848,400

IV. Ministers of the Methodist group, exclusive of local preachers, amount, according to the summary, to...................4112
Deduct for missionaries and professors.............................. 118
                                                                 ———
                                                                 3994
Supposing their salaries to be on an average 300 dollars each,
the result is...1,198,200
                                                                 ————————
                                   Grand total......4,480,200

The church edifices annually erected may be estimated, I consider, at about 880, rating them as follows:—

In the Episcopal Methodists, according to a good authority
" from 250 to 300,"—say...250
The Baptists, say as many as the Methodists.......................250
The Presbyterians and Congregationalists together, build at
least...160
The Lutheran Almanack mentions 76 new churches erected in
the year 1841. An imperfect report for 1840 mentions
47. Say then... 60
The German Reformed may be fairly estimated at.............. 30
The Protestant Methodists at....................................... 20
The Episcopalians at... 50
The Cumberland Presbyterians at.................................... 30
The Reformed Dutch at... 10
The Scotch Presbyterians of all kinds at........................... 20
                                                                 ———
Total new church edifices annually erected...880

The two last are perhaps too high, but the new churches of the Cumberland Presbyterians are probably understated. It is impossible to calculate to what extent this yearly increase meets the demands of a yearly increase of the population, now amounting to nearly half a million of souls. The whole population of the country under the influence of the evangelical denominations, being reckoned at about 13,000,000, and these being divided into about 43,700 congregations, the average number of souls in a congregation must be about 300, and as the number of churches already erected is calculated at about 26,200, the new ones must consist partly of those required for existing evangelical congregations not previously supplied, partly of those required for accessions to the evangelical churches from nearly 5,000,000 of souls not previously attached to evangelical congregations, and for the [gradual increase of evangelical congregations from births and emigration. If we suppose the evangelical proportion of the yearly increase of population to be as 13,000,000 is to 5,000,000, or about 360,000 souls, and this proportion to be divided into congregations of 300 souls each, the result would be an annual increase of 1200 congregations, requiring the same number of churches.

Such a result, however, is by no means probable, for many of these would no doubt join and be merged in existing congregations, and many would be found living in remote places, rendering it impossible for them to be gathered into congregations requiring churches.

Neither is it easy to calculate the cost of these 880 churches. Considering that from twenty to thirty at least are built in our large cities every year at an expense of from 10,000 to 50,000 dollars, and a few of them at even more, the whole cost is probably about 1,500,000 of dollars.

APPENDIX, NO. III.

INDIVIDUAL INSTANCES OF LIBERALITY IN EXTENDING AND SUPPORTING GOSPEL
INSTITUTIONS.

One of the most remarkable instances of liberality in the middle walks of life, is recorded in the memoirs of the late Normand Smith of Hartford, Connecticut. Mr. Smith was born in 1800 of pious parents, and seems himself to have become decided in his religious character at the age of twelve, during a revival. He learned the trade of a saddler, and commenced business himself at the age of two and twenty, on a small capital lent him by his father. He was remarkably prosperous in business from the first, so that he was soon able to repay this debt. But he did not allow his business to engross his time and thoughts. He frequently visited the poor with the view of inquiring into and relieving their necessities,—was a constant Sabbath school teacher, and for a long time was superintendent of a Sabbath school for Africans. In short, he was the foremost to encourage and support every good undertaking. But we must let the memoir[1] speak for itself:—

"In the early part of 1829, he had great doubts whether it was not his duty to relinquish his business, in part at least, that he might have more time to do good. At that time he called to converse on this subject with the writer. He said that he found his business engrossed too much of his time and attention ; he wished to be in a situation more favourable for the cultivation of personal religion and doing good to others; and as he had acquired property enough for himself and family, he felt a desire to retire that he might enjoy more quiet and leisure. In reply it was said to him, The Lord has plainly indicated how you are to glorify him in the world. He has greatly prospered you in your business ; the channels of wealth are open and their streams are flowing in upon you, and it would be wrong for you to obstruct or diminish them. Let them rather flow wider and deeper. Only resolve that you will pursue your business from a sense of duty, and use all that God may give you for his glory, and the good of your fellow men ; and your business, like reading the Bible, or worship on the Sabbath, will be to you a means of grace ; instead of hindering, it will help you in the divine life, and greatly increase your means of usefulness. The effect of the conversation was not known at the time, but from an entry made in a journal which he began to keep about that period, it appears that the purpose was then formed to continue his business, and to conduct it on the principles recommended.

"'The Lord,' says he, 'has made the path of duty plain before me. For a year I have been in much doubt as to the duty of continuing my present business. My mind has become settled ; I have determined to continue it, and I trust it is not in order to grow rich. "They that will be rich fall into temptation," &c. I believe the Lord has led me, and inclined me to pursue my business, not to increase in riches, but that I may have to give to him that needeth. It is therefore my purpose to engage in my business, that I may serve God in it, and with the expectation of getting to give.'

"From that time it was observable by all who knew him, that he made rapid progress in religion. There was a fervour and engagedness of spirit, a purity and elevation of aim, that could not be misunderstood or concealed. He rose toward heaven like the lark of the morning; his business was kept in its proper place, subordinate to the high purpose of serving God, and he found his path thenceforward plain and unobstructed.

"One subject seemed to engross his mind, that of *doing good*—and much good did God enable him to do. Besides many large donations made in aid of various objects previous to his death, he bequeathed at his decease nearly 30,000 dollars to the various benevolent societies of the day. The amount designated for these societies in his will was 13,200 dollars. But

[1] Written by his pastor the Rev. Dr. Hawes, of the First Congregational Church, Hartford, Connecticut, one of the most distinguished and useful ministers in America.

they were also made residuary legatees of property, which he would have distributed while living had it been practicable, without loss, to withdraw it from his business. To a brother, on his dying-bed, he said: ' Do good with your substance while living, and as you have opportunity; otherwise, when you come to die, you will be at a loss to know what distribution it is best to make of it. The trouble and care of such a distribution in a dying hour,' he thought, ' should be avoided by every Christian, by disposing of his property while in life and health, as the Lord should prosper him and present opportunities of doing good.' Sound advice. Strange that Christians should so often hold on upon their property till they come to die,—then, as if to snatch it from the hands of death, giving it in their last will to be distributed when they are gone.

" From the period above referred to, it became his established rule to use for benevolent distribution all the means which he could take from his business, and still prosecute it successfully, and to the best advantage. Hence, after making a moderate provision for his family, what property he had left became available only by the closing of his business. What were his customary contributions to benevolent societies, and to various objects of charity to which his attention was directed, it is impossible to tell. He was usually secret in regard to donations of a private or personal nature. A memorandum which he kept three or four years before his death, ' lest he should think that he gave more than he did,' shows, that his gifts were numerous and large,—sufficiently so to prove, that he adhered to his principle of holding all as consecrated to the Lord. A slip of paper taken from his vest-pocket after his death, mentions the amount of his contributions at the monthly prayer-meeting for missions among the heathen, to have been thirty dollars; or 360 dollars a year.

" In establishing a new church for the more destitute population of the city, and procuring a place of worship, he bore an active and generous part, and contributed largely of his means for its support, besides consecrating to it his devoted and prayerful efforts as one of its officers.

" In giving he was always careful to see that what he gave was needed; never bestowing charity in a way to release any from a sense of obligation to exert themselves to the utmost. He would give to encourage exertion, but never to relax it. In this respect he studied caution, as every one ought; judging rightly, that a man does better for the life that now is, and for that which is to come, by being impelled to put forth his own highest efforts.

" In personal and domestic expenditure he studied Christian economy. While he denied himself no reasonable comfort, it was his habit to consider what things he might dispense with, that he might have the more to give for charitable purposes. Modest and unassuming in his natural character, he thought it not consistent with the simplicity of the gospel for one professing godliness to follow the customs and fashions of the world. While others were enlarging their expenditures, he studied retrenchment in all things. As an example—the house in which he lived would not have been thought extravagant, considering his means; but he felt that his influence as a Christian would be impaired if he should be suspected of imitating the extravagance into which multitudes have been lured by prosperity. This led him to the determination to sell his house, and for some time previous to his death he held it at the disposal of providence, using it, while in his hands, for entertaining God's servants,[1] and for religious meetings.

"Though kind and amiable in his disposition, he was not *naturally* disposed to be liberal or free in the use of property. When he set out in the world, it was with the purpose to be rich. But grace opened his heart, and taught him that the only valuable use of money is to do good with it; a lesson which he emphatically exemplified in' practice, and which made him an instrument of good, the extent of which can never be known till it is revealed at the last day."

Such is the simple and yet interesting notice given by his biographer of Mr. Smith's views of the use of money proper for a Christian to make, and which he so admirably exemplified in his practice. Let us take another case; that of a contemporary of Mr. Smith, Mr. Nathaniel Ripley Cobb, at Boston, who died only seven months after him. Mr. Cobb was a merchant in that city, and a member of one of its Baptist churches. At the age of nineteen he publicly professed his faith in Christ, devoting himself to the service of God, in the sphere in which providence had placed him; considering himself under the same obligation to employ his business talent for the glory of his Saviour, that devolves on the minister of the gospel to consecrate the talents intrusted to him for the same great end.

At the age of twenty-three he drew up and subscribed the following remarkable document:—

"By the grace of God I will never be worth more than 50,000 dollars.

"By the grace of God I will give one-fourth of the net profit of my business to charitable and religious uses.

"If I am ever worth 20,000 dollars, I will give one-half of my net profits; and if I am ever worth 30,000 dollars, I will give three-fourths; and the whole after 50,000 dollars. So help me God, or give to a more faithful steward, and set me aside."

To these resolutions he attached his name, and the date of the transaction, November, 1821.

"To this covenant," says his memoir, "he adhered with conscientious fidelity. He distributed the profits of his business, with an increasing

---

[1] In no part of the United States will Christian families allow ministers of the gospel to remain at hotels. When these have occasion to travel, or to visit places even in their own neighbourhood, they are seldom allowed to stop, for any time at least, at inns, hospitable families being everywhere to be found who account it a privilege and a pleasure to entertain them at their houses. Meetings for prayer, reading the scriptures and exhortation, are often held in all parts of the country, in private houses, as being more comfortable in winter, or more convenient for assembling persons in the neighbourhood.

ratio, from year to year, till he reached the point which he had fixed as a limit to his property, and then gave to the cause of God all the money which he earned. At one time, finding that his property had increased beyond 50,000 dollars, he at once devoted the surplus, 7500 dollars, as a foundation for a professorship in the Newton Theological Institution. He held his property as really belonging to the cause of God. Here is the secret of that wonderful liberality which cheered so many hearts, and gave vigour to so many institutions and plans of benevolence. It sprung from steady religious principle. It was a fruit of the Holy Spirit. He always felt that God had bestowed on him a rich blessing, in enabling him thus to serve his cause. On his death-bed he said to a friend, in allusion to the resolutions quoted above, "By the grace of God—*nothing else*—by the grace of God, I have been enabled, under the influence of those resolutions, to give away more than 40,000 dollars. How good the Lord has been to me!"

Mr. Cobb,—such is the testimony of those who, like myself, knew him well,—was also an active, humble, and devoted Christian; seeking the prosperity of feeble churches; labouring to promote the benevolent institutions of the day; punctual in his attendance at prayer-meetings, and anxious to aid the inquiring sinner; watchful for the eternal interests of those under his charge; mild and amiable in his deportment; and in the general tenor of his life and character an example of consistent piety.

His last sickness and death were peaceful, yea, triumphant. "It is a glorious thing," said he, "to die. I have been active and busy in the world—I have enjoyed as much as any one—God has prospered me—I have everything to bind me here—I am happy in my family—I have property enough—but how small and mean does this world appear when we are on a sick-bed! Nothing can equal my enjoyment in the near view of heaven. *My hope in Christ* is worth infinitely more than all other things. The blood of Christ, the blood of Christ—NONE but Christ. O how thankful I feel that God has provided a way that I, sinful as I am, may look forward with joy to another world through his dear Son." "I can say with brother Lincoln, 'Should I live to the age of Methuselah, I do not think I should ever find a better time to die.'" Happy man! He had honoured God with his substance; he had lived to do good; he had put his trust in Jesus, the Author and Finisher of our faith; and his end was peace! How much better thus to live, than to live for self, and die without having been a benefactor to the world.

But I know not whether an instance of more systematic and long-continued benevolence, nor one that produced equal fruits from similar resources, ever came within my observation, than that of the late Mr. Solomon Goodell, of Vermont, who died when about seventy. Mr. Goodell was a farmer. The following notice of him, though long, will be read with interest. It is from a source worthy of all confidence.

"About the year 1800, the writer of these lines observed a donation of

100 dollars to the Connecticut Missionary Society, published in the annual accounts as from Mr. Goodell. Such donations were, at that time, very uncommon in this country, and in regard to that society, nearly or quite unprecedented. The thought occurred, that doubtless some gentleman of independent fortune had thought proper to take up his residence in the interior of Vermont, and that he considered the society just named a good channel for his pious beneficence. This conclusion was strengthened by seeing a similar donation from the same source, at the return of each successive year for a considerable period.

" When the American Board of Foreign Missions began its operations, Mr. Goodell did not wait for an agent to visit him; but sent a message, (or came himself), more than fifty miles, to a member of the board, saying that he wished to subscribe 500 dollars for immediate use, and 1000 for the permanent fund. He sent 50 as earnest money, and said he would forward the remaining 450 as soon as he could raise that sum; and would pay the interest annually upon the 1000 dollars till the principal should be paid. This engagement he punctually complied with, paying the interest, and just before his death, transferring notes and bonds secured by mortgages, which (including the 1000 dollars above mentioned) amounted to 1708 dollars, 37 cents; that is, a new donation was made of 708 dollars, 37 cents, to which was afterwards added another bond and mortgage of 350 dollars.

"Before this last transaction, he had made repeated intermediate donations. At one time he brought to the Rev. Dr. Lyman, of Hatfield, (the member of the Board above referred to), the sum of 465 dollars. After the money was counted, Dr. Lyman said to him, 'I presume, sir, you wish this sum endorsed upon your note of 1000 dollars.' 'O no,' was his reply, 'I believe that note is good yet. This is a separate matter.' He then expressed his wish, that the money might be remitted toward repairing the loss sustained by the Baptist missionaries at Serampore. He regretted that he had not been able to make the sum 500 dollars;—consoled himself with the thought, that he might do it still, at some period not very far distant; and said, that if any of the bank notes proved less valuable than specie, he would make up the deficiency.

"Mr. Goodell had made what he thought suitable provision for his children, as he passed through life. After consulting his wife, he left her such portion of his estate as was satisfactory to her, gave several small legacies, and made the Board his residuary legatee. He supposed that the property, left to the Board by will, would not be less than 1000 dollars; but as some part of it was, and still is, unsaleable, the exact amount cannot be stated.[1]

"On visiting Mr. Goodell at his house, you would find no gentleman with an independent fortune; but a plain man, in moderate circumstances, on one of the rudest spots in the neighbourhood of the Green Mountains,

[1] In the summary view of Mr. Goodell's donations in aid of missions to

every dollar of whose property was either gained by severe personal labour, or saved by strict frugality, or received as interest on small sums lent to his neighbours. His house was comfortable; but, with the farm on which it stood, was worth only between 700 and 1000 dollars. His income was derived principally from a dairy.

"When he took a journey of fifty miles to pay over 465 dollars of his hard earned property, for the circulation of the Scriptures on the other side of the world,—a donation which would have been acknowledged as generous from a British nobleman,—his whole appearance and equipage would indicate that he was in the plainest class of laborious farmers. All his wearing apparel, at the time of his death, did not equal in value what is often paid for a single garment by persons who *cannot afford* to expend any thing in the way of charity.

"Besides the donations above mentioned, Mr. Goodell made many smaller ones to missionary societies formed to send the gospel to new settlements. He paid [fifty dollars, or more, at one time to a missionary, whom he employed to preach in the destitute towns near him. He aided in the education of pious young men for the ministry, by furnishing them with money for their necessary expenses. He discovered no ostentation, so far as we have been able to learn, in his religious charities. Certain it is, that he always appeared to consider himself as the obliged party, and as obtaining a favour from societies, which he made the almoners of his bounty. Farthest of all was he from supposing that his charitable exertions could make any atonement for sin, or authorise any claims upon the divine mercy. He held to the most entire self-renunciation, and to dependence upon Christ alone.

" Were he on earth, how would he rejoice to see—or shall we not rather say, how *does* he rejoice, while surveying from on high the various efforts now made for the deliverance of men from sin and wrath, and reflecting that he gave his cordial assent to the divine word, before his assent would be unavailing,—that he proved his love of Christ and of his fellow-men,

the heathen, we find them acknowledged in the Panoplist to have been as follows:—

			Dollars.	
Feb. 6,	1812,		250	
July 20,	"		126	
Mar. 24,	1813,		123	
June 19,	"		200	
" "	"		14	
Jan. 7,	1814,		465	
May 27,	"		198	
July 25,	"		100	
Aug. 31,	"		1000	
Feb. 8,	1815,		51	
June 1,	"		207	
" 16,	"		92	
Aug. 31,	"		708	37 Cts.
" 20,	1816,		350	
Nov. 19,	Balance,			79 Cts.

Total,......3885 16 Cts.

by consecrating to God the increase of his flocks, and the labour of his hands."

One of the most remarkable instances of benevolence I have known was that of a coloured woman, who gave sixty dollars on one occasion to educate pious but poor young men for the ministry. She supported herself by her labour as a servant. When she offered the above sum, the agent refused to receive it all, until pressed by the humble donor, who said that she had reserved five dollars; that she had no one dependent on her, and that she hoped to earn enough to provide for her wants in her last sickness, and for her funeral: nor in this was she disappointed. She often gave large sums for one in her circumstances, and rejoiced to have it in her power to do anything for Christ and his cause.

Would that I could say that such benevolence is universal among the Christians of the United States. Alas! all that is done by too many of our merchants and others, who profess to love Him who died to save the world, is in reality nothing in comparison with the means which they have, or have had. Too many have indulged in a luxurious and expensive style of living, whilst they knew that men were dying in their sins, and ignorant of the gospel. It is for this sin, with others, that God has caused so many of our rich Christians to lose their riches in the dreadful commercial and financial crisis which has passed over the country during the last few years. Nevertheless, it is certainly true that the spirit of benevolence is extending itself more and more among the Christian portion of the community. May God hasten the day when Christian men, in all spheres, will deliberately act on the principle of glorifying God in their business, and live for the promotion of his glory, labouring as diligently to make money in order to glorify God with it as they do now to expend it for their own gratification. Such a day will come, or I see not how the world is ever to be converted to God.

APPENDIX, NO. IV.

ALLEGED IMMORALITY OF NEW YORK.

I HAVE read with great astonishment some remarks of Mr. Tait on Prostitution in New York, to be found in his recent work on Magdalenism, (p. 5,) and referred to by the Rev. Dr. Wardlaw in his Lectures on Prostitution. The sum of Mr. T.'s statement is, that "that city furnishes a prostitute for every six or seven adults of its male population." I have lived much in New York, and know well its moral state, and I affirm, that this statement, founded on an exaggerated Report published by the Magdalen Society of that city, about nine or ten years ago, is quite incorrect, and in no way approximates to the truth.

GLASGOW;—W. G. BLACKIE AND CO., PRINTERS.